Visual Basic® 2005

Your visual blueprint™ for writing dynamic applications

by Jim Keogh

Wiley Publishing, Inc.

Visual Basic® 2005: Your visual blueprint™ for writing dynamic applications

Published by
Wiley Publishing, Inc.
111 River Street
Hoboken, NJ 07030-5774

Published simultaneously in Canada

Library of Congress Control Number: 2006922505

ISBN-13: 978-0-471-79344-1

ISBN-10: 0-471-79344-2

Manufactured in the United States of America

10 9 8 7 6 5 4 3 2 1

1K/SU/QV/QW/IN

Trademark Acknowledgments

Contact Us

For general information on our other products and services, please contact our Customer Care Department within the U.S. at (800)762-2974, outside the U.S. at (317)572-3993 or fax (317)572-4002.

For technical support, please visit www.wiley.com/techsupport.

The Roman Aqueduct at Segovia, Spain

Legend claims that the aqueduct of Segovia appeared overnight, when a young water-girl sold her soul to the devil in exchange for having water delivered to her door. Sources disagree on the number of arches, the exact height, and when the aqueduct ceased to operate, but all concur on one point: The imposing structure has been held together for nearly 2,000 years by nothing more than gravity and spectacular architectural engineering. No concrete, mortar, or binder of any kind holds the massive granite blocks in place. Its image on coins and insignia has represented the city since the 15th century.

Discover more about Segovia in *Frommer's Spain 2006*, available wherever books are sold or online at www.frommers.com.

Sales

Contact Wiley
at (800) 762-2974
or (317) 572-4002.

Praise For Visual Books...

"This is absolutely the best computer-related book I have ever bought. Thank you so much for this fantastic text. Simply the best computer book series I have ever seen. I will look for, recommend, and purchase more of the same."

—David E. Prince (NeoNome.com)

"I have several of your Visual books and they are the best I have ever used."

—Stanley Clark (Crawfordville, FL)

"I just want to let you know that I really enjoy all your books. I'm a strong visual learner. You really know how to get people addicted to learning! I'm a very satisfied Visual customer. Keep up the excellent work!"

—Helen Lee (Calgary, Alberta, Canada)

"I have several books from the Visual series and have always found them to be valuable resources."

—Stephen P. Miller (Ballston Spa, NY)

"This book is PERFECT for me — it's highly visual and gets right to the point. What I like most about it is that each page presents a new task that you can try verbatim or, alternatively, take the ideas and build your own examples. Also, this book isn't bogged down with trying to 'tell all' – it gets right to the point. This is an EXCELLENT, EXCELLENT, EXCELLENT book and I look forward to purchasing other books in the series."

—Tom Dierickx (Malta, IL)

"I have quite a few of your Visual books and have been very pleased with all of them. I love the way the lessons are presented!"

—Mary Jane Newman (Yorba Linda, CA)

"I am an avid fan of your Visual books. If I need to learn anything, I just buy one of your books and learn the topic in no time. Wonders! I have even trained my friends to give me Visual books as gifts."

—Illona Bergstrom (Aventura, FL)

"I just had to let you and your company know how great I think your books are. I just purchased my third Visual book (my first two are dog-eared now!) and, once again, your product has surpassed my expectations. The expertise, thought, and effort that go into each book are obvious, and I sincerely appreciate your efforts."

—Tracey Moore (Memphis, TN)

"Compliments to the chef!! Your books are extraordinary! Or, simply put, extra-ordinary, meaning way above the rest! THANK YOU THANK YOU THANK YOU! I buy them for friends, family, and colleagues."

—Christine J. Manfrin (Castle Rock, CO)

"I write to extend my thanks and appreciation for your books. They are clear, easy to follow, and straight to the point. Keep up the good work! I bought several of your books and they are just right! No regrets! I will always buy your books because they are the best."

—Seward Kollie (Dakar, Senegal)

"I am an avid purchaser and reader of the Visual series, and they are the greatest computer books I've seen. Thank you very much for the hard work, effort, and dedication that you put into this series."

—Alex Diaz (Las Vegas, NV)

Credits

Project Editor
Dana Rhodes Lesh

Acquisitions Editor
Jody Lefevere

Product Development Supervisor
Courtney Allen

Copy Editor
Dana Rhodes Lesh

Technical Editor
Ken Davidson

Editorial Manager
Robyn Siesky

Business Manager
Amy Knies

Permissions Editor
Laura Moss

Manufacturing
Allan Conley
Linda Cook
Paul Gilchrist
Jennifer Guynn

Book Design
Kathryn Rickard

Production Coordinator
Adrienne L. Martinez

Layout
Jennifer Click
Sean Decker
Amanda Spagnuolo

Screen Artists
Ronda David-Burroughs
Jill A. Proll

Cover Illustration
Jake Mansfield

Proofreader
Vicki Broyles

Quality Control
Joe Niesen

Indexer
Richard T. Evans

Vice President and Executive Group Publisher
Richard Swadley

Vice President and Publisher
Barry Pruett

Composition Director
Debbie Stailey

About the Author

Jim Keogh is on the faculty of Columbia University and Saint Peter's College in Jersey City, New Jersey. He developed the e-commerce tract at Columbia University. Jim has spent decades developing applications for major Wall Street corporations and is the author of more than 70 books, including *Java Database Programming For Dummies, Unix Programming For Dummies,* and *Linux Programming For Dummies.*

Author's Acknowledgments

This book is dedicated to Anne, Sandy, Joanne, Amber-Leigh Christine, and Graaf, without whose help and support this book could not have been written.

TABLE OF CONTENTS

5 DECLARING VARIABLES, EXPRESSIONS, AND STATEMENTS 60

6 CREATING CONDITIONAL STATEMENTS 76

TABLE OF CONTENTS

TABLE OF CONTENTS

HOW TO USE THIS BOOK

Visual Basic 2005: Your visual blueprint for writing dynamic applications uses simple, straightforward examples to teach you how to create powerful and dynamic programs.

To get the most out of this book, I suggest that you read each chapter in order, from beginning to end. Each chapter introduces new ideas and builds on the knowledge learned in previous chapters. As you become familiar with Visual Basic .NET 2005, you can use this book as an informative desktop reference.

Who Needs This Book

If you are interested in writing applications for Windows computers and the Internet using the Visual Basic .NET 2005 programming environment, *Visual Basic 2005: Your visual blueprint for writing dynamic applications* is the book for you.

This book takes you first through the process of installing and using Visual Studio 2005 and then more specifically through the process of writing advanced Windows applications. This book also provides detailed coverage to develop reusable components and package your application or component.

Although this book requires no prior experience with Visual Basic programming, a familiarity with the Microsoft Windows operating system installed on your computer and programming languages in general is recommended.

Book Organization

Visual Basic 2005: Your visual blueprint for writing dynamic applications has 16 chapters.

Chapter 1, "Getting Started with VB.NET," covers the installation of Visual Studio .NET 2005 on your computer, the development environment that you will be using to build your Visual Basic .NET 2005 application.

Chapter 2, "Working with Windows Forms," shows you how to create a Windows form, which is used to interact with your application.

In Chapter 3, "Creating Windows Controls: Labels, Text Boxes, and Lists," you will learn how to use labels, text boxes, and lists on a Windows form — controls that you find on nearly every professional Windows application.

Chapter 4, "Creating Windows Controls: Buttons, Radio Buttons, and Check Boxes," describes using a variety of buttons.

In Chapter 5, "Declaring Variables, Expressions, and Statements," you will see how to write the center of your application by using variables and expressions to form statements that tell Visual Basic .NET what to do.

Chapter 6, "Creating Conditional Statements," shows you how to give Visual Basic .NET instructions on how to make decisions in your application.

Chapter 7, "Creating Loops," covers a great time-saver, the loop, which saves you from writing a statement multiple times. You write the statement once and use a loop to have Visual Basic .NET repeatedly execute it.

Chapter 8, "Declaring Arrays," covers using arrays to help organize your data.

Chapter 9, "Defining Subroutines and Functions," describes how to write code once in a subroutine or function and then call it by name whenever you want that chunk of code to execute.

Chapter 10, "Understanding Databases," discusses databases. You will see how to store and access database information from within your application.

Chapter 11, "Debugging Your Application," shows you how to use some useful tools to work out all the bugs in your application.

Chapter 12, "Using Classes," prepares you to incorporate an advanced feature of Visual Basic .NET — called a *class* — into your application.

Chapter 13, "Creating Components," shows you how to build components yourself.

Chapter 14, "Creating Graphics," covers how to display eye-catching graphics as part of your application.

In Chapter 15, "Providing Input and Output," you will learn how to link your application to access information on the Internet or on a business network. You will also see how to give your application the capability to print.

Chapter 16, "Packaging Your Application," describes packaging and distributing your application. You will learn how to use tools in Visual Studio .NET 2005 to create a professional installation wizard.

What You Need to Use This Book

To perform the tasks in this book, you need a computer with Microsoft Windows NT 4.0, 2000, or XP installed, as well as Microsoft Visual Studio 2005. You do not require any special development tools because all the tools are part of the Visual Studio 2005 development environment.

The Conventions in This Book

A number of styles have been used throughout *Visual Basic 2005: Your visual blueprint for writing dynamic applications* to designate different types of information.

`Courier Font`

Indicates the use of Visual Basic. NET code such as statements, operators, functions, objects, methods, and properties.

Bold

Indicates information that you must type.

Italics

Indicates a new term.

Apply It

An Apply It section takes the code from the preceding task one step further. Apply It sections enable you to take full advantage of Visual Basic. NET code.

Extra

An Extra section provides additional information about the preceding task. Extra sections contain the inside information to make working with Visual Basic. NET easier and more efficient.

Install Visual Studio 2005

Visual Studio 2005 is an integrated development environment (IDE) that enables you to build various kinds of applications using Visual Basic .NET and other Microsoft programming languages. An IDE contains all the tools that you need to write, test, build, and distribute your application.

The installation of Visual Studio 2005 is straightforward and should take an hour to an hour and a half. You begin the installation by closing down any applications that you opened on your computer. Next, place installation disc 1 into your CD drive. Windows automatically starts the Setup Wizard. The Setup Wizard walks you through the installation. The Setup Wizard is also used to uninstall Visual Studio 2005 and to add or remove components to the installation that have not been installed yet. During the installation process, you will have the opportunity to install all the components, select the components that you want to install, or accept the default components that Microsoft suggests you install. You probably will want to install the components that are selected by default. If you need a feature that you do not install now, some time in the future you can use the Setup Wizard again to install any component was not originally installed. You probably will not need to add a new component later, however, because nearly all the components that you need are part of the default installation.

Install Visual Studio 2005

INSTALL VISUAL STUDIO 2005

1. Insert disc 1.

Note: Make sure that all applications that were running have been shut down.

The Setup Wizard loads, and you are presented with different options.

2. Click Install Visual Studio 2005.

The Setup Wizard prepares temporary files.

The Welcome page appears, and the Setup Wizard says that it is loading installation components.

3. When the wizard is ready, click Next.

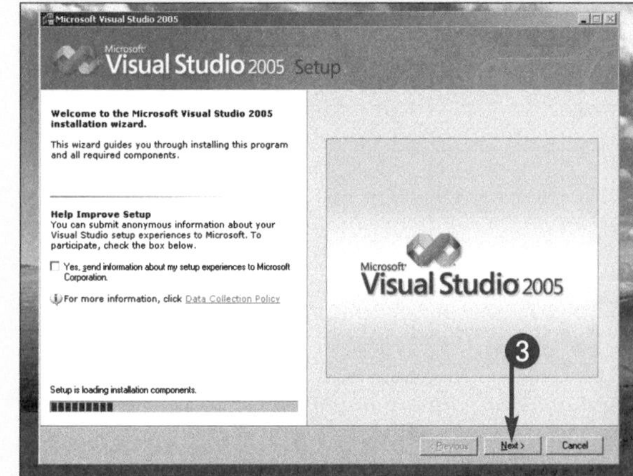

The license agreement appears.

4 Read the license agreement.

Note: The license agreement specifies the terms under which you can use the software.

5 Click I Accept.

Note: You will not be able to install the software unless you select this.

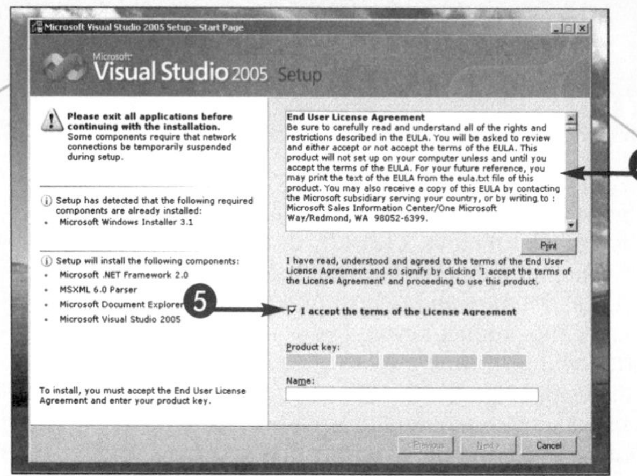

6 At the bottom of the page, type the product key.

Note: You will find this on an orange tag on the product cover of disc 1.

7 Type your name.

Note: Your name is used to identify that you own the software.

8 Click Next.

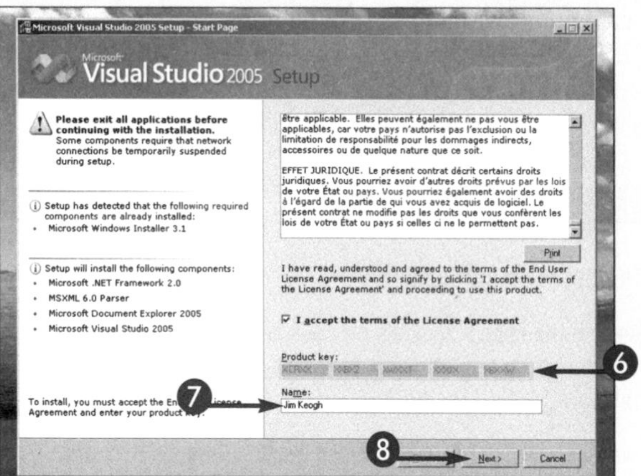

Extra

You can place the Visual Studio 2005 icon on your computer's desktop by creating a shortcut. You do this by clicking the Start button and then the Programs folder. Open the Visual Studio 2005 subfolder, and you will see the Visual Studio 2005 executable file. Select this file and click the right mouse button. Click Create Shortcut, and the shortcut for the Visual Studio 2005 executable files appears in the folder. Drag and drop the shortcut to the desktop, and the Visual Studio 2005 icon will appear on the desktop.

continued

Install Visual Studio 2005 *(continued)*

The Setup Wizard begins by giving you three options: install, add/remove a feature, or uninstall. Select install and then the Microsoft license agreement is displayed. Read it over and select I Accept. You will also need to enter the product key and your name before the Next button will turn from gray to black. Then click Next to display the Options page. The Options page shows the amount of disk space required to install components of Visual Studio 2005 and the available disk space on your computer. You will need to free up some disk space if the Options page indicates that there is insufficient space.

Click the Install button. The screen shows components that have been installed, are currently being installed, and components that still must be installed. The status of the list changes as the installation continues. After a few minutes, you will be prompted to insert disc 2 into your CD drive; then click the OK button to continue installation. The installation continues for a while. After the installation is finished, a screen is displayed indicating if the installation was successful or if not, and the screen lists components that failed to install. If the installation was successful, click the Finish button.

If the installation was not successful, double-check that you have shut down any application that may be running and reinsert disc 1 to begin the installation process again; however, this time select Add/Remove, then check only the component that did not install, and then select the Update button.

Install Visual Studio 2005 *(continued)*

The Options page appears.

9. Review the space available on your hard drive and the space requirements to install the software.

Note: You can remove files or unused applications to free hard disk space if you do not have sufficient space to install the software.

10. Click Install.

The installation process begins.

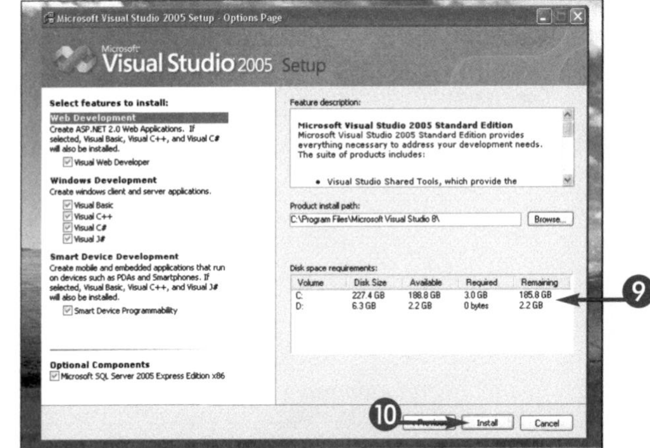

11. Replace disc 1 with disc 2 when prompted.

Note: Two discs are necessary to install the software for the Standard edition. Other editions may have different installation steps.

12. Monitor the installation process.

A check mark appears next to installed components. A blue arrow points to the component that is currently being installed. Components that appear in gray have yet to be installed.

13. Click Next.

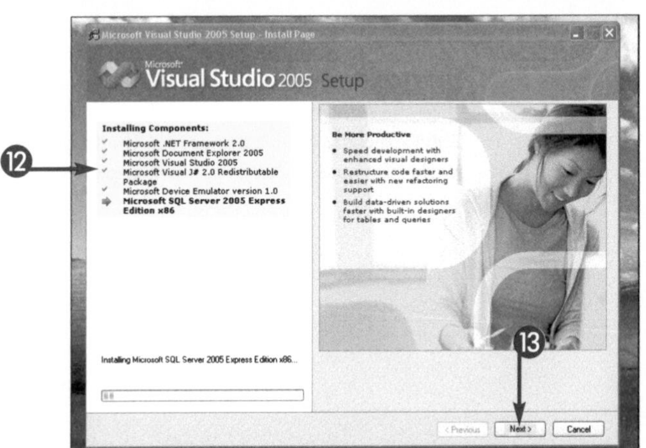

The results of the installation appear.

14 Click Finish.

You will be prompted to restart your computer.

15 Click Restart Now.

The installation is complete.

INSTALL A COMPONENT THAT FAILED

16 If any component failed to be installed, note the name of it and continue on to step 17 after you restart your computer.

17 Reinsert disc 1 if any component failed to install.

18 Click Add/Remove Component.

The Maintenance Mode page appears.

19 Click only the component that failed to install.

Note: Make sure that the other components are unchecked.

20 Click Update.

The process that begins with step 11 is repeated, but only the selected component is installed.

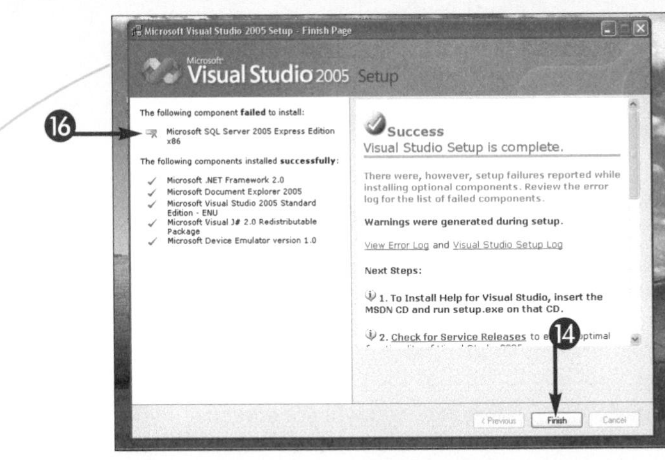

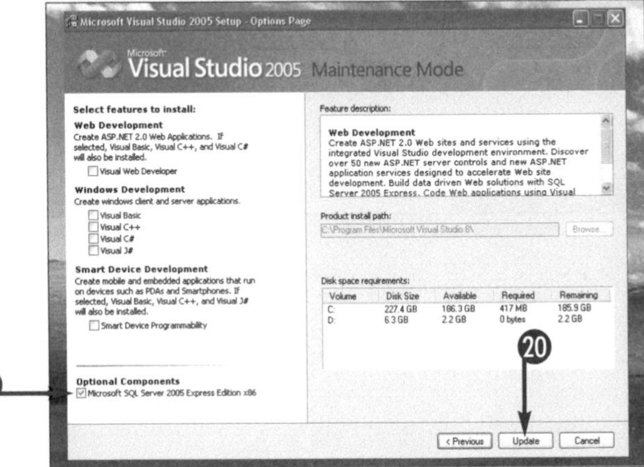

Extra

You can avoid frustrations when installing Visual Studio 2005 by first making sure that your system can run Visual Studio 2005. One of the most agonizing problems is to begin the installation only to have the Setup Wizard display the dreadful message that it cannot install the application because your computer is not capable of supporting it. Typically it is software — not hardware — at the center of your troubles. Visual Studio 2005 requires a 600MHz or faster CPU, 192MB or more of RAM, and 2GB of disk space. Your computer probably meets or surpasses these requirements if you purchased it within the past few years.

However, not everyone keeps up-to-date with Microsoft's latest service packs. A *service pack* is a group of enhances to Windows that usually patch security gaps in the original Windows release. Visual Studio 2005 requires you to have certain service packs installed on your computer before running the Setup Wizard. You can download service packs free of charge from www.microsoft.com. Here are the service packs you need: Windows 2000 with Service Pack 4 (SP4), Windows XP with Service Pack 2 (SP2), and Windows Service 2003 with Service Pack 1 (SP1).

Create a New Project

All applications are created as a project. It is fairly easy to create a new project, as the steps here show. You use the New Project dialog box, in which you select a project type and template. Visual Studio 2005 enables you to create projects in Visual Basic .NET and other programming languages, as well. Here, you will be selecting Visual Basic .NET as the project type.

In the New Project dialog box, you will see several templates displayed in the Templates window. A *template* contains the basic ingredients needed to create a specific kind of Visual Basic .NET program. You will see the templates Windows Application, Class Library, Windows Control Library, ASP.NET Web Application, ASP.NET Web Service, and others. You will be creating Windows applications for the examples in this book.

After you select Windows Application as the template for your project, a new Windows application project opens, showing a blank form and the Properties window. The blank form is where you create the screens that are used to interact with your application. The Properties window is used to define characteristics of the blank form. The default settings are sufficient for most applications that you build. However, you probably want to change the text that appears at the top of the form to something that better describes the purpose of the form.

Create a New Project

1. Click File.
2. Click New Project.

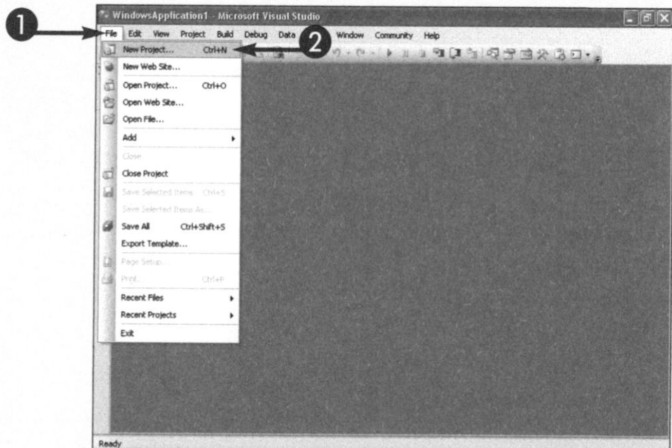

- The New Project dialog box appears.

3. Click the + next to Visual Basic under Project Types.

- The Visual Basic templates are displayed.

Note: Make sure that Windows is highlighted.

4. Click Windows Application.
5. Click OK.

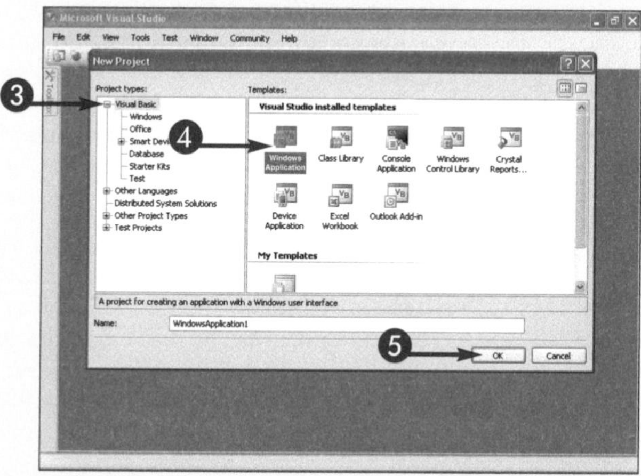

A blank Windows application form appears.

6 Click File ➔ Close Project.

A dialog box appears, asking if you want to save the project, discard the project, or cancel closing the project.

7 Click Save.

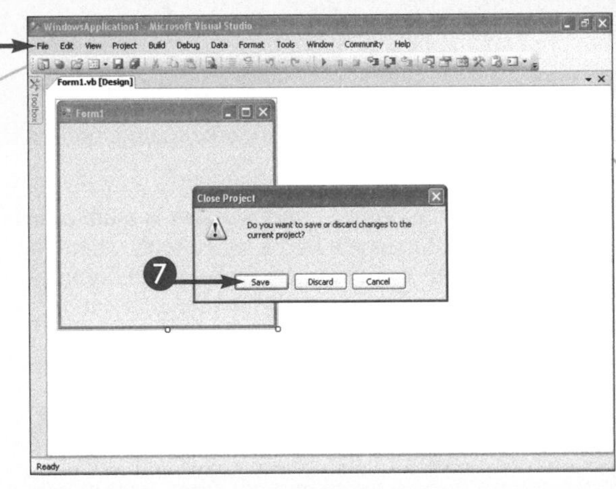

The Save Project dialog box appears.

8 Type a name for your project.

Note: The name should reflect the nature of your project.

9 Click Save.

The project files are saved to your project directory.

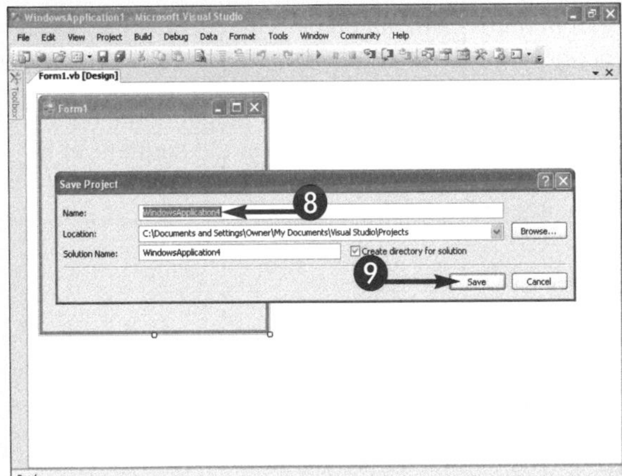

Extra

You can use Visual Studio 2005 to create other kinds of projects besides a Visual Basic .NET Windows Application project. You can also create an Excel workbook, a crystal report, add-in programs for Outlook, and many other projects that are beyond the scope of this book. Later on in Chapter 16, you will create a setup project, which is used to create a Setup Wizard much like the Setup Wizard used to install Visual Studio 2005, except your Setup Wizard will install your own Visual Basic .NET application.

Using Parts of a Project

On the left side of the project window is a tab called Toolbox that expands into a list of tools when you click the tab. You use these tools to transform a blank form into an interactive screen for your application. The tools are organized into groups. You select the name of the group to see a list of tools in that group. The Windows Forms tool group is used more than the other groups and contains buttons, check boxes, and other controls that are frequently seen in applications.

When you want to use a control on your form, you drag the control from the Toolbox and drop it on to the form. You can make adjustments to the control on the form by first selecting the control. Resize tabs will appear around the control. You can change the size of the control by dragging the resize tabs. You can reposition the control on the blank form by dragging the center of the control to the new location. You can remove a control by selecting it and pressing Delete.

Each control has a set of properties that define the characteristic or behavior of the control. The kinds of properties that are available depend on the type of control. For example, the `FontColor` property of the `Label` control sets the color of the label. The list of properties appears in the Properties window when you select the control. Throughout this book, you will learn how to work with the more commonly used controls.

Solution Explorer is a pane that contains all the elements of your project. The designer is where you create the user interface or form for the project that appears on the Design tab. If you do not see it, select the form from Solution Explorer.

Using Parts of a Project

1. Open a new project.

Note: See the section "Create a New Project."

A blank form appears.

2. Move the mouse cursor over the Toolbox.

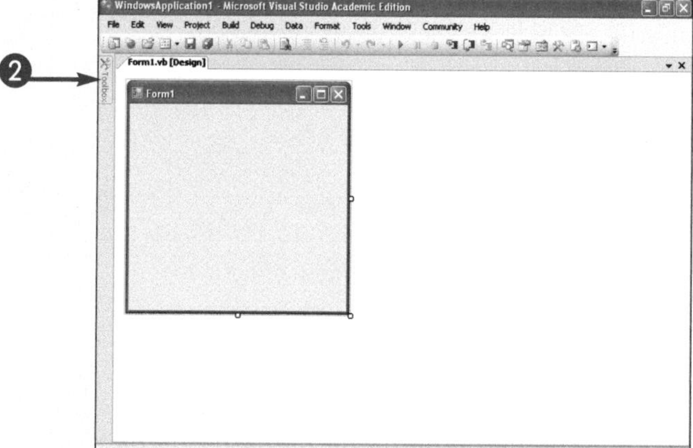

The Toolbox opens, showing a list of buttons and other controls that you use to build your application.

3. Move the mouse cursor away from the Toolbox.

The Toolbox returns to the left side of the window.

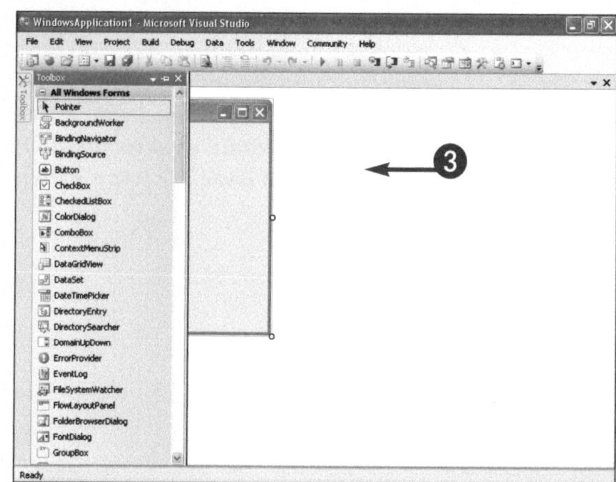

4 Press F7.

The Code tab is displayed. This is where you write instructions for Visual Basic .NET.

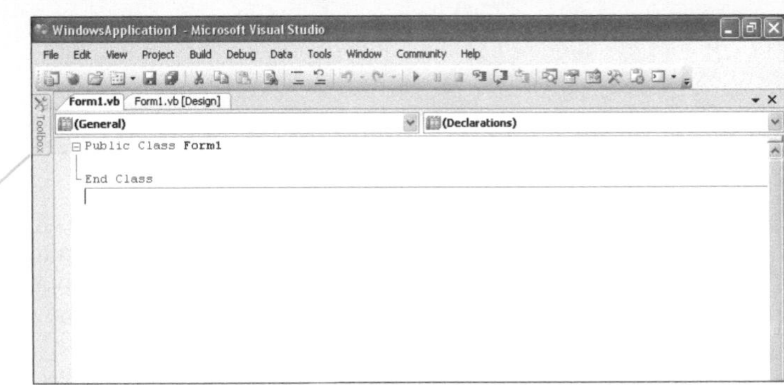

5 Click View ➔ Solution Explorer.

Solution Explorer appears, showing the components of your projects in a tree diagram.

- You can click a component to display it.

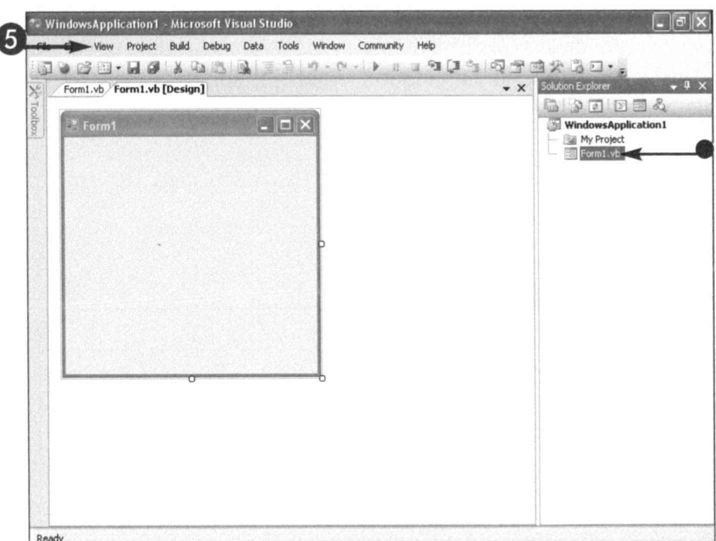

Extra

The Toolbox is usually hidden as a tab on the left, which opens when you place the cursor over it. You can keep the Toolbox open by first opening it with the mouse and then clicking the pin icon at the top of the Toolbox. You can then drag and drop tools onto your form without having to open and close the Toolbox each time. Click the pin again to return the Toolbox to its tab position.

Each control has a set of events that are associated with a subroutine. Double-click the control to display the class definition for the form. You create subroutines in the class definition for events that are important to your application. For example, if you click a `Button` control on your form, a subroutine called `Click` is created, which is executed when someone clicks the button. You place code in the subroutine that you want executed when the event occurs. The drop-down list box in the upper-right corner contains a list of all the events associated with the selected control. When you select an event, a corresponding subroutine is created in the class definition.

Create a "Hello World" Application

You probably want to jump in and start building a Visual Basic .NET application. Although there is much to learn before you can create a complete Visual Basic .NET application, you can get started by building a simple application that displays "Hello World" on your form.

First, make sure to have a new project opened; see the section "Create a New Project." The message "Hello World" will be displayed as a label on the form. A label is simply text. To change the text, you change the `Text` property in the Properties window.

You can open the Toolbox and select the Windows Forms group to see all the tools that you can use to build the form for your Windows application. The Label tool appears near the top of the Windows Forms group. When you drag and drop a label on to the blank form, the text of the label reads "Label1," which indicates that this is the first label on the form. If you select the label on the form, the Properties window will show the properties of the label. You will learn how to use these properties in Chapter 3.

Create a "Hello World" Application

1. Open a new Visual Basic .NET Windows application.

Note: See the section "Create a New Project."

2. Move the mouse cursor over the Toolbox tab.

   The list of tools appears.

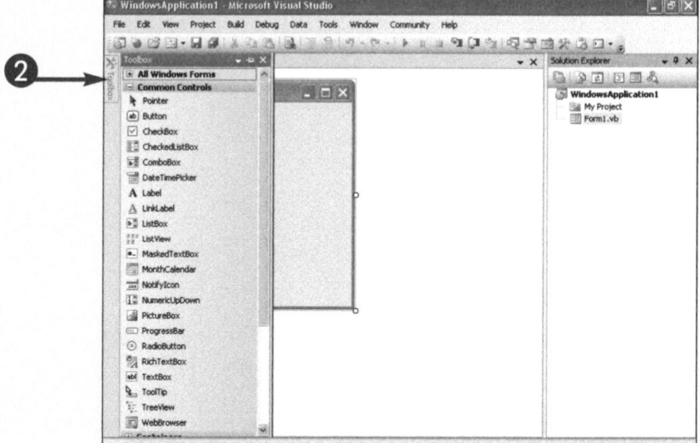

3. Drag and drop the `Label` control on to the blank form.

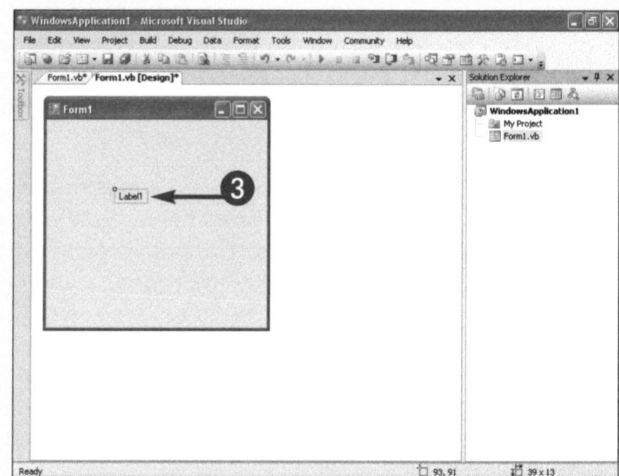

4 Click the label on the form and type **Hello World**.

- The Properties window is displayed, and "Hello World" appears alongside the `Text` property.

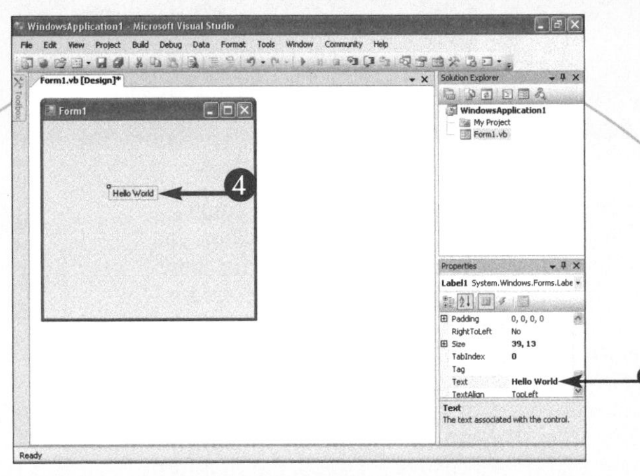

5 Press F5 to run the application.

The Hello World form is displayed on the screen.

6 Click the close box.

Your application stops running.

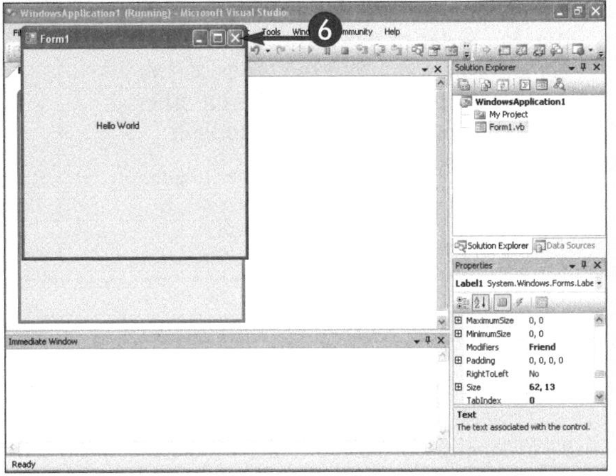

Extra

You can jazz up your "Hello World" application by changing the color and font of the text. Select the label and find `FontColor` and `Font` in the Properties window. Click `FontColor` to display a color chart. Double-click a new color on the color chart, and the text of the label automatically changes to that color. Click `Font` and choose from a list of available fonts. The text is redisplayed in the font that you selected.

SELECT THIS

```
FontColor Blue
Font Times New Roman
```

RESULT

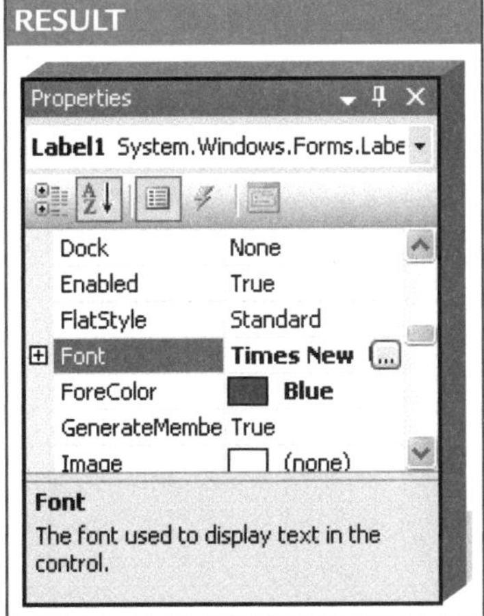

Create a New Form

A form enables users to interact with your application. A blank form appears when you create a new project; see Chapter 1 for more information. Many applications that you will create require more than one form. The first form typically is the form that is most useful to the person who uses your application. Other forms are used to enter or display specific types of information that do not appear on the first form. For example, if you are building an application that tracks customer orders, the first form probably will prompt the user to enter an order number. If the person enters an order number, the application displays summary information about the order on the first form, and detail information is available on other forms that can be displayed by selecting buttons or other controls on the first form.

Extra

You can create a second new form after you follow the steps here by clicking the Project menu bar option. From the Project submenu, click Add Windows Form to display the Add New Item dialog box, which contains an assortment of Visual Studio–installed templates for various items that you can add to your application.

When you select the Windows Form icon, a new blank form called Form2 appears on the screen. There are two tabs at the top of the screen below the menu bar. The active tab contains Form2, and the other tab contains Form1, which is the original form that was displayed when you created a new application. You can click these tabs to move between Form2 and Form1.

Create a New Form

1. Click File ➔ New Project.

   The New Project dialog box appears.

2. Click Visual Basic Projects.

   The New Project dialog box displays the Visual Basic templates.

3. Click Windows Application.
4. Click OK.

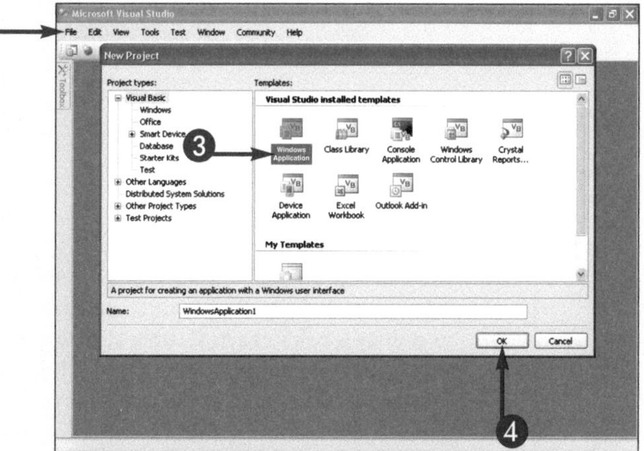

A Windows application template is displayed, along with a form.

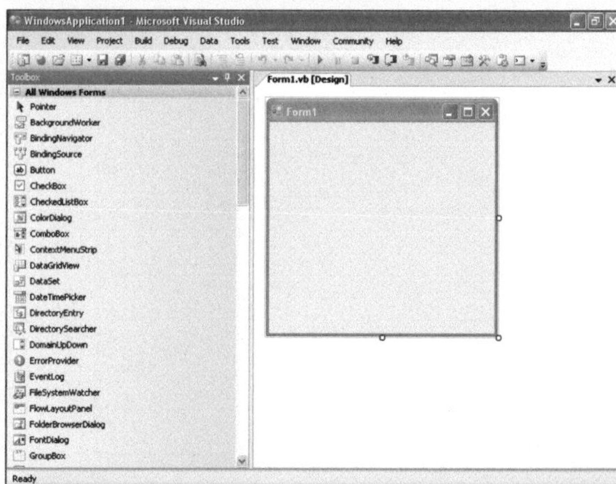

Add a Control to a Form

A control displays information on a form or is an item that a user uses to interact with the form. Controls are contained in the Toolbox that appears as a tab on the top left of the screen, just below the menu bar.

The Toolbox displays ten categories of controls. You select the category name to see the list of controls within that category. You can click the category name again to hide the list of controls. You will most often use controls in the Common Controls category, in which you find buttons, check boxes, labels, and other types of general controls. Throughout this book, you will learn how to incorporate many of these controls into your applications.

The Toolbox is very flexible. You can change the position of the Toolbox by moving the cursor over the Toolbox and pressing the right mouse button to display the pop-up menu. The menu includes the commands Float, Dockable, Tab Document, Auto Hide, and Hide. Float means that you can move the Toolbox anywhere on the screen. Dockable means that you can reposition the Toolbox at the top, bottom, or sides of the screen. Tab Document gives the Toolbox its own tab similar to the Form tab. Auto Hide places the Toolbox on a vertical tab; this is the default position. Hide removes the Toolbox from view.

Add a Control to a Form

1. Place the mouse pointer over the Toolbox tab and leave it there for a second.
   - Alternatively, you can click View ➔ Toolbox to display the Toolbox.

   The Toolbox opens.

2. Click Common Controls.

   A list of commonly used controls appears.

3. Drag and drop the control that you want on to the form.

   If you choose the `Label` control, a dotted line appears around the word *Label1* on the form.

4. Place the cursor on the control. Hold down the left mouse button while dragging the control into the position that you want it to appear on the form.

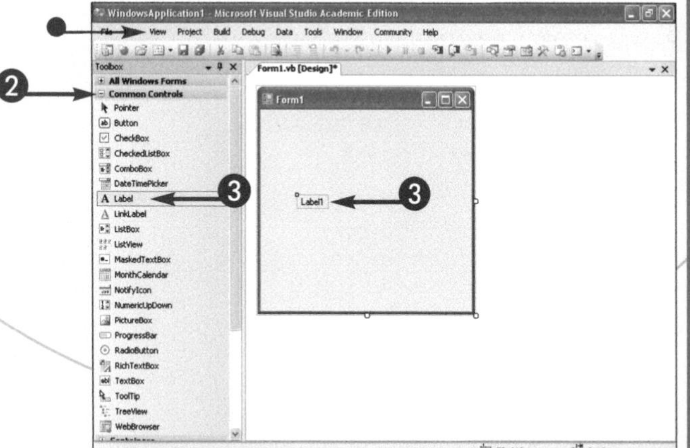

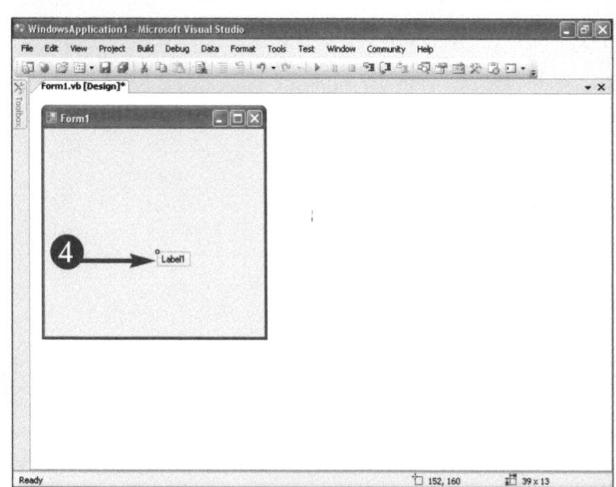

Set the Properties of a Control

Each control has several properties. A *property* is a characteristic that you can modify to alter the appearance or behavior of a control. For example, the `Label` control has a `Text` property that contains the text of the label. You modify the `Text` property of a label to change the label's text.

Some controls have the same property such as `Size`, which specifies the control's width and height on the form. Other controls have properties that are unique to the control such as `ImageKey`, which is used in the `Image` control to identify the image within a list of images to display in the control. You can assign text, a number, or `True` or `False` as a property value, depending on the nature of the property. For example, either `True` or `False` is assigned to the `Visible` property to indicate if the control should be shown on the form.

The Properties window contains a list of properties that are for the control that you select on your form. Changes to these properties affect only the selected control. Other similar controls on your form are not affected. This means that if you have two `Label` controls on your form, both have an identical list of properties; however, each property is unique to the label selected before opening the Properties list. If you want to modify the text for both labels, for example, you have to change the `Text` property for each label separately.

The Properties list is divided into two columns. The left column contains the names of the properties, and the right column contains the values that are assigned to the properties. You can change the value of a property by selecting the property from the Properties list and then entering the change in the value column. The change to the control takes effect immediately on your form.

Set the Properties of a Control

1. Drag and drop a control from the Toolbox on to your form.

   The control displays its default text, such as “Label1” for a `Label` control.

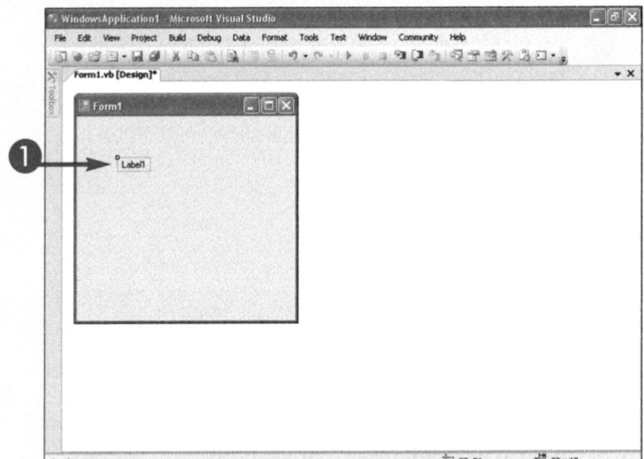

2. Click View ➔ Properties Window.

   The Properties window appears.

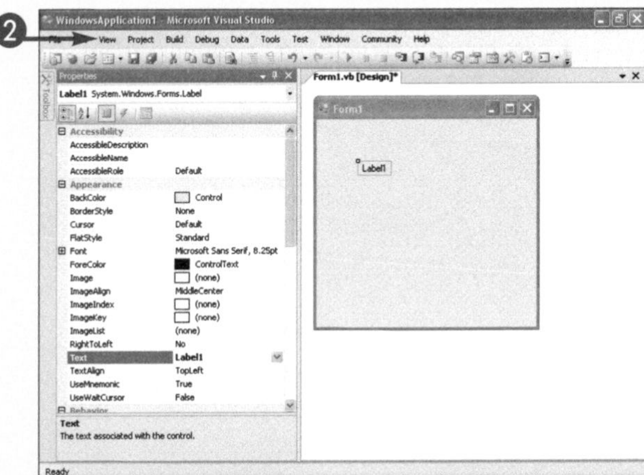

3. Click the property that you want to change.

4. Change the property according to your form's needs.

   For example, for the Text property, you would type the text that you want for the control and press Enter.

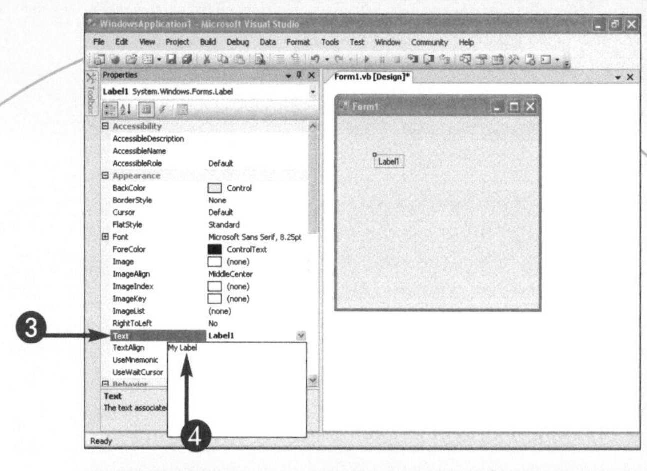

Your control is changed on the form according to how you set the property.

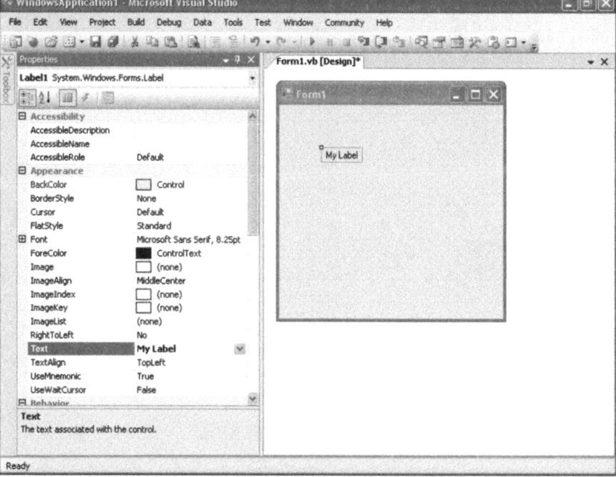

Extra

The following are the six properties that you will modify the most often.

PROPERTY	DESCRIPTION	POSSIBLE VALUES
`Name`	Uniquely identifies the control among other controls in your application	The name should reflect the nature of the control. For `FName` may be a good name for a example, `TextBox` control used to hold a person's first name.
`Text`	The text that appears on a control	This is used to input data. The `Text` property for a `Label` and other controls should have text that relates to the form such as `First Name` for a `Label` control used to describe a `TextBox` used to input a person's first name.
`Font`	Sets the font of text that appears in the control	Times New Roman is a commonly used font for Visual Basic .NET applications.
`ForeColor`	Sets the color of text appearing in the control	Black is a commonly used color. Other colors are used to call attention to the text.
`TabIndex`	Sets the order in which controls receive focus when the Tab key is pressed	The order should reflect the most convenient order for the user to enter data into the form.
`Location`	Specifies the coordinates of the upper-left corner	Values are set by dragging the control to the location usually using the mouse.

Resize a Control

You can adjust the size of a control on a form to fit your design by using the size handles that appear when you select the control. There are typically eight size handles around a control. One size handle is in each corner of a control, and another is in each side of the control.

The right- and left-side size handles move the corresponding size out and in to make the control wider or narrower. The top- and bottom-side size handles move the corresponding side up and down, making the control taller or shorter.

The corner size handles resize the control in any direction. This means that as a corner size handle is dragged on an angle, the sides of the control attached to that handle move up and out or down and in, depending on the direction that the size handle is dragged. The corner size handles are also used to drag one side up and down or out and in without affecting the other side.

Visual Basic .NET changes the size `Height` and `Width` properties of the control to reflect the new size as you resize the control.

Professional developers usually keep the size of the same type of control the same throughout an application. For example, all `Button` controls will be adjusted to the size of the `Button` control that has the longest button text, or the text that appears on the button.

Resize a Control

1. Drag and drop a control from the Toolbox on to your form.

   Size handles appear around the control.

2. Move the cursor over the size handle in the upper-left corner of the control.

   The cursor changes to a double-headed arrow drawn on an angle.

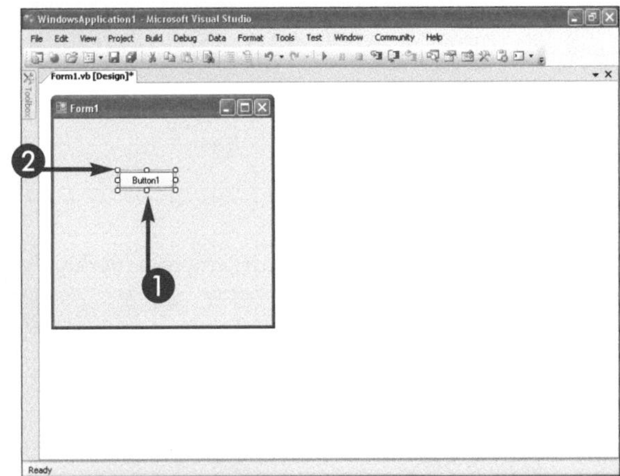

3. Hold down the left mouse button and drag the cursor towards the upper-right corner of the screen.

   The control increases in size.

Note: Moving the cursor inward decreases the size.

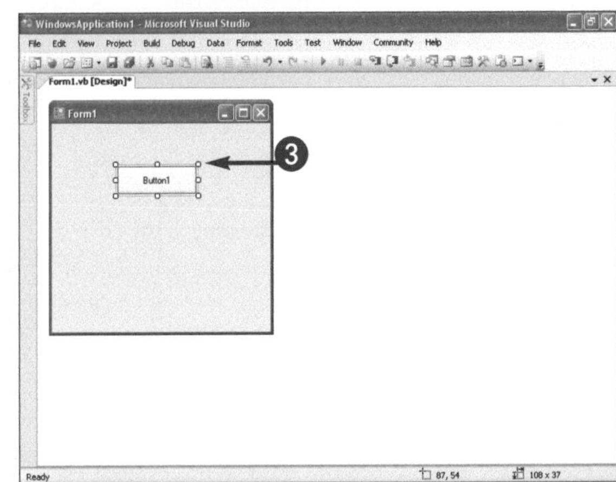

Create a Menu

You can add a menu to your form by using the `MenuStrip` control from the Toolbox. The `MenuStrip` control enables you to create a menu bar for your application and submenus that appear when a menu bar item is selected. Either the menu bar item or a submenu item can be linked to forms and other parts of your application. This means that the corresponding form is displayed when the menu item is selected.

The `MenuStrip` control first creates a menu bar item and automatically displays the first item on the submenu with the default text "Type Here." When you select the down arrow that appears when you move the cursor over the submenu item, you are given the option of creating another `MenuItem`, a `ComboBox` control, a separator, or a `Textbox` control. `MenuItem` is used to insert another item on the submenu. `ComboBox` inserts a `ComboBox` control as the menu item, which displays a list of items to select. The separator draws a line between the previous menu item and the next menu item. `Textbox` inserts a `Textbox` control as the menu item, enabling text to be entered into the menu item.

You can double-click a menu item to display the subroutine that is called when the menu item is selected; see the section "Write Code for an Event." This is where you insert the code that you want Visual Basic .NET to run when the menu item is selected by someone who uses your application.

Menus are key to making your application intuitive to use; therefore, organize your menus with an eye toward how the person is going to use your application. Find commonality among menu items and then group similar items under the same top-level menu item. For example, most Windows applications group file-related options under the top-level File menu item.

Create a Menu

1. Click Menus & Toolbars in the Toolbox.

   The selection of menus and toolbars is displayed.

2. Drag and drop a `MenuStrip` control from the Toolbox on to your form.

   The menu item Type Here is displayed on the menu bar.

3. Click the menu item and type the name that you want to use for the item.

4. Click the Type Here submenu item and type its name.

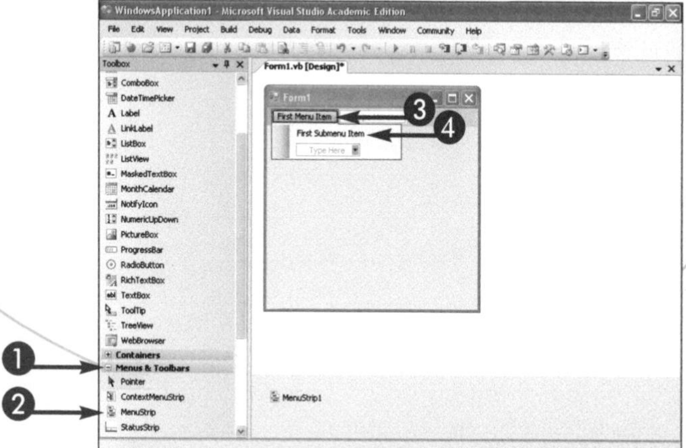

5. Click the down arrow for the next Type Here submenu item.

   A drop-down list is displayed.

6. Click Separator.

   A line appears below the first submenu item.

7. Repeat steps 3 to 6 for each additional menu and submenu item.

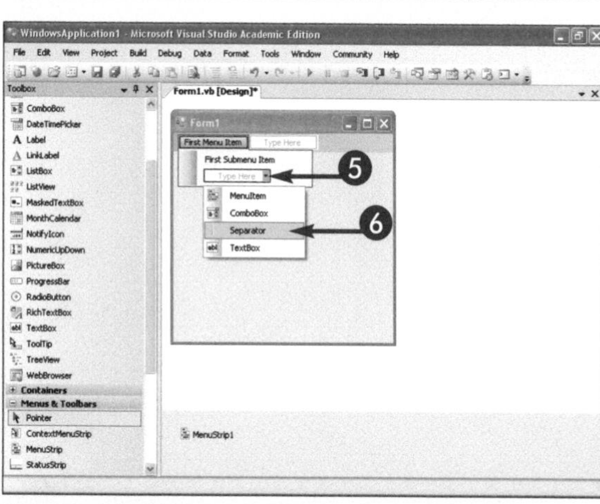

Create a Dialog Box

A dialog box is a pop-up window used to display information and receive information from the person who uses your application. Typically, a dialog box has at least two button controls. One button is labeled "OK," and the other is labeled "Cancel." The OK button is used to process information entered into the dialog box and closes the dialog box. The Cancel button is used to close the dialog box without processing information that was entered into the dialog box.

When you add a dialog box to your application, the dialog box appears on its own tab and displays the OK button and the Cancel button. You can add any control to the dialog box by dragging and dropping the control from the Toolbox on to the dialog box; see the section "Add a Control to a Form."

A dialog box is opened by calling the `ShowDialog()` function from your program. Many times, you have a button on your form that the user clicks to display a dialog box. For example, you could have a button labeled "Price" on your form. When the user clicks the Price button, code that you place in the button's click event calls the `ShowDialog()` function, causing the dialog box to appear on the screen. Clicking either the OK button or the Cancel button closes the dialog box and returns the user to the form.

You can have your code execute when someone selects the OK button or the Cancel button by placing code in the `Click` event of the OK button or the Cancel button.

Create a Dialog Box

1. Drag and drop a `Button` control from the Toolbox on to your form.
2. Click Project ➔ Add New Item.

   The Add New Item dialog box displays items that can be added to your project.
3. Click Dialog.
4. Click Add.

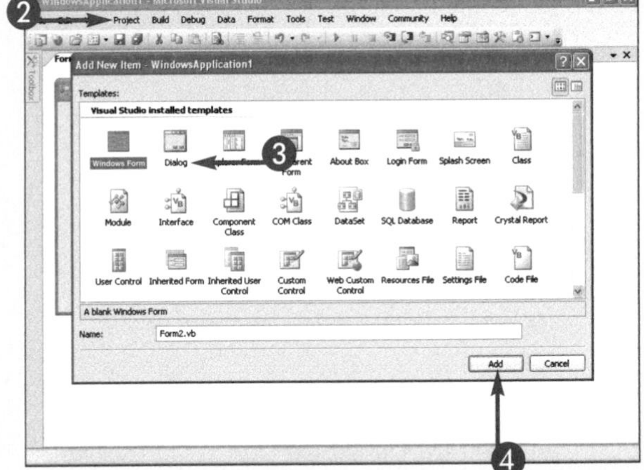

A blank dialog box appears, showing an OK button and a Cancel button.

5. Click the Form1.vb [Design] tab.

   `Form1` is displayed.

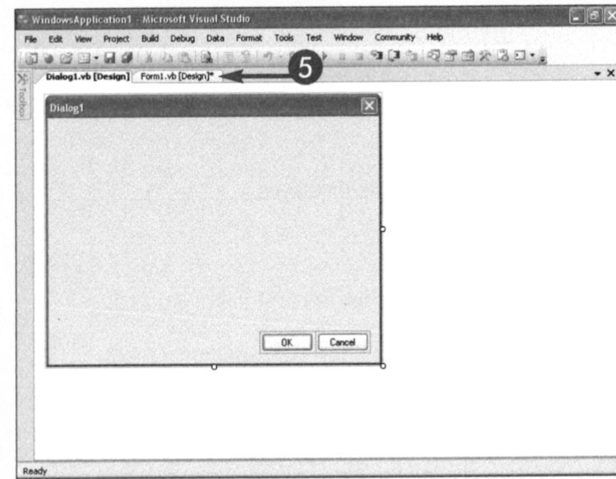

6 Double-click Button1.

The `Button1_Click` subroutine appears.

7 Call the `Dialog1.ShowDialog()` function.

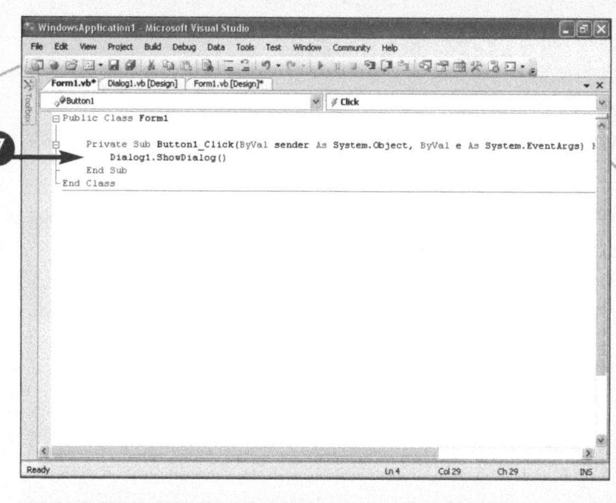

8 Press F5.

The application starts running, and Form1 appears on the screen.

9 Click Button1.

The dialog box appears.

10 Click OK or Cancel to close the dialog box.

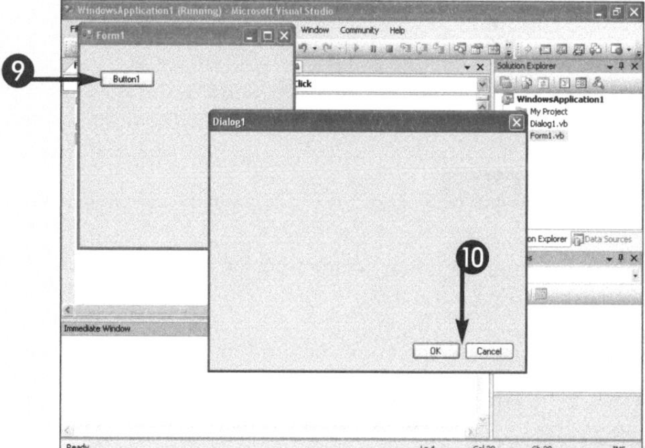

Extra

A dialog box can be used as an extra page on your form. Let's say that your form is an application for students to apply for a dorm room. The form has controls to input the student name, address, telephone, and other information that you expect to enter on a dorm room application. One of these controls is a group of two radio buttons — a single room or double room. If the student selects a double room, a dialog box can be displayed in which the student can enter information about his or her living style (that is, noisy, quiet, and so on). However, this dialog box will not be displayed if the student selects a single room because it is not relevant. You can drag any control from the Toolbox and drop it on to the dialog box, the same way as you do to create a form.

Set the Tab Key Order

The Tab key offers an alternative to using the mouse to select controls on a form. Each time that you press the Tab key, the focus moves from the current input control to the next input control in the tab index. An *input control* is a text box, button, or other control that enables a user to enter information into an application.

Focus is a term to describe when the cursor appears in the control or the control is highlighted. Pressing the Enter key causes the control that has the focus to be selected — just as if the user clicked the left mouse button when the cursor was over the control.

The tab index determines the order in which an input control receives focus when the Tab key is pressed. Each input control is automatically assigned a tab index value when the input control is placed on the form. The first input control is assigned a tab index value of 0. The second input control is assigned the tab index value of 1 and so on.

The order in which input controls are placed on a form does not always correspond to the best workflow for entering information into the form because you may reposition input controls on the form. You can change the order in which input controls receive focus by changing the `TabIndex` property of the input controls; see "Set the Properties of a Control."

You can have Visual Basic .NET skip over giving focus to an input control by changing the `TabStop` property of the input control from `True` to `False`. An input control's `TabStop` property is usually set to `True` by default.

Set the Tab Key Order

1. Drag and drop a `Button` control from the Toolbox on to your form.
2. Drag and drop two `Textbox` controls from the Toolbox on to your form.
3. Press F5.

   The application starts running, and Form1 appears on the screen. Button1 has focus.
4. Press the Tab key.

   The focus moves from Button1 to the first text box.
5. Click the close button of the form.

   Your application stops running.
6. Place the cursor in the first textbox and right-click.

   A pop-up menu appears.
7. Click Properties.

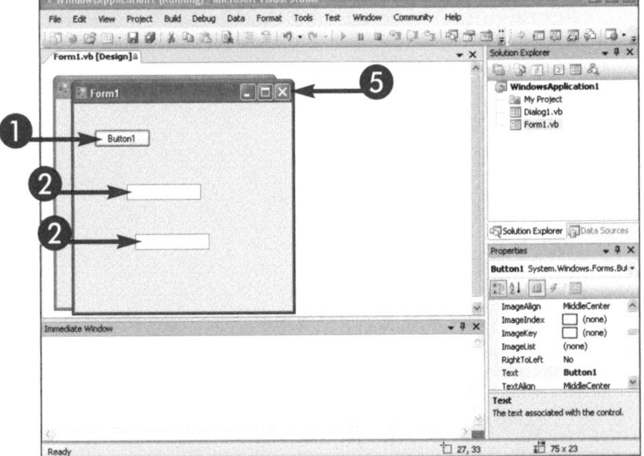

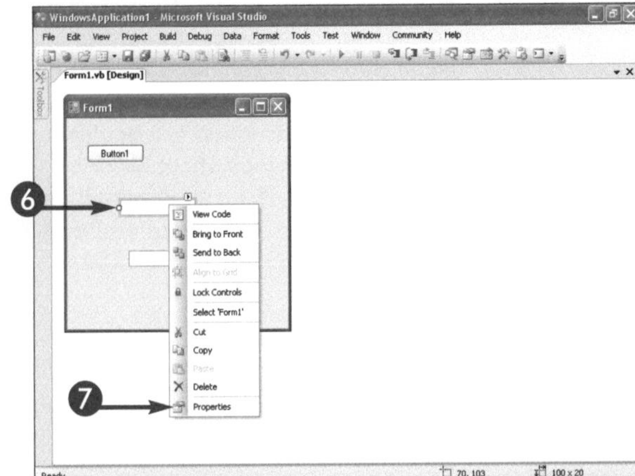

The Properties window appears.

8. Change the `TabIndex` property to **0**.

9. Change the `TabIndex` property for the second textbox to **1**.

10. Change the `TabIndex` property for the button to **3**.

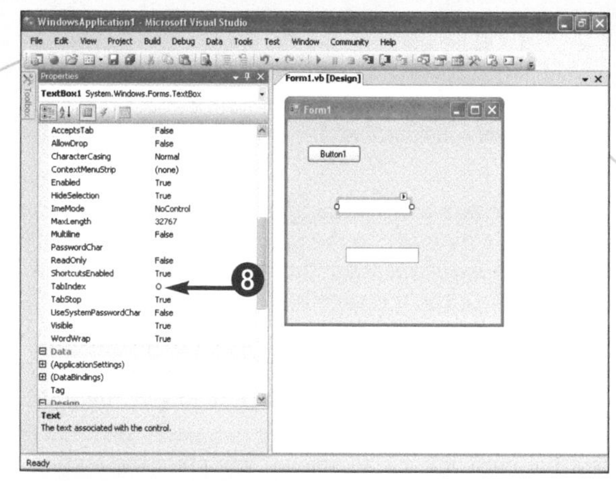

11. Press F5.

    The application runs, and Form1 appears on the screen with the focus given to the first textbox.

12. Press the Tab key.

    The focus moves from the first text box to the second text box.

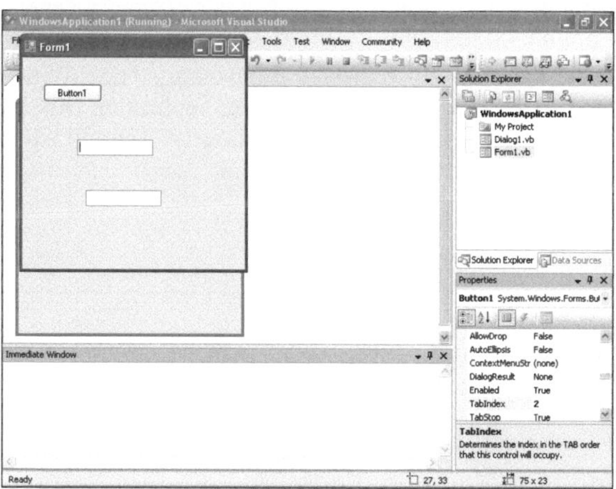

Extra

The tab order might seem trivial, but developers who build professional applications find the tab order critical to the success of their applications because this determines whether an application is easy to use for the person who has to enter data. Let's say that there is a form that has a `TextBox` for the first name, another for the last name, and still another for the street address, as well as other controls for city, state, and zip code. The tab order for the form is first name, street address, and then last name. When you press the Tab key after entering the first name, the cursor jumps to the street address `TextBox`. That is unexpected. The cursor should have moved to the last name `TextBox`. The user of the application cannot change the tab order; therefore, the developer must make sure that the tab order follows the logical sequence that a person would use to enter data into the form, or the application will be awkward to use.

Create a Message Box

A *message box* is a special type of dialog box that is used to display a message to the person who uses your application. It contains the message that you create and an OK button, which is used close the message box.

Visual Basic .NET already knows how to create the message box. All you need to do is tell Visual Basic .NET the message that you want displayed in the message box and when to display the message box.

You display a message box by writing `MessageBox.Show()` when you want the message box to appear. You place the text of the message within the parentheses of the `MessageBox.Show()` function within double quotations.

Let's say that you want to display the message "Login Successful" in a message box to tell the user of your application that he or she has successfully logged in to your application. Here is what you need to write in your code: `MessageBox.Show("Login Successful")`.

Extra

The button that the user selects is returned to your program by the `MessageBox .Show()` function. Let's say that the user tries to exit your application. You can display a message box with Yes and No buttons, asking the user to confirm the exit. Your program then exits only if the user selects Yes.

Here is what you need to write:

```
If (MessageBox.Show("Are you sure
you want to exit?", "Confirm Exit",
MessageBoxButtons.YesNo) =
DialogResult.Yes) Then
            Application.Exit()
End If
```

Create a Message Box

1. Drag and drop a `Button` control from the Toolbox on to your form.
2. Double-click the button on the form.

   The button click subroutine appears.
3. Write `MessageBox.Show("XXX")` in the subroutine, replacing `XXX` with the message that you want displayed in the message box.

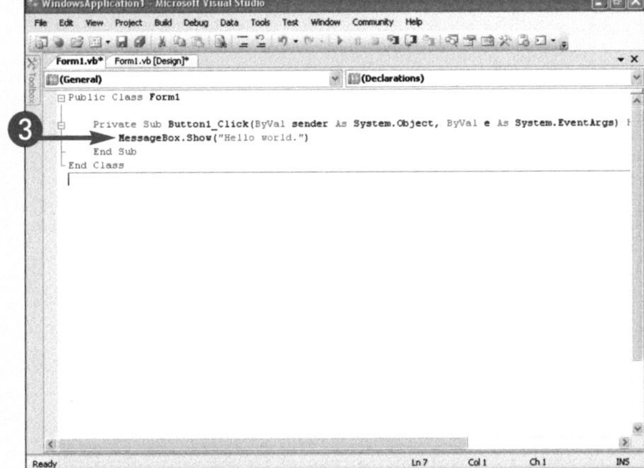

4. Press F5.

   The application starts running, and Form1 appears on the screen.
5. Click the button.

   The message box appears on the screen.

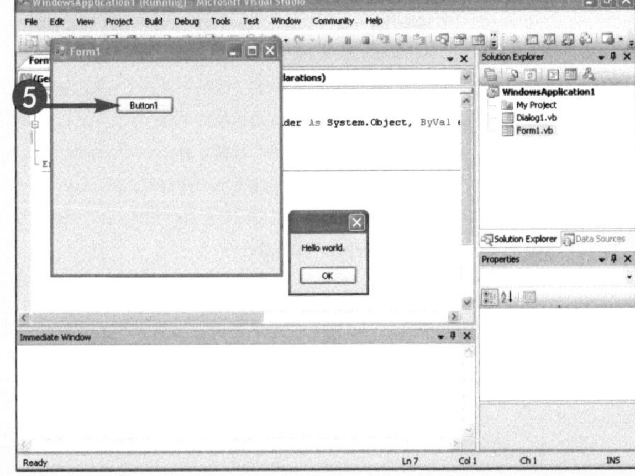

Write Code for an Event

A Visual Basic .NET application is an event-driven application. An *event* is something that happens when the application runs, such as the clicking of a button. There are thousands of events that can occur. You can write code to respond to an event that is important to your application and ignore other events because Visual Basic .NET has a default response for every event.

For example, you can write code that executes when the user clicks a button because that event is important to your application. You do not have to write code that executes when a form is loaded unless you want something special to happen when this event occurs.

Each form in your application has a class that contains subroutines for events related to the form and to controls placed on the form. You can see the class and subroutines by double-clicking the form or a control on the form. By default, Visual Basic .NET displays the most frequently used subroutine, such as the `Click` subroutine for a `Button` control.

The left drop-down box at the top of the window contains a list of objects on the form and the name of the form. The right drop-down box contains a list of events associated with the object in the left box. Select an event from the list, and Visual Basic .NET then displays the corresponding subroutine.

You place code that you want executed in response to an event in the event's subroutine.

When you double-click a control, a new event-handler function is created. You can avoid creating a new event-handler function by clicking View ➔ Code. The code page is then displayed without creating a new function. You use this method to modify code.

Write Code for an Event

1. Double-click the form.

   The `Form` class is displayed, showing the `Form1_Load` subroutine.

2. Click the top-right down arrow, which displays the word `Load`.

   A list of form events is displayed.

3. Click `Load` for this example.

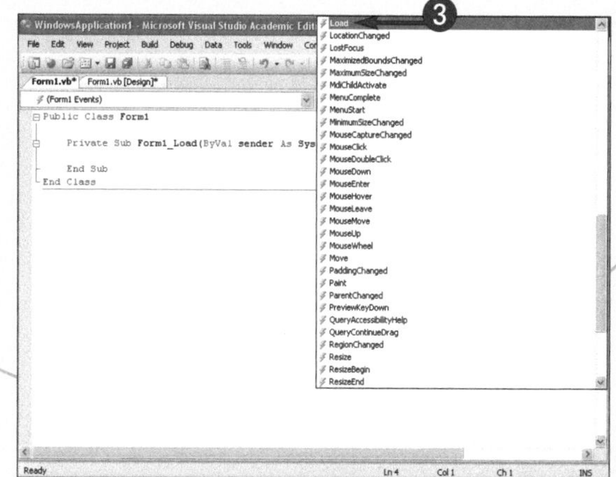

4. Write `MessageBox.Show("XXX")` in the subroutine, replacing XXX with the message that you want displayed in the message box.

5. Press F5.

   Form1 is loaded but does not appear until the message box is displayed and closed.

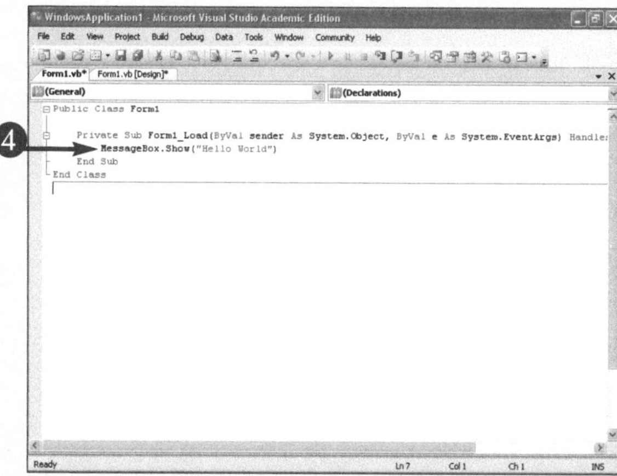

Add a TextBox Control to a Form

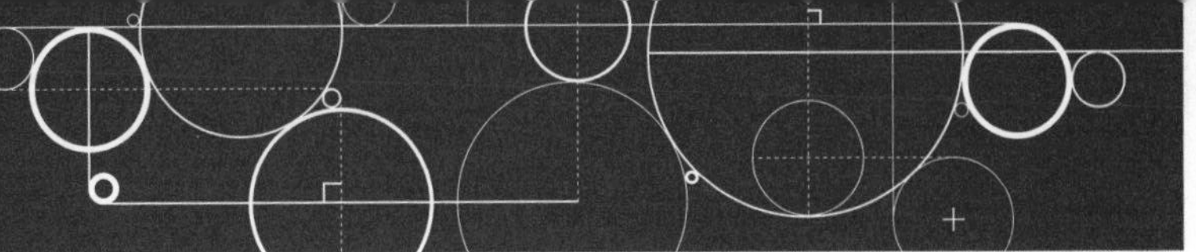

A TextBox control enables a user to enter text into the form of your application. Text can include letters, numbers, and other characters found on the keyboard. You should use a TextBox control any time that your application requires information that cannot be selected from other controls such as ListBox, RadioButton, ComboBox, and other similar controls used to display valid information on the screen.

When you add a TextBox control to your form by dragging and dropping one from the Toolbox, size handles appear on each end of the TextBox control. These are used to stretch the length of the TextBox. You can also reposition the TextBox by moving the cursor over the TextBox, holding down the left mouse button, and dragging the TextBox into position.

By default, the TextBox control accepts one line of text from the user. However, you can have the user enter multiple lines into the TextBox control by selecting the right arrow located near the upper-right corner of the text box. The Tasks pop-up menu appears. Select the Multiline check box to convert from a single line TextBox to a multiline TextBox. After making this selection, the eight size handles appear around the TextBox control. You use these to resize the TextBox control to display multiple lines of text.

Add a TextBox Control to a Form

1. Add a button to a form.

Note: See Chapter 4 for information about adding buttons.

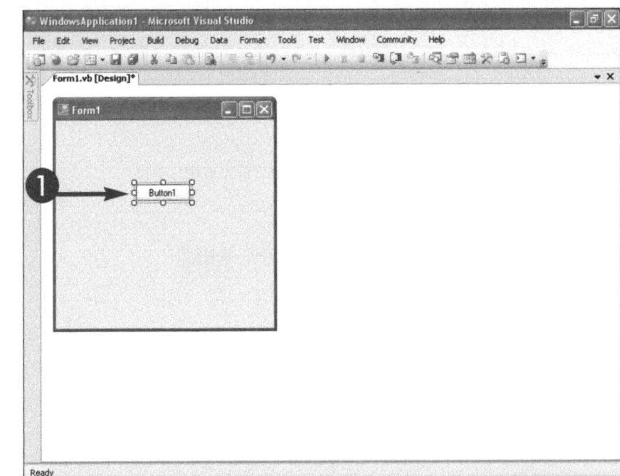

2. Add a TextBox control by dragging and dropping a TextBox control from the Toolbox on to the form.
3. Double-click the button.

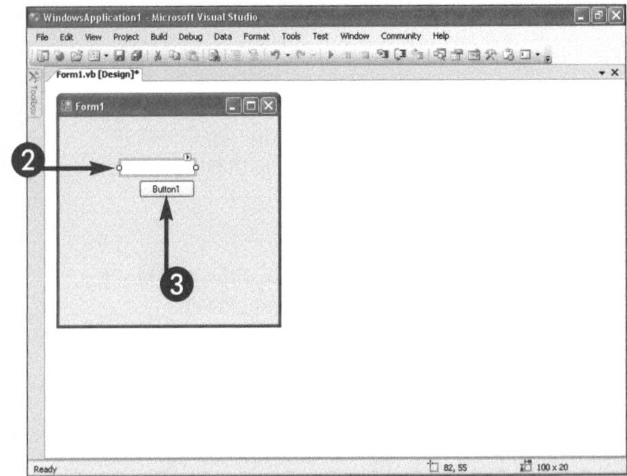

The code that executes when the button is clicked appears.

4 Call the `MessageBox()` function, using the `TextBox1.Text` property as the message for the `MessageBox()`.

5 Press Ctrl+S to save the code.

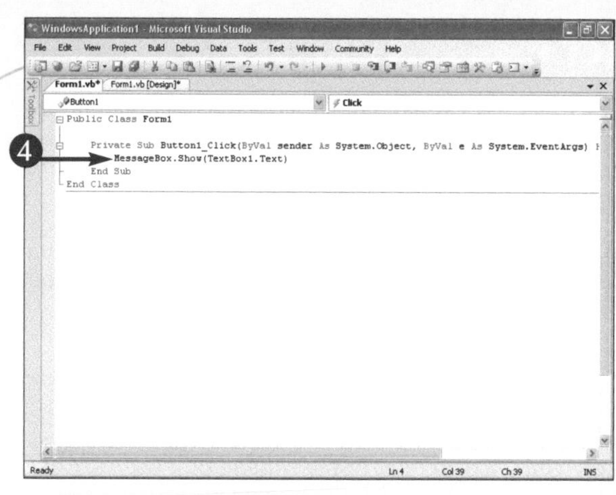

6 Press F5 to run the program.

7 Type text into the `TextBox` control.

8 Click the button.

The text in the `TextBox` is displayed in the `MessageBox()`.

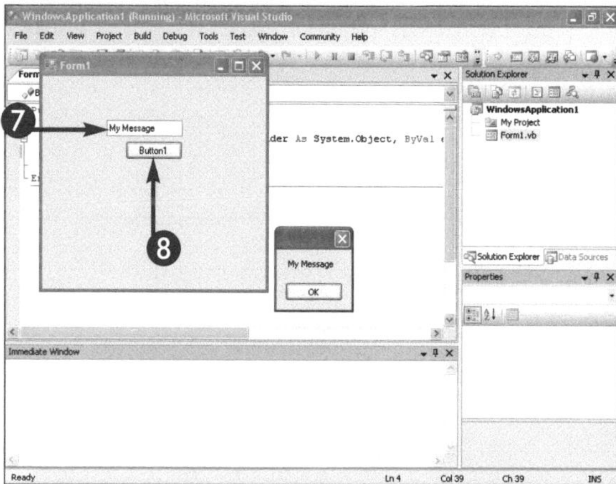

Extra

Each `TextBox` control should have a corresponding `Label` control that describes the kind of information that you want the user to enter into the `TextBox` control; see the section "Add a Label Control to a Form." The `Label` control should appear to the left or at the top of the `TextBox` control, depending on the design of your form. For example, a `Label` control to the left of a `TextBox` control may say, `"Customer First Name: "`, suggesting that the user enter his or her first name into the `TextBox` control.

You should rename the `TextBox` control using a name that reflects the content of the `TextBox`, such as `CustomerFirstName`, which you would use if the `TextBox` will contain the first name of a customer. This makes the `TextBox` control more meaningful to you when you refer to it in your code. You can change the name by selecting the `TextBox` control, right-clicking, and clicking Properties from the pop-up menu. Type the new name in the (Name) property.

Access a TextBox Control

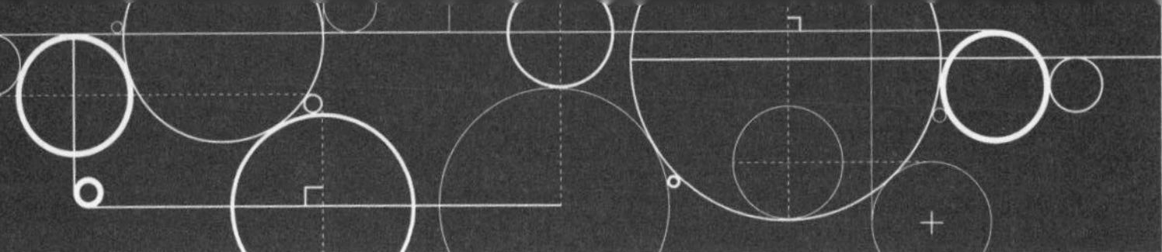

A TextBox control is accessed by using the TextBox control's Text property, TextBox1.Text. The name of the control appears on the left side of the period, and the name of the property is on the right side of the period.

There are two ways to use the Text property of a TextBox: to access the content of the TextBox and to place text in the TextBox. Use TextBox1.Text in your application wherever you want to refer to the content of a text box. Be sure to replace TextBox1 with the name of the TextBox control. Visual Basic .NET replaces TextBox1.Text with text that appears in the TextBox control when your application executes.

Sometimes you may want your application to enter text into a TextBox control. Suppose that your application retrieves a customer's telephone number from a database. The telephone number can be displayed in a TextBox where the user can then update this information.

You place text in a TextBox by assigning the text to TextBox1.Text, just as you assign text to a String variable; see Chapter 5 for more information. For example, TextBox1.Text = "201-555-1212" causes the telephone number 201-555-1212 to appear in the TextBox1 text box. You can place text into a TextBox either when you create the TextBox or anytime while your program is running.

Access a TextBox Control

1. Add a button to a form.

Note: See Chapter 4 for information about adding buttons.

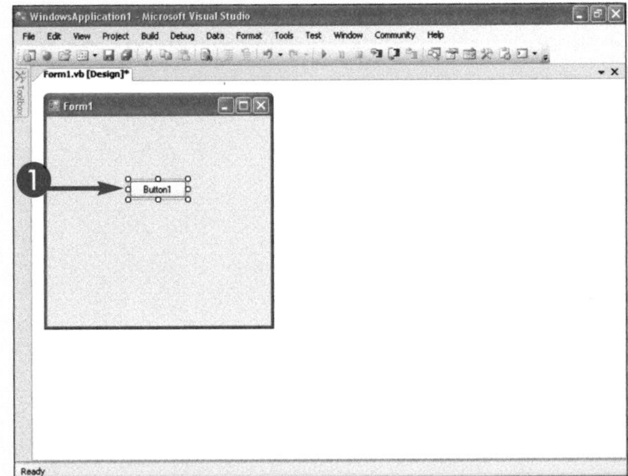

2. Add a TextBox by dragging and dropping a TextBox control from the Toolbox on to the form.
3. Double-click the button.

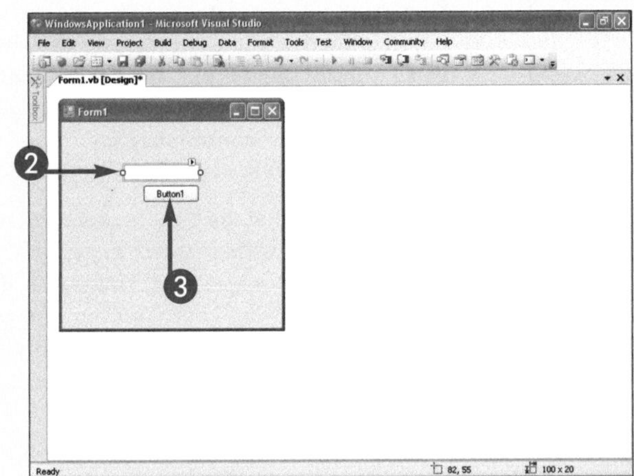

The code that executes when the button is clicked appears.

4. Assign text to `TextBox1.Text`, such as `"201-555-1212"` in this example.

5. Call the `MessageBox()` function, using the `TextBox1.Text` property as the message for the `MessageBox()`.

6. Press Ctrl+S to save the code.

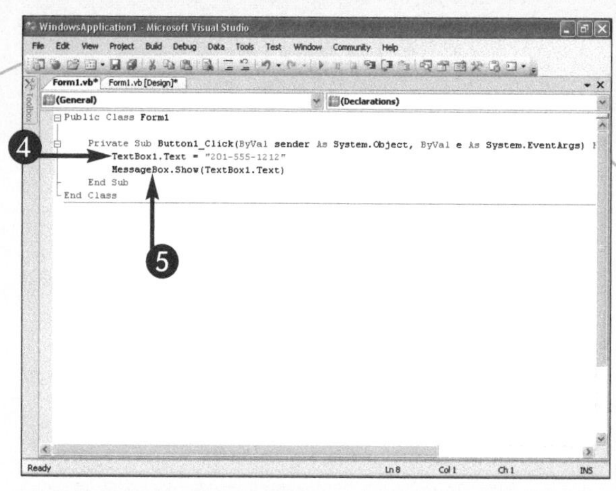

7. Press F5 to run the program.

8. Click the button.

The text in the `TextBox` is displayed in the `MessageBox()`.

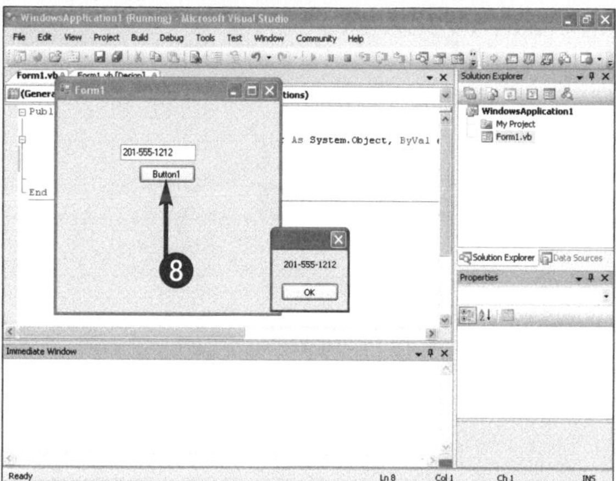

Extra

Sometimes you will place information into a `TextBox` control that you do not want the user to change, such as a customer account number. However, the user can edit the contents of a `TextBox` control by default. You can prevent the user from changing the contents of a `TextBox` control by changing the `ReadOnly` property of the `TextBox` control. The `ReadOnly` property tells Visual Basic .NET whether to permit changes to the contents of the `TextBox`. The `ReadOnly` property is set to `False` by default, meaning that the contents can be changed. You can change the `ReadOnly` property to `True` and thereby prevent the contents from being changed. You set the `ReadOnly` property by writing `TextBox1.ReadOnly = True`. The text can be edited by the user again only if you change the `ReadOnly` property back to `False`, such as `TextBox1.ReadOnly = False`.

Set Defaults for a TextBox Control

The default values of the TextBox control's properties may or may not be appropriate for your application, so you can change them. You can change the default values by using the Properties list. You highlight the property and then enter the new value for the property.

Some properties that are commonly changed are MaxLength, Multiline, Font, ForeColor, BackColor, TextAlign, and Cursor. The MaxLength property sets the maximum number of characters that can be entered into the TextBox. The Multiline property determines if one or multiple lines can be entered into the TextBox. Set the Multiline property to False for a single line or True for multiple lines. If you are allowing multiple lines, you may also want to enable either horizontal or vertical scrollbars. The Font property designates a font for text entered into the TextBox; you can choose from a listing of available fonts. ForeColor and BackColor set the foreground and background color for the TextBox, respectively; you can choose a color from a palette of available colors. The TextAlign property aligns text within the TextBox; options are Left, Center, or Right. The Cursor property sets the cursor that appears when the TextBox is selected. The IBeam is the default cursor; however, you can choose from a list of available cursors by selecting the Cursor property.

Set Defaults for a TextBox Control

1. Add a TextBox by dragging and dropping a TextBox control from the Toolbox on to the form.
2. Display the Properties list for the TextBox by right-clicking the TextBox and clicking Properties.
3. Click Font.

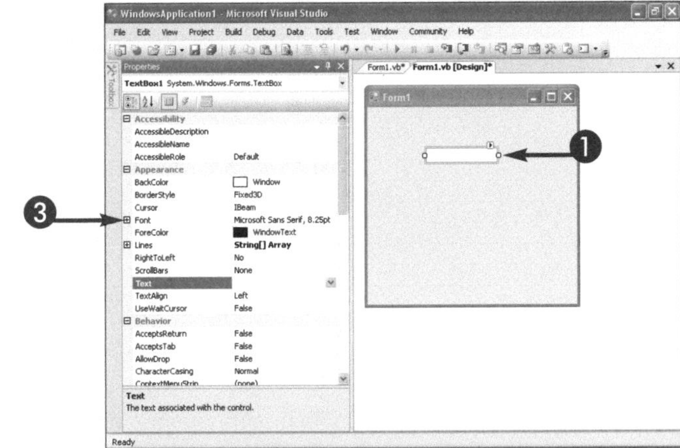

The Font dialog box appears.

4. Choose a font from the list of available fonts.
5. Click OK.

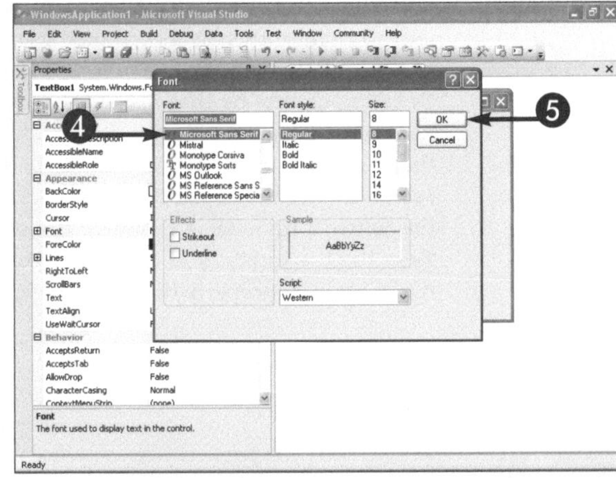

6. Click ForeColor.

   A drop-down palette appears.

7. Choose a foreground color from the palette.

8. Click MaxLength.

9. Change the maximum length, such as to 5.

10. Press Ctrl+S to save the code.

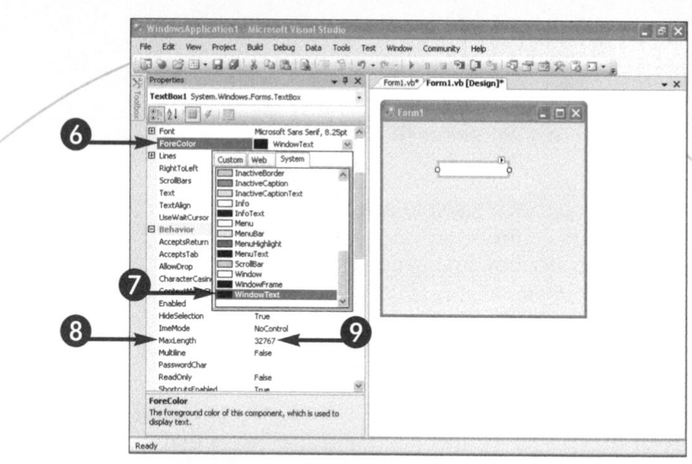

11. Press F5 to run the program.

12. Enter text into the `TextBox`.

Note: The number of characters that you can enter is limited to the value of the `MaxLength` property.

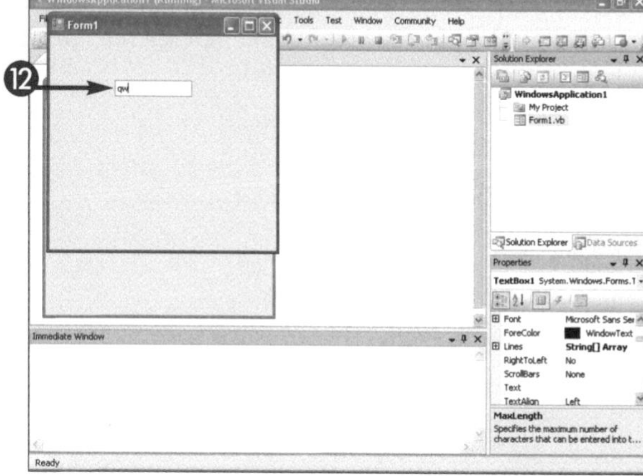

Extra

Typically, users of your application will want to tab to each control on your form, including the `TextBox` control. Each control that can be accessed by using the Tab key is referred to as a *tab stop*. The order in which the control is selected is called the *tab index*. You can enable a `TextBox` control to be selected with the Tab key by setting the `TextBox` control's `TabStop` property to `True`. You set the order in which the `TextBox` control is selected by setting the `TextBox` control's `TabIndex` property. The `TabIndex` property is assigned an integer value that represents the order in which the `TextBox` control is selected by using the Tab key. The value must be greater than or equal to 0. If you have four controls with `TabIndex` values of `0`, `8`, `20`, `40`, they will be selected in that order. If two or more controls have the same `TabIndex`, they will be selected according to where they are located on the screen, starting from the upper-left corner. Instead of setting this property for each control, you can click View ➔ Tab Order and then click the controls in the order that you want them selected.

Add a Label Control to a Form

A Label control is used to display text on a form that identifies controls, provides instructions for using your application, and generally communicates to the user. For example, a label is typically used to identify a TextBox control such as with the text "Customer First Name:," which is placed to the left of the TextBox control on the form.

After you add a Label control to your form, you can adjust the size of the control by dragging the resize boxes that appear around the outside of the Label control. You can reposition the Label control by moving the cursor over it, holding down the left mouse button, and moving the Label control into its new position on the form.

You can modify the appearance of the Label control by changing the Label control's properties in the Properties window. You can use the Text property to change the text of the Label control and the ForeColor and BackColor properties to change the foreground and background colors of the Label control, respectively. The Font property is used to change the font of the Label control's text.

You need to be very careful when changing the text of a label. When the label is placed onto the form, it has a height and width. If the new text for the label does not fit in this box, the text is cut off. You can either draw the label to accept the longest expected string, or you can change the height and width of the label in your program to make it big enough to accept the new text. For example, `Label1.Width() = 100` changes the width of the label to 100 pixels.

Add a Label Control to a Form

1. Add a Label control by dragging and dropping a Label control from the Toolbox on to the form.
2. Right-click the Label control and choose Properties from the pop-up menu to display the Properties list.
3. Change the Text property of the Label control to the text that you want for the label, such as My Label in this example.

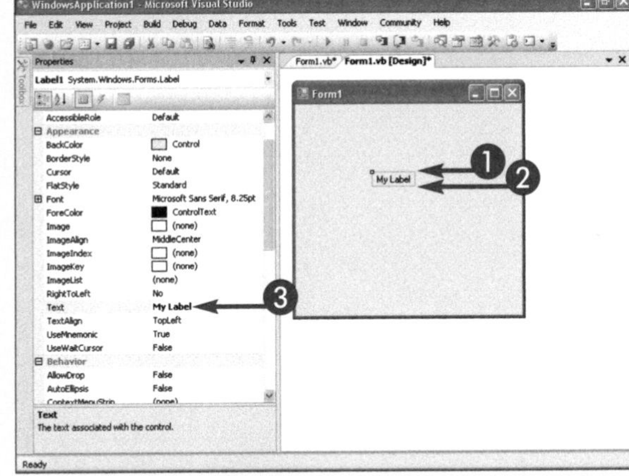

4. Add a button to a form.

Note: See Chapter 4 for information about adding buttons.

5. Double-click the button.

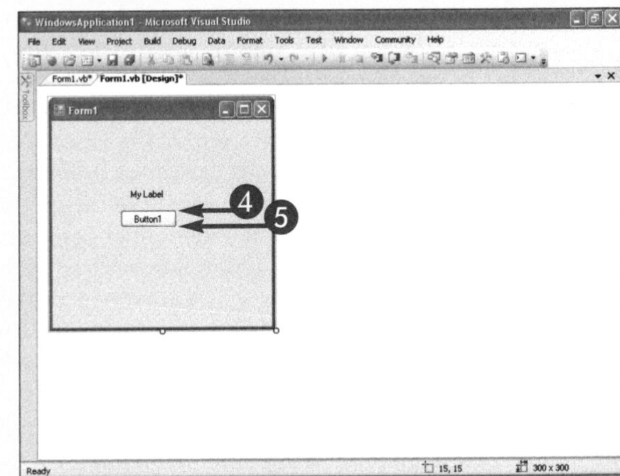

The code that executes when the button is clicked appears.

6. Write new text for the `Label` control using the format `Label1.Text = "XXX"`, where `XXX` is the new message, such as `New Text` in this example.

7. Press Ctrl+S to save the code.

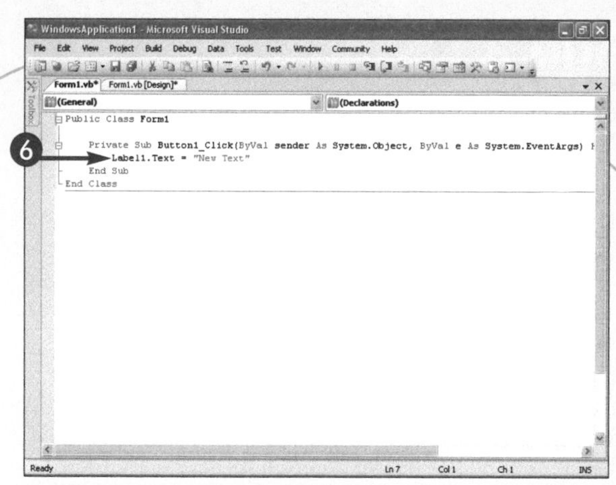

8. Press F5 to run the program.

   The label appears with the new text that you specified.

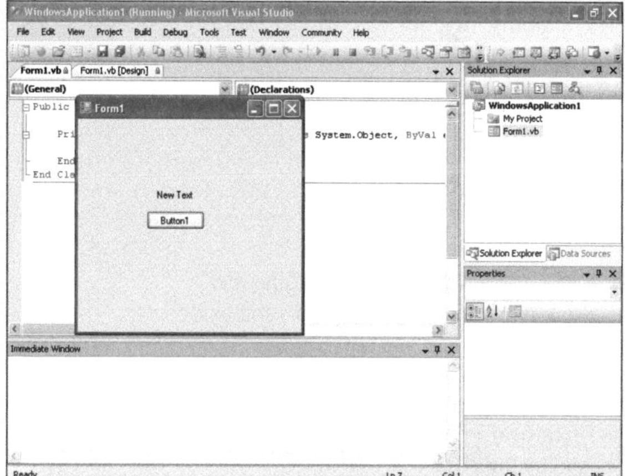

Extra

A good way to reduce the number of `Label` controls on a form is to reuse an existing `Label` control and change the control's text to reflect new information that you want to display on the form. For example, suppose a `Label` control displays instructions for completing the form. Your program validates information on the form, and any errors are displayed on the form in a `Label` control. The same `Label` control that displays instructions can be used to display the error by changing the `Text` property of the label. You can change the text of a `Label` control while your application is running by writing `Label1.Text = "XXX"`; `Label1` is the name of the `Label` control, and `XXX` is the text that you want displayed. Any property can be changed from within your application by writing `Label1.YYY = XXX`, where `YYY` is the name of the property and `XXX` is the new value of the property, as shown on the Properties list of the `Label` control.

Add a ListBox Control

A ListBox control is used to display a list of items that can be selected by the user. The user can select one item or multiple items from the list, depending on how you set the SelectionMode property; see the section "Set Defaults for a ListBox Control."

You add a ListBox control using the Toolbox. After you add the ListBox control, handles appear around the control that can be used to modify the size of the ListBox control. You can make the list as big or small as necessary for your application. You can also reposition the ListBox control on the form, placing it wherever works best.

The width of the ListBox control should be wide enough to fit the longest item on the list. The length of the ListBox control should be sufficient to display a reasonable number of items without taking an inordinate amount of space on the form.

Let's suppose that you are creating an online order form for toy cars. The visitor needs to choose the make, model, and color. You could provide a text box for each choice, but this method is prone with problems. The visitor may misspell an entry, use abbreviations, or otherwise enter a make, model, and color that is unlikely to be found in your inventory. A better way is to use three ListBox controls — one each for make, model, and color. You can fill these controls with the makes, models, and colors that are in your inventory.

Add a ListBox Control

1. Add a Label control by dragging and dropping the control from the Toolbox on to the form.
2. Right-click the Label control and choose Properties from the pop-up menu to display the Properties list.
3. Change the Text property of the Label control to the text that you want for the label, such as My PlayList in this example.

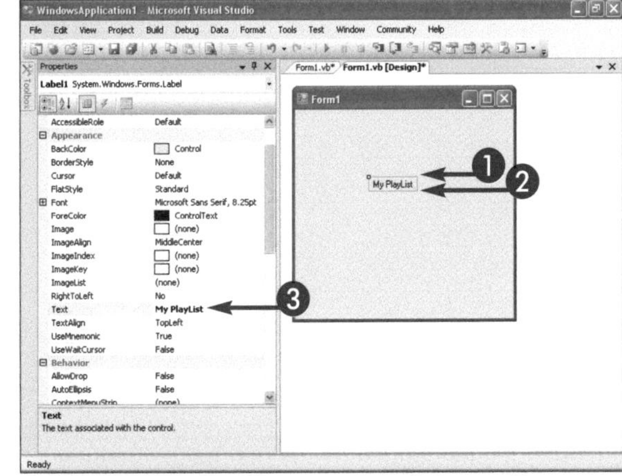

4. Add a ListBox control to a form by dragging and dropping the control from the Toolbox on to the form.

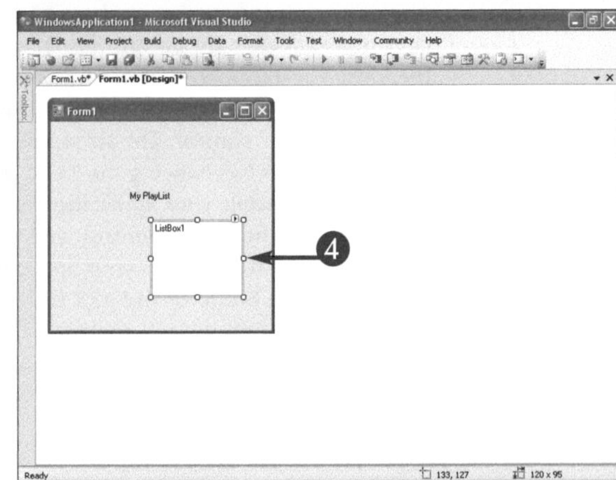

5 Reposition the `ListBox` control beneath the label by moving the cursor over the `ListBox` control, holding down the left mouse button, and dragging the `ListBox` control into position.

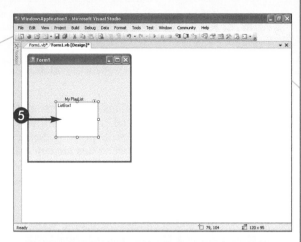

6 Resize the `ListBox` control by moving the cursor over a resize handle, holding down the left mouse button, and dragging the resize handle into the new position.

7 Press Ctrl+S to save the code.

8 Press F5 to run the program.

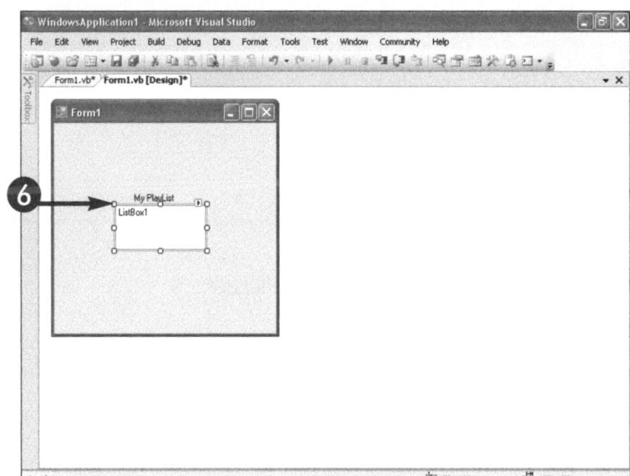

Extra

It is difficult to exactly determine the height and width of text that will be displayed in the `ListBox` control because with some applications, text comes from a database when the application runs. In other words, you do not know the size of the text when you place the `ListBox` control on your form. Fortunately, Visual Basic .NET displays a horizontal scrollbar at the bottom of the `ListBox` control if the text is too long to fit into the control. If you expect that you will need a horizontal scrollbar, you need to set the `HorizontalScrollBar` property to `True`; by default, it is `False`. The scrollbar is then used to scroll across the text. Likewise, Visual Basic .NET displays a vertical scrollbar in case there are more lines of text that can appear in the `ListBox` control. The user can always scroll the `ListBox` control to see items that are not displayed. However, no scrollbars are displayed if all the text cannot be displayed in the `ListBox` control.

Set Defaults for a ListBox Control

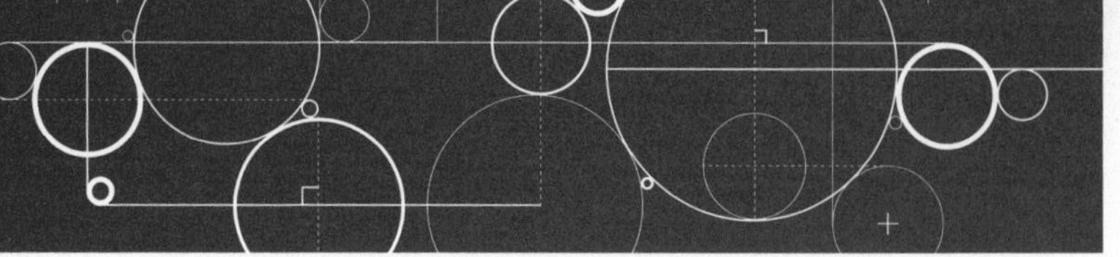

You can change the default settings of a `ListBox` control's properties by using the Properties window. You simply change the value of the property. Some values are chosen from a list, and other values are entered from the keyboard.

The `SelectionMode` property determines how many items the user can select from the `ListBox` control. The `None` option displays the list but does not permit the user to select an item. The `One` option enables the user to select one item from the list. `MultiSimple` enables the user to select one or more items. The `MultiExtended` option enables the user to use the Shift, Ctrl, and arrow keys to select multiple items from the `ListBox` control.

The `MultiColumn` property divides the `ListBox` control into two or more columns. Each column displays separate but related information such as Customer Account Number and Customer Name. The complete row is returned when the user selects an item from a multicolumn `ListBox` control.

The `Sorted` property determines if items are placed in sort order. You set this property to `True` to sort items. You set this property to `False` to display items in data entry order. Sometimes, you will want to display items based on the most selected item rather than in sort order.

The `TabStop` property is set to `True` if the `ListBox` control is to be selected using the Tab key. If this property is set to `True`, then set the `TabIndex` value to the order in which you want the `ListBox` control selected among other controls.

Set Defaults for a ListBox Control

1. Add a `Label` control to your application.

Note: See the section "Add a `Label` Control to a Form" for more information.

2. Change the `Text` property of the `Label` control.

Note: See Chapter 2 for more information.

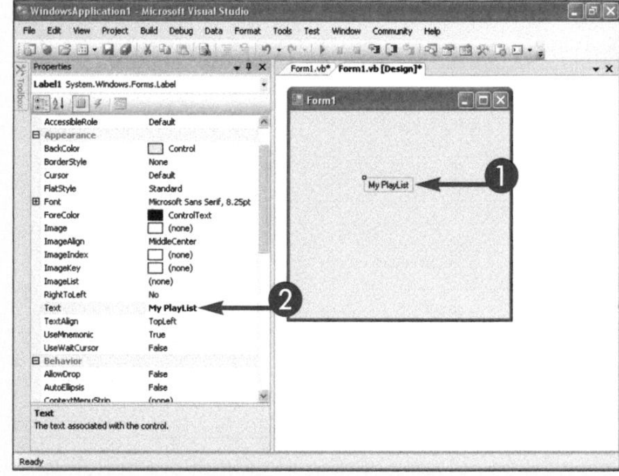

3. Add a `ListBox` control to the form.

Note: See the section "Add a `ListBox` Control."

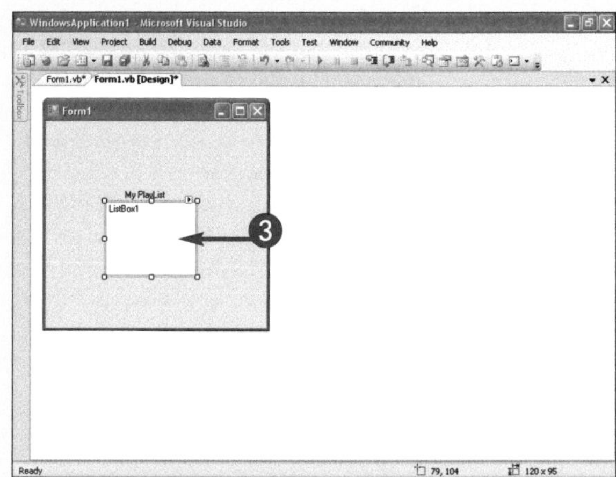

4. Display the Properties window by right-clicking the `ListBox` control and selecting Properties from the pop-up menu.

5. Click the property whose default that you want to set.

6. Change the value of the property.

Note: For example, you can make the `ListBox` control `MultiExtended`.

7. Repeat steps 5 and 6 for other properties whose defaults you want to set.

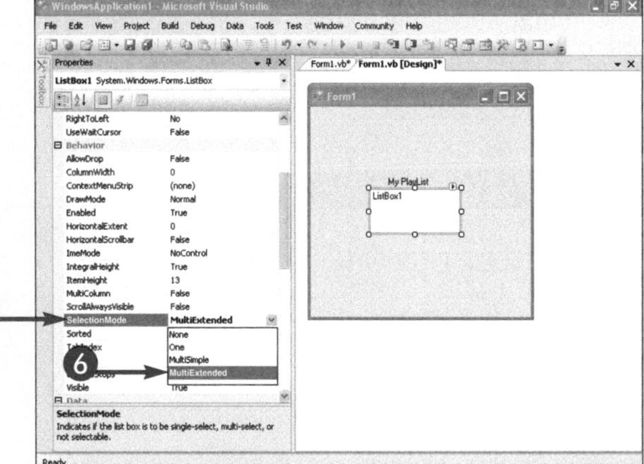

Extra

Sometimes items displayed in a list box need to be placed in a particular format, such as those used for date and time and the decimal places in a number. Instead of formatting items yourself, you can let Visual Basic .NET do it for you by setting the `FormatString` property. Select the `FormatString` property from the Properties list to display the Format String dialog box, in which you can choose from Numeric, Currency, Date and Time, and Scientific formats. Each of these displays a list of common formats to pick from. And if you do not find the form that you need on there, you can click Custom and create your own format. This is helpful if items in a list box have a proprietary format.

Write Items to a ListBox Control

There are two ways to add an item to a `ListBox` control: One way is to use the `Items ListBox` control property, and the other way is by writing `ListBox1.Items.Add("XXX")` in your program. `ListBox1` is the name of the `ListBox` control. `Items` means that you are referencing items associated with the `ListBox` control. The `Add("XXX")` method adds the item `XXX` to the `ListBox` control.

You can place `ListBox1.Items.Add("XXX")` anywhere in your program; however, many developers place this code in the application's `Load` event so that the code runs when the application is loaded. This means that items are added to the `ListBox` control when the application is loaded and before the form is displayed.

You can remove an item from a list box by calling `ListBox1.Items.RemoveAt(X)`, where `X` is the number of the item that you want to remove. The first item is 0, and the second item is 1. Therefore, if you want to remove the fifth item in a `ListBox` control, you would write `ListBox1.Items.RemoveAt(4)` because 4 is the number of the fifth item. You can remove all the items from a list box by calling `ListBox1.Items.Clear()`.

Earlier in this chapter, I mentioned an online order form example in which a visitor used three list boxes to choose the make, model, and color for toy cars. Let's say that you sold your last Ford Mustang from your inventory. You can use `RemoveAt()` to remove the Mustang from the model list to avoid having visitors order a product that is no longer in inventory. Likewise, you can use `Add()` to insert a new product onto the list after it arrives in inventory.

Write Items to a ListBox Control

USING THE ITEMS PROPERTY

1. Display the Properties window for your `ListBox` control.
2. Click `Items`.

   The String Collection Editor dialog box appears.
3. Add items to the `ListBox` control by typing them in the dialog box.
4. Click OK.
5. Press Ctrl+S to save the code.
6. Press F5 to run the program.

   The items that you added appear in the list box.

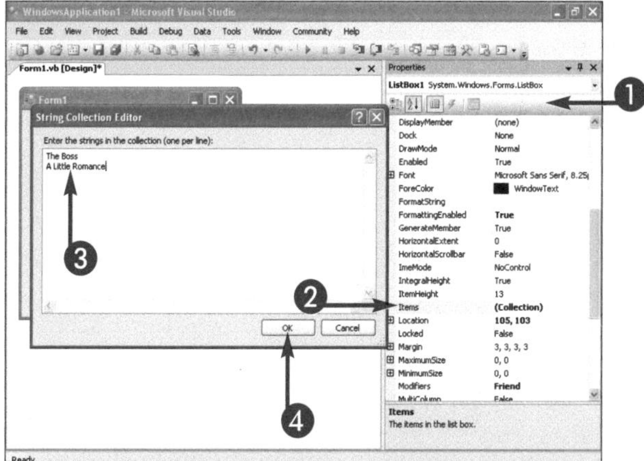

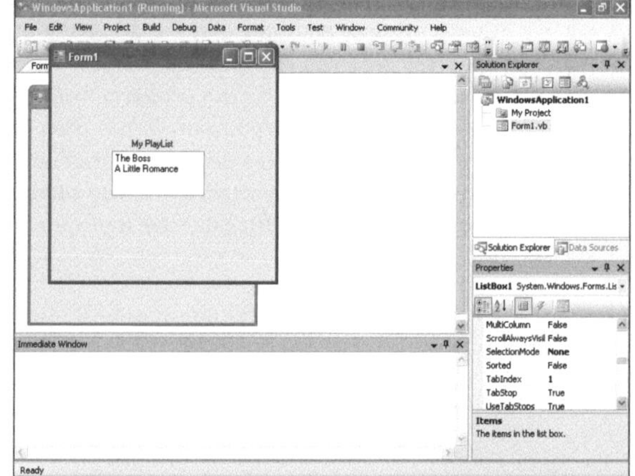

USING LISTBOX1.ITEMS.ADD()

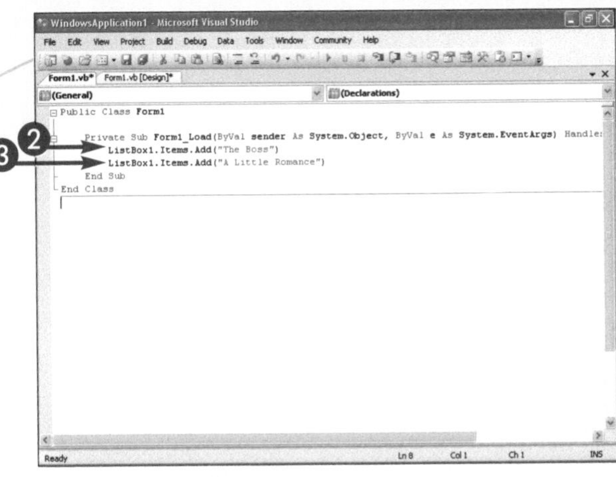

1. Double-click the form.

   The form `Load()` event is displayed.

2. Add `ListBox1.Items.Add("XXX")` to the code, replacing `XXX` with the item that you want to add to the list box.

3. Repeat step 2 for any additional items that you want to add.

4. Press Ctrl+S to save the code.

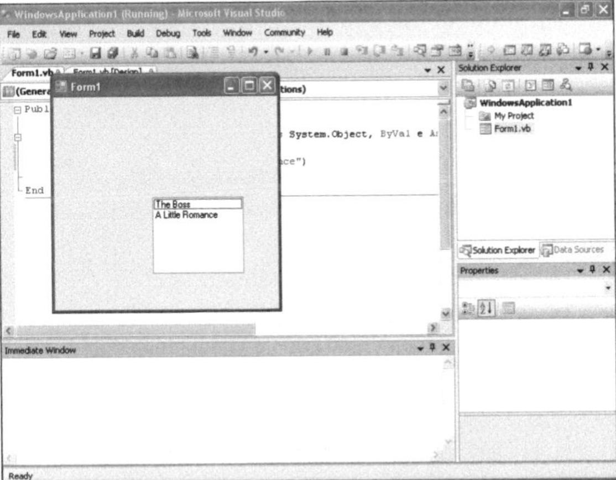

5. Press F5 to run the program.

   The items that you added appear in the list box.

Apply It

As you will learn in Chapter 8, a list of similar information such as colors can be stored in an array. Think of an array as a list in memory. Each item is assigned to an array element that is identified by the array name and a number such as `Colors(0) = "Blue"` and `Colors(1) = "Red"`. Sometimes you will want to copy items from an array to a `ListBox` control to make it easy for a visitor to select an item from the array. Copying is possible by using a `For` loop, which you will learn about in Chapter 7. Here is the code that you would use:

```
Dim counter As Integer
For counter = 0 To 1
    ListBox1.Items.Add(Colors(1))
Next
```

Access an Item Selected from a ListBox Control

There are two ways to access an item selected from a `ListBox` control. One way is to reference the `SelectedIndex` property of the `ListBox` control. The `SelectedIndex` property contains the index of the selected item. The first item on the list is index 0, and the second item is index 1, and so on. The `SelectedIndex` property is –1 if no item was selected from the `ListBox` control.

Let's say there are two items in a `ListBox` control — `Bob` and `Mary`. `Bob` is index 0, and `Mary` is index 1. If `Mary` is selected, the value of the `ListBox1.SelectedIndex` is 1. `ListBox1` is the name of the `ListBox` control, and `SelectedIndex` is the name of the property.

The other way to access the selected item is to reference the `Text` property of the `ListBox` control. The `Text` property contains the text of the selected item. Suppose `Mary` is the selected item. The value of `ListBox1.Text` is `Mary`. If the `ListBox` allows multiple selections, this will return the first selected item. Similarly, the `SelectedIndex` property will return the first selected index.

It is always best to determine if an item was selected from the `ListBox` control before trying to access the item from within your code. You do this by using an `If...Then` statement; see Chapter 6. The `If...Then` statement contains a logical expression that determines if the value of `ListBox1.SelectedIndex` is not equal to –1. This means that an item was selected. The code to access the value is placed in the `If...Then` code block and executes only if an item was selected.

Access an Item Selected from a ListBox Control

1. Begin with a list box with items already in it and a button on the form.

Note: See "Write Items to a `ListBox` Control" and Chapter 4.

2. Double-click the `Button` control to open the `Click` subroutine.

3. Add an `If...Then...Elseif` statement that determines which item is selected, as shown here.

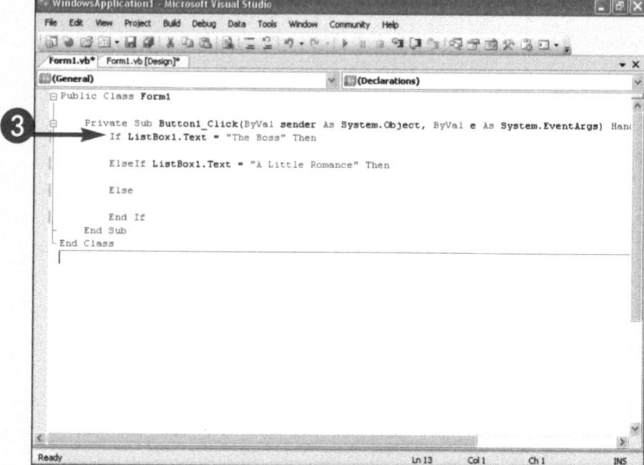

4. Use a `MessageBox("XXX")` function for the first item to display a message, only if the first item is selected, replacing `XXX` with the item name.

5. Use an individual `MessageBox("XXX")` function to display a message for all the other items, only if they are selected.

6. Press Ctrl+S to save the code.

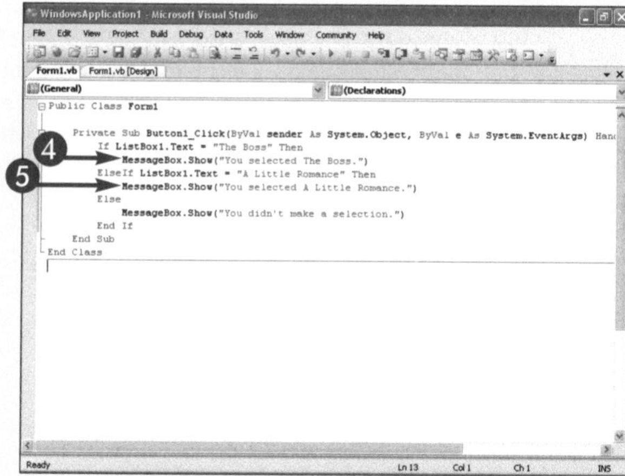

7 Press F5 to run the program.

8 Click an item from the list.

9 Click the button.

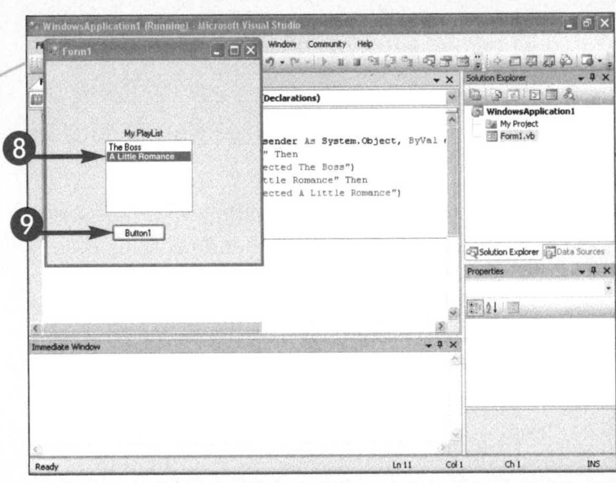

The message box displays which item you selected.

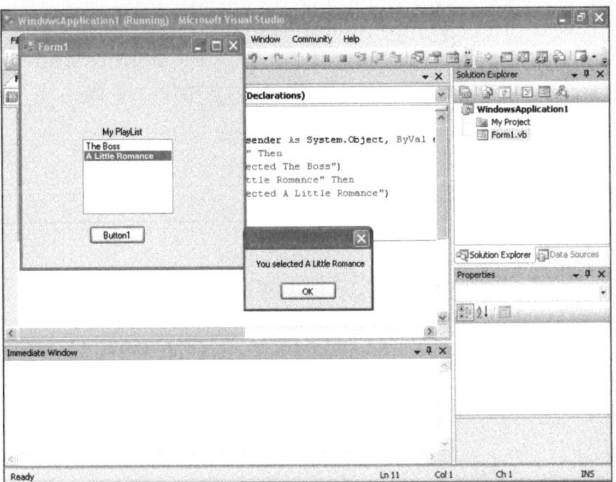

Extra

You can have Visual Basic .NET execute code whenever the visitor changes the item selected in the `ListBox` control by placing the code in the `SelectedIndexChanged()` subroutine. You create this subroutine by double-clicking the `ListBox` control and then inserting your code. This is handy to use when you want to validate the selected item. Let's say that your visitor is entering an address, and you decided to display a list of state abbreviations in a `ListBox` control. When the state is selected, you can execute code that determines if the zip code entered by the visitor corresponds to the state that the visitor picked from the `ListBox` control. If there is a mismatch, you can have code in the `SelectedIndexChanged()` subroutine display a warning in a message box, alerting the visitor to the problem before the form is submitted for processing. This gives the visitor time to correct the problem and reduces processing time to validate this information after the form is processed.

Add a ComboBox Control

A ComboBox control is a combination of a TextBox control and a ListBox control and contains one line of text. Text can be entered directly into the ComboBox control or selected from a ListBox that appears when the ComboBox control is selected. The selected item is automatically placed in the TextBox portion of the ComboBox control.

You add a ComboBox control to a form using the Toolbox. After you drag and drop the ComboBox on to the form, you can use resize handles to modify the size of the ComboBox control. You can reposition the ComboBox control on the form by placing the cursor on the ComboBox control and holding down the left mouse button as you move the control into place.

You use the Combo1.Items.Add("XXX") method to add an item to a ComboBox control. Combo1 is the name of the ComboBox control, Add() is the name of the method, and XXX is the text of the item being added to the ComboBox control list.

You can require the user to select an item from the ComboBox by changing the DropDownStyle ComboBox control property to DropDownList. You do this by placing the cursor over the ComboBox control and right-clicking. A pop-up menu is displayed. Click Properties to display the Properties window. The DropDown option appears on the list of options displayed when you select the DropDownStyle property.

Add a ComboBox Control

1. Add a ComboBox control by dragging and dropping the control from the Toolbox on to the form.
2. Double-click on the form.

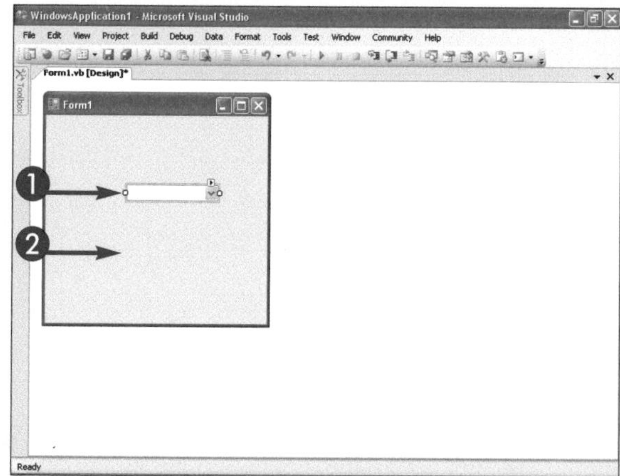

The Load event opens.

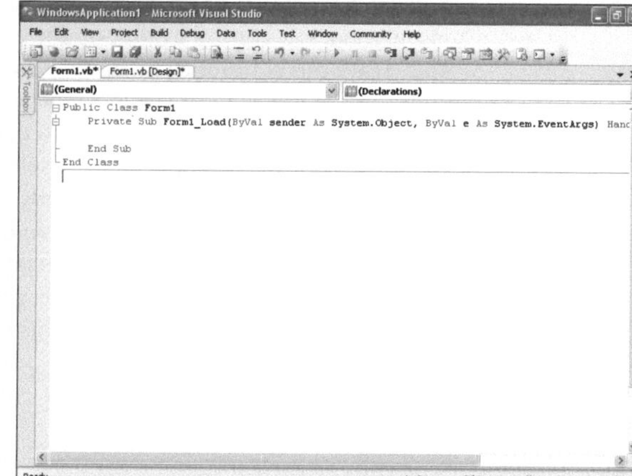

3 Add an item to the ComboBox control by writing `ComboBox1.Items.Add("XXX")`, replacing XXX with the item, such as Bob in this example.

4 Press Ctrl+S to save the code.

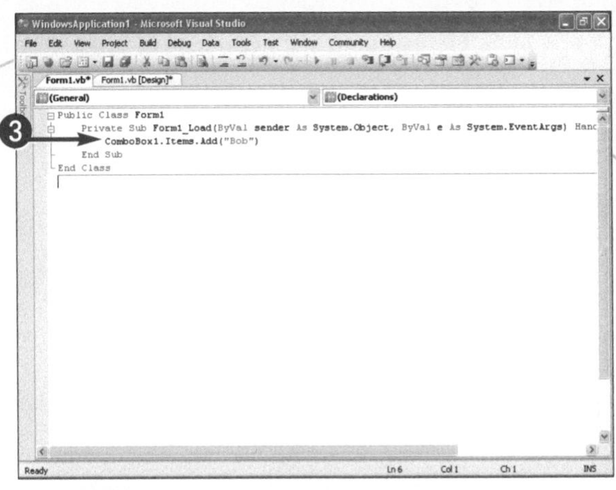

5 Press F5 to run the program.

- You can click the ComboBox control to display the item.

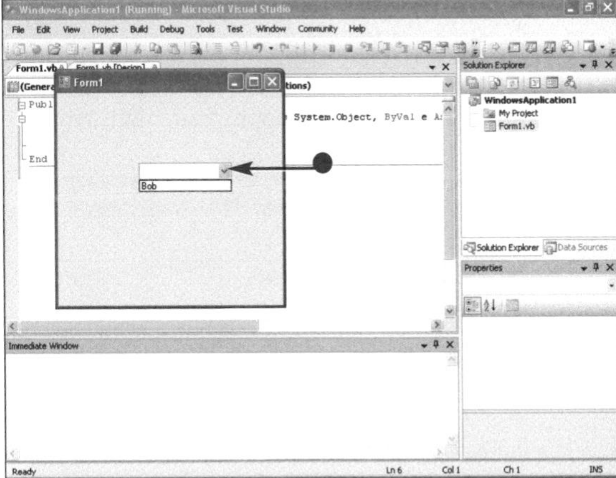

Extra

Programmers typically populate a ComboBox control when the form is loaded rather than when the ComboBox control is displayed on the form. This is made possible by using the form's Load event subroutine, which is called automatically every time that the form is loaded into memory. You can display the Load event subroutine by placing the cursor on the form and then double-clicking. Make sure that the cursor is not on a control; otherwise, you will display the control's subroutine. Enter the code that you want executed when the form is loaded into memory in the Load event subroutine, such as `Combo1.Items.Add("XXX")`.

In addition, you will typically want to preselect an item. If you do not preselect with a DropDownList, the control shows an empty string.

Access an Item Selected from a ComboBox Control

You access the item in a `ComboBox` control by referencing the `ComboBox` control's `Text` property from within your application. You do this by writing `ComboBox1.Text`. `ComboBox1` is the name of the `ComboBox`, and `Text` is the `Text` property.

You use `ComboBox1.Text` in your application whenever you want to refer to the item in the `ComboBox` control. The item can be text that the user directly enters into the `ComboBox` control or a selection from the `ComboBox` control list. The selected item is treated as if the user directly entered the item into the `ComboBox` control.

`ComboBox1.Text` always refers to a `String`, even if the `ComboBox` control contains a number. This means that you need to convert the `String` to an appropriate data type (see Chapter 5), as required by your application. For example, suppose that the `ComboBox` control contains a date. You probably want to convert the date to a `Date` data type using `CDate(ComboBox1.Text)`. `CDate()` is the function that converts a `String` to a `Date` data type. `ComboBox1.Text` references the contents of the `ComboBox` control.

Let's say that you are creating an online membership form that requires a visitor to enter her gender and the state where she lives, among other information. Because these are limited choices, you probably want to use a `ComboBox` control to gather this information. The gender `ComboBox` contains two choices — Male or Female. The state `ComboBox` contains a list of state abbreviations in alphabetical order.

Access an Item Selected from a ComboBox Control

1. Add a `ComboBox` control to your application.

Note: See the preceding section, "Add a `ComboBox` Control."

2. Add a button to the form.

Note: See Chapter 4 for information about adding buttons.

3. Double-click on the form.

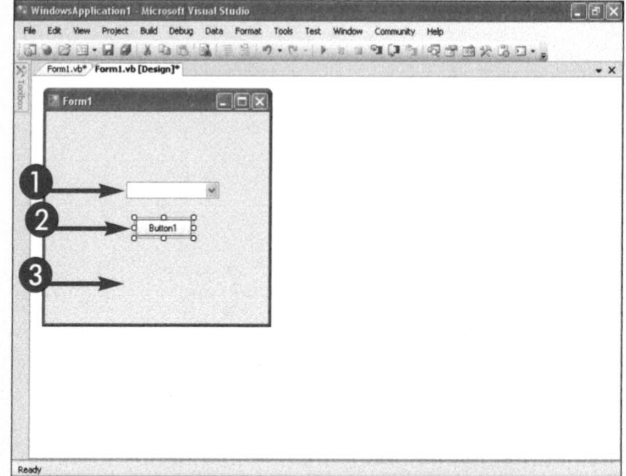

The `Load` event opens.

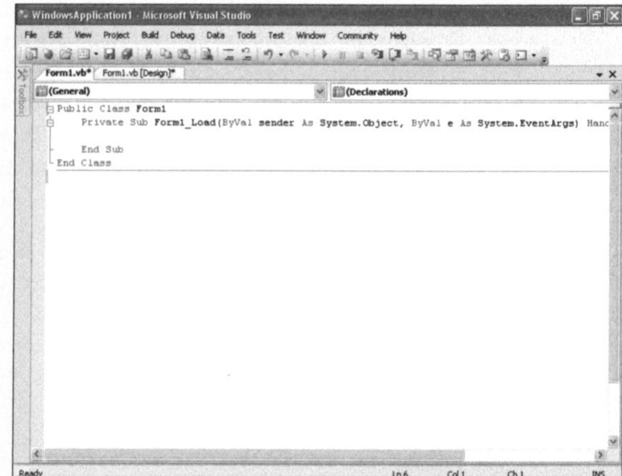

4 Add an item to the ComboBox control by writing ComboBox1.Items.Add("XXX"), replacing XXX with the item, such as Bob in this example.

5 Double-click the button.

The code that executes when the button is clicked appears.

6 Display the context of the ComboBox control in a MessageBox() by writing MessageBox(ComboBox1.Text).

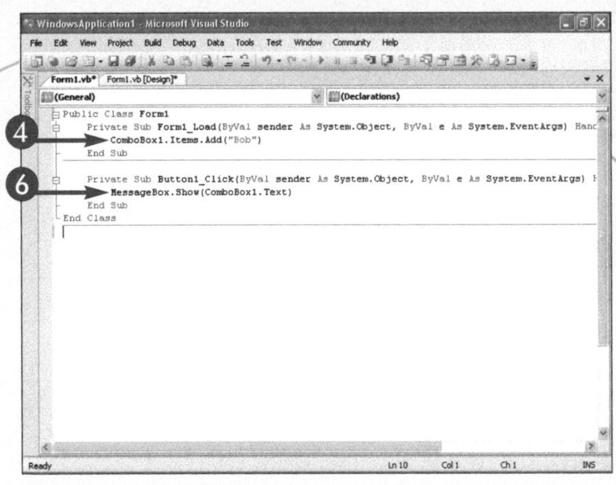

7 Press Ctrl+S to save the code.

8 Press F5 to run the program.

The application executes.

9 Click the ComboBox control and choose an item.

Your selection appears in the ComboBox control.

10 Click the button.

The ComboBox control text appears in the MessageBox().

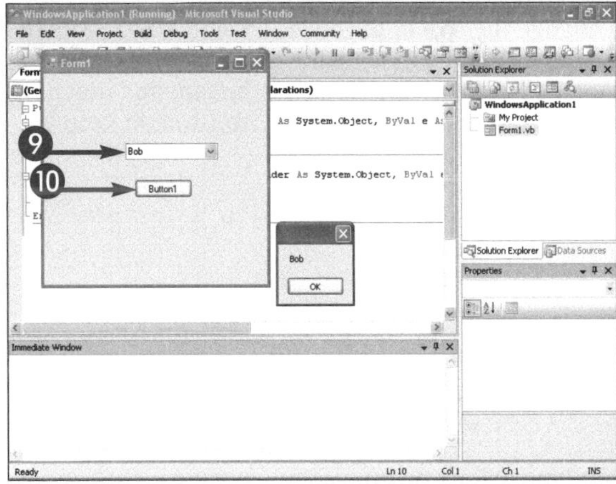

Extra

You can place text into a ComboBox control while your program is running by assigning the text to the ComboBox control's Text property. Let's say that you want to place the name Tom into the ComboBox control. To do so, you write `ComboBox1.Text = "Tom"`. The name Tom appears just as if the user entered **Tom** into the ComboBox control. Some programmers use this technique to set a default value for the ComboBox control based on entries made into other controls that appear on the form. For example, the form may have a bill-to address and a ship-to address and use a ComboBox control to select the state. When the user selects the state for the bill-to address, the program can use the same state to set the ship-to address state. Usually, state abbreviations are displayed in a ComboBox.

If you have two ComboBox controls (BillToState and ShipToState), you double-click the BillToState ComboBox control to display the SelectedIndexChanged() subroutine. This subroutine executes when the value in the BillToState ComboBox control changes. Type the following code to automatically copy the bill-to address:

```
ShipToState.Text = BillToState.Text
```

Add a Button Control

A Button control simulates a push button on a form and is used to start, confirm, or cancel an operation. For example, you can use a Submit button on an online order form; the customer submits the order form by clicking the Button control.

After you add a Button control to your form, you can reposition the control by moving the cursor over it, holding down the left mouse button, and dragging the Button control into the new position on the form.

The Button control displays resize handles that you can use to change the size of the Button control. You resize the Button control by moving the cursor over a resize handle, holding down the left mouse button, and dragging the Button control into its new size. You should keep all buttons the same size to give your form a professional look and feel. Also, avoid having too many buttons on your form.

You can prevent a Button control from being accidentally "pushed" by setting the Enabled property of the Button control to False. There are two ways to set the Enabled property: First, you can open the Properties window and change the Enabled property to False. Second, from within your code, you write `Button1.Enabled = False`. Button1 is the Button control name, and Enabled is the name of the property. You enable the Button control by changing the Enabled property to True or by writing `Button1.Enabled = True` in your code.

Add a Button Control

1. Open the Toolbox and click the Button control.

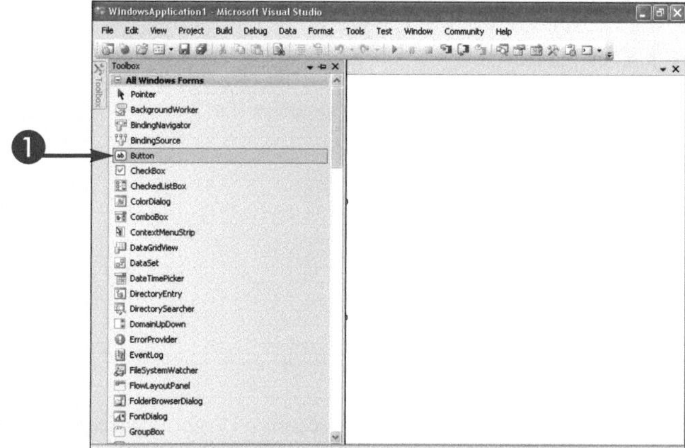

2. Drag and drop the Button control on to the form.

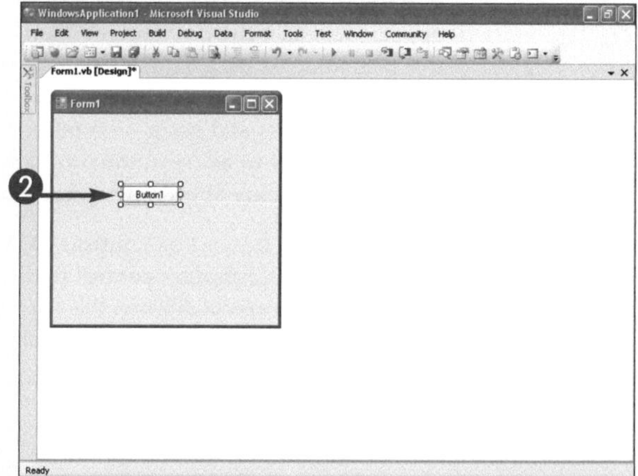

Write a Button Control Event

A Button control *event* is something that occurs when the user interacts with a Button control. Clicking the left mouse button while the cursor is over the button is a Button control event, as is releasing the left mouse button while the cursor is over the button. The more commonly used Button control events are a single MouseClick, MouseDoubleClick, MouseDown, and MouseUp.

Each Button control event is associated with a subroutine. A *subroutine* is a block of code that executes when the subroutine is called. Visual Basic .NET automatically calls the subroutine when the corresponding Button control event occurs. For example, there is a subroutine that is called when the user clicks the left mouse button while the cursor is over the Button control.

You place the code that you want to execute when a Button control event occurs into the Button control event's subroutine. This means that if you want a message box to display when a user clicks the Button control, you would place MessageBox.Show("Message") into the corresponding subroutine for that Button control event.

After displaying the subroutines associated with the events for a Button control, you enter your code between the Sub and End Sub lines. You can select other events by choosing them from the drop-down list. The Click event is the most commonly used event.

The Click subroutine is automatically created; however, you can use the ComboBox in the upper-right corner to create subroutines for other Button control events.

You can also display subroutines that you already created by pressing F7.

Write a Button Control Event

1. Double-click the Button control.

   The Click subroutine is displayed.

2. Write the code for the event that you want to occur.

Note: For example, to write a statement that displays a message box, you would write MessageBox.Show ("XXX"), replacing XXX with a message.

3. Press Ctrl+S.

   Your program is saved.

4. Press F5.

   Your program executes.

5. Click the Button control.

   The event occurs.

Note: In this example, a message box is displayed.

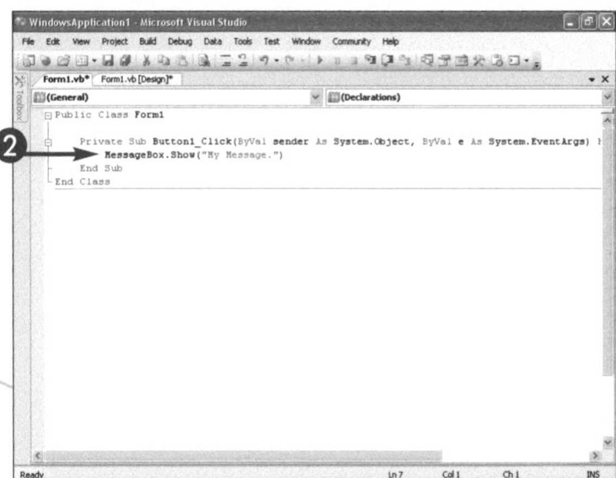

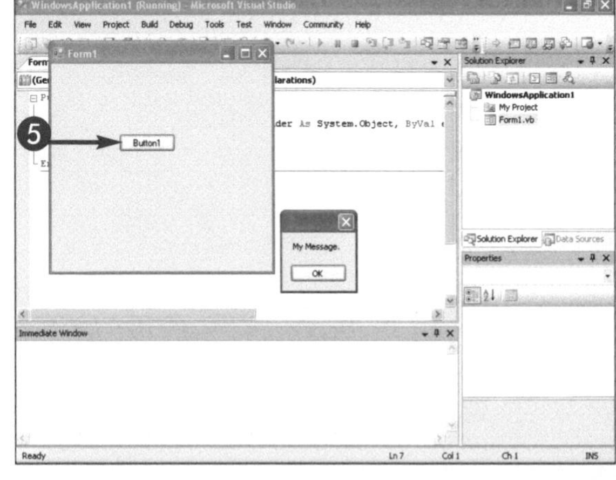

Change the Label of a Button Control

You change the text of the label on a `Button` control by using the `Button` control's `Text` property. The text on a `Button` control is `Button1` by default. The number represents the number of the `Button` control on the form that uses the default text, so `Button1` is the first `Button` control. The second `Button` control defaults to `Button2` and so on. You should rename the `Button` control to reflect the action of the button, such as Submit or Cancel, which submits the form for further processing or cancels the form, respectively.

You can modify the appearance of the label by changing other `Button` control properties. You change the font of the label by choosing a new value for the `Font` property. Click the `Font` property to display a list of other available fonts.

You can reposition a label on the `Button` control by using the `TextAlign` property. Click the `TextAlign` property to see a diagram illustrating where you can position the text. The choices are top, middle, or bottom and left, center, or right.

The user selects a `Button` control by clicking the mouse button while the cursor is over the `Button` control, pressing the Tab key until the `Button` control is highlighted and pressing Enter, or by using a keyboard shortcut. A keyboard shortcut enables the `Button` control to be selected by pressing the Ctrl key and the keyboard shortcut key, such as Ctrl+S to save the form to a file.

Change the Label of a Button Control

1. Right-click the `Button` control.
2. Click Properties.

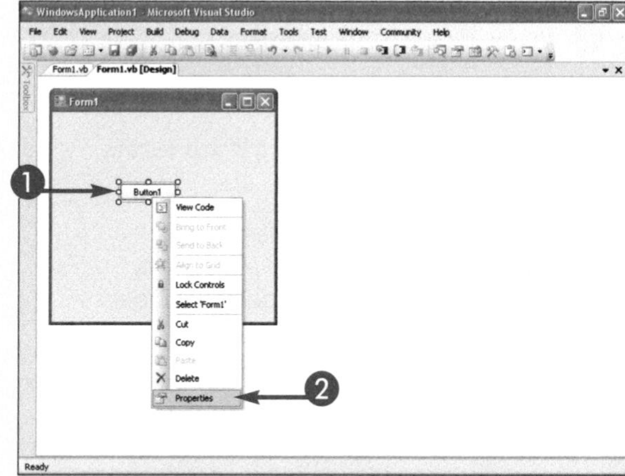

The Properties pane is displayed.

3. Click the `Text` property and enter a new label.

The text appears on the button.

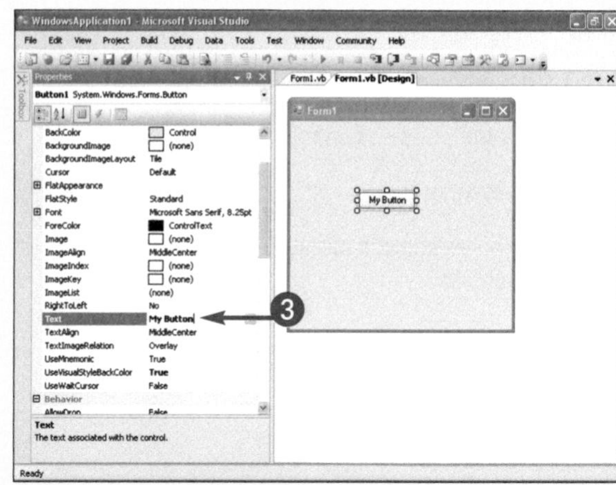

Using an Image for a Button Control

You can dress up a `Button` control by displaying an image on the button. You do this by assigning the image's filename to the `Button` control's `Image` property. There are two ways to do this: The first way is to import an image file using the Properties window and the `Image` property, as shown here.

You can also write code that assigns the image filename to the `Image` property. Here is how to assign the image `myimage.bmp` to a `Button` control's `Image` property. `MyImage` is an `Image` object that has the `FromFile()` method to link the image filename to the `Image` object and then to the `Image` property.

```
Dim MyImage As Image
Button1.Image = MyImage.FromFile("myimage.bmp")
```

Position the image within the `Button` control by using the `ImageAlign` property. Click the `ImageAlign` property in the Properties window and then pick a location for the image such as `TopCenter` or `BottomCenter`.

Extra

You can display both text and an image on a `Button` control by setting both the `Text` and `Image` properties. Make sure to align the text and the image to different positions on the button; otherwise, the text and image will overlap. There are two alignment properties — `TextAlign` and `ImageAlign`. Each works the same way but affects either the text or the image. For the best result, select `TopCenter` for the image and `BottomCenter` for the text. This causes the image to appear above the text in the center of the button.

Using an Image for a Button Control

1. Display the `Button` control's Properties pane.
2. Click the `Image` properties and select Import.

The Select Resource dialog box appears.

3. Browse images on your computer.
4. Click the image that you want to place on the `Button` control.
5. Click OK.

The image appears on the button.

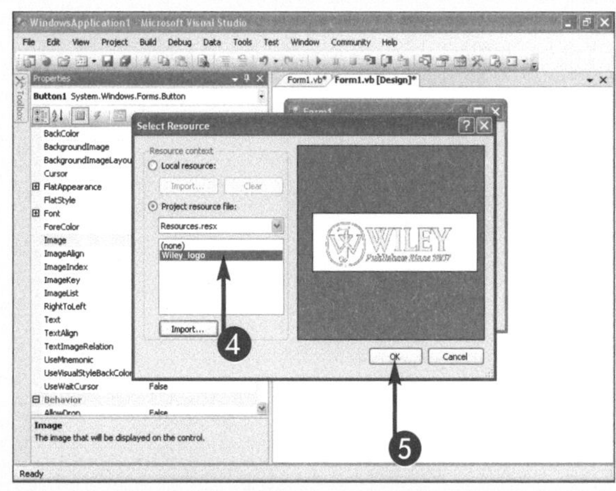

Make a Button the Default Button

Buttons are used to activate an action while a form is displayed on the screen. Many forms that you create will have at least two actions. One action is to process the form and is usually initiated by clicking a button labeled "Submit" or "Accept"; however, you can place any label on the button. The other action is to cancel the form and is usually activated by clicking a button labeled "Cancel." Good programming style requires that the Submit button be associated with the Enter key and the Cancel button be linked to the Esc key on the keyboard. When you do this, you are making the Submit button *the default button,* which is the button that is activated when the user presses the Enter key. Thus, the user can press Enter to submit the form or press Esc to cancel any form, regardless of who wrote the application.

You associate a button with the Enter key by setting the form's `AcceptButton` property to the name of the button. Likewise, setting the form's `CancelButton` property to the name of a button links the button to the Esc key. Once linked, code that you include in the corresponding `Click` subroutine executes when the user presses the Enter key or the Esc key.

When you press Enter, Visual Basic .NET calls the `Click` event of the `Button` control whose `AcceptButton` property is `True`, even if it is not selected. However, if another `Button` control is selected when the Enter key is pressed, its `Click` event will be executed.

Make a Button the Default Button

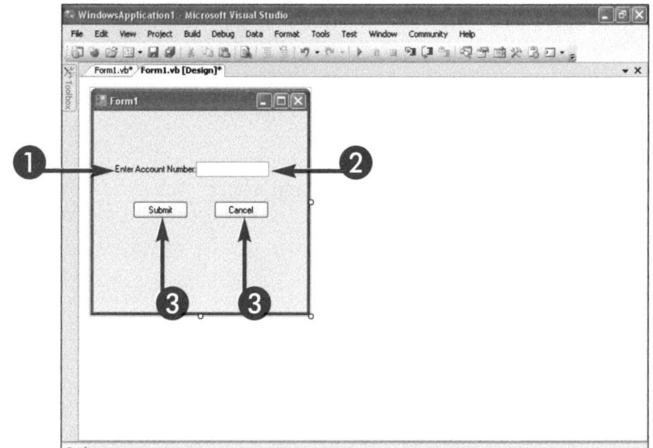

1. Add a `Label` control to your form and change its text.
2. Add a `TextBox` control to the form, placing it to the right of the `Label` control.
3. Add two button controls, changing the text of one button to `Submit` and the other button to `Cancel`.

Note: See the section "Change the Label of a Button Control."

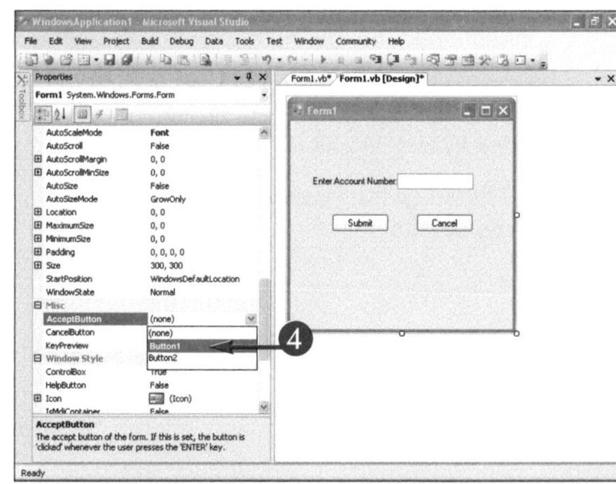

4. In the form's Properties window, change the form's `AcceptButton` property to `Button1`, which in this example is the Submit button.
5. Change the Submit button control's `TabStop` property to `True`.
6. Change the Submit button control's `TabIndex` property to `0`.

7 Change the form's `CancelButton` property to `Button2`.

8 Double-click the Submit button control.

The `Click` subroutine is displayed.

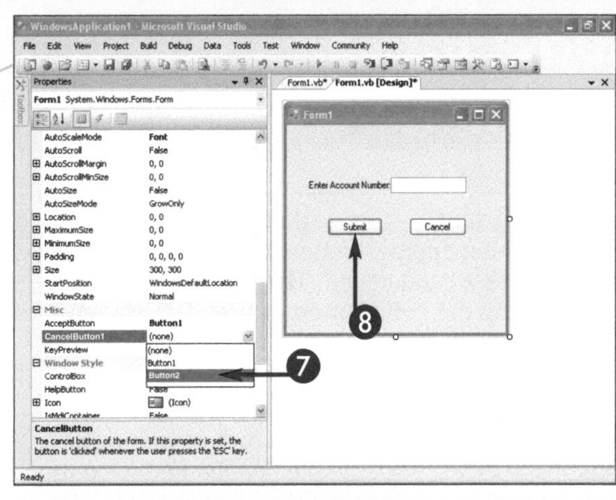

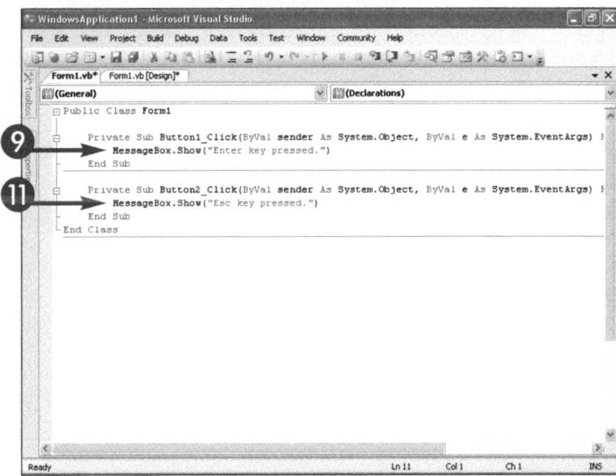

9 Enter code that displays a message box by writing `MessageBox.Show("XXX")`, replacing `XXX` with a message.

10 Double-click the Cancel button control.

11 Repeat step 9 for the Cancel button, writing a different message.

12 Press F5.

The program executes.

13 Press the Enter key.

The event for the Submit button occurs.

Note: If you run the program again and press the Esc key, the Cancel button's event will occur.

Extra

The most frequently used button on your form should be made the default control for the form. The default control is the first control that has focus when the form is displayed. For example, the Submit button is likely to be the most-used control on your form. Therefore, you should make the Submit button the default control. You do this by setting the button's `TabStop` property to `True` and setting the `TabIndex` property to 0. Let's say that you have a `TextBox` control, a Cancel button control, and a Submit button control on your form. You can assign the Submit button control an index value of 0 as long as the tab index value for the `TextBox` control and Submit button control are greater than 1.

Add a Radio Button

A *radio button* is a control that displays a button and a label that appears alongside the button. The label describes a valid option. The user chooses the option by clicking the radio button control. For example, radio button controls are typically used to choose gender — Male or Female.

Related radio buttons are organized into a radio button control group. Only one radio button control within the group can be selected. For example, a radio button control Male and a radio button control Female are related radio buttons that are frequently joined to form a group. The user can select either the Male radio button control or the Female radio button control but not both. When one radio button control is selected, the other radio button controls are automatically deselected.

After you create a radio button control, you can reposition it by placing the cursor over the control, holding down the left mouse button, and dragging it into position.

You change the label of the radio button and give the control a unique name using the Properties pane. Use a name that describes the particular radio button control. You use the name within your code to refer to this radio button control. The label of the button appears alongside the radio button on the form.

Radio buttons on a form are in the same group by default. You can split them into separate groups by using `GroupBox`, which is discussed later in this chapter in the section "Create a `GroupBox` Control."

Add a Radio Button

1. Add at least two radio button controls to your form by dragging and dropping them from the Toolbox.

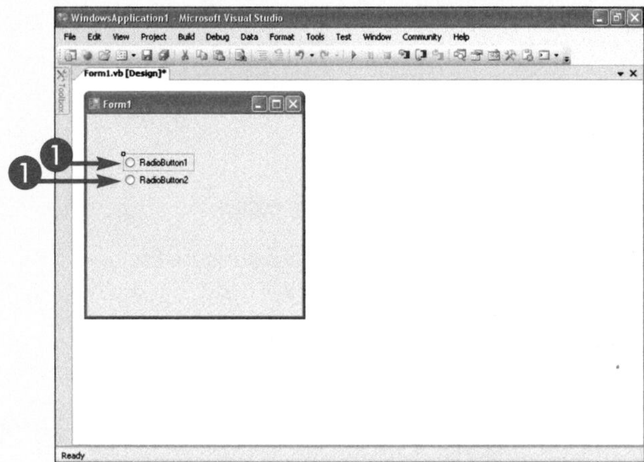

2. Change the label of each radio button control by assigning the text that you want to its `Text` property, such as `Male` or `Female`.

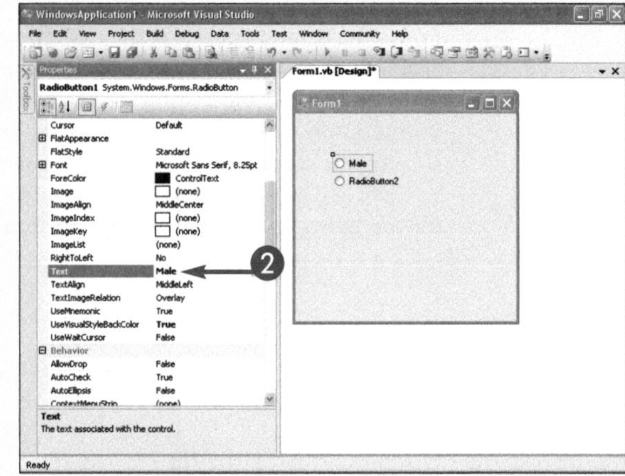

3 Change the name of each radio button control by assigning the name that you want to its `Name` property, such as `rbMale` or `rbFemale`.

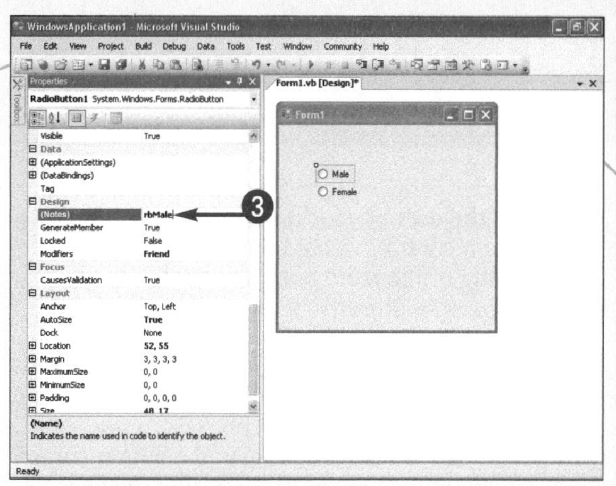

4 Press F5.

The program runs and displays the radio button controls.

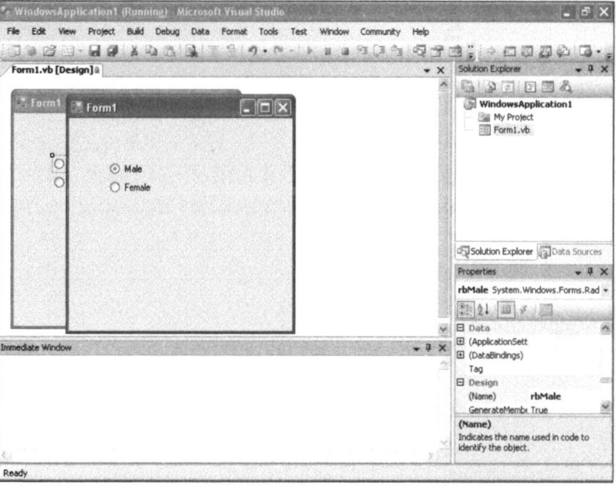

Extra

You should always select a radio button control to be the default selection within the radio button control group; otherwise, all radio button controls within the group will appear deselected. Good programming style requires that the most commonly selected radio button control is the first radio button control in the group and is selected as the default radio button control. You make a radio button control the default selection by setting the radio button control's `Checked` property to `True`. You do this by using the Properties pane or by writing in your code `XXX.Checked = True`, where `XXX` is the name of the radio button control.

Access a Radio Button

When the user of your application selects a radio button control, Visual Basic .NET reverses the setting of the radio button control's `Checked` property. The `Checked` property is set to `True` if the radio button is selected. You must write code that examines the `Checked` property of each radio button control to determine which radio button control the user selected. Typically, you place this code in the Submit button control's `Click` subroutine. The Submit button control is the button control that you designate to process information that the user enters on the form.

You examine the `Checked` property by using an `If...Then...ElseIf...Then` statement; see Chapter 6. Each radio button control must be examined individually by using the expression `XXX.Checked = True`, where `XXX` is the name of the radio button control and `True` tests if the button control was selected by the user. For example, you would write `If XXX.Checked = True Then`, which would execute one or more lines of code if the XXX radio button was selected, and then write `ElseIf YYY.Checked = True Then`, which would execute other lines of code if the YYY radio button was selected. You would write other `ElseIf...Then` statements if you had more than two radio buttons.

The `If...Then...ElseIf...Then` statement has two sections called *code blocks,* which is where you place code. The first code block executes if the expression in the `If...Then` statement is `True`. The second code block executes if the expression in the `ElseIf...Then` portion of the statement is `True`. Statements in a code block execute only if the corresponding expression is true; otherwise, the code block is skipped, and code within the code block is not executed.

Access a Radio Button

1. Add at least two radio button controls to your form by dragging and dropping them from the Toolbox.
2. Add a `Button` control to the form by dragging and dropping one from the Toolbox and on to the form.

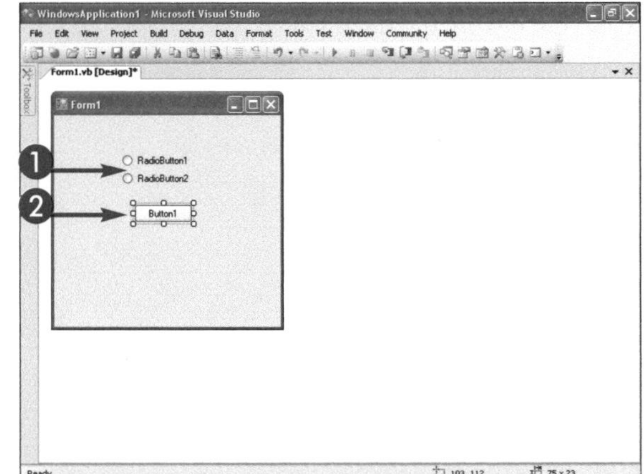

3. Change the label of each radio button control by assigning the text that you want to its `Text` property, such as `Male` or `Female`.
4. Change the name of each radio button control by assigning the name that you want to its `Name` property, such as `rbMale` or `rbFemale`.

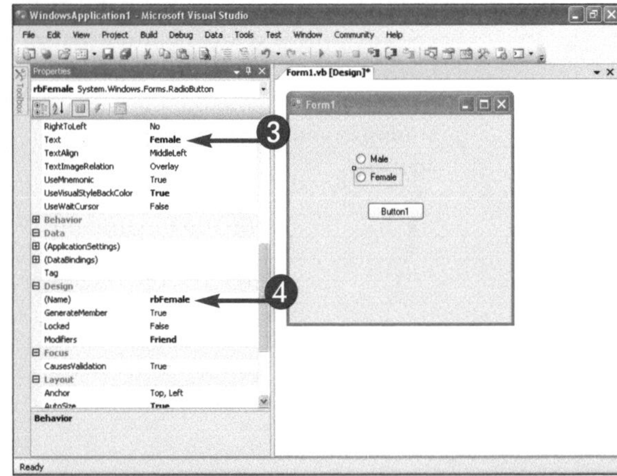

5 Create a `Click` subroutine for the `Button` control by first double-clicking control.

6 Write an `If...Then...ElseIf...Then` statement that examines all the radio button controls.

7 Display a message box on the screen showing which radio button the user selected by writing `MessageBox.Show("XXX")` in each code block, replacing `XXX` with the text of the radio button control.

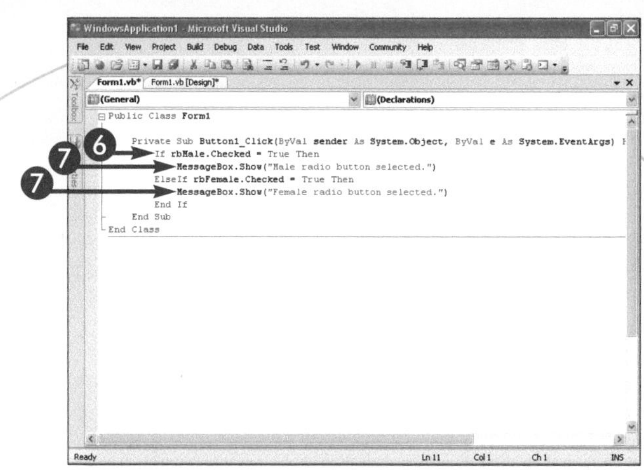

8 Press F5.

The program runs and displays the radio button controls.

9 Click a radio button control.

10 Click the `Button` control.

A message box is displayed, showing the radio button that you selected.

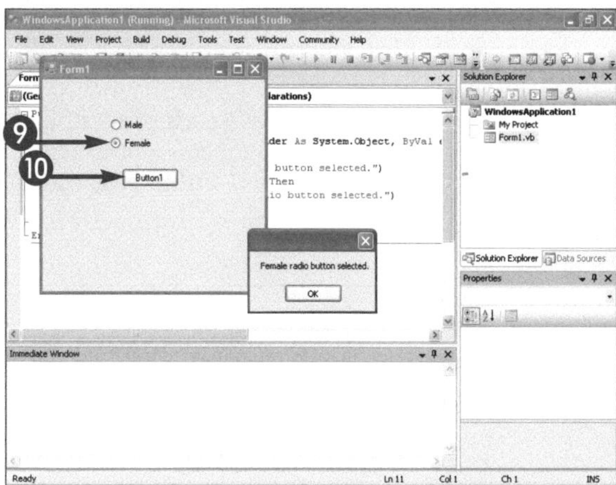

Extra

You can use multiple `ElseIf...Then` clauses in an `If...Then...ElseIf...Then` statement. Suppose you have three radio button controls named `rbAirplane`, `rbTrain`, and `rbCar`. You need to examine each to see which radio button control was selected. Here is what you need to write:

```
If rbAirplane.Checked = True Then
    'Place code here
ElseIf rbTrain.Checked = True Then
   'Place code here
ElseIf rbCar.Checked = True Then
   'Place code here
End If
```

Add a Check Box

A CheckBox control displays a check box and a label that appears to the right of it. The check box is used to select or deselect the CheckBox control. The label specifies an option such as New Customer. A check mark appears in the check box when the user selects the option. The CheckBox control is different from a RadioButton control because a CheckBox control operates independently of other CheckBox controls. If a user selects or deselects a CheckBox control, the status of other CheckBox controls remain unchanged. With a RadioButton control, there is no automatic way to deselect it except by selecting another RadioButton control. Also, you can select multiple check boxes but only one radio button.

When you name your check boxes, give each one a unique name. Note that you use the value of the Name property when referring to the CheckBox control within your code.

Make sure that you set a default value for each CheckBox control based on whether the user is likely to select the option. So if the user is going to select a CheckBox control more often than not, check the CheckBox control by default. You can set the default value by changing the CheckBox control's Checked property to True, which checks the box, or False to uncheck the box.

A check box has three possible display states — Checked, Unchecked, and Indeterminate. These are defined in the CheckState property. The Checked property is True for both the Checked and Indeterminate CheckState values. Indeterminate displays a gray check mark. You may have seen this on forms where the user has made a partial selection. You could use this to indicate that the user has selected all, some, or none of the items from a list.

Add a Check Box

1. Add at least two CheckBox controls to your form by dragging and dropping the controls from the Toolbox on to the form.

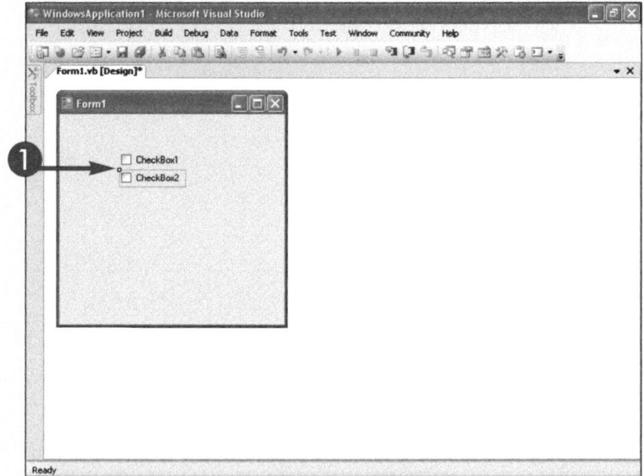

2. Rename the CheckBox controls by changing the values of their Name properties, with names such as cbNewCustomer and cbPrimaryCustomer.

3. Enter the option label for the CheckBox controls by changing the values of their Text properties with text such as New Customer and Primary Customer.

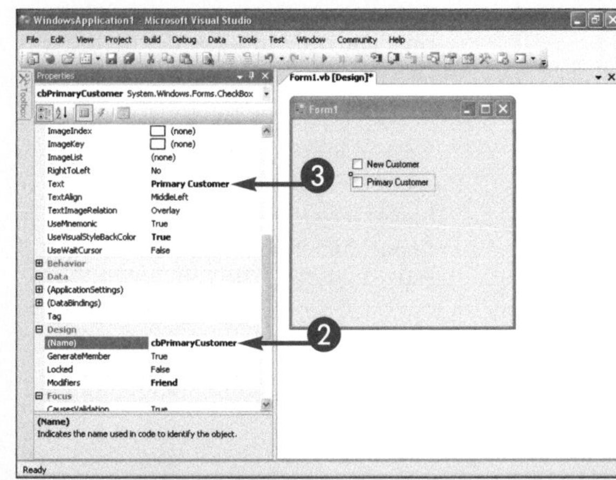

- You can change the second `CheckBox` control to a button by changing the `Appearance` property of the second `CheckBox` control to `Button`.

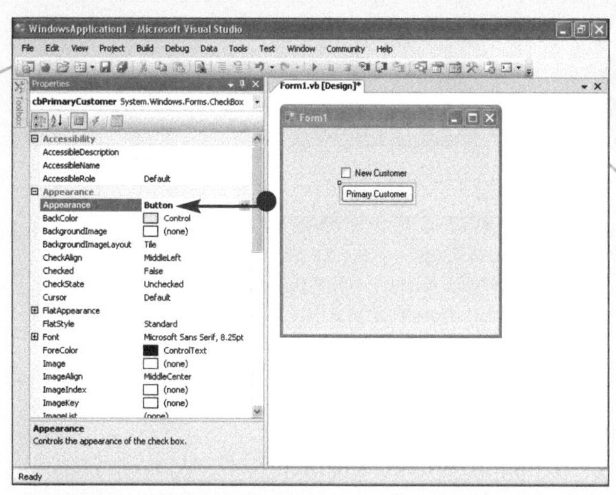

4 Press F5.

The program runs and displays your `CheckBox` controls — in this example, one as a check box and the other as a button.

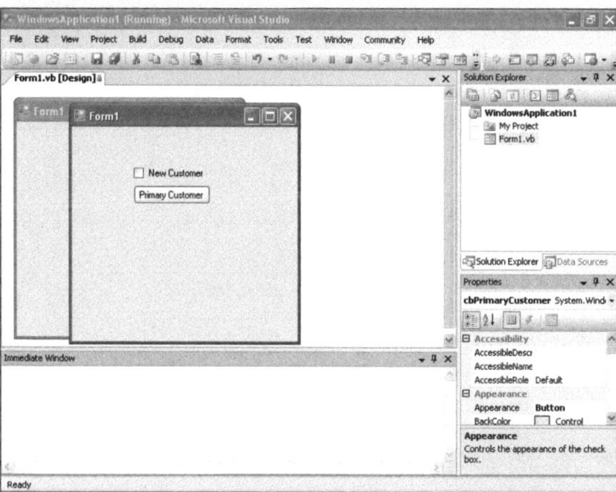

Extra

The `CheckBox` control can appear as a button rather than a check box and label. The button appears raised if the `CheckBox` control is deselected and appears in the down position when selected. The name of the option appears on the button. You can change the appearance of the `CheckBox` control from a check box to a button by changing the value of the `CheckBox` control's `Appearance` property from `Normal` to `Button`. The value of the `Text` property becomes the label for the button.

You can also change the appearance of a check box by changing the `FlatStyle` property. The `FlatStyle` property determines the appearance of the `CheckBox` control when the user moves the mouse cursor over it and clicks the mouse button. There are four choices — Flat, Popup, Standard, and System. Try the Popup selection. This gives your `CheckBox` control a classy look because it causes the check box to pop up when the cursor moves over it.

Access a Check Box

Whenever a user selects a CheckBox control, Visual Basic .NET changes the CheckBox control's Checked property to True. You can access the Checked property from within your code to determine if the CheckBox control was selected by the user. You do this by using the XXX.Checked = True expression in an If...Then statement (see Chapter 6), where XXX is the name of the CheckBox control.

The If...Then statement has one section called a *code block*. The code block contains code that executes if the expression is true. You write code that you want executed if the user selects the CheckBox control in the code bock. If the expression is false, meaning that the user did not select the CheckBox control, Visual Basic .NET does not execute code in the code block. Instead, Visual Basic .NET executes the code that follows the If...Then statement.

Typically, you will place the If...Then statement in the Click subroutine of the Submit button that the user clicks to submit the form for processing. It is in this subroutine where you validate information contained in the form.

You can also access a check box within your code to either check or uncheck it based on other information the visitor enters on your form. Let's say that you created an online order form that has a check box indicating that the visitor is a new customer. The visitor checks this box and then leaves the customer account text box empty. Your code can detect the absence of the customer account and then uncheck the check box.

Access a Check Box

1. Place a CheckBox control on your form.

Note: See the section "Add a Check Box."

2. Add a button control to the form.

Note: See the section "Add a Button Control."

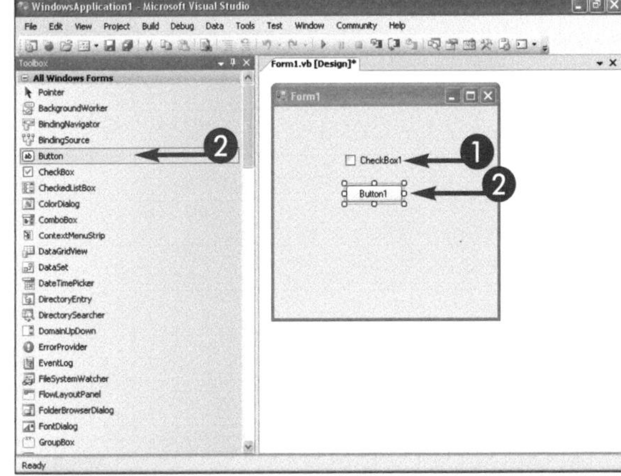

3. Change the text of the CheckBox control.

4. Change the name of the CheckBox control.

Note: See the section "Add a Check Box" for more information about steps 3 and 4.

5. Change the text of the button control, such as to Submit.

Note: See the section "Change the Label of a Button Control."

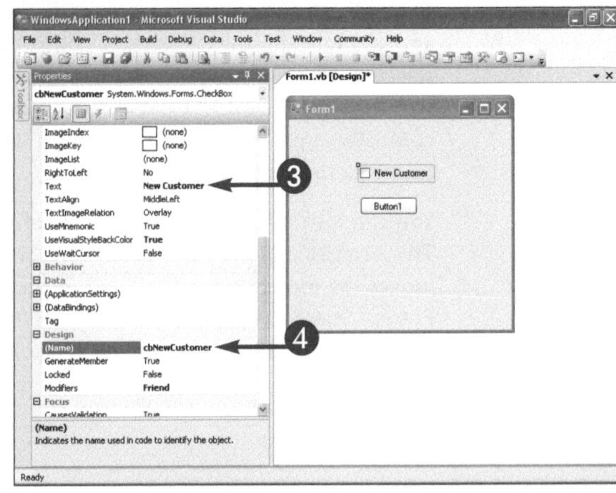

6 Enter an `If...Then...Else` statement in the button control's `Click` subroutine that displays a message box if the `CheckBox` control is selected and another message box if it is not selected.

- Write `XXX.Checked = True` as the expression for the `If...Then...Else` statement, replacing `XXX` with the name of the check box.

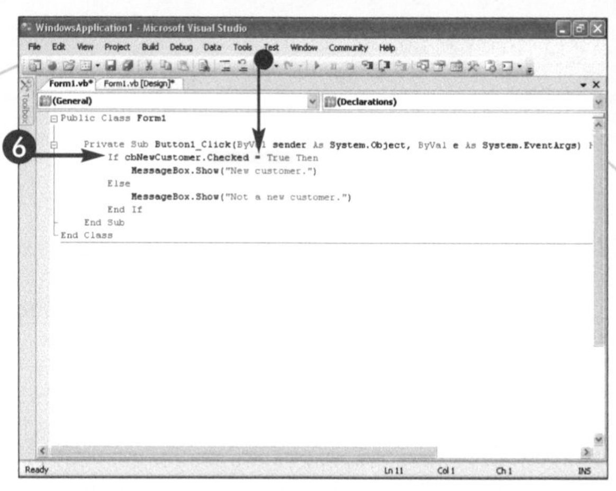

7 Press F5.

The program runs.

8 Click the `CheckBox` control.

9 Click the Submit button.

The message box for the checked option appears.

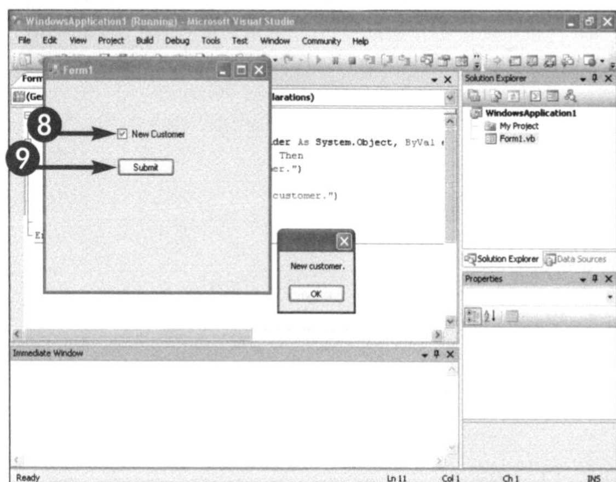

Extra

Sometimes you want your program to do something if a `CheckBox` is not selected. Let's say that a user enters customer information onto a form. The form has a `TextBox` control for the customer's account number and a `CheckBox` control used to indicate if the customer is a new customer. Either an account number must be entered in the `TextBox` control indicating that the customer is an existing customer or the `CheckBox` control must be selected signaling that the customer is a new customer. If no account number is entered and the `CheckBox` control is deselected when the form is processed, your code needs to catch this error.

You can trap this error by using an `If...Then...Else` statement instead of an `If...Then` statement. The `If...Then...Else` statement has two code blocks: The first executes if the expression is true (the `CheckBox` control is selected), and the other code block executes if the expression is false (the `CheckBox` control is not selected).

```
If CheckBox1.Checked = True Then
     'Enter code to execute if the CheckBox control is selected
Else
    'Enter code to execute if the CheckBox control is not selected
End If
```

Create a GroupBox Control

You can avoid cluttering a form with controls by organizing related controls into groups on the form, such as grouping together controls that contain information about a customer's address. You do this by using the `GroupBox` control. The `GroupBox` control is a frame called a *container* within which you place controls. At the upper-left corner of the `GroupBox` is a label that describes the controls contained within the group. For example, the label may say `Customer Address` for a `GroupBox` control that groups controls that contain a customer's address.

After you place a `GroupBox` control on the form, you will need to reposition it. You do this by first selecting the `GroupBox` control, which causes resize handles to appear around the box and a reposition handle to appear in the upper-left corner of the box. Place the cursor over the reposition handle, hold down the left mouse button, and then move the `GroupBox` control into its new position on the form. You can resize the `GroupBox` control by moving the cursor over a resize handle, clicking the left mouse button, and dragging the resize handle to the new size. The label can be changed using the `GroupBox` control's `Text` property.

After the `GroupBox` control is on the form, drag and drop controls from the Toolbox into the group box. Do not drag a `GroupBox` control over controls because although the controls look like they belong to the `GroupBox`, they will not. You can only place controls within the `GroupBox` control, not the other way around.

Create a GroupBox Control

1. Add a `GroupBox` control to your form by dragging and dropping a `GroupBox` control from the Toolbox on to the form.

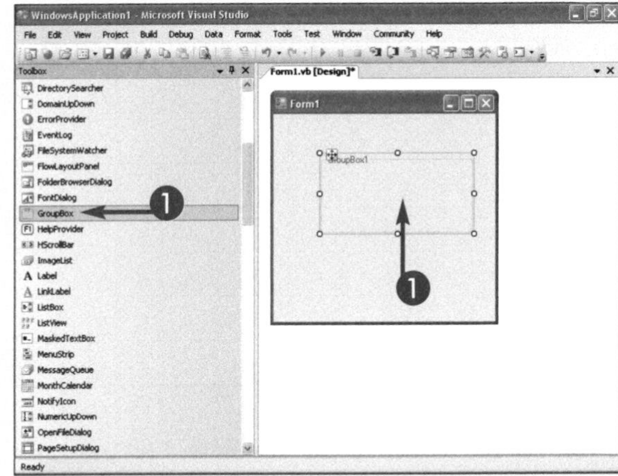

2. Change the label of the `GroupBox` control by changing its `Text` property to the text that you want to use for the group box, such as Gender.

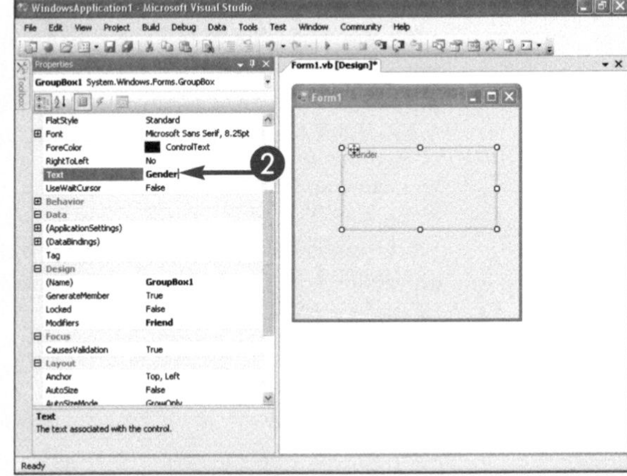

3 Add controls to the GroupBox control, such as RadioButton controls.

4 Change the labels of the controls that you added, such as labeling two RadioButton controls Male and Female.

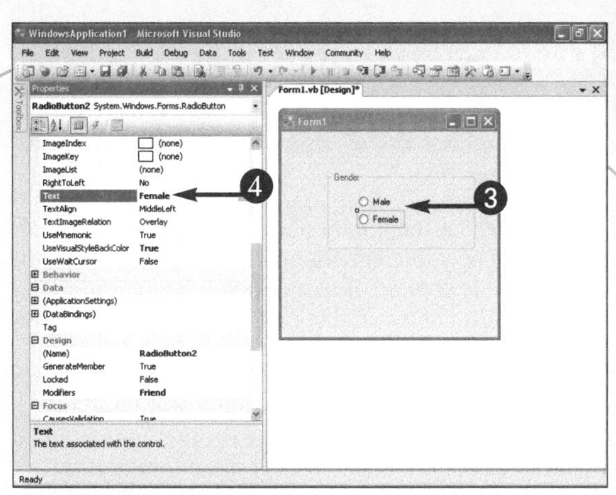

5 Press F5.

The program runs and displays the controls within the GroupBox control.

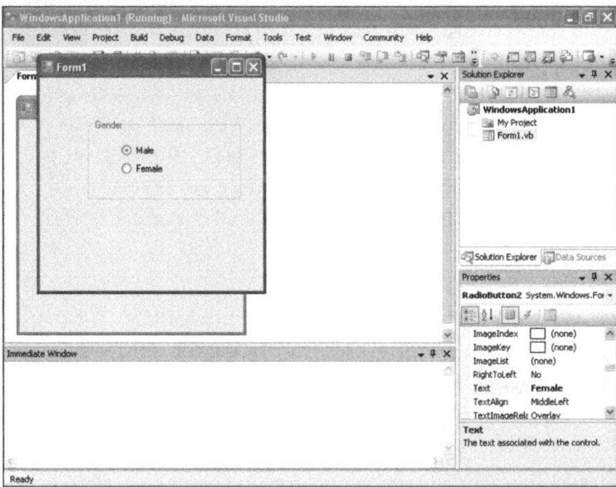

Extra

You can create two sets of radio buttons by placing each set in its own GroupBox control. Each set works independently from the other set. Let's say that you have two radio buttons in one GroupBox control. When the first radio button is selected, the other one is automatically deselected. You also have two other radio buttons in another GroupBox control. When you select the first radio button in the first GroupBox, radio buttons in the second GroupBox control remain unchanged.

You can enable or disable all the controls within a GroupBox control by setting the Enabled property to True or False. Setting Enabled to False grays the GroupBox control and all its controls, and setting it to True makes the GroupBox control and its controls available to the visitor. This is handy to use when a group of controls are used only sometimes. For example, suppose that some information on an online order form is required for new customers only. If the visitor checks the new customer check box, your code can set the GroupBox control's Enabled property to True; otherwise, it remains False.

Understanding Variable Types

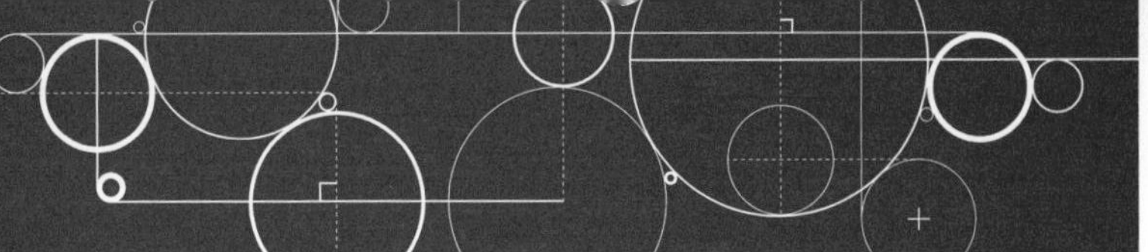

A *variable* is a temporary place in memory to hold a value. The value is assigned to a variable when the variable is created or at any point during the program. The value of a variable can be updated with a new value also at any time during the program. The variable is used in place of the value in mathematical equations, within subroutines and functions, in expressions, and in other places in the program where the value is otherwise used and is within scope; see Chapter 9 for more information.

You can assign a constant value to a variable. A *constant value* is a value that does not change during the program, such as a passing grade. For example, you can declare a variable named `const intPassingGrade As Integer` and assign the variable a value of `70`. You can refer to `intPassingGrade` within your code each time that you need to reference the passing grade. The reserved word `const` tells Visual Basic .NET that you are declaring a constant.

Using a variable is better than simply typing the value **70** because the variable name tells you the meaning of the value, which makes debugging and working with your code easier than if you typed **70** into your code. A good reason to use a constant variable is that you may be referencing the value in many places within your application. For example, if the passing grade dropped to 65, you only need to update the passing grade in one place within your program by assigning `65` to the constant variable.

Variable names must conform to VB.NET requirements. For example, you cannot use a reserve word such as `Dim` as a name because VB.NET tries to declare a variable every time `Dim` is encountered in the code. Likewise, 70 is not a good variable name because it can easily be confused by the value. A variable name cannot begin with punctuation marks or a space. Variable names can contain letters — both upper- and lowercase — numbers, and underscores. A variable name may contain digits but cannot start with a digit.

Variable names are not case-sensitive, which means that the variable name `INTMINUTESPERHOUR` is considered the same variable as the variable name `intMinutesPerHour`. Note that it is good programming style to make the first letter of a variable name lowercase. The first letter of the word contained in the variable name should be uppercase, such as the *M* in *Minutes.*

VB.NET has several types of variables based on the type of data that is stored in the variable. The variable type is called a *data type.* Date types include the following: `Boolean`, `Char`, `Date`, `Decimal`, `Double`, `Integer`, `Object`, and `String`.

Each data type requires a specific amount of memory to store data that is assigned to the variable. For example, a `Byte` data type requires the least amount of memory, and a `Decimal` requires the most memory. You choose the data type for a variable based on the size of the data that you want to store in the variable.

It is good programming style to begin a variable name with the data type and follow it by a name that represents the kind of data that is stored in the variable. For example, `intPassingGrade` is a variable name that conforms to good programming style. This variable name begins with `int`, which indicates that the value stored in this variable is an `Integer` data type. Although `int` is a reserved word, you can use a reserved word as part of the variable name.

Types of Variables

Boolean	Double
A `Boolean` variable holds the word `True` or `False` and is used to test the condition of a statement. The number 0 is used to represent the word `False`, and the number 1 represents the word `True`. `Boolean` variables are used as flags to indicate if part of your code should execute.	A `Double` variable holds a very large or very small value. A very small number is a decimal value requiring more than 28 decimal places. A `Double` variable is typically used in scientific and engineering calculations.
Char	**Integer**
A `Char` variable holds a character. A character can be any character on the keyboard, including numbers, punctuation, and characters that you do not see, such as a space or tab. A number represents each character from 0 to 65,535. The number that represents the character is stored in a `Char` variable. For example, the letter *A* is represented as the number 65. When you type the letter **A**, the number 65 is stored as the letter *A* inside your computer. The U.S. character set requires one byte; however, two bytes are necessary to accommodate the international character set.	An `Integer` variable holds a whole number. The whole number can be from –2,147,483,648 to 2,147,483,647 and is used for arithmetic and as counters for loops. An `Integer` variable is not used to store a value that contains a decimal. **Object** An `Object` variable holds any kind of value. `Object` data may reserve more memory than is required to store a value. It is good programming style to use a data type appropriate for the variable rather than an `Object` date type.
Byte	**Long**
A `Byte` variable holds a positive number from 0 to 255. `Byte` variables are commonly used to store small whole number and binary streams.	A `Long` variable holds a whole number from –9,223,372,036,854,775,808 to 9,223,372,036,854,775,807.
Date	**Short**
A `Date` variable holds date and time information. `Date` variables are commonly used to perform date calculations, such as subtracting a birth date from today's date to calculate the age of a person. Values assigned to a `Date` variable must appear in the format of a date.	A `Short` variable holds a whole number from –32,768 to 32,767.
Decimal	**String**
A `Decimal` variable holds a value that has a decimal. The value can be a decimal value, a whole number, or a mixed number. A `Decimal` variable can hold up to 29 decimal places. It is good programming style, however, to use an `Integer` variable instead of a `Decimal` variable if the value is a whole number because an `Integer` uses less memory than a `Decimal` value.	A `String` variable holds more than one character and is commonly used to store names such as a person's first name or last name. For example, `"Bob"` is a value that can be stored in a `String` variable. `String` values are enclosed in double quotation marks (`"`). A `String` variable can hold a space, such as `" "`.

Choose the Appropriate Variable Type

Selecting the best type of variable for your application is tricky because you may be unsure which variable type is the most efficient to use. Choosing a variable type that is too small to store your data causes subtle errors in your program known as *bugs*. When in doubt, use the variable type that will hold the most data. For example, you may prompt the user of your program to enter a whole number, which you will store in a variable. Do you use a `Byte`, `Short`, `Integer`, or `Long` variable type? An error occurs if you choose a `Byte` and the user enters the number 256 because a `Byte` can store numbers only from 0 to 255. Therefore, it is best to use a variable type that can store a larger number such as an `Integer`.

Declare a Variable

To declare a variable, you specify the `Dim` reserved word, the variable name, the `As` reserved word, and the data type of the variable. For example, in `Dim decProductPrice As Decimal`, `Dim` is the reserved word that tells VB.NET that you are declaring a variable. `As` tells VB.NET that you are declaring the variable as a particular data type, which in this example is a `Decimal`.

VB.NET knows how much memory to reserve for the variable because you specified the data type of the variable. Remember to use the appropriate data type for a variable so that you do not reserve more memory than is required to hold the value that you assign to the variable.

You can declare multiple variables on the same line of your code, as long as each variable is the same data type. A comma must separate variable names. For example, you can declare `decProductPrice` and `decSalesTaxRate` on the same line because both are the same data type — `Decimal`. You cannot declare `decProductPrice` and `strFirstName` on the same line because `decProductPrice` is a `Decimal` data type and `strFirstName` is a `String` data type.

Declaring multiple variables on the same line saves space in your code and is a convenient way to organize your variable names.

Make sure that you use good programming style when deciding on a name for your variable. A variable name should begin with an abbreviation of the variable's data type. The abbreviation is in lowercase. The remaining variable name should reflect the kind of data stored in the variable. The variable name can be a combination of words, such as `FirstName`. The first letter of each word should be uppercase.

Declare a Variable

DECLARE A SINGLE VARIABLE

1. Add a button to a form.

Note: See Chapter 4.

2. Double-click the button.

   The code that executes when the button is clicked appears.

3. Declare a variable at the beginning of the code such as `Dim XXX As DataType`, replacing `XXX` with the name of the variable and `DataType` with the variable type, such as `Decimal`.

4. Press Ctrl+S to save the code.

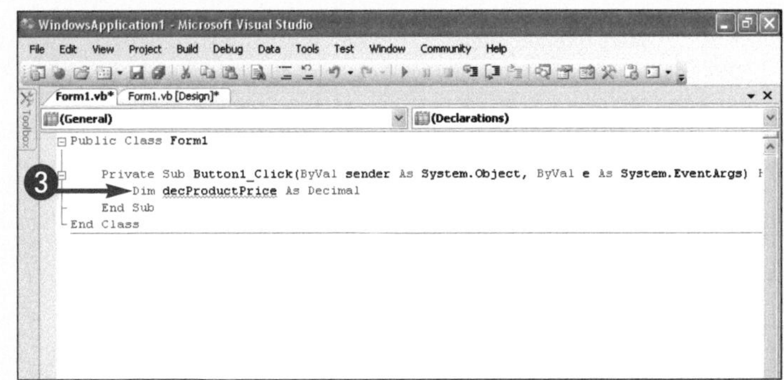

DECLARE MULTIPLE VARIABLES

1. Add a button to a form.

2. Double-click the button.

   The code that executes when the button is clicked appears.

3. Declare a variable by repeating the previous step 3.

4. Add a comma after the first variable and then add the next variable name, such as `Dim decProductPrice, decSalesTaxRate As Decimal`.

5. Press Ctrl+S to save the code.

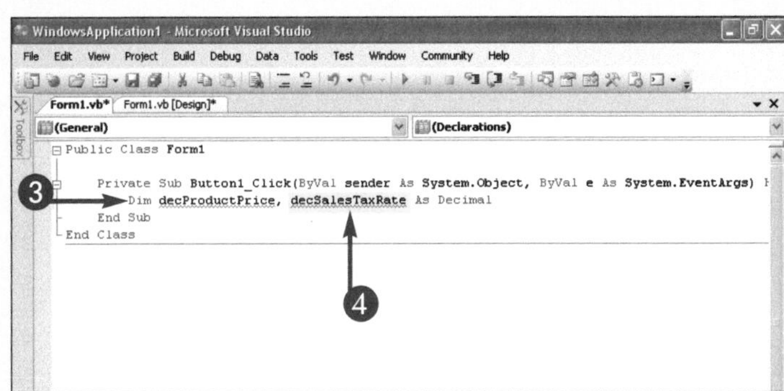

Initialize a Variable

A common error is to use a variable that has not been assigned a value. You can avoid this type of error by assigning an initial value to variables either when the variable is declared or shortly after the variable is declared. The process of assigning an initial value to a variable is called *initializing a variable.*

Any value can be the initial value assigned to a variable. Programmers typically use a value that cannot be confused with a typical value that is assigned to the variable. Zero is a good initial value for variables that are used to store a number such as `decProductPrice` because the actual value — the price of a product — is usually greater than zero.

You can initialize a variable when the variable is declared by using `Dim decProductPrice As Decimal = 0.` Alternatively, you can assign the initial value to the variable after the variable is declared, such as `decProductPrice = 0.` Do this immediately after you declare the variable at the beginning of your application.

The initial value that you assign to a variable remains until another value is assigned to the variable by a different line of code in your application.

You can initialize more than one variable when you declare multiple variables at the same time by separating each declaration with a comma. If you want to declare two decimal variables and initialize both to zero, you would write `Dim decProductPrice As Decimal = 0, decSalesTaxRate As Decimal = 0.`

Variables that are declared and initialized in the same `Dim` statement can be different data types. For example, VB.NET allows this: `Dim decProductNumber As Integer = 0, decSalesTaxRate As Decimal = 0.`

Initialize a Variable

1. Add a button to a form.

Note: See Chapter 4 for information about adding buttons.

2. Double-click the button.

The code that executes when the button is clicked appears.

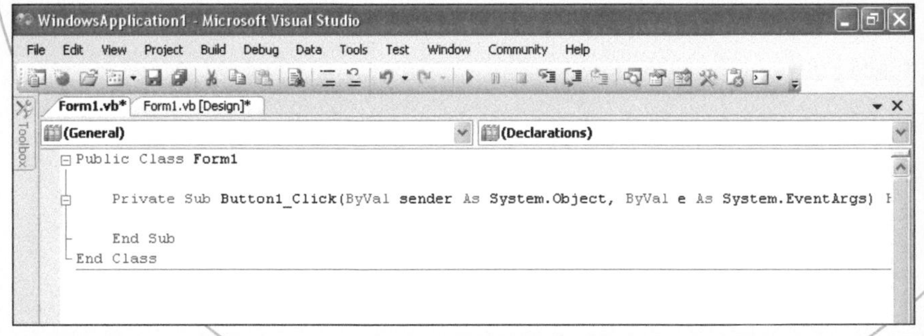

3. Declare a variable at the beginning of the code such as `Dim XXX As DataType`, replacing `XXX` with the name of the variable and `DataType` with the variable type, such as `Decimal`.
4. Initialize the variable by adding `= X` at the end of the line, replacing `X` with the value to be assigned to the variable.
5. Press Ctrl+S to save the code.

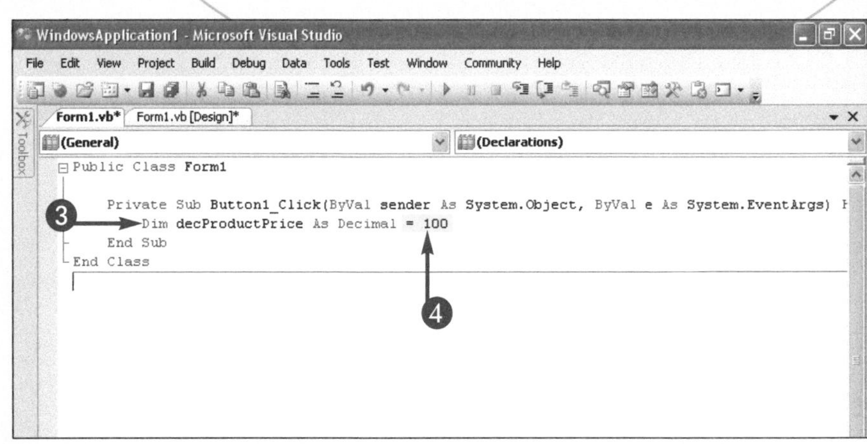

Assign a Value to a Variable

The assignment operator (=) is used to assign a value to a variable. The assignment operator is placed on the right side of the variable name. To the right of the = can be a value, a variable, or an expression. This right side must match the variable type; for example, a `Date` variable must be assigned a value in the format of a date.

You do not use quotations marks (" ") around numbers that are assigned to a variable that is a `Boolean`, `Decimal`, `Double`, or `Integer` data type. You do place quotation marks around numbers and characters that are assigned to a `String` variable or a `Char` variable.

If you assign a character or `String` data to an `Integer` variable without using quotation marks, an error message is displayed saying that the name is not declared. VB.NET assumes that the data is a name of a variable that you forgot to declare.

If you assign a number to a `Char` or `String` variable, you will receive an error message saying that an integer value cannot be converted to a character variable.

You can assign a value to a variable when you declare the variable by using the equals sign and the value to the right of the data type.

Assign a Value to a Variable

1. Add a `Button` control to a form.

Note: See Chapter 4 for more information.

2. Double-click the button.

The code that executes when the button is clicked appears.

3. Declare a variable at the beginning of the code, such as `Dim decProductPrice As Decimal`.

4. Assign a value to the variable on a new line of code.

5. Press Ctrl+S to save the code.

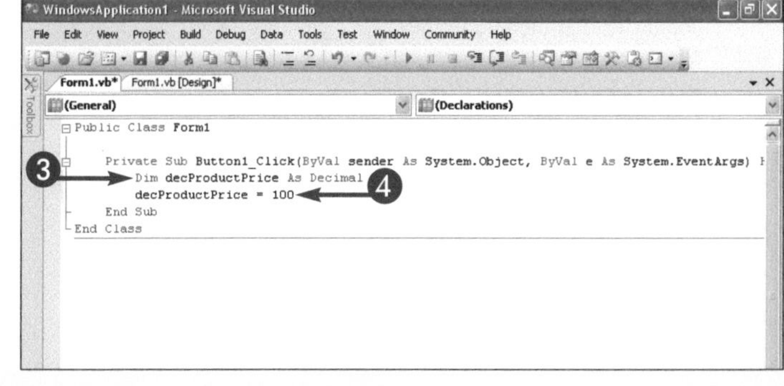

Using Variables

You use the name of a variable in your code whenever you want to use the value stored in the variable. When your program runs, the variable name is replaced by the value of the variable. You will not see the value replace the variable name because normally you cannot see your code when your program is running. A variable name can be used in any expression that can use a value.

Suppose that you want to calculate a 5% sales tax rate on a $100 purchase. The expression you need to write is 100 * 0.05. Instead of using actual values in your program, you can use variables to represent the purchase price and the sales tax rate by assigning 100 to the `decProductPrice` variable and 0.05 to the `decSalesTaxRate` variable. The variable names rather than the values are then used in the expression `decSalesTaxRate * decProductPrice`.

Make sure that you spell the variable name exactly the way the variable name is spelled when you declared the variable; otherwise, you will receive an error message when you try to run your program. For example, `decSalesTaxRate` and `SalesTaxRate` are two different variable names; although both contain `SalesTaxRate`, they may be different sales tax rates.

Never place a variable name within quotations. If you do, the variable name is treated as a string value rather than the name of a variable. Let's say that you wrote `"strCustomerFirstName"` in your program when you want to refer to the contents stored in the variable `strCustomerFirstName`. Visual Basic .NET will treat `"strCustomerFirstName"` as a value because the name is enclosed in quotations and will not replace `"strCustomerFirstName"` with the value stored in the variable `strCustomerFirstName`.

Using Variables

1. Add a `Button` control to a form.

Note: See Chapter 4 for more information.

2. Add a `TextBox` control to a form.

Note: See Chapter 3 for more information.

3. Double-click the button.

   The code that executes when the button is clicked appears.

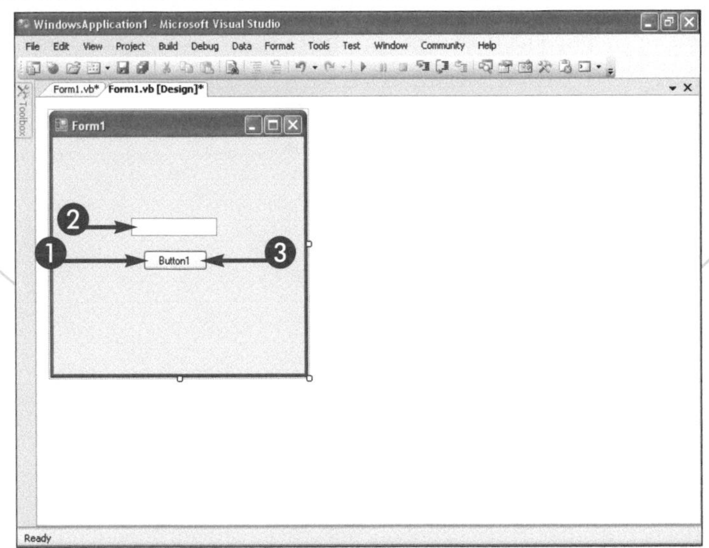

4. Declare variables at the beginning of the code.
5. Assign data to the variables on new lines.
6. Add a line to perform a calculation using the variables, such as calculating the sales tax, and display the result in the `TextBox` control.
7. Press Ctrl+S to save the code.
8. Press F5 to run the program.
9. Click the button when the dialog box appears to perform the calculation.

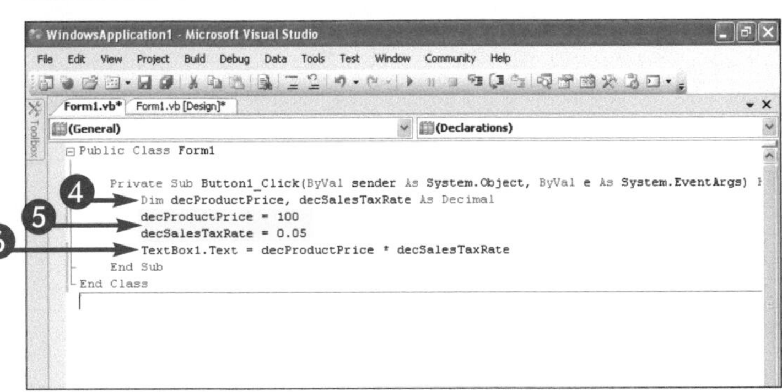

Change the Value of a Variable

You can change the value of a variable by assigning the variable a different value using the assignment operator (=). The assignment operator tells Visual Basic .NET to assign the value from the right side of the operator to the left side of the operator. The right side of the operator may be a value, a variable, or an expression.

Let's say that you want to change the price of a product that is represented as the variable `decProductPrice` in your program. The original price is $100. The new price is $200. You change the price by assigning `200` to the `decProductPrice` variable, such as `decProductPrice = 200`. The new value assigned to a variable overwrites the existing value stored in the variable. That is, `200` replaces `100` in the `decProductPrice` variable. After you change the value of a variable, you cannot revert back to the previous value of the variable because the previous value does not exist anymore.

The right side of the equals sign can be the name of a variable. For example, the value stored in the variable `decNewPrice` can be assigned to the variable `decProductPrice` by using `decProductPrice = decNewPrice`. Visual Basic .NET replaces `decNewPrice` with the value stored in the `decNewPrice` variable before assigning this value to the `decProductPrice` variable.

The value stored in a variable can be changed any number of times within your program after you declared the variable. The new value remains stored in the variable until you change the value or until the variable is destroyed by Visual Basic .NET at the end of a subroutine or function (see Chapter 9) and at the end of your program.

Change the Value of a Variable

1. Add a `Button` control to a form.

Note: See Chapter 4 for more information.

2. Double-click the button.

   The code that executes when the button is clicked appears.

3. Declare variables at the beginning of the code, such as `Dim decOldProductPrice, decNewProductPrice As Decimal`.

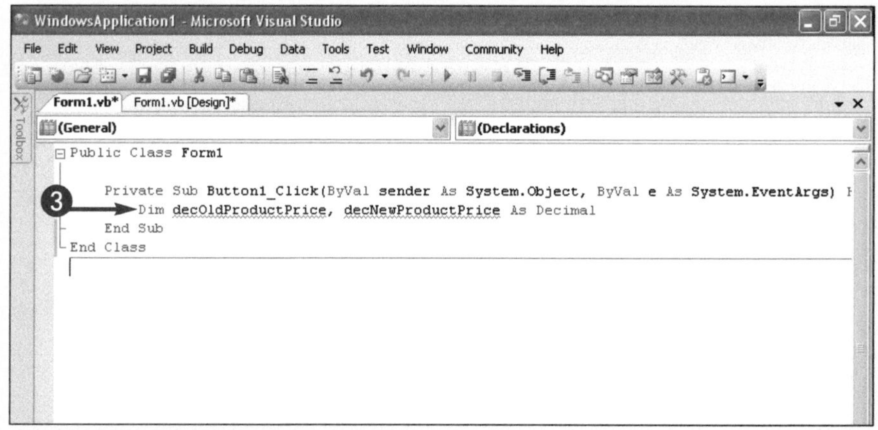

4. Assign data to one of the variables on a new line of code.

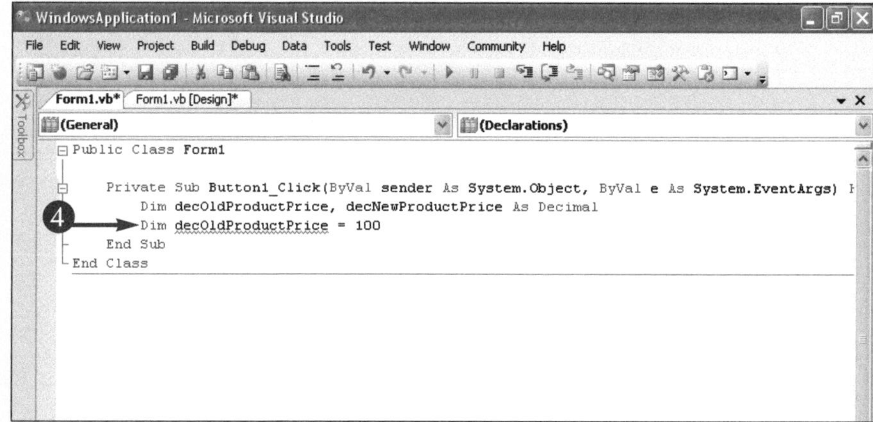

5 Assign data to the other variable on another new line of code.

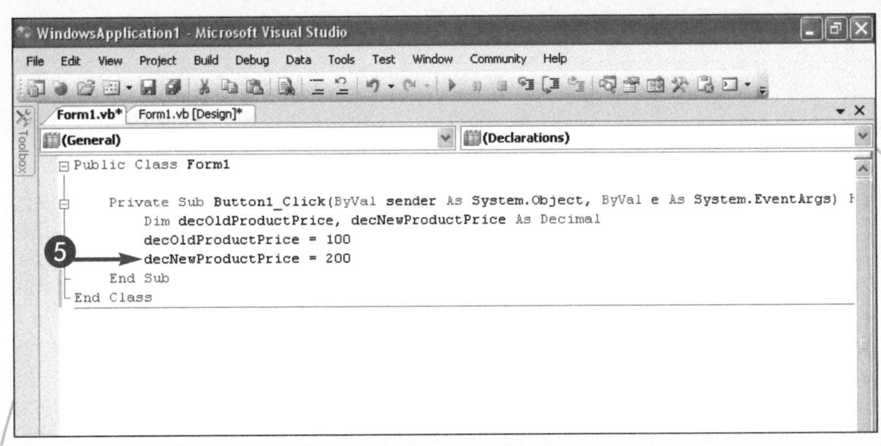

6 Add a line to assign the value of the second variable to the first variable.

7 Press Ctrl+S to save the code.

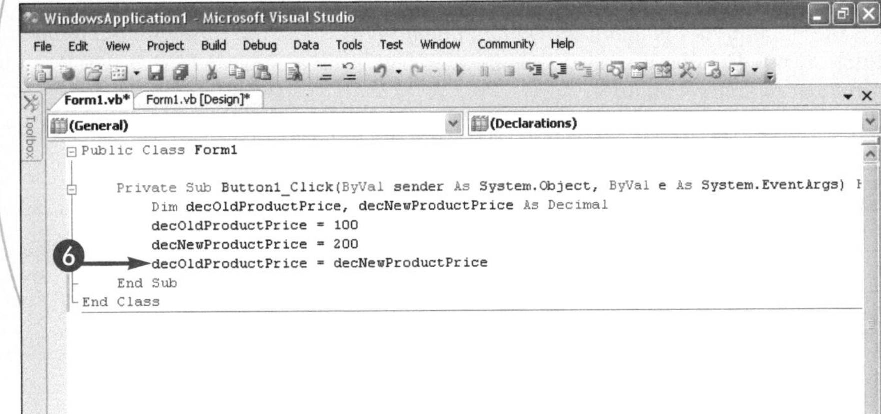

Extra

You can include the current value of the variable in the updated value by using the variable name. Let's say that you want to increase the current value of `decProductPrice` by 10% and then save the new price to the `decProductPrice` variable. The new price is 110% of the current price, which is stored in the `decProductPrice`.

TYPE THIS

```
Dim decProductPrice As Decimal = 100
decProductPrice = decProductPrice * 1.10
```

RESULT

Visual Basic .NET multiplies the value stored in the `decProductPrice` by 1.10, which is the current price plus 10%, and assigns the product of the calculation to the `decProductPrice`.

Convert Data Types

Sometimes within your program you will need to assign the value of a variable to another variable that is a different data type. You cannot do this using the assignment operator in most circumstances. Instead, you need to cast the value using a type conversion function.

For example, you may want to assign the price of a product stored in a `Decimal` variable to a `String` variable. A `Decimal` value is a number. A `String` value is a series of characters. A good way to understand the difference between these data types is that a number can be used in a calculation. A number that is a `String` is used as text, such as the number in a street address.

A type conversion function transforms a value from one data type to another data type. A type conversion function consists of a function name and parentheses. The function name describes the data type that the value is being converted to. The value being converted is placed within the parentheses. The type conversion function converts the value to the new data type and returns it to your program.

Here are the type conversion functions that you will need: `CBool()` converts to the `Boolean` data type, `CByte()` converts to `Byte`, `CChar()` converts to `Char`, `CDate()` converts to `Date`, `CDbl()` converts to `Double`, `CDec()` converts to `Decimal`, `CInt()` to `Long`, `CObj()` to `Object`, `CShort()` to `Short`, `CSng()` to `Single`, and `CStr()` to `String`.

Convert Data Types

1. Add a `Button` control to a form.

Note: See Chapter 4 for more information.

2. Double-click the button.

   The code that executes when the button is clicked appears.

3. Declare a `Decimal` variable at the beginning of the code, such as `Dim decProductPrice As Decimal`.

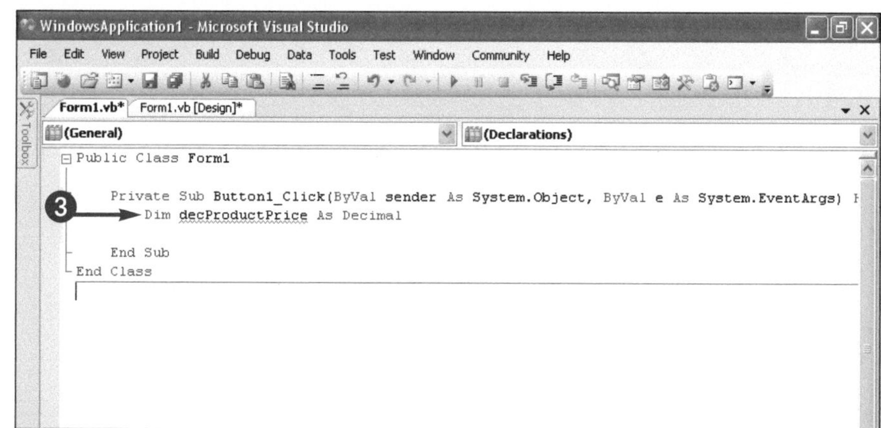

4. Declare a `String` variable after the `Decimal` variable, such as `Dim strCatalogPrice As String`.

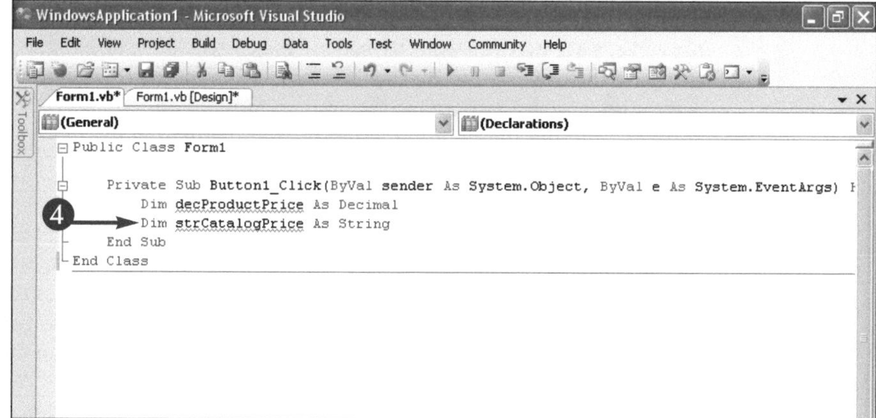

5 Assign data to the `Decimal` variable on a new line of code.

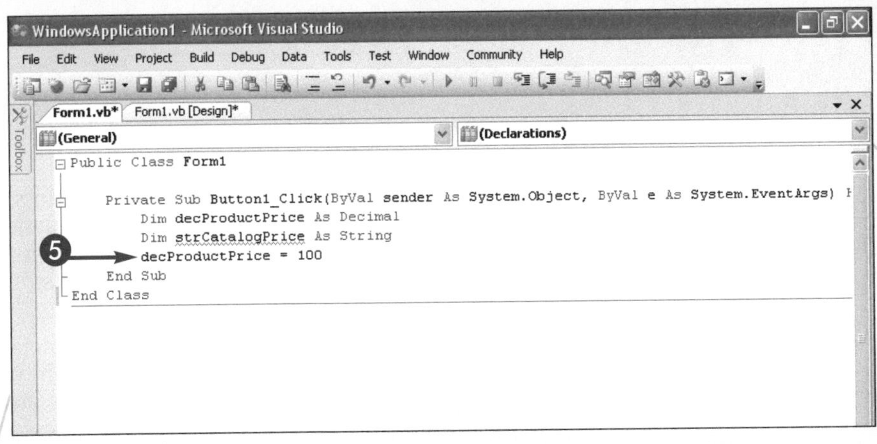

6 Add a line to convert the value of the `Decimal` variable to a `String` and assign the `String` to the `String` variable.

7 Press Ctrl+S to save the code.

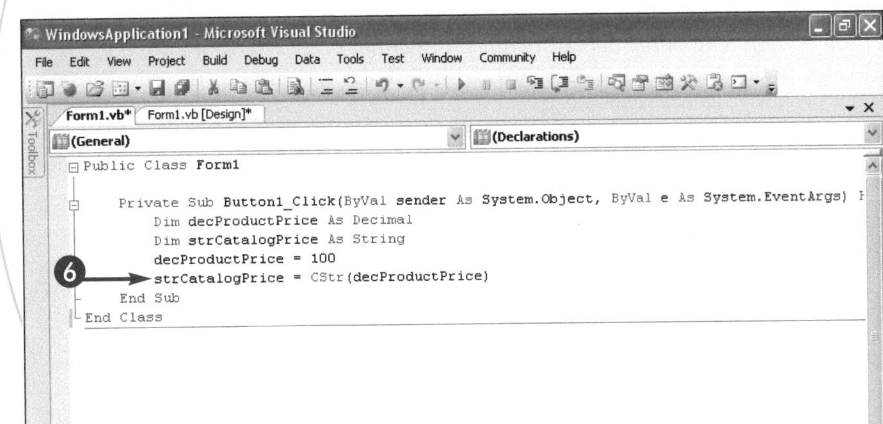

Extra

Most often, you will use a type conversion function to convert a value stored in a variable to a different data type. However, a type conversion function can also convert a value not stored in a variable to a different data type. You simply place the value and not the variable name within the parentheses of the function. Putting the value in parentheses is shorthand for converting a `String` to another data type. Visual Basic .NET creates an unnamed `String` variable and then converts the `String` to the other data type.

TYPE THIS

```
Dim strCatalogPrice As String
strCatalogPrice = CStr(100)
```

RESULT

Visual Basic .NET converts the `100`, which is an integer, to a `String` and assigns the converted 100 to `strCatalogPrice`.

Create a Simple Expression

An expression uses an operator to tell Visual Basic .NET to perform an operation using values on either side of the operator. These values are called *operands*. For example, `7 + 5` is an expression. The `+` is the symbol for the addition operator. `7` and `5` are operands.

There are basically three types of operators that you will use in your program. These are arithmetic operators, comparison operators, and logical operators. Arithmetic operators tell Visual Basic .NET to perform arithmetic. Comparison operators tell Visual Basic .NET to compare the operand on the left side of the operator with the operand on the right side of the operator. If they compare, then the operator returns a true; otherwise, the operator returns a false. Logical operators compare the results of two logical expressions and return a true or false.

The arithmetic operators are as follows: exponentiation (`^`), used for scientific notation; negation (`-`), used for a value less than zero; multiplication (`*`); division (`/`); addition (`+`); subtraction (`-`); and string concatenation (`&`), used for combining two strings.

The comparison operators are as follows: equals (`=`); left side is greater than the right side (`>`); left side is less than the right side (`<`); left side is greater than or equal to the right side (`>=`); and left side is less than or equal to the right side (`<=`).

The logical operators are as follows: `NOT`, which returns the opposite logical value of an expression (if the equation is true, `NOT` returns a false); `AND`, which returns a true if both expressions evaluate true; `OR`, which returns a true if either expression evaluates true; and `XOR`, which returns a true if one and only one expression is true (if both are true, a false is returned).

Create a Simple Expression

1. Add a `Button` control to a form.

Note: See Chapter 4 for more information.

2. Add a `TextBox` control to a form.

Note: See Chapter 3 for more information.

3. Double-click the button.

   The code that executes when the button is clicked appears.

4. Assign an expression to the `Text` property of the `TextBox1` control.

5. Press Ctrl+S to save the code.

6. Press F5 to run the program.

7. Click the button.

   The expression is calculated.

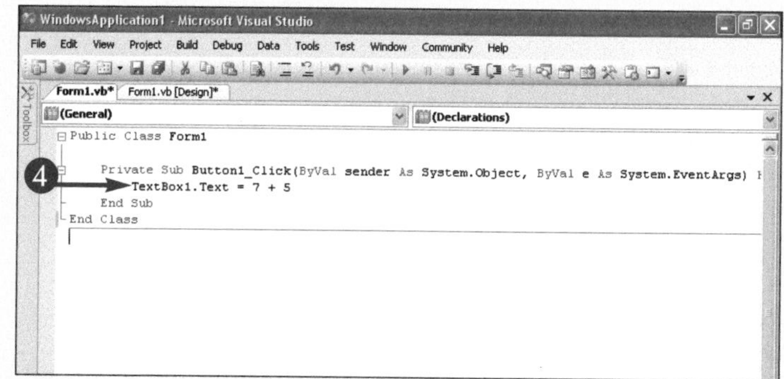

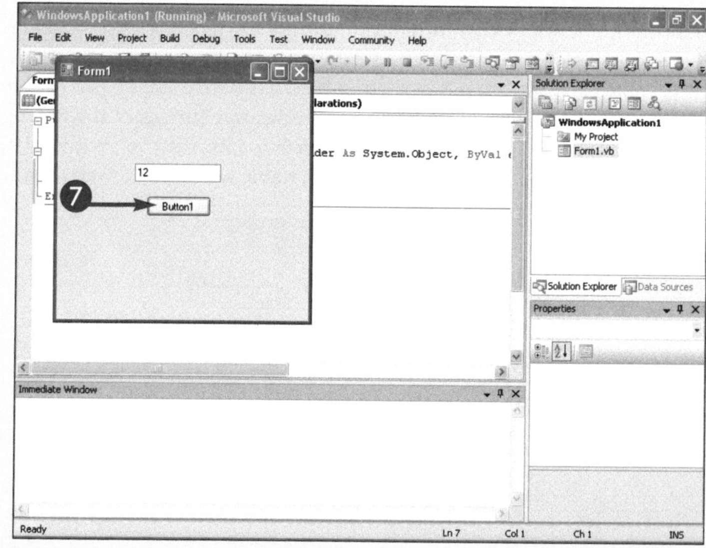

Create a Complex Expression

A complex expression has several operations that are performed in a single expression and can be used to combine multiple lines of code in your program to one line of code. A complex expression can contain arithmetic operations or logical operations.

For example, `7 + 5 * 2` is a complex expression that contains two arithmetic operations; each operation could be performed in its own equation on separate lines of code. Operations are placed one after the other in the expression. The result of one operation becomes the operand for the next operation. This means that the result of `5 * 2`, which is `10`, becomes part of `7 + 10`, which is the next operation; see the section "Using Operator Precedence."

A logical expression is `intMidTermExamGrade >= intPassingGrade AND intFinalExamGrade >= intPassingGrade`. The `intPassingGrade` is a variable that contains the grade value needed to pass both exams. The `intMidTermExamGrade` is a variable that contains the mid-term grade, and the `intFinalExamGrade` is the variable that contains the final exam grade. Visual Basic .NET is able to evaluate each operation in a complex expression separately. That is, Visual Basic .NET determines if the mid-term grade is greater than or equal to the passing grade. If so, this operation results in a true, and then Visual Basic .NET determines if the final exam grade is greater than or equal to the passing grade. If so, the expression is true. If either exam grade is less than the passing grade, the expression is false.

Sometimes you will find combining operations into one expression makes the line of code confusing for you to read. Although you may find a complex expression confusing, Visual Basic .NET will have no trouble reading it.

Create a Complex Expression

1. Add a `Button` control to a form.

Note: See Chapter 4 for more information.

2. Add a `TextBox` control to a form.

Note: See Chapter 3 for more information.

3. Double-click the button.

   The code that executes when the button is clicked appears.

4. Assign a complex expression to the `Text` property of the `TextBox1` control.

5. Press Ctrl+S to save the code.

6. Press F5 to run the program.

7. Click the button.

   The complex expression is calculated.

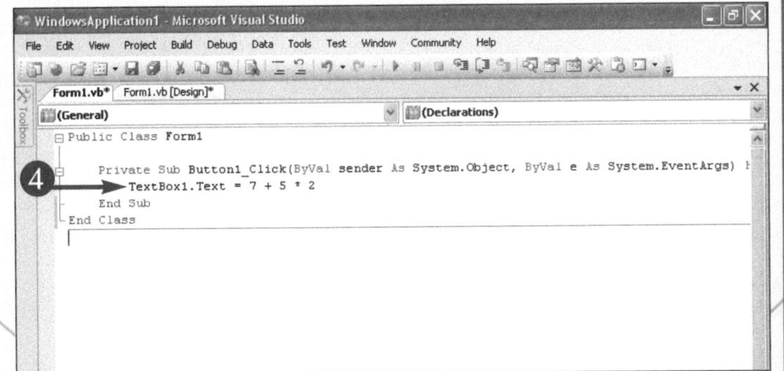

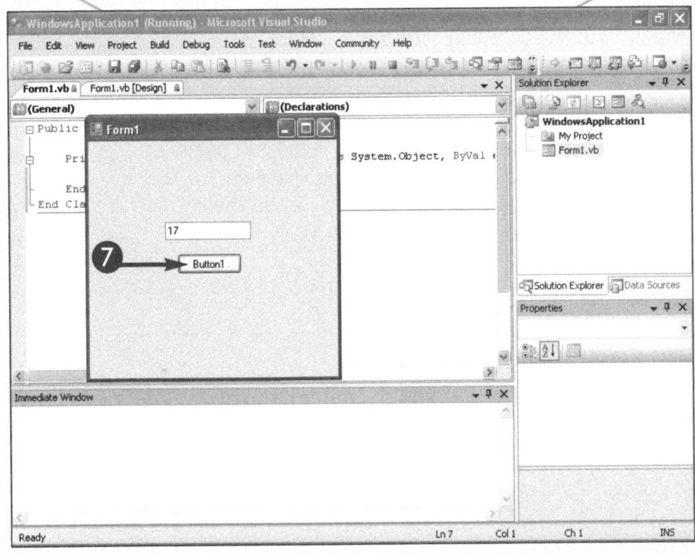

Using Operator Precedence

Visual Basic .NET performs each operation using operator precedence. Operator precedence determines the order in which to perform an operation.

For example, `7 + 5 * 2` could be evaluated two ways: The first way is `7 + 5 = 12` and then `12 * 2 = 24`. The other way is `5 * 2 = 10` and then `7 + 10 = 17`. Operator precedence requires that multiplication be performed before addition. Therefore, Visual Basic .NET evaluates this as `7 + 5 * 2 = 17`.

A common programming error is to create an expression without consulting the operator precedence and incorrectly assume the order in which Visual Basic .NET will evaluate your expression. The result is that your program generates an unexpected value when evaluating the expression. That is, you expected `7 + 5 * 2 = 24` when Visual Basic .NET evaluates this expression as `17`.

When an expression contains two operations that are equal according to the operator precedence, Visual Basic .NET evaluates the expression left to right. The left operation is performed first, followed by the second operation, then the third operation, and so on, until all the operations are performed.

Operator Precedence

Here is the operator precedence used by Visual Basic .NET, in order:

1. Exponentiation (`^`) and `NOT`
2. Negation (`-`) and `AND`
3. Multiplication(`*`), division (`/`), and `OR`
4. Modulus arithmetic (`Mod`)
5. Addition (`+`) and subtraction (`-`)
6. String concatenation (`&`)
7. Equals (`=`), less than (`<`), greater than (`>`), less than or equal to (`<=`), and greater than or equal to (`>=`)

Using Parentheses to Create Your Own Operator Precedence

You can use parentheses around equations in an expression to specify your own operator precedence. Visual Basic .NET performs an operation within parentheses before performing other operations in the expression. You can place parentheses within parentheses such as `(7 * (5 + 2))`. The operation in the inner-most parentheses will be performed first, followed by the operation in the next outer parentheses. After performing the operation within the parentheses, Visual Basic .NET replaces that equation with the value returned from the operation such as `(7 * 7)`.

TYPE THIS

```
(7 + 5)* 2
```

RESULT

Visual Basic .NET performs the addition, replaces the `(7 + 5)` with 12, and multiplies 12 by 2, resulting in the product of 24.

Create a Statement

A *statement* is an instruction that tells Visual Basic .NET to do something, which is similar to an English sentence. A statement can contain an equation, an expression, Visual Basic commands, or a combination of these. For example, you can use a Visual Basic .NET command to call a function and then pass an expression to the function; see Chapter 9.

A Visual Basic .NET *command* is a keyword that Visual Basic .NET understands, which is very similar in concept to words that you use to create an English sentence. For example, you may say, "Write 'I love to program in Visual Basic .NET' on a piece of paper." This is a sentence that tells someone to do something. The person hearing the sentence knows the definition of the words that you say and therefore can follow your direction.

In Visual Basic .NET, you write a statement with words that Visual Basic .NET knows; therefore, Visual Basic .NET can follow your direction. For example, in your program, you can write this statement: `Textbox1.Text = "I love to program in Visual Basic .NET"`. Visual Basic .NET understands the meaning of `Textbox1.Text =`. `Textbox1` is the name of a text box control on a form. `Text` is the name of the text property of that text box control. The assignment (`=`) operator tells Visual Basic .NET to assign the value on its right side to the left side. In this case, that means to assign the string "I love to program in Visual Basic .NET" to the `Text` property of the text box control.

Create a Statement

1. Add a `Button` control to a form.

Note: See Chapter 4 for more information.

2. Add a `TextBox` control to a form.

Note: See Chapter 3 for more information.

3. Double-click the button.

   The code that executes when the button is clicked appears.

4. Add text to the `TextBox1 Text` property.

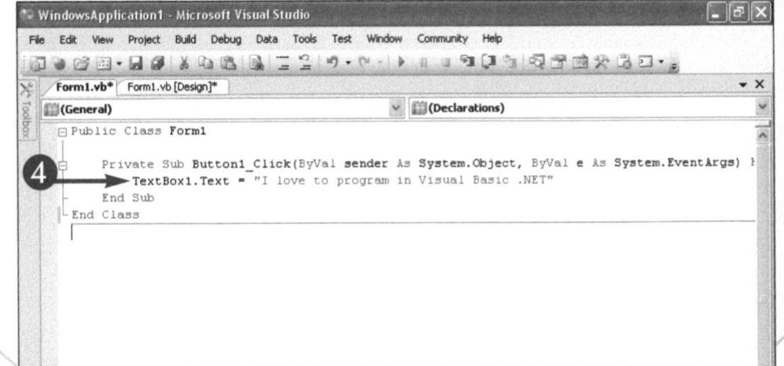

5. Press Ctrl+S to save the code.
6. Press F5 to run the program.
7. Click the button.

   The text is displayed.

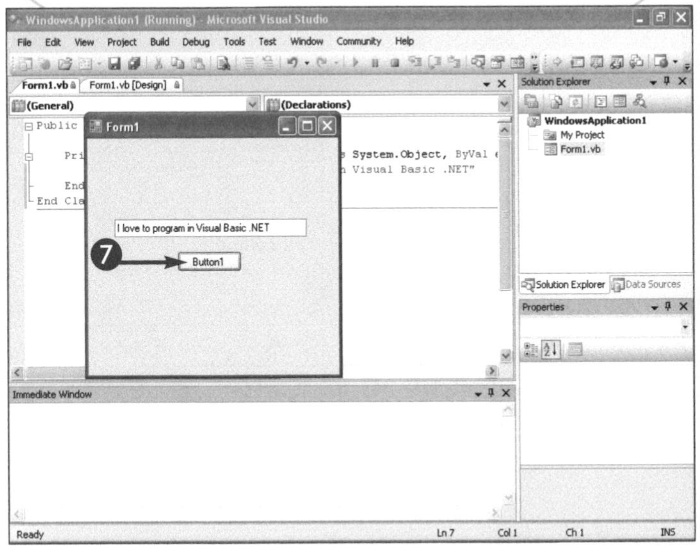

Create More Complex Expressions

You can place values and names of variables to form a complex expression. Visual Basic .NET replaces variable names with the value stored in the variable before performing the operation in the expression. You use the name of the variable in the expression where you would otherwise use the value stored in the variable.

Let's say that you need to calculate local and state sales tax for a product price. The local sales tax is assigned to the `decLocalSalesTaxRate` variable, and the state sales tax is assigned to the `decStateSalesTaxRate` variable. The price of the product is assigned to the `decProductPrice` variable. The expression to calculate the total amount the customer pays for the product is `decProductPrice + (decProductPrice * decLocalSalesTaxRate) + (decProductPrice * decStateSalesTaxRate).`

Remember that operations contained within parentheses are performed first before operations outside the parentheses. This means that the local sales tax is calculated first and then the state sales tax is calculated. The final operation adds together the product price and both sales taxes to arrive at the amount of money the customer pays for the product.

Sometimes a complex expression can give correct but unexpected results if you do not use parentheses to identify operations. For example, what is the result of 5 + 4 * 10? It could be 90 if the addition is performed before the multiplication, or 45 if the multiplication is performed first. The answer is 45 because of Visual Basic .NET's order of operations. You do not have to memorize the order of operations, though, if you use parentheses to clarify what expression you want calculated first. For example, the result of (5+4) * 10 is 90.

Create More Complex Expressions

1. Add a `Button` control to a form.

Note: See Chapter 4 for more information.

2. Add a `TextBox` control to a form.

Note: See Chapter 3 for more information.

3. Double-click the button.

The code that executes when the button is clicked appears.

4. Declare three variables such as `Dim decProductPrice, decLocalSalesTaxRate, decStateSalesTaxRate As Decimal`.

5. Assign values to these variables.

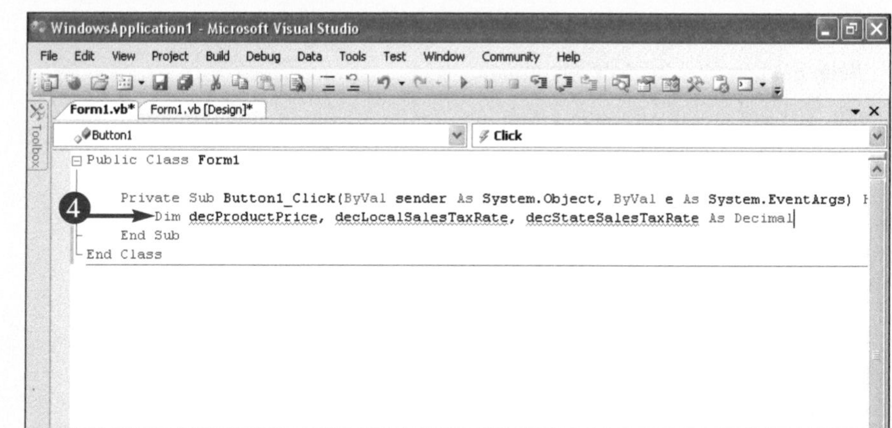

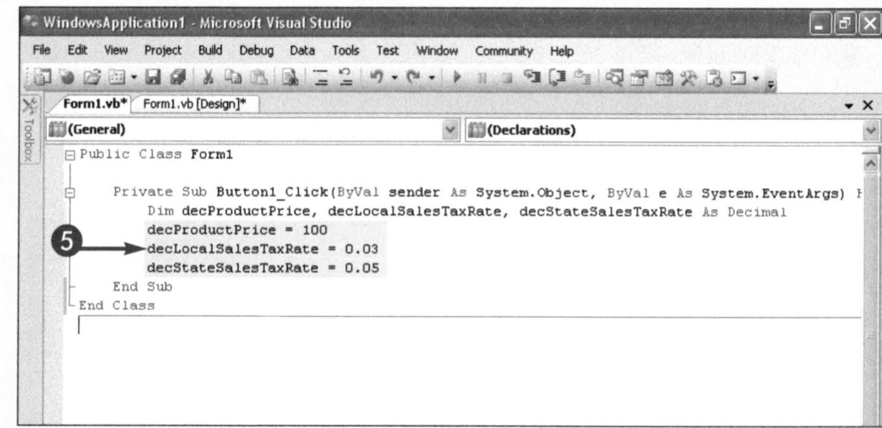

6 Assign a complex expression to the `Text` property of `TextBox1`.

Note: The expression appears on two lines to fit the expression in the figure. You should create an expression on one line.

7 Press Ctrl+S to save the code.

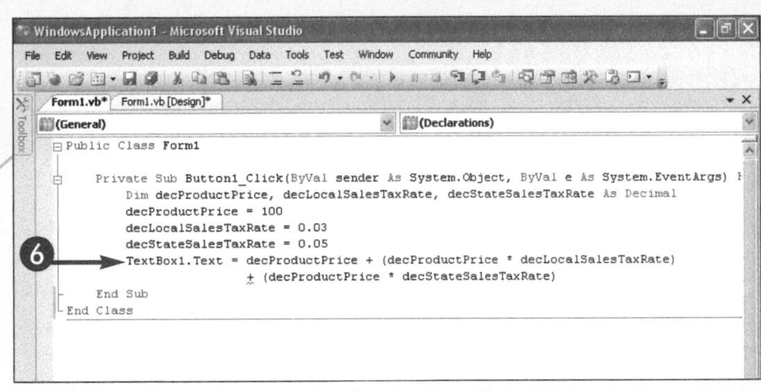

8 Press F5 to run the program.

9 Click the button.

The expression is calculated.

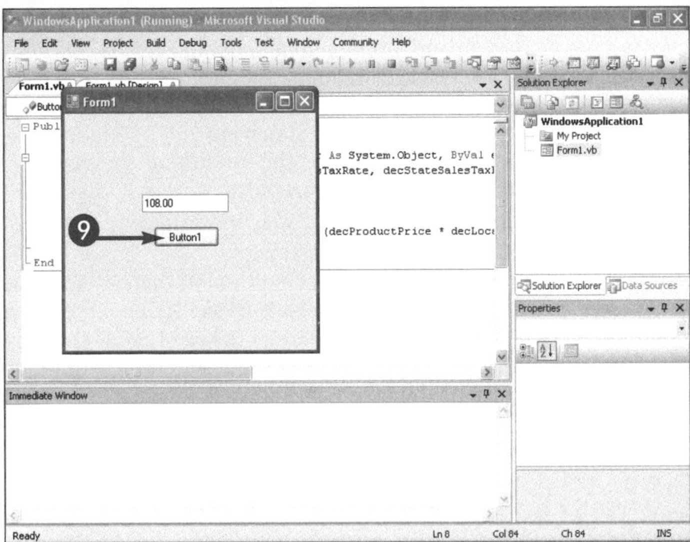

Extra

Parentheses must be balanced. For every open parenthesis, you must have a close parenthesis. It is easy to balance parentheses if you have a simple expression; however, you can easily lose track of open and close parentheses in complex expressions that contain many sets of parentheses inside other sets of parentheses. There are two ways to avoid unbalanced parentheses. First, place a close parenthesis into the expression when you insert an open parenthesis rather than insert the close parenthesis after you write the equation in the parentheses. Next, count the number of open parentheses and the number of closed parentheses. There should be an equal number. If the number is not equal, then the parentheses are unbalanced.

Understanding Conditional Statements

You use a conditional statement to have Visual Basic .NET make a decision while your program is running. Based on this decision, Visual Basic .NET either executes one or more lines of your program, called a *code block,* or skips them entirely. Those lines of code that are skipped are never executed.

A conditional statement evaluates a logical expression to decide to execute or skip a code block in your program. A *logical expression* is an expression that uses a logical operator to evaluate two values; see Chapter 5. If the expression evaluates true, the conditional statement executes the code block that you specify in the conditional statement; otherwise, the code block is not executed.

The logical operator tells Visual Basic .NET how to evaluate the values in the logical expression. For example, `decNewPrice > decOldPrice` is a logical expression that uses the greater than operator (>) to tell Visual Basic .NET to compare the values stored in the variables `decNewPrice` and `decOldPrice`. If the new price is greater than the old price, the expression is true; otherwise, the expression is false.

There are two general types of conditional statements. These are the `If... Then` statement and the `Select Case` statement. The `If... Then` statement simply tells Visual Basic .NET to execute one or more lines of code if the logical expression is true. The `Select Case` statement tells Visual Basic .NET to compare a test value with one or more `Case` values. Beneath each `Case` value is a code block that executes if the `Case` value matches the test value.

There are variations of an `If... Then` statement that you can use to have Visual Basic .NET make complex decisions. Let's say that you want some code to execute if a condition is true and another bunch of code to execute if the condition is false. You would use an `If...Then...Else` variation of the `If...Then` statement.

Now suppose that you want Visual Basic .NET to evaluate another condition if the first condition is false such as saying, "If the color is green, then go, else if the color is yellow, then slow down, else stop." This is another variation of the `If... Then` statement called an `If...Then...ElseIf...Then...Else` statement.

You can also combine `If...Then` statements by putting one `If...Then` statement inside the another. You can say, "If the person is a student, then determine if the student lives in the dorm." This is referred to as a nested `If...Then` statement because the second `If...Then` statement is nested inside the other `If...Then` statement.

Likewise, you can combine an `If...Then` statement with a `Select Case` statement by placing the `Select Case` statement inside the `If...Then` statement. This says, "If there is a traffic light, then test the color of the light to see if it is green, yellow, or red." These colors are `Case` values.

Types of Conditional Statements

If...Then The `If...Then` conditional statement executes a code block if the logical expression evaluates true; otherwise, the code block is not executed.	**If...Then (Inline)** The `If...Then` is an inline `If...Then` statement if it is written as `If a = b Then MessageBox.Show ("True")`. You can only execute one statement if the condition is true. This statement follows `Then` on the same line. You do not need to use an `End If` because there is a single statement executed if the condition is true.
If...Then...Else The `If...Then...Else` conditional statement has two code blocks. One code block executes if the logical expression evaluates true; otherwise, the second code block executes.	**If...Then...Else (Inline)** The `If...Then...Else` is an inline `If...Then` statement if it is written as `If a = b Then MessageBox.Show("True") Else MessageBox.Show("False")`. You can have one statement executed if the expression is true and a different single expression executed if the expression is false. You do not need an `End If`.
If...Then...ElseIf...Then The `If...Then...ElseIf...Then` conditional statement has two logical expressions and two code blocks. If the first logical expression is true, the first code block executes; otherwise, the second logical expression is evaluated. If the second logical expression is true, the second code block executes; otherwise, neither code block executes. This expression can have as many `ElseIf` conditions as you need.	**Select Case** The `Select Case` conditional statement compares a test value to one or more `Case` values. If there is a match, the code block beneath the matching `Case` value executes.
If...Then...ElseIf...Then...Else The `If...Then...ElseIf...Then...Else` conditional statement has two logical expressions and three code blocks. If the first logical expression is true, the first code block executes; otherwise, Visual Basic .NET evaluates the second logical expression. If the second logical expression is true, the second code block executes. If neither the first logical expression nor the second logical expression is true, then the third code block executes. This expression can also have as many `ElseIf` conditions as you need.	**Select Case...Case Else** The `Select Case...Else` conditional statement compares a test value to one or more `Case` values. If there is a match, the code block beneath the matching `Case` value executes. If none of the `Case` values match, the `Case Else` code block executes.

True and False

The concept of true and false is fairly straightforward to understand. Your program tells Visual Basic .NET to evaluate a conditional expression. The expression is either true or false. However, true is really any nonzero value, and false is zero. For example, you can place 1 as the conditional expression in an `If...Then` statement such as `If 1 Then`. At first glance, this does not look like a true value, but Visual Basic .NET treats this as a true. In fact, you can use 2, 3, 4, or another number other than 0, and Visual Basic .NET will consider it a true value and execute statements that you place within the code block of the `If...Then` statement. If you place a 0 in the `If...Then` statement, Visual Basic .NET will not execute those statements.

Why would you use a 0 or a 1 in an expression for an `If...Then` statement? Most times, you will simply use a conditional expression, so you do not have to worry about 0 and nonzeros. However, there may come a time when the nature of your application requires you to use a mathematical expression such as 6-5, which results in 1 — a true value.

Create an If...Then Statement

An If...Then statement begins with the keyword If, followed by a logical expression and the keyword Then all on one line. You place the line(s) of code that you want executed if the logical statement is true on the next line(s). The last line in the If...Then statement is End If.

For example, If decNewPrice > decOldPrice Then is the beginning of an If...Then statement. This statement tells Visual Basic .NET to make a decision — is the new price greater than the old price? If this expression is true, Visual Basic .NET executes the code that follows the beginning of the If..Then statement.

End If is the end of the If...Then code block. Code that appears between If...Then and End If executes if the logical expression is true. Code that appears before If...Then and after End If executes whether or not the logical expression is true or false.

If the logical expression is false, Visual Basic .NET skips the code block and executes code that appears on the line following End If. If the logical expression is true, Visual Basic .NET executes code in the code block and then executes the code that follows End If.

The code block of an If...Then statement can contain any valid statement as if the statement were written outside the code block. You can even include other If...Then statements within the code block of an If..Then statement. This is referred to as a nested If...Then statement; see the section "Create a Nested If...Then Statement." However, variables declared inside an If...Then code block are only accessible by statements within the If...Then code block.

Create an If...Then Statement

1. Add a button to a form.

Note: See Chapter 4 for information about adding buttons.

2. Double-click the button.

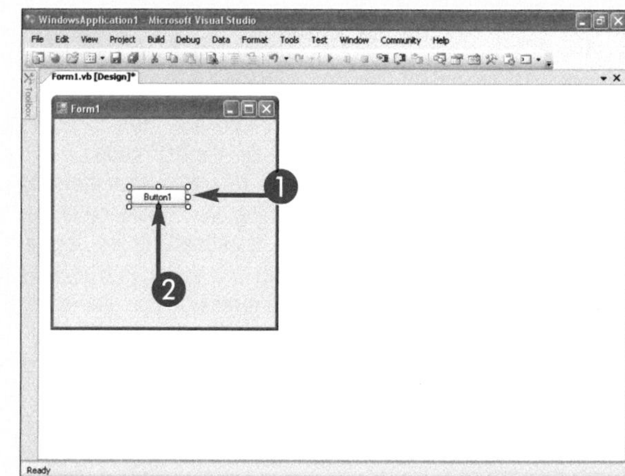

The code that executes when the button is clicked appears.

3. Declare and initialize a variable at the beginning of the code, such as Dim XXX As Decimal = YYY, replacing XXX with the variable name such as decOldPrice and replacing YYY with a value such as 3.99.

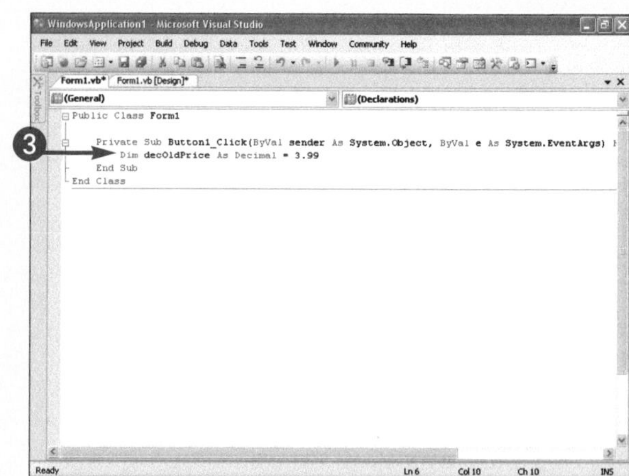

4 Write an `If...Then` statement with a logical expression that determines if the variable is greater than `xxx`, replacing `xxx` with a value such as `2.95`.

5 Add a line that calls `MessageBox.Show("XXX")` if the variable is greater than the value, replacing `xxx` with a message such as `"The old price is greater than $2.95."`

6 Press Ctrl+S to save the code.

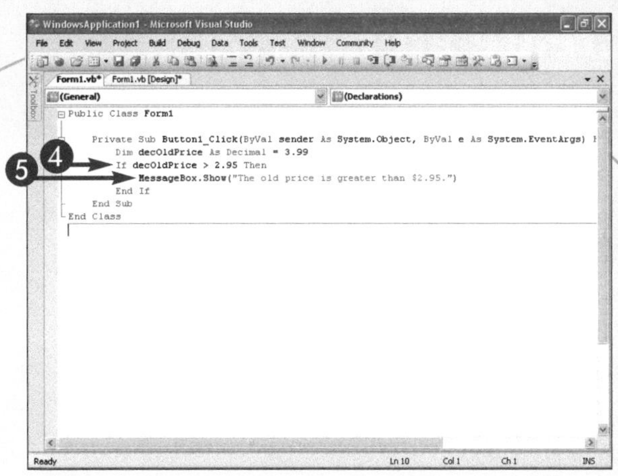

7 Press F5 to run the program.

8 Click the button.

The message box appears.

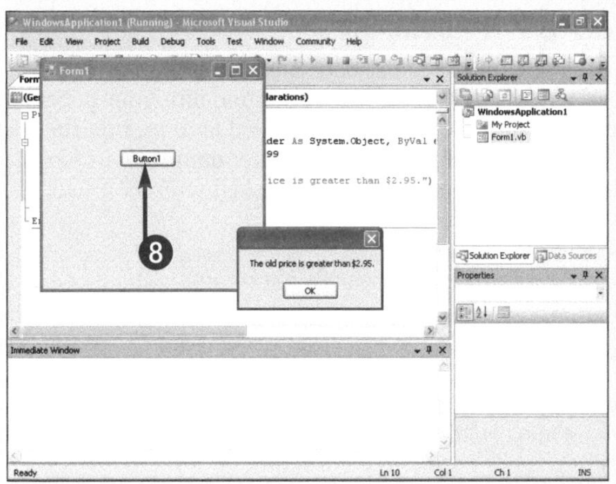

Extra

Variables declared within the `If...Then` code block cannot be used by statements outside the code block. These variables are said to be *out-of-scope* of the rest of the program and are sometimes referred to as *local* to the code block. Variables declared within the `If...Then` code block can be used by statements within the code block.

Statements within the code block can also use variables declared outside the `If...Then` code block as long as those variables were not declared in another code block. For example, variables declared at the beginning of your program can be used by statements within the `If...Then` code block.

An error occurs in the following example because "Hello World" is assigned to a variable that is not declared. There is not an error assigning "Goodbye" because the variable was declared within its code block.

```
Dim intA, intB As Integer
intA = 1
intB = 1
If intA = intB Then
    Dim strC as String
    strC = "Goodbye"
End If
strC = "Hello World"
```

Create an Equivalent Logical Expression

A common part of many programs is to have Visual Basic .NET determine if an expected condition exists while the program is running. You can do this by creating an equivalent logical expression in an `If...Then` statement.

A condition can be a number or one or more characters that you establish when you write your program. For example, a valid user ID is a condition, which must be met before a person is permitted to access the main portion of your program. A valid user ID typically consists of all numbers, all characters, or a mixture of both.

Your program must acquire data that Visual Basic .NET compares to the condition that you wrote into your program. The most common way data is acquired is to prompt the person who uses your program to enter data into a `TextBox` control. For example, the person is asked to enter a user ID.

An equivalent logical expression is used to have Visual Basic .NET compare the data against the condition. Here is the expression you can use to compare the user ID that is entered into your program to the valid user ID: `TextBox1.Text = "ValidUserID"`.

If they are the same, the equivalent logical expression is true and Visual Basic .NET executes lines of code that you place within the `If...Then` statement's code block; otherwise, the code block is skipped. The code following the `End If` is then executed.

Many times the condition is not directly written into your program but instead retrieved from a database (see Chapter 10) and stored in a variable. Therefore, the equivalent logical expression is written as `TextBox1.Text = ValidUserID`, where `ValidUserID` is a variable whose value is the condition retrieved from a database.

Create an Equivalent Logical Expression

1. Add a button to a form.

Note: See Chapter 4 for information about adding buttons.

2. Double-click the button.

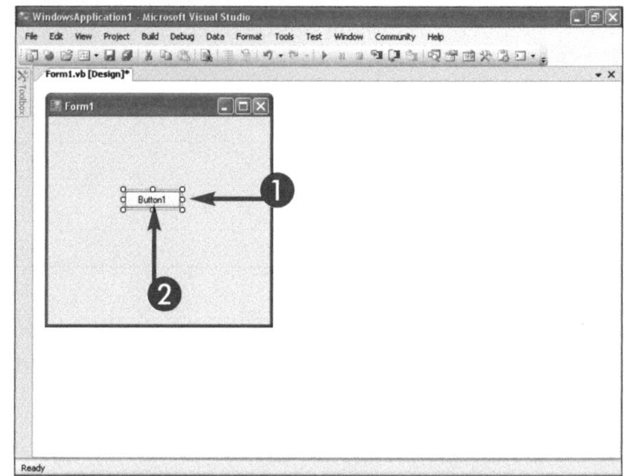

The code that executes when the button is clicked appears.

3. Declare and initialize a variable at the beginning of the code such as add `Dim XXX As Decimal = YYY`, replacing `XXX` with the variable name such as `decOldPrice` and replacing `YYY` with a value such as `3.99`.

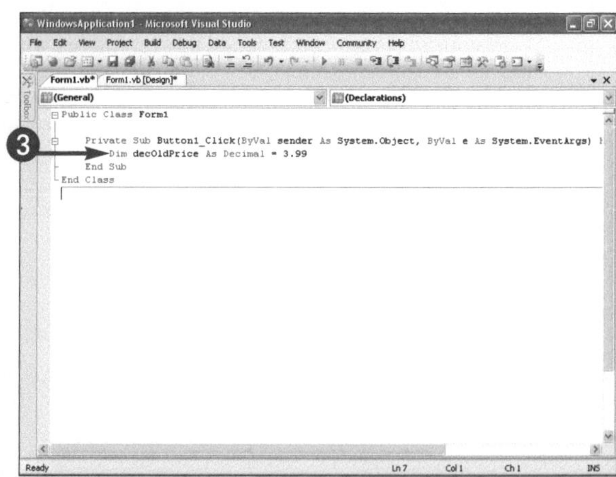

4 Write an `If...Then` statement with a equivalent logical expression that determines if the variable is equal to `xxx`, replacing `xxx` with a value such as `3.99`.

5 Add a line that calls `MessageBox.Show("XXX")` if the variable is equal to the value, replacing `xxx` with a message such as `"The old price is equal to $3.99."`

6 Press Ctrl+S to save the code.

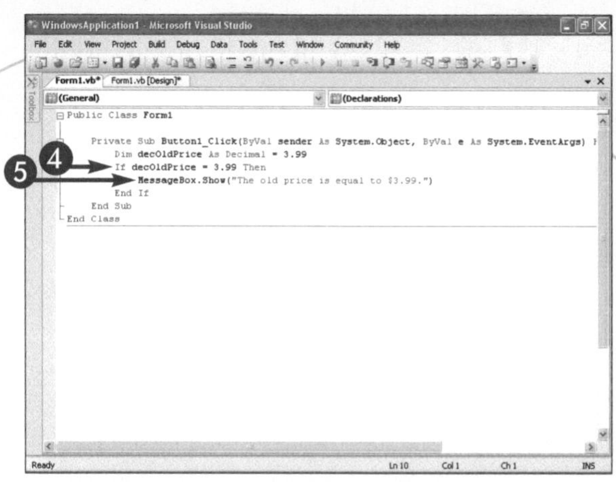

7 Press F5 to run the program.

8 Click the button.

The message box appears.

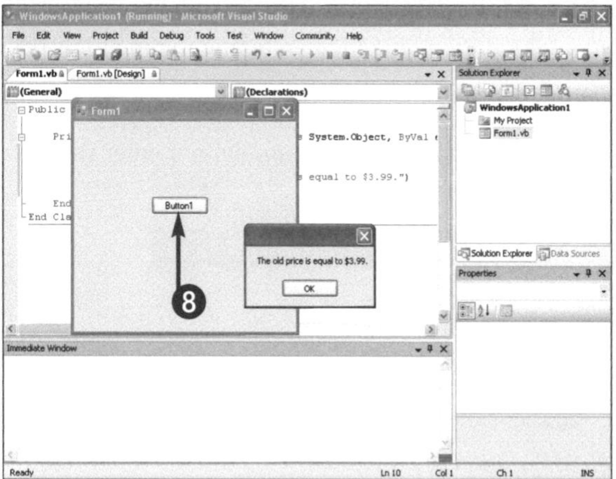

Extra

You can use the value 1 in place of a logical expression in an `If...Then` statement. The value 1 is the same as if the logical expression is true.

Example

```
Dim intStatus As Integer = 1
```

Use the variable `intStatus` as the logical expression for the following `If...Then` statement.

Example

```
If intStatus Then
    MessageBox.show("Status is true.")
End If
```

The statement in the `If...Then` code block executes. However, if you change the value of the `intStatus` variable to zero, the `If...Then` code block is not executed because the zero value is treated as false.

Create a Not Equivalent Logical Expression

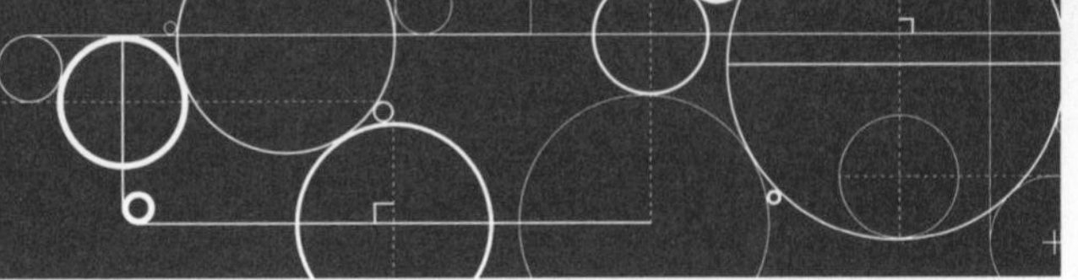

A common occurrence is to execute code within your program when a condition does not exist. For example, you can prevent your program from processing incorrect data by validating the data before processing begins.

To do this, you use a not equivalent logical expression within an `If...Then` statement. If the condition is not met, Visual Basic .NET executes codes within the `If...Then` code block; otherwise, the code block is not executed.

A not equivalent logical expression reverses the outcome of an equivalent logical expression. Let's say that your program prompts a person to enter a zip code into a `TextBox`. The number of characters in the `TextBox` should be five because that is the length of a valid zip code. Your program needs to know if the person did not enter five characters into the `TextBox`.

Here is what you need to do. First, write an equivalent logical expression that determines if the person entered five characters such as `TextBox1.Text.Length = 5`. Next, replace the equivalent operator (`=`) with the not equivalent operator (`<>`) such as `NOT TextBox1.Text.Length <> 5`. This means if the person enters 6 characters as the zip code, the logical expression `TextBox1.Text.Length <> 5` is true. In other words, it is true that the length of the zip code entered into `TextBox1` does not equal 5.

When you use a not equivalent logical expression in an `If...Then` statement, the `If...Then` statement code block executes when this expression is true. That is, `If TextBox1.Text.Length <> 5 Then` is true, the code in the `If...Then` statement code block executes.

Create a Not Equivalent Logical Expression

1. Add a button to a form.

Note: See Chapter 4 for information about adding buttons.

2. Double-click the button.

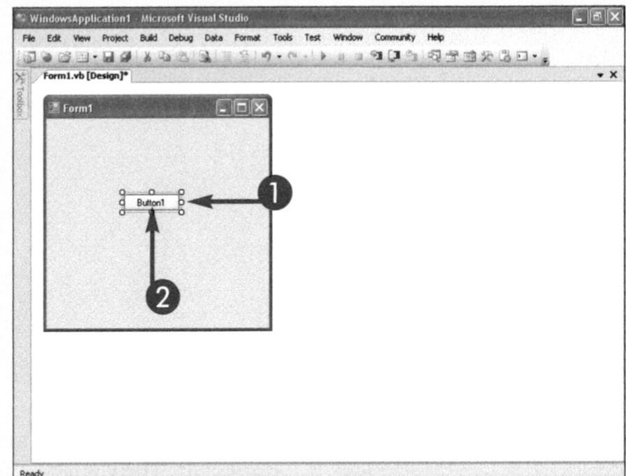

The code that executes when the button is clicked appears.

3. Declare and initialize a variable at the beginning of the code, such as `Dim XXX As Decimal = YYY`, replacing `XXX` with the variable name such as `decOldPrice` and replacing `YYY` with a value such as `3.99`.

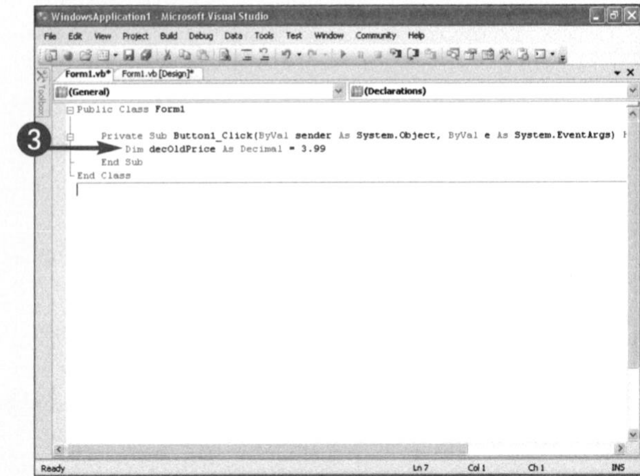

4. Write an `If...Then` statement with a not equivalent logical expression that determines if the variable is not equal to XXX, replacing XXX with a value such as `2.99`.

5. Add a line that calls `MessageBox.Show("XXX")` if the variable is not equal to the value, replacing XXX with a message such as `"The old price is not equal to $2.99."`

6. Press Ctrl+S to save the code.

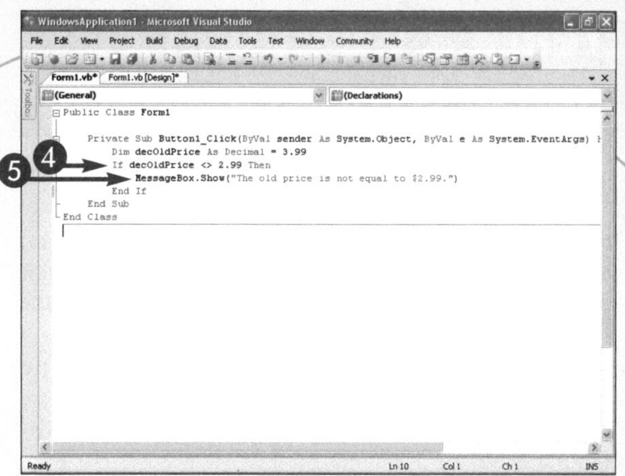

7. Press F5 to run the program.

8. Click the button.

   The message box appears.

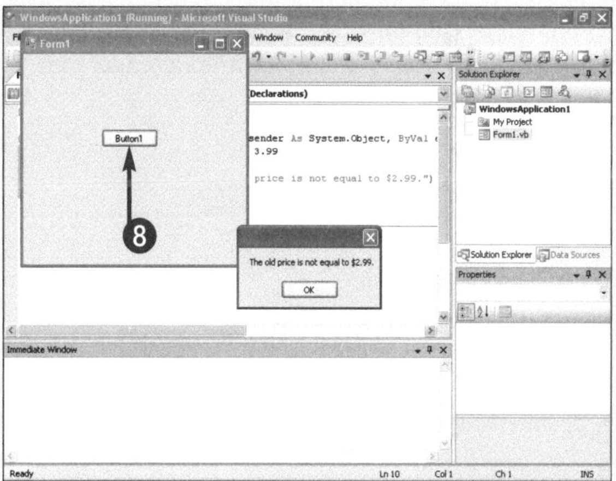

Extra

You can use an arithmetic expression in place of a logical expression in an `If...Then` statement. An arithmetic expression uses addition, subtraction, multiplication, and/or division operators to arrive at a numeric value. If this numeric value is 1, then the value is considered true and statements within the `If...Then` code block execute. If the value is zero, then the value is considered false and statements within the `If...Then` code block are not executed.

Example

```
Dim decA As Decimal = 10, decB As Decimal = 11
If decB - decA Then
   MessageBox.show("The difference is 1.")
End If
```

When Visual Basic .NET subtracts `decA` from `decB`, the result is one, which is considered true, causing the `MessageBox()` to be displayed on the screen.

Create a Compound Logical Expression

A compound logical expression is used in an `If...Then` statement to make a decision based on the results of two or more logical expressions such as deciding if both a user ID and password entered into the program by the user are valid.

You create a compound logical expression by combining two or more logical expressions. Visual Basic .NET evaluates each logical expression and then evaluates the compound logical expression.

Say that you write a program that initiates a purchase if the product you want sells for $100. Two decisions are made. The item's product number must match the product that you want to buy, and the price must be $100. If both conditions are true, your code executes steps to purchase the product. If one condition is false, the code is not executed.

This compound expression is written as

```
If intProductNumber = 1234 AND
decProductPrice = 100 Then
```

The AND operator (see Chapter 5) combines both logical expressions into a compound expression.

A compound expression can also be created by using the OR operator. The OR operator states that the compound expression is true if either the first or second logical expression is true.

Create a Compound Logical Expression

1. Add a button to a form.

Note: See Chapter 4 for information about adding buttons.

2. Double-click the button.

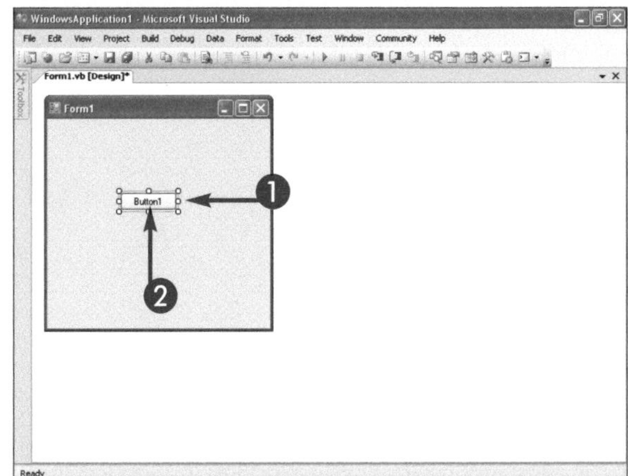

The code that executes when the button is clicked appears.

3. Declare and initialize a variable at the beginning of the code, such as `Dim XXX As Decimal = YYY`, replacing `XXX` with the variable name such as `decOldPrice` and replacing `YYY` with a value such as `3.99`.

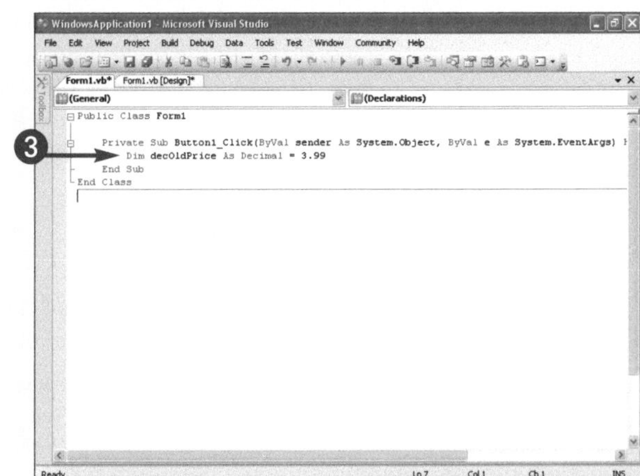

4. Write an `If...Then` statement with a compound logical expression that determines if the value is greater than one value, such as 2.99, and less than another value, such as 4.00.

5. Add a line that calls `MessageBox.Show("XXX")` if the value is greater than the first value and less than the second one, replacing `XXX` with a message such as `"The old price is greater than 2.99 and less than 4.00."`

6. Press Ctrl+S to save the code.

7. Press F5 to run the program.

8. Click the button.

The message box appears.

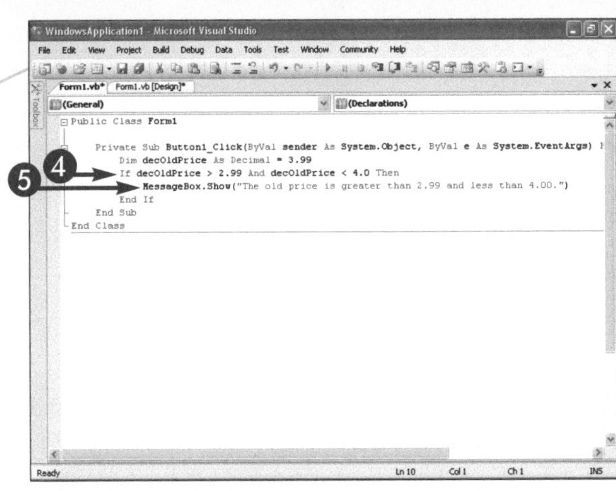

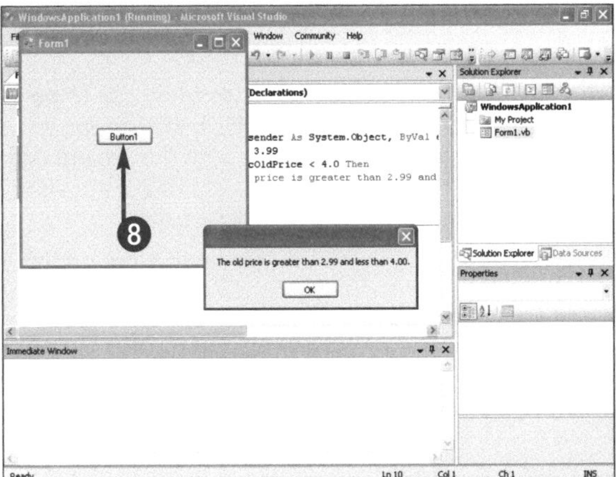

Extra

Sometimes you want statements in the `If...Then` code block to execute only if one or another logical expression is true but not if both are true. You can do this by using the `XOR` operator to create a compound logical expression.

Example

```
If intAirplaneTicket = 1 Xor intCruiseTicket = 1 Then
   MessageBox.show("Pack your bags. You're going on a vacation.")
Else
   MessageBox.show("Better check your ticket.")
End If
```

Let's say that 1 means that you were sent a ticket. You were sent both tickets if both the plane ticket and the cruise ticket are set to 1. If so, then the `XOR` operator causes the compound expression to be treated as false and executes statements in the `Else` code block.

Create an If...Then...Else Statement

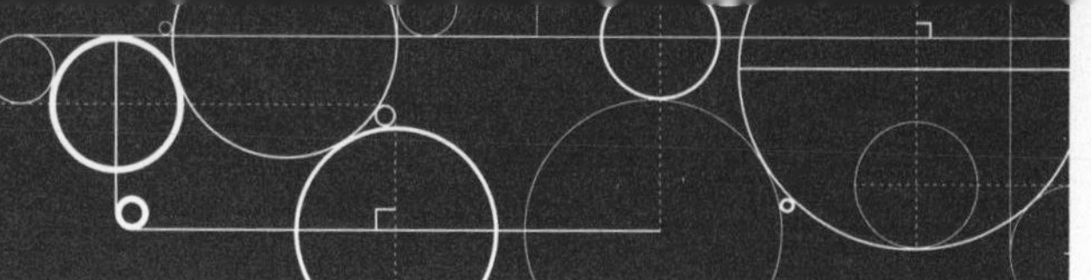

Think of an `If...Then...Else` statement as telling Visual Basic .NET to test a condition. If the condition is true, then do *this;* otherwise, do *that.* *This* is the first code block, which is identical to the `If...Then` statement. *That* is another code block that executes if the logical expression is false.

You create an `If...Then...Else` statement practically the same way as you created an `If...Then` statement. First you open the statement with `If` *`logical expression`* `Then` and follow it with code that you want executed if the logical expression is true. This is referred to as the *first* code block.

Next, you tell Visual Basic .NET where to find code to be executed if the logical expression is false by using the `Else` keyword. The `Else` keyword is followed by the second code block. Code that you place in the second code block executes only if the logical expression is false; otherwise, Visual Basic .NET skips this code block. The `If...Then...Else` statement ends with `End If`.

Either the first or second code block executes each time the `If...Then...Else` statement executes.

If the logical expression is true, the code in the first code block executes, and Visual Basic .NET skips the second code block and executes the next line of code beneath the `End If`.

If the logical expression is false, Visual Basic .NET skips the code in the first code block and executes the code in the second code block. The code that follows the `End If` is then executed.

Create an If...Then...Else Statement

1. Add a button to a form.

Note: See Chapter 4 for information about adding buttons.

2. Double-click the button.

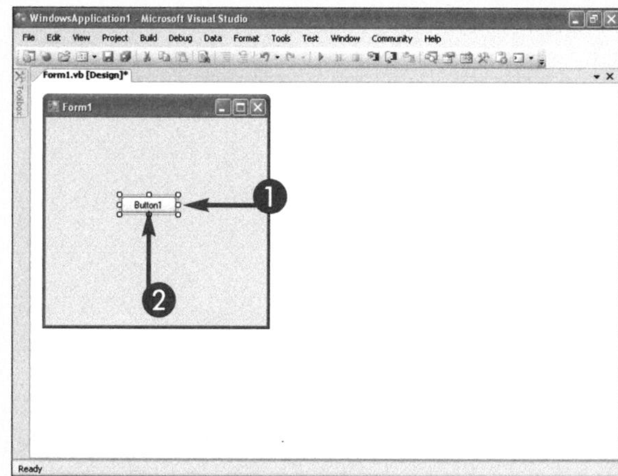

The code that executes when the button is clicked appears.

3. Declare and initialize a variable at the beginning of the code, such as `Dim XXX As Decimal = YYY`, replacing `XXX` with the variable name such as `decOldPrice` and replacing `YYY` with a value such as `3.99`.

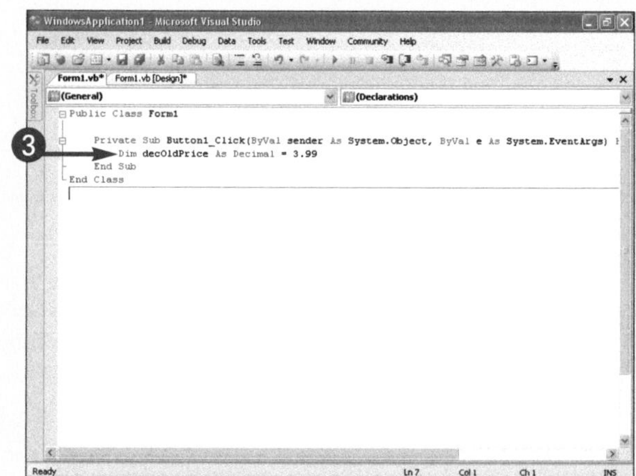

4. Write an `If...Then ...Else` statement with a equivalent logical expression that determines if the value is greater than 2.99.

5. Add a line that calls `MessageBox.Show("XXX")` if the value is greater than 2.99, replacing `XXX` with a message such as `"The old price is greater than 2.99."`

6. Add a line that calls `MessageBox.Show("YYY")` if the value is not greater than 2.99, replacing `YYY` with a message such as `"The old price is not greater than 2.99."`

7. Press Ctrl+S to save the code.

8. Press F5 to run the program.

9. Click the button.

   The message box appears.

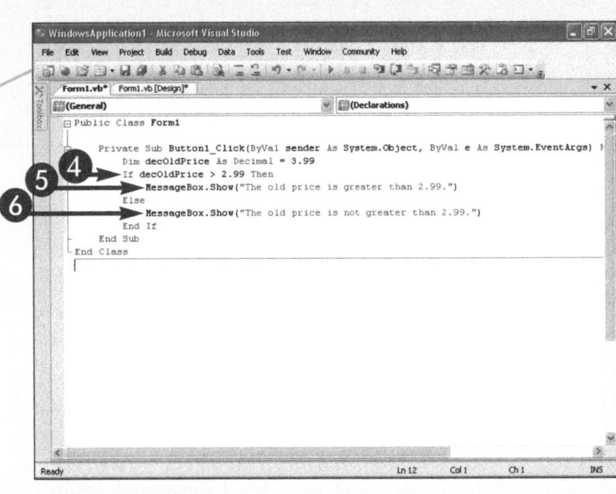

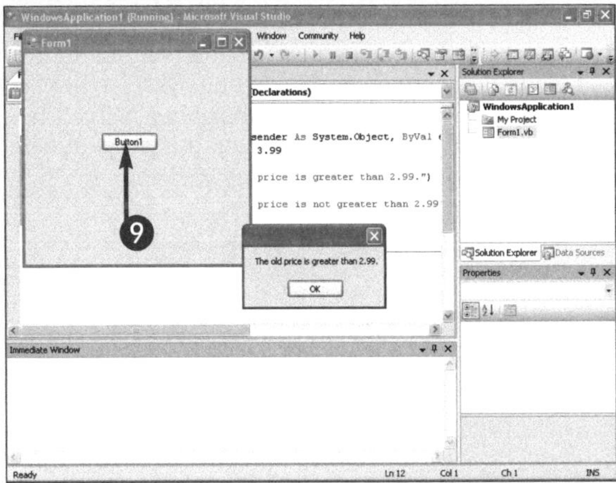

Extra

A way to eliminate bugs in your program is to write code to handle any condition that may arise while your program is running. At first this seems like an enormous task because you have to identify all the possible conditions that could happen, much too many to identify. However, there is an easy way to address these conditions without having to identify them. Reduce all the possible conditions down to two. That is, the condition is either true, or the condition is false. After you simplify it this way, you can write an `If...Then...Else` statement to handle each condition. The `Else` portion of the `If...Then...Else` statement responds to all those conditions that are not true without having to identify all those conditions.

Create an If...Then... ElseIf...Then Statement

The `If...Then...ElseIf...Then` statement first tells Visual Basic .NET to evaluate a logical expression. If the expression is true, the code in the first code block is executed. If the expression is false, a second logical expression is evaluated. If the second logical expression is true, the code in the second code block is executed.

For example, the `If` may be "Did the sale representative meet her sales quota?" If this is true, the `Then` will execute, such as calculating her sales bonus. If this is false, the `Elseif` will be evaluated, such as "Does she receive a guaranteed sales bonus regardless if she meets her sales quota?" If this is true, the `Elseif`'s `Then` will execute, such as calculating her sales bonus; then the program will continue with the next set of instructions. If the `Elseif` is false, the bonus will not be calculated (neither `Then` will execute), and the program will continue with the next set of instructions after the `If...Then...ElseIf...Then` statement.

There are two parts of an `If...Then...ElseIf...Then` statement. The first part is `If...Then` followed by the first code block. You place the first logical expression between the `If` and `Then`. The second part is the `ElseIf...Then` followed by the second code block. You place the second logical expression between the `ElseIf` and `Then`.

Code in the first code block executes only if the first logical expression is true. Code in the second code block executes only if the first logical expression is false and the second logical expression is true. If both logical expressions are true, only the first code block executes. If neither logical expression is true, Visual Basic .NET skips both code blocks and executes the statement that follows `End If`.

You can use a single logical expression or a compound logical expression for either the `If...Then` or the `ElseIf...Then` portion of the `If...Then...ElseIf...Then` statement.

Create an If...Then...ElseIf...Then Statement

1. Add a button to a form.

Note: See Chapter 4 for information about adding buttons.

2. Double-click the button.

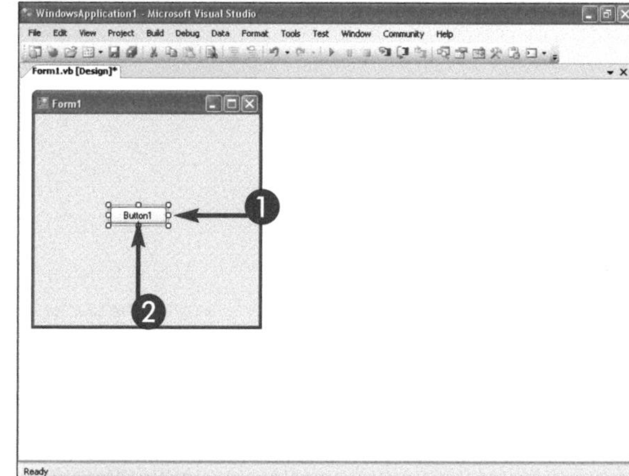

The code that executes when the button is clicked appears.

3. Declare and initialize a variable at the beginning of the code such as `Dim XXX As Decimal = YYY`, replacing `XXX` with the variable name such as `decOldPrice` and replacing `YYY` with a value such as `3.99`.

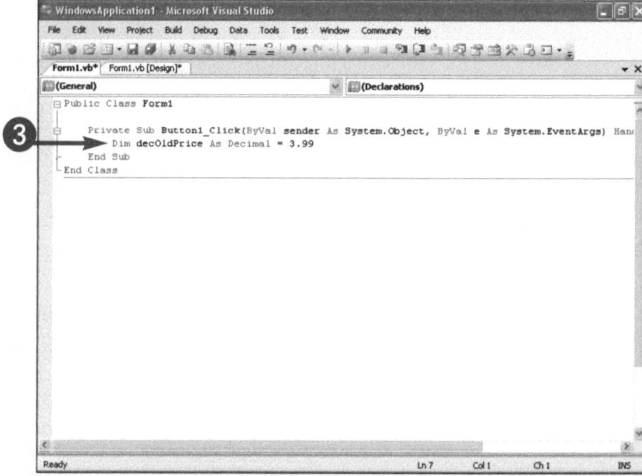

4. Write an `If...Then...ElseIf...Then` statement with two equivalent logical expressions that first determines if the value is greater than 4.0 and then determines (`Elseif`) if the value is greater than 3.0.

5. Add a line that calls `MessageBox.Show("XXX")` if the value is greater than 4.0, replacing `XXX` with a message such as `"The old price is greater than 4.0."`

6. Add a line that calls `MessageBox.Show("YYY")` if the value is greater than 3.0, replacing `YYY` with a message such as `"The old price is greater than 3.0."`

7. Press Ctrl+S to save the code.

8. Press F5 to run the program.

9. Click the button.

   The message box appears.

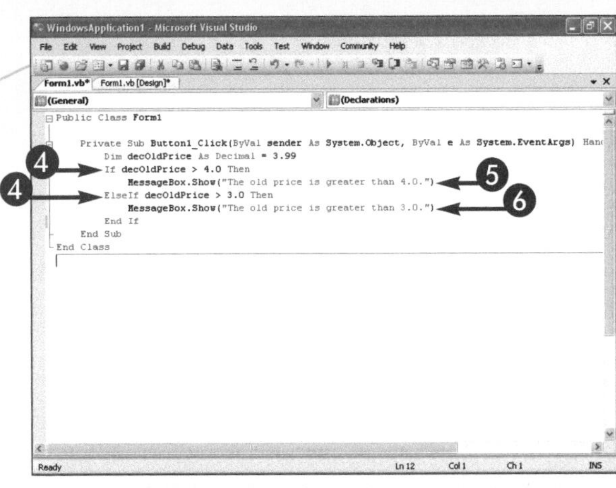

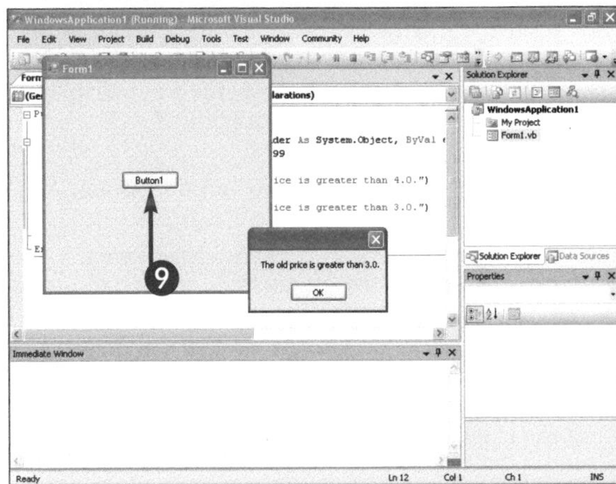

Extra

A short way for writing an `If...Then` statement is to place the statement on one line. Each statement that executes if the condition is true is separated by a colon. Let's say that your program is setting the price and inventory for new products. Here is what you write:

Example

```
If intProductNumber = 1234 Then decProduct123Price =  14.99:
intProduct123Inventory = 50
```

This may look confusing at first, but look carefully and you will see that this is really an `If...Then` statement. `intProductNumber = 1234 Then` evaluates the logical condition. The first statement that executes if the condition is true is `decProduct123Price = 14.99`. The second statement that executes if the condition is true is `intProduct123Inventory = 50`. Notice that a colon (:) separates these statements.

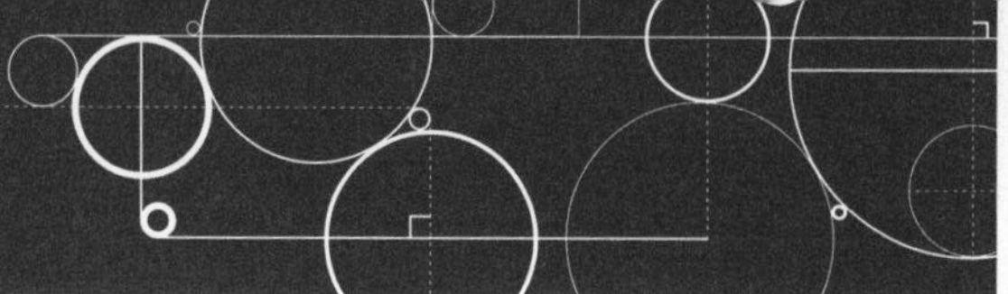

Create an If...Then...ElseIf... Then...Else Statement

The `If...Then...ElseIf...Then...Else` statement tells Visual Basic .NET to evaluate a condition. If the condition is true, the first code block is executed. If the condition is false, a second condition is evaluated. If the second condition is true, the second code block is executed. If the second condition is false, the third code block located below `Else` is executed.

For example, the `If` may ask, "Did the sale representative meet her sales quota?" If the answer is yes, her sales bonus is calculated. If the answer is no, the `ElseIf` may ask, "Does she receive a guaranteed sales bonus regardless if she meets her sales quota?" If the answer is yes, her sales bonus is calculated. If the answer is no, the `Else` displays the message, "You do not qualify for a bonus."

There are three parts to the `If...Then...ElseIf...Then...Else` statement. The first part is `If...Then`, which contains the initial expression evaluated by Visual Basic .NET. The second part is `ElseIf...Then`, which contains an expression evaluated by Visual Basic .NET only if the first expression is false. The third part is `Else`, which executes if both the first and second expressions are false.

If the first expression is true, the first code block executes and then Visual Basic .NET executes the next statement after `End If`. The second and third code blocks are skipped.

If the first expression is false, the second expression is evaluated. If the second expression is true, the second code block executes, and then Visual Basic .NET executes the next statement after `End If`. The third code block is skipped.

If the second expression is false, the third code block executes, and then Visual Basic .NET executes the next statement after `End If`.

Create an If...Then...ElseIf...Then...Else Statement

1. Add a button to a form.

Note: See Chapter 4 for information about adding buttons.

2. Double-click the button.

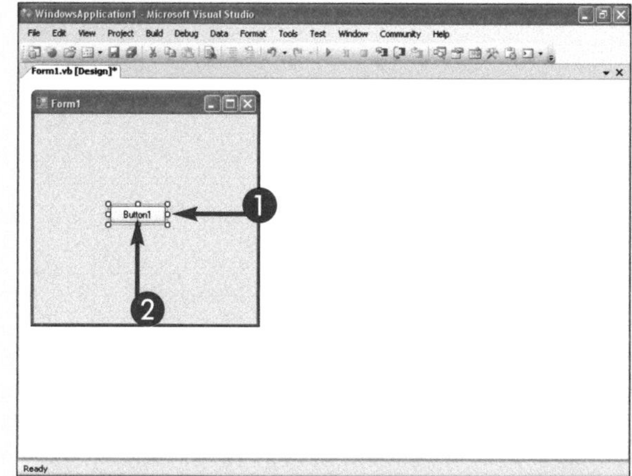

The code that executes when the button is clicked appears.

3. Declare and initialize a variable at the beginning of the code such as `Dim XXX As Decimal = YYY`, replacing `XXX` with the variable name such as `decOldPrice` and replacing `YYY` with a value such as `3.99`.

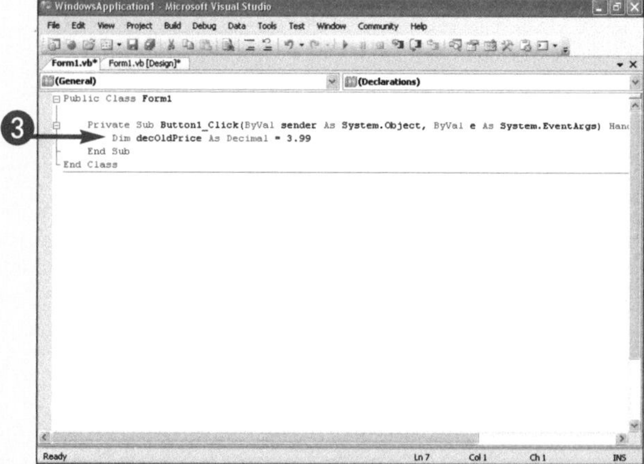

4. Write an `If...Then ...ElseIf...Then...Else` statement that determines if the value is greater than 4.00 and 3.00.
5. Add a line that calls `MessageBox.Show("XXX")` if the value is greater than 4.00, replacing `XXX` with a message.
6. Add a line that calls `MessageBox.Show("YYY")` if the value is greater than 3.00, replacing `YYY` with a message.
7. Add a line that calls `MessageBox.Show("ZZZ")` if the value does not meet either condition, replacing `ZZZ` with a message.
8. Press Ctrl+S to save the code.
9. Press F5 to run the program.
10. Click the button.

The message box appears.

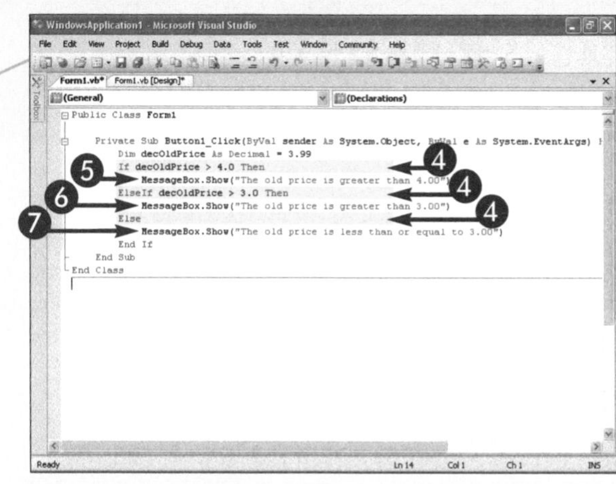

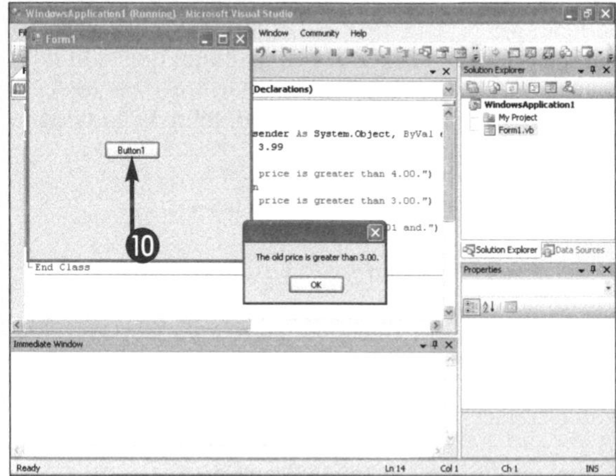

Extra

You may realize that the `Select Case ...Case Else` statement is very similar to the `If...Then...ElseIf...Else` statement because both let you make multiple decisions using one statement. The question is which of these is the best to use in your program? The answer depends on the nature of your program. The `Select Case ...Case Else` statement works well if you are comparing one value to various conditions such as a menu selection in which you compare the user input to possible menu options. The `If...Then...ElseIf...Else` statement is the best choice if different values are used to make a decision.

Example

```
If intDoor1 = 1 Then
   MessageBox("Alarm: Door 1 is open.")
ElseIf intWindow1 = 1 Then
   MessageBox("Alarm: Window 1 is open.")
Else
   MessageBox("Alarm: Unknown source")
End If
```

Create a Nested If...Then Statement

You use a nested `If...Then` statement to make two decisions. A nested `If...Then` statement consists of two `If...Then` statements. The first `If...Then` statement is referred to as the *outer* `If...Then` statement. The second `If...Then` statement is called the *nested* or *inner* `If...Then` statement because this is located in the code block of the first `If...Then` statement.

Visual Basic .NET is told to evaluate the expression in the outer `If...Then` statement first. If this is true, the expression in the nested `If...Then` statement is evaluated.

For example, the first `If` may ask, "Is this product qualified for sales tax?" If the answer is yes, a second question is asked, such as, "Is the customer a resident of New Jersey?" If the answer to the first question is no, there is no need to ask the second question.

There can be levels of nested `If...Then` statements. That is, a nested `If...Then` statement can have its own nested `If...Then` statement, and its nested `If...Then` statement can have a nested `If...Then` statement, and so on.

To further the earlier example, the first `If` may ask, "Is this product qualified for sales tax?" If the answer is yes, a second question is asked, such as, "Is the customer a resident of New Jersey?" If the answer to this question is also yes, a third question is asked, such as, "Is the customer qualified for New Jersey sales tax?" The first question is the outer `If...Then` statement. The second question is a nested `If...Then` statement and also an outer `If...Then`. The third question is nested within the second question.

Create a Nested If...Then Statement

1. Add a button to a form.

Note: See Chapter 4 for information about adding buttons.

2. Double-click the button.

The code that executes when the button is clicked appears.

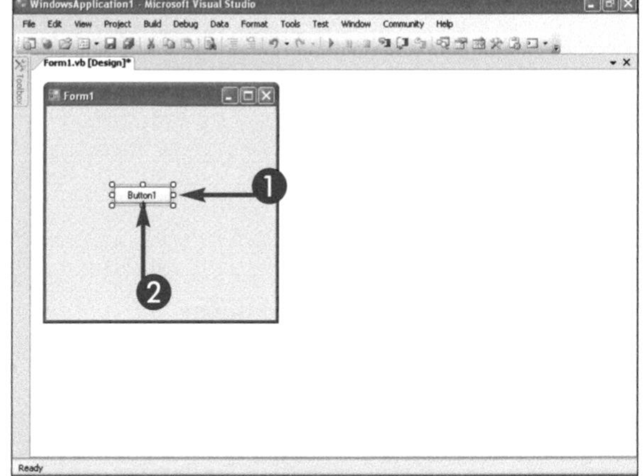

3. Declare an integer variable `xxx`, replacing `xxx` with the variable name such as `intCustomerNumber`.
4. Declare an integer variable `xxx`, replacing `xxx` with the variable name such as `intOrderNumber`.
5. Declare an integer variable `xxx`, replacing `xxx` with the variable name such as `intProductNumber`.
6. Assign a value to the first integer variable.
7. Assign a value to the second integer variable.
8. Assign a value to the third integer variable.

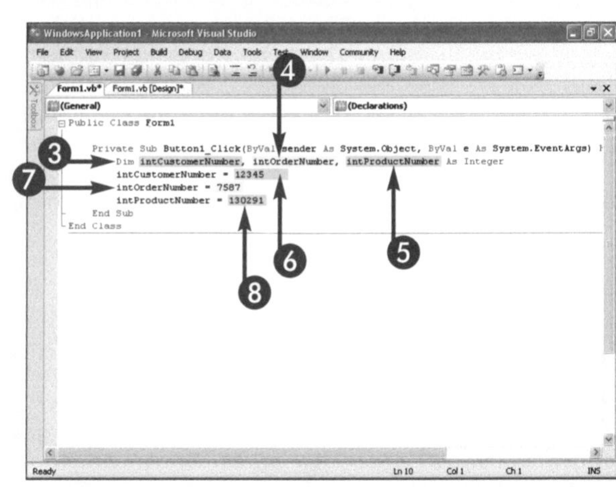

9 Write the `If XXX Then` statement, replacing `XXX` with a logical expression.

10 Write a nested `If XXX Then` statement, replacing `XXX` with a logical expression.

11 Write `MessageBox.Show("XXX")` in the code block of the innermost nested `If...Then` statement, replacing `XXX` with a message such as `"Nested If...Then statement executed"`.

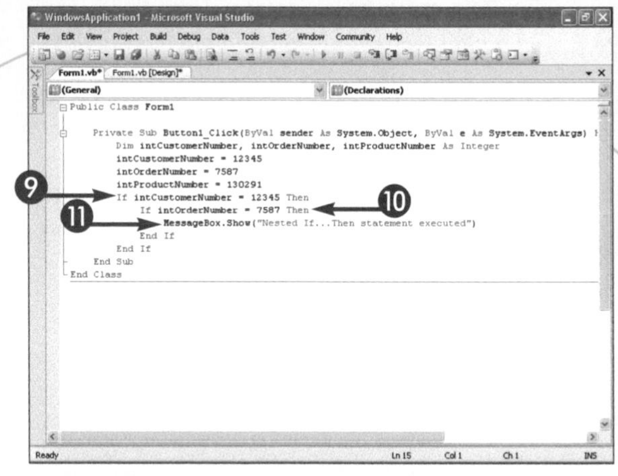

12 Press Ctrl+S to save the code.

13 Press F5 to run the program.

14 Click the button.

A message box appears telling you which code block executed.

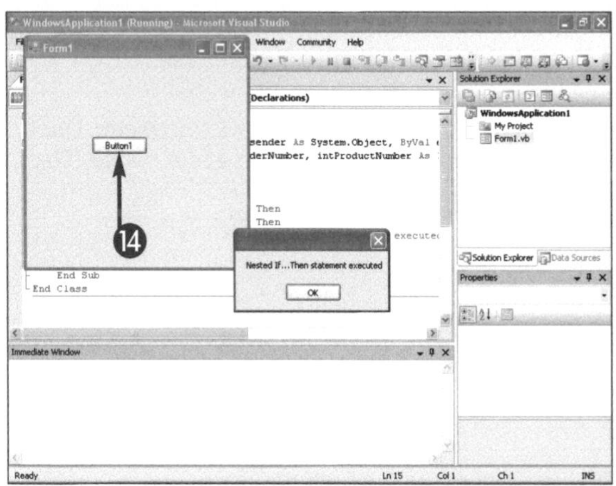

Extra

It is always best to avoid too many levels of nested `If...Then` statements because your code will be difficult to read. However, if you find yourself needing many nested `If...Then` statements, then begin each level with a comment that describes the level.

Example

```
'Determine student's status
If strStudentStatus = "Active" Then
     'Determine student's academic rank
     If strStudentAcademicRank = "Graduate" Then
         'Determine student's major
         If strStudentMajor = "MBA" Then
           MessageBox("Please visit the Business School's library.")
         End If
   End If
End If
```

Create a Select Case Statement

A `Select Case` statement compares a `Select` value to one or more `Case` values. Each `Case` value has a code block that executes when the `Case` value matches the `Select` value. You can have any number of `Case` values.

Your application may prompt the user to enter a user ID into a `TextBox`. When the user clicks the login `Button` control on the form, the text of the `TextBox` becomes the `Select` value of a `Select Case` statement and is compared to valid user IDs, each represented as a `Case` value. If there is a match, the code block beneath the matching user ID is executed. If there is not a match, Visual Basic .NET executes the statement that follows `End Select`.

There are three parts to a `Select Case` statement. The first part is `Select Case` followed by the `Select` value. The second part contains one or more `Case` values and its corresponding code block. The third part is `End Select`, which signifies the end of the `Select Case` statement.

The `Select Case` statement should be used in place of many `If...Then` statements because a `Select Case` statement can achieve the same objective but in a more readable format.

The `Select` value can be a value, variable, or logical expression. The value must evaluate to one of the elementary data types; see Chapter 5. An expression must evaluate to either true or false. If you specify a variable, it must be one of these data types. A `Case` value can be a value or a variable, but not an expression. Visual Basic .NET compares the `Select` value to each `Case` value in order until a match occurs; then the remaining `Case` values are skipped.

Create a Select Case Statement

1. Add a button to a form.

Note: See Chapter 4 for information about adding buttons.

2. Add a `TextBox` control to the form.

Note: See Chapter 3 for more information.

3. Add a `Label` control to the form and change the `Text` property to `XXX`, replacing `XXX` with the text of the label, such as "User ID."

4. Double-click the button.

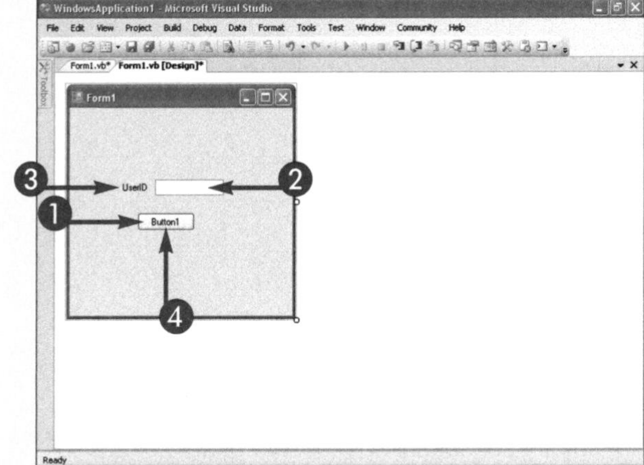

The code that executes when the button is clicked appears.

5. Declare a `String` variable `XXX`, replacing `XXX` with the variable name, such as `strUserID`.

6. Assign the `Text` property of the `TextBox` to the `String` variable using the `Trim()` function, such as `Trim(TextBox1.Text)`.

Note: Text entered into the `TextBox` is trimmed of blank characters and assigned to the `String` variable.

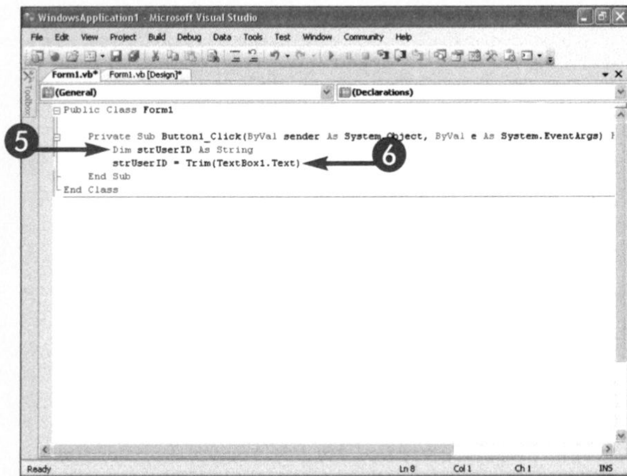

7. Write a `Select Case XXX Case YYY` statement, replacing `XXX` with the `String` variable and replacing `YYY` with a valid user ID such as `"JK1234"`.

8. Write several `Case` values, as necessary for your application.

9. Write `MessageBox.Show("XXX")` in the code block for each `Case`, replacing `XXX` with a message such as `"JK1234 Login successful."`

10. Press Ctrl+S to save the code.

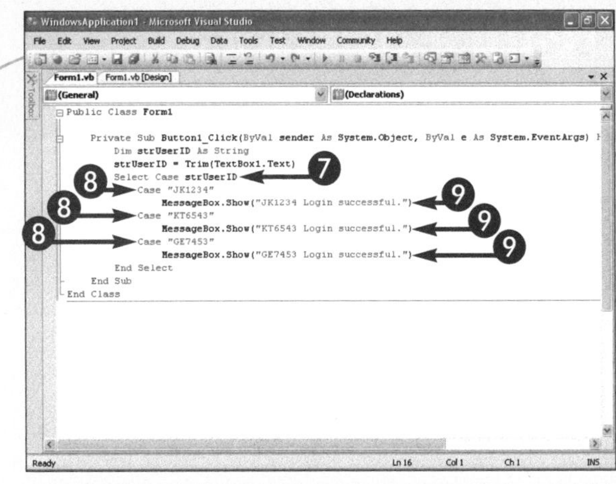

11. Press F5 to run the program.

12. Enter a user ID.

13. Click the button.

A message box appears, telling you if the login is successful.

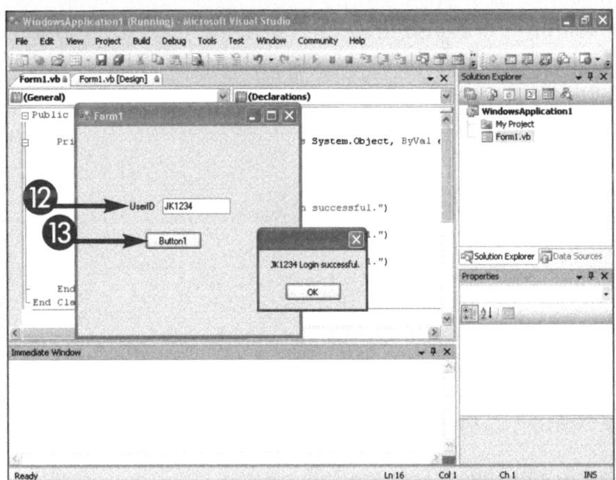

Extra

If you want the same statements executed for multiple `Case` values, one solution is to repeat the statements for each `Case` value. However, a better approach is to use multiple values for one `Case` because you do not have to repeat statements.

Do not write this:

```
Select Case intTicket
Case 1
MessageBox.show("You are going on a cruise.")
Case 2
MessageBox.show("You are going on a cruise.")
Case 3
MessageBox.show("You are going on an airplane trip.")
End Select
```

Instead, write this:

```
Select Case intTicket
Case 1, 2
MessageBox.show("You are going on a cruise.")
Case 3
MessageBox.show("You are going on an airplane trip.")
End Select
```

Create a Select Case...Case Else Statement

The Select Case...Case Else statement is identical to the Select Case statement, except there is a code block that executes if none of the Case values match the Select value. This default code block is located below Case Else, which is positioned as the last Case in the Select Case statement.

Suppose an invalid user ID is entered into your program. Visual Basic .NET compares this user ID to the list of valid user IDs in the Select Case statement. If none match, Visual Basic .NET executes the Case Else code block, which displays a message saying that the user ID is invalid. The Case Else code block is not executed if the Select value matches one of the Case values.

There are four parts of a Select Case...Case Else statement: The first part is Select Case, followed by the Select value. The second part contains one or more Case values and their corresponding code blocks. The third part is Case Else, under which is the code block that executes if the Select value does not match any Case value. The fourth part is End Select, which signifies the end of the Select Case...Case Else statement.

It is good programming practice to use a Select Case...Case Else statement rather than a Select Case statement because the Select Case...Case Else statement gives your program the capability of addressing a condition that matches or that does not match the Select value.

Create a Select Case...Case Else Statement

1. Add a button to a form.

Note: See Chapter 4 for information about adding buttons.

2. Add a TextBox control to the form.

Note: See Chapter 3 for more information.

3. Add a Label control to the form and change the Text property to XXX, replacing XXX with text of the label, such as "User ID."

4. Double-click the button.

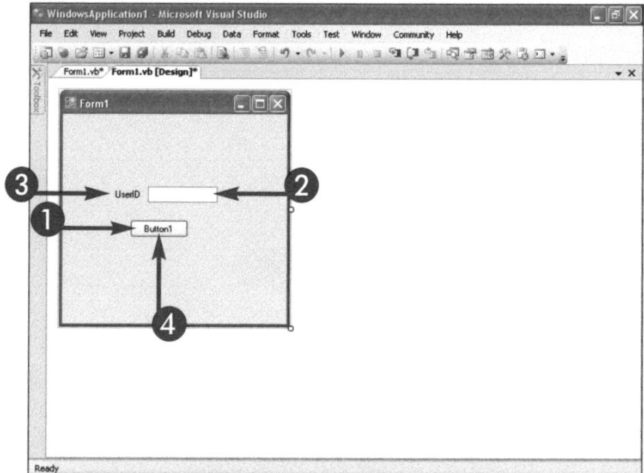

The code that executes when the button is clicked appears.

5. Declare a String variable XXX, replacing XXX with the variable name such as strUserID.

6. Assign the Text property of the TextBox to the String variable using the Trim() function, such as Trim(TextBox1.Text).

Note: Text entered into the TextBox is trimmed of blank characters and assigned to the String variable.

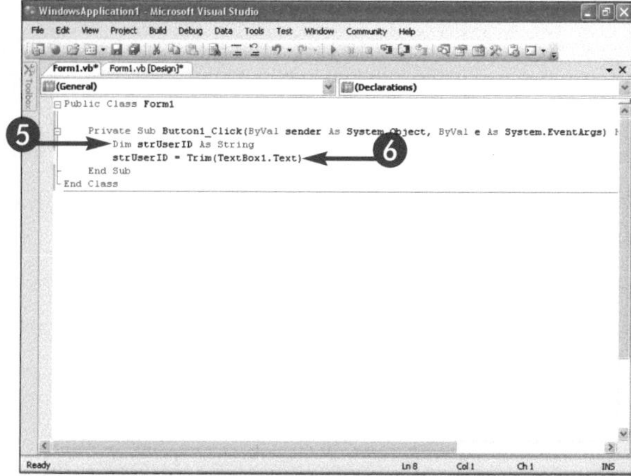

7. Write `Select Case XXX Case YYY`, replacing `XXX` with the `String` variable and replacing `YYY` with a valid user ID such as `"JK1234"`.

8. Write several `Case` values, as necessary.

9. Write a `Case Else` statement.

10. Write `MessageBox.Show("XXX")` in the code block for each `Case`, replacing `XXX` with a message such as `"JK1234 Login successful."`

11. Write `MessageBox.Show("XXX")` in the code block for `Case Else`, replacing `XXX` with a message such as `"Login Failed."`

12. Press Ctrl+S to save the code.

13. Press F5 to run the program.

14. Enter an invalid user ID.

15. Click the button.

    A message box appears telling you that the login failed.

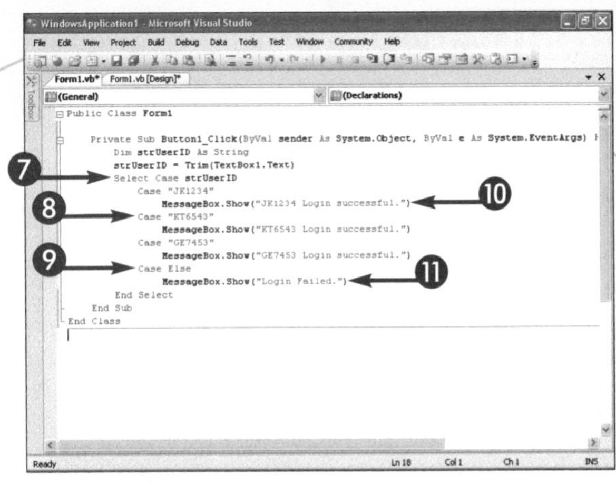

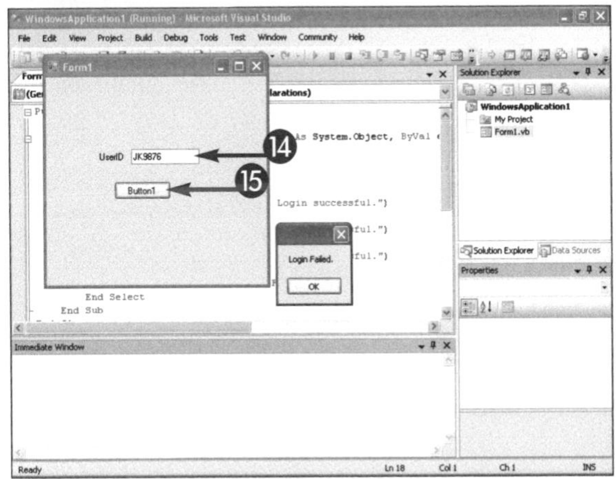

Extra

Complex applications typically require you to write code to make a lot of decisions. Intuitively, some developers pick a series of `If...Then` statements or one of its many variations. `If...Then` statements are straightforward to write until there are many decisions being made within the same `If...Then` statement. For example, you may have several `ElseIf` statements and nested `If...Then` statements. Although Visual Basic .NET will not have a problem understanding a complex `If...Then` statement, you may become confused reading it. You can avoid this confusion by using a `Select Case` statement instead of a complex `If...Then` statement because a `Select Case` statement has all the possible conditions in a list of `Cases`.

Create a For Loop

Sometimes you will encounter situations in which you want to execute the same statements for a specific number of times. Let's say that you want to display the 8 times table from 0 to 12. Instead of writing 13 statements of `8 * 0`, `8 * 1`, and so on, you can place one statement such as `8 * intCounter` in the code block of a `For` loop. `intCounter` is a variable whose initial value is zero and is incremented by the `For` loop.

The `For` loop has three parts: the header, the code block, and the `Next` statement. The header contains information that tells Visual Basic .NET how many times to execute statements. The statements that are executed are contained in the code block. The `Next` statement tells Visual Basic .NET to go to the header again.

The header is composed of a counter variable, a start value, and an end value. The counter variable is assigned the current number of times that statements are executed. The start value is the starting number that is assigned to the counter variable. The end value tells Visual Basic .NET when to stop executing statements. After statements within the code block execute, Visual Basic .NET automatically increments the counter variable by one. When the value of the counter variable equals the end value, Visual Basic .NET stops executing the statements in the code block and executes the statement that follows `Next`.

The `For` loop terminates when the counter is greater than the end value, so `For n = 1 To 10` stops executing when `n` is incremented to 11.

Create a For Loop

1. Add a `Button` control to a form.

Note: See Chapter 4 for information about adding buttons.

2. Double-click the button.

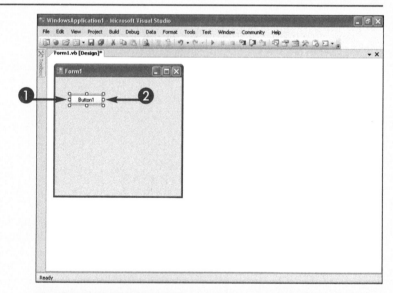

The code that executes when the button is clicked appears.

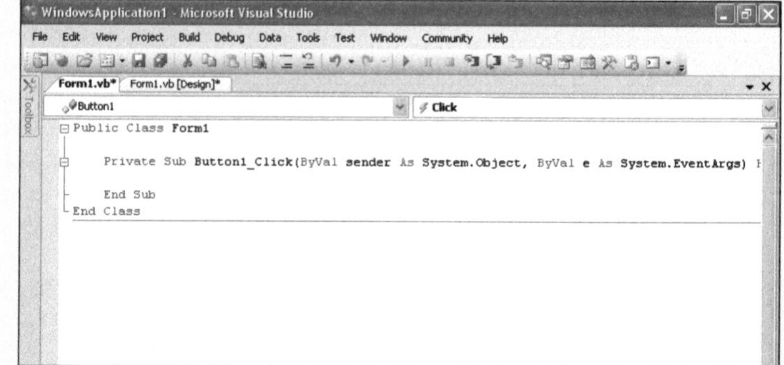

3. Declare an integer variable such as `intCounter`.

4. Write a `For` loop that shows a message box three times by assigning the variable a start value of `0` and an end value of `2`.

5. Have the message display the value of the counter variable by writing `MessageBox.Show ("Counter value is " + CStr(intCounter))`.

6. Remember to include `Next` at the end, followed by `intCounter`, which will tell Visual Basic .NET to use the next value of the `intCounter`.

7. Display a message box after Visual Basic .NET leaves the `For` loop by writing `MessageBox.Show("Exit For Loop")`.

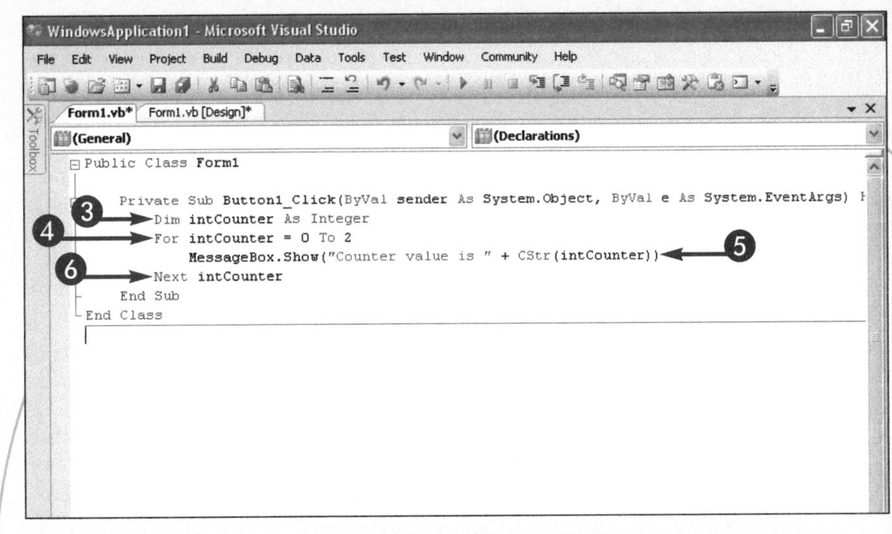

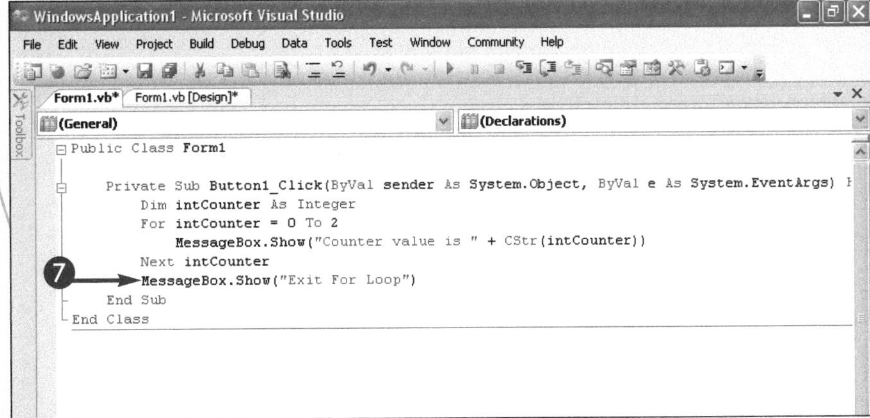

Extra

A nested `For` loop is a `For` loop inside the code block of another `For` loop. The nested `For` loop is called the *inner* `For` loop, and the other is called the *outer* `For` loop. After the inner `For` loop reaches its end value, the outer `For` loop's counter variable is incremented by one. If the outer `For` loop's counter is not greater than the outer `For` loop's end value, the inner `For` loop executes again.

Example

```
Dim counter1, counter 2 As Integer
For counter1 = 0 To 3
      For counter2 = 0 To 4
            'Place statements here
      Next counter2
Next counter1
```

Increment a For Loop by a Set Value

By default, Visual Basic .NET increments the value of the counter variable by one each time that statements within the code block of the `For` loop execute. In some situations, you may want Visual Basic .NET to increment by two or another value other than one. You can specify how Visual Basic .NET increments the value of the counter variable by using a `Step` value in the header. The `Step` value specifies the value of each increment.

Suppose that you want to increment the value of the counter variable by two. To do this, you set the `Step` value to `2`. Let's say that the start value for the counter variable is `0`. After executing statements in the code block, Visual Basic .NET adds 2 to the counter variable because the `Step` value is `2`. Visual Basic .NET continues to add 2 to the counter variable until the value of the counter variable is greater than the end value.

The `Step` value is placed in the header following the end value, such as `counter = 0 To 4 Step 2`. If you exclude the `Step` value, Visual Basic .NET increments the counter value by 1. If you include the `Step` value, Visual Basic .NET adds the `Step` value to the counter value after statements in the code block execute.

Increment a For Loop by a Set Value

1. Add a `Button` control to the form.

Note: See Chapter 4 for information about adding buttons.

2. Double-click the button.

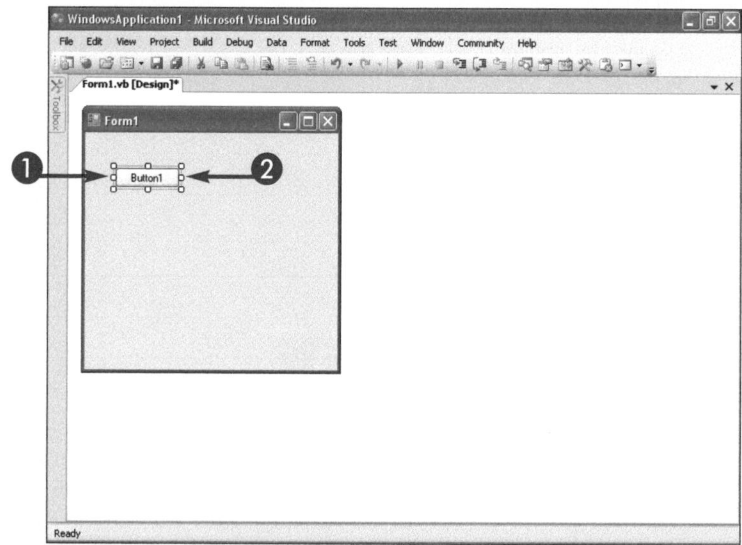

The code that executes when the button is clicked appears.

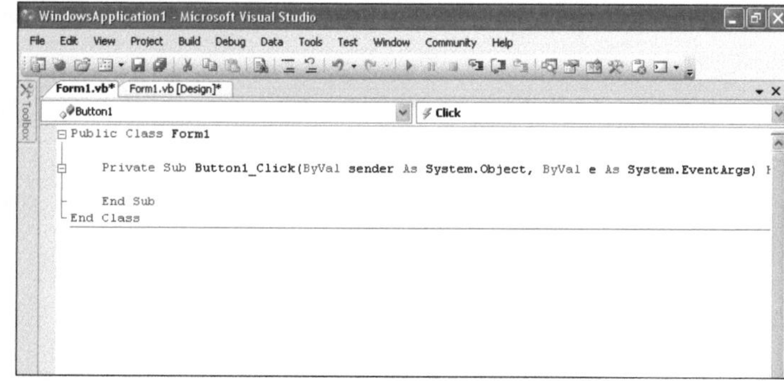

3 Declare an integer `intCounter`.

4 Write a `For` loop with a start value of `0`, an end value of `12`, and a `Step` value of `2`, using `intCounter` as the counter variable.

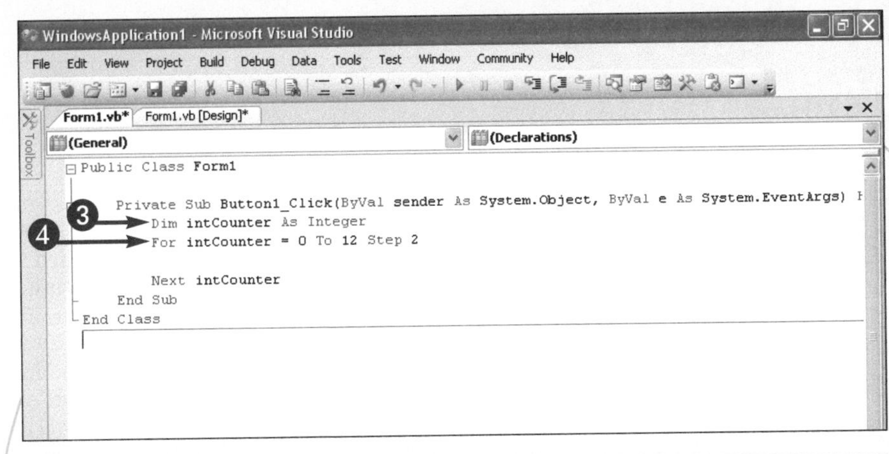

5 Display a message box showing the current value of the counter variable by writing `MessageBox.Show("Counter value is "+ CStr(intCounter))`.

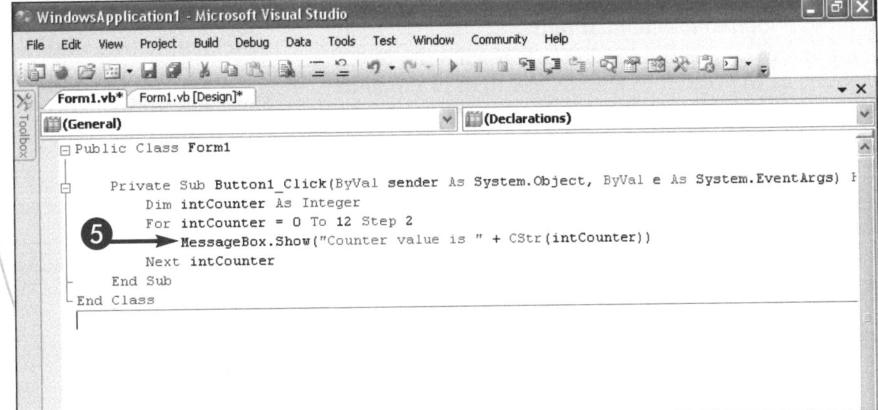

Extra

You can have a `For` loop count down by using a negative `Step` value. Let's say that you want your program to count down from 10. Set the starting value at `10` and the end value at `0`. You then need to set the `Step` value to `-1`. This means that Visual Basic .NET will subtract 1 from the counter value. The counter value is 10 when the `For` loop begins. After statements within the code block execute, Visual Basic .NET subtracts 1 from the counter value. The counter value is then 9. This process continues until the counter value is less than the end value.

Use the `Exit For` statement inside the code block of a `For` loop if you ever need to break out of a `For` loop before it finishes. For example, you can use an `If...Then` statement in the code block of the `For` loop to test a condition each time it loops. If the condition is true, you may want to stop looping, so you place the `Exit For` statement inside the `If...Then` statement's code block to exit the loop.

Create a Do While Loop

A `Do While` loop is a simple loop that starts with the `Do While` keywords and defines the condition that must be true for statements inside the loop to execute. The condition is a statement that must evaluate to true or false; it can be a variable, an operation, or calling a function that returns a `True` or `False` value. If the condition is true, statements in the loop execute. If the condition is false, the loop is skipped. The statement that follows the loop executes.

Here is how you write the beginning of the loop if you want the `Do While` loop to execute ten times: `Do While count <=10`. `count <= 10` is the condition that asks the question "Is the value of the counter variable less than or equal to 10?" If so, the condition expression is true; otherwise, the condition expression is false.

Write the beginning of the loop and then define the body of the loop. The body of the loop is where you place statements that you want executed when the condition is true. These statements stop executing when the condition is false. For example, you can increment the `counter` variable in the body of the loop by writing this statement: `counter = counter + 1`. 1 is added to the value of the `counter` variable each time this statement executes. After the tenth time the statement executes, the value of `counter` is `10`. The condition statement evaluates the value of the `counter` variable each time the loop executes. The condition statement is true until the last time the `counter` variable is incremented. The condition statement is then false, and the statement in the body of the loop no longer executes.

Create a Do While Loop

1. Add a `Button` control to a form.

Note: See Chapter 4 for information about adding buttons.

2. Double-click the button.

The code that executes when the button is clicked appears.

3. Create a `counter` variable and set the value to `1` by writing `Dim intCounter As Integer = 1`.

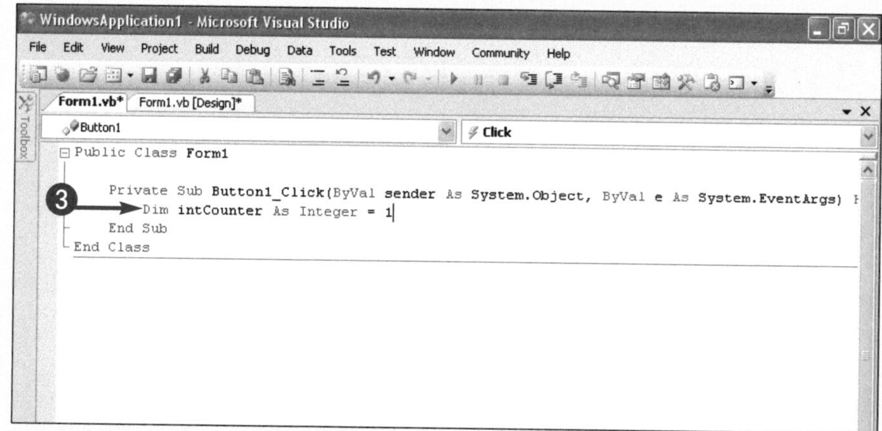

4. Insert a `Do While` loop and loop two times by setting the logical expression to `intCounter < 3`.

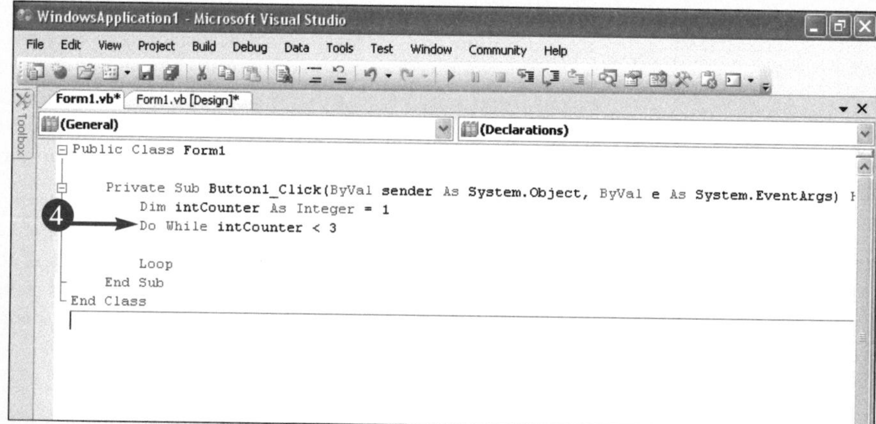

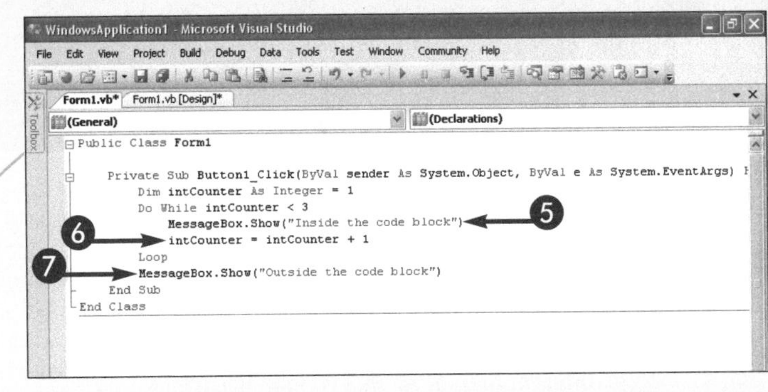

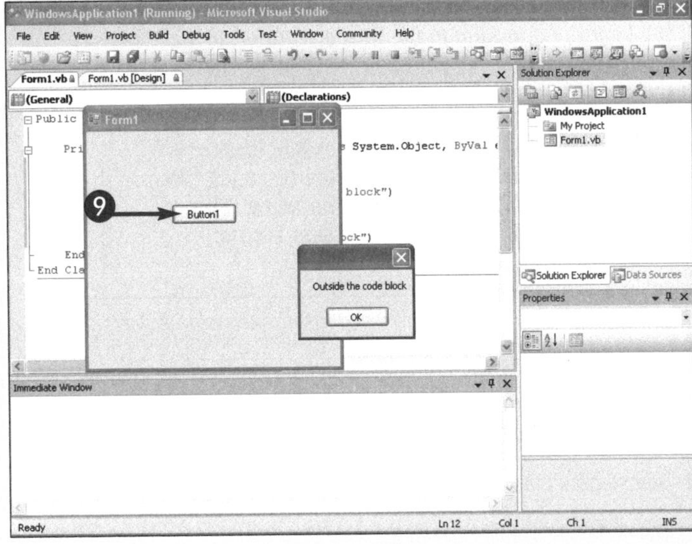

5. Write a statement in the code block of the `Do...While` loop that displays a message box, such as writing `MessageBox.Show("Inside the code block")`.

6. Increment the counter variable after the message box is displayed, such as writing `intCounter = intCounter + 1`.

7. Write a statement after the `Do...While` loop that displays a message box, such as writing `MessageBox.Show("Outside the code block")`.

8. Press F5 to run the application.

   The Form1 window appears.

9. Click the `Button` control.

   A message box is displayed each time Visual Basic .NET executes the statements in the code block. Afterward, a final message box is displayed.

Extra

You can place one `Do While` loop inside the code block of another `Do While` loop to create a *nested,* or inner, `Do While` loop. The inner `Do While` loop executes as long as the condition of the outer `Do While` loop is true.

Example

```
Dim intCounter1 As Integer = 0
Dim intCounter2 As Integer = 0
Do While intCounter1 < 2
   MessageBox.Show("Outer Do While loop")
   Do While intCounter2 < 2
      MessageBox.Show("Inner Do While loop")
      intCounter2 = intCounter2 + 1
   Loop
   intCounter2 = 0
   intCounter1 = intCounter1 + 1
Loop
```

Create a Do Until Loop

A `Do Until` loop is similar to a `Do While` loop because both have a header and a code block. The header contains a logical expression that evaluates to either true or false. The code block is defined between the header and the `Loop` keyword.

A `Do Until` loop is different than a `Do While` loop because statements within the code block of a `Do Until` loop execute only if the logical expression in the header is false. If the logical expression is true, Visual Basic .NET skips statements within the code block and executes the statement that follows the `Loop` keyword. If the logical expression is false, Visual Basic .NET executes the statements in the code block; afterwards, Visual Basic .NET returns to the `Do Until` loop header and evaluates the logical expression again. This process continues until the logical expression is true.

You should include a statement in the code block of a `Do Until` loop that at some point causes the logical expression to be true and therefore causes Visual Basic .NET to exit the loop. Let's say that your program continues to ask the user questions until the user answers a question incorrectly. Statements that ask questions and correct answers are placed inside the code statement of a `Do Until` loop. A `Boolean` variable such as `bAnswerIncorrect` can be set to `True` or `False` depending on the user's answer. The variable is initialized to false, which causes statements within the code block to execute one time, enabling the program to ask the user at least one question. After the user answers a question incorrectly, a statement within the code block assigns the value `True` to the variable. This causes Visual Basic .NET to exit the `Do Until` loop.

Create a Do Until Loop

1. Add a `Button` control to the form.

Note: See Chapter 4 for information about adding buttons.

2. Double-click the `Button` control.

The code that executes when the button is clicked appears.

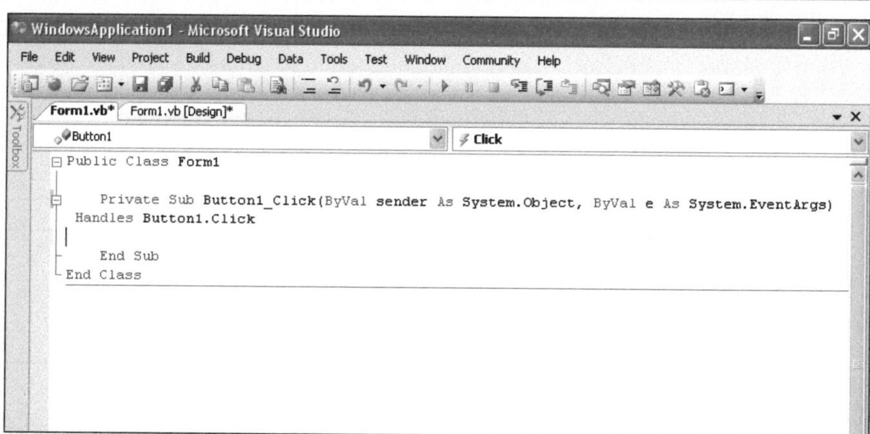

3. Declare a Boolean variable `bAnswerIncorrect`, initializing the Boolean variable to `True`.

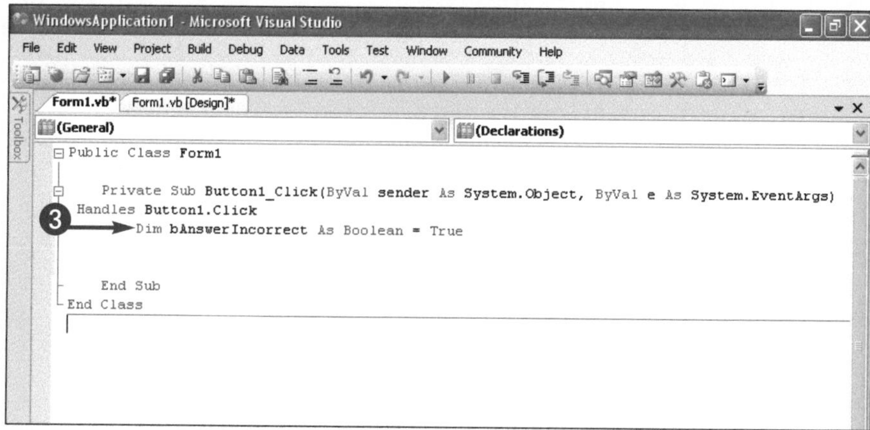

4 Insert a `Do Until` loop that executes if `bAnswerIncorrect` is `False`.

5 Display a message box that asks a question and prompts the user for a yes or no answer, including `MessageBoxButtons.YesNo` in the `MessageBox.Show()` method.

6 Write a caption following the question in the `MessageShow()` method.

7 Display a question mark icon in the message box by writing `MessageBoxIcon.Question`.

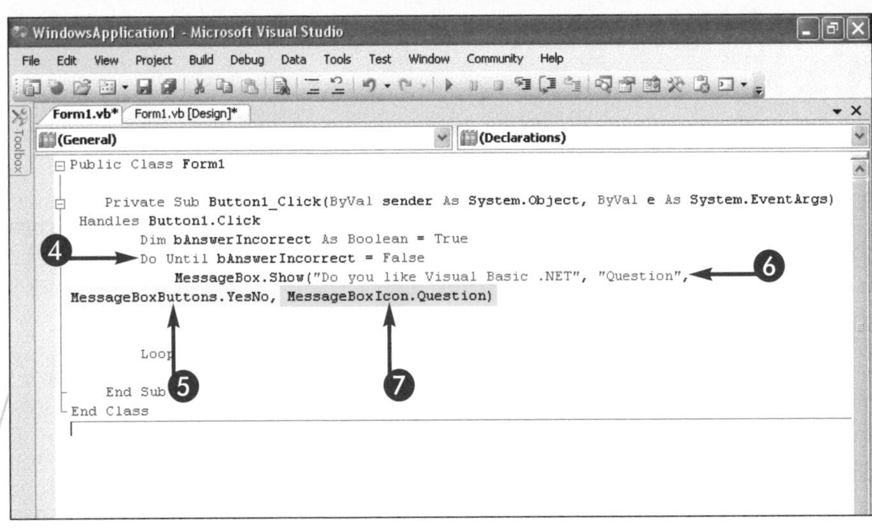

8 Use an `If...Then` statement to evaluate the response from `MessageBox.Show()`.

9 Create a logical expression that compares the return value of `MessageBox.Show()` with the `DialogResult.Yes` property.

Note: A `DialogResult.Yes` is returned if the user clicks Yes, and a `DialogResult.No` is returned if No is clicked.

10 Exit the `Do Until` loop if the user selects no.

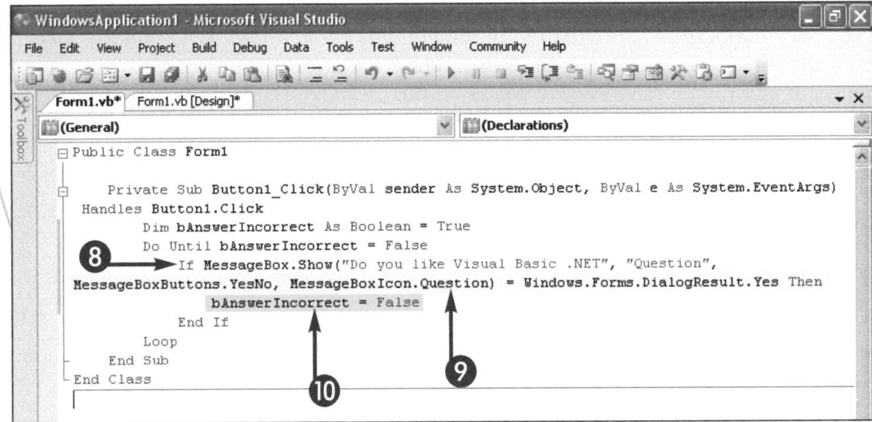

Extra

The `Do` loop is different than other loops because statements within a `Do` loop always execute until you tell Visual Basic .NET to exit the loop. The `Do` loop does not have a logical expression in its header that tells Visual Basic .NET when to stop executing statements in the `Do` loop's code block. Instead, you must place the `Exit Do` keywords in the code block of the `Do` loop when you want Visual Basic .NET to exit the loop. The `Exit Do` keywords can also be used in a loop that has a logical expression in its header to exit the loop without evaluating the logical expression.

Example

```
Do
     'Place statements here
     Exit Do
Loop
```

Create a Do Loop While Loop

Do...Loop While is a loop in which statements in the code block execute at least once before Visual Basic .NET evaluates the logical expression that determines if the code block should be executed again. The `Do...Loop While` loop begins with the `Do` keyword, which signifies the beginning of the code block. The `Loop` keyword signifies the end of the code block. You place statements that you want to execute between the `Do` and the `Loop` keywords. The `While` keyword is followed by a logical expression that must be true if the code block is to execute another time. The code block is skipped if the logical expression is false, and the statement that follows the `Loop While` is executed.

You will notice that the `Do...Loop While` loop is very similar to the `Do While...Loop` loop. Both cause statements to execute more than once based on the evaluation of a logical expression. The `Do...Loop While` loop executes those statements at least once regardless of the logical expression because the logical expression is placed at the bottom of the loop and is evaluated after statements execute.

You will find the `Do...Loop While` loop handy to use when you need to have statements executed before the logical expression is evaluated. Let's say that your program needs to locate a name in a list of names. The program reads the first name from the list and then determines if it is the correct name. If not, the program reexecutes the statement and reads the next name on the list. If the name is correct, the logical expression is set to false, and the program exits the loop.

Create a Do Loop While Loop

1. Add a `Button` control to a form.

Note: See Chapter 4 for information about adding buttons.

2. Double-click the `Button` control.

The code that executes when the button is clicked appears.

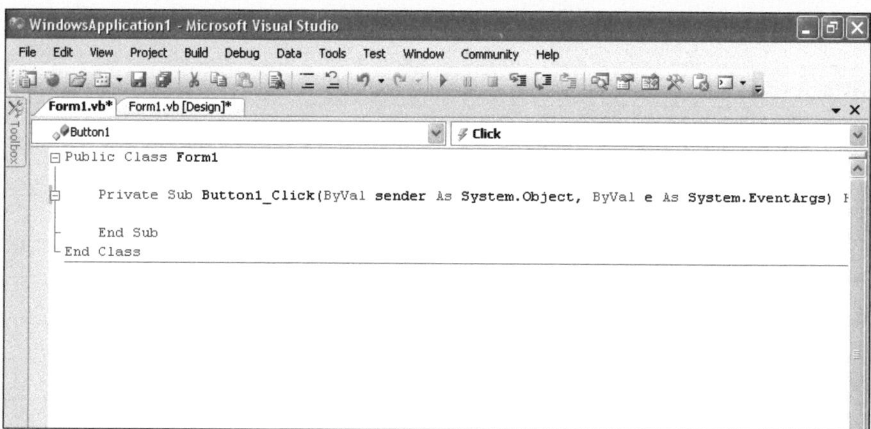

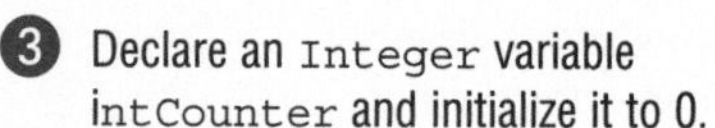

3. Declare an `Integer` variable `intCounter` and initialize it to 0.

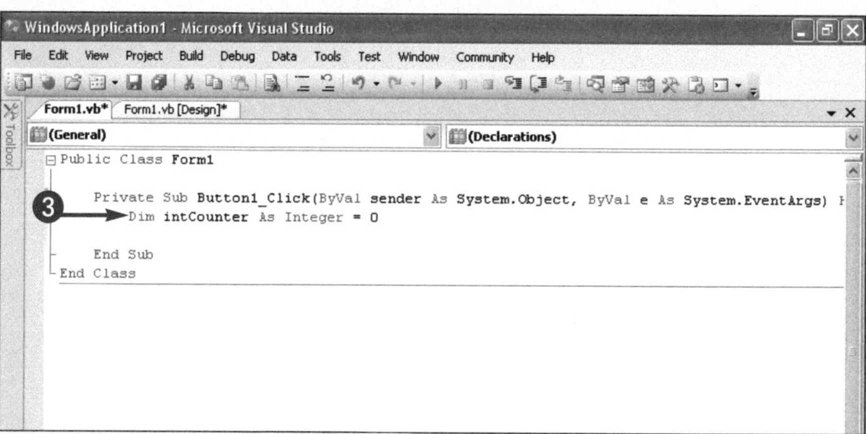

4. Insert a `Do...Loop While` loop that continues to execute statements in the code block as long as the integer variable is 1, writing the expression as `intCounter = 1`.

5. Display a message box in the code block of the `Do...Loop While` loop with a message such as `"Inside the code block"`.

6. Display a message box after the `Do...Loop While` loop with a message such as `"Outside the code block"`.

7. Press F5 to execute your program.

8. Click the `Button` control.

   The message box in the code block is displayed even though the logical expression is false.

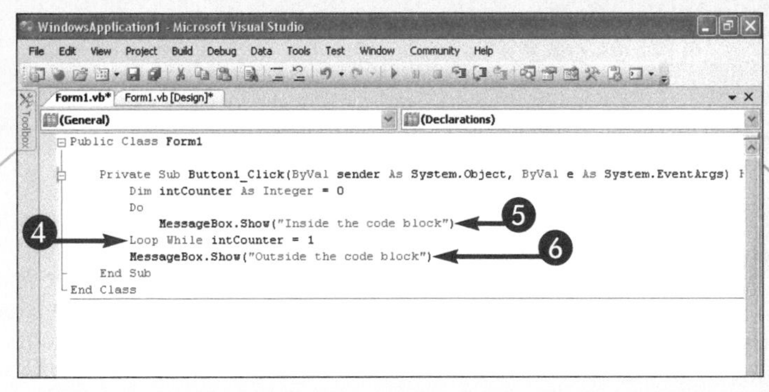

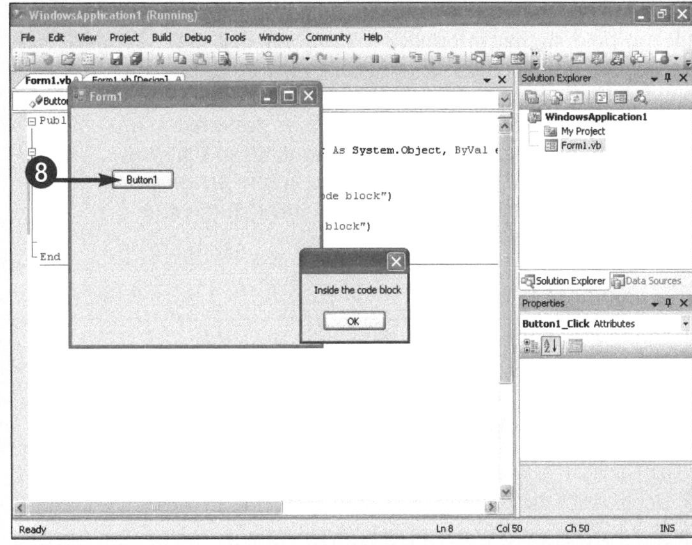

Extra

The `Do...Loop Until` loop is similar to the `Do...Loop While` loop in that statements in both their code blocks execute at least once before the logical expression is evaluated. However, the difference between these loops is the action taken when the logical expression is true. In the `Do...Loop While` loop, statements in the code block execute another time if the logical expression is true. In the `Do...Loop Until` loop, these statements execute again only if the logical expression is false. That is, Visual Basic .NET continues to execute statements in the code block until the logical expression is true.

Example

```
Dim intCounter As Integer = 0
Do
   MessageBox.Show("Inside Code Block")
intCounter = intCounter + 1
Loop Until intCounter > 2
```

Declare an Array

An *array* is a series of variables of the same data type that have the same name. Each variable in the series is called an *array element* and is identified by its position in the series, which is referred to as an *index*. The first array element is index 0, the second array element is index 1, and so on.

An array is used whenever your program requires many variables to hold similar information. Let's say that you need to display ten messages throughout your program. You could declare ten variables, but you will need to create ten unique names — one for each variable. A preferred alternative is to declare an array of ten elements so that you need only one name. It is more efficient to access array elements than a variable because you can use the index to loop through each element of the array.

You create an array similarly to the way a variable is declared by using the `Dim` keyword, followed by the array name and the data type. In addition, you must define the dimension of the array. The *dimension* is the number of elements that are contained in the array. The dimension is placed in parentheses following the name of the array. This is referred to as the *upper bound* of the array.

Let's say that you want to declare a `String` array of 10 elements. You would write `Dim strMessages(9) As String` in your program before you write statements that reference the array. This array is named `strMessages`, but you can use any unique name for your array.

Declare an Array

1. Add a `Button` control to a form.

Note: See Chapter 4 for information about adding buttons.

2. Double-click the button.

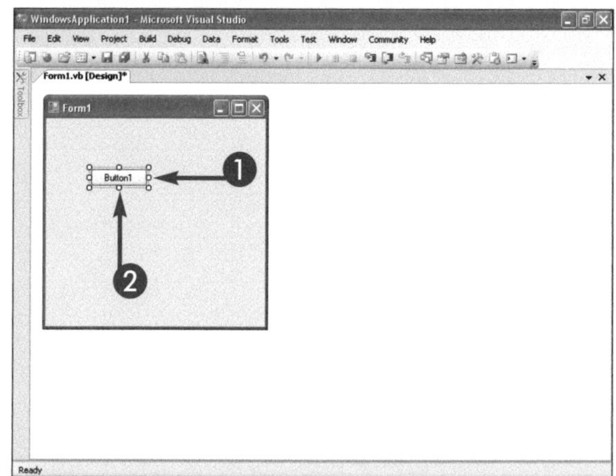

The code that executes when the button is clicked appears.

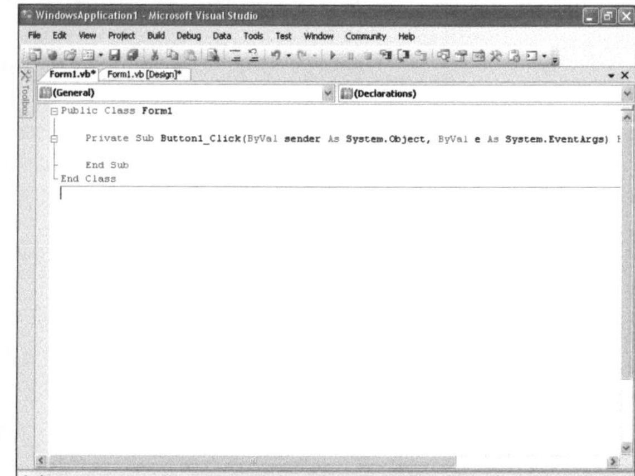

3 Declare a `String` array as shown here.

Note: The array in this example has 11 elements (see the Extra for more information).

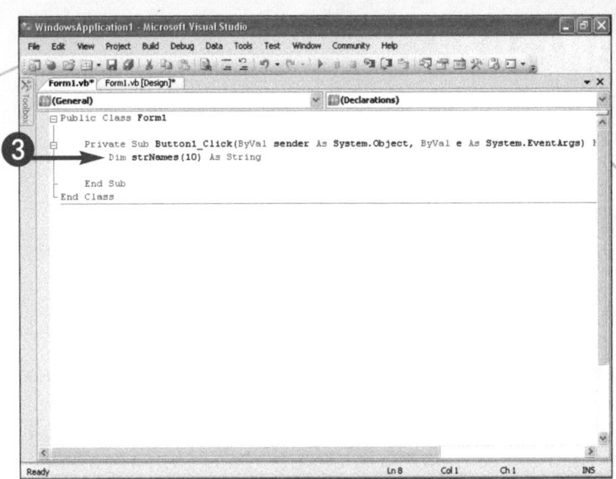

4 Declare an `Integer` array as shown here.

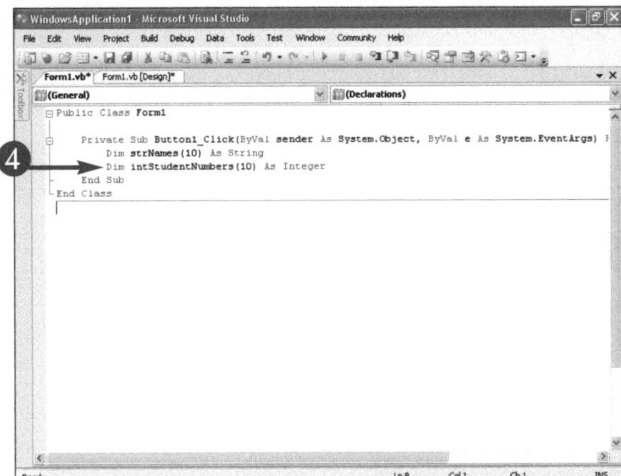

Extra

Declaring an array can be confusing. New programmers sometimes mix up the index with the dimension of the array. For example, if you want an array with ten elements, you might guess that you place 10 as the dimension of the array such as `Dim myArray(10) As Integer`. However, this statement actually declares 11 array elements — not 10. Both the dimension of the array and array index begin with zero — not 1. A simple way to avoid confusion is to subtract 1 from the number of array elements that you need and use the difference as the dimension for the array. So if you want 10 elements, subtract 1 and use 9 as the dimension for the array such as `Dim myArray(9) As Integer`.

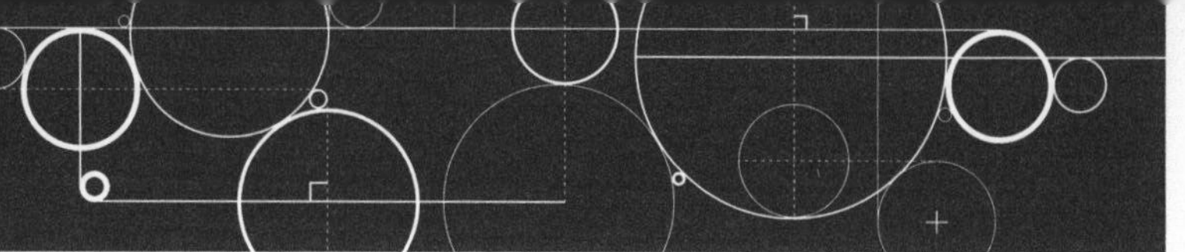

Initialize an Array

There are two ways to assign a value to array elements. The first way is to assign an initial value when you declare the array. The other way is to assign a value to an array element elsewhere in your program after you declare the array.

You initialize array elements when the array is declared by using the assignment operator (`=`) and placing the initial value for each element within French braces following the declaration of the array, such as `Dim strName() As String = {"test1", "test2"}`. A comma must separate each value.

Values used to initialize an array must conform to the array's data type. That is, `String` values must be enclosed within double quotations. Non-`String` values are not placed within double quotations. You cannot mix values of different data types in an array.

You do not specify the dimension of the array if you initialize the array when the array is declared. Visual Basic .NET determines the dimension of the array based on the number of values that you specified within the French braces. For example, `Dim strName() As String = {"test1", "test2"}` creates an array that contains two elements.

Visual Basic .NET flags as an error any array declaration that specifies an array dimension and initial values within French braces. For example, `Dim strName(2) As String = {"test1", "test2"}` generates an error. You can specify either an array dimension or initial values, but not both.

Initialize an Array

1. Add a `Button` control to a form.

Note: See Chapter 4 for information about adding buttons.

2. Double-click the button.

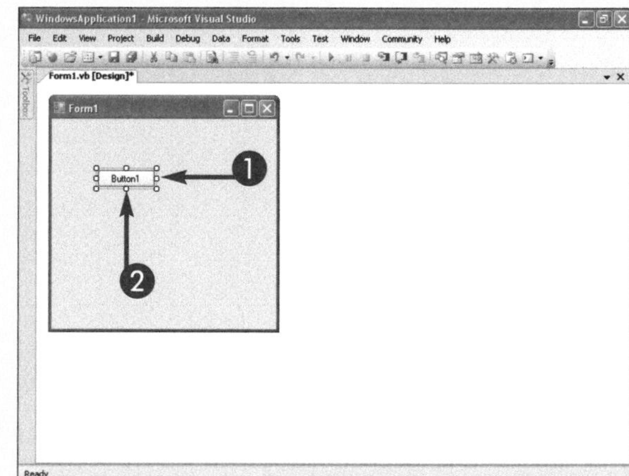

The code that executes when the button is clicked appears.

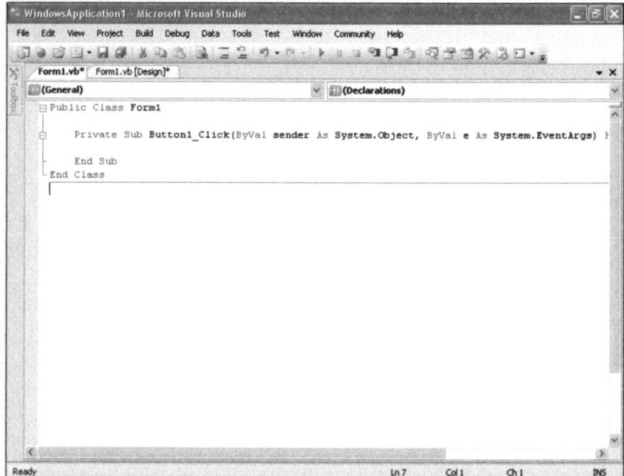

3. Declare a `String` array as shown here.

Note: The array in this example is named `strNames`.

4. Initialize the `String` array with names, such as `"Bob Smith", "Mary Jones", "Tom Adams"`.

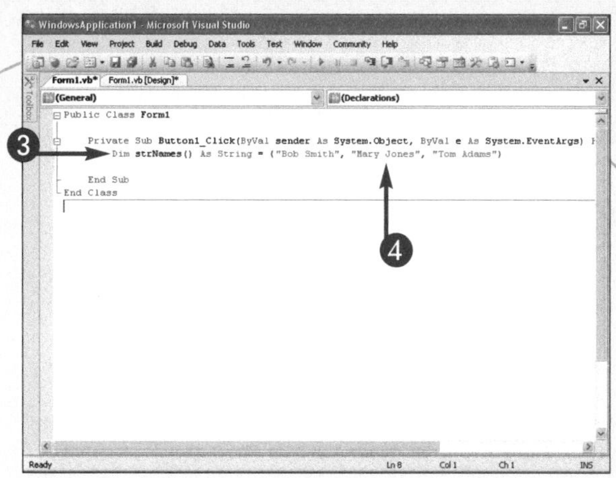

5. Declare an `Integer` array as shown here.

Note: The array in this example is named `intStudentNumbers`.

6. Initialize the array with numbers, such as `5432, 9887, 1432`.

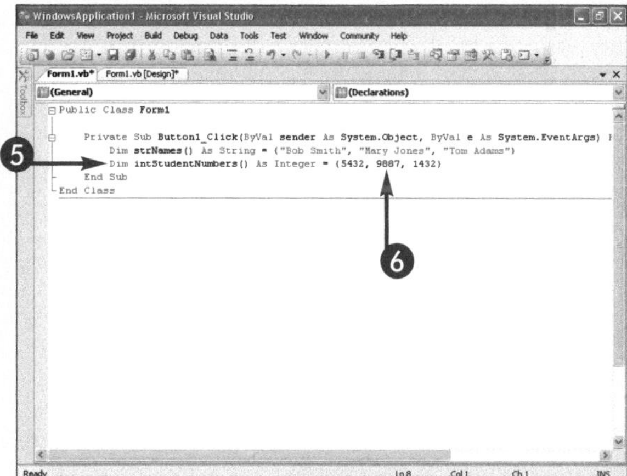

Extra

Let's say that you need three elements for an array, but you have initial values for only two of those elements. You may think that you can write `Dim strName() As String = {"test1", , "test2"}`, inserting a comma to indicate an array element. However, Visual Basic .NET flags this as an error because it expects you to place a value to the left of each comma. You can work around this problem by writing using a temporary value. For example, for a `String` array, you can write `Dim strName() As String = {"test1", "" , "test2"}`, in which two double quotes are used as the value. For a numeric array such as an `Integer` array, you can write `Dim strName() As String = {52, 0 , 75}`, in which zero is used as the unknown value.

Assign a Value to an Array

You can assign a value to an element of an array anywhere within your program regardless if the array is initialized when you declare it. Values are assigned to array elements by specifying the name of the array and the index of the element in a statement. The statement must be within the scope of where the array is declared. *Scope* refers to the level within your program where the array (or variable) can be seen. For example, an array declared in a code block can be seen only within the code block. That is, the statement that accesses an element of the array must be written within the code block where the array is declared. A code block is defined within an `If...Then` statement, a loop, or a subroutine such as the `Click` subroutine that is called by a `Button` control when it is selected.

Let's say that you want to assign a value to the first element of the `strStudentName` array. You write `strStudentName(0) = "Bob Smith"`. `strStudentName` is the name of the array. `0` is the index of the first element of the array; remember that the index of the first element of an array is `0`, not `1`. The index must be placed within parentheses to the right of the array name.

Think of the array name and index combination as the name of a variable. You can use this combination in the same way as you use a variable. For example, suppose that you declare a variable using `Dim strName As String`, and you want to assign it a value. You would write `strName = "Bob Smith"`. This is very similar to how a value is assigned to an array element.

Assign a Value to an Array

1. Add a `Button` control to a form.

Note: See Chapter 4 for information about adding buttons.

2. Double-click the button.

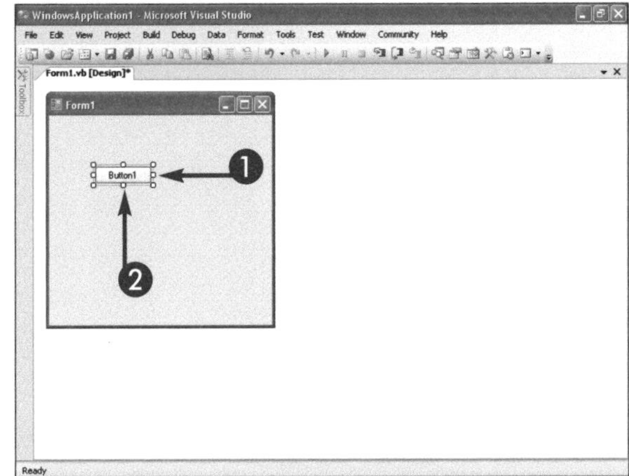

- The code that executes when the button is clicked appears.

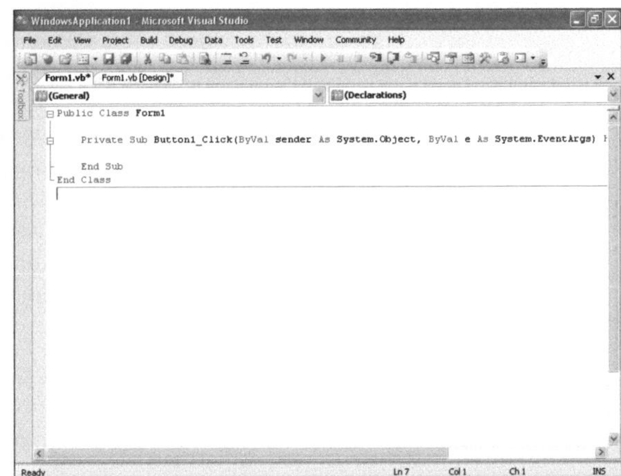

3. Declare an `Integer` array with a dimension of 10 elements, such as this `intStudentNumbers` array.

4. Declare two `Integer` variables, such as `intCounter` and `intNumber` shown here.

5. Assign a starting value of `0` to the `intNumber` variable.

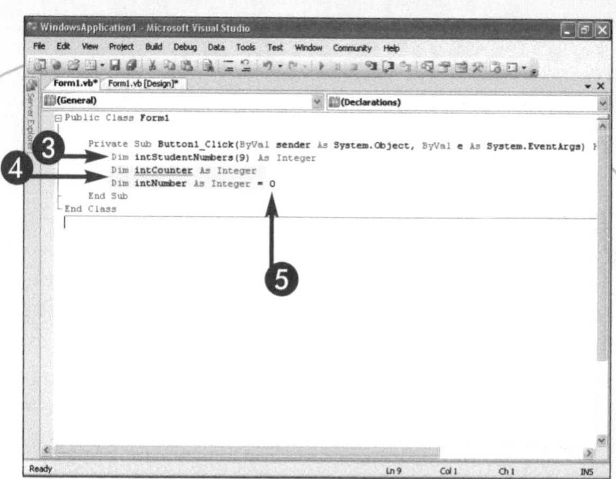

6. Write a `For` loop to assign values to array elements, using the `intCounter` variable and assigning it `0` to `9`.

7. Write a statement that increments the variable for each iteration of the loop.

Note: In this example, you increment the `intNumber` variable and assign the sum to the current array element.

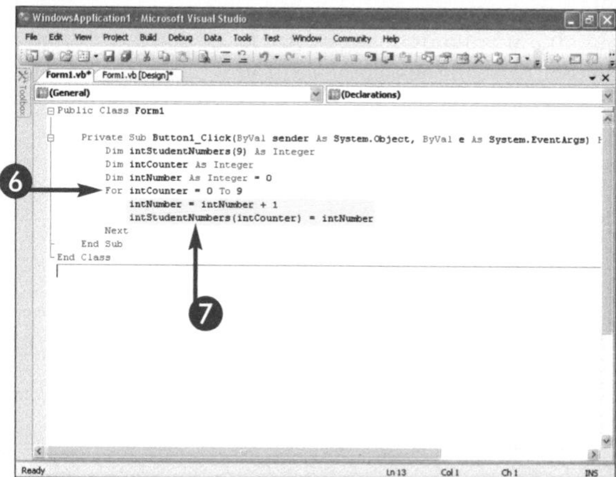

Extra

A `For` loop can be used to efficiently assign values to elements of an array because the loop repeatedly executes the statement that assigns values to array elements. The counter variable of the `For` loop is used to step through each element of the array. The value of the counter variable is used as the index of the array element. Therefore, you should set the initial value of the counter variable to `0` and not `1` because the index of the first element of the array is `0`. If you set the initial value to `1`, your code begins with the second array element, skipping the first.

Example

```
For intCounter = 0 To 9
   IntStudentNumber(intCounter) = intCounter
Next intCounter
```

Access the Value of an Array Element

Values that are assigned to an element of an array can be accessed by using the array name and referencing the index of the array element such as `strStudentNames(0)`, which accesses the value of the first element of the array called `strStudentNames`.

The combination of array name and index can be used to access information the same way as you use the name of a variable. Use the array name and index in a statement any time that you want to use the value assigned to that array element.

Let's say that `strStudentNames(0)` is assigned the name `Bob Smith`. Any time that you want to refer to `Bob Smith` in your program, you can use `strStudentNames(0)`.

When Visual Basic .NET sees `strStudentNames(0)`, it will replace `strStudentNames(0)` with the name `Bob Smith`.

In order to access an array element, the array element must be within scope. As discussed in the section "Assign a Value to an Array," the scope refers to the level within your program where the array can be seen. Visual Basic .NET generates an error message if you try to access an array element that is out-of-scope. This error may be confusing to understand because it will state that the array is not declared when in fact you declared the array elsewhere in your program. Visual Basic .NET is saying that it cannot see the declaration of the array because the array was declared outside the current code block.

Access the Value of an Array Element

1. Add a `Button` control to a form.

Note: See Chapter 4 for information about adding buttons.

2. Double-click the button.

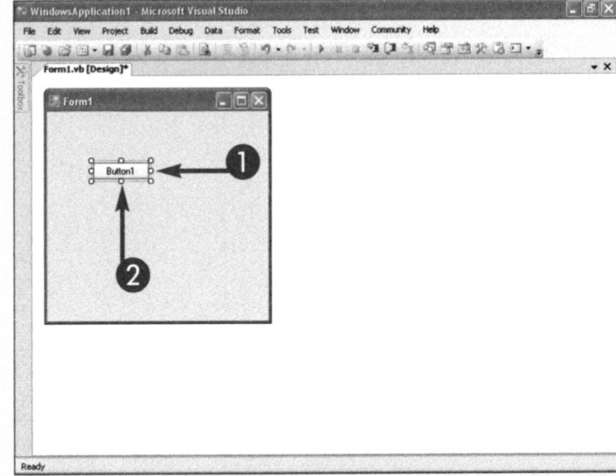

The code that executes when the button is clicked appears.

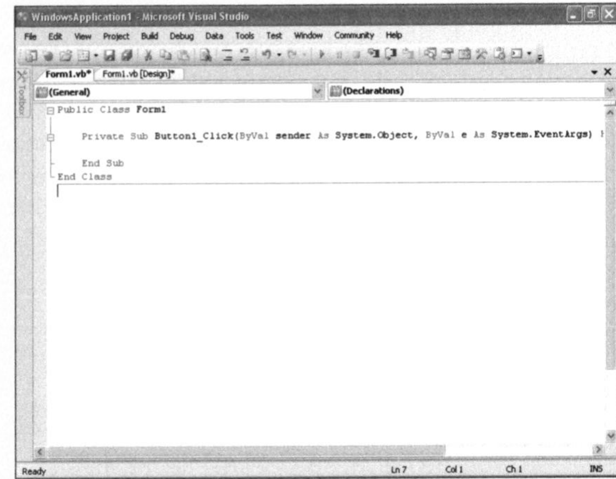

3. Declare a `String` array, such as the `strStudentNames` array in this example.

4. Declare an `Integer` variable, such as `intCounter` here.

5. Assign values to elements of the array, such as `"Bob Smith", "Mary Jones"` here.

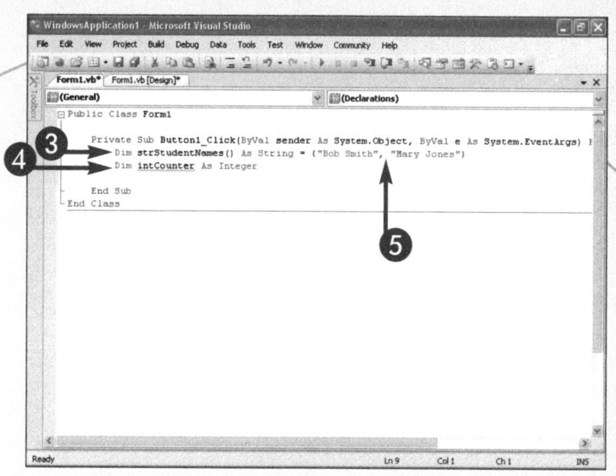

6. Write a `For` loop, using the `intCounter` variable and assigning it `0` to `1`.

7. Write a statement that displays a message box welcoming each student by writing `"Hello, "` and then the array element.

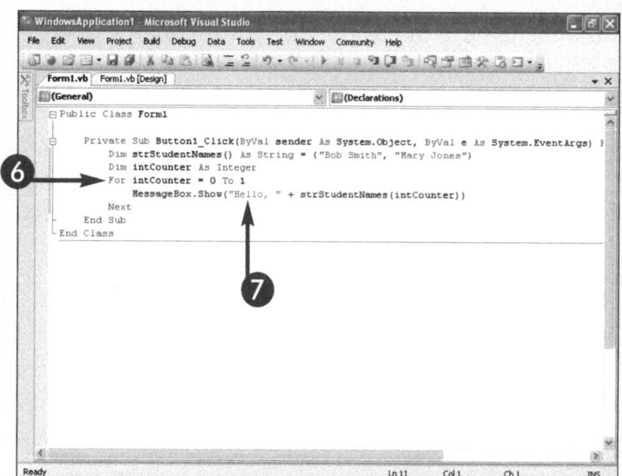

Extra

You can use a `For` loop to efficiently access each element of an array by placing the statement that accesses the element inside the `For` loop code block and using the `For` loop counter variable as the index for each array element. The starting value of the `For` loop counter variable must be zero to coincide with the index of the first array element. With each iteration of the `For` loop, the counter variable is incremented, which increments the index in the statement that references the array element.

Example

```
For intCounter = 0 To 2
   MessageBox.Show("Hello, " + strStudentNames(intCounter)
Next intCounter
```

Declare a Multidimensional Array

The arrays that you created previously in this chapter are called *single-dimensional arrays* because each array element contains one value. A *multidimensional array* is similar to a single-dimensional array in that both have array elements. However, each array element in a multidimensional array is itself another array.

A multidimensional array has one name and multiple dimensions, such as `intTestGrades(3,4)`, in which `intTestGrades` is the array name and `(3,4)` is the multiple dimensions. This example has two dimensions. The first dimension is similar to the dimension of a single-dimensional array because it defines the number of array elements. The array `intTestGrades(3,4)` has four array elements. The second dimension defines a second set of array elements. Each first dimension array element has a second set of array elements. This means that array `intTestGrades(3,4)` has 4 first dimension array elements and five second dimension array elements. For each first dimension array element, there are 5 second dimension array elements.

Consider a two-dimensional array as columns and rows of a spreadsheet. This first dimension represents the number of columns, and the second dimension is the number of rows. Each column has the same number of rows. That is, each first dimension array element has its own set of second dimension array elements. In the array `intTestGrades(3,4)`, there are four columns, each having five rows.

You declare a multidimensional array by specifying the array name followed by dimensions. A comma separates each dimension. You must also specify the data type. All the dimensions have the same data types. Here is how you declare the `intTestGrades(3,4)` multidimensional array: `Dim intTestGrades(3,4) As Integer.`

Declare a Multidimensional Array

1. Add a `Button` control to a form.

Note: See Chapter 4 for information about adding buttons.

2. Double-click the button.

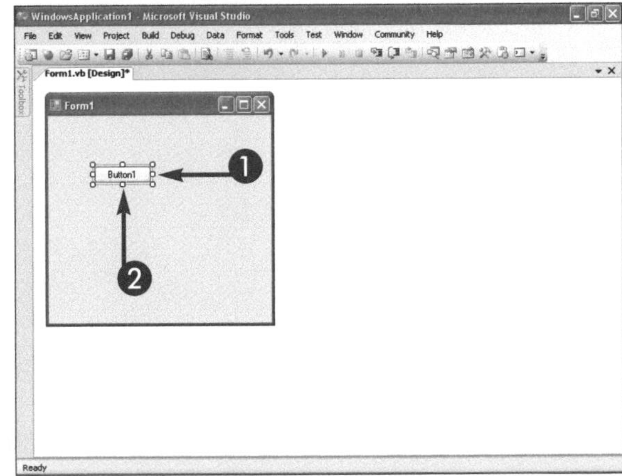

The code that executes when the button is clicked appears.

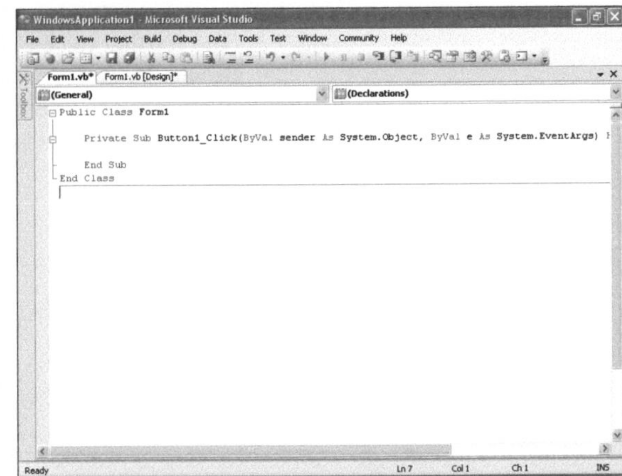

3 Declare a two-dimensional `Integer` array.

Note: The array `intStudentGrades` in this example holds 25 students (the first dimension). For each student, there are four numbers (the second dimension). The first number is the class number, and the other three are test grades.

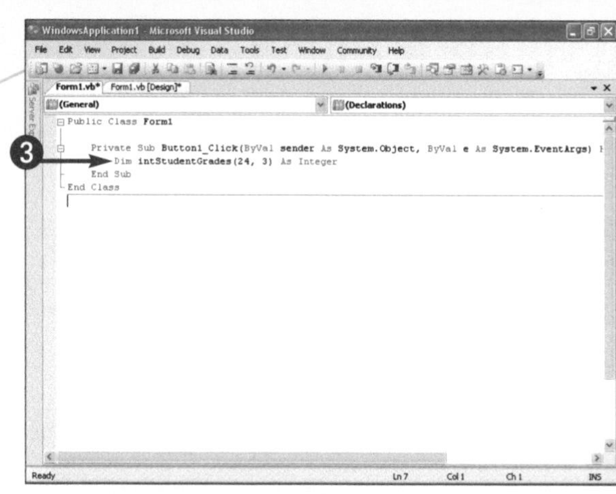

4 Declare a three-dimensional `String` array.

Note: The array `strStudents` in this example holds 25 students (the first dimension). For each student, there are two classes (the second dimension). And for each class, there are two grades (the third dimension).

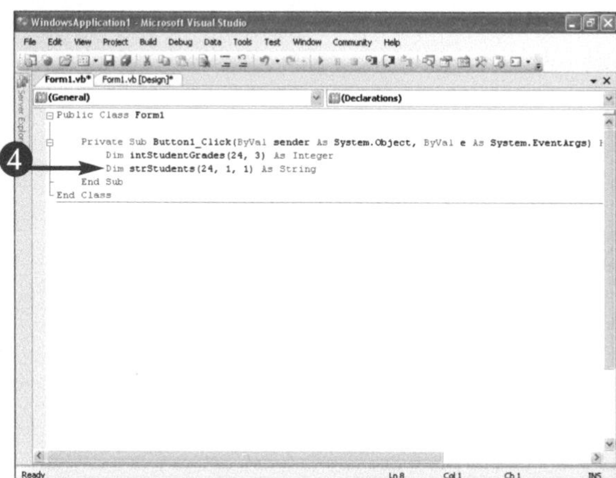

Extra

You can create a multidimensional array that has more than two dimensions by placing additional dimensions in the declaration statement. Let's say that you want to create a three-dimensional array; you could write `Dim intTestGrades(3,4,2) As Integer`. Think of this as a three-dimensional spreadsheet that has four columns, each having five rows. Each of the five rows has three cells. Another way to look at this is that there are four students. Each student takes five tests. Each test has three grades. No doubt this is a little confusing to understand. It is for this reason that many programmers rarely use more than a three-dimensional array. However, Visual Basic .NET enables you to create a maximum of 32 dimensions for an array.

Assign a Value to a Multidimensional Array

Values are assigned to a multidimensional array by specifying the array name and the index for each dimension of the array. Let's say that you declared a two-dimensional array. Think of the first dimension as columns and the second dimension as rows for each column. You want to assign a value to the first row of the first column. Remember that an index begins with `0` and not `1`. Therefore, the first column has the index `0`, and the first row of the first column has the index `0`. If the array name is `intTestGrades`, then the first column and first row is specified as `intTestGrades(0,0)`.

Suppose that this multidimensional array is declared as `intTestGrades(3, 2)`, meaning that there are four columns, each having three rows. If you want to specify the second row of the third column, you write `intTestGrades(2,1)`. Assume that the first dimension represents a student, and the second dimension represents test grades. You can assign test grades for the third student by writing `intTestGrades(2,0) = 98` and `intTestGrades(2,1) = 95`. Keep in mind that `2` as the first dimension refers to the third array element because the index of the first array element is `0`. The index of the second dimension refers to the first and second array elements.

Steps used to assign a value to a two-dimensional array also are used to assign values to any multidimensional array. That is, you specify the array name followed by the index for each dimension of the array. For example, an element of a three-dimensional array is specified as `intTestGrades(3,1,1) = 78`. Think of this as having two grades for each test taken by a student. This assigns 78 as the second grade for the second test taken by the fourth student.

Assign a Value to a Multidimensional Array

1. Add a `Button` control to a form.

Note: See Chapter 4 for information about adding buttons.

2. Double-click the button.

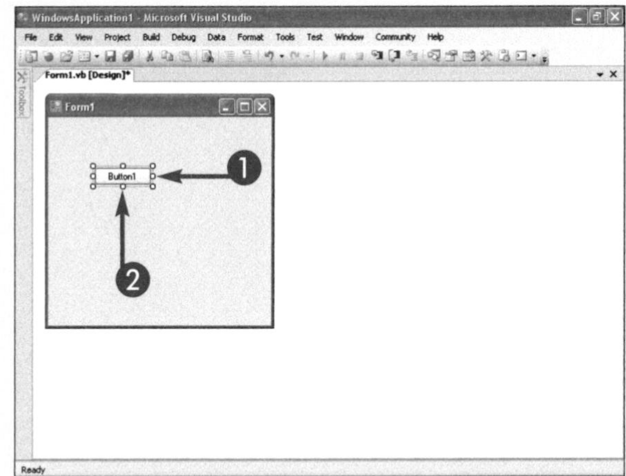

The code that executes when the button is clicked appears.

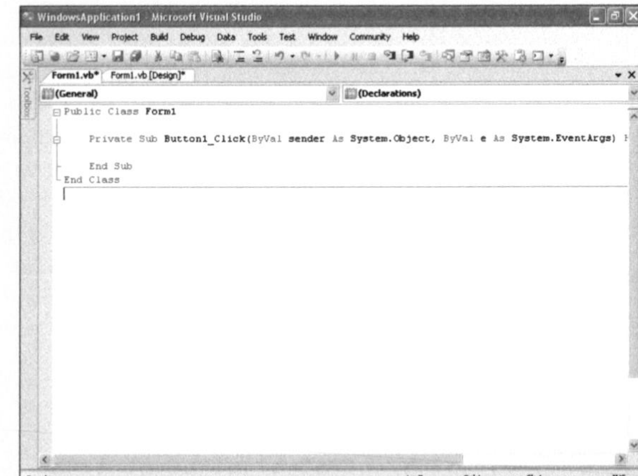

3 Declare a two-dimensional `Integer` array.

Note: The array `intStudentGrades` in this example holds 4 test grades for 25 students.

4 Declare two `Integer` variables to be used as counter variables, such as `intCounter1` and `intCounter2` here.

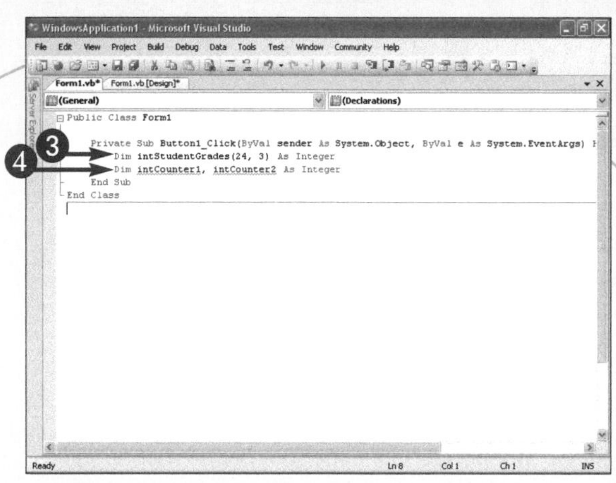

5 Write a nested `For` loop, using `intCounter1` for the outside `For` and assigning it `0` to `24` and using `intCounter2` for the inside `For` and assigning it `0` to `3`.

6 Assign `0` to each array element in the code block of the inside `For` loop.

7 Write a message box at the end of the outside loop.

8 Press F5 to run your program.

9 Click the `Button` control to initialize the two-dimensional array.

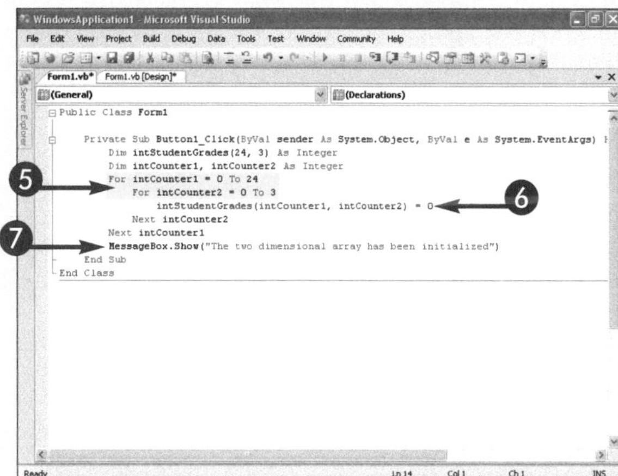

Extra

You can efficiently initialize a multidimensional array by using a nested `For` loop. Recall that a nested `For` loop consists of two `For` loops — an outside `For` loop and an inside `For` loop. The inside `For` loop is placed in the code block of the outside `For` loop. Suppose that you want to initialize a two-dimensional array. The counter variable for the outside `For` loop is used as the index for the first dimension, and the counter variable for the inside `For` loop is used as the index for the second dimension.

Example

```
For intCounter1 = 0 to 3
   For intCounter2 = 0 to 1
      IntTestGrades(intCounter1, intCounter2) = 0
   Next intCounter2
Next intCounter1
```

Access Elements of a Multidimensional Array

Elements of a multidimensional array are accessed similarly to how you access an element of a single-dimensional array, except you reference the index of both dimensions. The array name and indexes of the dimensions are treated as one unit and used within your program the same way as you use the name of a variable.

Let's say that you declared the two-dimensional array `intTestGrades(3,2)`. The first dimension refers to a student by number, and the second dimension refers to the student's three test grades. Suppose that you want to display the second student's first test grade. The second student is index `1` of the first dimension of the array. The first test grade is assigned to index `0` of the second dimension. Therefore, `(1,0)` are the indexes you need to specify the second student's first test grade. You need to combine these indexes with the array name to access the student's first test grade from within your program, such as `intTestGrades(1,0)`.

Whenever you want to refer to the second student's first test grade, you write `intTestGrades(1,0)`. For example, you can assign this grade to a variable by writing `intCurrentStudentSecondTestGrade = intTestGrades(1,0)`. Visual Basic .NET copies the value assigned to array element `intTestGrades(1,0)` to the variable `intCurrentStudentSecondTestGrade`.

If you are accessing an element of a multidimensional array that has more than two dimensions, you must specify the index of each dimension. Let's suppose that you declare a three-dimensional array because there are two grades for each test. The first grade is for multiple choice and the other for an essay. The array may be `intTestGrades(3,1,1)`. In order to access the third student's first test's essay grade, you type `intTestGrades(2,0,1)`, in which `2` identifies the student (the first dimension), `0` identifies the test (the second dimension), and `1` identifies the essay grade (the third dimension).

Access Elements of a Multidimensional Array

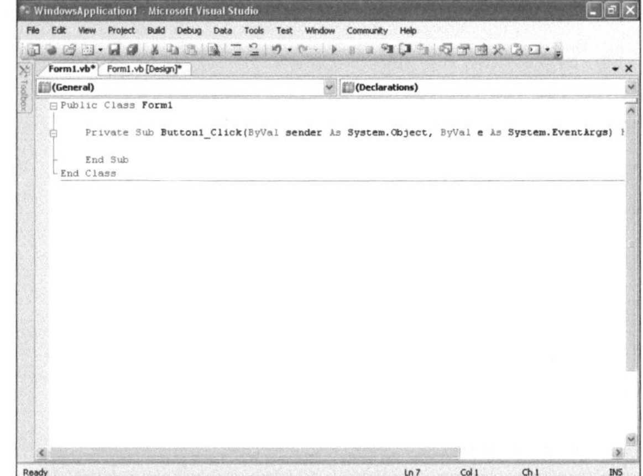

1. Add a `Button` control to a form.

Note: See Chapter 4 for information about adding buttons.

2. Double-click the button.

   The code that executes when the button is clicked appears.

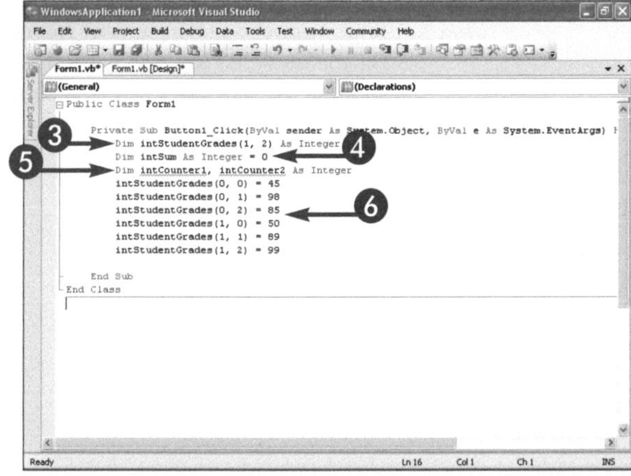

3. Declare a two-dimensional `Integer` array.

Note: The array `intStudentGrades` in this example holds 3 test grades for 2 students.

4. Declare an `Integer` variable `intSum`.
5. Declare two `Integer` variables, `intCounter1` and `intCounter2`, to be used as counter variables.
6. Initialize array elements for the first and second student, assigning the first student `45`, `98`, and `85` and assigning the second student `50`, `89`, and `99`.

7. Write a nested `For` loop, using the `intCounter1` variable for the outside `For` loop and assigning it `0` to `1` and using `intCounter2` for the inside `For` loop and assigning it `0` to `2`.

8. Assign `0` to `intSum`.

9. Sum up the grades for each student and assign the sum to `intSum`.

10. Display each student's average grade in a message box.

11. Add 1 to the counter of the outer `For` loop and use the sum as the student number.

12. Press F5 to run your program.

13. Click the `Button` control to display the average grade for each student.

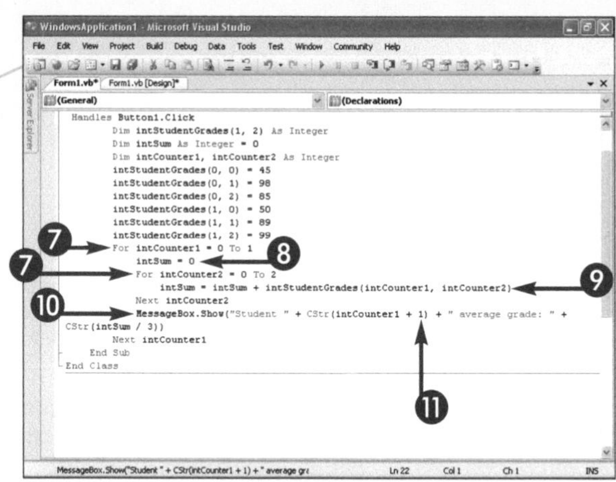

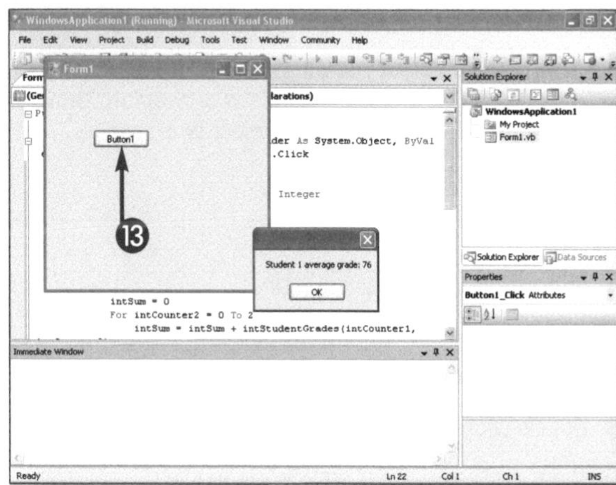

Extra

Many programmers use nested `For` loops to access values stored in elements of a multidimensional array. The outer `For` loop is used to access the first dimension of the array, and each nested `For` loop is used to access the second and subsequent dimensions. Here is how to use nested `For` loops to access a three-dimensional array.

Example

```
For intCounter1 = 0 To 3
   For intCounter2 = 0 to 1
      For intCounter3 = 0 to 1
        IntCurrentGrade = intTestGrades(intCounter1,intCounter2,intCounter3)
      Next intCounter3
   Next intCounter2
Next intCounter1
```

Sort an Array

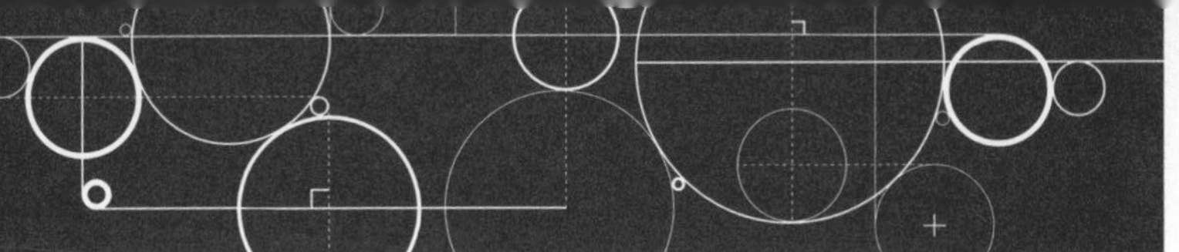

Values assigned to elements of an array can be sorted by using the `Sort()` function of the `Array` class. The `Sort()` function requires that you pass it the name of the array. The function then rearranges values into the sort order and reassigns these values to elements of the array.

Let's say that you declare a `String` array called `strNames` that has three elements. You assign values to each element such as `strNames(0) = "Mark"`, `strNames(1) = "Bob"`, and `strNames(2) = "Adam"`. These values are not in sort order.

You can sort these values by writing `Array.Sort(strNames)`. `Array` is the name of a class. A *class* is a template that defines an object. In this case, the object is an `Array`.

A class specifies data and functions that are associated with the object. `Sort()` is a function that is specified in the `Array` class. The `Sort()` function requires that you pass it the name of the array to be sorted. You do so by placing the array name between the parentheses of the `Sort()` function. The name of the array is said to be *passed* to the `Sort()` function.

After the `Sort()` function finishes sorting, the `strNames` array looks like this: `strNames(0) = "Adam"`, `strNames(1) = "Bob"`, and `strNames(2) = " Mark"`. These values are in sort order.

Sort an Array

1. Add a `Button` control to a form.

Note: See Chapter 4 for information about adding buttons.

2. Double-click the button.

The code that executes when the button is clicked appears.

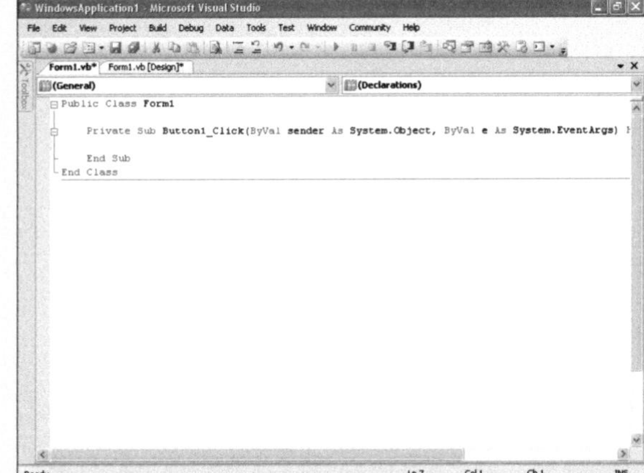

3. Declare a `String` array that has a dimension of three elements, such as this `strStudents` array.
4. Declare a `String` variable, naming the variable `strNames` and initializing it with the value `" "`.
5. Declare an `Integer` variable `intCounter1` to be used as a counter variable.
6. Initialize the array elements with the values `"Mark", "Adam", "Bob"`.

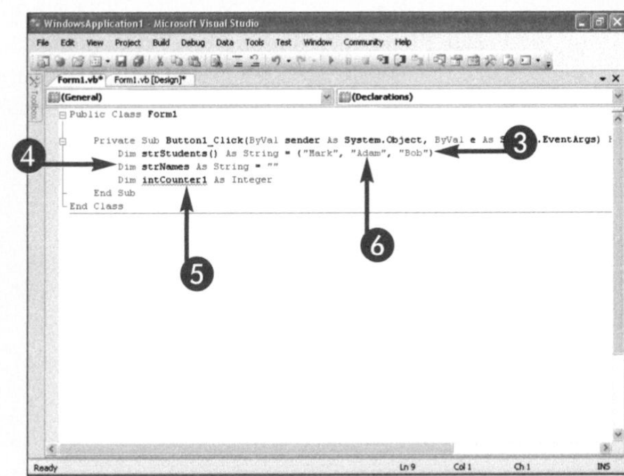

7. Write a `For` loop, using the `intCounter1` variable and assigning it `0` to `2`.

8. Append each element of the array to the `strNames` variable in the code block of the `For` loop by writing `strNames = strNames + "  "+ strStudents(intCounter1)`.

9. Display the `strNames` value by writing `MessageBox.Show(strNames)`.

10. Sort the `strStudents` array by writing `Array.Sort(strStudents)`.

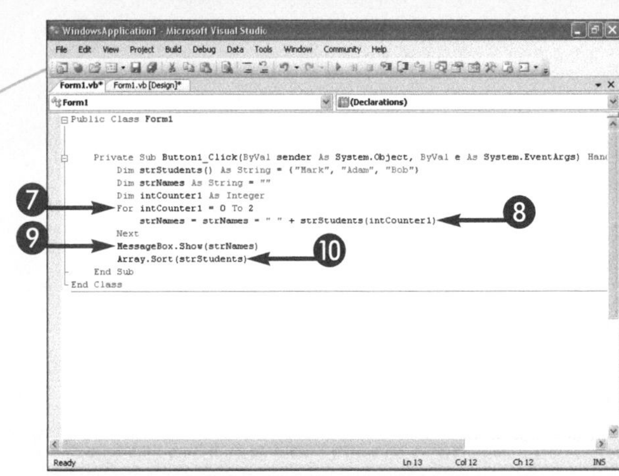

11. Assign `"  "` to the `strNames` variable.

12. Write a `For` loop, using `intCounter1` and assigning it `0` to `2`.

13. Append each array element to `strNames` in the `For` loop by writing `strNames = strNames + "  "+ strStudents(intCounter1)`.

14. Display `strNames`.

15. Press F5.

16. Click the `Button` control to display the unsorted names.

17. Click the message box.

The second message box displays sorted names.

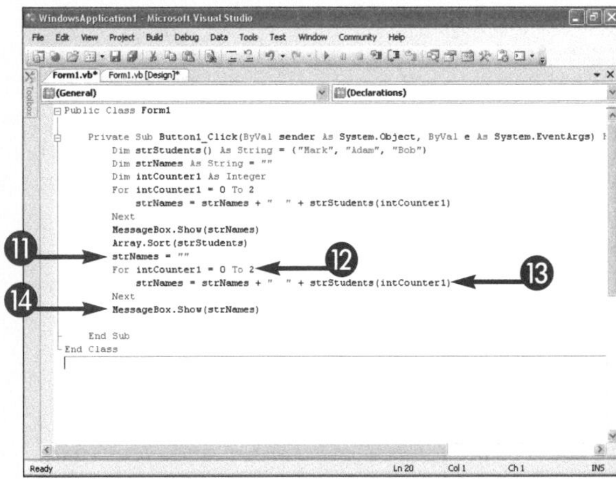

Extra

Sometimes you will come across a situation when values assigned to a variable are already in sort order, but your application needs to use them in reverse order. This means that you start with the last value first and then work your way back to the first value. There are a number of ways to do this. You could use `intCounter = 10 to 0 step -1` in a `For` loop and then use `intCounter` as the index value for each array element. You would start at the last array element and work your way to the first.

A more efficient solution is to reverse the order by calling the `Reverse()` function of the `Array` class. The `Reverse()` function requires that you pass it the name of the array whose elements you want to reverse the order. Suppose the `strNames` array looks like this: `strNames(0) = "Adam"`, `strNames(1) = "Bob"`, and `strNames(2) = "Mark"`, and you want to place values in reverse `sort` order. You write `Array.Reverse(strNames)`. Here is how these array elements appear after the `Reverse()` function finishes: `strNames(0) = "Mark"`, `strNames(1) = "Bob"`, and `strNames(2) = "Adam"`.

Search Array Elements

A fast way to determine if an array contains a particular value is to use the `BinarySearch()` function of the `Array` class. The `BinarySearch()` function performs a binary search of an array, looking for the search value that you specify. A binary search is a technique to find a search value without having to compare it to each element of the array. As a result, the `BinarySearch()` function can find a search value in an array of a million array elements within a few seconds. You can use this function only on one-dimensional arrays. If the search is too slow, sort the array before calling the `BinarySearch()` function.

The `BinarySearch()` function compares the search value to the value assigned to an array element. If there is a match, `BinarySearch()` returns the index of the first array element whose value matches the search value; you may have the same element value defined more than once, but later matches are not returned. The `BinarySearch()` function returns a `-1` if the search value is not found in the array.

The `Array.BinarySearch()` function requires two pieces of information in order to conduct the search. These are the name of the array to search and the search value. Both of these are placed between the parentheses. Let's say that `strNames` is a `String` array, and you want to search for `"Bob"`. You would write `Array.BinarySearch(strNames, "Bob")`.

The `Array.BinarySearch()` function returns an integer that represents the index if the search value is found. Typically, you will assign the return value from the `Array.BinarySearch()` function to an `Integer` variable such as `intSearchResult = Array.BinarySearch (strNames, "Bob")`. You then use the `Integer` variable in your program any time that you want to refer to the index of the search value.

Search Array Elements

1. Add a `Button` control to a form.

Note: See Chapter 4 for information about adding buttons.

2. Double-click the button.

The code that executes when the button is clicked appears.

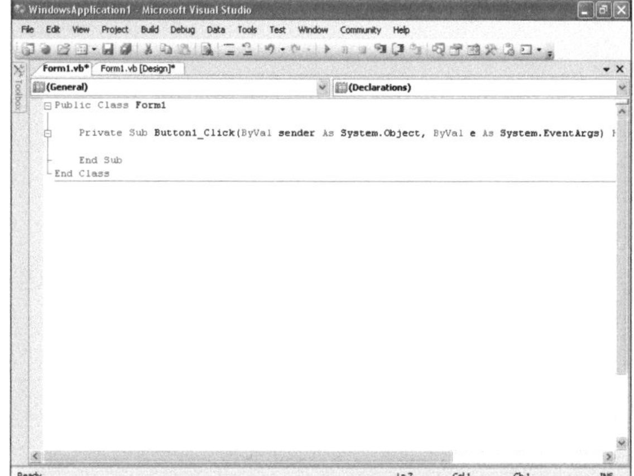

3. Declare a `String` array `strStudents` that has a dimension of three elements.
4. Initialize the array elements, using the values `"Mark", "Adam", "Bob"`.
5. Declare an `Integer` variable `intSearchResult`.

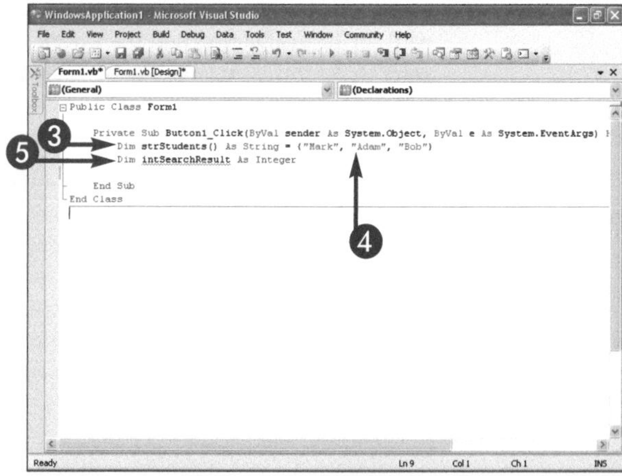

6 Write a statement that searches the `strStudents` array and assigns the result of the search to the `Integer` variable, searching for `Adam`.

7 Write an `If...Then...Else` statement that displays a message box showing the index of the search value if found or displays a message box saying that the search value was not found.

- You compare the value of the `Integer` variable to `-1`. If it equals `-1`, the search value was not found.

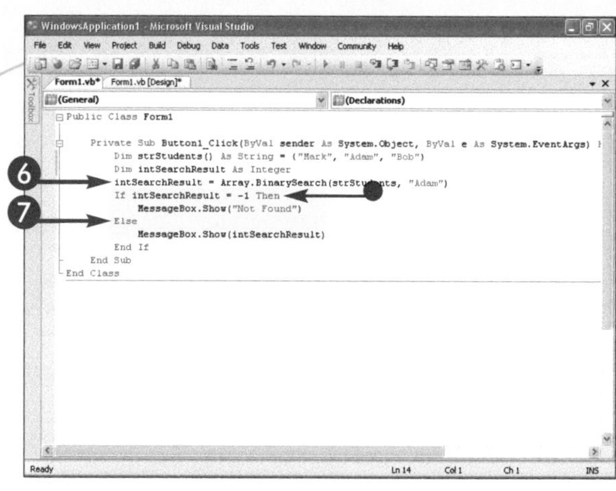

8 Press F5 to run your program.

9 Click the `Button` control to search the array.

The message box displays the index of the array element whose value is `Adam`.

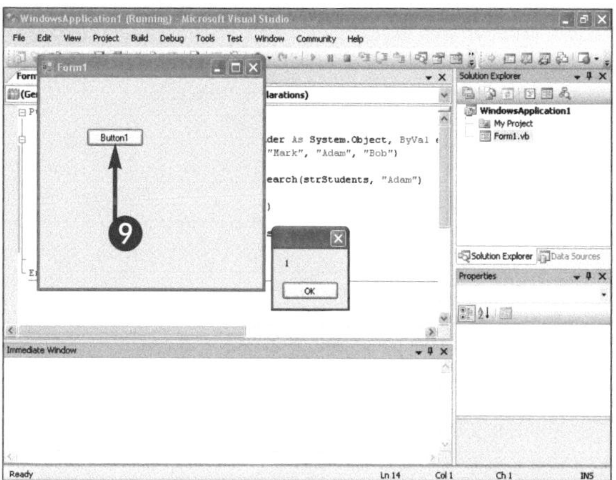

Extra

Each array that you create has its own data and functions that you will find useful in your program. Two of these that are more commonly used are `Length` and `Initialize()`. `Length` represents the number of elements in the array, and `Initialize()` is a function that assigns initial values to each element of the array.

You reference data or functions of the array by specifying the name of the array, followed by a period and the name of the data or function. Let's say that you created an array called `strNames`. If you wanted to determine the length of the array, you would write `intSize = strNames.Length`. This assigns the length of the array to the `intSize` variable.

You initialize this array by writing `strNames.Initialize()`. The `Initialize()` function assigns `vbNULL` values to each element of the `String` array. `vbNULL` means nothing – not even a space. `Integer` arrays are initialized to zero, and `Boolean` arrays are initialized to `False`. If an element has a value, the `Initialize()` function leaves the value unchanged.

Size an Array

There are times when you are developing Visual Basic .NET applications that you will need to write code that needs to reference either the length of an array or an index of the last array element. Some developers refer to the declaration statement that created the array to learn these values. A better approach is to use the array's `length` property or call the `UBound()` function.

Every array that you create has a property called `length` whose value is the number of elements of the array. You access this property by using `XXX.length`, where `XXX` is the name of the array. Let's say that you declare an array called `strStudentNumber` and want to know how many elements are in the array. You write `strStudentNumber.length` to find out.

The length of an array is not the same as the index of the last array element. The index of the last array element is referred to as the array's *upper boundary*. You can determine the upper boundary of an array by calling the `UBound()` function. The `UBound()` function requires one parameter, which is the name of the array. It returns an integer that is the index of the last array element.

Suppose that you want to determine the upper boundary of the `strStudentNumber` array. You write `UBound(strStudentNumber)`. The `UBound()` function is typically used as the maximum value assigned to the counter variable in a `For` loop. The counter variable is then used in statements within the code block of the `For` loop to access array elements.

Size an Array

1. Add a `Button` control to a form.

Note: See Chapter 4 for information about adding buttons.

2. Double-click the button.

   The code that executes when the button is clicked appears.

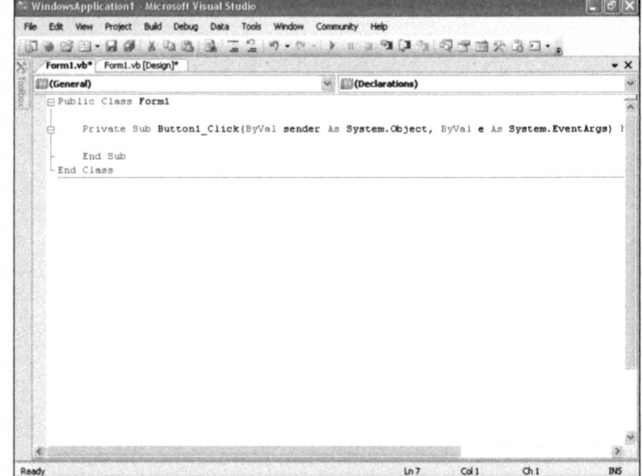

3. Declare a `String` array `strStudents` that has a dimension of three elements.

4. Initialize the array elements, using the values `"Mark", "Adam", "Bob"`.

5. Write a statement that displays the length of the array using `MessageBox.Show(strStudents.length)`.

6. Write a statement that displays the index of the last array element using `MessageBox.Show(XXX)`, replacing `XXX` with the name of the array such as `UBound(strStudents)`.

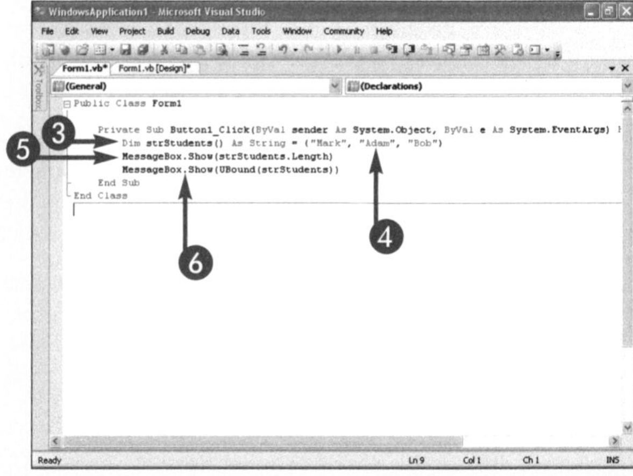

7. Declare a counter value `intCounter` as an `Integer`.

8. Write a `For` loop that uses the `UBound(XXX)` function as the maximum value of the counter variable, replacing `XXX` with the name of the array.

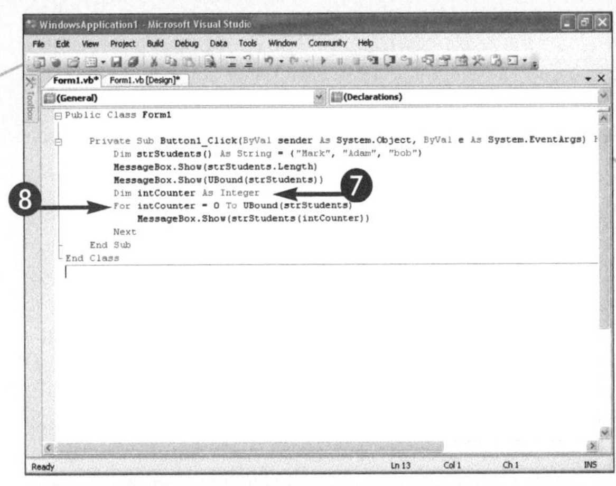

9. Press F5 to run your program.

10. Click the `Button` control to display the length upper boundary of the array and the contents of the array.

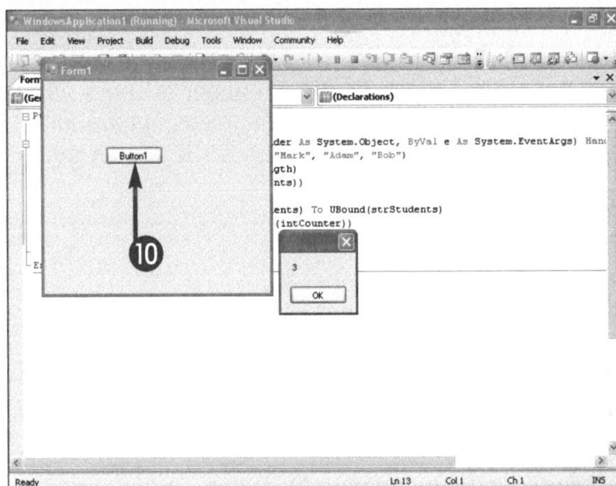

Extra

The index of the first array element is called the array's *lower boundary*. The lower boundary is always `0`. However, you can use the `LBound()` function to return the lower boundary of the array instead of using the number 0. The `LBound()` function requires the same parameter as `UBound()`, which is the name of the array.

Let's say that you want to refer to the lower boundary of the `strStudents` array; you write `LBound(strStudents)`. The most common use of the `LBound()` function is in a `For` loop.

Example

```
For intCounter = LBound(strStudents) To UBound(strStudents)
   MessageBox.Show(strStudents(intCounter))
End For
```

Create a Dynamic Array

Sometimes you will run across a situation in which you will need several arrays of the same data type within your code, but not simultaneously. Instead of creating three arrays, you can create one dynamic array. When you declare a *dynamic array,* you declare it without setting its dimension. The dimension is set outside the declaration by using the `ReDim` keyword. This means that you can set the array to one dimension and then reset it to another dimension later in your code. Let's say that you have an array called `strTests`. You declare it as `strTests()` and then set its dimension as `ReDim strTests(3)` in a different statement.

A dynamic array can be resized any number of times within your code. However, values assigned to elements are lost when the array is resized. This means that if you wrote `strTests(0) = "90"` and then wrote `ReDim strTests(4)`, the value of `strTests(0)` is no longer `"90"`.

The purpose of a dynamic array is to reuse memory that has previously been allocated that is no longer needed by the application. Let's say that you needed three arrays but not simultaneously. You could declare three dimensional arrays at the beginning of your application, and those arrays will remain in memory until your application ends. Alternatively, you could declare one dynamic array and then redimension the array. Memory used by the previous array is freed, and new memory is allocated for the redimensioned array.

Create a Dynamic Array

1. Add a `Button` control to a form.

Note: See Chapter 4 for information about adding buttons.

2. Double-click the button.

The code that executes when the button is clicked appears.

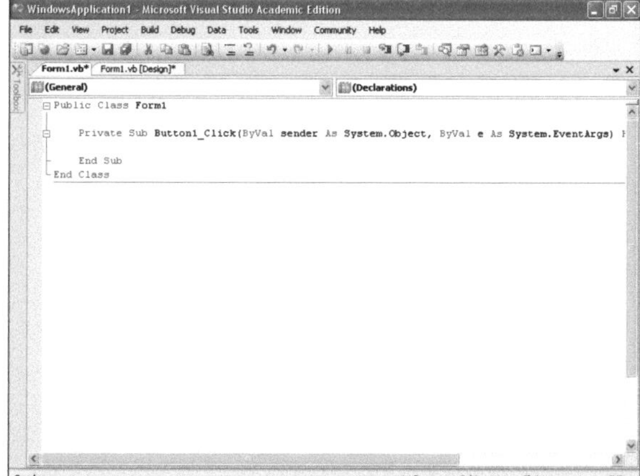

3. Declare a dynamic `String` array `strStudents`.
4. Use the `ReDim` keyword to set the dimension to 4 elements.
5. Display the length of the array using the `Length` property of the array.

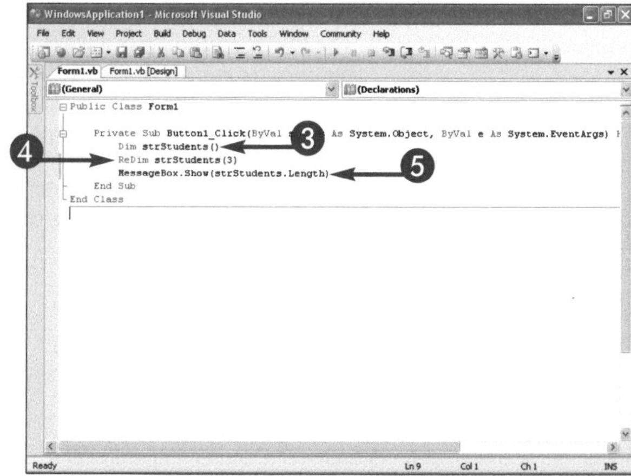

6 Use the `ReDim` keyword to reset the dimension for the `strStudents` array to 12 elements.

7 Display the length of the array using the `Length` property of the array.

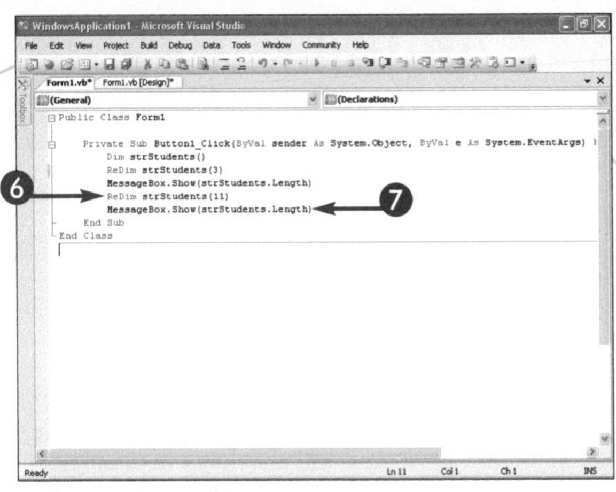

8 Press F5 to run your program.

9 Click the `Button` control to search the array.

The first message box displays the first dimension of the array, and the second message box displays the length of the redimensional array.

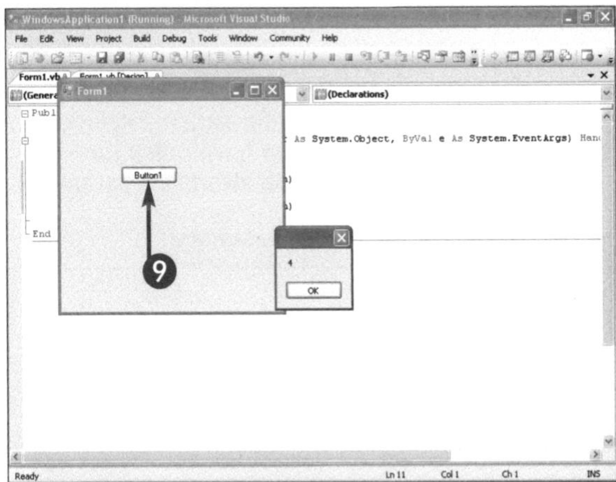

Extra

Although many developers create a dynamic array by declaring an array without a dimension and then setting the dimension later in the code, you can set the dimension when you declare the array and then reset it in another statement. When Visual Basic .NET encounters the `ReDim` keyword, it simply destroys the original array and replaces it with the redimensional array.

This means that you can write the following, and you will not experience an error.

Example

```
Dim strStudents(4) As String
MessageBox.Show(strStudents.Length)
ReDim strStudents(11)
```

Pass an Array to a Subroutine or Function

In Chapter 9, you will learn how to break up your application into segments called subroutines and functions. Think of a *segment* as a block of code that has a name. Each time you want that block of code to execute, you call its name. Sometimes that block needs information to execute. This information is called a *parameter* and is passed to it when the code block is called. And there are times when the code block returns a value to the statement that calls it. You will also learn in Chapter 9 that a parameter can be passed to both a subroutine and a function. However, only a function can return a value.

For example, suppose that you have written `MessageBox.Show(XXX)` many times. `Show(XXX)` is a subroutine, and `XXX`, which is the information displayed on the screen, is the parameter. You also have called the `UBound(XXX)` function. This function also has a parameter, which is the array name and returns an integer, which is the index of the last element of the array.

Now that you have an idea of how subroutines and functions work, let's see how you can pass an array as a parameter to a subroutine and function. There are two things that must be done. First is to define the function, which you will learn about in Chapter 9. In this definition, you must declare a dynamic array as the parameter. Second, you pass the name of the array when you call the subroutine or function.

Visual Basic .NET sets the dimension of the dynamic array to the dimension of the array that is passed to the subroutine or function. It then copies the value of each element to the dynamic array so that the dynamic array can be used in statements with the subroutine or function's code block.

Pass an Array to a Subroutine or Function

1. Add a `Button` control to a form.

Note: See Chapter 4 for information about adding buttons.

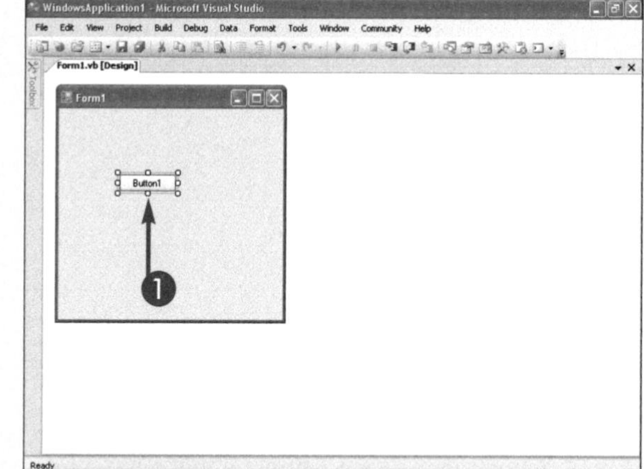

2. Add a module to your project by clicking Project ➔ Add Module and then clicking the Add button in the dialog box.
3. Define a subroutine `DisplayStudents` by copying the code here.

Note: You will learn more about defining a subroutine in Chapter 9.

4. Declare an array parameter `strStudents`, copying this example.
5. Display the value of the first array element, using `MessageBox.Show (strStudents(0))`.

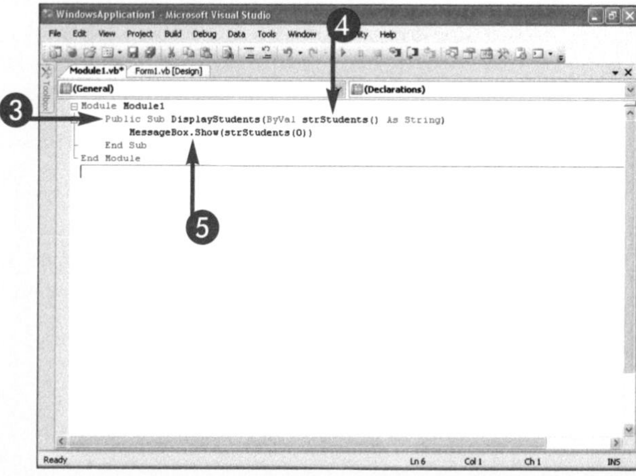

6 Double-click the button.

The code that executes when the button is clicked appears.

7 Declare a `String` array called `strStudents` that has four elements.

8 Assign a value to the first array element by writing `strStudents(0) = "Bob"`.

9 Call the `DisplayStudents()` subroutine and pass it the name of the array by writing `DisplayStudents (strStudents)`.

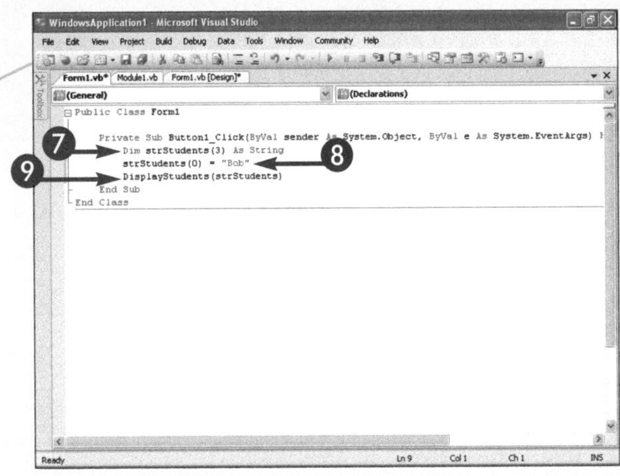

10 Press F5 to run your program.

11 Click the `Button` control to display the first element of the array.

The value is assigned to the array outside the subroutine, and the subroutine receives the array and displays the first array element.

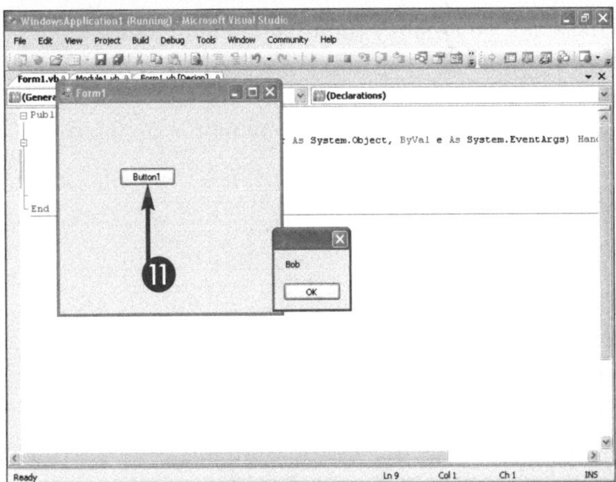

Extra

Any dimensional array can be passed to a subroutine and function because you do not set the dimension of this array. The dimension of the array declared as a parameter is automatically set to match the dimension of the array passed to it. This means that you can redimension an array in your code without having to change the array that is a parameter to the subroutine or function. This is illustrated in the following example. Notice that the dimension of the `strStudents` array is different each time the `DisplayStudents()` subroutine is called.

Example

```
Dim strStudents(3) As String
strStudents(0) = "Bob"
DisplayStudents(strStudents)
ReDim strStudents(5)
strStudents(0) = "Tom"
DisplayStudents(strStudents)
```

Return an Array from a Function

A *function* is a segment of your application whose code executes when the function is called from a statement elsewhere in your application. A function, unlike a subroutine, can return a value when it is finished executing its code. The value is returned using the `Return` statement, which you will learn more about in Chapter 9. A function can return an array by using the array name with the `Return` statement.

Let's say that you created a function called `GetStudents()` that returned an array of students. Whenever you want a list of students, you simply call this function, and the list is returned in an array.

The values of array elements that are returned by the function are assigned to another array that is declared in the part of your application that called the function. This is done by using the assignment operator. Suppose that you want to assign the list of students returned by the `GetStudents()` function to the `strStudents` array. You would write `strStudents = GetStudents()`. This tells Visual Basic .NET to execute the code in the `GetStudents()` function and then copy the returning values to elements in the `strStudents` array.

The array that is being assigned the values must be declared prior to calling the function; otherwise, Visual Basic .NET will not have any placed within your code to copy the returning values.

Return an Array from a Function

1. Add a `Button` control to a form.

Note: See Chapter 4 for information about adding buttons.

2. Double-click the button.

The code that executes when the button is clicked appears.

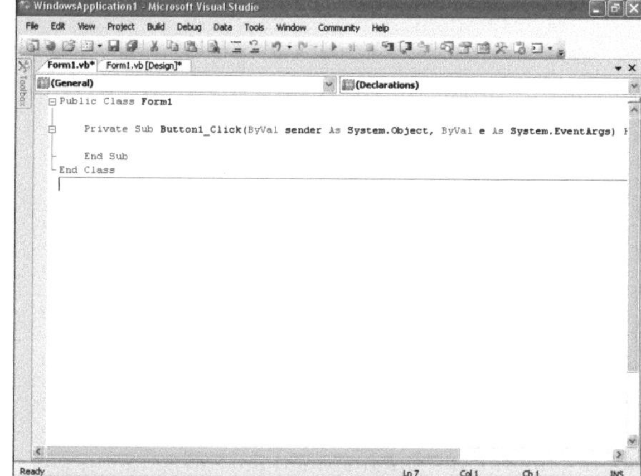

3. Declare a `String` array `strStudents` that has a dimension of four elements.
4. Call the `GetStudents()` function and assign the returning values to the `strStudents()` array.
5. Display the first element of the array using `MessageBox.Show()`.

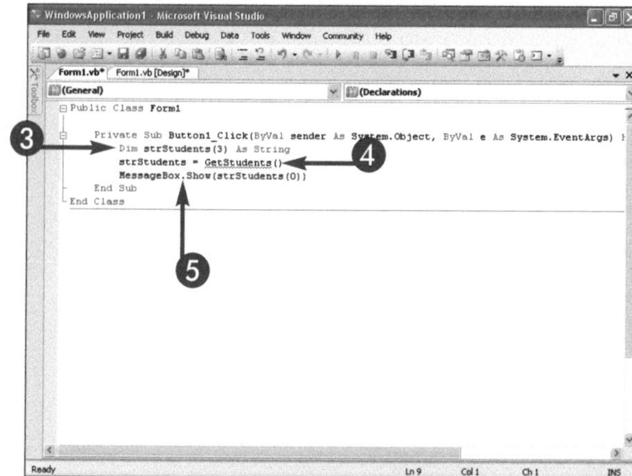

6. Add a module to your project by clicking Project ➔ Add Module and then clicking the Add button in the dialog box.

7. Define a function called `GetStudents` by copying the code here.

Note: You will learn more about defining a function in Chapter 9.

8. Declare a `String` array `strStudents` that has four elements.

9. Assign a value to the first array element.

10. Use the `Return` statement to return the array.

11. Press F5 to run your program.

12. Click the `Button` control to display the first student in the array.

    Notice that the value assigned by the function is displayed in a different part of the application.

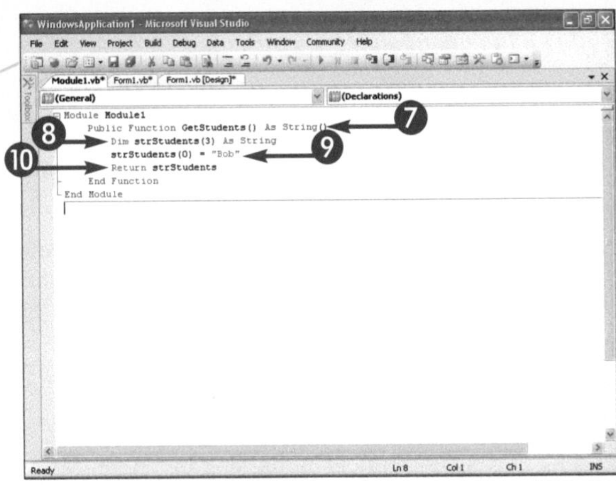

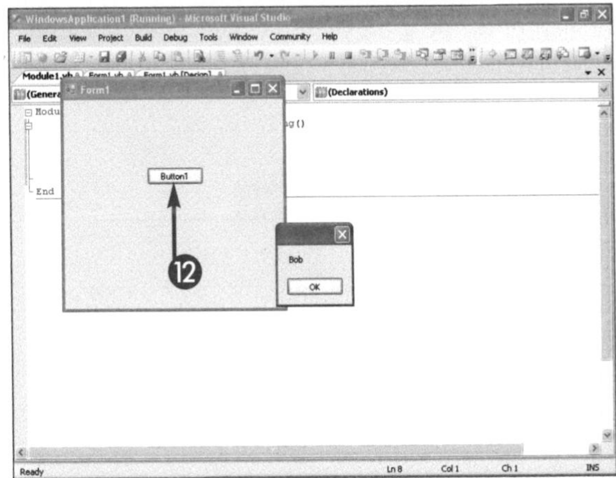

Extra

One problem with calling a function that returns an array is that you will not know the size of the array that is returned unless it is defined in the function. This happens whenever you call a function written by another developer or one from the Visual Basic .NET library. You can work around this problem by declaring an array without specifying a dimension. The dimension will be set dynamically when Visual Basic .NET returns the array from the function. Visual Basic .NET first sets the array's dimension and then copies values returned by the function.

Example

```
Dim strStudents() As String
strStudents = GetStudents()
MessageBox.Show(strStudents(0))
```

Change an Array Value Using ByRef

You probably noticed in previous examples that we used the keyword `ByVal` when passing an array to a subroutine. This also holds true for functions. Visual Basic .NET copies the value of the array from the part of the program that calls the subroutine to the subroutine's parameter. This means that there are two arrays each with the same values. As you will learn in Chapter 9, this is referred to as passing *by value.*

Another way to pass an array is by passing by reference using the `ByRef` keyword. Passing *by reference* means that both the part of the program that calls the subroutine and the subroutine itself both refer to the same value instead of each having its own copy of the value. As a result, both portions of your program can change the value.

You still need to declare an array in the part of your program that calls the subroutine and as the subroutine's parameter. Each can have a different array name. When the subroutine is called, Visual Basic .NET points the parameter array to the other array. So when you refer to the first element of the array within the subroutine to assign it a value, you are actually referencing the corresponding element in the other array.

Change an Array Value Using ByRef

1. Add a `Button` control to a form.

Note: See Chapter 4 for information about adding buttons.

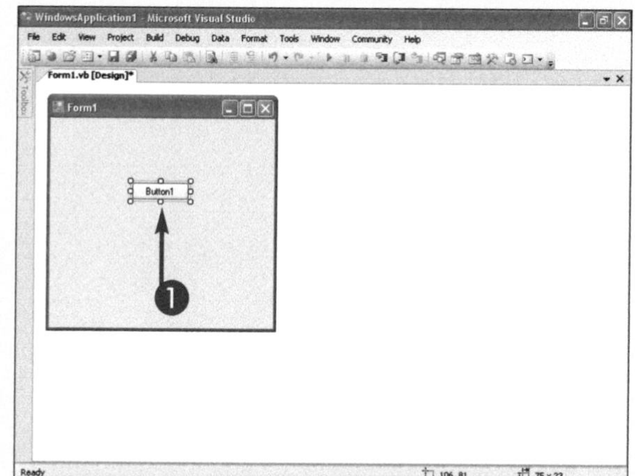

2. Add a module to your project by clicking Project ➔ Add Module and then clicking the Add button in the dialog box.
3. Define a subroutine `GetStudents` by copying the code here.

Note: You will learn more about defining a subroutine in Chapter 9.

4. Declare an array parameter called `strStudents`, copying this example.
5. Assign `"Bob"` to the first element of the array.

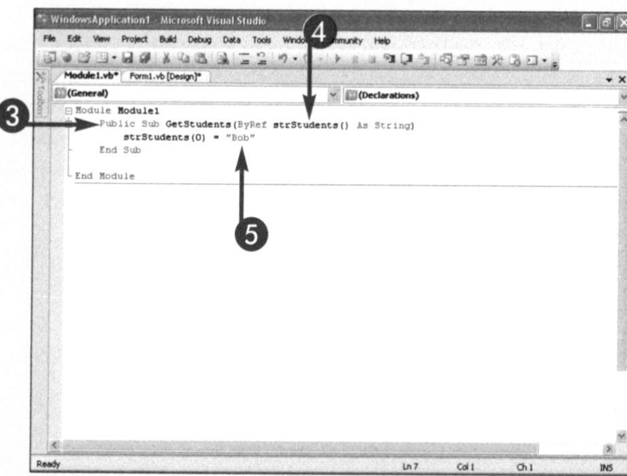

6 Double-click the button.

The code that executes when the button is clicked appears.

7 Declare a `String` array called `strStudents` that has four elements.

8 Call the `GetStudents()` subroutine and pass it the name of the array.

9 Display the value of the first array element using the `MessageBox.Show()` method.

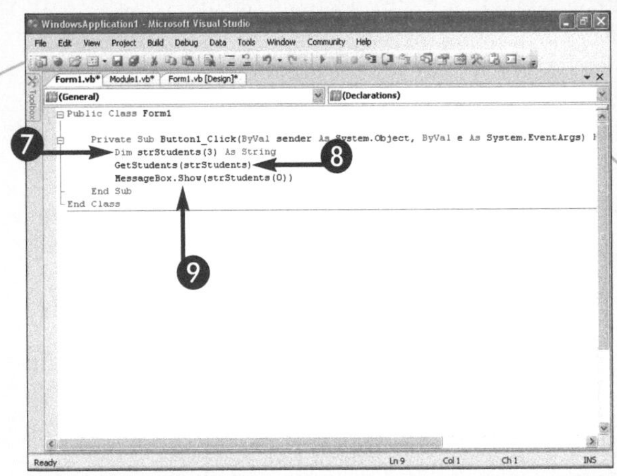

10 Press F5 to run your program.

11 Click the `Button` control to display the first element of the array.

The value assigned this array element in the subroutine is displayed by the part of the program that called it without returning a value.

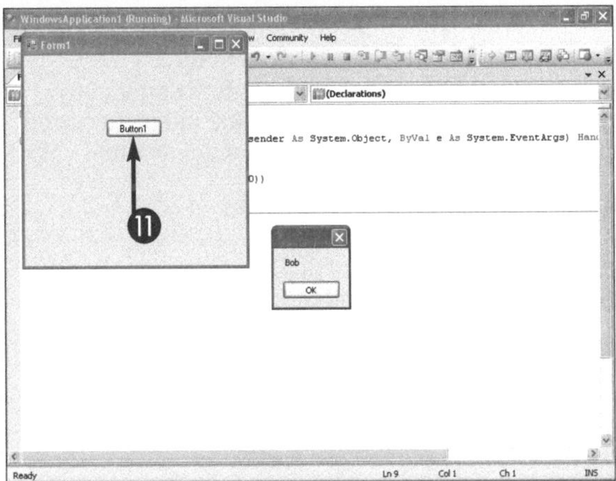

Extra

Sometimes you may develop an application that requires fast access to data, faster than accessing data from a hard disk. To do this, copy the data into a large array in memory. Accessing memory is more efficient than accessing a disk drive because the read/write head of a disk drive is relatively slow when compared to retrieving data in memory.

Passing a large array to a subroutine or function by value is less efficient than passing by reference because Visual Basic .NET must make a copy of all the values assigned to the array and store them in a second array. Furthermore, this requires double the memory.

However, passing by reference is a very efficient way to manipulate large arrays because the same values are shared among subroutines and functions and the parts of your program that call them.

Define a Subroutine

Statements that you want called more than once from various parts of your code are grouped together under one name. This group is referred to as a *procedure.* You refer to the name of the procedure — known as *calling* the procedure — any time that you want to execute statements that are contained in the procedure. Think of this like the procedure for stopping your car for a red light. *Stop* is like the name of the procedure, and the steps that you perform to stop the car are similar to statements in the procedure. When you see a red light, part of your brain says, "Stop," and another part of your brain moves your body through the motions to cause the car to stop.

There are two types of procedures — a function and a subroutine. A function can return a value, after executing statements within the function, to the statement that called the function. A subroutine cannot return a value. A subroutine has three parts. These are the header, the code block, and the end. The header consists of the keyword `Sub` and the name of the subroutine. The name should reflect the action performed by the subroutine. Following the name is a list of parameters that are placed within parentheses. A *parameter* is information the subroutine needs to execute its statements, much like the `String` that you place in the parentheses of the `MessageBox.Show()` function. Nothing is placed in the parentheses if the subroutine does not require a parameter.

The code block is where you place statements that you want executed when the subroutine is called. The end of the subroutine is defined by the keywords `End Sub`.

Define a Subroutine

1. Add a module to your project.

Note: See the Extra section for more information.

The Module tab appears on the screen.

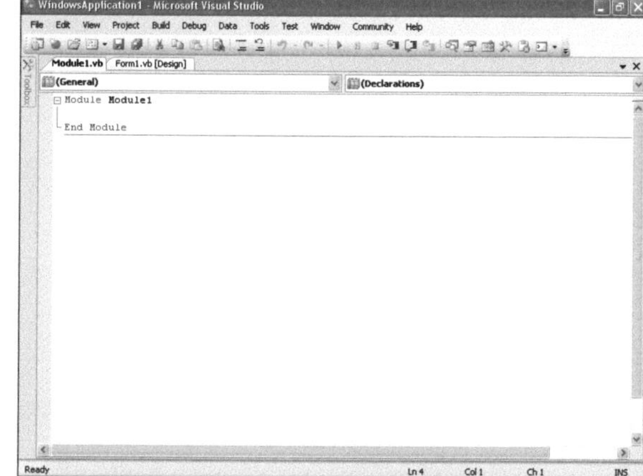

2. Define a subroutine that does not have any parameters such as `Sub HelloWorld()...End Sub.`

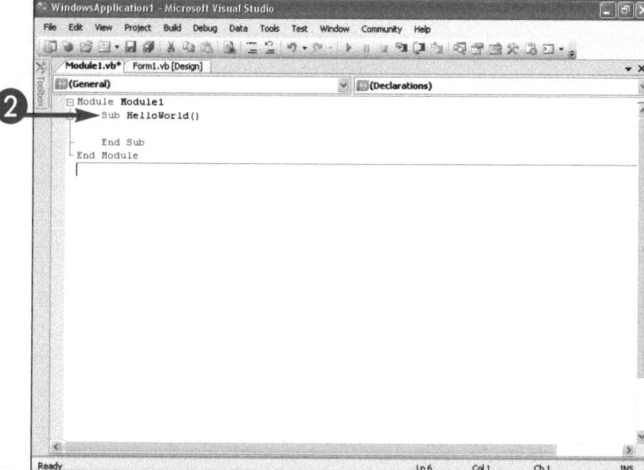

3 Write a statement that displays `"Hello World"` on the screen when the subroutine is called by writing `MessageBox.Show("Hello World")`.

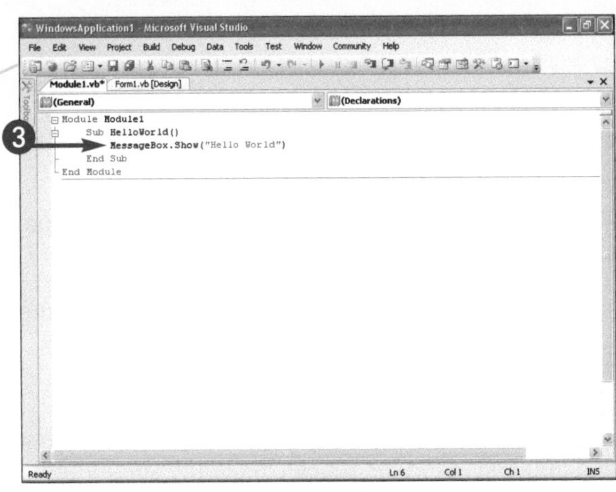

4 Press F5 to run your program.

An error message will be displayed if Visual Basic .NET is unable to successfully run your program, such as if you defined a subroutine but did not call it.

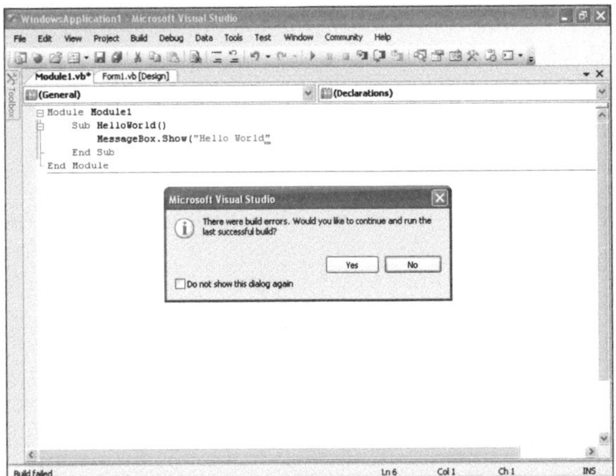

Extra

The definition of a subroutine and a function are placed in a module. A *module* is a separate part of your project that contains code that is accessible from other parts of your project. You can place all your procedures in one module, although in a large project you can group together procedures that do similar things in their own module.

For example, you may have a group of subroutines or functions that save, retrieve, update, and delete data from a database and another group that validates information that is entered into a form. VB.NET developers typically create separate modules, one for each group so that it is easier to maintain these subroutines and functions.

You add a new module to your project by clicking Project from the menu bar and then clicking Add Module from the submenu. A dialog box appears. Click the Add button to open a tab for the module. Place the definition for your procedures in this module.

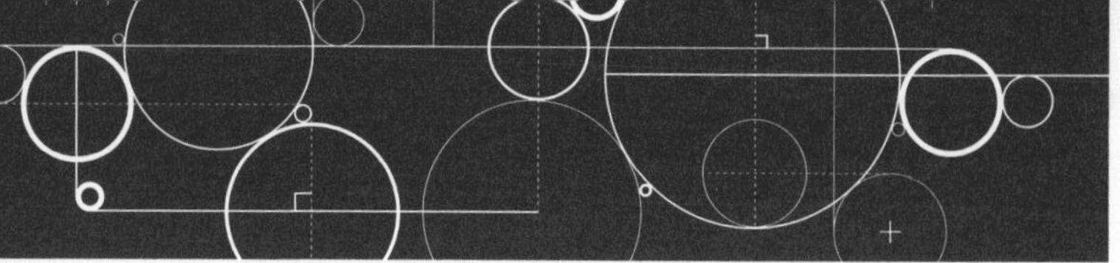

Call a Subroutine

You can reference the name of a subroutine any time that you want Visual Basic .NET to execute the statements contained in the subroutine. The name must be followed by open and close parentheses even if the subroutine does not require parameters. For example, you write `HelloWorld()` to call the `HelloWorld` subroutine.

When Visual Basic .NET reads a statement that calls a subroutine, Visual Basic .NET searches for the subroutine's definition and then executes statements in the subroutine. When the end of the subroutine is reached, Visual Basic .NET executes the statement that follows the statement that called the subroutine.

Visual Basic .NET displays an error message if the subroutine's definition cannot be found. If you see this error message, double-check that you spelled the name of the subroutine correctly in the statement that calls the subroutine. If the spelling is correct, examine the scope of the subroutine by looking at the scope designator in the subroutine's definition; see the Extra section for more information.

A different error message is displayed if you included a parameter when calling the subroutine and the subroutine did not require a parameter. This happens because the name and parameters in the statement that calls a subroutine must match the name and parameters in the subroutine's definition.

Call a Subroutine

1. Perform steps 1 to 3 from the section "Define a Subroutine."

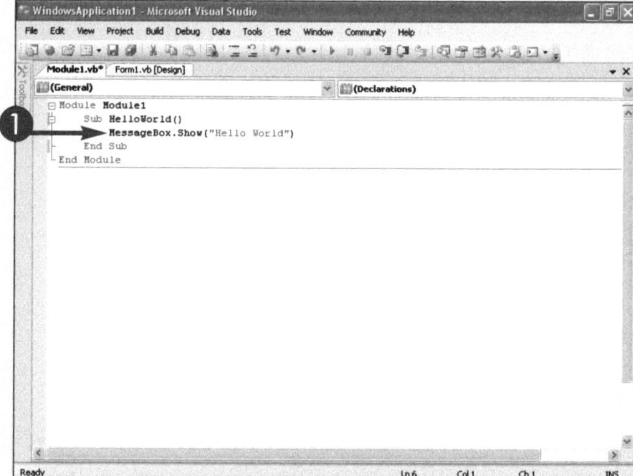

2. Add a `Button` control to the form.

Note: See Chapter 4 for information about adding buttons.

3. Double-click the `Button` control to create a `Click` subroutine for it.

The `Click` subroutine appears.

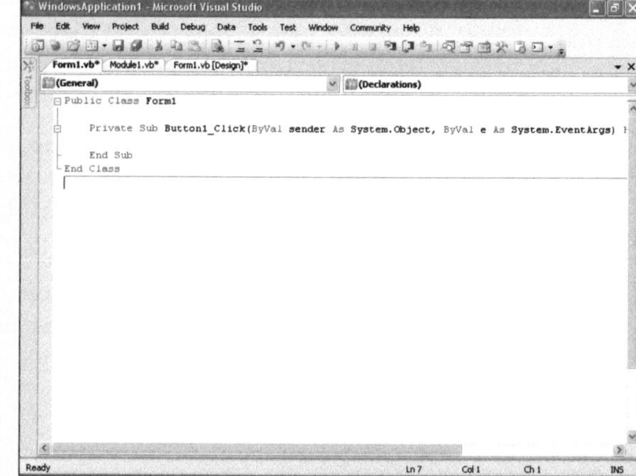

4. Call the subroutine from within the `Button` control's `Click` subroutine by writing `HelloWorld()`.

5. Press F5 to run your program.

6. Click the `Button` control.

   The `"Hello World"` message is displayed on the screen.

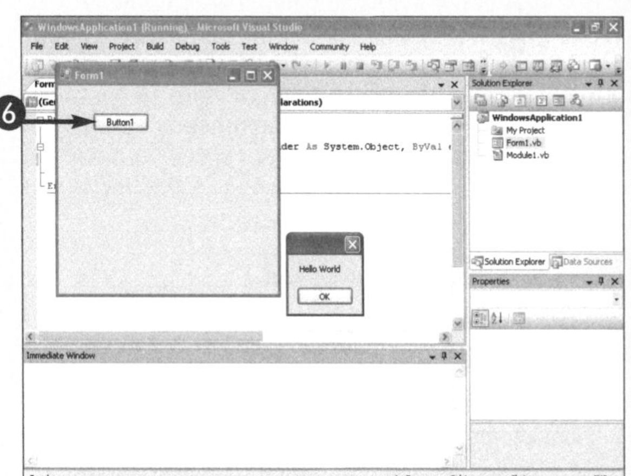

Extra

A *scope designator* determines where in your code you can call a procedure. The scope designator is chosen when the procedure is defined, and two of the scope designators are `Public` and `Private`. If designated as `Public`, such as `Public Sub HelloWorld()`, a procedure can be called from anywhere in your program. If designated as `Private`, such as `Private Sub HelloWorld()`, a procedure can be called only from a procedure that is defined in the same module, but not from anywhere else in your program. If there is not a scope designator specified in the procedure's definition, Visual Basic .NET assumes that the procedure is `Public`.

It is important to master scope designators. Failure to do so can lead to hours of frustration debugging your application, trying to find why a statement is unable to call a subroutine or function. Typically, the statement is written correctly, and so is the subroutine or function. However, the subroutine or function is out of scope of the statement.

Create Parameters for a Subroutine

There will be times when a subroutine requires information that is only available when the subroutine is called. For example, you may want to personalize the message displayed by the `HelloWorld` subroutine, such as `"Hello, Bob"`. At the time you define the `HelloWorld` subroutine, you know that the message will say `"Hello, "`. However, you do not know the person's first name until you call the `HelloWorld` subroutine.

Information that is not available when a subroutine is defined can be provided as a subroutine parameter. Think of a parameter as a variable that is used within the subroutine in place of the missing information. A parameter is declared within the subroutine's parentheses, similarly to how you declare a variable. That is, you specify a name and a data type such as `strName As String`. A parameter can be any data type.

You must also specify how Visual Basic .NET is handling the value assigned to the parameter. You do this by placing either `ByVal` or `ByRef` before the name of the parameter. `ByVal` means that a copy of the data placed in parentheses when the subroutine is called is assigned to the parameter. `ByRef` means that the subroutine is using the same data as the statement that called the subroutine — not a copy. This means that if the subroutine changes the value of the parameter, the value is also changed in the statement that called the subroutine.

You can declare multiple parameters for a subroutine by placing them within the parentheses of the subroutine definition, separating each with a comma. Let's say that you define a subroutine that enrolls a student in your school. The header is `Enroll(ByVal intStudentNumber As Integer, ByVal strFirstName As String, ByVal strLastName As String)`. Notice that the parameters are separated by a comma.

Create Parameters for a Subroutine

1. Add a module to your project.

Note: See the section "Define a Subroutine" for more information.

- You can rename the module by double-clicking the name on the module tab and then typing a new name.

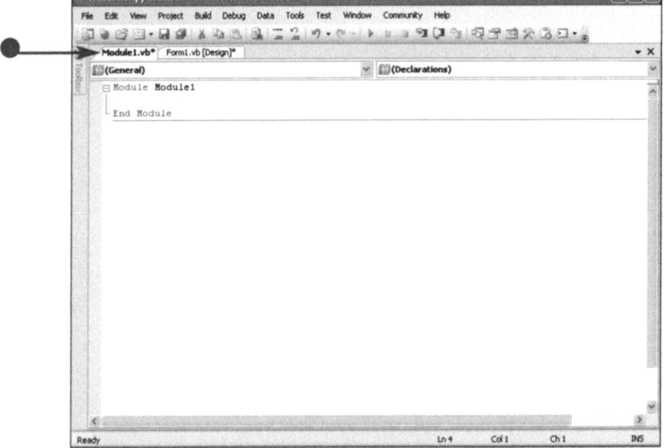

2. Define a public subroutine that does not have any parameters, such as `Sub HelloWorld()...End Sub`.

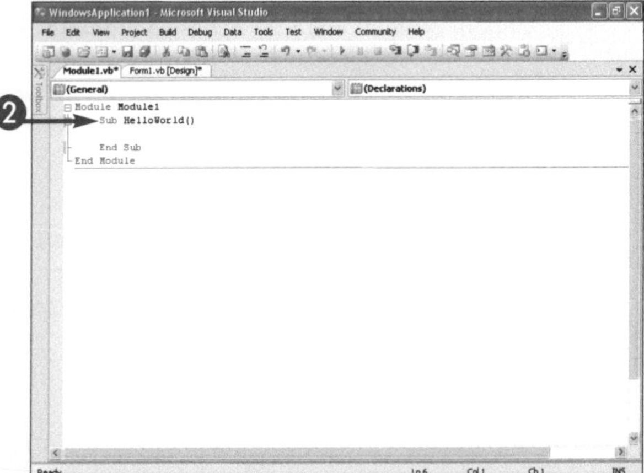

3. Declare a `String` parameter by writing `ByVal strName As String`.

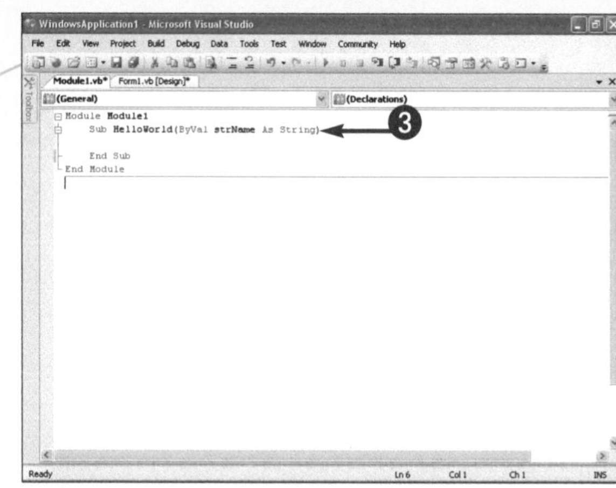

4. Display the parameter in a message on the screen by writing `MessageBox.Show("Hello, " + strName)`.

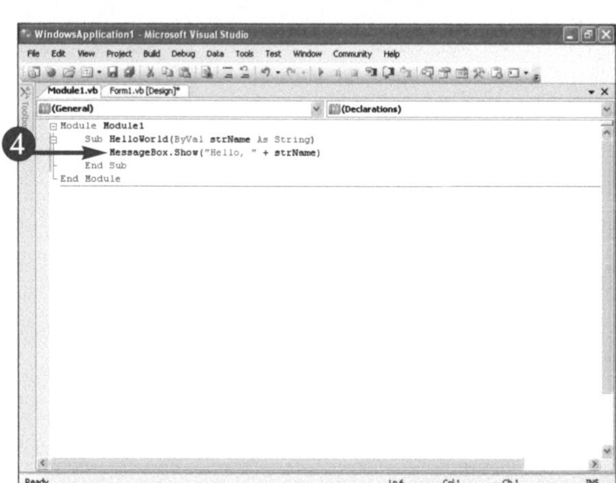

Extra

Occasionally, you will want a subroutine to use an array that is provided by the statement that calls the subroutine. In order to use the array, you must declare the array as a parameter. One problem that you will encounter is that you are unable to set the dimension of the array because you do not know the dimension until the subroutine is called. The solution is not to specify the dimension. Instead, write `ByVal strStudents() As String`. Visual Basic .NET sets the dimension of the array when the subroutine is called.

Let's say that you have an array of ten student numbers that you want passed to the `DeansList()` subroutine. The parameter is defined as `DeansList(ByVal strStudents() As String)`. When your program runs, Visual Basic .NET counts the number of elements in the array and then creates an array called `strStudents` with the same number of elements in the `DeansList()` subroutine definition. Student numbers are then copied to the `strStudents` array.

Pass Parameters to a Subroutine

Missing information that a subroutine needs to execute its statement is placed between the parentheses when the subroutine is called. This is referred to as *passing parameters.* You can use values such as `"Bob"` or `1234`; alternatively, you can use a variable or an element of an array as the parameter passed to the subroutine.

Suppose that you want to pass a name to the `HelloWorld` subroutine. You can write `HelloWorld("Bob")`, or you can write `HelloWorld(strName)`, in which `strName` is a `String` variable. The value of the variable is passed to the subroutine.

You pass multiple parameters to a subroutine in much the same way as you pass a single parameter, except you must separate them with a comma. For example, you can call the `Enroll` subroutine by writing `Enroll(1234, "Bob", "Smith")`, assuming that parameters for `Enroll` subroutine are defined as `intStudentNumber As Integer, ByVal strFirstName As String, ByVal strLastName As String`.

There are three things that you must keep in mind when passing parameters to a subroutine. The value that you pass must be the same data type as the parameter declared in the subroutine's definition. An error occurs if they are different data types. You must pass the same number of parameters as are declared in the subroutine's definition. If there are three parameters declared and you pass two of them, you will see an error message. Parameters must be passed in the same order in which they are declared. For example, you will see an error message if you call `Enroll(True, "Bob", "Smith")`. Although the number of parameters is correct, the first parameter is declared as an `Integer`, and a `Boolean` value is passed when the subroutine is called.

Pass Parameters to a Subroutine

1 Perform steps 1 to 4 from the section "Create Parameters for a Subroutine."

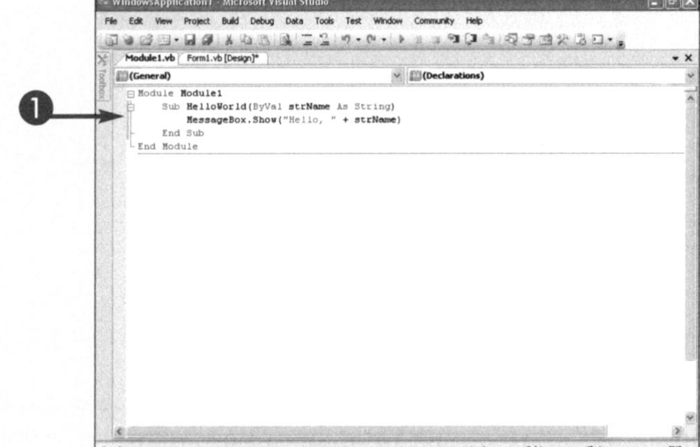

2 Add a `Button` control to the form.

Note: See Chapter 4 for information about adding buttons.

3 Double-click the `Button` control to create a `Click` subroutine for it.

The `Click` subroutine appears.

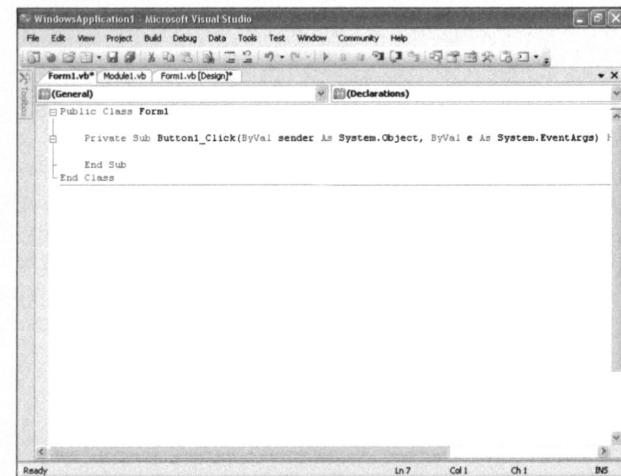

4 Call the subroutine from within the `Button` control's `Click` subroutine and pass a `String` as the parameter by writing `HelloWorld("Bob")`.

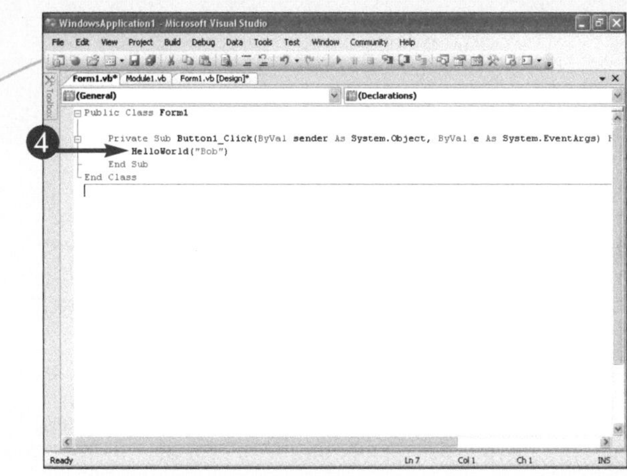

5 Press F5 to run your program.

6 Click the `Button` control.

The `"Hello, Bob"` message is displayed on the screen.

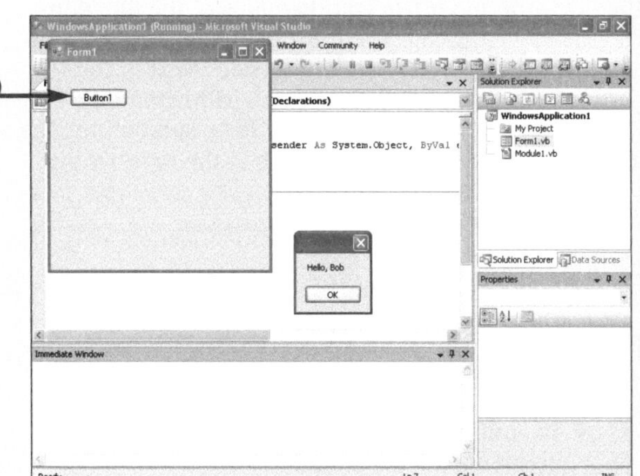

Extra

Make sure that the values are passed in the correct order when passing multiple parameters to a subroutine; otherwise, you may receive unexpected results from the subroutine. Visual Basic .NET passes values in order. If the data type of the value is not compatible with the matching parameter, Visual Basic .NET displays an error. This happens if the statement that calls a subroutine or function passes a `Boolean` value (that is, true or false) when the matching parameter has a `String` data type. This is fine because you can fix the problem when you notice the error message.

However, a hidden problem may not materialize until your program is in use if the value and the parameter are the same data type but different data. Let's say that you defined two parameters for the `Enroll()` subroutine. The first parameter is the student's last name, and the second parameter is the student's first name. Both are strings. When calling your program, you switch values and pass them as `Enroll("Bob", "Smith")`. `"Bob"` will be treated as the student's last name and `"Smith"` as the first name. No error message is displayed because the values and the parameters are the same data type.

Define a Function

A *function* is a procedure that returns a value to the statement that calls the function. For example, you could define a function called `NewSalary`, which would apply a percentage increase to an employee's current salary and return the new salary.

You define a function in a module similarly to how a subroutine is defined. There are three parts to a function definition — the header, the code block, and the trailer. The header consists of four components. The first two of these are the keyword `Function` and the name of the function, which follows `Function`. The function name should represent the action taken by the function. Next in the header is the declaration of parameters within parentheses. You declare these the same as you do for a subroutine. The last part of the header is the data type of the return value. You do not specify a name for the return value — only its data type.

Place statements that you want executed when the function is called inside the function's code block, which is between the header and trailer. The trailer is the `End Function` keywords that define the end of the function's definition.

To return a value from a function, you place a `Return` statement in the code block. There are two parts of a `Return` statement — the keyword `Return` and the value that the function is to return. For example, here is how you return the value `10`: `Return 10`. The return value must be the same data type as you defined in the header; otherwise, Visual Basic .NET displays an error. You can return a value, a variable, or an array element.

Define a Function

1. Add a module to your project.

Note: See the section "Define a Subroutine" for more information.

- You can rename the module by double-clicking the name on the Module tab and then typing a new name.

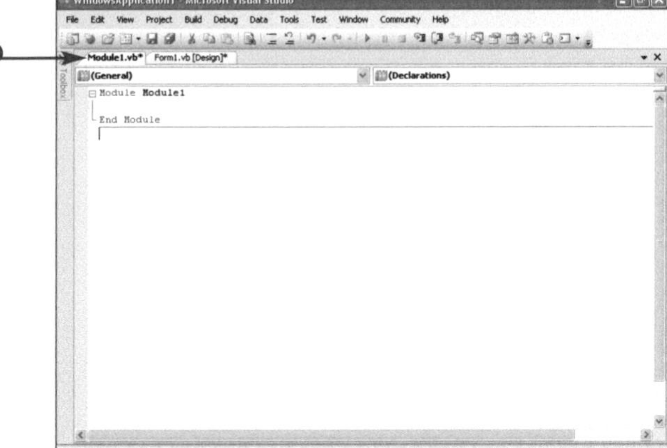

2. Define a function that has an `Integer` parameter and returns a `String` by writing `Function PassFail(ByVal intGrade As Integer) As String...End Function`.

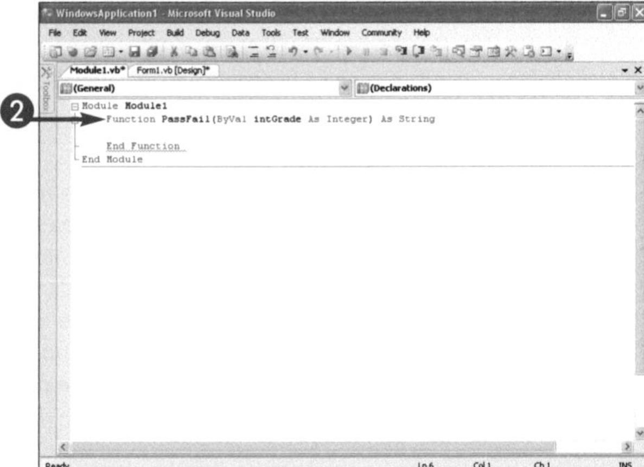

3 Write an `If...Then...Else` statement in the code block that compares the parameter to the passing grade, using the logical expression `intGrade >= 85`.

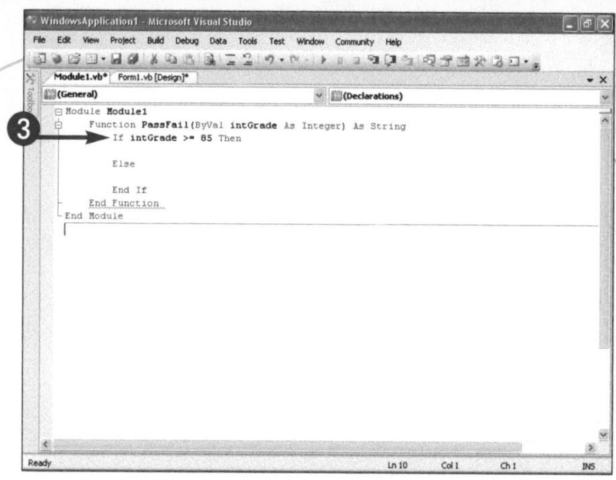

4 Return `"Pass"` if the grade is passing and `"Fail"` if the grade is failing, using multiple `Return` statements.

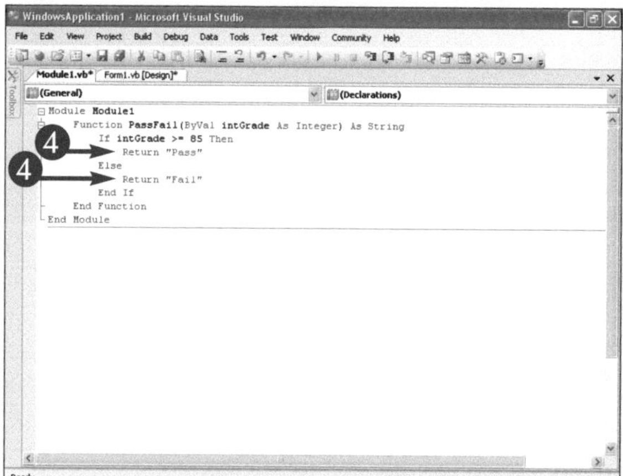

Extra

You can use multiple return statements in the code block of a function definition. This is helpful if the value you return depends on conditions tested by statements in the function. For example, suppose that you want to return `0` if a condition is true and `-1` if the condition is false. You would write the following:

Example

```
If bResults = True Then
    Return 0
Else
    Return -1
End If
```

Call a Function

You call a function by using the function's name and passing the function the proper parameters, if the function has any parameters. Like subroutines, functions can be defined without declaring parameters. Visual Basic .NET finds the function definition, executes its statements, and returns to the statement that called the function.

The assignment operator is used to access the value returned by the function. You place the assignment operator to the right of the function name in the statement that calls the function. Let's say you call the `NewSalary` function and pass it the old salary of $500 and a percent increase of 3.5%, such as `NewSalary(500, 3.5)`. You would write `dCurrentSalary = NewSalary(500,3.5)`. Visual Basic .NET uses these parameters to calculate the new salary using statements in the `NewSalary` function definition. The new salary is returned using the `Return` statement. Visual Basic .NET assigns the return value to the `dCurrentSalary` variable. The data type of the variable that is assigned the return value must be the same data type or a compatible data type as the data type of the return value.

You do not have to use the value returned by a function. You can simply call the function and ignore the return value. For example, you could write `NewSalary(500, 3.5)`. The `NewSalary` function calculates and returns the new salary, but the statement that calls the `NewSalary` function simply ignores the return value. Whether or not you ignore a return value depends on the nature of the function.

Call a Function

1. Perform steps 1 to 4 from the section "Define a Function."

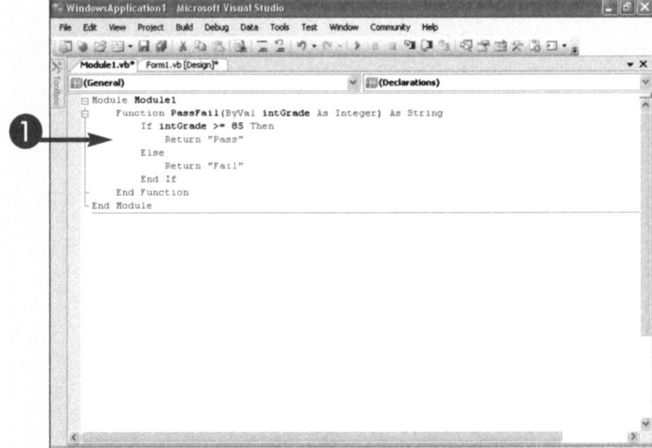

2. Add a `Button` control to the form.

Note: See Chapter 4 for information about adding buttons.

3. Double-click the `Button` control to create a `Click` subroutine for it.

The `Click` subroutine appears.

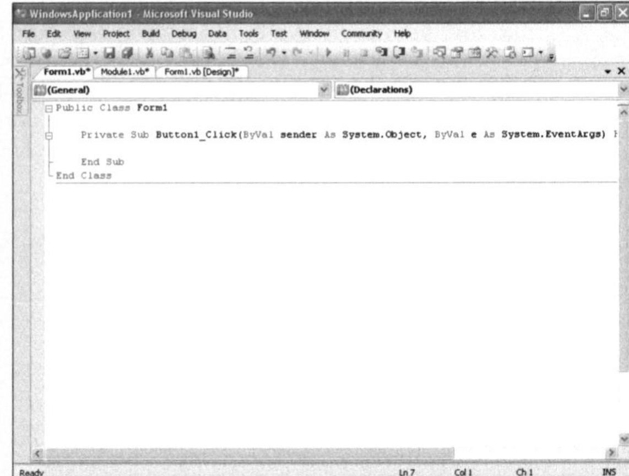

4 Call the function from within the `Button` control's `Click` subroutine and pass an `Integer` as the parameter by writing `MessageBox.Show(PassFail(90))`.

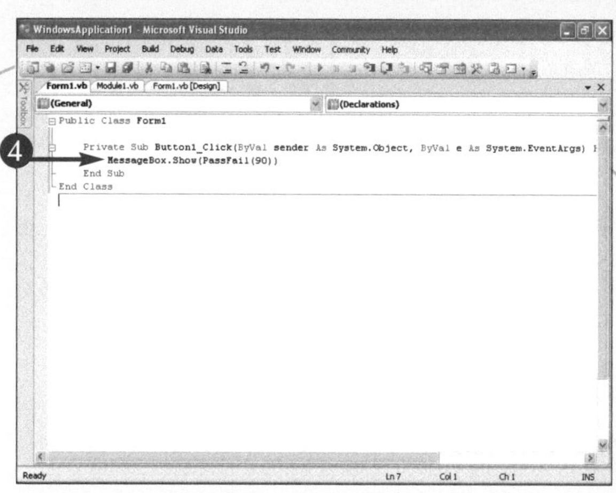

5 Press F5 to run your program.

6 Click the `Button` control.

The `"Pass"` message is displayed on the screen.

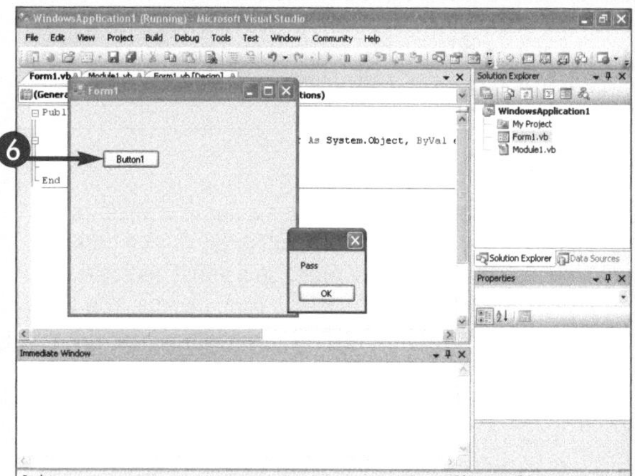

Extra

In some situations, you will want to pass the function's return value to another function or subroutine as a parameter. You do this by placing the call to the function in the parentheses of the other function or subroutine. Let's say that you want to pass the return value of the `NewSalary` function to the `ModifyPayroll` function. Here is what you need to write:

Example

```
ModifyPayroll(NewSalary(500, 3.5))
```

Visual Basic .NET calls the `NewSalary` function first and then after the `NewSalary` function finishes, the return value is used when calling the `ModifyPayroll` function.

Understanding Database Design

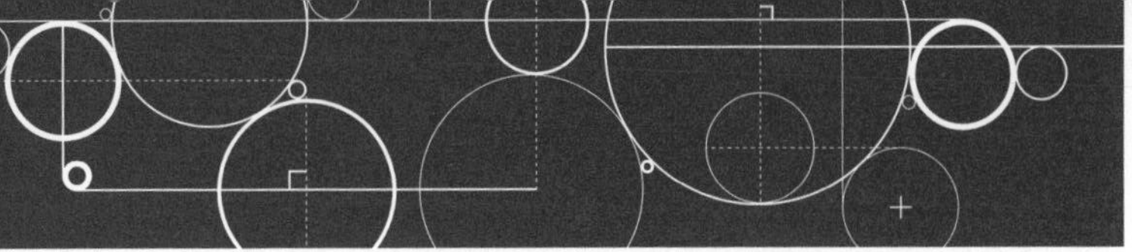

For many of your applications, you will be responsible for automating a process such as placing an order, which requires that order information entered into a form be stored into a database. One of your tasks is to design the database. Database design entails grouping order information into tables.

Decomposing Data Elements

The initial step in designing a database is to extract data elements from the process that is being automated using a technique called *decomposition*. Imagine an order form. It has product IDs, quantities, unit prices, prices for the items purchased, the customers' first and last names, addresses, and other information that you normally find on an order form.

Each of these items is called a *data element*. In the decomposition process, you will make a list of the data elements on a sheet of paper or in a word-processing document. For each data element, you determine the type of data, the minimum and maximum value, and whether or not the data is required.

The Type of Data

The type of data refers to whether it is a numeric value (such as a quantity), currency, alpha characters (such as a person's name), an alphanumeric value (such as a street address), a logical value (such as true or false), a date, or time. You will need to identify the type for each data element on the list. This information is used to define the column for the data element in a table of a database.

Minimum/Maximum Values

The minimum and maximum values refer to the number of characters that make up the data element. This is used to set up data entry rules for your database. Some data elements have both a minimum and maximum number of characters such as a state abbreviation, which has a minimum and maximum of two characters. Data elements that are not required usually do not have a minimum value. This means that it can be left out of the database. However, every data element has a maximum value because this determines the width of the column used to store the information in the database.

Grouping Data Elements

After all data elements are decomposed, they must be organized into logical groups. Database designers do this by using a sophisticated process called *normalization.* This concept is advanced for this book, so I will simplify the process for you. First, remove repeating data elements. For example, a customer can place many orders. The customer's ID, name, and address appear on each order. However, you want to store this information only once in the database — not for every order that the customer places. This means that you place all the customer's information into its own group. Likewise, a product ID, product description, and unit price can appear on multiple orders. It makes sense to put these into their own group as well.

Primary Keys

There must be a way to uniquely identify each group of a data element such as a customer ID, a product ID, and an order number. This means that information about a customer is associated with a unique customer ID. Likewise, information about a product is associated with a product ID. And an order number is used to identify information about an order. These are referred to as a *primary key.*

The Database Schema

A *database schema* is a diagram that describes tables that make up a database. Tables are described by a unique name and by its columns. Each column is identified by name, type of data, minimum/maximum values, and whether or not the data must be entered into the column. There are other ways to describe a column, but these are the most commonly used in popular database software. As you probably surmised, groups of data elements become tables of the database.

Relating Tables

Data elements are dispersed into multiple tables. You are probably wondering how they are reassembled into meaningful information such as an order. This is accomplished by creating a relationship among tables using a foreign key. A *foreign key* is another table's primary key.

Let's say that there are two tables, one for customers and one for orders. A customer ID identifies each row in the customer table, which is that table's primary key. An order number identifies each row in the order table, which is its primary key. However, the order table also has a column called *Customer ID* that has the ID of the customer who placed the order.

Suppose that a person enters an order number into your application to display an order. Your application finds the order number in the order table and then uses the value of the Customer ID column to find the customer ID in the customers table to retrieve the customer's name and address.

An Introduction to ADO.NET

The latest evolution in Microsoft's database technologies, ADO.NET provides support for new functionality and programming methods. ADO.NET functions inside the .NET framework, allowing any .NET application to access its features in a similar way.

Features

Many developers now develop new client applications based on the Web application model. Many applications use XML to encode data to pass over network connections. Web applications use HTTP to communicate and therefore must maintain state between requests. *State* is the persistence of data across parts of an application. This new model differs from the connected, tightly coupled style of programming in which a connection was held open for the duration of the program's lifetime and no special handling of state was required.

ADO.Net was designed to meet the needs of this new programming model: disconnected data architecture, tight integration with XML, and common data representation with the ability to combine data from multiple and varied data sources and optimizations for accessing data in different ways.

Consistency

Consistency is one of ADO.NET's major features. Microsoft database technology can work with multiple data sources consistently, thus providing consistent access to data sources such as Microsoft SQL Server and any data sources exposed via OLE DB. ADO.NET also includes inherent support for XML datasets. You can use ADO.NET to connect to data sources and retrieve, manipulate, and update data.

A Powerful Object Model

ADO.NET provides an object model with database features. This enables you to use the objects together with a database provider or individually to work with custom application data.

In addition, you still have the option to work with the database provider using SQL to execute commands and retrieve results directly.

Similarities to ADO

The design for ADO.NET maintains as many similarities to ADO as possible, while still addressing requirements necessary to support new disconnected functions.

ADO.NET coexists with ADO. Although you commonly write new applications with ADO.NET, ADO remains available to the .NET programmer.

N-Tier Programming

ADO.NET provides support for the disconnected, n-tier programming environment for which many Visual Basic .NET programmers need to develop. *N-tier programming* involves developing separate levels of the application — the presentation tier, the business logic tier, and the data access and storage tier — that work together to provide the complete user experience.

XML Support

To access data in a standard way, XML serves to encode and format data into a standards-compliant format. As a fundamental part of their applications, developers need XML to function as a data source. For this reason, XML builds its support into ADO.NET at a very fundamental level. The core of the entire .NET Framework, the XML class framework enables you to cross between the two libraries easily.

Features *(continued)*

Disconnected Recordersets

Although previous versions of ADO added disconnection as an afterthought, ADO.NET, through major changes in design, focuses its functionality around disconnected data. When you connect to a database, you actually load all the data in tables of the database into the client application's memory. ADO.NET performs all the data manipulation to these in-memory copies of the table information. When the user finishes with the form or application and makes changes to the database, you can reconnect to the database. ADO.NET looks through the in-memory data and makes changes to synchronize the two.

Because of the disconnection, you must carefully design your database. Large tables may perform poorly when you load them into memory. To improve speed, you must filter only necessary data down to a particular client. Also, multiple users can connect to a database, retrieve a table, make changes, and update the same records.

The Object Model

In ADO.NET, the object model re-creates all the functionality present in a database system. The object model must replicate the database contents because the database does not stay connected to the client. The `DataTable` object represents a single table of a database and consists of `DataColumn` objects, which define the fields and `DataRow` objects, which store the records of the table. A `DataTable` object resides in a `DataSet` object, which is the main wrapper control and can hold any number of tables. The `DataSet` object also enables you to create relationships between tables using `DataRelation` objects. These objects, the core set of data for storage and manipulation, enable you to bind the data to controls, whether the components connect to an actual database or not.

ADO.NET Objects

The connection and adapter components provide the basic ability for connecting to a database, while the `DataSet` object provides storage in memory for everything that makes up tables and relationships. The table, row, and column objects provide underlying data and manipulation abilities for the `DataSet` object.

DbConnection

To attach a database to your application, you first create a data connection object. Microsoft includes two components that implement the `DbConnection` interface, `OleDbConnection` and `SqlConnection`. The `OleDbConnection` components enable you to connect to any database that the OLEDB interface supports, and `SqlConnection` enables you to connect to a Microsoft SQL Server database.

DataAdapter

A data adapter provides the conduit for connecting a `DbConnection` to the objects in ADO.NET that actually store and manipulate the database information. For a particular connection component, you must have a specific adapter that understands how to communicate with the connection. Microsoft provides `SqlDataAdapter` and `OleDbDataAdapter`, depending on which `DbConnection` you use.

DataSet

The `DataSet` component is the major component for retrieving and manipulating information. The `DataSet` object stores a set of tables from the database, including their field definitions and all the associated data. Controls can bind to the `DataSet` object or contain tables to view or modify the data.

DataTable

The `DataTable` object represents a single database table. Because the database source disconnects, this object must provide all the capabilities of an actual database table. The `DataTable` object relies on `DataColumn` objects to define the fields of the table and `DataRow` objects to store the actual data of the table.

Understanding Data, Tables, and a Database

A *database* can be used to quickly store information of any type and then search, filter, and manipulate that data according to the needs of your application. Visual Basic .NET uses a database system called Active Data Objects (ADO.NET). ADO.NET contains a standard set of functionality that you will need to interact with a database.

Database Software

Visual Basic .NET uses common database packages such as Microsoft Access, Microsoft SQL, and Oracle. Contact the vendor of your database software to determine if the vendor provides a native .NET data provider or an OLEDB-compatible provider, which will enable you to access its database using Visual Basic.

Microsoft Access is best suited for creating small databases, and Microsoft SQL Server is best for large databases that require heavy access from multiple users such as occur in Web development.

Database Structure

A database consists of one or more tables. A table contains one or more rows. Each row has one or more columns. Each column contains information referred to as *data*. Data can be a string, a number, or a date. For example, you can store customer information in a table of a database. Each record represents one customer. Columns can hold a customer number, customer first name, customer last name, and so on. Think of a database as an Excel workbook and a table as a spreadsheet. A row is a row of the spreadsheet, and a column is a column of the spreadsheet.

Designing the database is a critical part of building an application. The design must accommodate the data storage needs of the application and provide the flexibility to be expanded as your application evolves into a more complex application.

Structured Query Language

The common language used to interact with an ADO.NET data source is the Structured Query Language (SQL). SQL is used with Visual Basic .NET to communicate with the database. SQL consists of simple English-like instructions that you use in your Visual Basic .NET application to interact with a database.

SQL Features

SQL through ADO.NET enables your application to be used with different databases with the minimum of changes to your application. This means that you can develop your Visual Basic .NET application using Microsoft Access and then move to Microsoft SQL in the future.

SQL is used to combine tables, filter data, and create procedures that are used by your Visual Basic .NET application to manipulate data stored in a database. This chapter presents major SQL commands that you will need to retrieve, update, and modify records in a database. You can read *Microsoft SQL Server 2005 For Dummies* by Andrew Watt (Wiley Publishing, 2006) for more information about other SQL commands.

SQL Clauses

The `WHERE` clause is used to specify rows to select for the `SELECT`, `UPDATE`, and `DELETE` commands. You create a filter expression for the `WHERE` clause by using equal, less than, greater than, less than or equal, greater than or equal, or `LIKE` operators. The `LIKE` operator is used to return data that partially matches a test string value that contains a wildcard character. A wildcard character such as `%` matches zero to many characters, and _ matches exactly one character. Filter expressions can be combined using `AND`, `OR`, and `NOT`. These are just some of the most common things that you can do with the `WHERE` clause.

SQL Clauses *(continued)*

Here are some examples of the `WHERE` clause:

```
WHERE Test1Grade >= 85

WHERE StudentLastName LIKE 'To%'

WHERE StudentFirstName LIKE 'M_ _E' AND LastName =
'Adams'
```

The `ORDER BY` clause is used to specify the column or columns used to sort rows returned by the SQL query. The sort order is ascending unless the `DESC` keyword is used to specify a descending sort order. Here is an example:

```
SELECT StudentNumber, Test1Grade

FROM Students

ORDER BY Test1Grade
```

Here is another example:

```
SELECT StudentNumber, Test1Grade

FROM Students

ORDER BY StudentNumber DESC
```

SQL Statements

The `SELECT` statement is used to specify column names that you want retrieved from the table. The `FROM` clause specifies that name of the table that contains column names listed in the `SELECT` statement. The `WHERE` statement specifies the filter used to select rows. If the `WHERE` statement is not used, columns specified in the `SELECT` statement are returned from all rows in the table. Here is an example:

```
SELECT Test1Grade

FROM Student

WHERE StudentNumber = 12345
```

The `INSERT` statement places a row into a table. The `INSERT` statement requires the `INTO` keyword, which identifies the table into which the new row is inserted. The row names are placed in parentheses following the name of the table. The `VALUES` clause is used to specify values for each column specified in the `INSERT` statement. Values are placed within parentheses. Here is an example:

```
INSERT INTO Student

(StudentNumber, Test1Grade)

VALUES (123456, 95)
```

The `UPDATE` statement replaces data in a table with data that you specify. The `WHERE` clause is used to identify rows that you want changed. The `SET` clause specifies the column name and the new data for the column. Here is an example:

```
UPDATE Students

SET Test1Grade = 96

WHERE StudentNumber = 123456
```

The `DELETE` statement deletes a row from a table. The `WHERE` clause specifies rows to delete from the table. Here is an example:

```
DELETE from Students

WHERE StudentNumber = 123456
```

Connect to a Database

Before your application can interact with a database, you must connect to the database. This is like calling your friend's telephone before being able to speak with your friend. You can create a database and its tables by using database management software such as Microsoft Access. Alternatively, you can use a Microsoft Access database that someone else created. Simply copy the database file onto your hard drive. Your application should not create databases and tables; however, you could using the proper SQL query.

After you have created or acquired the database, you then connect to it. The database connection is made by using Server Explorer. Server Explorer opens as a pane that lists servers and databases that are already connected. If you do not see your database listed, you will need to connect to the database by following the steps here.

In addition to Microsoft Access, your application can connect to practically any database that is used in a typical business. This includes Oracle, Sybase, DB2, and MySQL. The database that you pick must be available either locally such as on your hard disk or on a network connected to your computer. For learning Visual Basic .NET, you will probably use a copy of Microsoft Access or MySQL on your hard drive. The advantage is that you will have total control over the database; however, you have the responsibility to maintain and secure it.

A network database is usually used for applications developed at work. The advantage of connecting to a network database is that a database administrator maintains and secures it. However, you do not control the database nor the network. Either may not be available when you want to develop or test your application.

Connect to a Database

1. Click View ➔ Server Explorer.

   The Server Explorer pane appears.

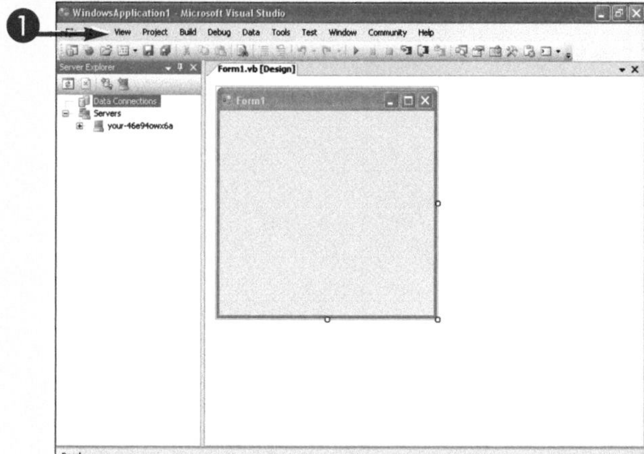

2. Click the Connect to Database button.

   The Choose Data Source dialog box appears.

3. Click Microsoft Access Database File.
4. Click Continue.

   The Add Connection dialog box appears.

5. Click Browse.

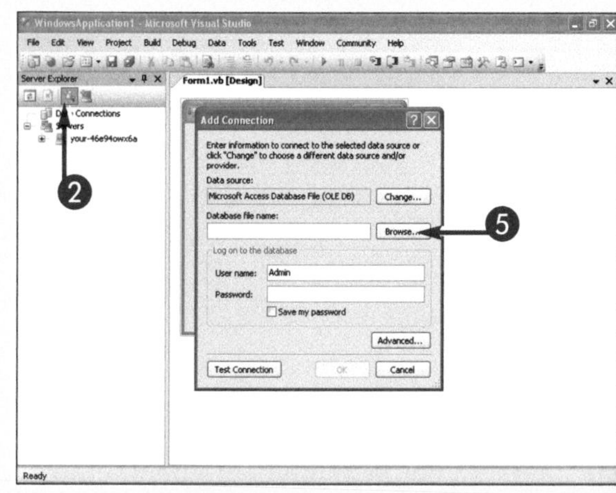

The Select Microsoft Access Database File appears.

6 Locate and click the database file.

Note: You can use the sample Access database file located at Program Files\Microsoft Office\Office\Samples\Northwind.mdb.

7 Click Open.

- A reference to the database appears in the Server Explorer pane.

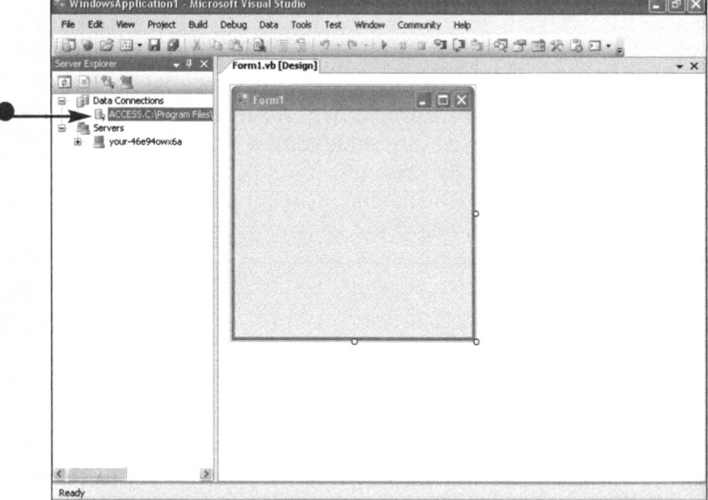

Extra

Here is a time-saving tip. After selecting the database filename, you can click the Test Connection button. Visual Basic .NET attempts to connect to the database file. A message box is displayed indicating if the connection was successful or not. If the connection is successful, you know that you will be able to connect to the database. If the connection is not successful, you need to use the database software to determine any problems that may exist with the database file.

A network problem can be one reason that Visual Basic .NET is unable to connect to the database. Think of the network as the highway linking your computer to the database. If there is a traffic jam, accident, or a pothole, then the flow along the highway is disrupted. The same is true with a network. Too many computers may be sending data, causing a traffic jam. A circuit along the network may have malfunctioned (a traffic accident), or there could be a loose cable (a pothole). Whatever the network problem, Visual Basic .NET's message to the database is not getting through; therefore, it cannot make a connection to the database.

Configure the Data Source

The database is referred to as the *data source.* After connecting to the database, you must configure the data source by using the Data Source Configuration Wizard. The Data Source Configuration Wizard walks you through the configuration process. You will notice that the Data Source Configuration Wizard dialog box contains several icons. You only need the Database icon to begin the configuration; it tells the wizard that the data source will be a database.

When the wizard displays the database that is currently connected to your application, you will have an opportunity to change to a different database connection. However, you will only need to do so if the current connection is not the database you need for your application.

When you have the data file copied to your project, the wizard creates a connection string. The connection string is what you use in your code to reference the database. The connection string usually is the database filename, followed by the words *ConnectionString.* You can change this to a different name if you want to; however, many programs choose to use the default connection string.

On the Choose Your Database Objects page, the wizard displays a list of objects that are available with the database. These can include tables, views, and other objects specific to the database. You will probably want to start by accessing a table, but you can select multiple objects that you want your application to access.

Configure the Data Source

1. Click Data ➔ Add New Data Source.

   The Data Source Configuration Wizard appears.

2. Click Database.
3. Click Next.

   The Choose Your Data Connection page of the wizard appears.

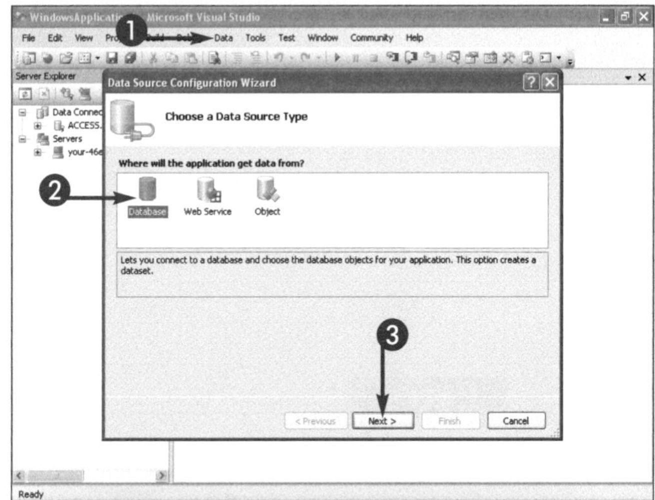

The current connection is displayed, which is likely the connection that you want selected.

4. Choose the database connection.
5. Click Next.

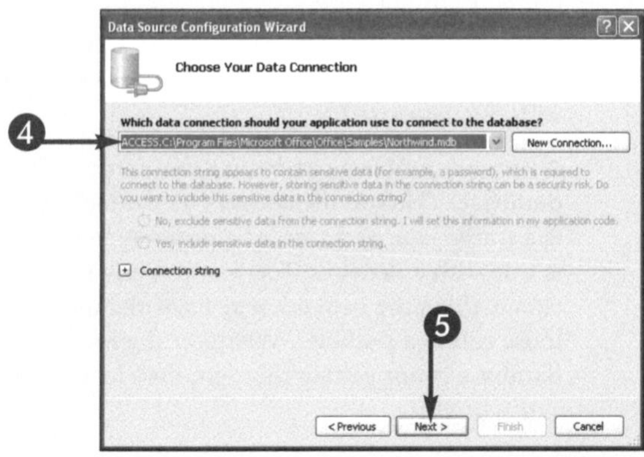

The Save the Connection String to the Application Configuration File page of the wizard appears.

6 Click Yes.

This copies the data file to your project.

7 Enter the connection string.

Note: The default connection string is likely acceptable, so you will not need to change it.

8 Click Next.

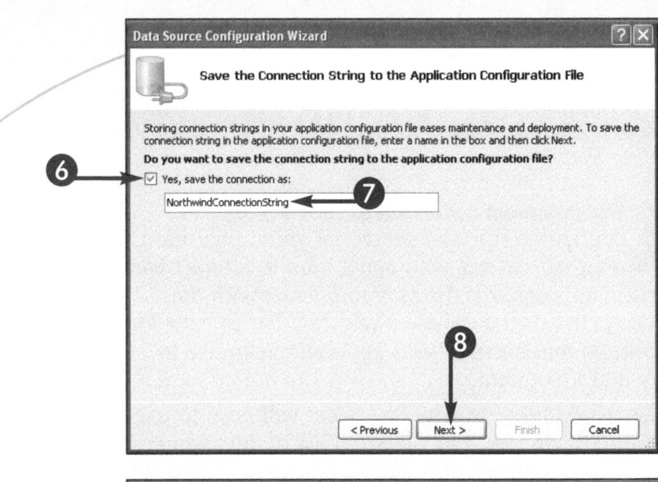

The Choose Your Database Objects page of the wizard appears.

9 Click Tables.

Note: You can select additional tables or other objects if they are displayed.

10 Click Finish.

The data source is now configured.

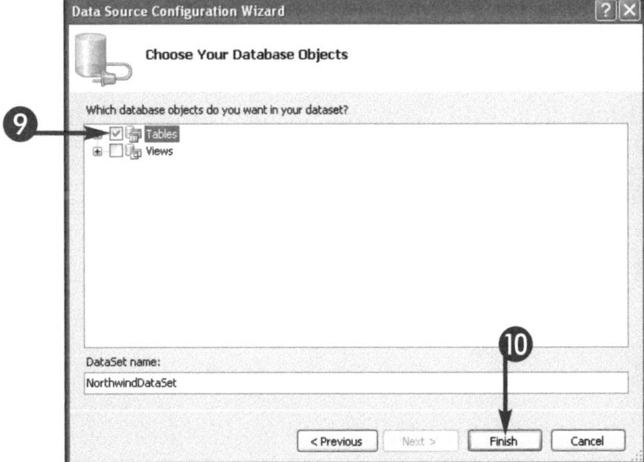

Extra

You do not have to access an entire table, especially if the table contains a long list of columns. You can select only the columns of the table that are important to your application. Here is how to do this. Click Tables on the Choose Your Database Objects page of the Data Source Configuration Wizard, and a list of columns appears on the screen. Columns may be referred to as *fields* on this list. Each column has a check box. Select the check boxes of the columns that you want to access from within your application.

Before making a selection, you should review the data requirements for all parts of your application. Scan the specifications for your application, looking for routines that need to retrieve or save data to a database. Make note of the data used by those routines. Look at the tables in the database and note the table and column that contain the required data. Then make sure that those columns or tables are selected when you connect your application to the database.

Using the Data Sources Window

After you have connected to the database and configured the data source for your application, you are ready to use your application to interact with the data. The most effective way to interact with the database is to add a database navigation bar to your form and controls that users of your application can use to display and input data.

In order to add these to your form, you will need to use the Data Sources window. You will see a list of data sources that you have configured for your application. One of these data sources is the name of the database and a list of tables contained in the database.

When you drag and drop a table on to the form, a spreadsheet-like grid is displayed. Column names are the names of the columns in the table. Typically, you want to display a few columns rather than all of them.

Visual Basic .NET automatically places the database navigation bar at the top of the form when you drag either a table or column from the Data Sources window to the form. The navigation bar displays the number of the current row and the total number of rows in the table. On the left side are the Move Previous and Move First buttons, and to the right are the Move Next and Move Last buttons, which are used to move up and down the rows. To the right of the Move Last button are a plus sign, a red X, and a disk. The plus sign is used to add a new row to the table. The X deletes the current row, and the disk icon saves changes to the current row to the database.

Data does not appear until you run the application.

Using the Data Sources Window

1. Click Data ➔ Show Data Sources.

   The Data Sources window appears.

2. Click the + next to the Customers table.

   The names of the columns of the Customers table appear.

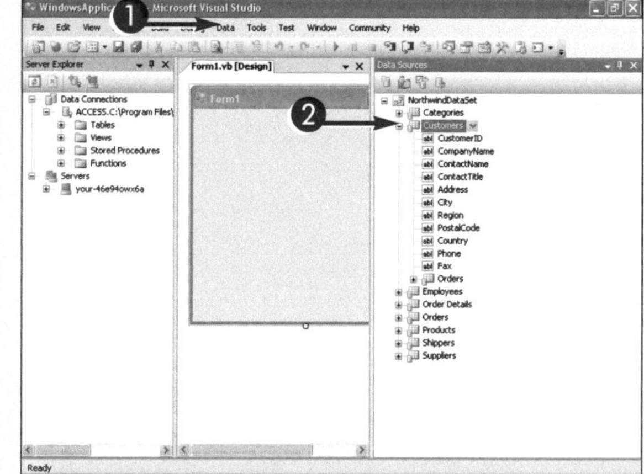

3. Drag and drop the Company Name column on to the form.

   A `Label` control containing `Company Name` and an empty `TextBox` control are displayed. The database navigation bar is also displayed.

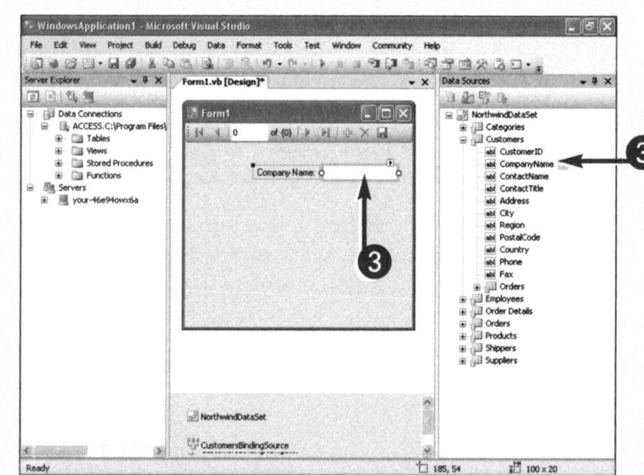

❹ Drag and drop the Contact Name column on to the form.

A `Label` control containing `Contact Name` and an empty `TextBox` control are displayed.

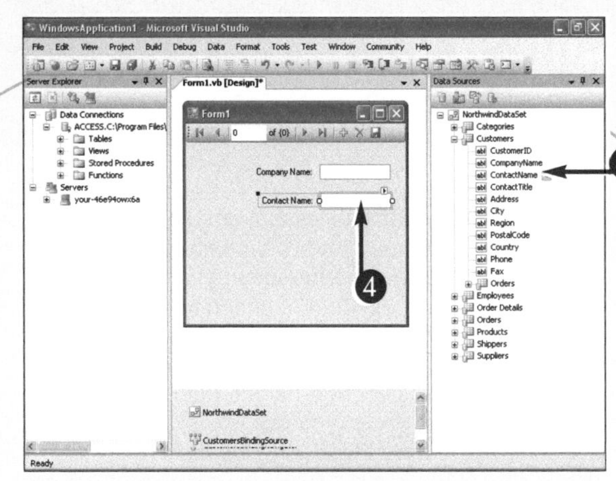

❺ Press F5 to run your program.

The company name and contact name for the first row of the table are displayed.

- You can use the database navigation bar to scroll through the table.

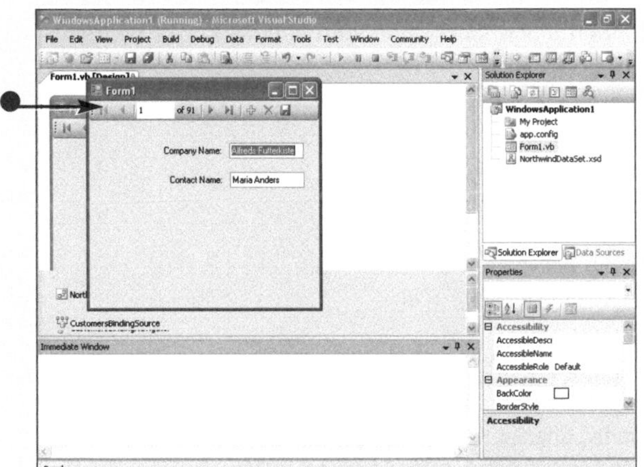

Extra

Data can be presented in other ways than a `TextBox` control by changing the control type in the column in the Data Sources window before dragging and dropping the column on to the form. A down arrow appears when you select a column in the table. Click the down arrow to see a list of other controls that you can use to display the column. These are `TextBox`, `ComboBox`, `Label`, `LinkLabel`, and `ListBox`. Simply change the control type and then drag and drop the column on to the form. For example, you may want a list of product names displayed in a `ListBox` control. Select the product names' column and change the control type to `ListBox`. Drag and drop the control on to the form and then use the size handles to resize the `ListBox` control. Product names automatically fill the `ListBox` control when your application runs.

Using SQL Statements

One of the many advantages of a database is that you can see just rows and columns of data that you need and exclude other data by writing a SQL query. SQL is a query language that is understood by database management software. Database management software is the application that manages databases such as Microsoft Access and Microsoft SQL Server. SQL is beyond the scope of this book; however, you can learn SQL by reading *Microsoft SQL Server 2005 For Dummies* by Andrew Watt (Wiley Publishing, 2006).

You can insert a SQL query into your application by using the Search Criteria Builder. First you need to add a control that displays the data such as a `TextBox` on your form and then bind the control to a column of tables from the database. You do this by dragging and dropping columns from the Data Sources window on to the control on your form. When you do this, Visual Basic .NET links together the control and the column, which you can see in the control's Data Bindings `Text` property.

Visual Basic .NET displays data contained in the selected column in the control of rows that meet the requirements of the SQL query. You will notice that the maximum rows shown on the database navigation bar reflect the number of rows that meet the SQL query requirements. The Move First and Move Last buttons move to the first and last row of the rows that meet requirements of the SQL query.

Using SQL Statements

1. Perform steps 1 to 8 in the section "Configure the Data Source."

Note: The Northwind.mdb sample database is used in this example.

2. On the Choose Your Database Objects page of the wizard, click the Tables + and select the Customers table.
3. Click Finish.
4. Click Data ➔ Show Data Source.

   The Data Sources window appears.

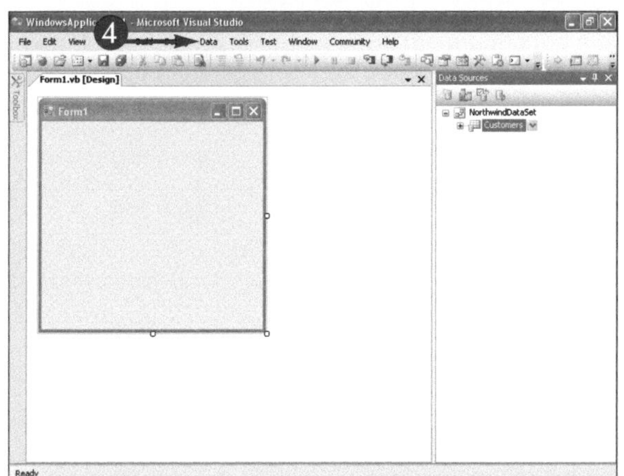

5. Click the + next to the Customers table.

   A list of fields is displayed.
6. Drag and drop the CompanyName, ContactName, and Phone columns on to the form.

   A label and `TextBox` control are displayed for each column.
7. Click the Company Name `TextBox` control.
8. Click Data ➔ Add Query.

   The Search Criteria Builder dialog box appears.

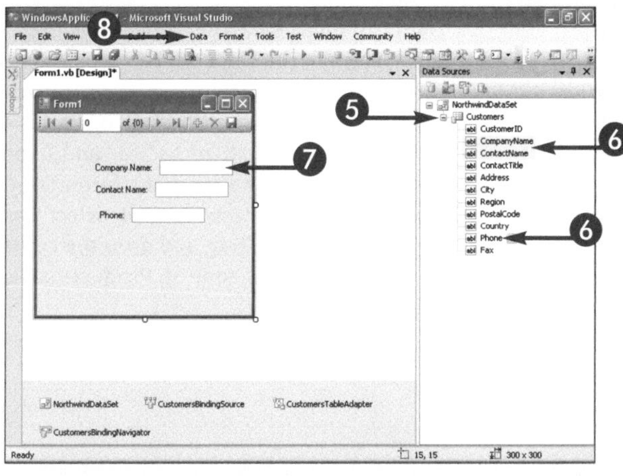

9 Change the New Query name to Germany.

The query displays information about German companies.

10 Click the Query Builder button.

The Query Builder appears.

11 Scroll down to the Country row and type **Germany** in the Filter column.

12 Click the mouse in the query.

The SQL query appears.

13 Click OK.

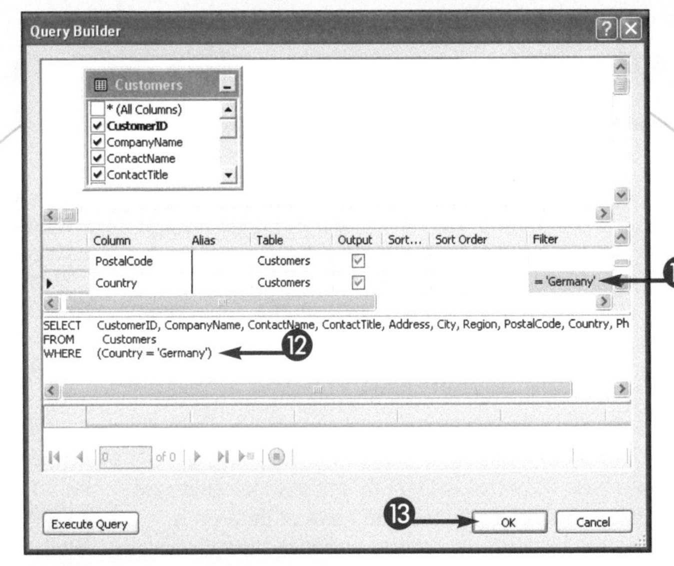

You are returned to the Search Criteria Builder.

14 Click OK.

The query button Germany appears below the data navigation bar.

15 Press F5.

The first row appears on the form.

16 Click the Germany query button.

The first row that contains information about a German company is displayed. The data navigation bar indicates that there are 11 rows because only 11 rows have information about German companies.

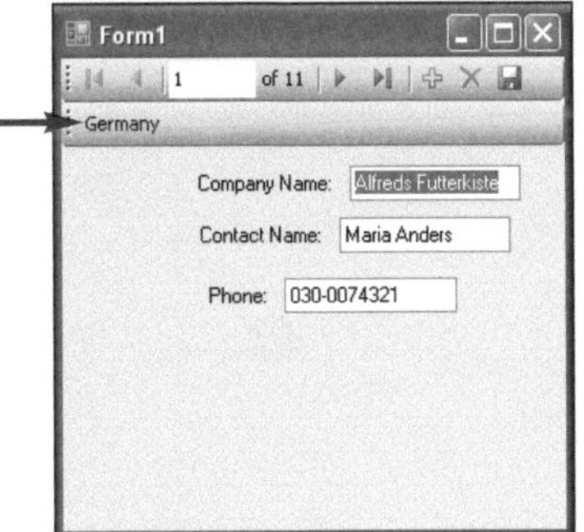

Extra

You do not have to be a whiz at SQL to write a SQL query because Visual Basic .NET has a feature called Query Builder that helps you create a SQL query interactively. You launch the Query Builder by clicking the Query Builder button located at the bottom of the Search Criteria Builder dialog box. You form the SQL query by dragging and dropping table names and columns on to the query form and then creating an expression to filter rows of data. The Query Builder enables you to relatively easily create complex SQL queries that involve accessing columns from multiple tables. After you click the OK button, Visual Basic .NET places the SQL query in the Search Criteria Builder dialog box.

Using the DataGridView Control

The `DataGridView` control displays data in a grid of rows and columns, similar to an Excel table. There are two ways to create a `DataGridView` control on a form: The first way is to drag the control from the Toolbox, and the second, much easier, way is to drag the name of a table from the Data Sources window on to the form. If you drag this control from the Toolbox, you will have to link it to the data source yourself. However, dragging the table name from the Data Sources window automatically links the control and the data source.

The `DataGridView` control is ideal to use anytime that you need to display multiple columns and rows of data on a form at one time because the control provides the navigation tools that enable the user to intuitively manipulate data in the grid.

When you drag the table name from the Data Sources window, Visual Basic .NET automatically displays a navigation bar at the top of the form. The navigation bar displays the current row number and the total number of rows in the grid. It also has buttons that can be used to move through the rows. The `DataGridView` control also displays horizontal and vertical scrollbars if all the columns and rows are unable to be displayed in the control.

Besides a table, a `DataGridView` control is also used to display a view of the data. A view is like a table in that both contain rows and columns of data. However, a *table* is a database component that contains a group of similar data such as student information or registration information, whereas a *view* is a combination of columns and rows from two or more tables. A view is stored in the database.

Using the DataGridView Control

1. Perform steps 1 to 8 in the section "Configure the Data Source."
2. On the Choose Your Database Objects page of the wizard, click the Tables +.
3. Click Customers.

Note: This makes the Customers table available to your application.

4. Click Finish.

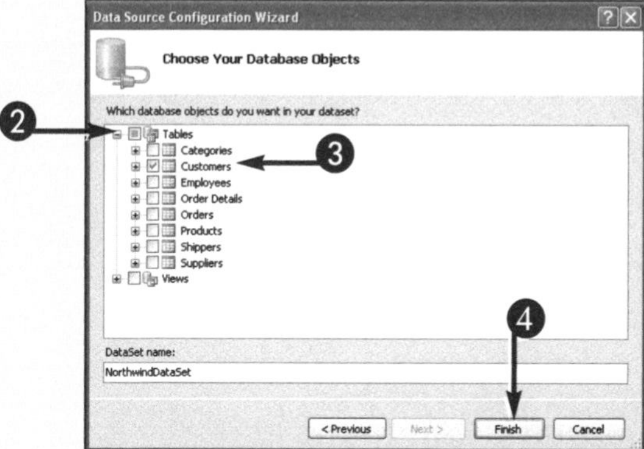

5. Click Data.
6. Click Show Data Sources.

The Data Sources window is displayed, showing the NorthwindDataSet and the Customers table.

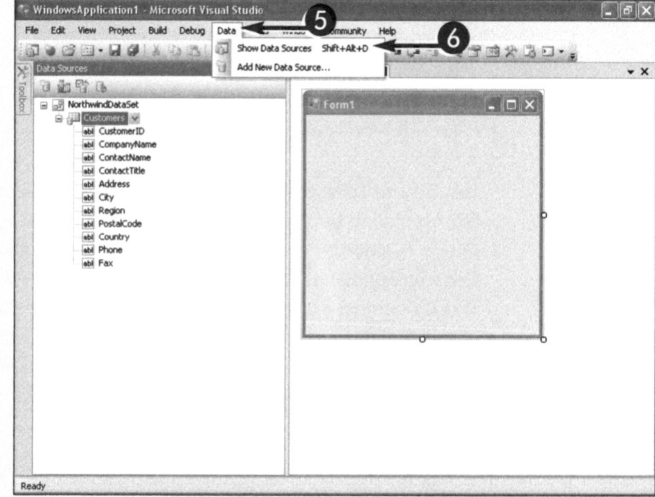

7 Drag the `DataGridView` control from the Toolbox and drop it on to the form.

8 Position the control on the form.

9 Drag the Customers table on to the Data Grid view.

The Data Grid view is filled with columns of the Customers table.

10 Resize the form and the Data Grid view to show several columns from the Customers table.

A scrollbar is automatically displayed so that the user can scroll to other columns.

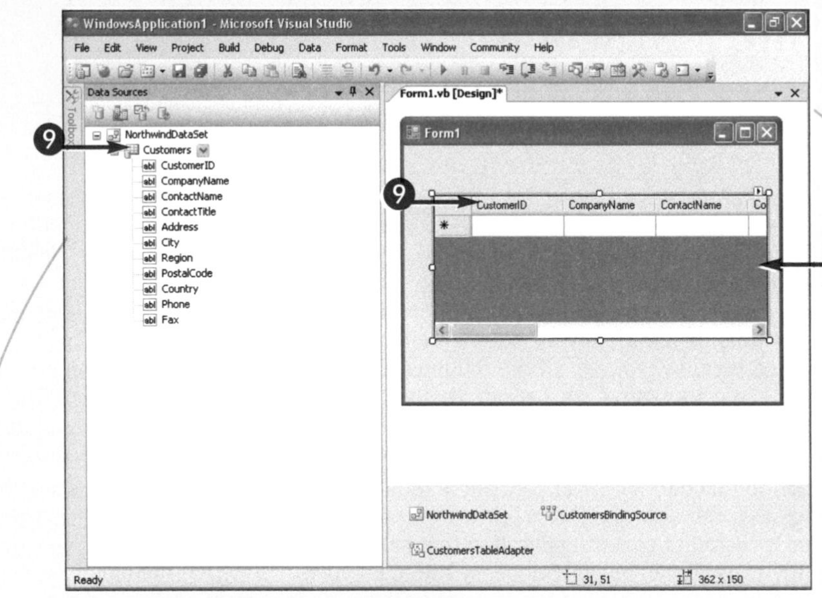

11 Press F5 to run your application.

- Data from the Customers table automatically fills the Data Grid view.

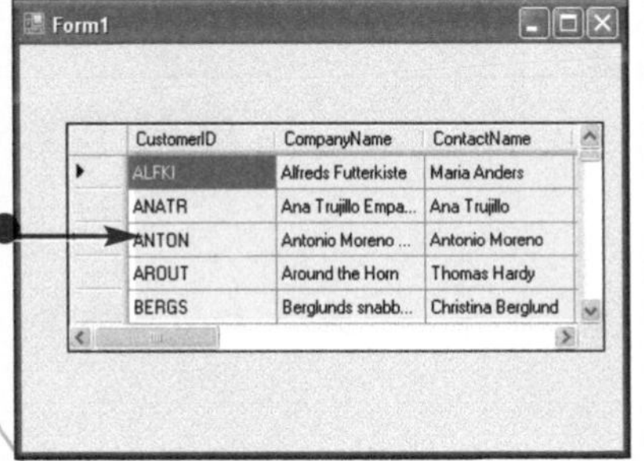

Extra

The order in which rows appear depends on a number of factors. Initially, rows are in data entry order unless modified by the person who creates the database. *Data entry order* means that rows appear in the order that they were entered into the table. You can reorder rows using a SQL query that is bounded to the `DataGridView` control. For example, your application may require data to appear alphabetically by company and contact name. You can write a SQL query that sorts by these columns before displaying data in the `DataGridView` control.

Example

```
SELECT      CustomerID, CompanyName, ContactName, ContactTitle, Address, City,
Region, PostalCode, Country, Phone, Fax
FROM         Customers
ORDER BY CompanyName, ContactName
```

After your application runs, the user can re-sort the table by clicking the name of the column. Clicking it once places the column in ascending order, and clicking it a second time reverses the order.

Remove a Column from the Data Grid View

Data overload is one drawback to dragging a table name from the Data Sources window to the form because Visual Basic .NET assumes that you want to display all the columns in the table. This can overwhelm your user because this is simply too much information to digest at one time. In addition, your presentation of data looks cluttered because typically all the columns will not fit in the `DataGridView` control. As a result, the user needs to scroll the other columns into view. Sometimes the data seems endless if the table contains a lot of columns.

One solution to this data overload problem is to display just the columns that the user needs to work with. Let's say that you created a customer contact application that sales representatives use to set up appointments with customers. There is a lot of information about customers in the Customers table; however, the sales representative needs only some information to contact the customers, such as company name, customer name, telephone number, and e-mail address.

If you drag the Customers table into the Data Grid view, you get all the columns; however, you can easily remove columns that you do not want displayed by using the Edit Columns feature of the `DataGridView` control. This feature lists all the column names in a list box, from which you can select the columns that you want to remove.

Columns are removed from the `DataGridView` control and not from the table. This means that you are free to modify the `DataGridView` control as required by your application without having to worry about causing permanent changes to the table.

Remove a Column from the Data Grid View

1. Add the Customers table to your application.

Note: See the section "Using the `DataGridView` Control."

2. Click Data ➔ Show Data Sources.

   The Data Sources window appears, showing the NorthwindDataSet and the Customers table.

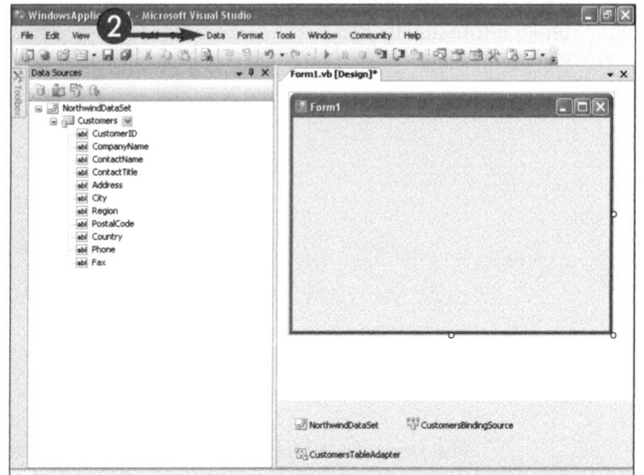

3. Drag the `DataGridView` control from the Toolbox and drop it on to the form.

   A gray box and the Data Grid view Tasks box are displayed.

4. Drag the Customers table from the Data Sources window on to the Data Grid view.

   The Data Grid view is filled with columns of the Customers table.

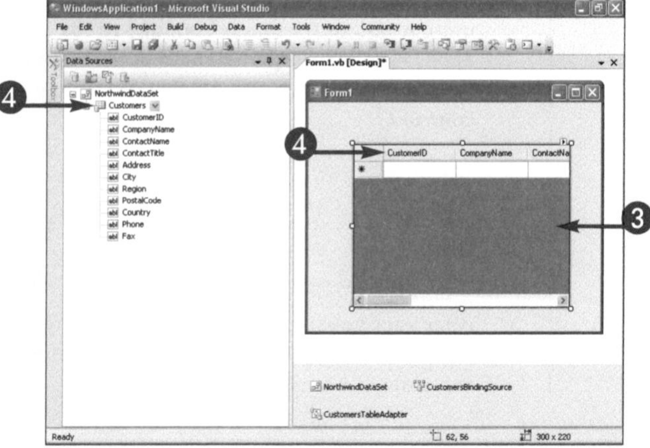

5. Right-click the `DataGridView` control and click Edit Columns.

   The Edit Columns dialog box appears.

6. Click the ContactTitle column.

   The ContactTitle column is highlighted, and its properties appear in the property list.

7. Click Remove.

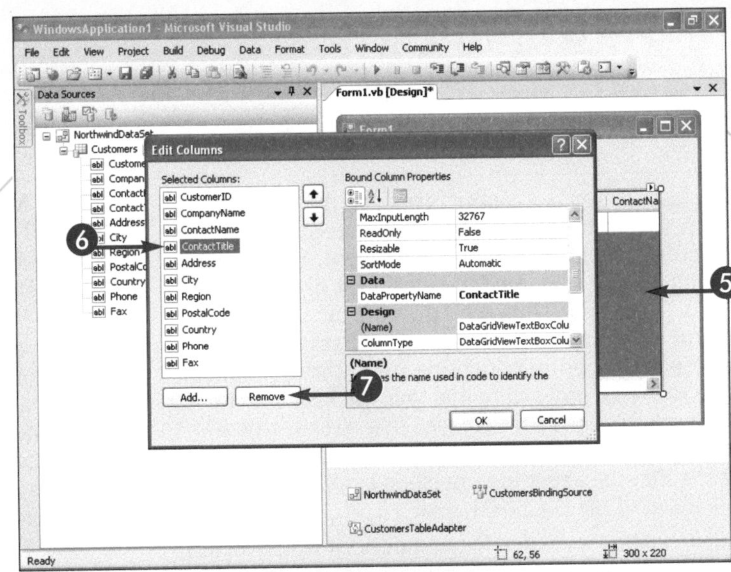

The ContactTitle column is removed from the list.

8. Click OK.

   The ContactTitle column is removed from the Data Grid view.

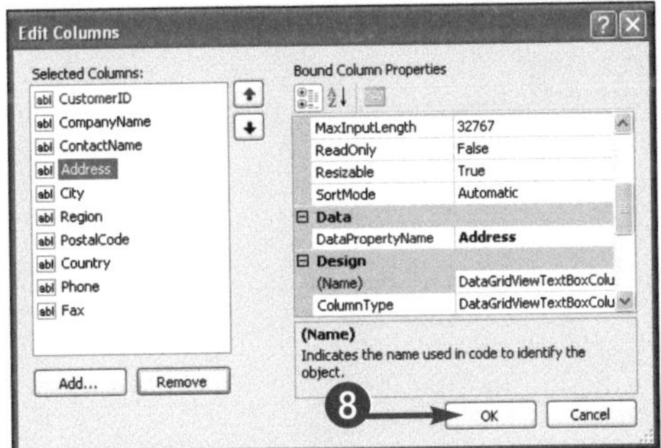

Extra

You can reduce the number of columns that will be displayed when you add a data source to your application. As your learned earlier in this chapter, you select the tables that you want to include in the data source for your application when you add the data source. If you expand the table name by clicking the plus sign, a list of the table's columns is displayed. Alongside each column name is a check box. Simply check the columns that you need. Only those columns become the data source for your application. The table name still appears in the Data Sources window; however, when you drag the table name on to the form, only those columns are displayed in the `DataGridView` control.

The downside of using this technique is that only those columns are available to your application. This is different than removing columns from the `DataGridView` control because in this situation, all columns in the table are available to your application. You pick and choose the columns you need each time that you place the `DataGridView` control on the form.

Add a Column to the Data Grid View

The DataGridView control gives you the flexibility to experiment with data, which is the freedom you require when designing an application. You probably have a good idea of what the forms will look like when you design your application. However, the ultimate judge is the user of your application, who no doubt will ask for changes after she has an opportunity to begin using the application. And there is a high probability that you will be asked to have more columns of data displayed in a DataGridView control than were in the original application specifications. This means that the application must be modified and new columns added to the Data Grid view.

Fortunately, adding a column is not a difficult task because the DataGridView control is designed to let you do this with the click of a few buttons. You can add any column by using the Add Column feature. This feature lists all the columns in the table, including those that you may have previously removed from the DataGridView control. Simply select the new column, and Visual Basic .NET displays the column in the Data Grid view.

Here are a couple of points to remember: First, the list contains columns that you originally selected from the table when you added the data source to your application. You will not find a column on the list if you did not select the column when you added the data source to your application. The other point to remember is that you cannot use this feature to add a column to the table. This feature only adds a column to the DataGridView control. You will need to write a SQL query to add a column to the table.

Add a Column to the Data Grid View

1. Add the Customers table to your application.

Note: See the section "Using the DataGridView Control."

2. Click Data ➔ Show Data Sources.

   The Data Sources window appears, showing the NorthwindDataSet and the Customers table.

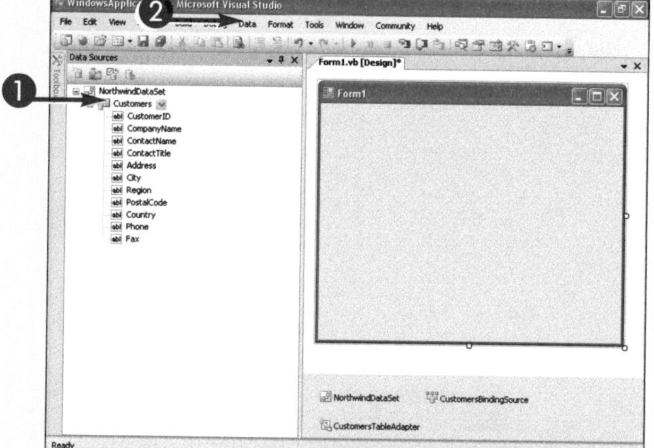

3. Drag the DataGridView control from the Toolbox and drop it on to the form.

   A gray box and the Data Grid view Tasks box are displayed.

4. Drag the Customers table from the Data Sources window on to the Data Grid view.

   The Data Grid view is filled with columns of the Customers table.

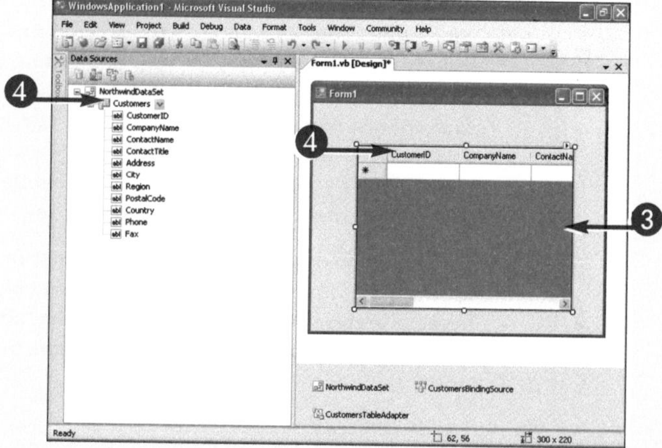

5 Right-click the `DataGridView` control and click Add Column.

The Add Column dialog box appears.

6 Click ContactTitle.

7 Click Add.

The ContactTitle column is added to the Data Grid view.

8 Click the close button.

The Add Column dialog box closes.

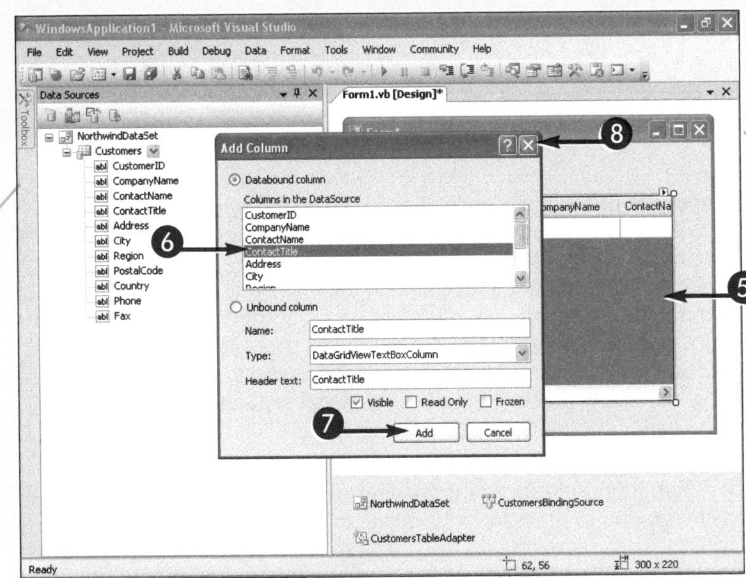

9 Press F5 to run your application.

10 Scroll across the columns, and you will see that the ContactTitle column has been added to the Data Grid view.

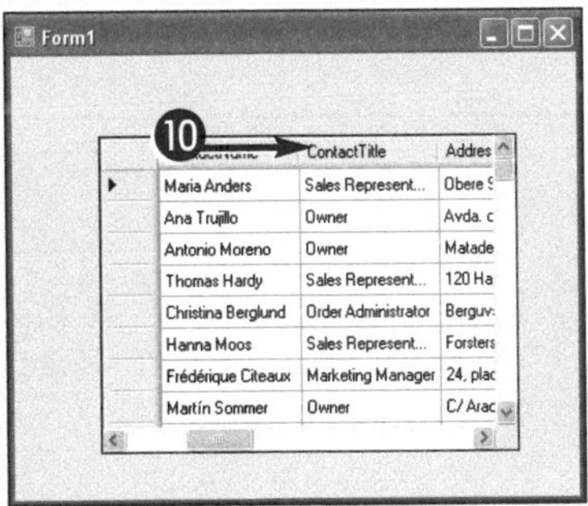

Extra

The Add Column dialog box displays the name of columns that are available from the data source that you connected to your application. When you select a column from the list, Visual Basic .NET assumes that you want to use the column name as the column name in the Data Grid view and places that name in the Header Text text box. You can name the column anything you want by overwriting the name in the Header Text text box. Whatever appears in the Header Text text box appears at the column name in the Data Grid view.

Sometimes you will want a column displayed but not edited. For example, suppose that you do not want the user to change a customer's ID because the customer ID is used to uniquely identify the customer in your application. You can prevent someone from changing the value of a column by selecting the Read Only check box in the Add Column dialog box.

Change the Color of Every Other Row

Designers of financial applications realize that after reading rows upon rows of tabular data for a few hours, it becomes difficult to focus on the data, which raises the risk that the data could be misread. One solution to this problem is to use grid lines to make each row distinct. A better solution is to use green bar paper for the report. Green bar paper, a staple in many businesses, colors every other row green, giving a clear visual separation of rows and making a tabular report easy to read.

You can create the green bar effect on a `DataGridView` control by changing the color of every other row to green. This is a classy way to dress up your application while making it easy to read the rows of the data in the Data Grid view.

The `DataGridView` control makes changing colors easy because of its built-in CellStyle Builder. The CellStyle Builder is a tool that you can use to modify the way data appears in the `DataGridView` control. One of those ways is to color every other row. When you open the CellStyle Builder, you will see a list of properties for the `DataGridView` control. Look for the `AlternatingRowsDefaultCellStyle` property and set this property to green, and Visual Basic .NET changes the color of every other row.

Change the Color of Every Other Row

1. Add the Customers table to your application.

Note: See the section "Using the `DataGridView` Control."

2. Click Data ➔ Show Data Sources.

   The Data Sources window appears, showing the NorthwindDataSet and the Customers table.

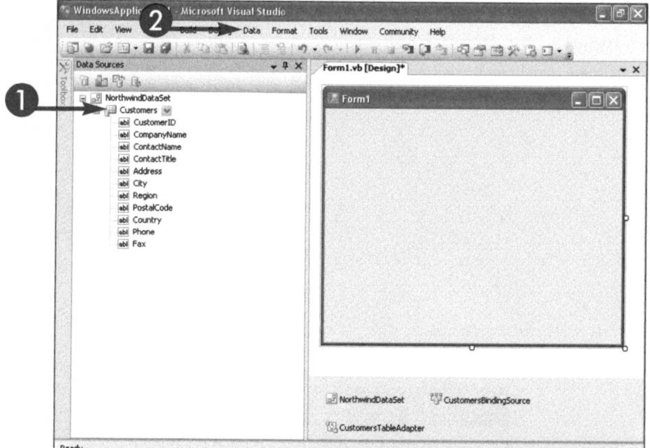

3. Drag the `DataGridView` control from the Toolbox and drop it on to the form.

   A gray box and the Data Grid view Tasks box are displayed.

4. Drag the Customers table from the Data Sources window on to the Data Grid view.

   The Data Grid view is filled with columns of the Customers table.

5. Right-click the `DataGridView` control and click Properties.

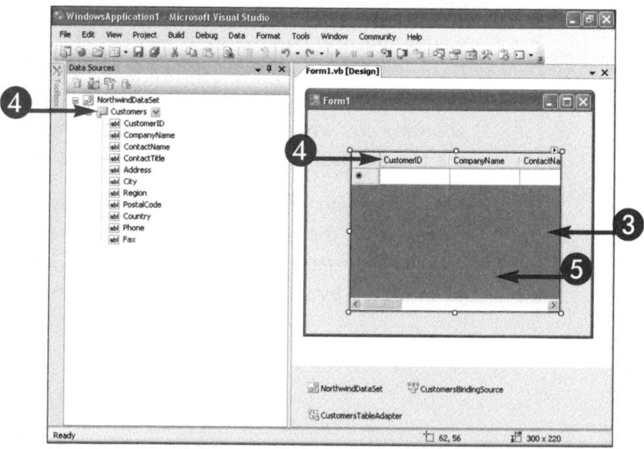

The Properties dialog box appears.

6. Select the `AlternatingRowsDefaultCellStyle` property and click the dot box.

   The CellStyle Builder opens.

7. Click BackColor.
8. Click the down arrow.

   A palette of colors appears.

9. Click a color.

   The color appears in the BackColor box.

10. Click OK.
11. Press F5 to run your application.

    Every other row appears in the color that you selected.

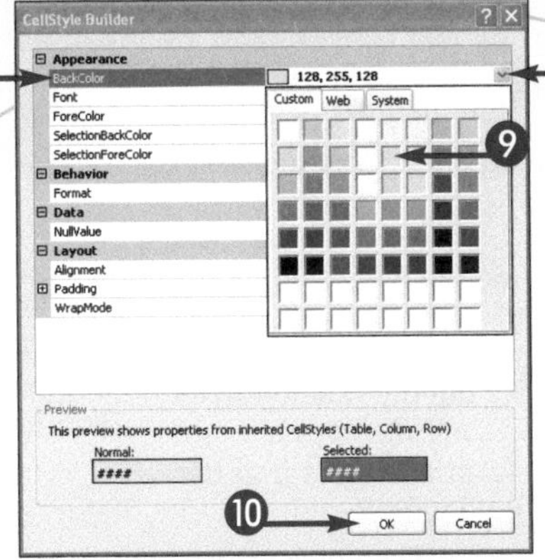

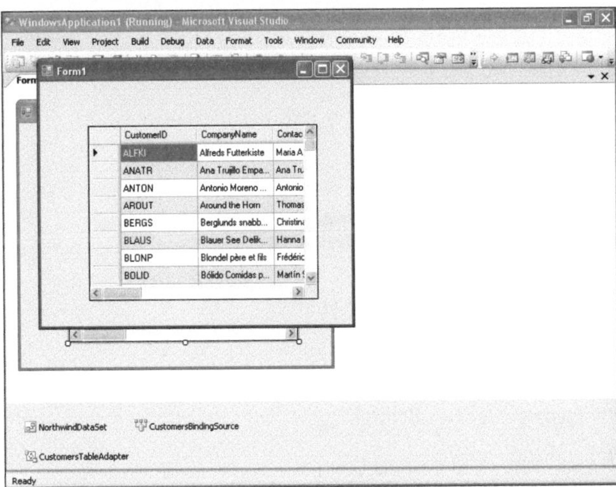

Extra

You have great latitude in designing the grid using the `DataGridView` control's Properties dialog box. For example, you can change the color of the grid lines by using the `GridColor` property. Click this, and you will have a wide selection of colors to choose from. The same color choices are available for the `BackgroundColor` property.

The `CellBorderStyle` property has a variety of different looks that you can give cells. You can make them appear raised, sunken, or some variation of these. Similar styles are available with the `ColumnHeaderBorderStyle` and `RowHeaderBorderStyle` properties to give headers a classy look and feel.

Save Changes Made to the Data Grid View

When a data source is added to your application, Visual Basic .NET creates a dataset of the data. A *dataset* is a copy of the data stored in a table. When you drag the table name from the Data Sources window to a form, Visual Basic .NET displays a `DataGridView` control on the form and links it to the dataset — not to the table in the database.

Therefore, the `DataGridView` control shows a copy of the data and not the actual data that is in the database. This is not a problem unless the user changes the data in the `DataGridView` control, such as inserting a new row into the table. The change is made to the copy of the data and does not change the corresponding data in the database.

Changes to the data in the `DataGridView` control are transferred to the database only when the user clicks the disk icon (the Save button) on the navigation bar to save the changes. All changes are lost if the user exits your application before clicking the Save button.

Save Changes Made to the Data Grid View

1. Add the Customers table to your application.

Note: See the section "Using the `DataGridView` Control."

2. Click Data ➔ Show Data Sources.

   The Data Sources window appears, showing the NorthwindDataSet and the Customers table.

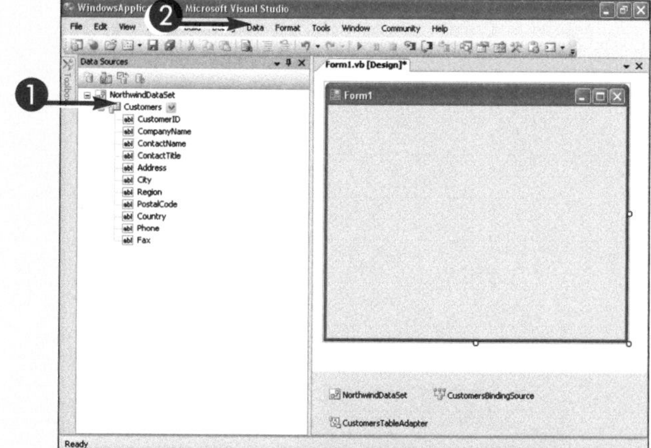

3. Drag the Customers table from the Data Sources window to the form.

   The `DataGridView` control is added to the form, and a navigation bar is placed at the top of the form.

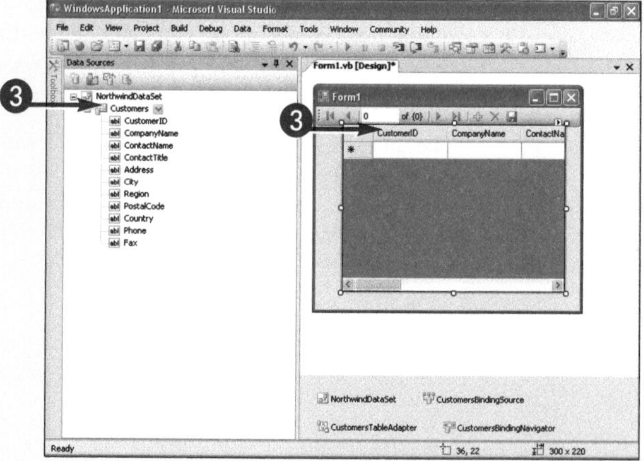

4. Press F5 to run the application.

   The `DataGridView` control is filled with data from the Customers table.

5. Change the value of the CompanyName column in the first row.

6. Click the Save button.

   The changes are saved to the Customers table of the database.

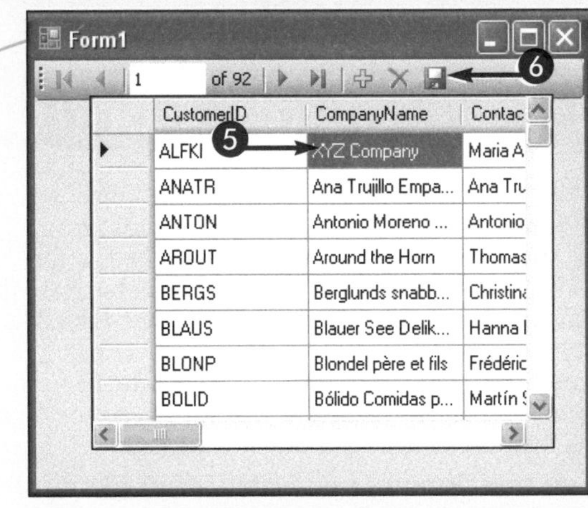

7. Close your application.

8. Press F5 to run your application.

   - Notice that your change appears in the CompanyName column of the first row.

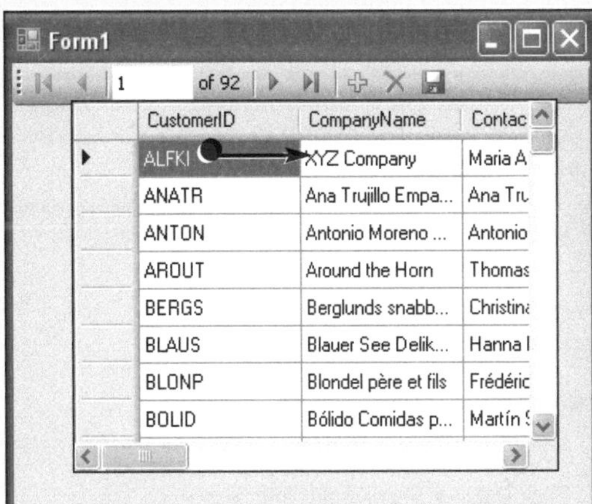

Extra

The user of your application can insert data into a new row in the `DataGridView` control by dragging the vertical scrollbar to the bottom of the control. A new row appears with an asterisk in the leftmost column. Simply enter new information into each column of the row. Visual Basic .NET will enforce any data entry rules by displaying error messages on the screen. For example, the CustomerID column requires four characters. An error message is displayed when the data is saved if there are fewer characters than four entered into that field. The user can insert additional rows by pressing the down-arrow key when the cursor is in the last row.

The user can delete a row by clicking the mouse cursor in the leftmost column of the row to be deleted and then clicking the red X on the navigation bar or pressing the Delete key on the keyboard.

Remember that these changes affect only the `DataGridView` control and not the database until the Save button is clicked to save the data to the database.

Save Changes to a Database Using a Button Control

Although the disk icon (the Save button) on a toolbar is generally recognized as the tool for saving a file, some developers prefer to create their own Save button to save changes made to the Data Grid view. The biggest advantage that this has over using the disk icon is that you control when data is actually saved to the database. This is valuable if you need to do something such as data validation before saving the data.

When the user clicks the Save button, she thinks that the data is immediately being saved to the database. However, all this does is call the `Click` event subroutine. As you have learned in previous chapters, statements that you place in the `Click` event subroutine give you control over what happens when the button is clicked. You do not have this capability using the disk icon.

You will need two statements in the `Click` event subroutine to save data from the dataset to the corresponding table in the database. The first statement calls the `Update()` method of the `TableAdapter` object. The `TableAdapter` object contains the table dataset, and the `Update()` method updates the database dataset and the database with the table dataset. The `Update()` method requires that you pass a reference to the database dataset as a parameter.

The second statement calls the `AcceptChanges()` method of the database dataset object. This confirms that you want to update the database dataset. The database is updated after you call this method. Until then, changes are in the table dataset.

Save Changes to a Database Using a Button Control

1. Add the Customers table to your application.

Note: See the section "Using the `DataGridView` Control."

2. Click Data ➔ Show Data Sources.

   The Data Sources window appears, showing the NorthwindDataSet and the Customers table.

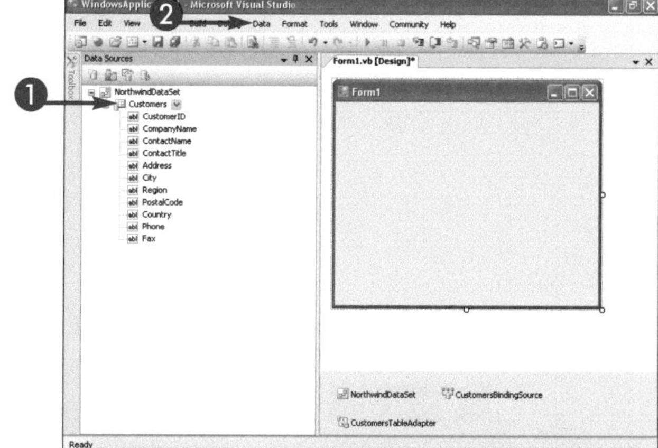

3. Drag the Customers table from the Data Sources window to the form.

   The `DataGridView` control is added to the form, and a navigation bar is placed at the top of the form.

4. Drag a `Button` control from the Toolbox and drop it on to the form.

5. Change the Button control's `Text` property to **Save**.

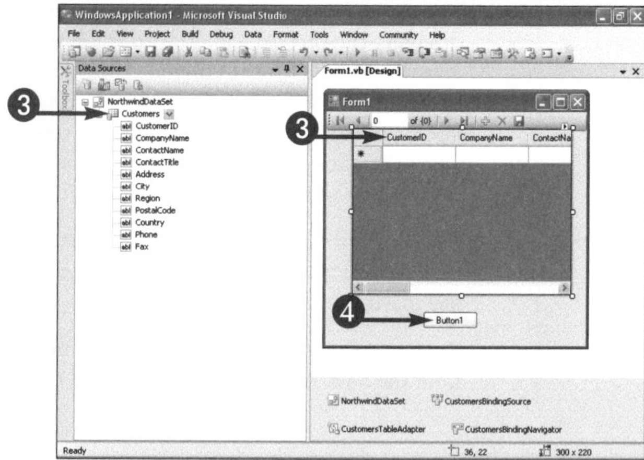

6 Double-click the `Button` control.

An empty `Click` subroutine appears.

7 Type **Me.CustomersTableAdapter.Update(Me.NorthwindDataSet)**.

Note: This copies the dataset to the database.

8 Type **Me.NorthwindDataSet.AcceptChanges()**.

Note: This confirms that you want to update the database.

9 Press F5 to run the application.

The `DataGridView` control is filled with data from the Customers table.

10 Change the value in the CompanyName column of the first row.

11 Click the Save button.

The changes are saved to the Customers table of the database.

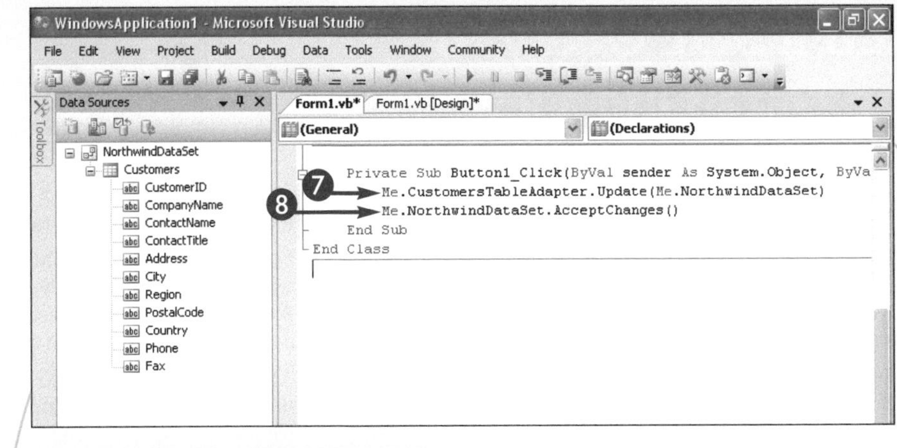

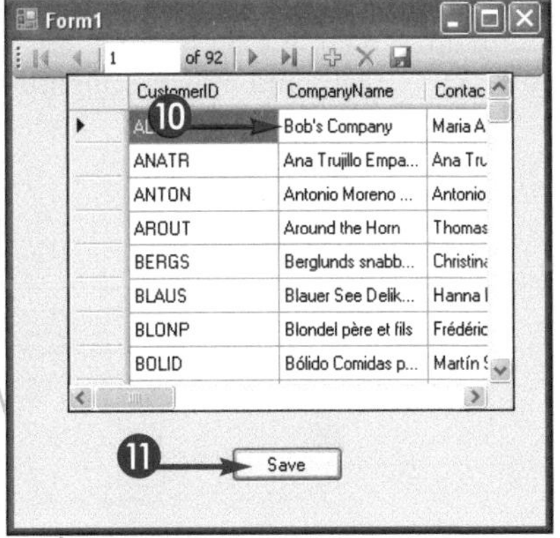

Extra

When designing your application, determine alternative ways that the data will be used. Sometimes you will want the data to be used only by your application and not shared with other applications. This means that you do not want the user to electronically copy data that appears in the `DataGridView` control. Other times, you may not care if the user electronically copies data.

You can use the `ClipboardCopyMode` property to control if data can be electronically copied. Select Disabled to prevent data from being copied to the Clipboard. Other options let the Clipboard be used to copy data. You can specify that just the data be copied or that the data and column headings be copied.

The user highlights the cells he wants copied and presses Ctrl+C to place the selected data on the Clipboard. Pressing Ctrl+V or selecting Paste from the menu copies data from the Clipboard into another application.

Add a SQL Query to the Data Grid View

All the rows in a table are displayed when you drag the table name from the Data Sources window on to the form to create a `DataGridView` control. This is fine if the user expects to see all the data, but chances are good that this is a data overload — more data than the user requires to do his job.

You can reduce the number of rows that appear in the grid by writing a query that filters out unnecessary rows and then link the query to the `DataGridView` control. Linking is done by inserting the query into the `DataGridView` control's Search Criteria Builder that is displayed when you click the Add Query hyperlink in the `DataGridView` Tasks box. A query is written using SQL. SQL enables you to select columns and rows to display and otherwise manipulate data in the table.

For example, say that the user wants to display customers who are in Spain. You would write a query that tells Visual Basic .NET to show rows where the value of the country column is `Spain`. Other rows are hidden from view.

After the query is linked to the grid, Visual Basic .NET displays the query on the navigation bar. The user simply clicks it, and Visual Basic .NET executes the query showing only those rows that meet the criteria set in the query. You can link as many queries to the `DataGridView` control as required by your application.

Add a SQL Query to the Data Grid View

1. Add the Customers table to your application.

Note: See the section "Using the `DataGridView` Control."

2. Click Data ➔ Show Data Sources.

The Data Sources window appears, showing the NorthwindDataSet and the Customers table.

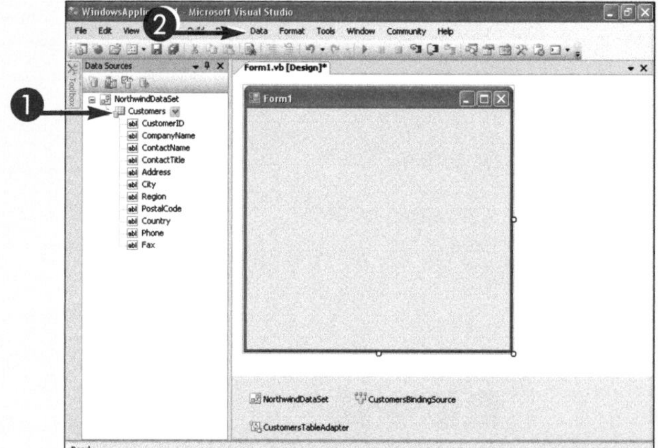

3. Drag the Customers table from the Data Sources window to the form.

The `DataGridView` control is added to the form, and a navigation bar is placed at the top of the form.

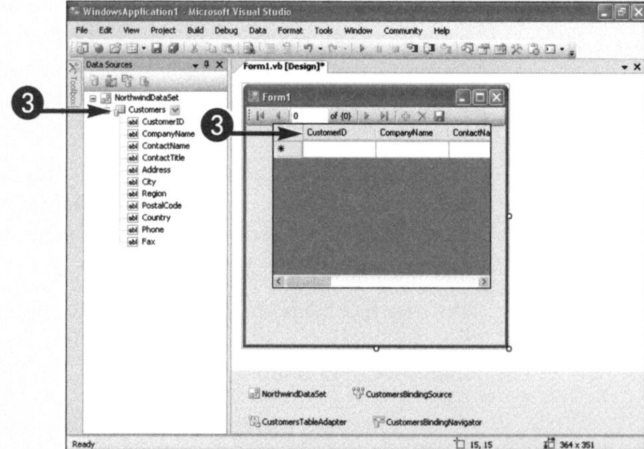

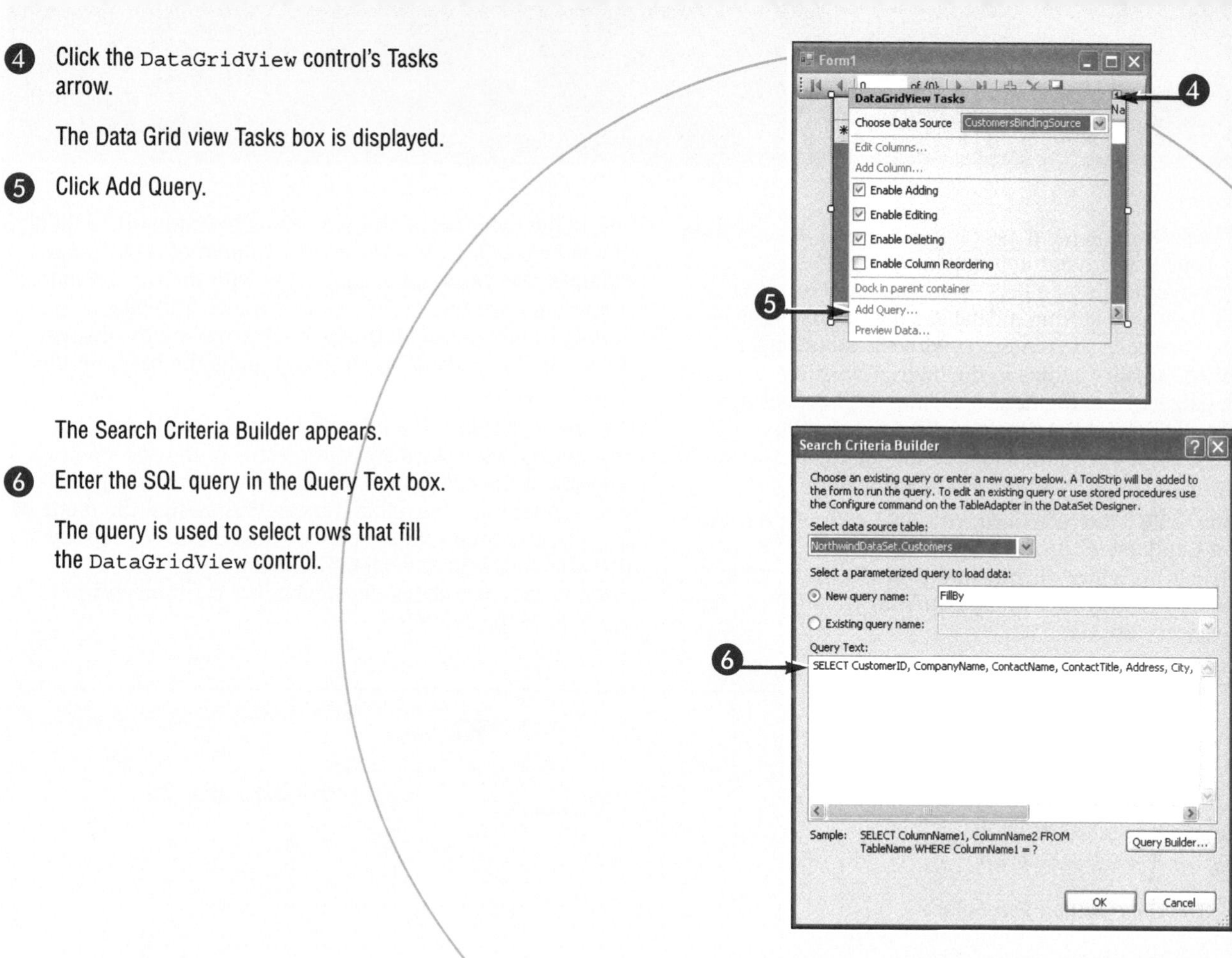

4. Click the `DataGridView` control's Tasks arrow.

   The Data Grid view Tasks box is displayed.

5. Click Add Query.

   The Search Criteria Builder appears.

6. Enter the SQL query in the Query Text box.

   The query is used to select rows that fill the `DataGridView` control.

Extra

Do not be concerned if you do not know how to write queries using SQL because the `DataGridView` control's Search Criteria Builder has a built-in tool that will build the query for you. It is called Query Builder, and you start it by clicking the Query Builder button in the Search Criteria Builder dialog box. The Query Builder is an interactive tool that lists all the columns in the table linked to the `DataGridView` control. Click the check box alongside the names of the columns that you want to appear in the grid. The Query Builder displays a table. Each row is a column of the table shown in the grid, and each column is where you enter the criteria for selecting rows.

For example, if you place the word *Spain* in the column alongside Country, the Query Builder will write a query that shows only rows where the value of the country column is `Spain`. Click the Execute Query button to show the results of your query. This is the data that appears in the grid when your query executes. Click OK to return to the Query Builder; then click OK to have the Query Builder build your query.

Using Code to Bind Data to a Combo Box

Tables from a database can be accessed directly from code within your application by using a `TableAdapter` object. A `TableAdapter` object is used to copy a table from a database dataset to a table dataset. Your code then interacts with the table dataset to display and modify values in the table. You load a table into a table dataset from the database dataset by calling the `TableAdapter`'s `Fill()` method. The `Fill` method requires that you pass the name of the table that you want to copy as a parameter to the `Fill()` function.

After the table dataset is filled with data, you will need to create a DataView of the data in the table dataset. A DataView is an image of rows and columns in the table dataset. You then reference the DataView from within your code to access its data.

One of the more common uses of this technique is to fill a combo box with values stored in a column of a table. For example, you could fill a combo box with the contact names of all your customers. This enables the user to pick a contact from a list of all contacts. The combo box always shows the latest contacts because it pulls the list from the Customers table.

In order to display a column of data in a combo box, you must assign the DataView as the value of the `DataSource` property of the combo box. This tells Visual Basic .NET where to look for the data. You can then assign the name of the column to the combo box's `DisplayMember` property after the data source is identified. Visual Basic .NET automatically populates the combo box with the entire contents of the column.

Using Code to Bind Data to a Combo Box

1. Add the Customers table to your application.

Note: See the section "Using the `DataGridView` Control."

2. Click Data ➔ Show Data Sources.

   The Data Sources window appears, showing the NorthwindDataSet and the Customers table.

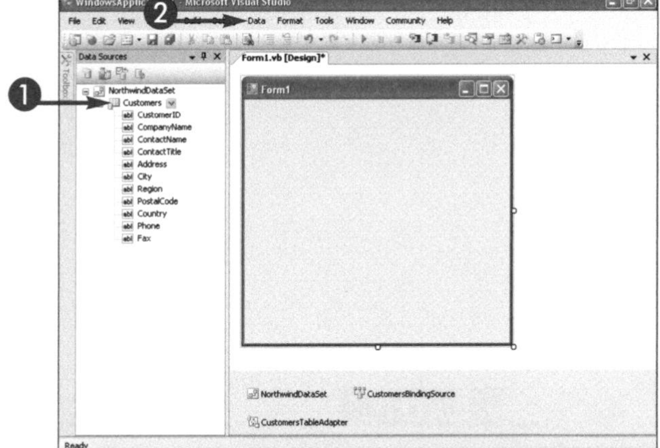

3. Drag a `ComboBox` control from the Toolbox to the form and position it where you want it.
4. Drag a `Button` control from the Toolbox to the form and position it where you want it.
5. Double-click the `Button` control.

   The `Click` subroutine is displayed.

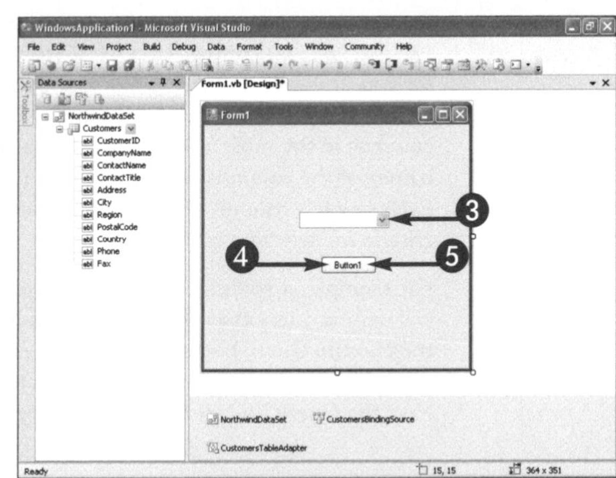

6 Type **Dim dv As DataView = NorthwindDataSet.Tables ("Customers").DefaultView**.

Note: This creates a DataView of the Customers table.

7 Type **ComboBox1 .DataSource = dv**.

Note: This assigns the DataView as the data source for the combo box.

8 Type **ComboBox1 .DisplayMember = "ContactName"**.

Note: This assigns data in the ContactName column of the DataView as the data for the combo box.

9 Press F5 to run your application.

The form showing the combo box and button appears.

10 Click the button.

Contact names from the Customers table fill the combo box.

11 Click the down arrow.

A list of contact names from the Customers table appears.

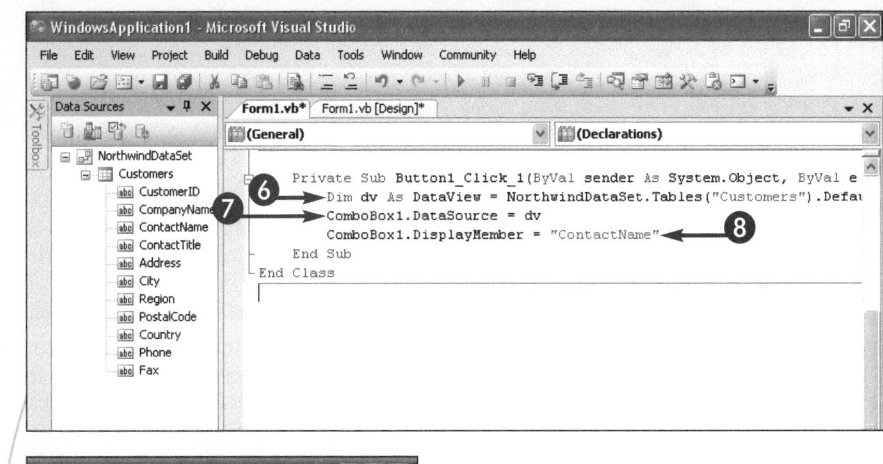

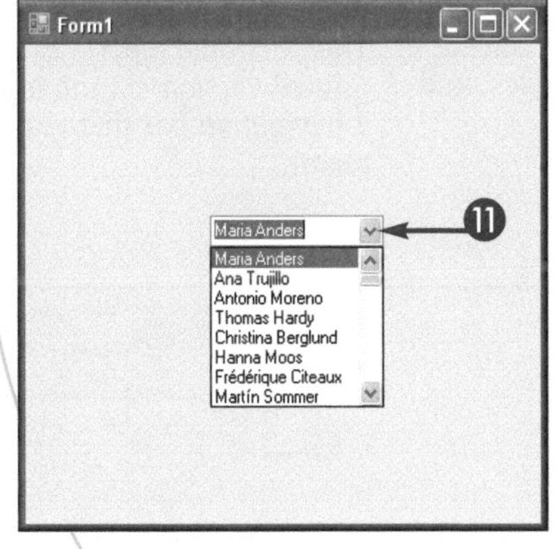

Extra

The same technique for populating a combo box with a column of data from a table can be used to populate other controls from within your code. Another common use for this technique is to fill a `ListBox` control with data. Let's say that your application can send bulk e-mails to your customers. You could display all your customers in a list box so that the user of your application can select those customers who should receive the e-mail. To do this, you follow the same steps used to fill a combo box with contact names; however, you assign the Customer column to the `DisplayMember` property of the list box instead of the combo box:

```
ListBox1.DisplayMember = "Customer"
```

Filling a control with data from a table automatically keeps your controls up-to-date because data in the table reflects the latest information available. The table is always updated whenever customer information is updated or when a new customer does business with the firm.

Using the ReportViewer Control

The paperless office has almost arrived for many businesses whose reports traditionally were printed on paper but are now displayed electronically — saving time, money, and trees. You can have your applications display an electronic report by using the `ReportViewer` control. Think of a report viewer as an electronic display for paper reports.

These reports are created using the report designer that comes with Visual Studio 2005. The report designer is very similar to other popular report designers that you may have used with other applications. It consists of a grid of anchor dots that are used to help position columns, text boxes, and other objects on a form.

The Toolbox contains standard objects used to design the report. These include a text box for displaying text. You will use this for text not generated from a database. There are also images, lines, lists, charts, and a variety of other objects that dress up your report.

In addition to objects from the Toolbox, you can use columns from the data source that is connected to your application. You can position columns or any object on the report by holding down the left mouse button and dragging it into position.

The electronic reports can be multiple pages just like the printed version. At the top of the `ReportViewer` control is a navigation bar that enables the user to page through the report.

Using the ReportViewer Control

1. Add the Customers table to your application.

Note: See the section "Using the `DataGridView` Control."

2. Click Data ➔ Show Data Sources

The Data Sources window appears.

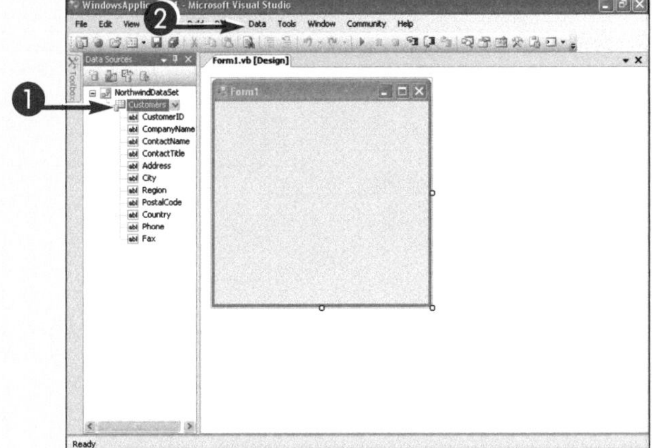

3. Drag the `ReportViewer` control from the Toolbox and drop it on to the form.

Note: The `ReportViewer` control may be larger than the form. If so, you will need to adjust the size of the form using the form's size handles.

4. Click the Report Viewer Tasks arrow.

The `ReportViewer` Tasks box opens.

5. Click Design a New Report.

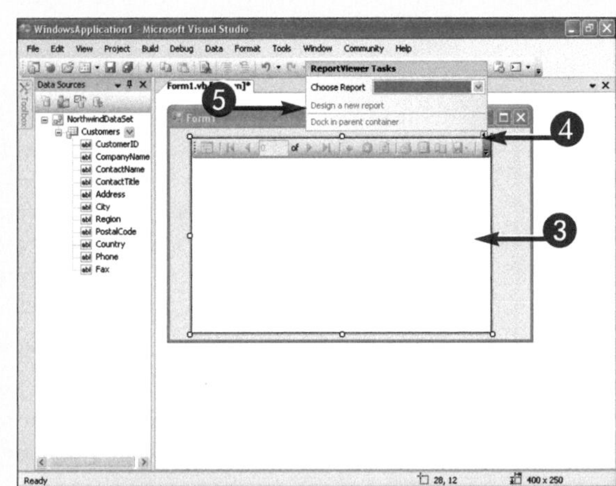

The report designer appears.

Note: You can also open the report designer by clicking Project ➔ Add New Item ➔ Report.

6 Drag and drop controls from the Toolbox and columns from the Customers table in the Data Sources window on to the report.

Note: For example, you can use a text box to place text on the form.

7 Click the Form Design tab.

The form is displayed.

8 Click the `ReportViewer` Tasks arrow.

The `ReportViewer` Tasks box opens.

9 Select Choose Report and pick the report that you created.

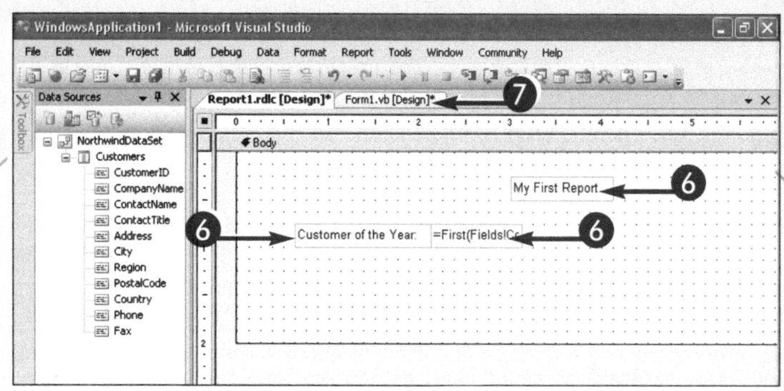

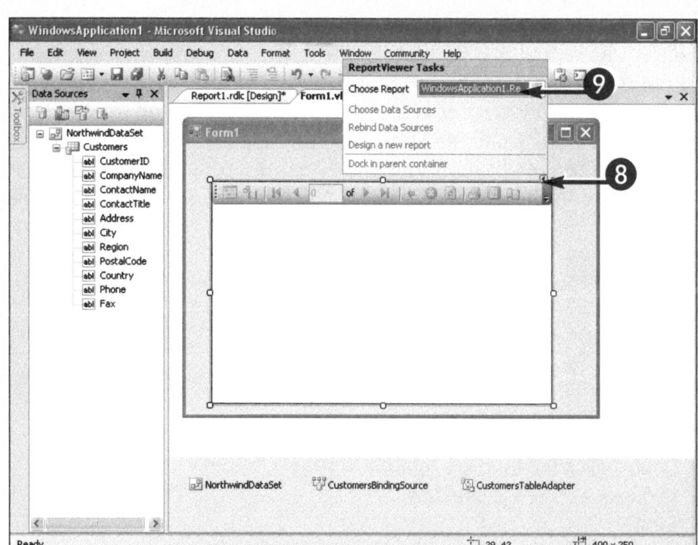

Extra

The fact is that some people still like to have reports on paper, so you can expect some users of your application to want paper reports. This is not a problem because the `ReportViewer` control is also used to print a paper version of the report.

The navigation bar contains several printing tools that are common to many applications. These include a Print icon that immediately prints the report. There is also a Print Layout icon that displays a snapshot of the layout of the printed version of the report. There is also a Page Setup icon, which is used to display the Page Setup dialog box, in which the user can select the paper size, landscape or portrait orientation, and other common printer options. Also on the navigation bar is a Refresh button. This refreshes the data elements on the report so that the user is assured that the report contains the latest information.

Set Breakpoints

One of the most challenging aspects of building a Visual Basic .NET application is identifying a logical error in your application. A *logical error* occurs when your application produces unexpected results, such as when you expect the application to display the message "Invalid user ID or password" and the message "Valid login" is displayed. Somewhere in your code you gave Visual Basic .NET wrong instructions.

A breakpoint is used to help you identify logical errors in your application. A *breakpoint* is a place in your application where you tell Visual Basic .NET to pause the application while executing the application and show you the code. You then can execute each statement in the code by hand and see the immediate result of the statement to determine if the statement caused the error.

You set a breakpoint at the spot in your program where the error is likely to occur. For example, the statement that causes the wrong message to be displayed is likely several lines of code previous to the statement that displays the message, so that is where you set the breakpoint.

In the Code Editor, Visual Basic .NET displays the value of a variable or control on the current statement when you place the cursor over a variable or property. You can also highlight a conditional expression in an `If...Then` statement or a loop, and Visual Basic .NET will evaluate the expression, showing you if it is true or false. In this way, you can determine if the value is what you expected.

Set Breakpoints

1. Add a `Button` control to a form.

Note: See Chapter 4 for information about adding buttons.

2. Double-click the `Button` control to create a `Click` subroutine for it.

The `Click` subroutine appears.

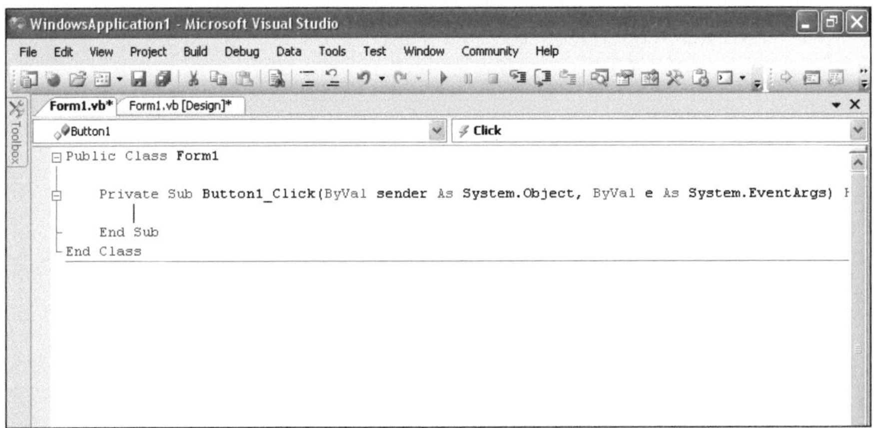

3. Declare an `Integer` variable, calling it `intAge` and initializing it with the value `18`.

4. Create an `If...Then...Else` statement with a conditional statement of `intAge > 18`.

5. Display a message in the code block of the `If...Then` statement by writing `MessageBox.Show("You can vote.")`.

6. Display a message in the code block of the `Else` statement by writing `MessageBox.Show ("You cannot vote.")`.

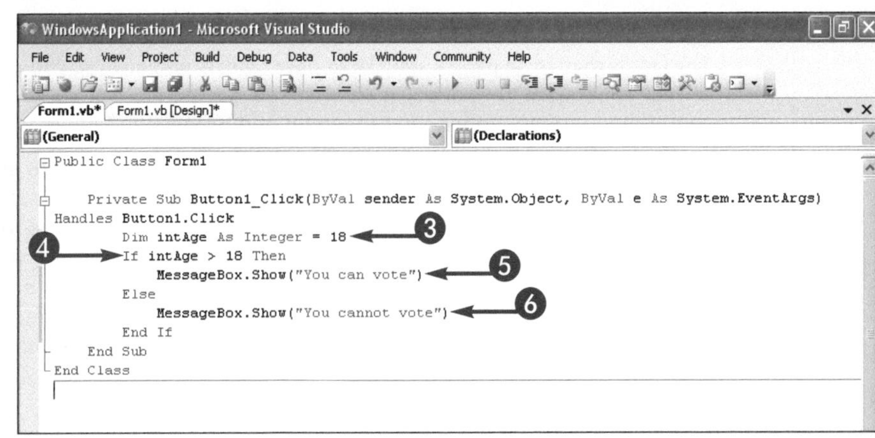

7 Set a breakpoint at the beginning of the `If...Then...Else` statement by clicking the left mouse button in the left margin of the `If...Then` statement.

The statement is highlighted, and a red dot appears in the margin indicating that a breakpoint is set for the statement.

Note: You can click the red dot to remove the breakpoint.

8 Press F5.

The application runs in the debugger.

9 Click the `Button` control.

The application pauses, and statements are shown in the Code Editor.

10 Highlight the conditional statement in the `If...Then` statement.

The conditional statement is shown to be false. A person must be older than 17 — not older than 18 — to vote. This is the source of the error.

Note: You can press F5 to continue and execute the next statement in your code, or you can press Ctrl+Alt+Break to stop the debugger.

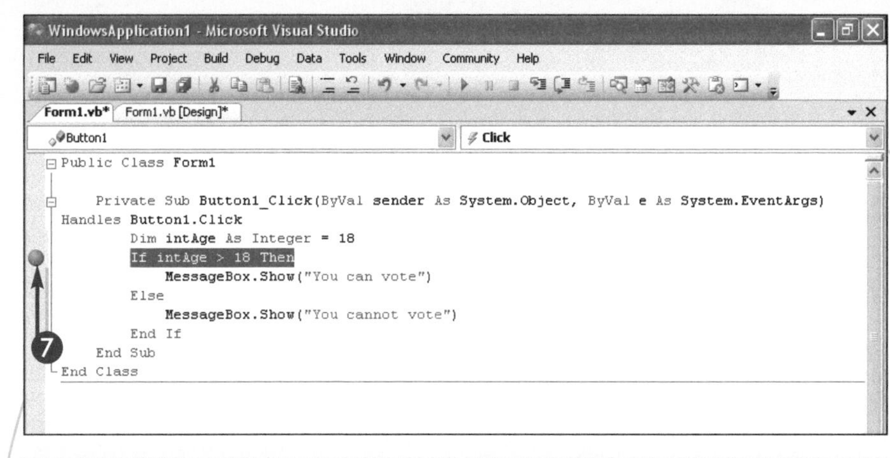

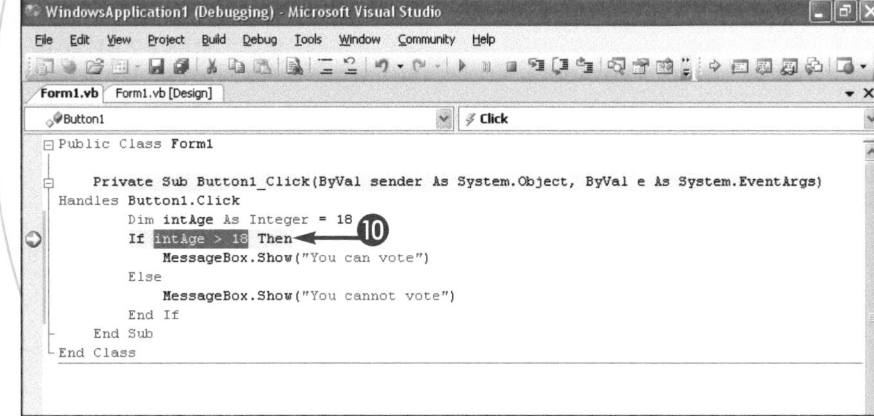

Extra

The Standard toolbar and the Debug toolbar can be used to interact with your code while running your application in the debugger. You can display these toolbars by clicking View ➔ Toolbars ➔ Standard and View ➔ Toolbars ➔ Debug. Here are the toolbars:

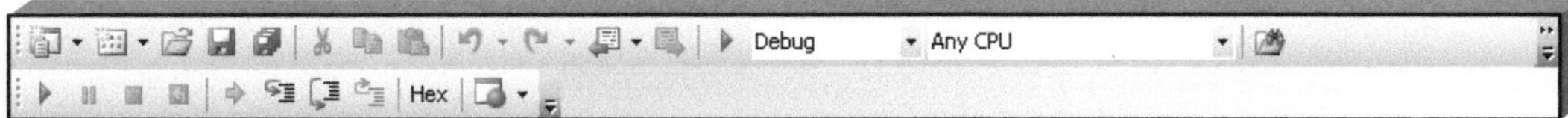

Using the Watch Window

You can watch variables and control properties change values as your application is running by using a Watch window. A Watch window is displayed at the bottom or on the left of your Code Editor while your application runs in the debugger. You can place a variable or a control property in the Watch window to monitor its value. The value represents the current state of the variable or property of a control such as the text of a `TextBox` control based on the statement in your application that is currently being executed. The currently executed statement is highlighted in your code.

The default value for a variable or control property appears alongside it in the Watch window if the application has not assigned a value to the variable or control property. For example, `0` is the value of an uninitialized `Integer` variable in the Watch window, and an empty string (`""`) is the value for an uninitialized `String` variable. Pressing F10 steps you through each line of the application beginning with the breakpoint. As statements change the value of the watched variables and control properties, their values change in the Watch window. When you see an unexpected value assigned to one of them, you can stop the debugger by pressing Ctrl+Alt+Break and then examine the statement that changed the value to locate the error.

Using the Watch Window

1. Add a `Button` control to a form.

Note: See Chapter 4 for information about adding buttons.

2. Double-click the `Button` control to create a `Click` subroutine for it.

The `Click` subroutine appears.

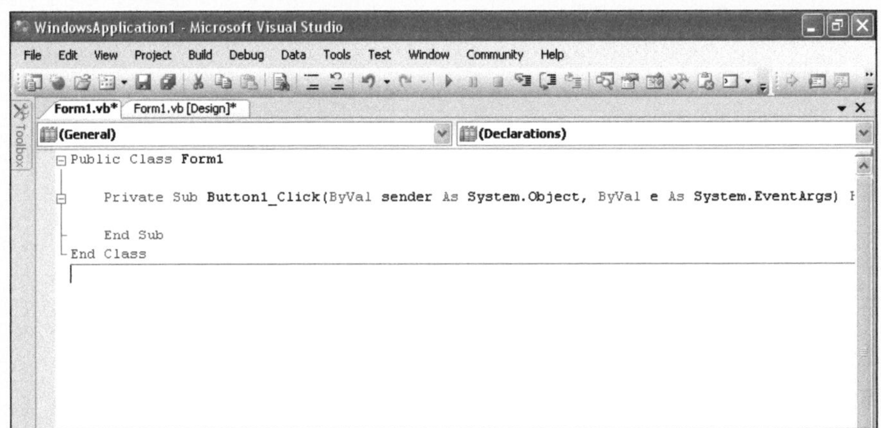

3. Declare two `Integer` variables, calling one `intCounter` and the other `intValue`.
4. Create a `For` loop that loops three times by using `intCounter = 0 to 2`.
5. Assign the value of `intCounter` to `intValue` in the code block of the `For` loop by writing `intValue = intCounter`.

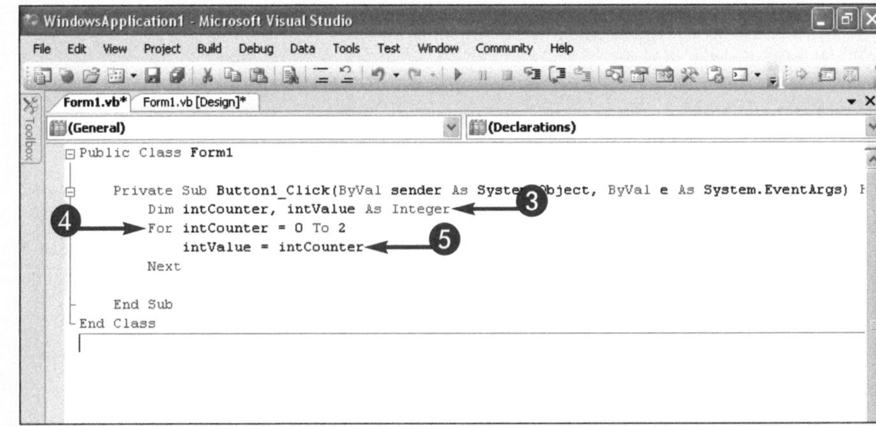

6. Set a breakpoint at the beginning of the `For` loop by clicking in the left margin of the `For` Loop.

7. Press F5.

   The application runs in the debugger.

8. Click the `Button` control.

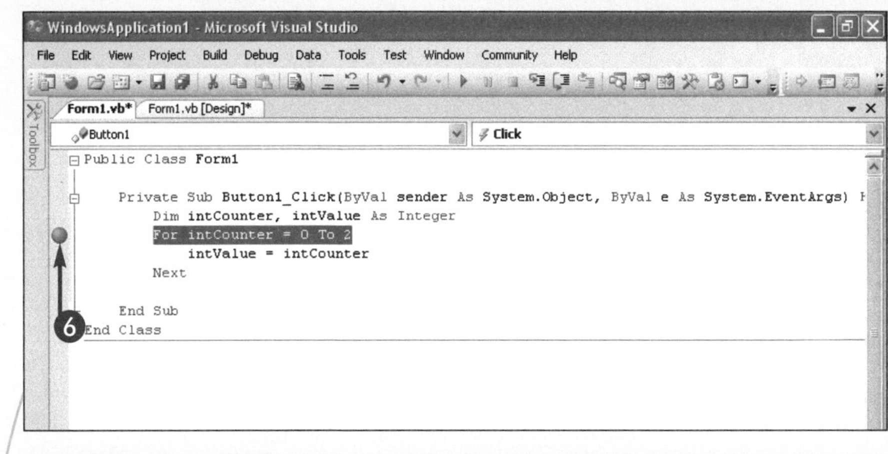

   The application pauses, and statements are shown in the Code Editor.

9. Highlight the `intCounter` variable and right-click.

10. Click Add Watch.

    The `intCounter` variable is added to the Watch window.

11. Repeat steps 9 and 10 for the `intValue` variable.

12. Press F10.

    - Notice that the value of each variable in the Watch window changes as the program executes the loop.

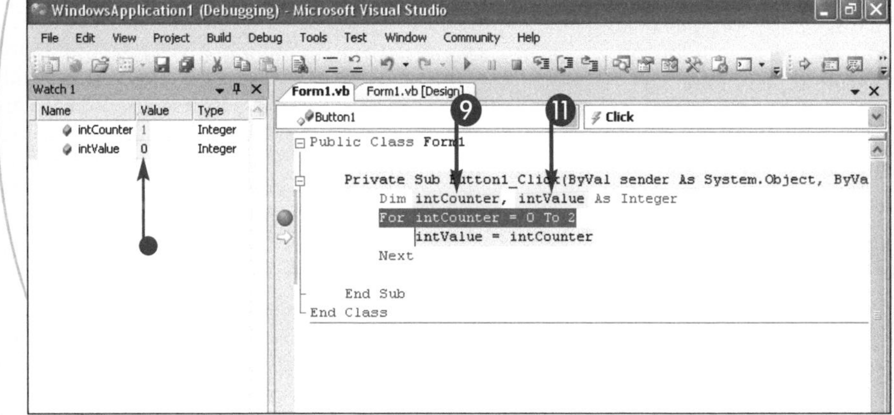

Extra

You can change the value in the Watch window, and the program will then use that new value. The new value will take effect on the line of code following where the cursor is currently located. Oftentimes, you get many steps into an application and realize that you initialized something to the wrong value, so you can change it on-the-fly without having to restart everything. You can also use this to test out all parts of an `If...Then...Else` statement.

Sometimes you will be developing an application that displays information to the console rather than to a form by calling the `Console.WriteLine("xxx")` function in a statement. The console is the command prompt that you will find in Accessories in the Programs folder. This means that you will not see anything written to the console when you run your application in the debugger unless you open the Output window. You do this by selecting Debug ➔ Windows ➔ Output. The Output window appears at the bottom of the screen.

Using a Visualizer

Some data is enclosed within metadata. *Metadata* describes data such as HTML and XML tags or column names of a table. Applications that use data enclosed within metadata strip away the metadata and just use the data. For example, a Web page consists of HTML tags (metadata) and text that is to be displayed on the Web page. The browser reads the HTML tags to understand how to display the text and then strips away those tags, only displaying the text of the Web page on the screen.

When you are debugging your code, you want to monitor data values and ignore metadata. However, this can become difficult to do because information assigned to a variable or to a control property may have data enclosed within metadata. You do not want to see the metadata. Instead, you want to see the data. This is what you use a Visualizer window for.

A *Visualizer* window is an enhancement to a Watch window in that it displays the current value of a variable or control property. However, a Visualizer window strips away metadata and displays only the data. So if the control property has an HTML document, the HTML Visualizer removes the HTML code and displays the text as it would appear on a browser. There are four types of Visualizer windows — text, HTML, XML, and dataset. Text, HTML, and XML Visualizers use a string, and the Dataset Visualizer is used for seeing `DataSet`, `DataView`, and `DataTable` objects.

To use a Visualizer window, you add a variable or control property to the Watch window. If there is a magnifying glass icon in the Watch window, this indicates that a Visualizer window is available for the variable or property. When you open the Visualizer window, the value of the variable or control property is displayed as readable text without metadata.

Using a Visualizer

1. Add a `Button` control to a form.

Note: See Chapter 4 for information about adding buttons.

2. Double-click the `Button` control to create a `Click` subroutine for it.

The `Click` subroutine appears.

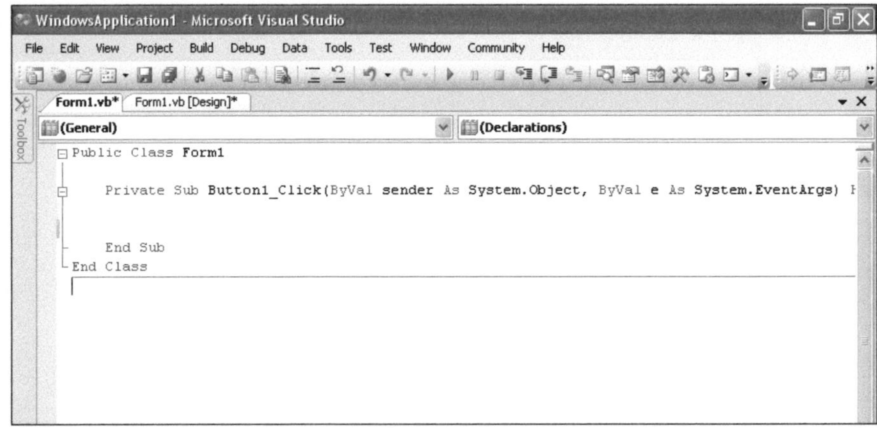

3. Declare two `String` variables, calling one `strLine1` and the other `htmlLine1`.

4. Assign HTML code to the first string variable, such as `<b>This is a test.</b>`.

5. Assign the first string variable to the second string variable by writing `htmlLine1 = strLine1`.

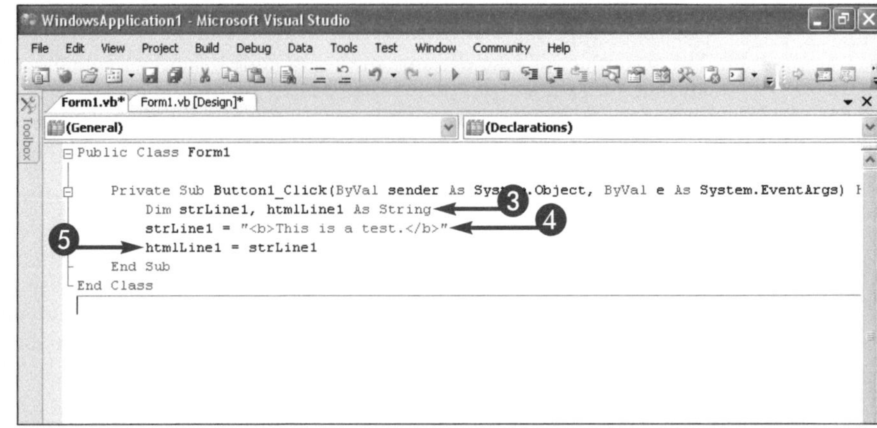

6. Set a breakpoint on the line that assigns one string to the other string by clicking in the left margin of the assignment statement.

7. Press F5.

   The application runs in the debugger.

8. Press the `Button` control.

   The application pauses, and statements are shown in the Code Editor.

9. Highlight the `strLine1` variable and right-click.

10. Click Add Watch.

    The `strLine1` variable is added to the Watch window.

11. Click this down arrow.

    The HTML Visualizer opens, and the text is displayed according to the HTML code.

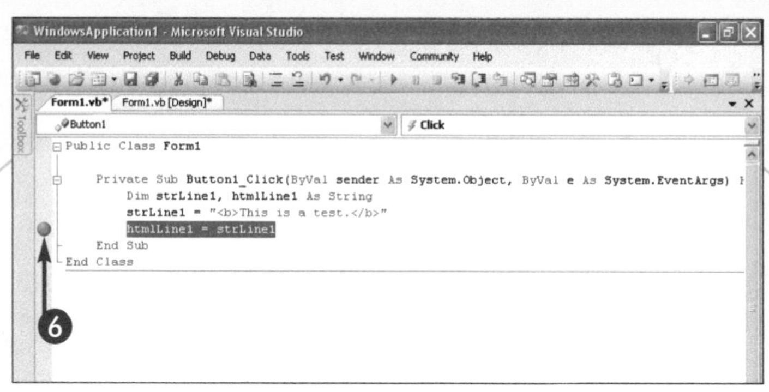

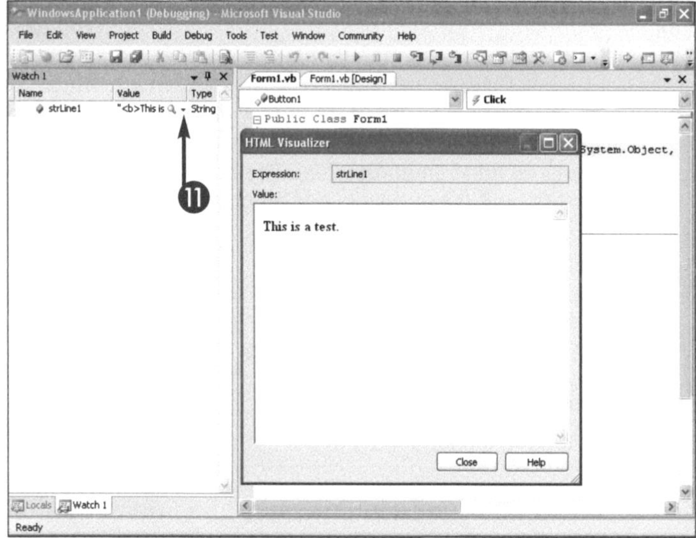

Extra

You can display a Visualizer window in debugging mode by pointing the mouse cursor at a variable or control property in the Code Editor while running your application in the debugger. This causes Visual Basic .NET to display a DataTip. The DataTip contains a Visualizer window, which is used to display the value of the selected variable or control property.

The debugger has an assortment of windows that enable you to peer into your application when it runs. To explore each window, press F5 to run your application in the debugger. Click Debug ➔ Windows and then select one of the many windows from the menu. You will notice that more windows are available to you when debugging an application than there are when you click Debug ➔ Windows when not debugging. Each window that you select appears at the bottom of the screen. Multiple windows can be selected. Each will appear in its own tab.

Create a Class and Declare an Object

A *class* is like a template that describes an object such as a student. The description consists of data and functionality such as a student number and registering for courses. Data is referred to as a *property,* and functionality is called a *method.* A class is created by adding an empty class to your project. You then declare the properties and methods within the empty class. Properties and methods of a class are referred to as being *encapsulated* by the class. That is, they are members of the class and can be accessed only by an object of the class. An *object* is an instance of the class. Think of a class definition as telling Visual Basic .NET how to build an object, just like a blueprint tells how to build an automobile. The blueprint is the class definition, and the automobile is an object.

Your program must declare an object of a class in order to access the class's properties and methods. An object is declared in the same way as you declare a variable, using `Dim name As Object`. Replace `name` with a unique name for the object. The next step is to create an object of a class and assign it to the object variable. You do this by using `name = New ClassName()`. `ClassName` is the name that you gave to the class when you defined the class, and `name` is the name of the object variable. You use the `name` of the object variable within your code to access properties and methods of the class.

You can have multiple objects of the same class. Each object has its own copy of the class's properties. However, you can have them share the same copy of a property by using the keyword `Shared`.

Create a Class and Declare an Object

1. Add a form to a new project.

Note: See Chapter 2 for more information.

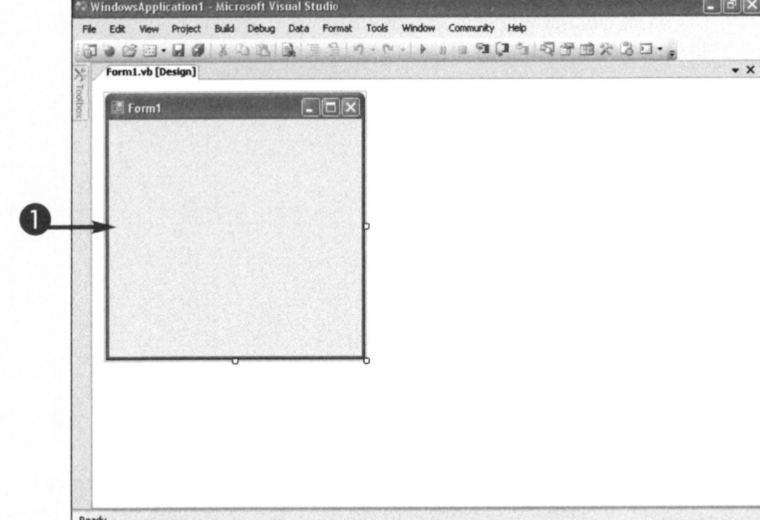

2. Click Project ➔ Add Class.

   An empty class definition appears.

3. Change the name of the class to a name that describes the purpose of the class, such as `Student`.

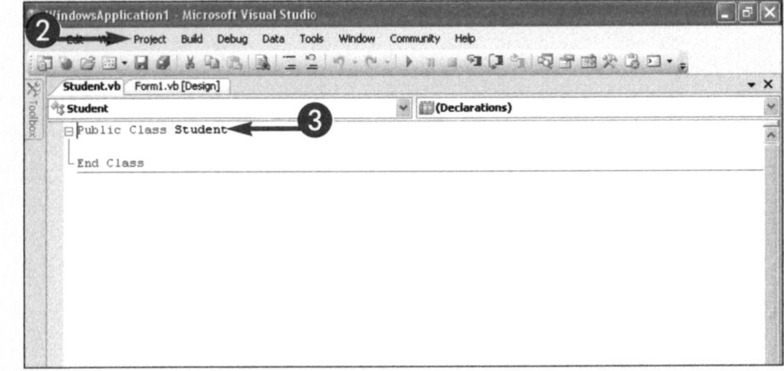

4. Click the Design tab.

   The blank form is displayed.

5. Drag and drop a `Button` control from the Toolbox on to your form.

   The `Button` control appears as `Button1` on the form.

6. Double-click the button on the form.

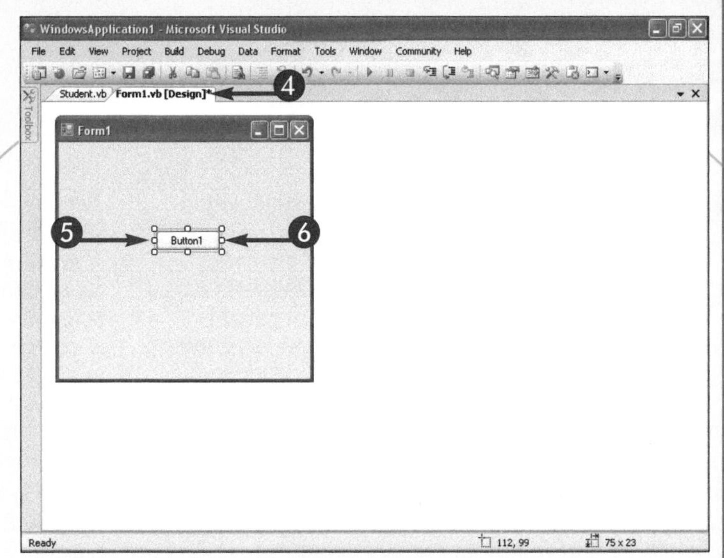

   The button `Click` subroutine appears.

7. Declare an object by typing `Dim XXX As Object`, replacing `XXX` with a name used for the object, such as `student1`.

8. Create an instance of the class and assign it to the object by writing `XXX = New YYY`, replacing `XXX` with the name of the object, such as `student1`, and replacing `YYY` with the name of the class, such as `Student`.

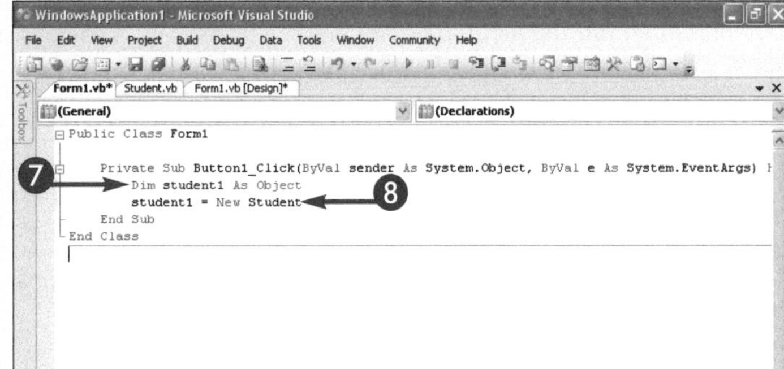

Chapter 12: Using Classes

Extra

Many applications are assembled from classes that are either built by the application's programmer or by other programmers. Each control that you learned about is defined in a class. For example, the `Button` control is a class that is built by programmers at Microsoft. Dragging the `Button` control from the Toolbox and dropping it on to your form is creating an instance of that class that is automatically called `Button1` to refer to it as the first instance of the `Button` control on the form. In fact, the form itself is a class that Microsoft built. Most of your applications will be built using classes built by Microsoft; however, you will also build your own classes to handle situations that are unique to your application. Programmers in large development groups such as those found in major corporations build classes that are shared among programmers in the group. They do this to avoid everyone having to build the same class. For example, a programmer may develop a class to retrieve customer information from the database. Other programmers who need this functionality for their application simply use that class rather than spending time building their own class to retrieve this information.

Create a Sub Method for a Class

A *method* is functionality that is associated with a class, such as a student registering for a class. A class can have no methods or many methods, depending on the nature of the class. Most classes that you will create with have at least one method. A method is defined as either a subroutine or as a function, depending on whether you want the method to return a value to the code that calls the method. A subroutine does not return a value, and a function returns a value.

You can define a method to accept one or more parameters from the code that calls the method. A *parameter* is a value that is given to the method when the method is called and used by statements within the method definition. Statements that you want executed when the method is called are placed within the method's code block. These statements can access variables declared within the code block and properties that are declared outside the method's code block but within the class definition.

A method can be public or private. A public method is accessible to code inside the class and outside the class by using an object of the class. A private method is accessible to code within the class. You specify the accessibility of a method by preceding the method with either the keyword `Public` or `Private`. You can also have `Shared` methods. A `Shared` method is called using the class name. It is not associated with a specific instance of the class, so it can only access `Shared` properties.

A method that does not return a value is defined by writing `Public Sub` *`name`*`()...End Sub`. You place statements that execute when the method is called between `Sub` *`name`*`()` and `End Sub`.

Create a Sub Method for a Class

1. Open a new project.

Note: See Chapter 1 for more information.

A blank form is displayed.

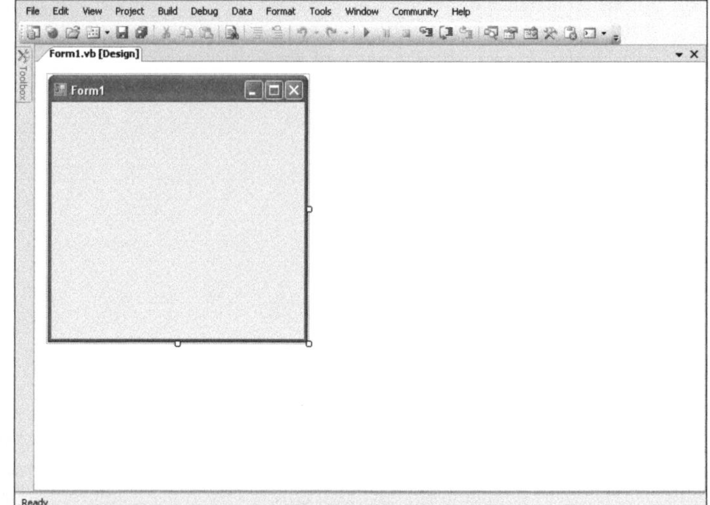

2. Click Project ➔ Add Class.

An empty class definition is displayed.

3. Change the class name to a name such as `Student`.

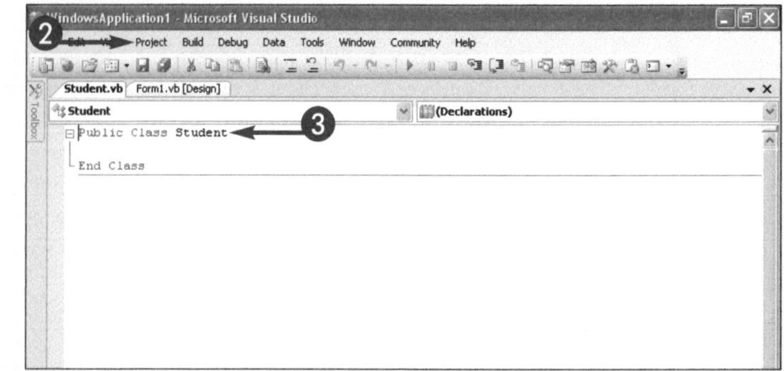

4 Create a public method that does not return a value by typing `Public Sub XXX()` followed by `End Sub`, replacing `XXX` with the name of the method, such as `Welcome`.

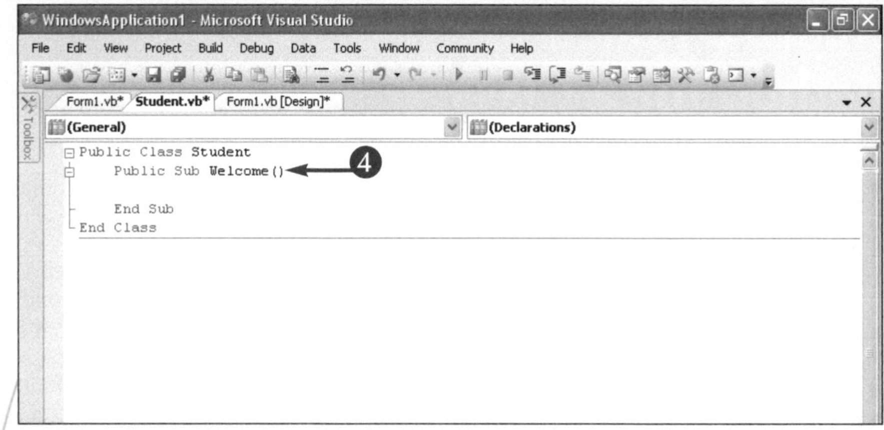

5 Insert a message box inside the method to display a welcome message by typing `MessageBox.Show("XXX")`, replacing `XXX` with a message such as `"Welcome to college."`

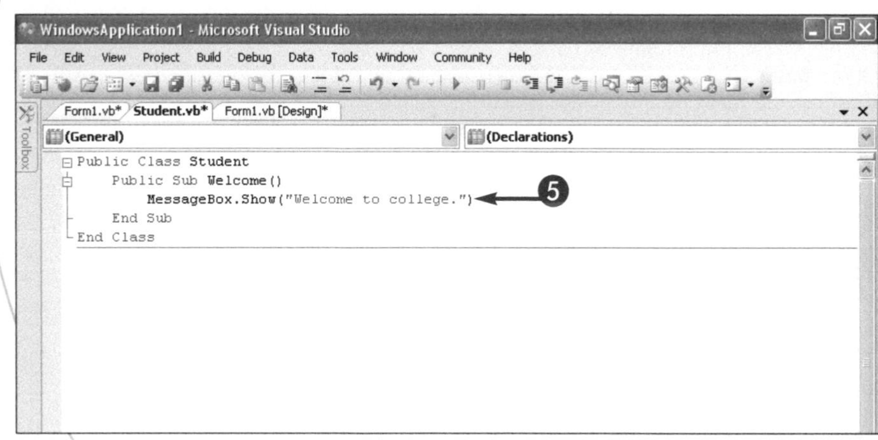

Extra

You can create one or more parameters for the subroutine method if statements within the method require information supplied by the code that calls the method. For example, you can have other parts of your application pass the message that the `Welcome()` method displays. Each parameter is declared within the parentheses of the method by specifying the name of the parameter and its data type. Each parameter must be separated by a comma. You must also specify if the data is passed by value or reference. By value is when Visual Basic .NET passes the method a copy of the data. By reference is when the same data is used.

Example

```
Public Sub Welcome (ByVal mesg As String)
```

You then use the name of the parameter in place of its value in statements within the definition of the method such as

```
MessageBox.Show (mesg)
```

Create a Function Method for a Class

You can define a method that returns a value to the code that called the method by creating a function method. A function method is practically the same as a function, which you learned about in Chapter 9, except that it is defined within the definition of a class. You can define a function method with or without parameters based on the need of your application. However, all function methods must return a value to the code that called the method.

You define a function method by writing `Public Function` *`name`*`()` `As` *`data type`* followed by `End Function`. The *`name`* is the name that you give to the function method and should reflect the functionality of the function, such as `getMessage()` for a function method that returns a message displayed by the code that calls the method. The *`data type`* is the data type of the return value, such a `String` if the method returns a message.

You place statements that you want executed when the method is called between the function method's name and `End Function`. The `Return` statement is used within the function method to tell Visual Basic .NET to stop executing the function method and return the value in the `Return` statement to the code that called the method. For example, `Return "Welcome to college."` is the string returned to the code that called the method.

The value in the `Return` statement must be compatible with the data type specified at the beginning of the function method definition; otherwise, an error will occur. The `Return` statement can use a literal value such as `"Welcome to college."`, a variable, a parameter, or a value returned from another function method.

You define parameters for a function method the same way as you defined parameters for a `Sub` method in the previous section.

Create a Function Method for a Class

1. Open a new project.

Note: See Chapter 1 for more information.

A blank form appears.

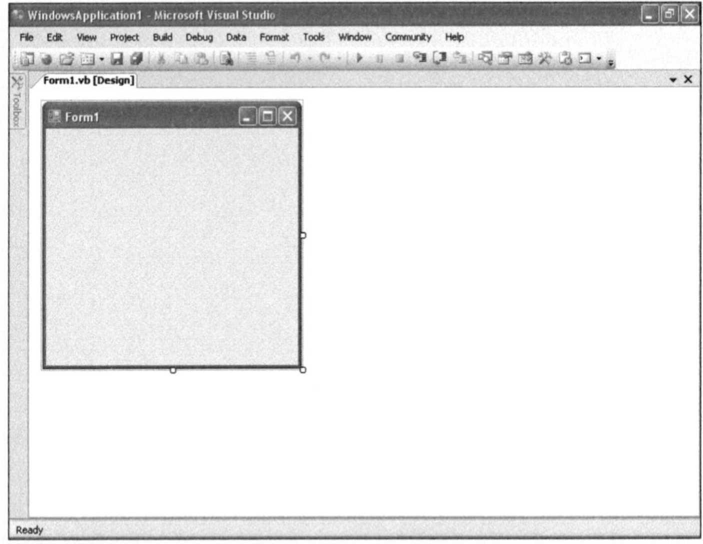

2. Click Project ➔ Add Class.

An empty class definition appears.

3. Change the class name to a name such as `Student`.

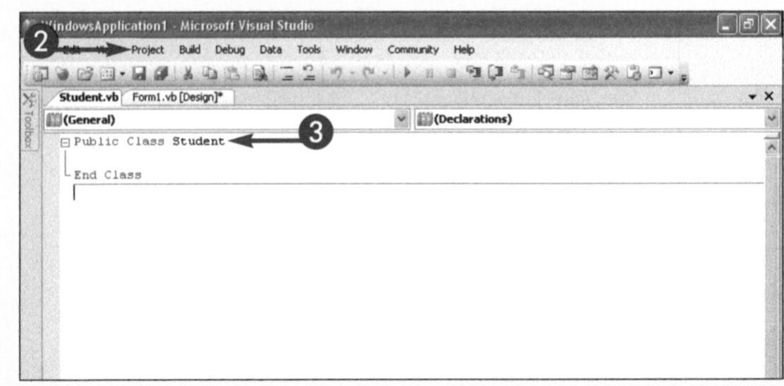

4 Create a public method that returns a value by typing `Public Function XXX() As YYY` followed by `End Function`, replacing `XXX` with the name of the method, such as `GetMessage()`, and replacing `YYY` with the data type of the return value, such as `String`.

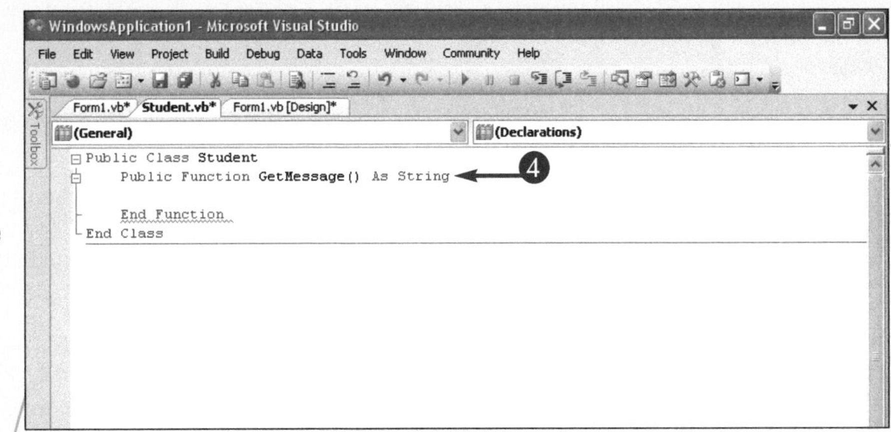

5 Insert in the function method a `Return` statement by typing `Return XXX`, replacing `XXX` with a message such as `"Welcome to college."`

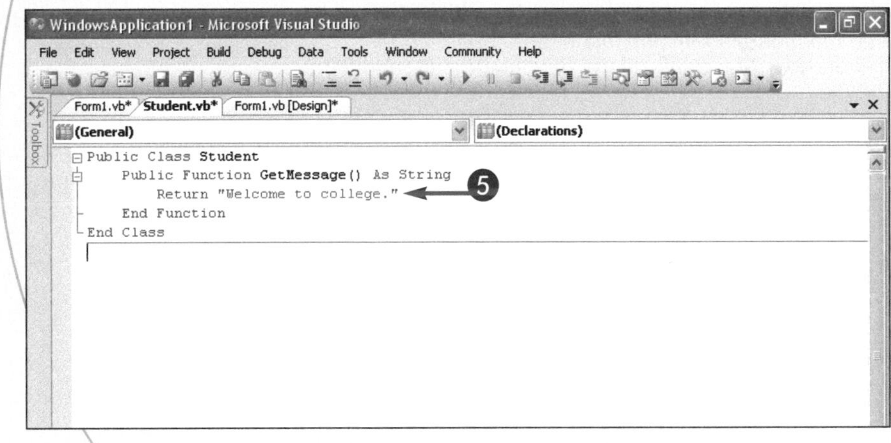

Extra

The other option besides a return statement is to set the function name to the return value.

Example

```
GetMessage = "Welcome to college."
```

The code after this statement will continue executing. This can be useful when you know the return value, but you want some more code to execute before you stop executing the function. A return statement causes it to terminate immediately.

You can have multiple `Return` statements in a function method depending on the needs of your application. After a `Return` statement executes, the other `Return` statements in the function method are ignored. You can use an `If` statement to determine which value to return.

Example

```
If grade > 69 Then
    Return "You passed."
Else
    Return "You'll do better on the next test."
End If
```

Create a Private Method

A private method is functionality of a class that can only be accessed from within the class by either a public or private method of that class. This is used by program designers to restrict the use of functionality that may be vulnerable to misuse if allowed to be accessed publicly. This is referred to as *hiding the functionality.* For example, some program designers use a private method when accessing a database. They create a public method that a programmer calls to save data, but that public method does not directly access the database. Instead, it calls a private method that handles interactions with the database. In this way, details about the database are hidden from programmers who use the class. You may need to do this for security purposes.

You create a private method similar to how a public method is created, except you use `Private` instead of `Public`. You write `Private Function` or `Sub` followed by the name that you give to the method. A private method can accept parameters and return a value.

A private method can access public, private, and protected (see the following section, "Create a Protected Method") methods and properties. However, a private method cannot access private members of the base class.

Create a Private Method

1. Open a new project.

Note: See Chapter 1 for more information.

A blank form appears.

2. Drag a `Button` control from the Toolbox to the form.

A button called `Button1` appears.

3. Click Project ➔ Add Class.

An empty class definition appears.

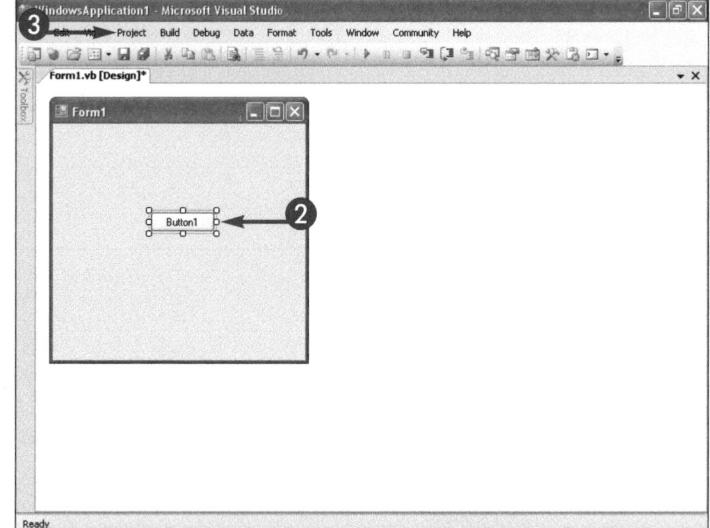

4. Change the class name.

5. Create a private method that does not return a value by typing `Private Sub XXX()` followed by `End Sub`, replacing `XXX` with the method name.

6. Insert a message box using `MessageBox.Show()`.

7. Create a public method that does not return a value by typing `Public Sub XXX()` followed by `End Sub`, replacing `XXX` with the method name.

8. Call the private method inside this method by typing the name and `()`.

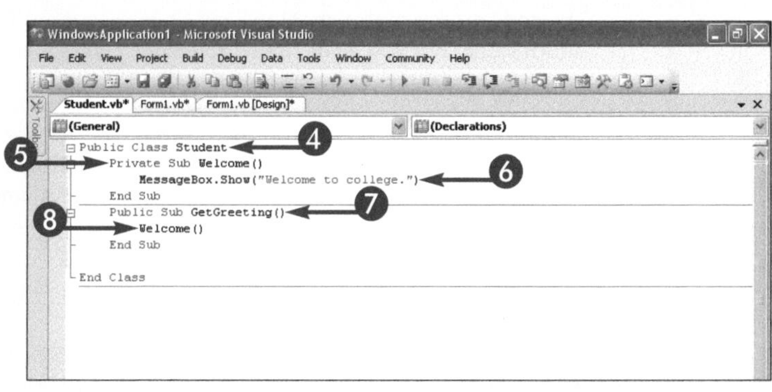

9 Double-click the `Button` control on the form.

The `Button1 Click` subroutine appears.

10 Declare an object by typing `Dim XXX As Object`, replacing `XXX` with the name of the object.

11 Create an instance of the class and assign it to the object by typing `XXX = New YYY`, replacing `XXX` with the object name and `YYY` with the class name.

12 Call the `GetGreeting` method by typing `XXX.GetGreeting()`, replacing `XXX` with the object name.

13 Press F5 to run the program.

14 Click the button to display the message.

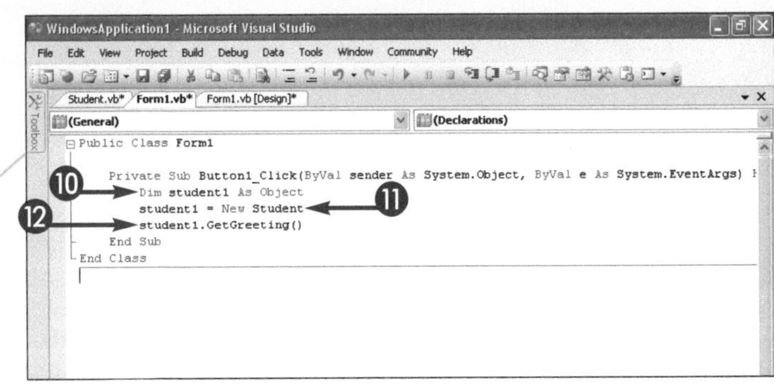

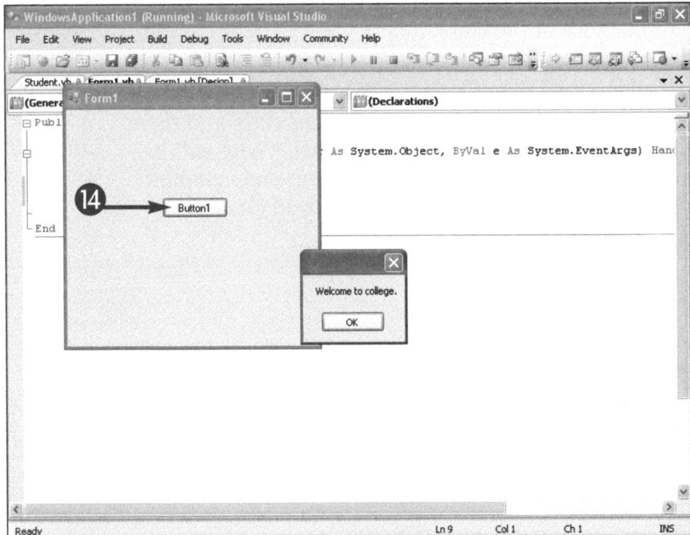

Extra

As a rule of thumb, limit the use of private methods and properties to situations in which you need to restrict or hide data or a particular functionality from parts of the application that use the class. Why would you want to hide these from the application because you are writing those parts? This is a question that some programmers raise when learning about classes. In the real world of building applications, some classes are shared among other programmers who are working on the same or similar applications. This means that the programmer who builds the class may not be the same person who writes part of the application that calls the class. Another member of the programming team may incorporate a class into his or her piece of the application. Using a private method helps to simplify the use of a class. Let's say that another programmer needs to retrieve customer information from the database. You provide a public method that retrieves customer information. The other programmer never directly accesses the information. If the database structure is changed, you can change the private method without having to change all the code that uses the class.

Create a Protected Method

A *protected member* of a class is a method or a property that can be accessed by methods defined within the class definition and by a derived class. A *derived class* is a class that inherits another class. However, a protected member cannot be accessed from outside these classes. This means that they are unable to be called directly from other parts of your application that create an instance of the class.

The most common purpose for creating protected members is that it allows you to put common functionality in one place. For example, you could have a person class and then derive teacher and student classes from that. There will be common things such as name, ID, and so on and common functionality that can be used by both derived classes.

Let's say that a new campus security system is installed. The new system no longer uses a Social Security number as a person's ID. The system generates a random 10-character ID that is a mixture of numbers and characters as the new ID. Only properties and methods in the person class need modification. Those modifications are automatically inherited by the teacher and student classes when the application is compiled. This means that you update the common functionality in one place without having to change the derived classes.

You create a protected method the same way as you create any method, except you use the word `Protected`, such as `Protected Function` or `Sub` *`methodname`*`()`.

Create a Protected Method

1. Open a new project.

Note: See Chapter 1 for more information.

A blank form appears.

2. Drag a `Button` control from the Toolbox to the form.

A button called `Button1` is displayed.

3. Click Project ➔ Add Class.

An empty class definition is displayed.

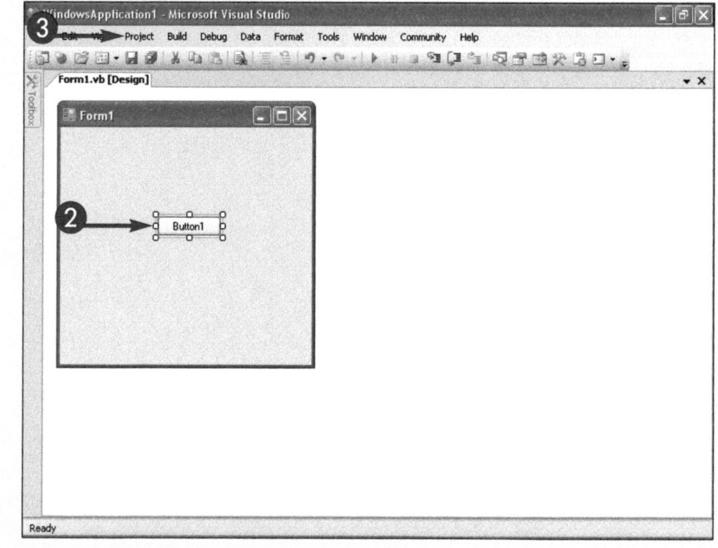

4. Change the class name to a name such as `Message`.
5. Create a protected method that does not return a value by typing `Protected Sub XXX()` followed by `End Sub`, replacing `XXX` with the name of the method, such as `DisplayMessage`.
6. Insert a message box inside the method by typing `MessageBox.Show("XXX")`, replacing `XXX` with a message such as `"Welcome to college."`
7. Click Project ➔ Add Class.

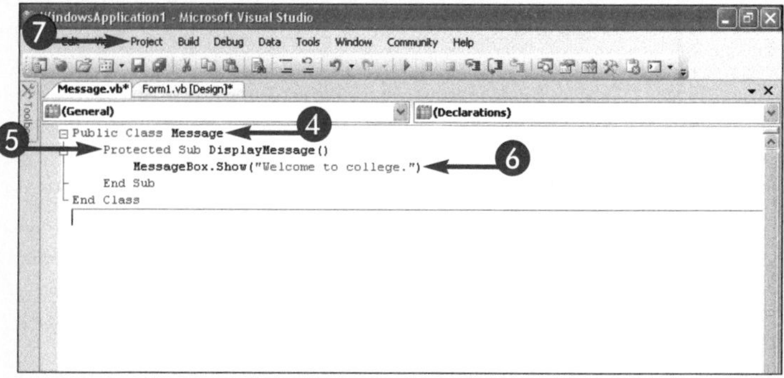

An empty class definition is displayed.

8. Change the class name.

9. Inherit the `Message` class by writing `Inherits Message`.

Note: This class now has access to the protected method in the `Message` class.

10. Create a public method that does not return a value by typing `Public Sub XXX()` followed by `End Sub`, replacing `XXX` with the method name.

11. Insert the call to the `DisplayMessage()` method.

12. Double-click the `Button` control to display its `Click` subroutine.

13. Declare an object by typing `Dim XXX As Object`, replacing `XXX` with the object name.

14. Create an instance of the class and assign it to the object by typing `XXX = New YYY`, replacing `XXX` with the object name and `YYY` with the class name.

15. Call the `GetGreeting` method by typing `XXX.GetGreeting()`, replacing `XXX` with the object name.

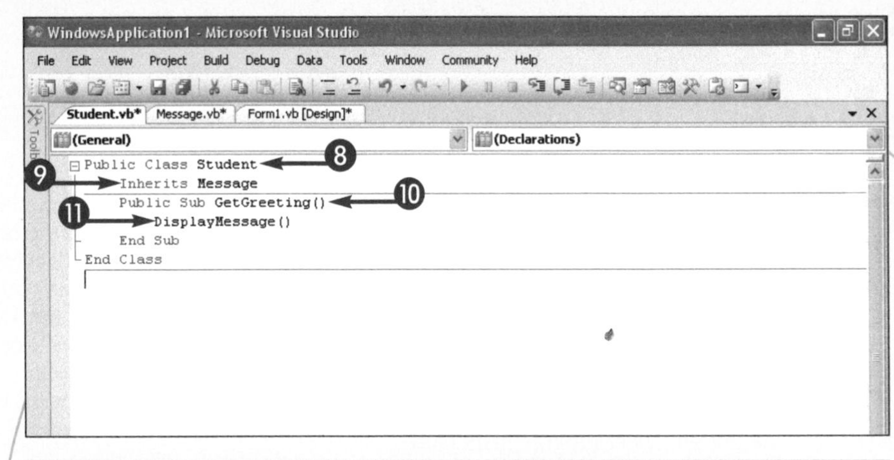

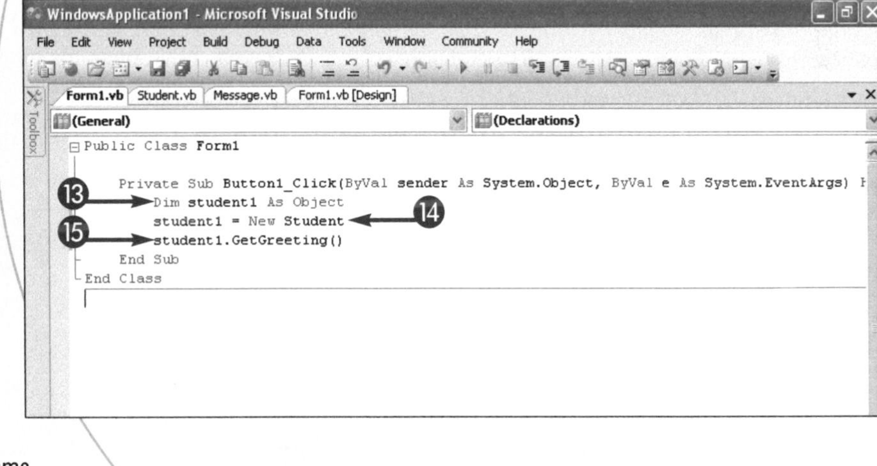

Extra

Protected methods are key elements when designing an object-oriented application because they enable you to build a portion or all parts of a class that is designed for use by other classes rather than directly by the application. Let's say that you are on a design team that develops applications for a college. Many applications require categories of information that is generic among staff, students, and faculty, such as name, address, phone number, emergency contacts, and so on. However, some applications deal with staff, others students, and still others faculty. Each of these has its own categories of information. For example, faculty will have an academic rank such as instructor and professor, department, degrees, and so on. These are in addition to the generic categories of information. The design team creates a class that has protected properties and methods used for generic information. This class is not directly used by an application. Instead, it is designed to be inherited by a class that defines properties and methods for faculty, students, or the staff.

Create a New() Method

The `New()` method is a special method that you can define within a class definition that executes automatically when an instance of the class is created. Although you probably will not need a `New()` method in every application, sometimes you will come across a situation when this method comes in handy.

Some programmers use the `New()` method to set initial values for properties or variables that are accessible from within the class definition. Other programmers place statements in the `New()` method that open connections to resources such as other applications on the network or to the database that will interact with the class's object.

You create a `New()` method by writing `Public Sub New()` followed by `End Sub`. You then insert statements that you want executed when an instance of the class is assigned to an object. The `New()` method can be defined with or without parameters, depending on the nature of your application. Sometimes you will have all the information that you need to execute statements, and therefore you will not require parameters. For example, you may know the Web location of a resource that interacts with the object. Other times you will want the programmer who uses your class to pass your class this information as a parameter to the `New()` method.

Parameters are created for the `New()` method the same way as you create them for other methods. You write `Public Sub New(ByVal` *`parametername`* `As` *`datatype`*`)`. You then use the parameter name within the definition of the `New()` method to refer to the value passed to the method.

Create a New() Method

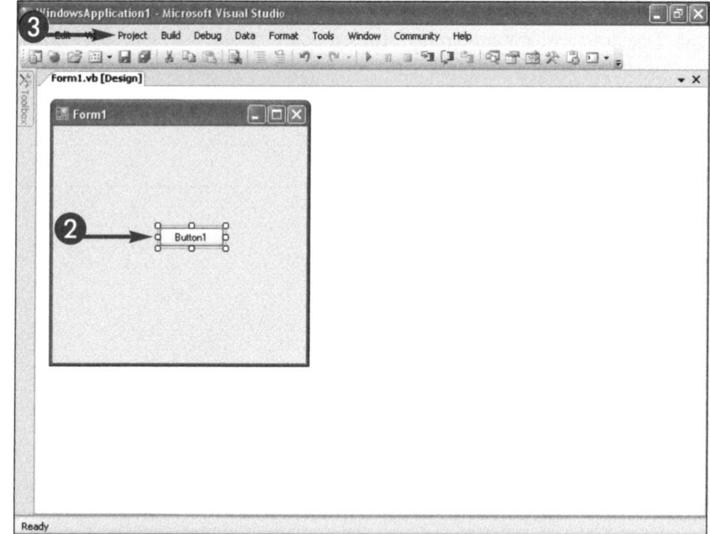

1. Open a new project.

Note: See Chapter 1 for more information.

A blank form appears.

2. Drag a `Button` control from the Toolbox to the form.

A button called `Button1` is displayed.

3. Click Project ➔ Add Class.

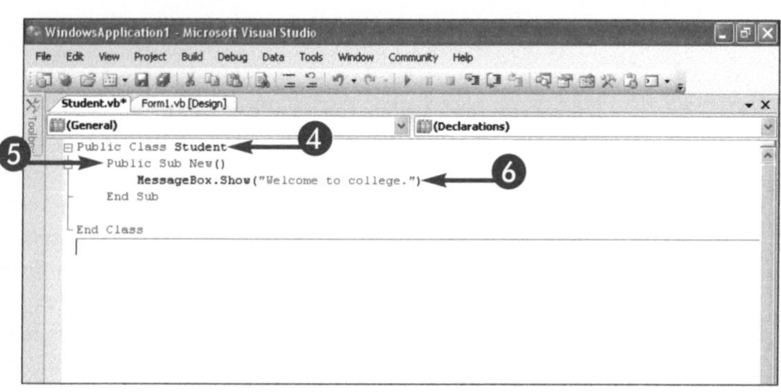

An empty class definition is displayed.

4. Change the class name to a name such as `Student`.

5. Create a `New()` method by typing `Public Sub New()` followed by `End Sub`.

6. Insert a message box inside the method to display a welcome message by typing `MessageBox.Show("XXX")`, replacing `XXX` with a message such as `"Welcome to college."`

7 Double-click the `Button` control on the form.

The `Button1 Click` subroutine is displayed.

8 Declare an object by typing `Dim XXX As Object`, replacing `XXX` with the name of the object, such as `student1`.

9 Create an instance of the class and assign it to the object by typing `XXX = New YYY`, replacing `XXX` with the name of the object, such as `student1`, and replacing `YYY` with the name of the class, such as `Student`.

10 Press F5 to run the program.

11 Click the button to display the message.

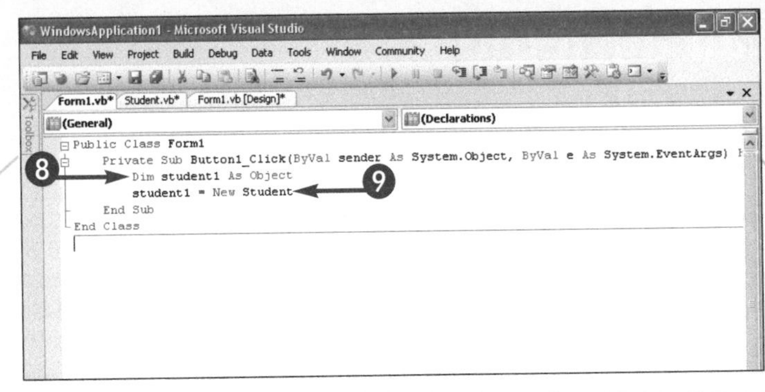

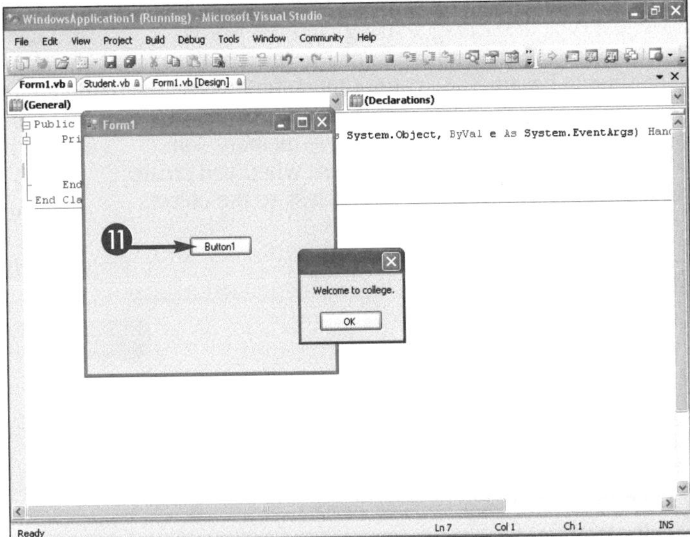

Extra

You can also define a `Finalize()` method in a class definition. The `Finalize()` method is called when the object goes out of scope. You will recall from Chapter 9 that scope defines the part of the program that can access a variable or object. Access is limited to statements within the code block where the variable or object is defined. A code block is defined by a set of open and closed French braces ({ }). Visual Basic .NET leaves a code block when the last statement in the code block is executed or when Visual Basic .NET encounters the `Return` statement. When either of these happen, the variable or object goes out of scope, making it no longer accessible. It is at this point when Visual Basic .NET executes the `Finalize()` method of a class. The `Finalize()` method is not used often except to release connections such as to a database that were used by the class. This is because Visual Basic .NET uses a technique referred to as *garbage collection*, in which it destroys anything left over and no longer needed such as variables and objects.

Call a Method of a Class

In order to call a method, first declare an object and then assign the object an instance of the class, unless you are calling a `Shared` method. The term *object* is sometimes confusing to understand because it is not as definitive as a `String`, `Integer`, or other data types that you can directly relate to a type of data. Think of an object as the real thing that a class describes. This is the same as a `String` data type describing a string, and the words `"Hello world."` are the real `String`. The term *real* may also be confusing because you cannot touch an object. Think of a class describing how much memory to reserve for properties, but a class does not reserve memory. You reserve the memory described by the class when you create an object and assign an instance of the class to the object.

You create an object by writing `Dim` *`name`* `As Object`, where *`name`* is the name that you give to the object. This creates an object, but you still must create an instance of the class and assign the instance to the object. An instance is created and assigned to an object by writing *`name`* `= New` *`classname`*`()`, where *`name`* is the object's name and *`classname`*`()` is the name of the class.

You use the name of the object to access public members of the class. A public member is a property or method that is defined using the keyword `Public`. Properties and methods that are defined using the keyword `Private` are private members and cannot be accessed by the object.

The dot operator is used between the object name and the class member to access the class member. For an object called `student1`, to call the `DisplayMessage()` method, you write `student1.DisplayMessage()`.

Call a Method of a Class

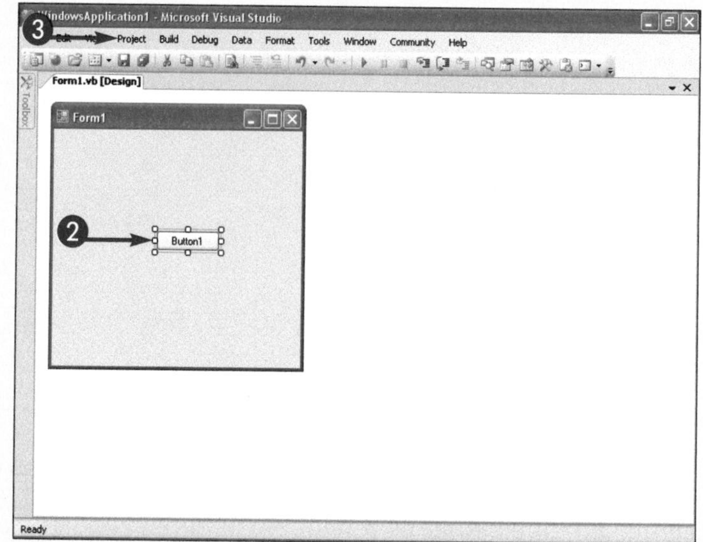

1. Open a new project.

Note: See Chapter 1 for more information.

A blank form appears.

2. Drag a `Button` control from the Toolbox to the form.

A button called `Button1` is displayed.

3. Click Project ➔ Add Class.

An empty class definition is displayed.

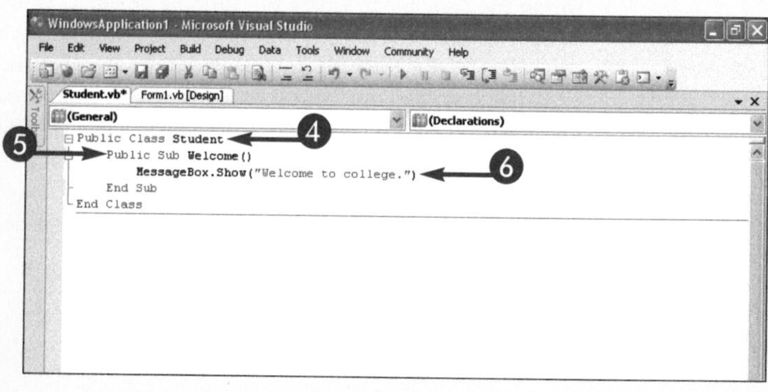

4. Change the class name to a name such as `Student`.

5. Create a public method that does not return a value by typing `Public Sub XXX()` followed by `End Sub`, replacing `XXX` with the name of the method, such as `Welcome`.

6. Insert a message box inside the method by typing `MessageBox.Show("XXX")`, replacing `XXX` with a message such as `"Welcome to college."`

7. Double-click the `Button` control on the form.

The `Button1 Click` subroutine is displayed.

8. Declare an object by typing `Dim XXX As Object`, replacing `XXX` with the object name.

9. Create an instance of the class and assign it to the object by typing `XXX = New YYY`, replacing `XXX` with the object name and `YYY` with the class name.

10. Call the `Welcome` method by typing `XXX.Welcome()`, replacing `XXX` with the name of the object such as `student1`.

11. Press F5 to run the program.

12. Click the button to display the message.

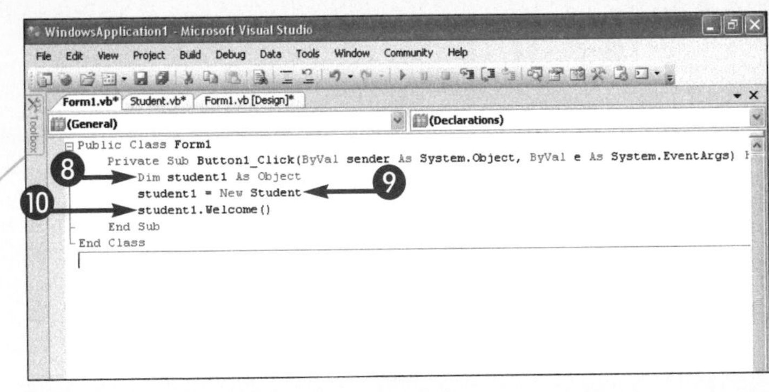

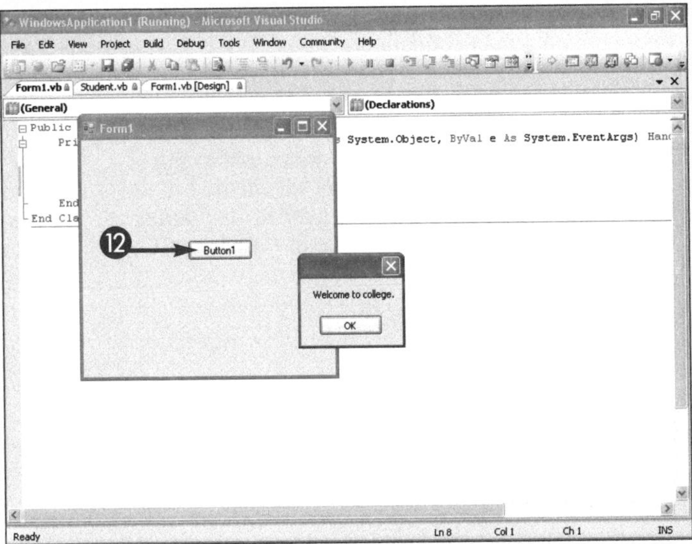

Extra

A method can also be called from a statement within a method defined in the class itself. Let's say that you define two methods in the class definition. These are a method called `CalculateRaise()`, which calculates a pay raise, and `CalculatePayrollTax()`. A statement in `CalculatePayrollTax()` can call the `CalculateRaise()` method before calculating the new payroll tax. When calling a method member of a class from within another method member, you do not have to declare an object or create an instance of the class. Therefore, you also do not have to use the dot operator. Instead, you simply call the method as you would call a function or subroutine elsewhere in your program.

Example

```
Public Sub CalculateRaise()
End Sub
Public Sub CalculatePayrollTax()
CalculateRaise();
End Sub
```

Pass a Value to a Method of a Class

Sometimes a method has all the information that it needs to execute, such as in the previous example where the `Welcome()` method displayed a message that was written into the definition of the method. However, there will be many situations when the method needs additional information that is not available when you define the method. This information becomes available only when the method is called by a statement elsewhere in your application.

In this situation, you define a method to accept one or more values that are passed to it by the statement that calls the method. As you will recall, these values are automatically assigned to parameters that you define for the method in the method's definition. A parameter is very similar to a variable and is used as a placeholder for the value in statements within the method.

You pass a value to the method when the method is called within your application by writing `name.methodname(value)`, where `name` is the name of the object, `methodname` is the name of the method, and `value` is the value that is being passed to the method.

The value must be compatible with the data type of the parameter defined in the method; otherwise, an error occurs. If the method requires multiple parameters, each value passed to the method must appear in the same sequence as its corresponding parameter is defined in the method. Each value must be separated by a comma.

You can pass literal values such as `"Hello world."` and numeric values to the method, or you can use a variable. You can even pass properties of an object of another class to the method.

Pass a Value to a Method of a Class

1. Open a new project.

Note: See Chapter 1 for more information.

A blank form appears.

2. Drag a `Button` control from the Toolbox to the form.

A button called `Button1` is displayed.

3. Click Project ➔ Add Class.

An empty class definition is displayed.

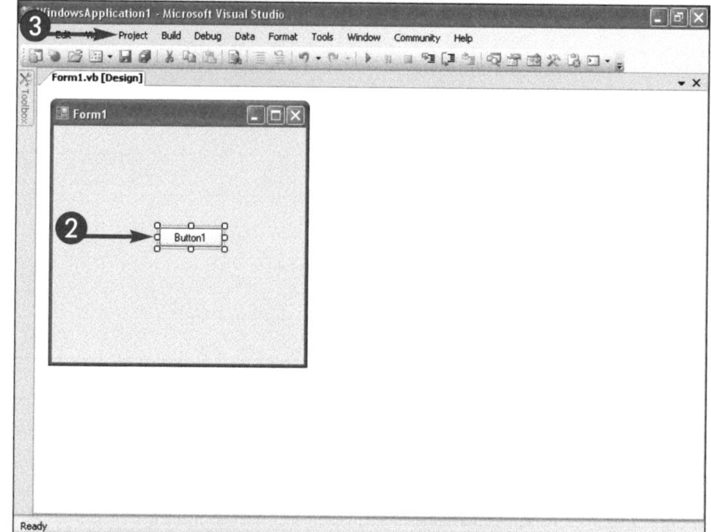

4. Change the class name.

5. Create a public method that does not return a value by typing `Public Sub XXX(ByVal YYY As ZZZ)` followed by `End Sub`, replacing `XXX` with the method name, `YYY` with the parameter name, and `ZZZ` with the data type of the parameter.

6. Insert a message box inside the method by typing `MessageBox.Show(YYY)`, replacing `YYY` with the parameter name.

7. Double-click the `Button` control on the form.

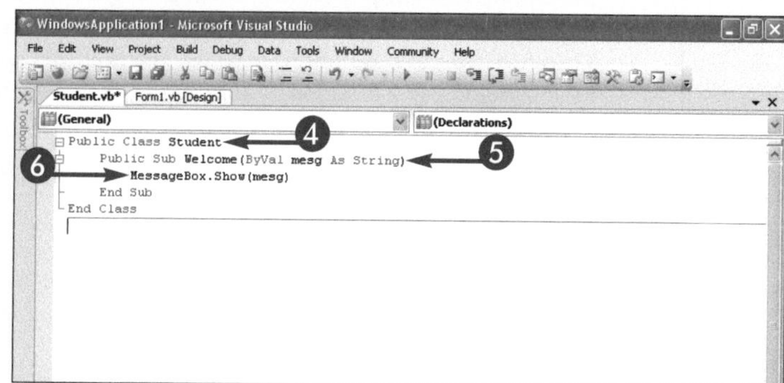

The `Button1 Click` subroutine is displayed.

8. Declare an object by typing `Dim XXX As Object`, replacing `XXX` with the object name.

9. Create an instance of the class and assign it to the object by typing `XXX = New YYY`, replacing `XXX` with the object name and `YYY` with the class name.

10. Call the `Welcome` method by typing `XXX.Welcome(YYY)`, replacing `XXX` with the object name and `YYY` with the value being passed to the method.

11. Press F5 to run the program.

12. Click the button to display the message.

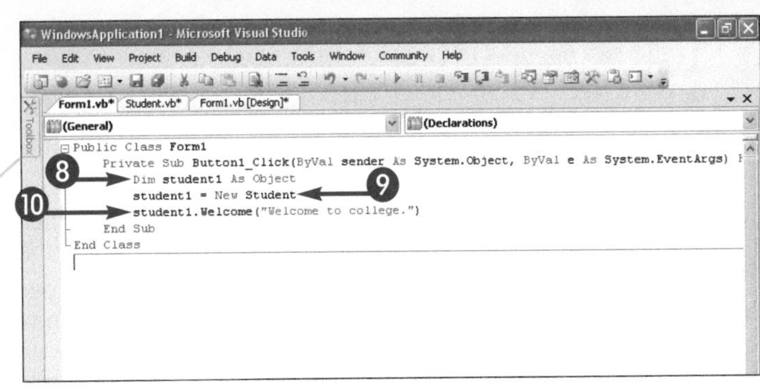

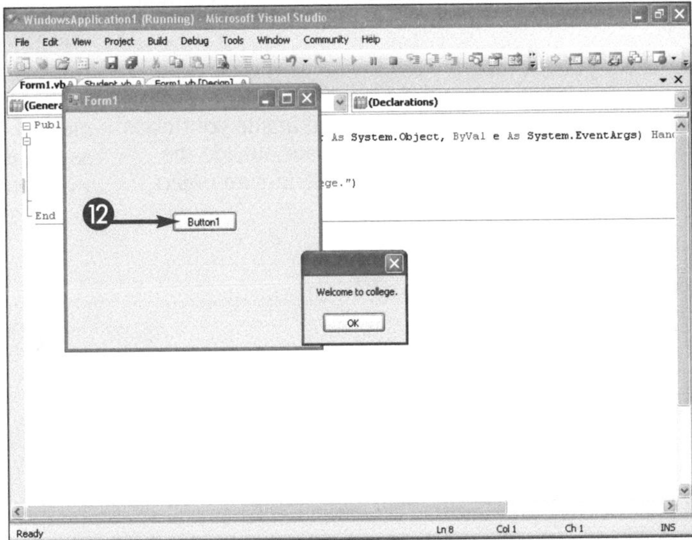

Extra

Objects that you drag from the Toolbox and drop on to the form are instances of predefined classes. For example, when you drag and drop the `TextBox` control, you are creating an instance of the `TextBox` class. The instance is automatically called `TextBox1`, if this is the first `TextBox` on the form. You can pass a property of one of these objects to your own method by using the instance name, the dot operator, and the name of the property. Let's say that you defined the `Welcome()` method, which displays a message passed to it by code in your application. This message can be entered by the user into a `TextBox` control on the form, and you can pass the `Text` property of that control to the `Welcome()` method such as `name.Welcome(TextBox1.Text)`, where `name` is the name of the object of your class and `TextBox1` is the name of the `TextBox` control object on the form.

Assign a Value to a Public Property

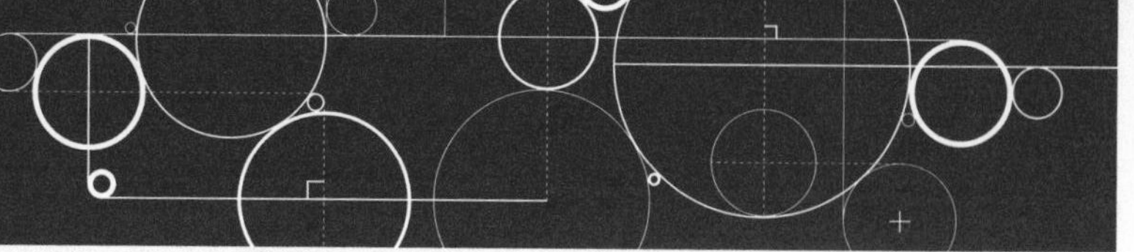

A public property of a class is similar to a variable that you declare in your application, except a public property is declared within the definition of a class. You declare a public property by writing `Public` *`propertyname`* `As` *`data type`*. The property name is similar to the name that you use for a variable. The data type describes the kind of data that can be assigned to the property.

You can use a public property both inside your class and outside the class just as you would use a variable. A public property can be used by a method declared inside your class definition. It can also be used by a statement outside the class definition; however, you first must declare an object and then assign it an instance of the class before accessing the public property.

A value is assigned to a public property using the assignment operator. Let's say that the public property `FirstName` is declared as a `String`. You assign a value to it by writing *`objectname`*`.FirstName = "Bob"`. You will need to replace *`objectname`* with the name of the object that you declared in your application.

However, you do not need to declare an object if you are assigning the value to the public property within a method defined in your class definition. Instead, you assign it as you would assign any variable by writing `FirstName = "Bob"`.

Assign a Value to a Public Property

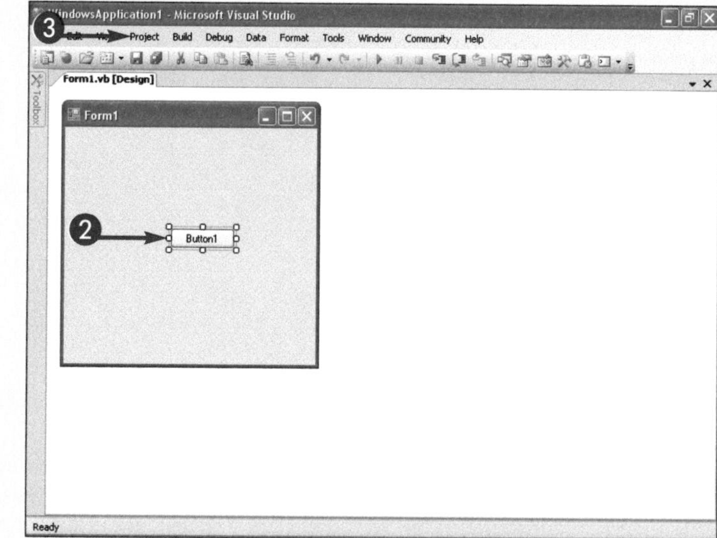

1. Open a new project.

Note: See Chapter 1 for more information.

A blank form appears.

2. Drag a `Button` control from the Toolbox to the form.

A button called `Button1` is displayed.

3. Click Project ➔ Add Class.

An empty class definition is displayed.

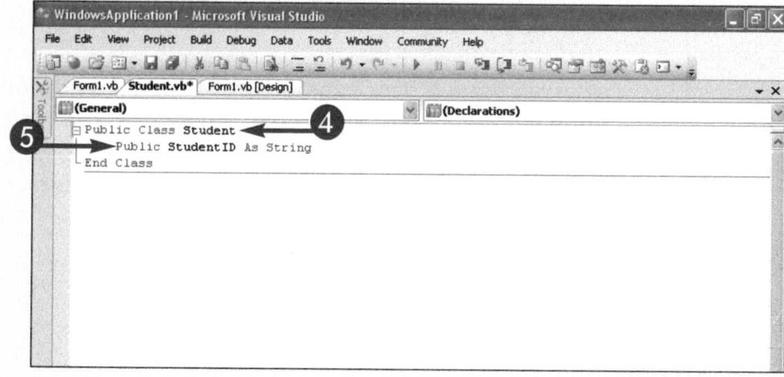

4. Change the class name to a name such as `Student`.

5. Declare a public property by typing `Public XXX As YYY`, replacing `XXX` with the name of the property, such as `StudentID`, and replacing `YYY` with its data type, such as `String`.

6. Double-click the `Button` control on the form.

The `Button1 Click` subroutine is displayed.

7. Declare an object by typing `Dim XXX As Object`, replacing `XXX` with the object name.

8. Create an instance of the class and assign it to the object by typing `XXX = New YYY`, replacing `XXX` with the object name and `YYY` with the class name.

9. Assign a value to the public property by typing `XXX.YYY = ZZZ`, replacing `XXX` with the object name, `YYY` with the name of the public property, and `ZZZ` with a value.

10. Display the public property like this.

11. Press F5 to run the program.

12. Click the button to display the message.

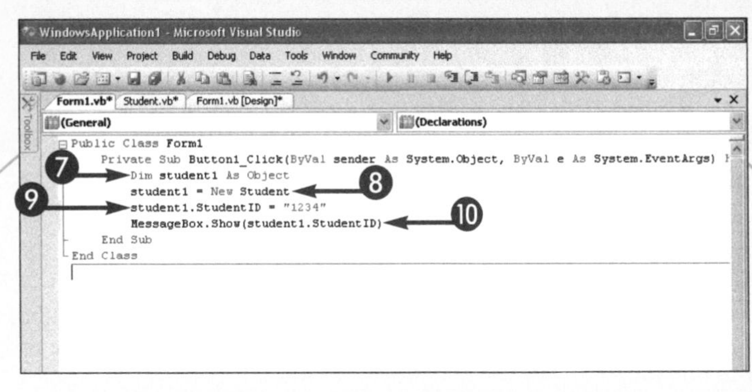

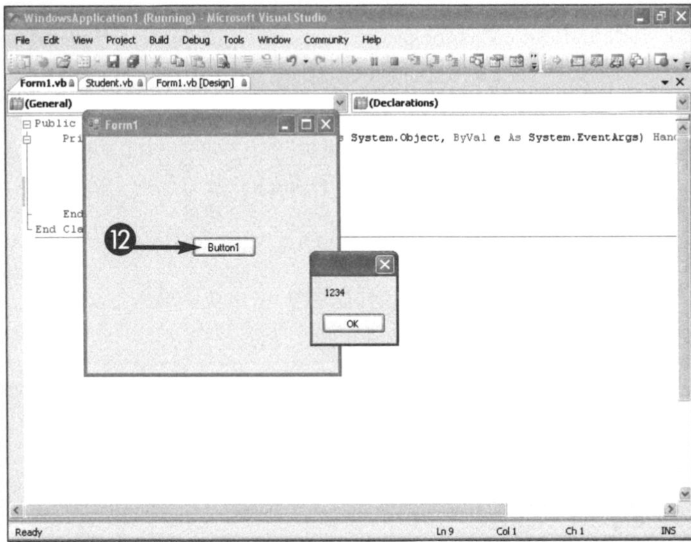

Extra

Although a statement anywhere in your application can assign a value to a public property after an instance of the class is assigned to an object, it cannot assign a value to a protected or private property of a class. You can assign a value to a protected property in one of two ways. First, a method defined in the class definition that also defined the protected property can assign a value to the protected property. Also, a method defined in a class that is derived from the class that defined the protected property can assign it a value. A *derived class* is a class that inherits the class where the protected property is defined. You can assign a value to a private property by using a method that is a member of the same class. When you are updating a private member of a base class, you do not create an instance of the class, and therefore you do not need to use the dot operator.

Create a Property Procedure for a Class

A *property* is data encapsulated within the class definition. A property is created by defining a property procedure. A *property procedure* consists of two constructs called `Get` and `Set`. The `Get` construct is used to get a value of a read-only property. Code that accesses this property can use its value but cannot modify it. The `Set` construct is used to assign a value for a write property. Code that accesses the property can change the value of the property. If both the `Get` and `Set` constructs have values, the property is referred to as a *read-write property.* Code that accesses a read-write property can read data assigned to the property and modify it.

A property procedure can be `Public` or `Private`. A `Public` property procedure is accessible from code that creates an object of that class. A property procedure is created within a class definition by writing `Public Property` *`name`*`()` `As` *`data type`* followed by `End Property`. `Public` specifies which code can access the property. The *`name`* is the name of the property. The *`data type`* specifies the data type of the property.

You place the `Get` and `Set` constructs between the name of the property and `End Property`. The `Get` construct is written as `Get` followed by the `Return` statement and a value that is assigned to the property. It closes with `End Get`. The `Set` construct has a parameter that is assigned a value by the code that accesses the property. You write a `Set` construct as `Set (ByVal` *`name`* `As String)` followed by `End Set`. The *`name`* is whatever name that you assign as the parameter. You can use this name within the body of the `Set` construct.

You can make the property read-only or write-only by using the keyword `ReadOnly` or `WriteOnly` in the property definition.

Create a Property Procedure for a Class

1. Open a new project.

Note: See Chapter 1 for more information.

A blank form appears.

2. Click Project ➔ Add Class.

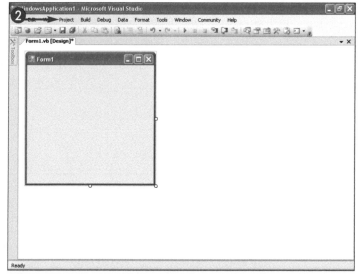

An empty class definition is displayed.

3. Change the class name to a name such as `Student`.

4. Create a `Private` property as a `String` data type, such as `mesg` here.

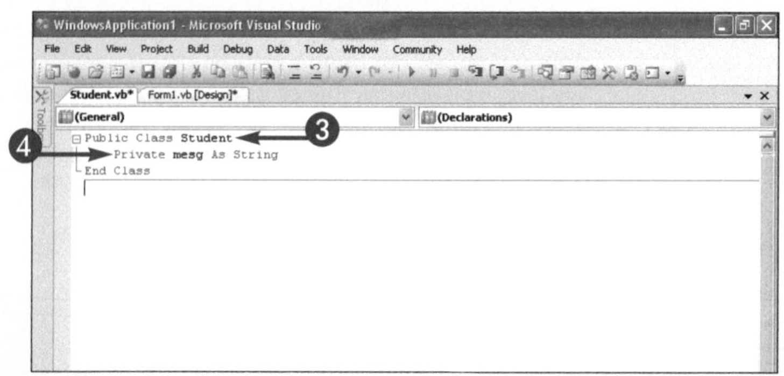

5 Create a property procedure by typing `Public Property XXX() As YYY`, replacing `XXX` with the name of the property, such as `Message()`, and replacing `YYY` with the data type of the property, such as `String`.

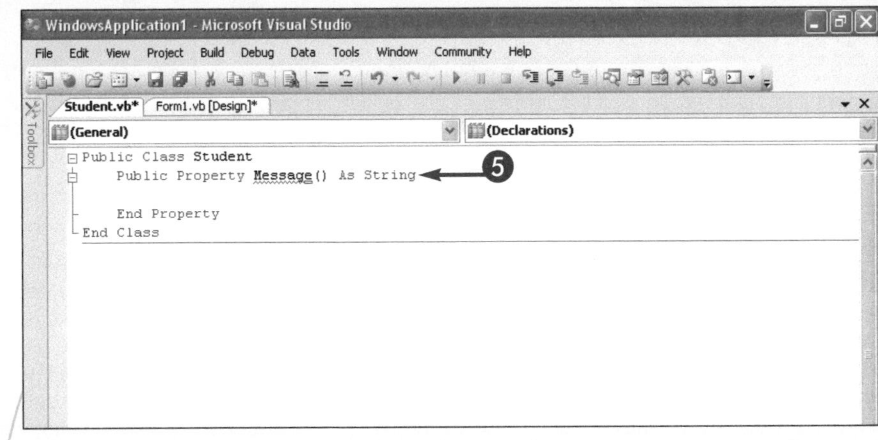

6 Create a `Get` that returns an empty `String` by typing `Get Return ""` and `End Get`.

7 Create a `Set` by typing `Set (ByVal value As String)` followed by `End Set`.

Note: The code that accesses this property assigns data to it that is represented within the `Set` as the `value` parameter.

8 Inside the `Set`, assign the `value` parameter to the `mesg` property.

Note: The `mesg` property is `Private` and therefore accessible by code from within the class definition.

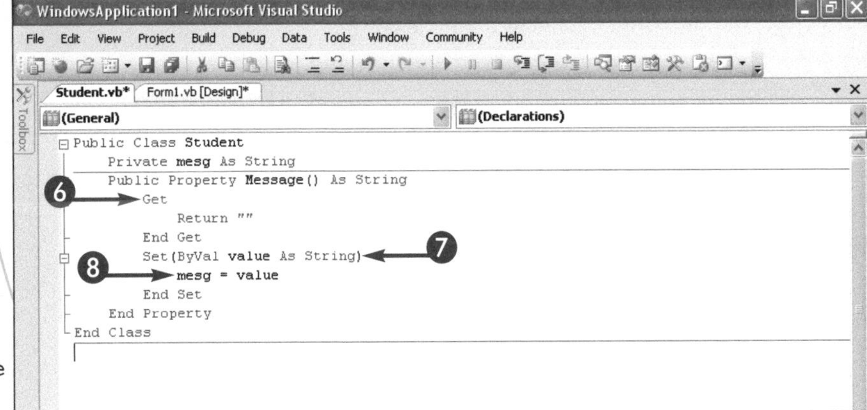

Extra

You can declare a property as a non-property procedure by declaring it similarly to how a variable is declared. You write `Private name As data type`, in which you replace `name` with the name of the property and `data type` with the data type of the property. This property can be accessed by a property procedure by writing the following:

```
Private mesg As String
Public Property name() As String
        Get
            Return mesg
        End Get
        Set(ByVal Value As String)
            mesg = Value
        End Set
    End Property
```

Get a Value of a Property Procedure

A property is a data member of a class. You can access public properties by declaring an object and then assigning it an instance of the class. You cannot access private properties of a class from outside the class definition. As you will recall, there are two ways to access a property. These are reading the value assigned to the property or assigning a value to the property. In order to do either, the property must be defined as a property procedure as described earlier in this chapter. The `Get` construct of the property procedure lets your object read the current value of the property, and the `Set` construct lets your object assign a value to the property.

You access a property of the class by writing *`name.propertyname`*, where *`name`* is the name of the object of the class and *`propertyname`* is the name of the property. You can use *`name.propertyname`* to represent the value of the property in statements just as you use the name of a variable to reference the value of the variable. It is important to remember the data type of the property so that you do not use the property in a statement that has an incompatible data type.

Get a Value of a Property Procedure

1. Open a new project.

   Note: See Chapter 1 for more information.

   A blank form appears.

2. Drag a `Button` control from the Toolbox to the form.

   A button called `Button1` is displayed.

3. Click Project ➔ Add Class.

   An empty class definition is displayed.

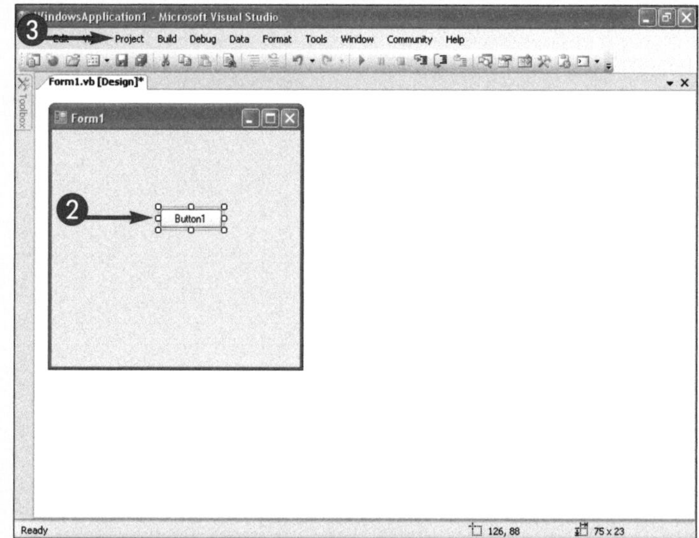

4. Change the class name.

5. Create a public property procedure by typing `Public Property XXX As YYY` followed by `End Property`, replacing `XXX` with the name of the property and `YYY` with the data type of the property.

6. Insert a `Get` inside the property procedure by writing `Get Return XXX End Get`, replacing `XXX` with the value of the property.

7. Insert a `Set` inside the property procedure by writing `Set (ByVal value As String) End Set.`

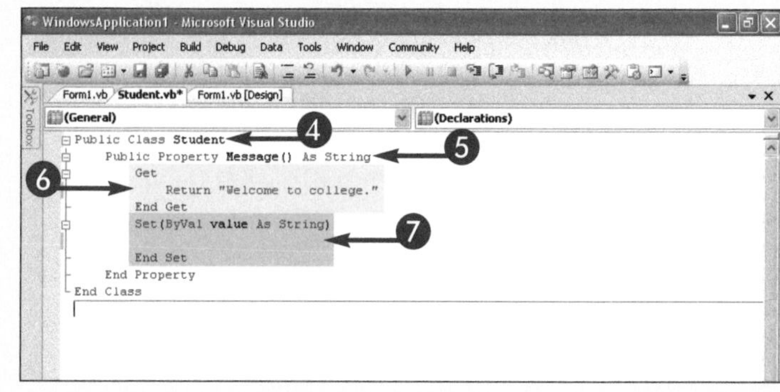

8. Double-click the `Button` control to display the `Click` subroutine.

9. Declare an object by typing `Dim XXX As Object`, replacing `XXX` with the object name.

10. Create an instance of the class and assign it to the object by typing `XXX = New YYY`, replacing `XXX` with the object name and `YYY` with the class name.

11. Display the value of the property by writing `MessageBox.Show(XXX.YYY)`, replacing `XXX` with the object name and `YYY` with the property name.

12. Press F5 to run the program.

13. Click the button to display the message.

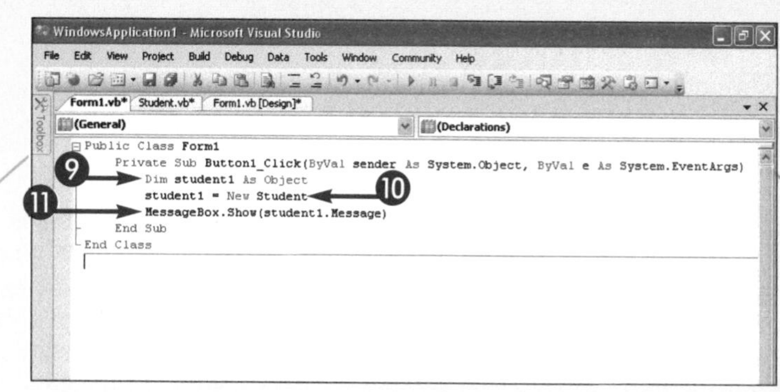

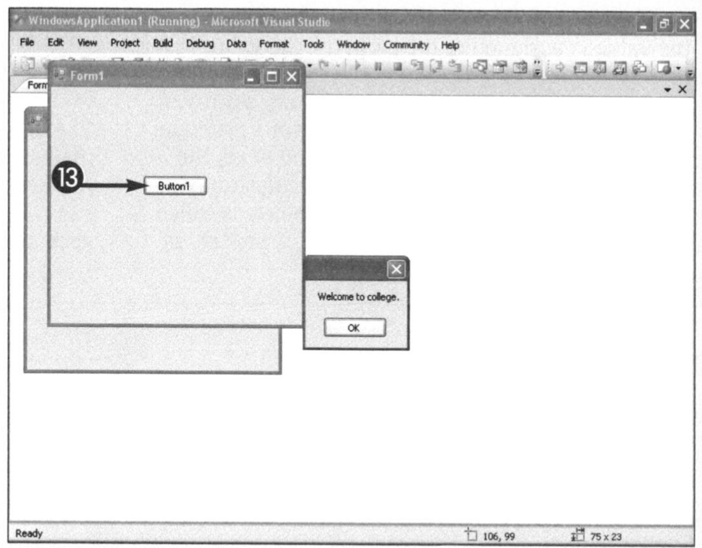

Extra

The `Get` construct can execute one or more statements whenever a statement from the application accesses the property's value. Let's say that a property is called `Salary` and its value is either the current salary or the new salary, if permission was granted to give the employee a raise. Before returning the value, the `Get` construct can determine if permission was granted by using an `If...Then` statement.

Example

```
Get
    If RaiseApproved = True Then
        Return Salary * (1 + Raise)
    Else
        Return Salary
    End If
End Get
```

Set a Value of a Property Procedure

A public property that is defined as writable can be assigned a value from an object of its class. The value can then be used internally within the class, depending on the nature of your application. For example, the value can be assigned to a private property by a statement within the `Set` construct, or statements within the `Set` construct can be used to validate the value.

After the value is assigned to the property, the value remains with the property until the object goes out of scope. *Out of scope* means that Visual Basic .NET has destroyed the object and its properties. Let's say that you created an object within a function. The object is created when the function is called and goes out of scope — is destroyed — when the function stops executing. A new object is called the next time the function is called, creating a new set of properties. Values assigned to the previous object are no longer available.

You can assign a value to the property the same way as you assign a value to a variable, except that you must use both the object name and the property name separated by the dot operator. Let's say that you want to assign a `String` to the `Message` property. You write `student1.Message = "Welcome to college."` In this example, `student1` is the name of the object, and `Message` is the name of the property.

The value assigned to the property must be compatible with the property's data type; otherwise, an error occurs. You can assign a property a literal value such as `"Welcome to College."`, a variable, or the property of another object, such as the `Text` property of an object of the `TextBox` class.

Set a Value of a Property Procedure

1. Open a new project.

Note: See Chapter 1 for more information.

A blank form appears.

2. Drag a `Button` control from the Toolbox to the form.

A button called `Button1` is displayed.

3. Click Project ➔ Add Class.

An empty class definition is displayed.

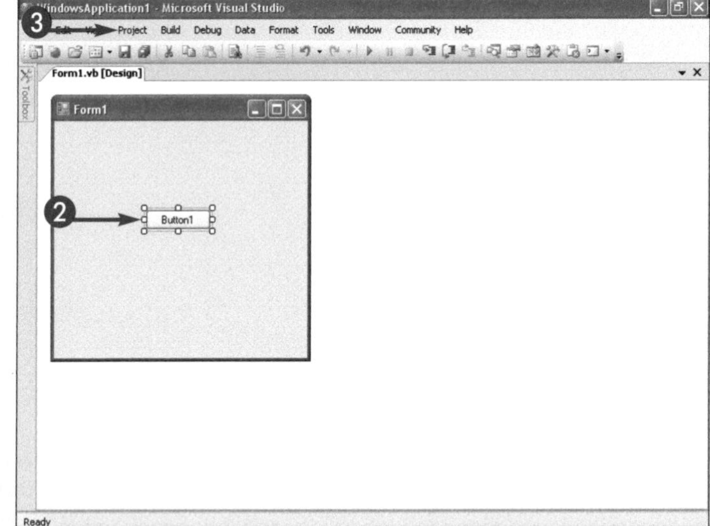

4. Change the class name.
5. Create a private property by writing `Private XXX As YYY`, replacing `XXX` with a property name and `YYY` with the data type.
6. Create a public property procedure by typing `Public Property XXX As YYY` followed by `End Property`, replacing `XXX` with the property name and `YYY` with the data type.
7. Insert a `Get` construct by writing `Get Return "" End Get`.

Note: This returns an empty `String`.

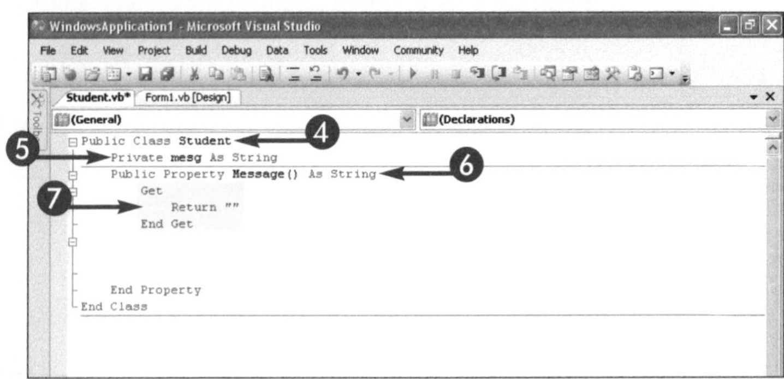

8 Insert a `Set` construct inside the property procedure by writing `Set (ByVal value As String) End Set`.

Note: This is where you make the property writable by the object.

9 Insert into the `Set` construct the statement that assigns the `value` to the private property by writing `XXX = value`, replacing `XXX` with the name of the private property, such as `mesg`.

10 Double-click the `Button` control on the form.

The `Button1 Click` subroutine is displayed.

11 Declare an object by typing `Dim XXX As Object`, replacing `XXX` with the object name.

12 Create an instance of the class and assign it to the object by typing `XXX = New YYY`, replacing `XXX` with the object name and `YYY` with the class name.

13 Assign a value to the property by writing `XXX.YYY = ZZZ`, replacing `XXX` with the object name, `YYY` with the property name, and `ZZZ` with value assigned to the property, such as `"Welcome to college."`

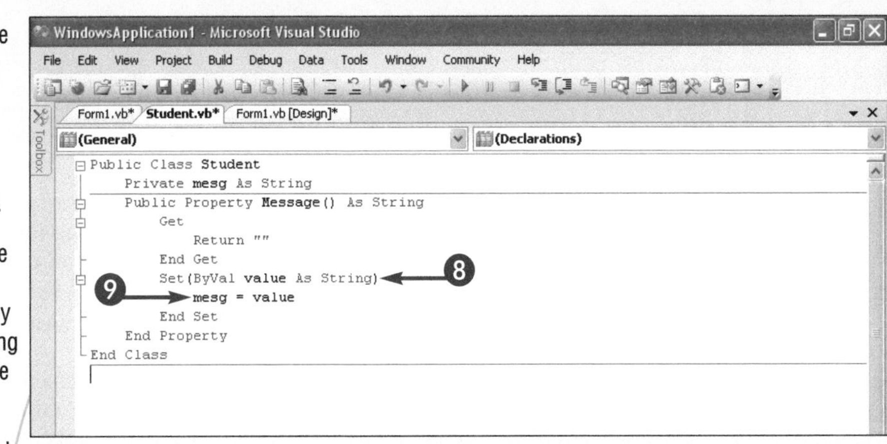

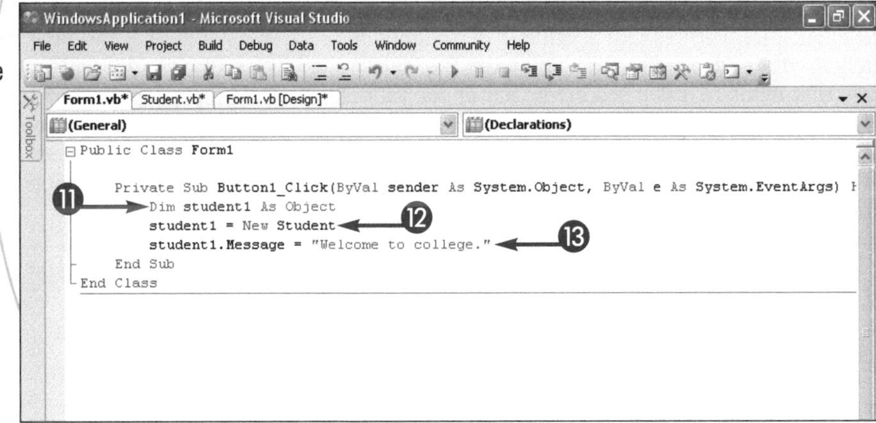

Extra

Sometimes you will find yourself in a situation where the value assigned to a property must be also assigned to other properties, variables, or controls on the form. The `Set` construct is perfect for this purpose because you can insert statements within the `Set` construct to do something when a statement assigns it a value. You can do this by placing statements within the `Set` construct and using the value as required by your application. For example, here is how you assign the value to a `TextBox` control. First, you must place the control on the form and then be sure to reference the instance of the form (Form1) in the statement; otherwise, Visual Basic .NET will not know where to find the `TextBox` control. If you type **Form1.**, a pop-up menu appears where you can choose the control. After the control is chosen, insert a dot operator, and another pop-up menu appears listing the properties for the control such as `Text`.

Example

```
Set(ByVal value As String)
      Form1.TextBox1.Text = value
End Set
```

Validate a Property Value

You can place statements with the `Set` construct of a property procedure to do something with the value assigned to the property by the object declared outside the class definition. They execute automatically whenever another part of your application assigns a value to the property.

Sometimes you will simply write a statement to assign the value to another public or private property. Other times you may want to perform more complex operations using the value, such as validating it. *Validation* is when a part of your application verifies that a value is reasonably or definitely accurate, depending how you write the code. Let's say that items that you sell are priced under $100. You could validate a new price assigned to a property by determining if the new price is under $100. This means that the price is probably valid. Similarly, you can write code to decide the accuracy of a zip code assigned to a property by comparing the zip code to a list of valid zip codes. This means that the zip code is valid if it is on the list.

You validate a value assigned to a property by using a conditional statement — either an `If...Then` statement or a `Select Case` statement — both of which you learned about in Chapter 6. Your choice depends on the number of valid items. If you have many items, a `Select Case` statement is best to use; otherwise, use an `If...Then` statement or a variation of it.

Place the conditional statement inside the `Set` construct of the property procedure. Use the value assigned to the property in the conditional expression. You will recall that the conditional expression is used by Visual Basic .NET to determine if the value is valid.

Validate a Property Value

1. Open a new project.

Note: See Chapter 1 for more information.

A blank form appears.

2. Drag a `Button` control from the Toolbox to the form.

A button called `Button1` is displayed.

3. Click Project ➔ Add Class.

An empty class definition is displayed.

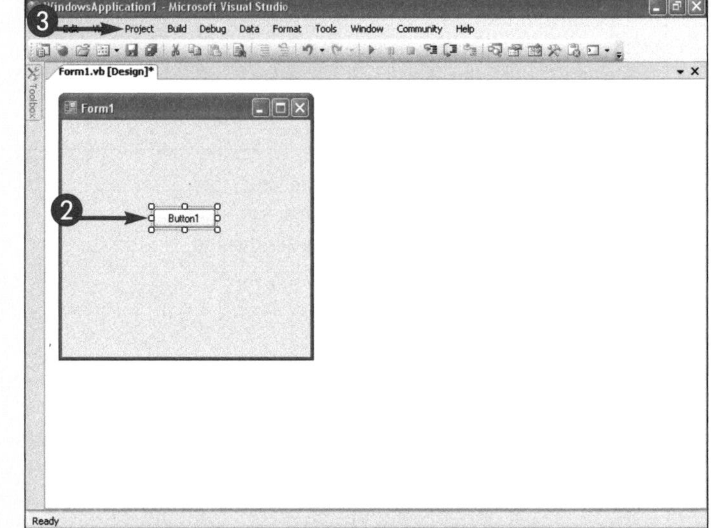

4. Change the class name to a name such as `Student`.
5. Create a public property procedure by typing `Public Property XXX As YYY` followed by `End Property`, replacing `XXX` with the property name such as `Housing` and `YYY` with the data type of the property such as `String`.
6. Insert a `Get` construct inside the property procedure by writing `Get Return "" End Get`.

Note: This returns an empty `String`.

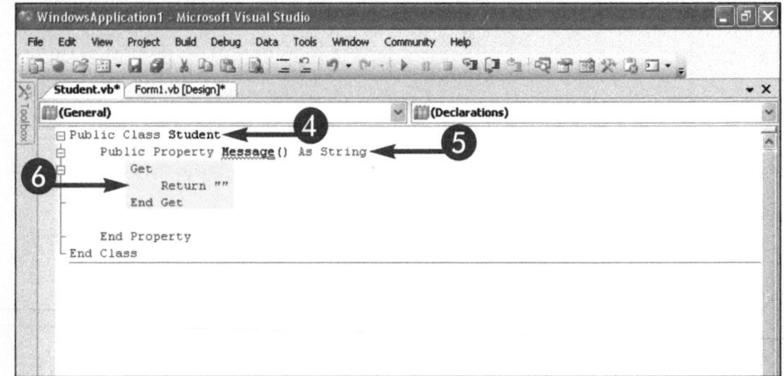

7 Insert a `Set` construct procedure by writing `Set (ByVal value As String) End Set`.

Note: This is where you make the property writable by the object.

8 Insert into the `Set` construct an `If...Then` statement that compares `value` to a value such as `"Dorm"`.

9 Insert a message box into the code block of the `If...Then` statement by writing `MessageBox.Show("XXX")`, replacing `XXX` with a message.

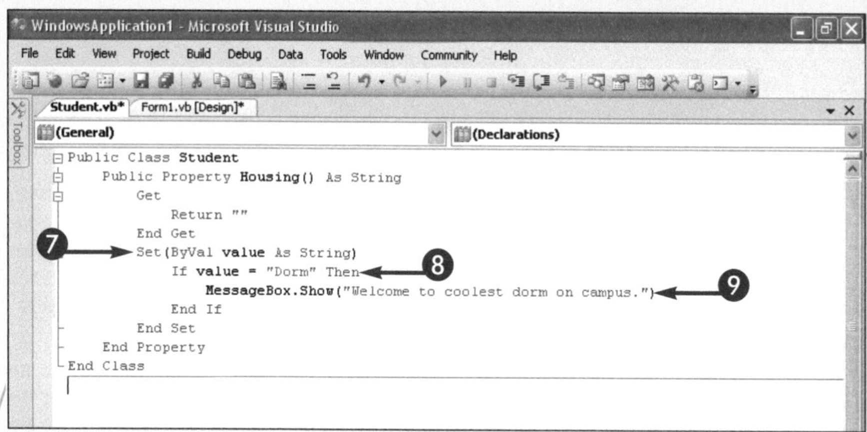

10 Double-click the `Button` control to display its `Click` subroutine.

11 Declare an object by typing `Dim XXX As Object`, replacing `XXX` with the object name.

12 Create an instance of the class and assign it to the object by typing `XXX = New YYY`, replacing `XXX` with the object name and `YYY` with the class name.

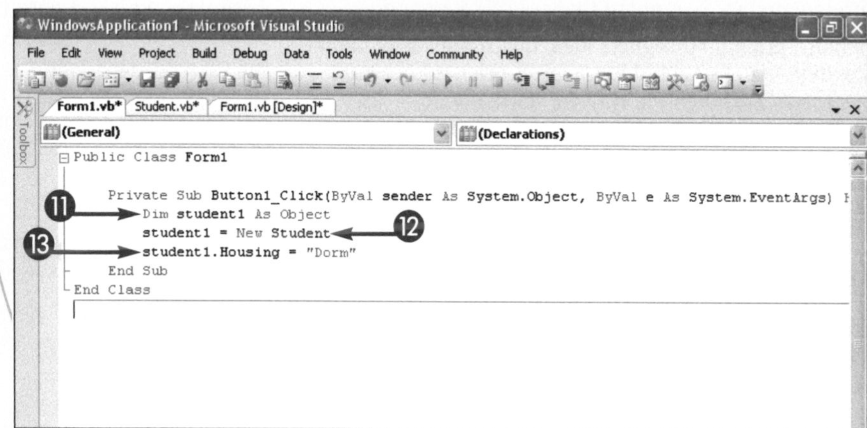

13 Assign a value to the property by writing `XXX.YYY = ZZZ`, replacing `XXX` with the object name, `YYY` with the property name, and `ZZZ` with value assigned to the property.

Extra

You can use values already entered into a control on the form to validate the value of a property. Let's say that the user enters city, state, and zip code on an address form. A zip code is entered into a `TextBox` rather than picked from a long list. This risks that the user will enter the wrong zip code. Therefore, the application should compare the zip code and the city to a database of zip codes. One way to do so is to place code in the `Set` construct of the property. Statements in the `Set` construct can use the zip code to look up the name of a city in a database and then compare the city to the city entered in the City `TextBox` on the form.

```
Set(ByVal value As String)
   'Place statements to search the zip code database here
    If Form1.City.Text <> dbCity Then
       MessageBox.Show("Invalid Zip Code.")
    End If
End Set
```

Inherit a Class

You probably heard that Visual Basic .NET is an object-oriented programming language, but you may not be familiar with the term *object-oriented.* This term refers to how programs are designed. We look at things in the real world as objects such as a student rather than data and functionality. We say there is a person. We do not say 6 feet tall, brown hair, blue eyes, and walks and talks. The person's height and colored hair and eyes are data. Walking and talking are functions. Data and functions are encapsulated into an object that we call a *person.*

Traditionally, program designers looked at things as data and functionality — not as an object. Object-oriented program designers look at things the way we normally do — as objects. They use a class definition to define an object in a program.

The term *object* has two meanings in object-oriented programming. It is used to describe a real-world thing such as a student — called an *object* in the everyday sense of the word. The term is also used to refer to an instance of a class — called an *object* in the object-oriented programming sense of the word.

Real-world things are made of other objects. An object that is made from another object inherits the characteristics of that other object. The class that is being inherited is called a *base* class, and the class that inherits the base class is called the *derived* class. A class is inherited by writing in the derived class `Inherits XXX`, where `XXX` is the name of the base class. An object of the derived class can access the public and protected members of the base class just as if those members were defined in the derived class.

Inherit a Class

1. Open a new project.

Note: See Chapter 1 for more information.

A blank form appears.

2. Drag a `Button` control from the Toolbox to the form.

A button called `Button1` is displayed.

3. Click Project ➔ Add Class.

An empty class definition is displayed.

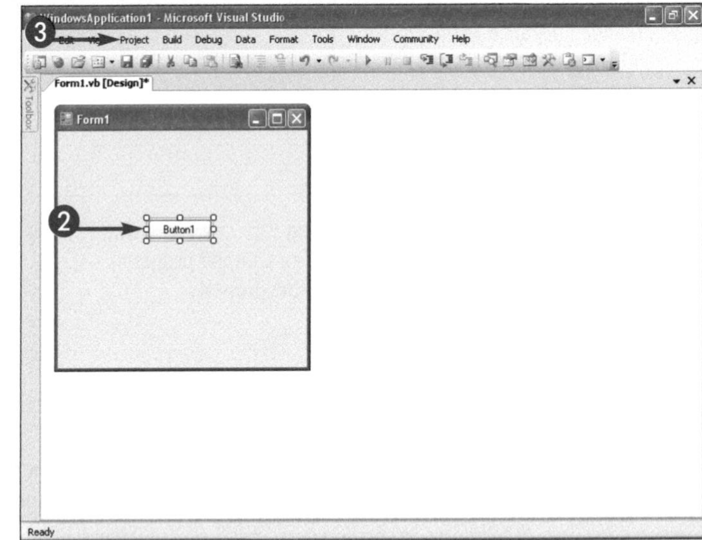

4. Change the class name to a name such as `Class1`.
5. Create a public method that does not return a value by typing `Public Sub XXX()` followed by `End Sub`, replacing `XXX` with the method name such as `Welcome`.
6. Insert a message box inside the method by typing `MessageBox.Show("XXX")`, replacing `XXX` with a message such as `"Welcome to college."`

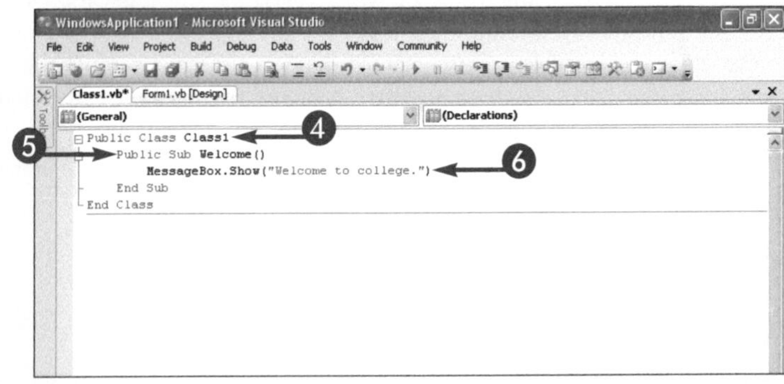

7 Click Project ➔ Add Class.

An empty class definition is displayed.

8 Change the class name to a name such as Class2.

9 Inherit Class1 by writing Inherits Class1.

Note: Class2 has access to the method in Class1.

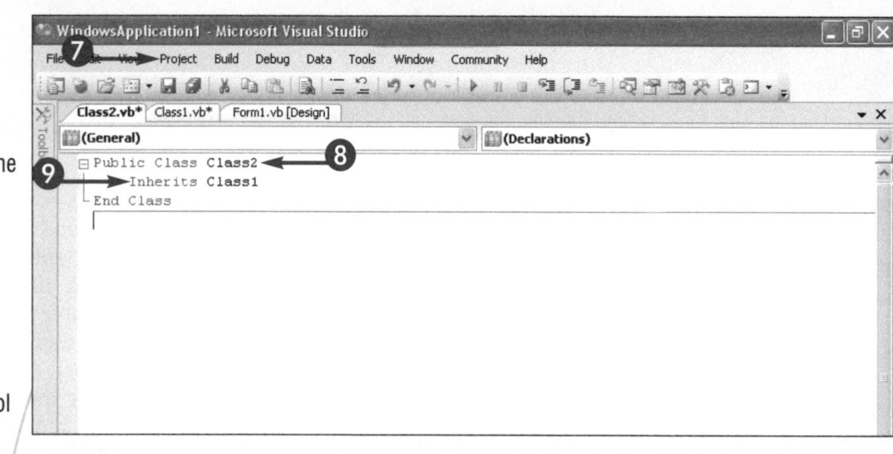

10 Double-click the Button control on the form.

The Button1 Click subroutine is displayed.

11 Declare an object by typing Dim XXX As Object, replacing XXX with the object name.

12 Create an instance of the class and assign it to the object by typing XXX = New Class2, replacing XXX with the object name.

13 Call the Welcome method by typing XXX.Welcome(), replacing XXX with the object name.

14 Press F5 to run the program.

15 Click the button to display the message.

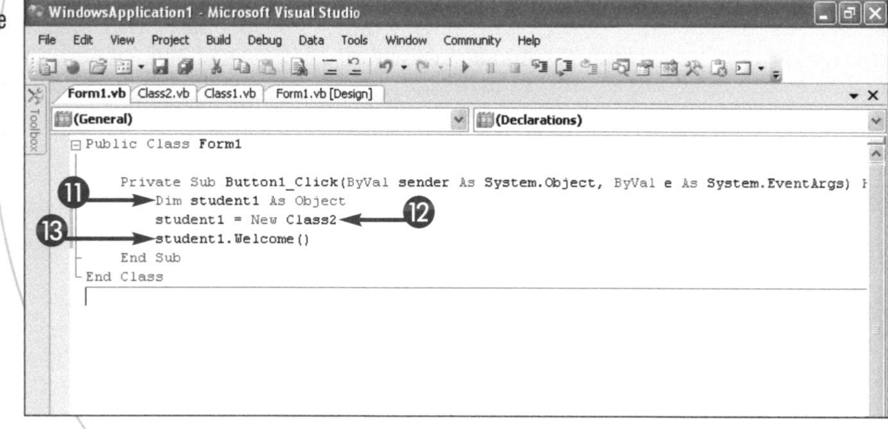

Extra

Object-oriented program designers create classes that can be inherited by other classes to mimic the relationships of real-world objects. For example, these designers may create a person class that encapsulates data (properties) and functionality (methods) that are associated with a person. Likewise, they may create a student class that inherits the person class and encapsulates its own data and functionality that are associated only with a student. For example, a person object has characteristics of height and colored hair and eyes and walks and talks. A student inherits these characteristics from the person object.

Some classes are designed to be base classes and not used directly by an application. For example, you may have a class that defines characteristics of a person such as name, address, phone number, and so on. However, you only want this class accessed by other classes that define characteristics of a type of person such as a faculty member or student. You can prevent a statement from creating an instance of a class by designating the class as MustInherit by writing

```
MustInherit Class Class1.
End Class
```

Using Overloading

Overloading is a term that you may have heard when reading about object-oriented programming, but you may not have fully understood its meaning. Literally, *overload* simply means that a method can have the same name and various sets of parameters, depending on the nature of the application. Let's say that you created a `WelcomeMessage()` method that displays a message on the screen. One version of this method has no parameters, which means that the message is contained in the method definition. You can have another version called `WelcomeMessage(ByVal msg As String)`. The message is passed as a parameter. And you can have still another version called `WelcomeMessage(ByVal msg As String, name As String)`. This version personalized the message by combining the `name` and `msg` parameters.

So why would you use overloading? You use it to make it easy for a programmer to use your methods. In the days before object-oriented programming languages, each method had to have a different name. This means that we would have had to have three different names for the `WelcomeMessage()` method — and the programmer would have to remember each of them. Thanks to overloading, you can use the same name, making it easier for the programmer. All that the programmer needs to remember are the parameters, if any, to use.

Visual Basic .NET identifies a method by a combination of its name and parameters. You can have a variation of parameters by data type and by position, and each variation is considered by Visual Basic .NET as a different method.

Using Overloading

1. Open a new project.

Note: See Chapter 1 for more information.

A blank form appears.

2. Drag a `Button` control from the Toolbox to the form.

A button called `Button1` is displayed.

3. Click Project ➔ Add Class.

An empty class definition is displayed.

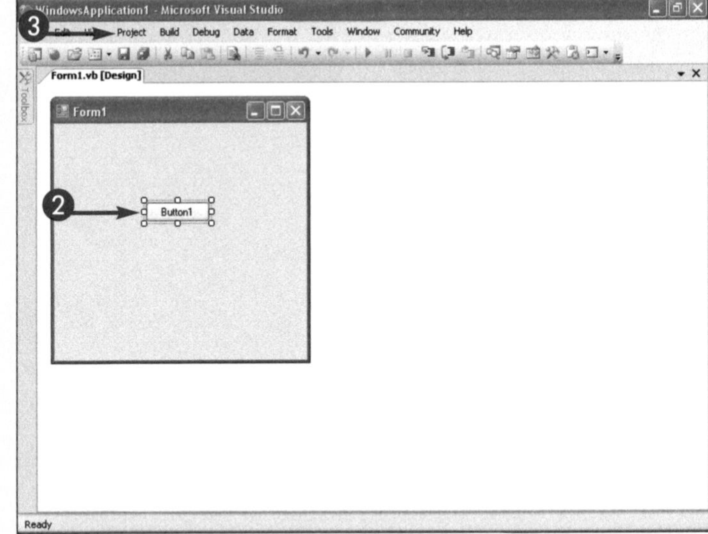

4. Change the class name.
5. Create a method without parameters by typing `Public Sub XXX()` followed by `End Sub`, replacing `XXX` with the method name.
6. Insert a message box.
7. Create a method with the same name with a `String` parameter by typing `Public Sub XXX(ByVal YYY As String)` followed by `End Sub`, replacing `XXX` with method name and `YYY` with the parameter name.
8. Insert another message box.

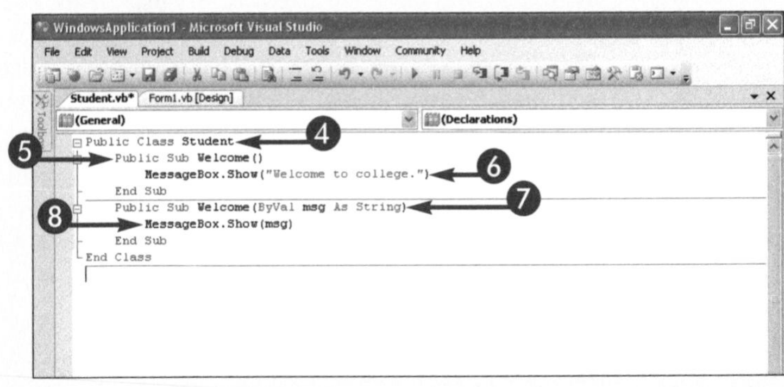

9 Double-click the `Button` control to display its `Click` subroutine.

10 Declare an object by typing `Dim XXX As Object`, replacing `XXX` with the object name.

11 Create an instance of the class and assign it to the object by typing `XXX = New YYY`, replacing `XXX` with the object name and `YYY` with the class name.

12 Display the default message by calling the method without a parameter.

13 Display the default message by calling the method with a parameter.

14 Press F5 to run the program.

15 Click the button to display the default message.

16 Click OK.

The `"Welcome aboard!"` message appears.

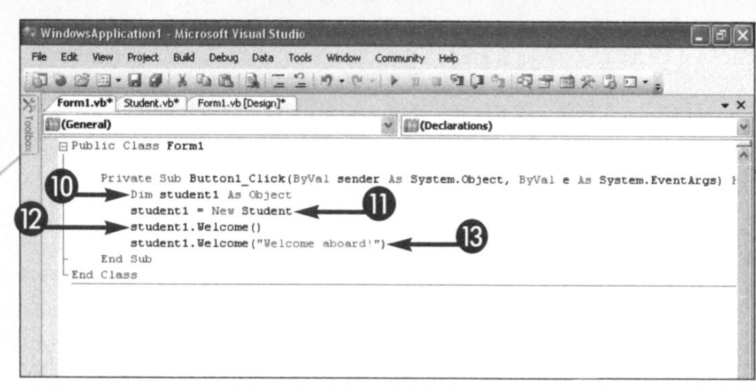

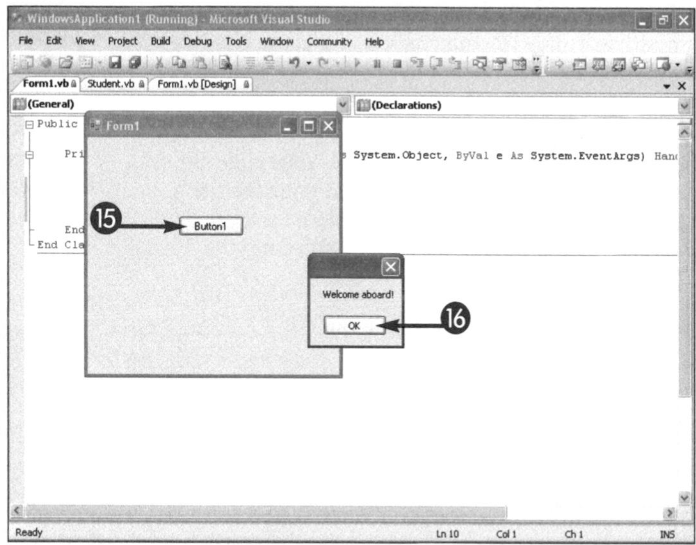

Extra

A derived class can define a member that has the same name and parameter list as a member of the base class. For example, a base class can define the method `GetName()`, and there can also be a `GetName()` method defined in the derived class. Both do not require a parameter. The redefine method in the derived class is called an *overload* of the same method in the base class. This means that the `GetName()` method of the derived class overloads the `GetName()` method of the base class. Programmers do this to enhance the base class's method. That is, the overload `GetName()` method does things differently than the base class's `GetName()` method based on the nature of the application. You can overload a base class's method by using the `Overloads` keyword.

Example

```
Public Class Class2
   Inherits Class1
   Public Overloads Sub GetName()
   End Sub
End Class
```

Using Multiple Inheritance

Inheritance is a way of sharing characteristics of a class (properties and method) with another class. You will recall that the class being inherited is called a *base class*, and the class that inherits the base class is referred to as a *derived class.*

A class can inherit characteristics from multiple classes by using multiple inheritance. Visual Basic .NET does not permit multiple `Inherits` statements in a class, nor does it permit you to place two classes in an `Inherits` statement. However, you can use levels of inheritance to enable a derived class to inherit from more than one class.

Think of level inheritance as your family. Your child inherits your characteristics, just as you inherited your mother's characteristics. Each generation is considered a level. The same holds true when using level inheritance in your Visual Basic .NET application.

The first level is a base class. The second level is the derived class that inherits the base class. Remember that the second level's class has characteristics of the base class plus its own characteristics. The third level inherits the second level's class. This means that the third level's class has characteristics of the second level's class, which also consists of characteristics of the first level's class.

The second level's class is both a derived class (inheriting the first level's class) and a base class because the second level's class is being inherited by the third level's class.

You create multiple inheritance by writing `Inherits` *`classname`* at the beginning of each class and using the appropriate class name to create the level inheritance effect.

Using Multiple Inheritance

1. Perform steps 1 to 3 from the preceding section.
2. Change the class name to a name such as `Person`.
3. Create a method without parameters by typing `Public Sub XXX()` followed by `End Sub`, replacing `XXX` with the method name, such as `WelcomeMessage`.
4. Display a message by writing `MessageBox.Show("XXX")`, replacing `XXX` with a message such as `Welcome`.

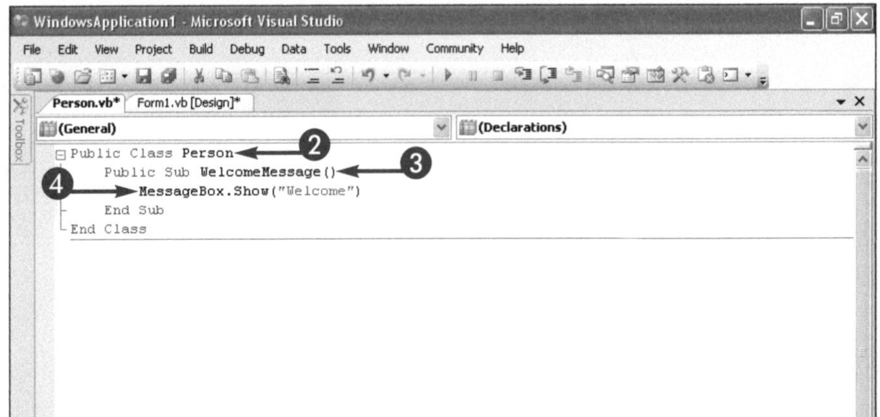

5. Click Project ➔ Add Class.

   An empty class definition is displayed.

6. Change the class name to a name such as `Student`.
7. Inherit the first class by typing `Inherits XXX`, replacing `XXX` with the name of the first class, such as `Person`.

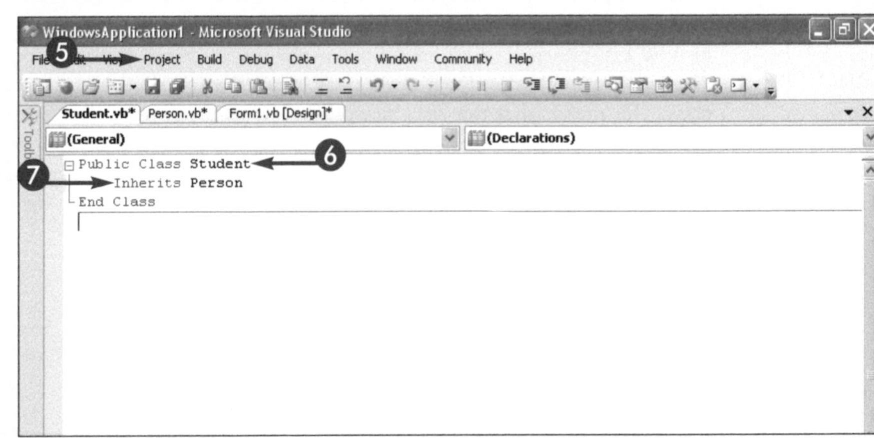

8 Click Project ➔ Add Class.

An empty class definition is displayed.

9 Change the class name to a name such as GradStudent.

10 Inherit the second class by typing Inherits XXX, replacing XXX with the name of the second class, such as Student.

11 Double-click the Button control on the form.

The Button1 Click subroutine is displayed.

12 Declare an object by typing Dim XXX As Object, replacing XXX with the object name.

13 Create an instance of the third class and assign it to the object by typing XXX = New YYY, replacing XXX with the object name and YYY with the class name.

14 Display the default message by calling the method defined in the first class.

15 Press F5 to run the program.

16 Click the button to display the message.

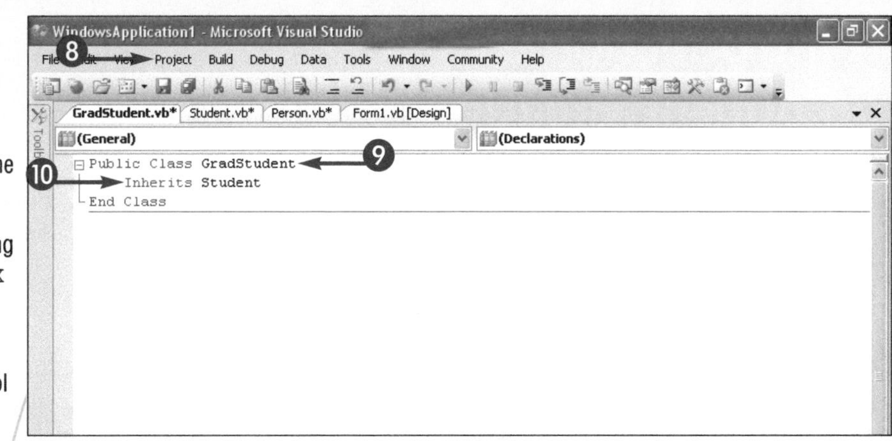

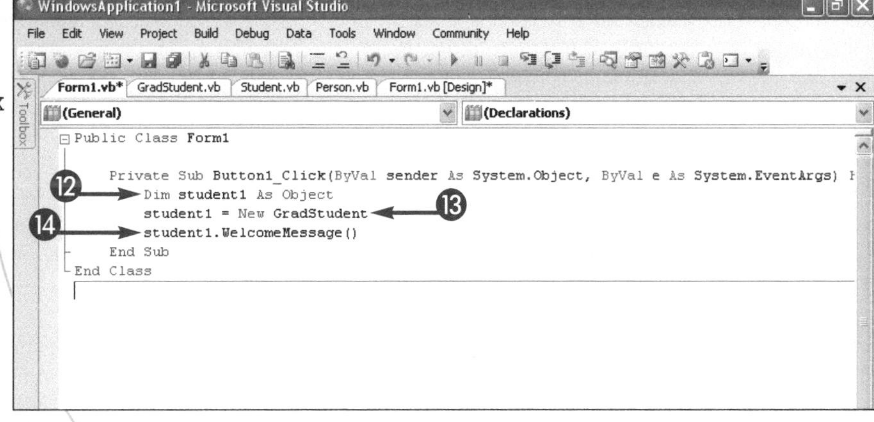

Extra

An interface is another feature of object-oriented programming, but beyond the scope of this book. You may want to look up *interface* using the Help feature of Visual Basic .NET. An *interface* is like a class in that it defines methods and other class members. However, an interface differs from a class in that no code is provided. For example, a method definition has a name, parameter, and a code block but no code. At first this sounds strange. Why define a method that does not do anything? The reason is to require functionality and then leave it to another programmer to define that functionality when the application implements the interface. For example, an interface may have a method called ValidateZipCode(ByVal ZipCode As String). When a programmer calls the ValidateZipCode() method, he expects it to validate the zip code. The class that implements this interface must define a ValidateZipCode() method that contains statements that actually validate the zip code.

Example

```
Public Interface Class2
    Function ValidateZipCode(ByVal ZipCode As String)
End Interface
```

An Introduction to Component Creation

Visual Basic .NET enables you to create components that you can use and reuse throughout your Windows, console, Web, and service applications. *Components* are classes that work more effectively as design tools in application development.

Ease of Use

You can easily create your own components in code or assemble them from the existing components in the .NET Framework classes, using either Visual Basic .NET or C#. You can use nonvisual components and associated features to easily incorporate resources such as message queues, event logs, and performance counters into your applications.

The .NET Framework classes greatly expand the component programming capabilities of Visual Studio .NET 2005. Instead of a limited set of base classes, you have a large library of sophisticated components that you can use to assemble applications or to derive high-quality components of your own.

Component Visual Development

The new rapid application development, or RAD, supports makes authoring controls and nonvisual components as easy as creating forms. You start with inheriting from an existing component and add other components to build in the functionality that you need.

Component Types

You can build components that service a variety of purposes based on the needs of a particular project or for reuse throughout multiple projects. All the components support working within the visual designer of the Development Studio, enabling you to use drag and drop to add components to your projects and to modify properties visually with the Properties window.

You can also create a specialized type of component known as *controls.* You can create controls that offer functionality to a form just like the controls provided by the .NET Framework. You can create both Windows and Web controls that offer their own visual interface and enable you to drag and drop them into their respective forms.

Create a Component Class

A basic component enables you to create an object very similar to a class, which adds support for the designer. Standard components work in all types of applications, including console applications where no visual interface is available.

You can use components to create objects that offer important functionality to forms, which you manipulate more easily than a typical class. You can modify the properties of the component visually instead of setting up a class in code. For example, you can easily add the timer control to a form or any other application type and modify its properties in the Properties window, but the timer itself provides no graphical interface.

Project Type

You can add a component to a class library or a Windows Control Library project. You can then build this library and reference it in applications that need to use the components.

Component Base

You create components by inheriting from the `System.ComponentModel.Component` class or implementing the `IComponent` interface.

Create Windows Controls

You can build a Windows control, a specialized type of component, to create custom and reusable graphical interfaces. As with Visual Basic .NET and third-party controls, you can create controls that you can drag and drop on to Windows forms and work with in the Properties window.

Your control can expose properties and methods and use a GDI+ drawn graphical interface or use a combination of one or more standard controls. Your control's properties appear in the Properties tool window, and you can visually manipulate your component in the designer. For example, you can create a custom button control that provides special visual effects. You can build a Windows custom control to create a specialized `ListView` control that displays the contents of a directory.

Project Type

You can build Windows controls either by creating them directly inside an existing Windows application project or using a Windows Control Library project.

If you add the control directly to a project, you can use it only within the project. The Windows Control Library builds a DLL that you can reuse across multiple Windows application projects easily by referencing the library as necessary.

Component Base

Visual Basic .NET creates a `UserControl` class that inherits from `System.Windows.Forms.UserControl`. The `UserControl` object provides a design surface to build a complex control easily and inherits from the `ContainerControl` class to add all the standard properties and functions that you expect in a Windows `Forms` control.

Create Web Controls

A powerful feature of Visual Basic .NET Web forms, Web controls enable you to create server-side applications that maintain their state and provide advanced functionality. You can create Web user controls that encapsulate functions of Web forms for reuse and ease of development.

You can build two types of Web controls. Web user controls enable you to define a visual layout combining multiple existing user controls. For example, you can create a Web user control that defines the top border of your Web site and then import the control in the various parts of your site. Web user controls embed into the page at runtime, so you cannot see the control at design time or manipulate its properties using the designer.

The other type of Web controls, Web custom controls, work only in Web Control Library projects. You generate the actual HTML these controls send to the browser, and the controls cannot use existing Web controls on which to build. You can reference these controls in a Web forms project and work with them just like the actual controls provided by the .NET Framework. Custom controls let you drag and drop the control directly on to the form from the Toolbox and use a full set of properties and events.

Project Type

You add Web user controls directly into an existing Web application project.

You use Web custom controls by building a Web Control Library project and referencing the library in a Web application project.

Component Base

Visual Basic .NET provides a Web Control Library project template, which automatically creates a `WebControl` class that inherits from the `System.Web.UI.WebControls.WebControl` class.

Create a Component

Components provide reusable code in the form of objects. *Components* are a special type of class that you can add to the Toolbox and manipulate using the designer. Components provide a visual interface on a form and appear in the component tray. The ability to work with the component using the designer means that the developer can quickly and easily modify component properties in a point-and-click manner.

To create a component, you use the Component Class template provided by Development Studio. The template provides a constructor and initialization routine for you.

To define a component, you add public methods, properties, and events to the component just as you would with a class. Unlike a normal class, you can define extra information about properties and events of the component that a designer can use when the user manipulates the components at design time. To specify a description for a property, place the attribute `Description()` inside angle brackets (`<>`) before the `Property` statement or accessibility keyword with the description as the parameter. You can hide a property by specifying the `Browsable()` attribute with `False` as the parameter.

To add your component to an application after you reference the library that contains the component, you simply double-click the component in the Toolbox. You can then use the Properties window to manipulate public properties of the component. Because the component is a specialized kind of class, you can also create an instance of the component in code using the `New` operator.

When you create a set of components in a library, you can use namespaces to help locate components more easily for reuse.

Create a Component

1. Create a new Class Library project or open an existing project.
2. Click Project.
3. Click Add Component.

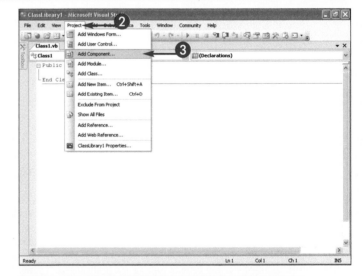

The Add New Item dialog box appears.

4. Type a name for the component.
5. Click Add.

The component appears in designer mode.

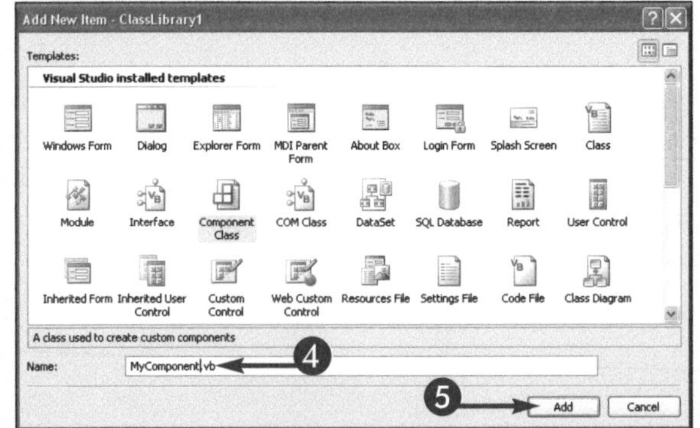

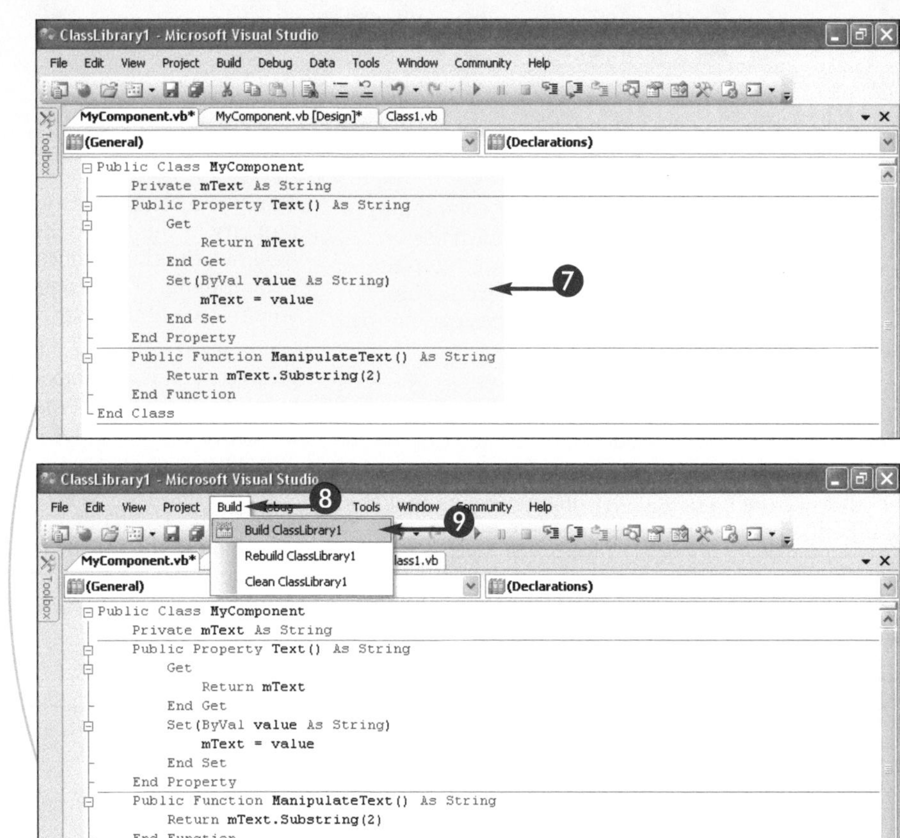

6 Double-click the designer area.

The Code Editor opens.

7 Add any desired properties, methods, and events to the component.

Note: This example adds a property to store a text string and a method to manipulate the string.

8 Click Build.

9 Click Build *ClassLibrary1.*

Visual Basic .NET builds the library. You can now use your component by referencing it in another application and adding the component to the Toolbox.

Extra

You can use the various attributes available to components to provide helpful information to the user and provide setup information to the designer. You can separate multiple attributes using commas. You need to import the `System.ComponentModel` namespace for attributes to work.

Example

```
<Description("Sets the timer length.",
DefaultValue(1000)>
Public Property timerInterval() As Integer
   Get
      Return mTimerInterval
   End Get
   Set (value As Color)
      MTimerInterval - value
   End Set
End Property
```

ATTRIBUTE	DESCRIPTION
`Browsable (Boolean)`	Specifies whether a property or an event should be displayed in the property browser.
`Category (String)`	Specifies the category to display the property if the user uses the categorical property display.
`Description (String)`	Specifies a description for the component.
`Bindable (Boolean)`	Specifies whether a property is useful to bind a database field.
`Default Property (String)`	Specifies the default property that the designer shows when the user clicks the control. Insert this attribute before the class declaration.
`Default Event Attribute (String)`	Specifies the default event that is selected in the property browser when a user clicks the component. Insert this attribute before the class declaration.

Create a Windows Forms Control

You can create a Windows `Forms` user control into which you can add a set of controls for reuse throughout a project. Alternatively, you can place the control in a library to use in multiple projects. The `UserControl` object provides the ability to design your own controls.

When you add a user control to a project, the Windows Control Designer, similar to the Windows Forms Designer, gives you a designer space without a title bar. You can use the Toolbox to add any number of controls to the user control.

You can also use the `UserControl` object's events that the control inherits from to paint onto the service and create your own user control that does not rely on combining other controls. This capability lets you create any sort of control by providing a custom painting method and your own event model.

To name a control that you create, change the `Name` property of the `UserControl` object. The `Name` property modifies the class name, so this name functions as the default name of the control that is displayed in the Toolbox when you add the user control to a form.

If you want to use a control or a set of controls in multiple projects, you can create a Windows Control Library project to hold the controls. When you create this project, Visual Basic .NET builds a .NET-compliant DLL that you can reference in other projects. To create a Windows Control Library project, you select the template from the Add Project dialog box. The name that you give the project functions as the name of the assembly for referencing. The template provides one `UserControl` automatically, but you can add any number of controls to the project.

Create a Windows Forms Control

1. Open a Control Library or Windows application project.

Note: To create a Control Library project, select the Windows Control Library template when you create a project.

2. If you are using a Windows application project, click Project ➔ Add User Control.

Note: The Control Library project already contains a `UserControl` that you can use.

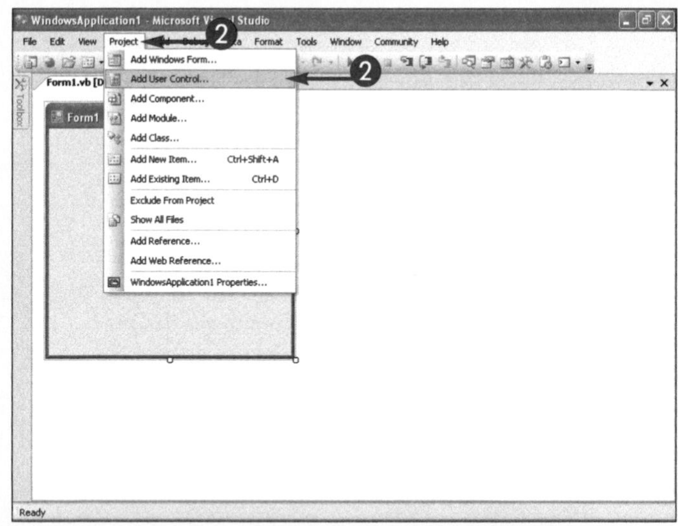

The Add New Item dialog box appears.

3. Type a name for the new user control.
4. Click Add.

The visual designer for the new control appears.

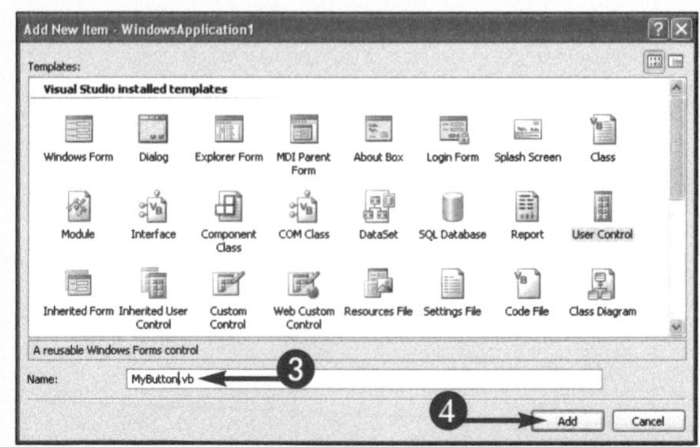

5. Add any necessary controls to the visual designer.

6. In the Code Editor, add necessary members to the control.

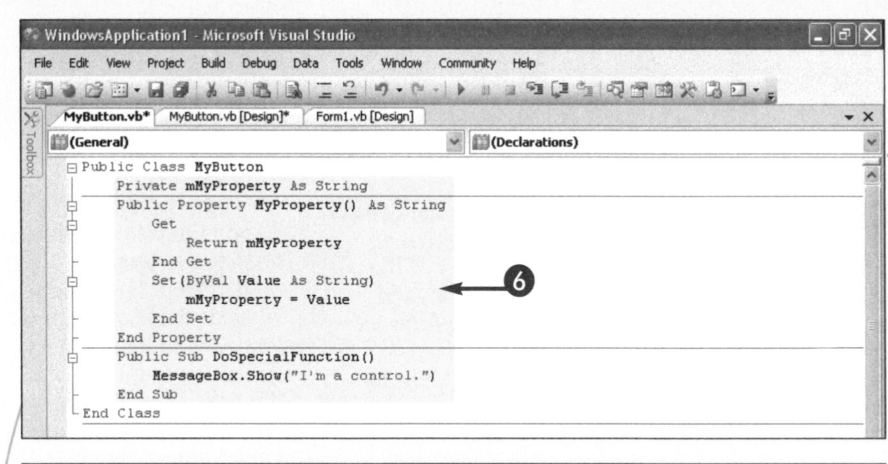

7. Click Build.

8. Click Build *WindowsApplication1.*

If the control exists in a control project, you can now reference the library. If you created the control in a Windows application, go to a form and add it to the form.

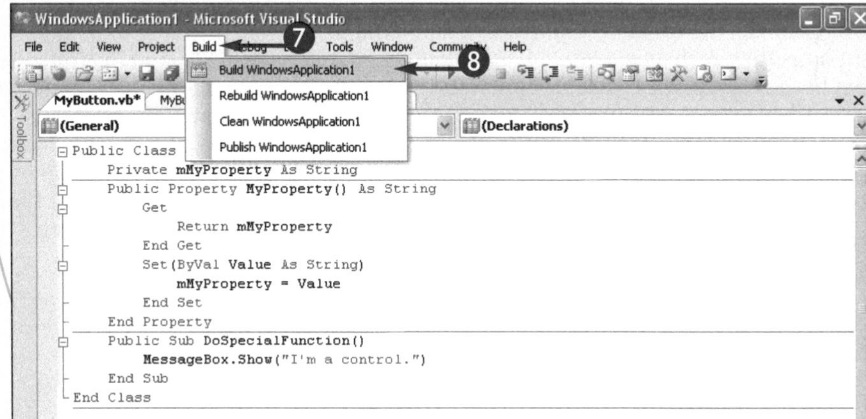

Extra

The `UserControl` also contains a number of default properties that it inherits from the `ContainerControl` class, which is the class that lets controls contain other controls inside of it. The `ContainerControl` inherits from `ScrollableControl`, which inherits from `Control` to provide the basic functions of all parts of the Windows `Forms` hierarchy. Properties such as `BackColor`, `ForeColor`, `Tag`, `Enabled`, and `AutoScroll` automatically apply to your user control through the various classes that the `UserControl` inherits.

You cannot create a `UserControl` that the user uses as a container. When developing the `UserControl`, you can add any necessary properties. The user cannot add controls to the `UserControl`, so you cannot replicate the function of a `GroupBox` or `Panel` control. You may want to create your own versions of these container controls directly instead of building a `UserControl`. To inherit from existing controls, search Visual Basic .NET help by typing **Inherit from existing Windows Forms controls.**

Handle Default Properties

When you create a user control using the Control Designer, Visual Basic .NET uses the `UserControl` class to manage many of the details of the control's placement, communication, and architecture requirements for it to function on a form. A user control inherits from the standard `ContainerControl` class that all container controls on a form and the form itself inherit. Because of this, containers of your control can access a number of properties that exist within the `ContainerControl` class without your explicitly defining them. For example, the container can retrieve and modify standard properties such as `BackColor`, `Tag`, and `Visible`. For some of these properties, such as appearance properties, you can handle changes specifically.

Most of the controls that you add to a user control automatically respond to formatting changes on the user control. For example, controls with `BackColor` set to `Control` contained in the `UserControl` automatically respond to color changes made by the `UserControl`'s `BackColor` property. If you change the `UserControl` properties in the designer, the container control can still override these settings. To force a particular property value, you need to handle the `On`*`Property`*`Changed` event, where *`Property`* is the name of the standard property, available in the Base Class Events section of the `UserControl`. If you set a value for the property inside this event handler, the value cannot change.

Another way to handle the base class's properties and methods is to override them. Because your `UserControl` is little more than an inherited version of the class, you can use standard inheritance techniques to override properties and other members. Inside the overridden method or property, do not assign a new value to the property or invoke the method of the same name because doing so causes an infinite loop.

Handle Default Properties

1. Open an existing user control and double-click the control to go to the Code Editor.
2. To monitor property changes, select (Base Class Events) from the components list.
3. Select a *`Property`*`Changed` event, where *`Property`* is the property to monitor.

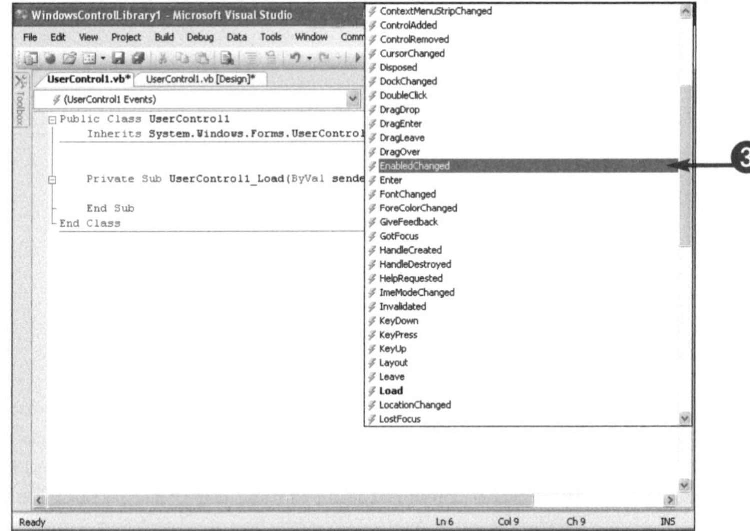

4. Add code to check the property against criteria.
5. Type `Me.` followed by the property name.
6. Type = followed by an appropriate value.

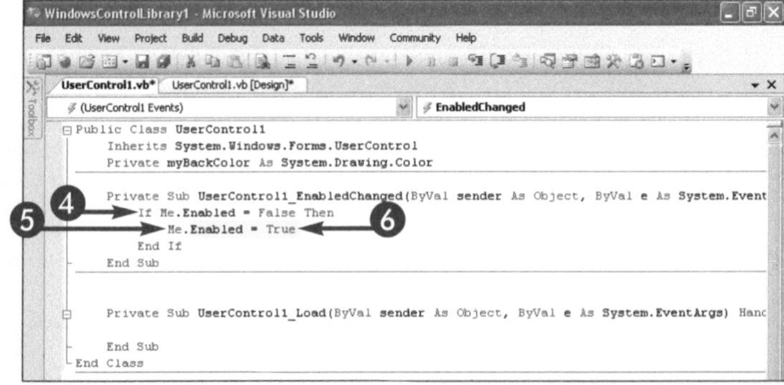

7 To override the property or event functionality, select (Overrides) from the components list.

8 Select a property or method to override.

9 Add code to provide the new functionality for the property or method.

Note: This example overrides the background color and paints a gradient using the selected color.

10 Click Build ➔ Build to build the project.

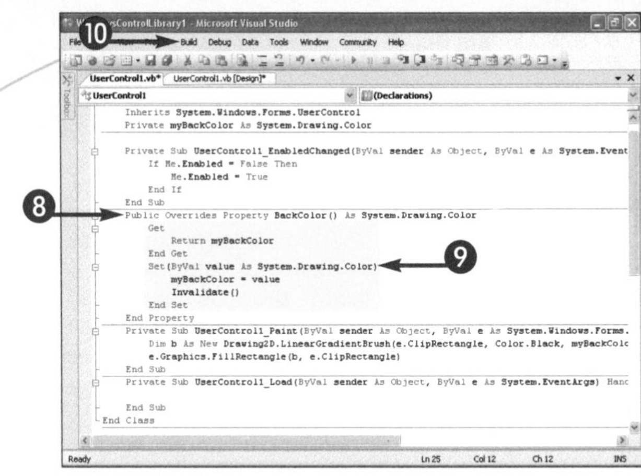

When you add the control to a form and attempt to modify a property, the appropriate code either monitors or overrides the function.

Note: If you use a control library, you must reference the control library.

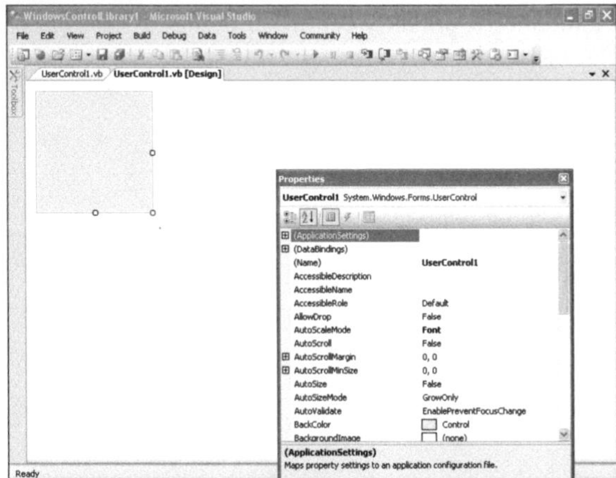

Extra

As with properties, you can override methods and events of the User Control class. For example, the control provides a click event that fires whenever the user clicks part of the `UserControl` that does not contain a constituent control. You may not want the containing application to provide code for clicking in the blank areas of the code. You can override the `OnClick` method to prevent this event from researching the parent control.

Example

```
Protected Overrides Sub Onclick(ByVal e As System.EventArgs)
    'do nothing...hide the event from the parent.
End Sub
```

You can also use the `OnEvent`, where `Event` is the name of a particular event, to modify certain information and pass the event along as usual. Because the events exist in the `Control` class, you cannot raise them normally. Instead, you must define the event again in your `UserControl` class using the `Shadows` keyword.

Example

```
Public Shadows Event click (ByVal sender As Object, ByVal e As System.EventArgs)
Protected Overrides Sub Onclick(byVal e As System.EventArgs)
    'perform necessary preprocessing
     ' raise the normal event
      RaiseEvent Click(Me, e)
End Sub
```

Add a Member

You can provide properties and methods in your user control that interact with its container to customize the appearance and functionality of your control. You can create properties that modify the appearance and functionality of your control like the `Text` property of the `Button` control, which sets the caption that is displayed on the button. You can also add custom methods, which allow the container to send commands and specify the control's actions.

To add a property to your user control, you access the Code Editor and add the property definition to the existing class that defines the user control. You define properties for your control's container as `Public` to give the container access to them.

To add a method to your user control, define the method inside the existing user control class. Define the method `Public` to let the control's container invoke the method. If you want to create an inherited version of the control, make sure that necessary properties contain the `Overridable` keyword.

When you build a control and add it to a form, you can access the properties that you define inside the Properties window. You can also manipulate both the property and methods in code. The Properties window determines the type of properties and uses the most appropriate selection system. For example, if you create a property of type `Color`, the Properties window automatically provides a color selector drop-down list for your property. If you have a property of type `Size` or `Point`, the designer shows the properties of the object as a subsection of your property.

Add a Member

ADD A PROPERTY

1. Open an existing user control and double-click the surface of the user control to go to the Code Editor.
2. Define a private member variable.
3. On an empty line of the class, type `Public Property` followed by the name of the property.
4. Press Enter.

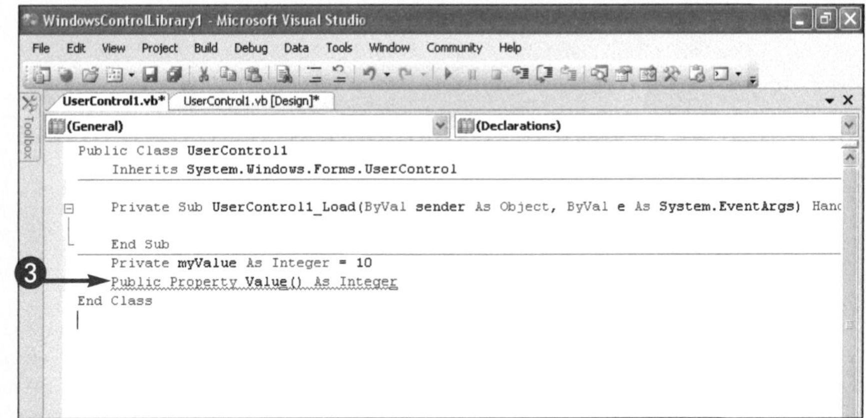

5. Type code inside the property to set and retrieve the value that the property specifies.
6. Click Build.
7. Click Build *WindowsControlLibrary1*.

You can now add the `UserControl` to a form and access properties of the control.

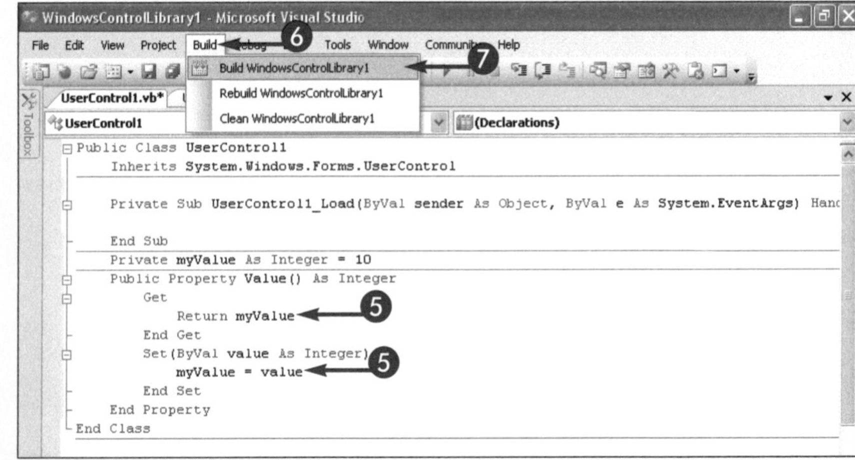

ADD A METHOD

1. Open an existing user control.
2. Double-click the surface of the user control to go to the Code Editor.
3. On an empty line of the class, type `Public` followed by `Sub` or `Function` and the name of the method.
4. For a `Function`, add the return type after the `As` keyword at the end of the line and then press Enter.

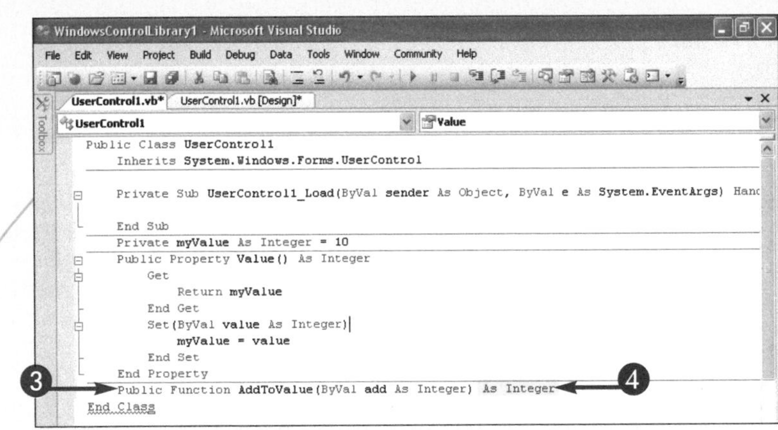

5. Type code inside the method to modify the function of the `UserControl`.
6. Click Build.
7. Click Build *WindowsControlLibrary1*.

You can access the methods of the control.

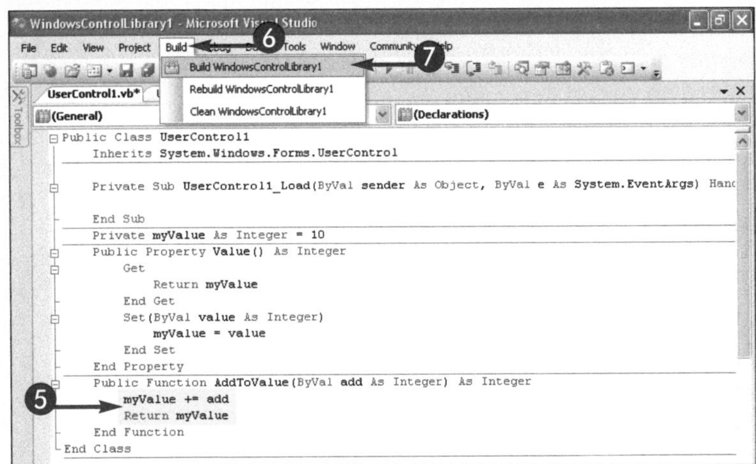

Extra

You can add read-only methods to your component, control, or class to provide information to the control's container. If your control maintains a collection of objects, you can use a `ReadOnly` property to allow access to the items without allowing direct changes to the objects.

Example

```
Private items As new Collection()
Public ReadOnly Property Item(ByVal index As
Integer)
   Get
      Return items(index)
   End Get
End Property
Public Sub Add(ByVal item As Object)
   Items.Add(item)
End Sub
```

You can make your property take on a range of values specified by an enumeration of constants using the `Enum` block. Use the type name of the enumeration block for the property, and the designer loads the list and provides a drop-down list of constants.

Example

```
Public Enum SelectionsStyles
   ByColor
   ByName
End Enum
Public Property SelectionStyle() As
SelectionStyles
...
```

Add an Event

You can add events to your user control that the containing form can catch to provide event handlers. You can create custom events that you can raise when necessary. For example, a `Button` control provides the `Click` event that raises when the user clicks a button.

To define an event, add a standard event definition in the existing `UserControl` class's declarations. Define the event as `Public` to allow the user control's container to handle the event. You raise the event in the container by calling `RaiseEvent`.

Because the `UserControl` inherits from the `Control` class, it provides a number of events that fire when actions occur on the user control's surface. For example, if the user clicks the `UserControl` where no control exists, the `UserControl`'s `Click` event fires. The `UserControl` class and the containing form receive this event automatically. You can override these events to prevent the container from automatically receiving them. See the section "Handle Default Properties" for more information. You can also use these events in a control where you draw on the surface. See the section "Create a Control from Scratch" for more information.

The controls you place on the user control fire events that you can handle inside the control. If you want to pass back a control's event, define an event and raise it in the event handler of the control's `UserControl`. For example, if your `UserControl` uses a `ListBox` control, you can alert the form when the user selects an item in the list. First, create a public event of your user control; then, in the `ListBox`'s `SelectedIndexChanged` event, fire your public event for the user control's container to handle.

Add an Event

1. Open an existing user control.
2. Double-click the surface of the user control to go to the Code Editor.
3. Define an event as `Public` for the control.

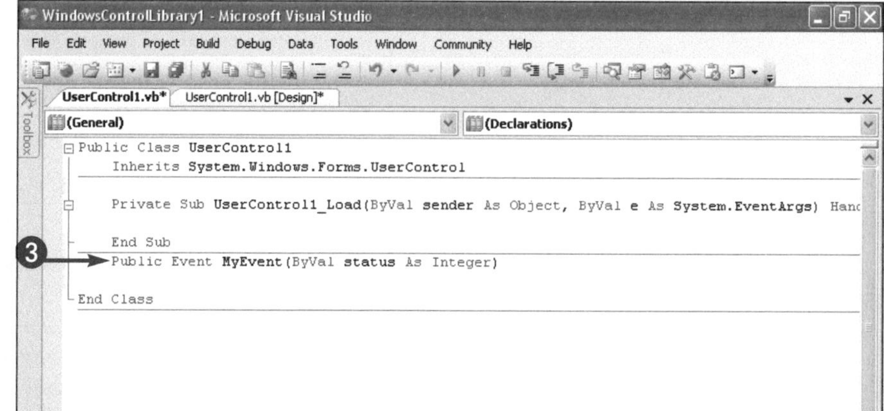

4. Type `RaiseEvent` in the method or internal event handler where you want to raise the event.

Note: The example raises the event in the method called `MyMethod`.

5. Type the name of the event that you defined followed by any necessary parameters in parentheses.
6. Click Build.
7. Click Build *WindowsControlLibrary1*.

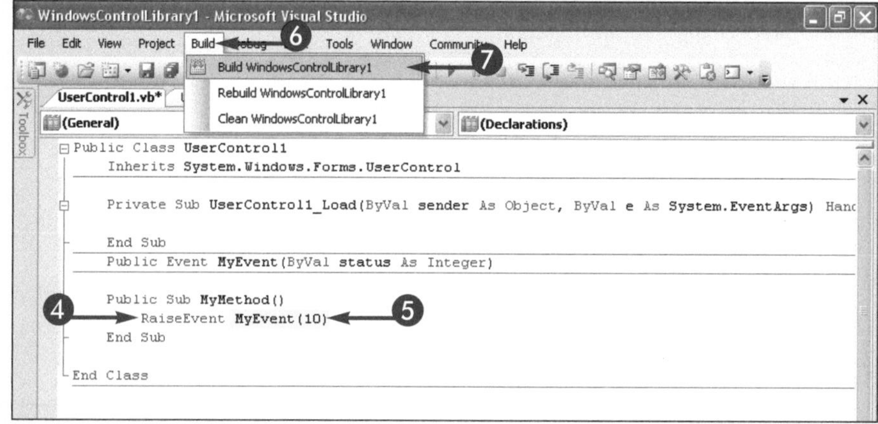

8. Add the control to a form.
9. In the Code Editor for the form, type code to cause the event to fire.
10. Select your control from the component list.
11. Select your custom event.
12. Add code to handle the appropriate event that you created.

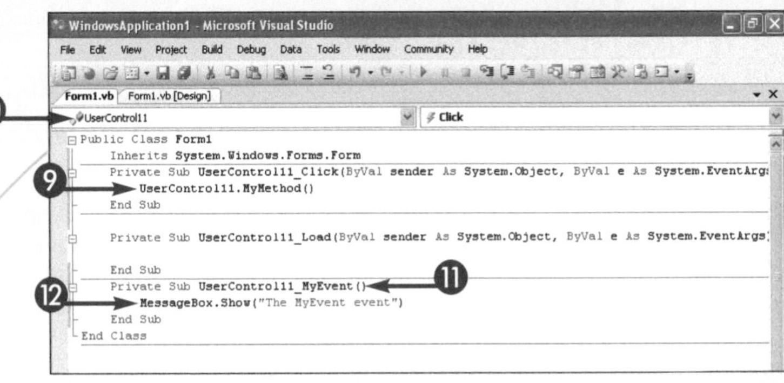

13. Press F5 to run your application.

The user control raises the event when necessary, and the form the control resides on handles the event.

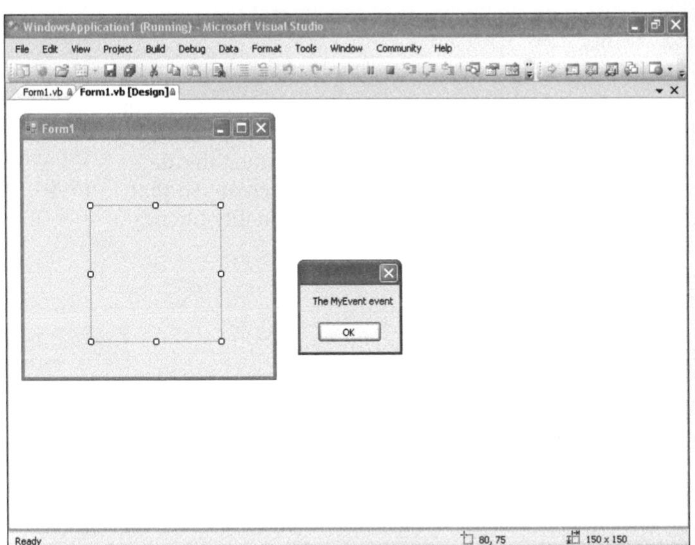

Extra

You can override the default events the `UserControl` provides to function as events for specific controls you contain in the `UserControl`. For example, the control automatically raises the `Click` event on the `UserControl`'s container when the user clicks the control's blank areas. You can add a button to the user control that fires the `Click` event instead. To do this, you must shadow the existing event in the base `Control` class and then raise your event as necessary. You can disable the default click event on the `UserControl` as well.

Example

```
Public Shadows Event click (ByVal sender As Object, ByVal e As System.EventArgs)
Private Sub Button1_Click(ByVal sender As System.Object, ByVal e As
System.EventAgs) Handles Button1.Click
    'Raise standard click event
     RaiseEvent Click(Me, e)
End Sub
Protected overrides Sub OnClick (ByVal e As System.EventArgs)
    'Hide event from parent
End Sub
```

Using Standard Controls

You can build a custom user control with the standard controls available in Visual Basic .NET and other custom controls. These composite controls function like a single control when you add them to a form, which enables you to build a layout with certain reusable controls. You can set properties of the controls, and they remain constant across various instances of the control that you create on forms.

You can use the Windows Control Designer to drag a control on to the surface of the `UserControl`. Note that you cannot access the properties, events, and other members of controls you add from outside the `UserControl`. You must decide what members to add to the `UserControl` to create so that you can replace, modify, or extend the functionality already available in the controls.

For example, your user control may consist of a button that you modify with a particular color and font to make a standard appearance for your program. But when the user clicks the button inside the user control, the form does not receive the button's `Click` event. Your user control receives the event, and you have the choice of adding an event to your user control to alert the form to the event. To alert the form, you need to create an event definition and, in the `Button_Click` event of the user control, raise the defined public event of the user control.

Keep in mind that you must give a `UserControl` the capability to resize. You can use the `Dock` and `Anchor` properties to make the controls that you use on the form resize to the size of the user control.

Using Standard Controls

1. Open an existing user control.
2. Click controls in the Toolbox and then click and drag the control on the surface of the user control to pick the appropriate size and location.
3. Double-click the surface of the user control.

   The Code Editor appears.

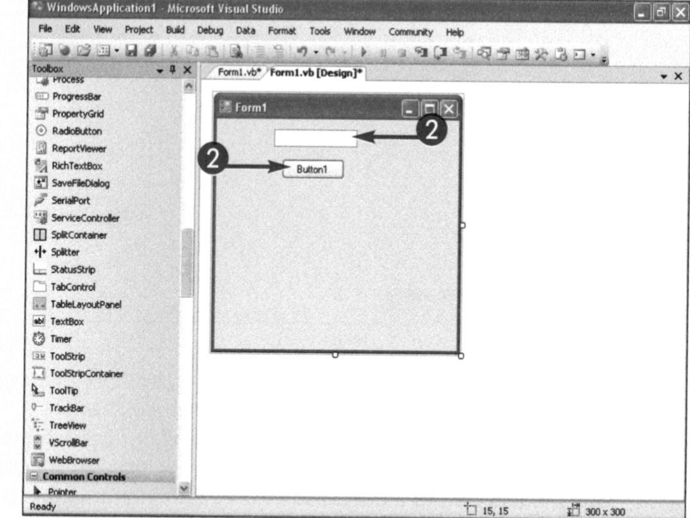

4. Add a property to the control that relates to a property of a control on the surface.

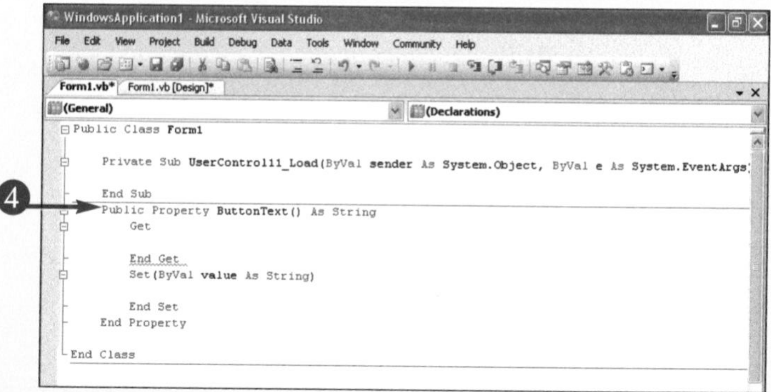

5. Return the property of the control on the `UserControl` in the `Get` routine.
6. Set the property of the control on the `UserControl` in the `Set` routine.
7. Build the control.

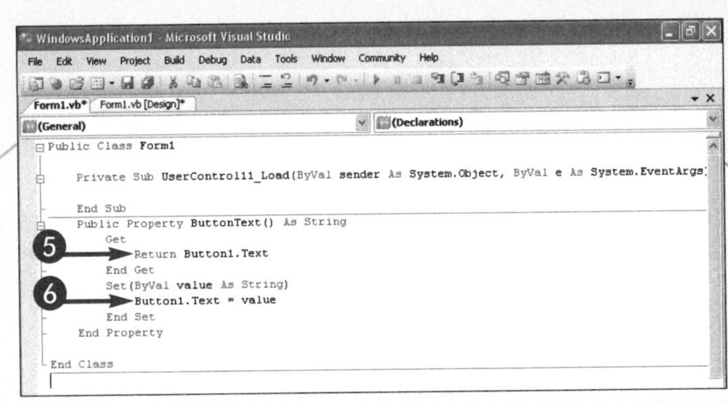

The control is ready for use.

You can add it to a form and alter the property of the control embedded in the `UserControl`.

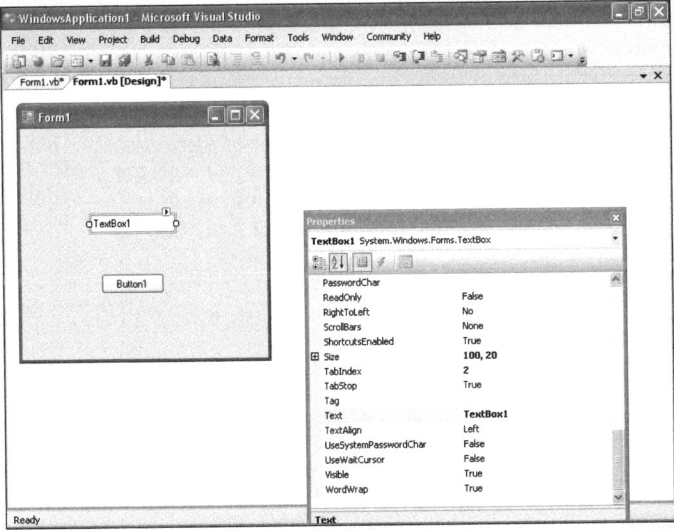

Apply It

You can use standard controls in your project by directly inheriting from them. This provides very specific support for building a control, because you must base your control on a single existing control. You can control functions of an inherited control by overriding their event methods such as `OnPaint`. If you want the base control to perform its function, call `MyBase.OnEvent`, where `Event` is the name of the event in the base to invoke. Follow this with the appropriate parameters. To use your customer control, place it in a control library and then reference the control in a project.

TYPE THIS

```
Public Class CustomControl1
   Inherits Systlem.Windows.forms.Button
   Public Sub New()
         MyBase.New()
   End Sub
   Protected Overrides Sub OnPaint(ByVal pe As
MyBase.OnPaint(pe)
         'Draw a red border around the edge
of a button.
         pe.Graphics.DrawRectangle(Drawing.Pens.Red,
pe.ClipRectangle)
   End Sub
End Class
```

RESULTS

The inherited button draws a red border over the standard border of a button. All functions perform the same.

Create a Control from Scratch

Typically, you can simply make a customized version of an existing control to ease development. But in cases where the standard controls do not offer the functionality that you want for a control, you can create a control completely from scratch. For example, you can create a highly stylized button control that a standard control cannot provide.

To create a control from scratch, you must rely heavily on the graphics command layer to draw the image of your control on the surface of the `UserControl`.

Providing interactivity is essential to the usefulness of your control. The `UserControl` provides a number of properties to monitor mouse and keyword actions and movement. For example, to create a customized button, you may want to draw one style for the inactive button, one for a pressed button, and a third for the active button. Add code to paint the surface of the control in the `Paint` event handler. Make sure that your `Paint` event uses the dimension specified by the `UserControl`.

All the drawing code in the control should exist in the `Paint` event. Placing painting code for interactivity such as mouse clicks in the mouse events can cause the control to draw improperly when the control repaints. To avoid this, call the `Invalidate` method to fire the paint `Resize` event to enable your control to redraw with the new dimensions.

The `UserControl` provides the `Click` event when the user clicks its surface and the `MouseDown` and `MouseUp` events for the user pressing and releasing the mouse on your control, respectively. You can use `KeyPress`, `KeyDown`, and `KeyUp` events to monitor for key presses.

Create a Control from Scratch

1. In the Code Editor of an existing user control class, add necessary member variables to the control.

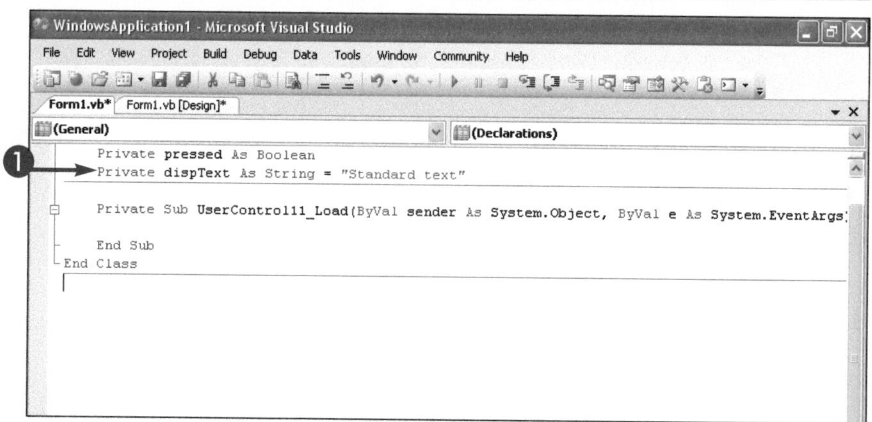

2. Type code to respond to any necessary events raised by the `UserControl`.

Note: This example adds code to respond to mouse clicks.

3. In any method that changes the appearance of the control, type `Me.Invalidate()`.

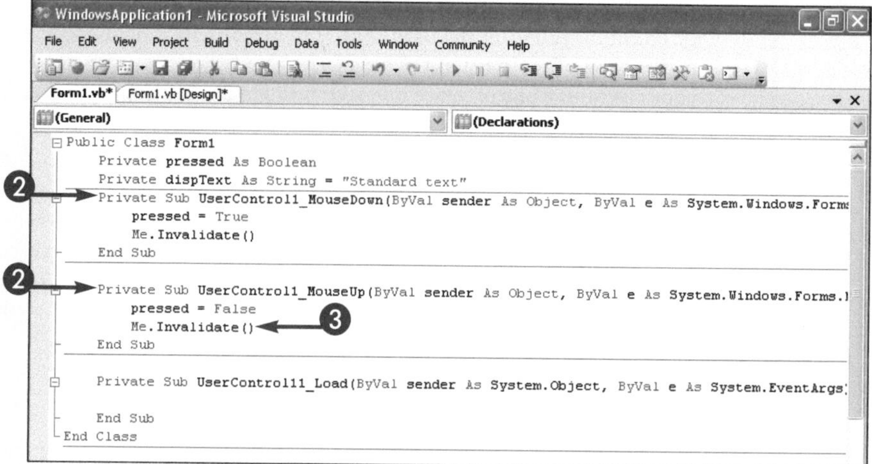

4 Add necessary events, properties, and methods to the control.

5 Select (Base Class Events) in the component list and select the `Paint` event.

6 Type code to paint the control.

7 Build the control.

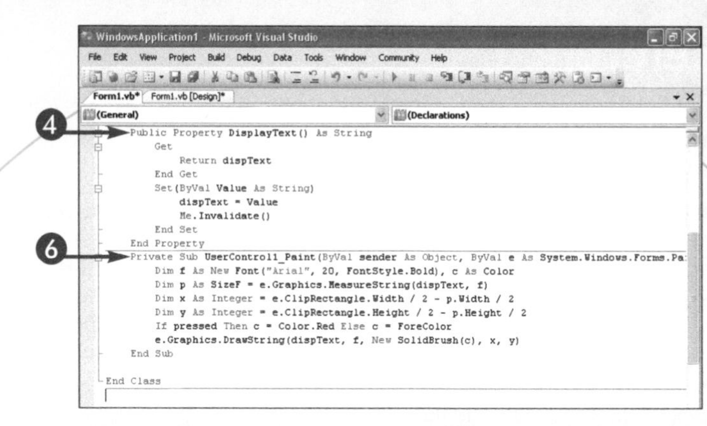

The control draws itself and functions like a standard control when you add it to a form.

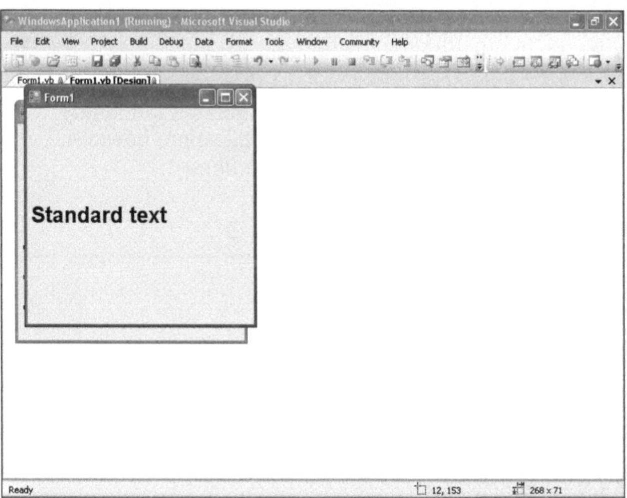

Apply It

You can provide drawing functions that appear like the pop-up style of the `Button` control to monitor for the user pressing the mouse in the `UserControl`.

TYPE THIS

```
Private Enum ButtonState
   Normal
   Pressed
   Hover
End Enum
Private myState As ButtonState - ButtonState.Normal
Private Sub UserControl1_MouseDown(...) Handles MyBase.MouseDown
   MyState = ButtonState.Pressed: Me.Invalidate()
End Sub
Private Sub userControl1_MouseEnter(...) handles MyBase.MouseEnter
   MyState = ButtonState.Hover: Me.Invalidate()
End Sub
Private Sub UserControl1_MouseLeave(...) Handles MyBase.MouseLeave
   MyState = ButtonState.Normal: Me.Invalidate()
End Sub
Private Sub userControl1_MouseUp(...) Handles MyBase.MouseUp
   MyState = ButtonState.Normal: Me.Invalidate()
End Sub
```

RESULTS

The control responds graphically to the user's mouse.

Reference a Library

The Windows Control Library project builds a DLL that contains a set of `UserControl` controls, which you can reuse in your applications. The Class Library project also builds a DLL that normally contains components and classes that you can reuse across projects. These projects build the same library type. The template only varies in the type of component that it initially provides when you create the project.

To use a library in another project, you indicate the compiled DLL library to reference in your project. Referencing a component library means that you now can access the classes, components, and controls that the library exports. The library is not part of your application, however, and you cannot access private parts of the library.

To reference a component or class library in an application, you use the Add Reference dialog box. A reference makes all the classes in the component library available, but you cannot use the controls automatically. You must customize the Toolbox and select from the library which controls and components you want available in the Toolbox.

Each assembly resides within its own namespace. Therefore, to add a library to another application, you must remember your library project's namespace to access the components and controls inside the library. Unless you change the root namespace of the library project, the namespace is the same as the name of the project.

Because the reference you make saves into the assembly of your application, you can create a setup project that automatically installs the appropriate component library DLL with your application.

Reference a Library

ADD A REFERENCE

1. Create a new Windows Application project or open an existing one.
2. Click Project.
3. Click Add Reference.

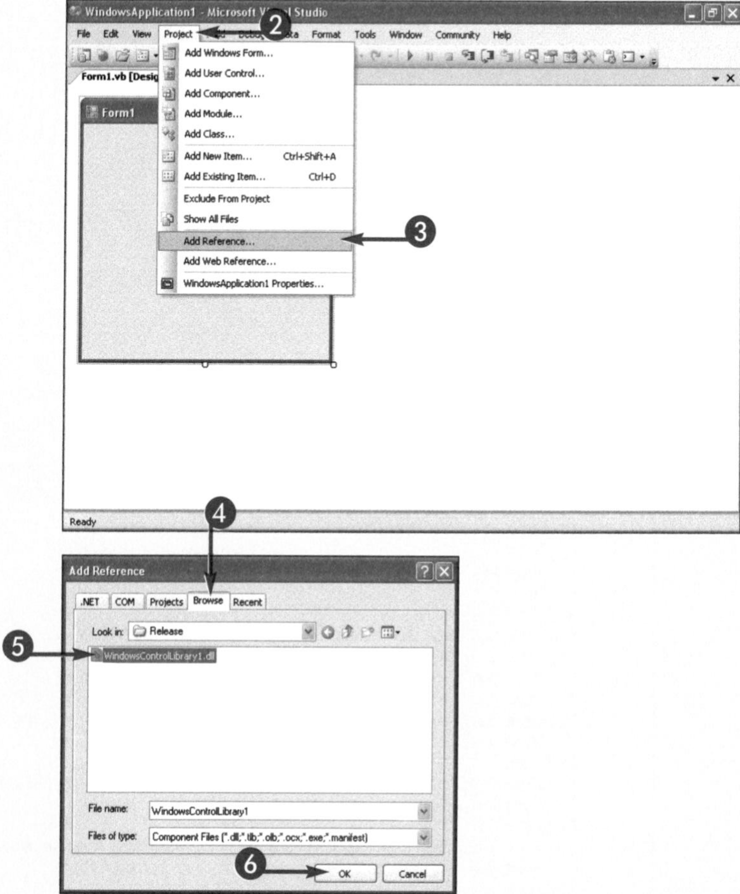

- The Add Reference dialog box appears.

4. Click Browse.
5. Click the DLL file.

- The library project places the built DLL in the `bin\` subdirectory of the project directory.

6. Click OK.

ADD ICONS TO THE TOOLBOX

7. Scroll to the General section of the Toolbox.
8. Right-click General.
9. Click Choose Items.

   The Choose Toolbox Items dialog box appears.

10. Click Browse and locate the user control.
11. Click Open.

    The user control appears in the Choose Toolbox Items dialog box.

12. Click OK.
13. Add controls or components in the Toolbox to the form of the application.

    The components load from the library DLL and let you manipulate them like other controls and components.

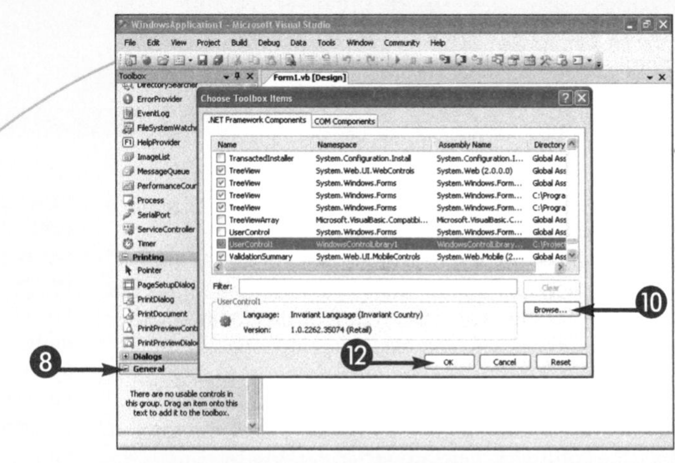

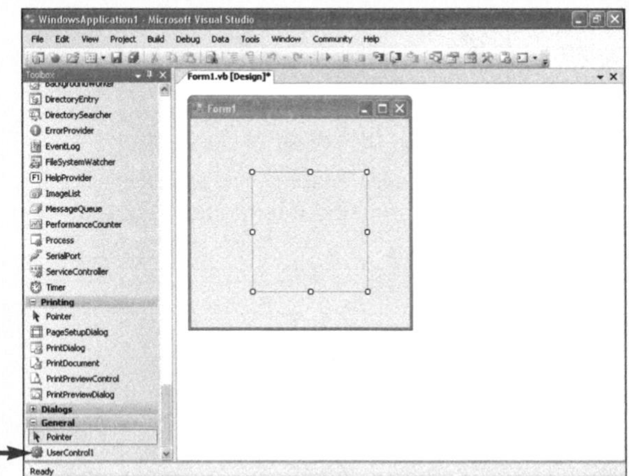

Extra

The .NET component model does not require components to register with the system before you use them in other assemblies. The COM interface, however, does require components to register before use. You can register your .NET components with COM to provide backward compatibility for other development environments that rely on COM, such as Microsoft Office and ASP applications. To register your library DLL, use the regasm.exe utility where the system .NET Framework files install, typically `C:\WINNT\Microsoft.NET\Framework\v\`, where `v` is the version of the software that you are using. Run this utility, and pass the pathname and filename of the .NET DLL assembly to register. If you do want to register the file on the current machine, pass `/regfile:` followed by the filename of a Registry file to generate. You can then import this file on any computer that contains the DLL.

Example

Register a Component

```
Regasm.exe MyLibrary.DLL
```

Generate a Registry Import File

```
Regasm.exe MyLibrary.DLL /regfile:MyLibrary.REG
```

Add a Picture to a Form

Many Windows applications use pictures to make a window more attractive and easier to understand. You can add a picture to a Windows form with the `PictureBox` control. The `PictureBox` control appears in the Windows Forms section of the Toolbox. After adding it to the form, you can assign a single picture file to its `Image` property. Use the `SizeMode` property to determine how the control draws the image. `Normal` makes the `PictureBox` draw the image in its actual size at the top-left corner of the control. When you set `SizeMode` to `StretchImage`, the control stretches the image to fill the entire control space. `AutoSize` makes the control size to the actual image size. When you set `SizeMode` to `AutoSize`, you can no longer resize the control. `CenterImage` draws the image at actual size in the center of the control.

The `PictureBox` control also enables you to place a border around the edge. Set `BorderStyle` to `FixedSingle` to draw a one-pixel black border. Use `Fixed3D` to draw a more traditional 3D sunken border around the control. `None` removes the borders completely. You can also load another image into the control using the standard control property `BackgroundImage`. Because Visual Basic .NET does not allow you to align the foreground image like many other controls, you may not find this property useful. You can use `BackgroundImage` to draw a frame around an image with `SizeMode` set to `CenterImage`.

You can use standard control events with `PictureBox`, such as `Click`, `MouseDown`, `MouseMove`, and others to respond to actions of the user. Use the `Paint` event to draw on the control. If you need to create an interactive picture control, a `Button` control enables you to use an image and provide interactive cues.

Add a Picture to a Form

1. Create a new Windows application project or open an existing project and create or open the form to load onto the control.
2. In the Toolbox, click the `PictureBox` control.
3. Drag the control to the form.

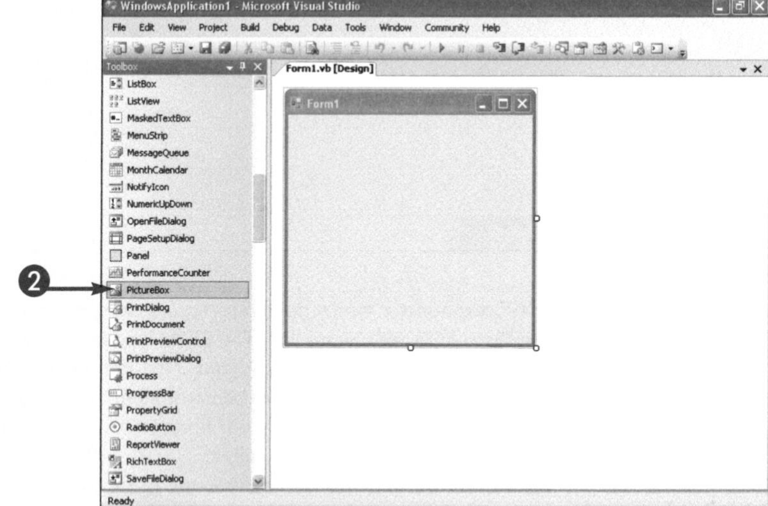

The control appears on the form.

4. Edit any necessary properties.
5. In the Properties Windows, click the `Image` property.
6. Click the ... link button.

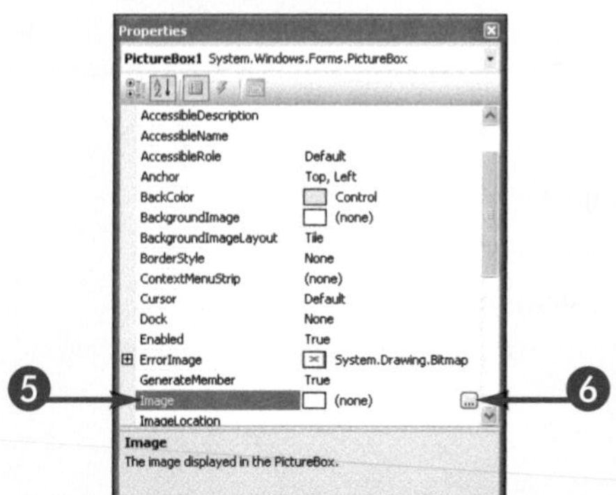

The Open dialog box appears.

7 Click an image file from disk.

8 Click Open to load the image into the control.

Note: This example sets `SizeMode` to `CenterImage`.

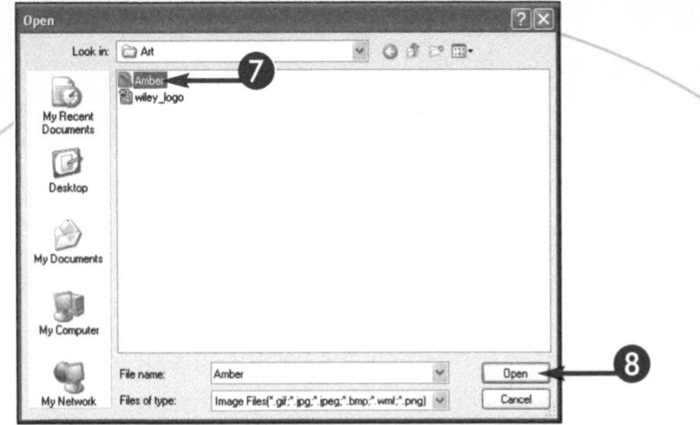

9 Press F5 to run the project.

The `PictureBox` control displays the picture file appropriately.

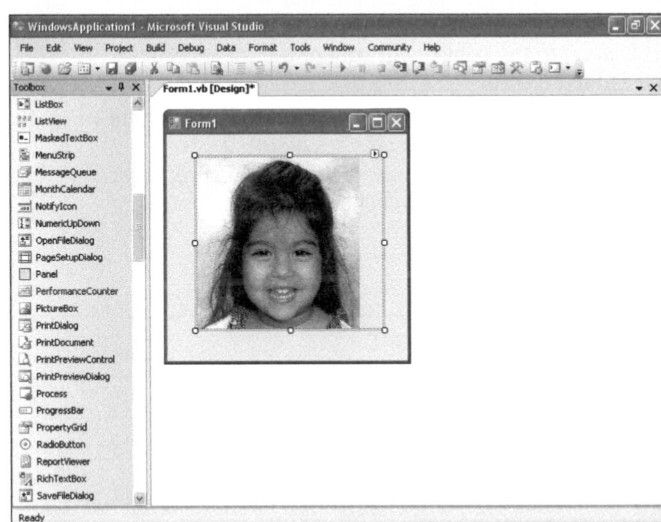

Extra

When you load an image into a `PictureBox` control, it saves the image into the executable, which can balloon in size unnecessarily in an application in which a variety of forms may include the same image. To prevent this, you can use a resource file to store only a single copy of the file in the executable. You can then load the appropriate resource image in the `PictureBox` control in the `Form_Load` procedures. The `ResourceManager` class contains the necessary functions to access a resource file.

Example

```
PictureBox1.Image = Ctype(ResourceManager.GetObject("flag"),
System.Drawingin.Image)
```

The `PictureBox` control accepts drawing commands such as the `Form` and many other controls. This means that the tasks later in the chapter explaining the `Graphics` object work using a `PictureBox` as well. Just place the code from a `Form_Paint` routine into a `PictureBox_Paint` routine. The `PictureBox` contains all the same drawing methods and properties.

Using the Color Dialog Box

When editing colors in an application or simply changing the colors on your desktop, the common Color dialog box supplies the standard method of selecting a color. You can use the `ColorDialog` control in your application to provide color selection abilities to your user.

The `ColorDialog` control is located in the Windows Forms section of the Toolbox. When you place the control on a form, it loads into the component tray of the form because it is in a hidden control.

The most important property for the Color dialog box is the `Color` property because it controls the color that you display in the box. When the user clicks OK, this property stores the selection. If the user clicks Cancel, the control does not alter the property value.

The `AllowFullOpen` property enables or disables the custom color section of the dialog box where the full color box is available. If you set `FullOpen` to `True`, the custom color area appears automatically when the dialog box opens. The `SolidColorOnly` property determines whether the dialog box selects only solid colors. This only affects 256 color or less displays, which must blend multiple colors. This blending creates a dotted appearance and makes text reading difficult. If you plan to have small-to-normal size text over the area where the selected color is in use, set `SolidColorOnly` to `False`. The `CustomColors` property stores an array of the stored custom colors.

As with other dialog boxes, you use the `ShowDialog` method of the control to make the dialog box appear. The method returns a `DialogResult` variable indicating either OK or Cancel, depending on the button that the user clicks.

Using the Color Dialog Box

1. Create a new Windows application project or open an existing one.
2. In the Toolbox, double-click the `ColorDialog` item to add it to the form.

   The control opens in the component tray.

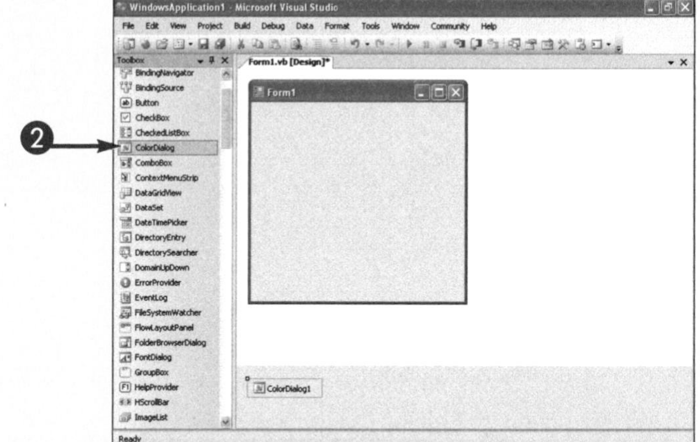

3. In the Properties window, change any necessary properties.
4. Double-click the control for which you want to display the dialog box.

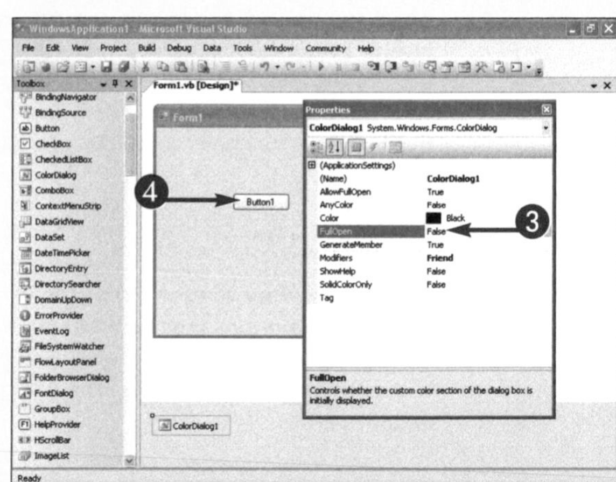

5 In the method where you want the dialog box to appear, declare a variable to store the DialogResult.

6 Type res=ColorDialog1.ShowDialog() replacing res with the variable name and ColorDialog1 with the control name.

7 Type code to process the result of the dialog box using the Color property to retrieve the selected color.

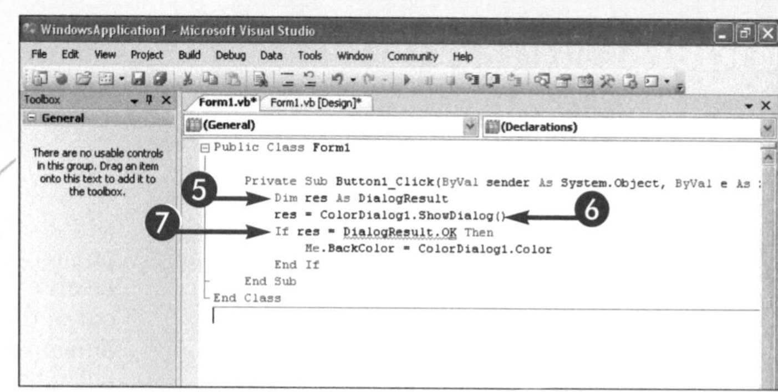

8 Press F5 to run the project.

The Color dialog box allows color selection. When the user selects a color, your application responds by using his or her color choice.

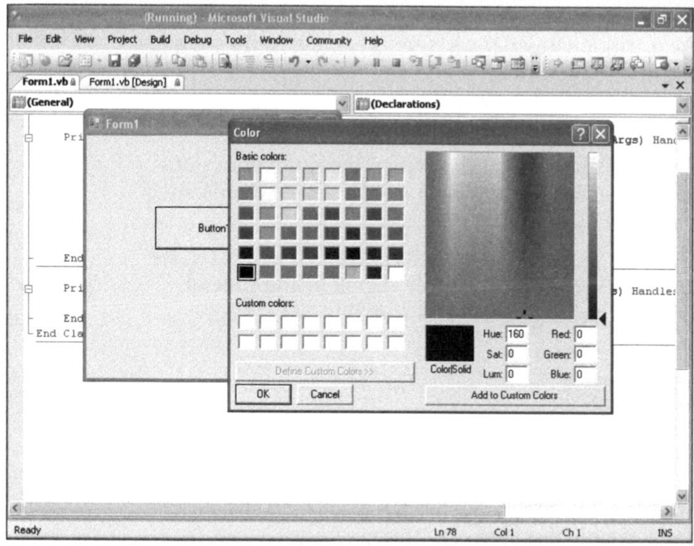

Extra

You can use the CustomColors property to both provide your own set of colors to the user or to store the user's own selection of colors. The variable types of the property are an integer array. You can use the For Each loop to run through the list and store the user's settings.

Example

```
ListBox1.Items.Clear()
Dim myColor As Integer
For Each myColor In ColorDialog1.CustomColors
   ListBox1.Items.Add(myColor)
Next
```

To store an entire set of new values in the CustomColors array, create a new array of size fifteen. Fill the sixteen values (0 to 15) and assign the array to the property.

Example

```
Dim counter As Integer
Dim red As Integer = 100
Dim newColors(15) As Integer
For counter = 0 to 15
   New Colors(counter) = red
   Red = red + 10
Next
ColorDialog1.Customercolors = newColors
```

Understanding the Graphics Object

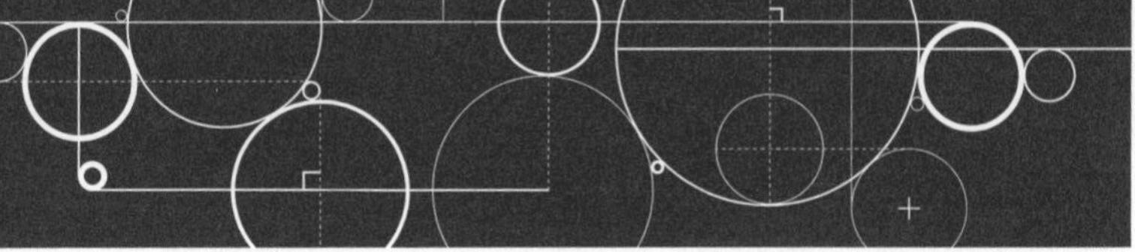

Using controls and forms creates simple interfaces. But for some applications, you may want to draw custom art, not a form or control. To do so, you can use the `Graphics` object that forms and controls provide.

Use the `Paint` event of a component to draw onto the component's surface. When a control needs to be redrawn because a window overlaps it, the `Paint` event fires when the control redraws itself. The `Paint` event provides the `Graphics` object in the event arguments. In most cases, this means that you access the object using `e.Graphics`.

The `Dpix` and `Dpiy` properties return the number of dots per inch, or resolution, available on the device represented by the `Graphics` object.

The `VisibleClipBounds` property returns a `RectangleF` structure that specifies the visible region of the control available for drawing. This class contains `Left`, `Top`, `Width`, and `Height` properties. The `Graphics` object's `Clip` property enables you to set a `Region` of the control where pixels can appear. When graphic methods attempt to draw out of the clip region, only the section inside the region draws. Retrieve the current `Clip` region as `RectangleF` using the `ClipBounds` property.

A number of properties combine to specify the total quality of the image drawn. The `CompositingMode` property specifies how pixels draw into the `Graphics` object. It provides two constants: `SourceCopy` to overwrite background pixels and `SourceOver` to combine with background pixels. Set `CompositingMode` to `SourceOver` to create a more realistic blend when overlapping translucent objects. `SmoothingMode` determines the quality of antialiasing that you use when drawing curves and diagonals. `TextRenderingHint` sets the antialiasing mode for text. `InterpolationMode` determines how Visual Basic .NET calculates intermediate values between two endpoints.

The Paint Event

By default, the `Paint` event invalidates the area that changes. For example, if the user makes the form larger, Visual Basic .NET allows only the part of the form that did not exist prior to that to repaint. This means that if your code relies on the size of the form and resizes graphics as the form resizes, Visual Basic .NET does not redraw the entire surface.

Also, when a `Panel` or other scrolling container scrolls, only the invisible part of the control invalidates. For a form or control that resizes, you can place the name of the object followed by `.Invalidate()` to invalidate the entire contents and draw on the entire surface.

The Point Object

The `Point` object specifies a set of two pixel values that make up a particular coordinate onscreen. To create a new instance of the `Pen` object, pass the `X` coordinate followed by the `Y` coordinate. The properties `X` and `Y` store the values that you specify.

Example:

```
'define a point that represents the (100, 100) position.
Dim pt As New Drawing.Point(100, 100)
```

The Size Object

The `Size` object represents the size of a particular object. To create an instance of the `Size` object, pass the width and height to the constructor. The properties `Width` and `Height` store the values that you specify.

Example:

```
'define a size of 200 pixels across and 100 pixels in height
Dim sz As New Size(200, 100)
```

The Rectangle Object

The `Rectangle` object specifies a set of four coordinates to define the size of a rectangle. Many of the graphics primitives throughout the chapter use the `Rectangle` object. To create a new instance of a `Rectangle` object, pass the left (`X`) coordinate, the top (`Y`) coordinate, and the width and height. The properties `Left`, `Top`, `Width`, and `Height` store each of the values that you specify.

Example:

```
'define a rectangle that starts at position
(100, 100), is 200 pixels across and 50 in
height
Dim rect As New Drawing.Rectangle(100, 100,
200, 50)
```

The Color Object

The `Graphics` object works with colors in the ARGB format. A value of 0-255 represents transparency (alpha-blending), and a range of 0-255 for each red, green, and blue value combines to create the full set of 32-bit colors. To create a custom color, call the `Color.FromArgb` method and either specify the combined `ARGB` integer or separate each of the four values by commas. The function uses the color given or generates the appropriate combined number and returns a `Color` object.

Visual Basic .NET makes a large variety of colors available to you by name in the `Drawing.Color` object. Colors range from `AliceBlue` to `YellowGreen`. Below is a partial list of the available colors in the `Color` object. For the complete list, search Visual Basic .NET help by typing **Color members**.

SAMPLE SYSTEM.DRAWING.COLOR MEMBERS

AliceBlue	AntiqueWhite	Aqua	Beige
Black	Blue	BlueViolet	Brown
CadetBlue	Chartreuse	Chocolate	Coral
CornflowerBlue	Crimson	Cyan	ForestGreen
Fuchsia	GhostWhite	Gold	Goldenrod
Gray	Green	GreenYellow	Honeydew
Indigo	Ivory	Khaki	Lavender
Lime	LimeGreen	Linen	Magenta
Maroon	MidnightBlue	Navy	OldLace
Olive	Orange	OrangeRed	Orchid
Peru	Pink	Plum	PowderBlue
Purple	Red	RoyalBlue	Salmon
SandyBrown	SeaGreen	Sienna	Silver
SkyBlue	SlateBlue	SlateGray	Snow
SpringGreen	SteelBlue	Tan	Teal
Thistle	Transparent	Turquoise	Violet
White	WhiteSmoke	Yellow	YellowGreen

Create a Brush

You use a Brush class to tell Visual Basic .NET how to fill an area. Each of the filled primitives, such as filled rectangles, requires you to use a Brush to specify how to fill the area. To produce a brush for use in Visual Basic .NET, create an instance of type Brush using the New operator. Visual Basic .NET provides a number of Brush classes depending on the style that you need. Each brush has a particular size. If the shape to fill is larger than the brush, the brush tiles to fill the entire space.

The System.Drawing namespace holds both the SolidBrush and TextureBrush classes. SolidBrush paints an area in a single color. Pass the color to use the brush as the only parameter. Because these brushes are a solid color, the brush is only 1 x 1 in size.

The System.Drawing.Drawing2D namespace contains a number of more complex brushes. HatchBrush creates a brush based on a pattern; Windows provides a collection of 2-bit hatch patterns. Visual Basic .NET provides constants for each of these patterns in the HatchStyle enumeration, ranging from BackwardDiagonal to ZigZag. To create the brush, declare an instance of the HatchBrush class and pass the constructor the pattern to use, followed by the foreground color as the second parameter, and the background color as the third parameter.

LinearGradientBrush fills in a steady range from one color to another, at any angle. For the constructor, pass an instance of a Rectangle class filled with the size of the gradient brush to create. The next parameter specifies the start color, and the third parameter specifies the end color. The last parameter is the angle in degrees of gradient. An angle of zero creates a horizontal gradient, and an angle of 90 creates a vertical gradient.

Create a Brush

CREATE A SOLID BRUSH

1. Create a new project or open an existing one.
2. Click the class list and select (Base Class Event) or the control on which to draw.
3. Click the method name list and select the Paint event.
4. Type Dim redBrush As New Drawing.SolidBrush(Color.Red), replacing redBrush with the name for the brush and Color.Red with the color.

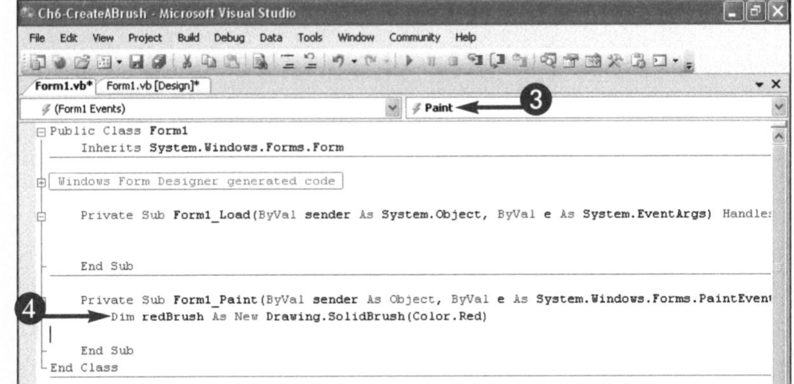

CREATE A HATCH BRUSH

5. Type Dim confettiBrush As New Drawing2D.HatchBrush(), replacing confettiBrush with the name of the brush.
6. Inside the parentheses, type the hatch pattern to use followed by the foreground and background colors, all separated by commas.

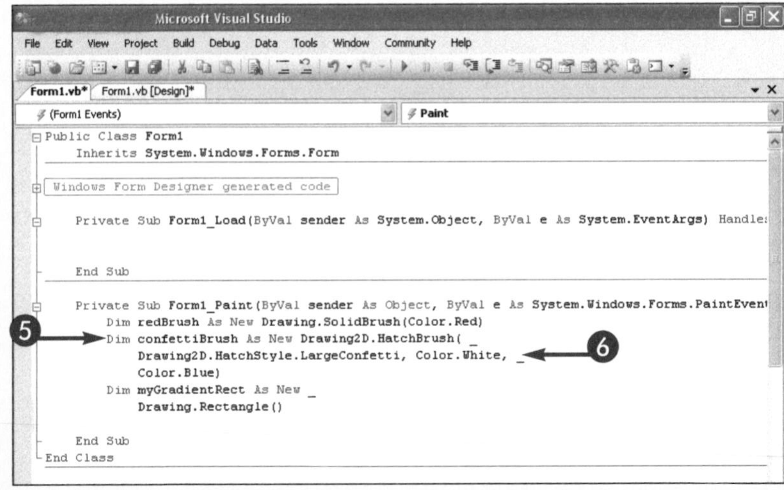

CREATE A LINEAR GRADIENT

7. Declare a `Rectangle` object.
8. Type `Dim gradient As New Drawing2D.LinearGradientBrush ()`, replacing `LinearGradient` with the name of the brush.
9. In the parentheses, type the `Rectangle` name, the start and end color, and the angle of rotation separated by commas.
10. Type the code to use the brushes.

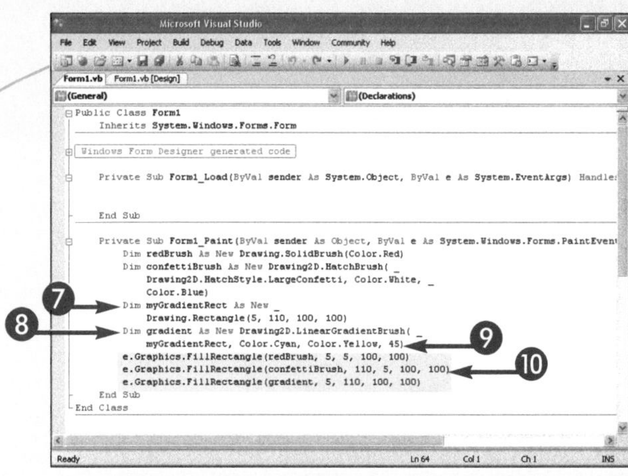

11. Press F5 to run the project.

    The brush draws into the area to fill, tiling if necessary.

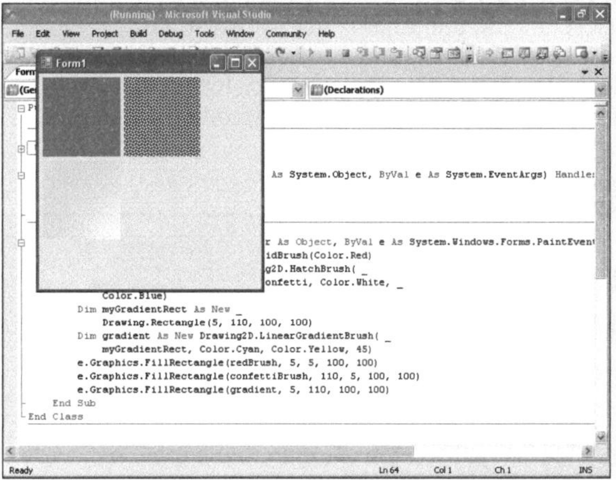

Extra

If you need a simple solid-color brush, you may find it time-consuming to constantly create custom brush objects. However, you can use a precreated brush to save you the trouble of creating a new instance of a `SolidBrush` class. The `System.Drawing.Brushes` class provides a set of brushes for each color in the standard color list.

Example

```
Dim myPlum As Drawing.SolidBrush - Drawing.Brushes.Plum
```

In Windows, the user sets a variety of colors in Desktop preferences, and all Windows applications respond in the same way. You may want to draw onto the form, but you need to follow the Windows colors the user selects. You can use the `SystemBrushes` class to fill in an area in a particular system color. The `SystemBrushes` class is part of the `System.Drawing` namespace. For example, `SystemBrushes.Desktop` returns a brush in the color of the current user's desktop. You can also retrieve the individual color values that each brush relies on using the `SystemColors` class. You can type **SystemBrushes members** in Help to search for a full list of the available system colors.

Example

```
Dim myControlColor As Drawing.SolidBrush = Drawing.SystemBrushes.Control
```

Create a Pen

You use a `Pen` to tell Visual Basic .NET the style, color, and thickness of a line to draw for the various primitives. For example, a variety of outlined primitives use a `Pen`, such as rectangles, ellipses, and curves. A `Pen` specifies details for Visual Basic .NET to know how to draw these shapes. Use a `Brush` to fill a primitive object or the inside of a `Pen`.

To produce a single-color pen, create a new instance of the `Pen` class using the `Dim` command and the `New` operator. Visual Basic .NET stores the `Pen` class in the `System.Drawing` namespace. For the most basic constructor of the `Pen`, pass a color as the single parameter. The second constructor expects a color for the first parameter and the line width as the second parameter.

To create a `Pen` object based on a `Brush`, create a new instance of the `Pen` class and provide the `Brush` as the first argument. To specify the width of the pen, use the alternate constructor that expects a `Brush` and a line width passed in as a `Single`.

After you create a `Pen` instance, a number of properties allow for editing its appearance. The `StartCap` and `EndCap` properties expect a constant from the `LineCap` enumeration. The properties specify the type of end caps to put on the pen. A primitive without ends — for example, a rectangle or ellipse — ignores the values. Instead, the `LineJoin` property specifies how to connect corners of lines and expects a value from the `LineJoin` enumeration. To create different styles of dashed lines, set the `DashStyle` value that represents the style to use for dashes.

Create a Pen

1. Open an existing user control.
2. Click the class list and select (Base Class Event) or the control on which to draw.
3. Click the method name list and select the `Paint` event.

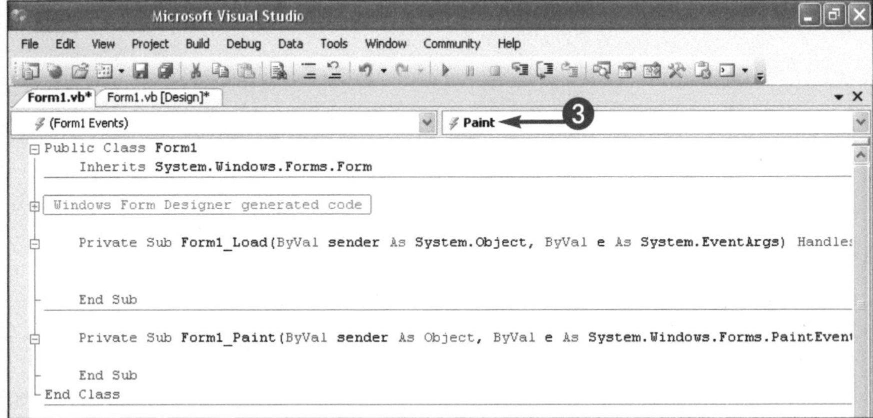

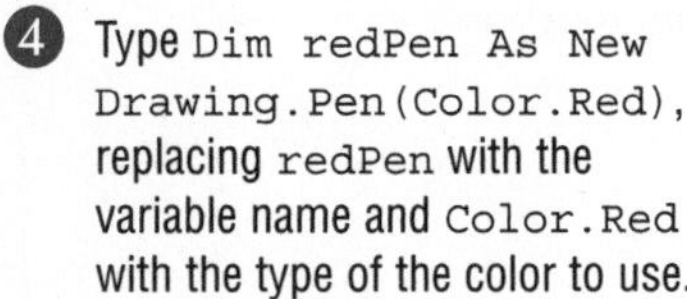

4. Type `Dim redPen As New Drawing.Pen(Color.Red)`, replacing `redPen` with the variable name and `Color.Red` with the type of the color to use.

Note: This example uses the `Color` class to provide a supplied color `Red`.

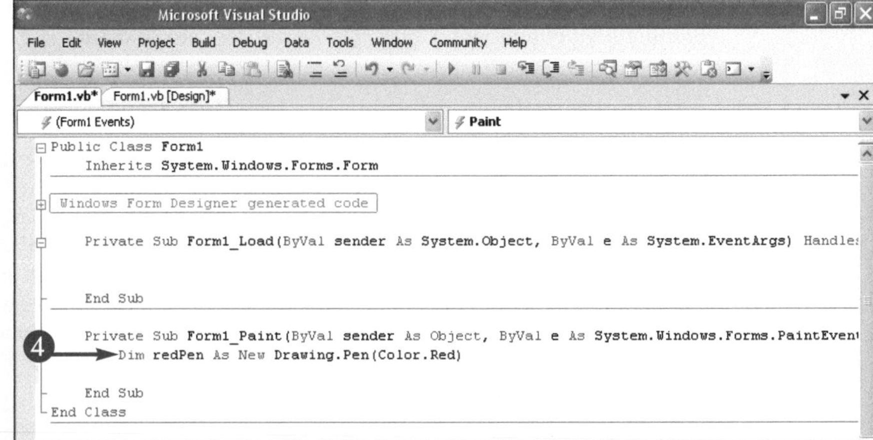

5. Type `e.Graphics.DrawLine(redPen, 5, 5, 200, 200)`, replacing `DrawLine` with the `Graphics` method to use the pen, `redPen` with the variable name of the `Pen` object, and `5, 5, 200, 200` with the appropriate parameters.

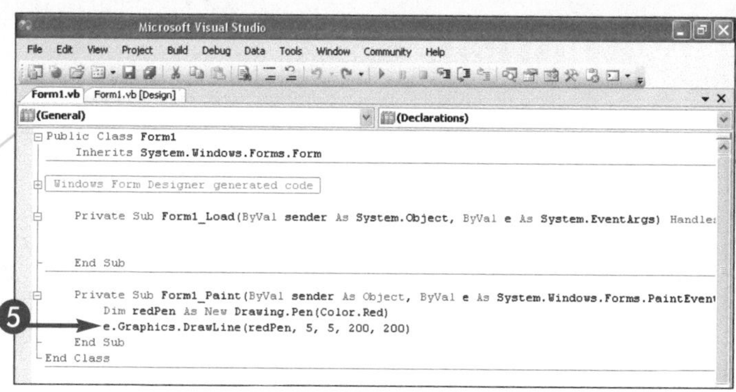

6. Press F5 to run your project.

   The graphics method runs and draws using the selected color.

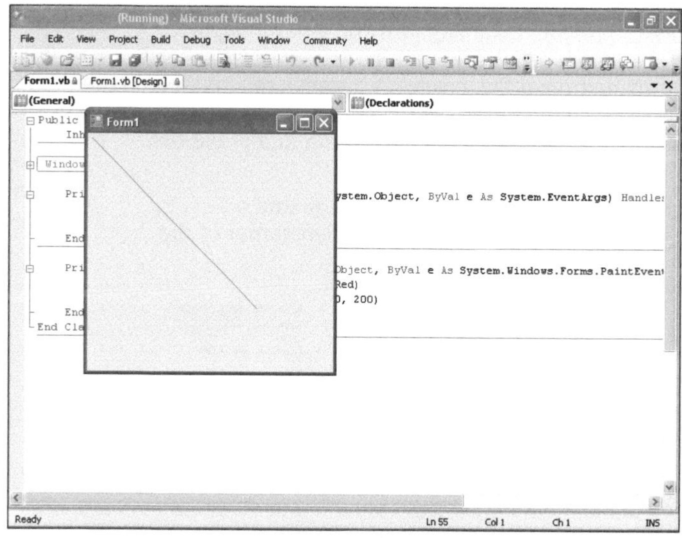

xtra

se the following constants to v a pen draws.

ing.Drawing2D.LineCap Enumeration

MEMBER	DESCRIPTION
`AnchorMask`	A mask used to check a line cap
`ArrowAnchor`	Arrow-shaped anchor cap
`Custom`	A custom line cap
`DiamondAnchor`	Diamond anchor cap
`Flat`	Flat line cap
`NoAnchor`	No anchor
`Round`	Round line cap
`RoundAnchor`	Round anchor cap
`Square`	Square line cap
`SquareAnchor`	Square anchor line cap
`Triangle`	Triangular line cap

Drawing.Drawing2D.DashCap Enumeration

MEMBER	DESCRIPTION
`Flat`	Squares off ends of each dash
`Round`	Rounds off ends of each dash
`Triangle`	Points ends of each dash

Drawing.Drawing2D.LineJoin Enumeration

MEMBER	DESCRIPTION
`Bevel`	Beveled join
`Miter`	Angled miter join
`MiterClipped`	Clipped miter join
`Round`	Smooth, rounded join

Draw Bitmaps and Images

You can add images to a form in conjunction with drawing commands. The `PictureBox` control provides a simple way to load an image on the form, but you cannot draw around the `PictureBox` unless you contain all the drawing inside. You can use commands from the `System.Drawing` namespace to draw images onto the form without using a control.

Two classes provide the ability to work with bitmapped images. You more commonly use the `Bitmap` class to load a raster image from a file, create an instance of a `Bitmap` class, and pass the filename as the parameter to the `Bitmap` constructor. The class stores the pixel data and properties of the image.

The simplest constructor expects an `Image` and a `Point`, which specifies the position for the top-left corner of the image. By providing an array of three `Point` classes that form a parallelogram, `DrawImage` skews the image to fit the shape. By passing a `Rectangle` as the second parameter, `DrawImage` scales the image to fit the dimensions of the rectangle starting from the top-left corner of the rectangle.

You can use `TextureBrush` to paint an image onto a shape. This enables you to create an image that has shaped edges and lets you place the image inside an ellipse or more advanced shapes. The first parameter of the available constructors accepts an `Image` or `Bitmap` class. For the simplest constructor, you need only this parameter. Another constructor of the `TextureBrush` class expects a `Rectangle` as the second parameter that specifies the section of the image to use as the brush. The width and height of the rectangle determine the size of the brush.

Draw Bitmaps and Images

1. Create a new Windows application project or open an existing one.
2. Open the method or event where the image needs to draw.
3. Type `Dim myPic As New Drawing.Bitmap("C:\WINNT\CoffeBean.bmp")` with the path to a supported raster image file.

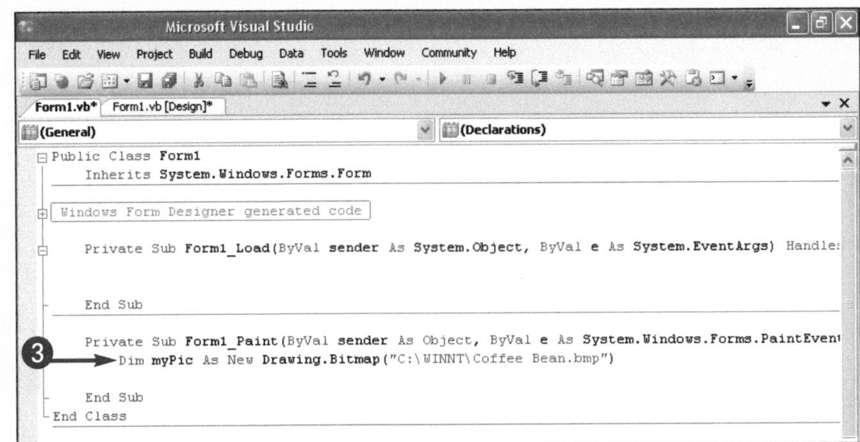

4. On a new line, type `e.Graphics.DrawImage(myPic)`, replacing `e.Graphics` with the name of the `Graphics` object and `myPic` with the variable name of the `Bitmap` object.

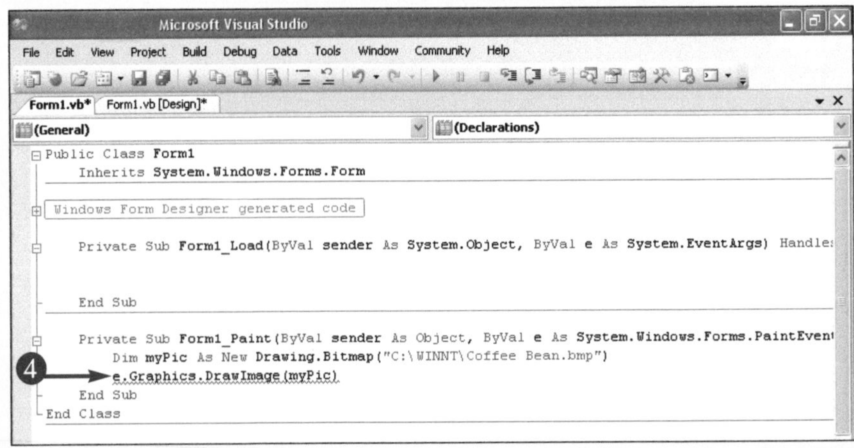

5 Type a comma and follow it with `New Drawing.Point(50, 50)`, replacing `50, 50` with the coordinates to draw the image.

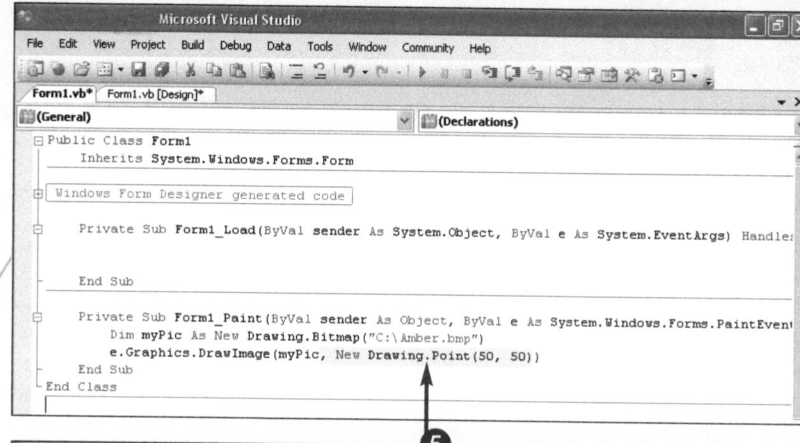

6 Press F5 to run your project.

The image draws onto the form.

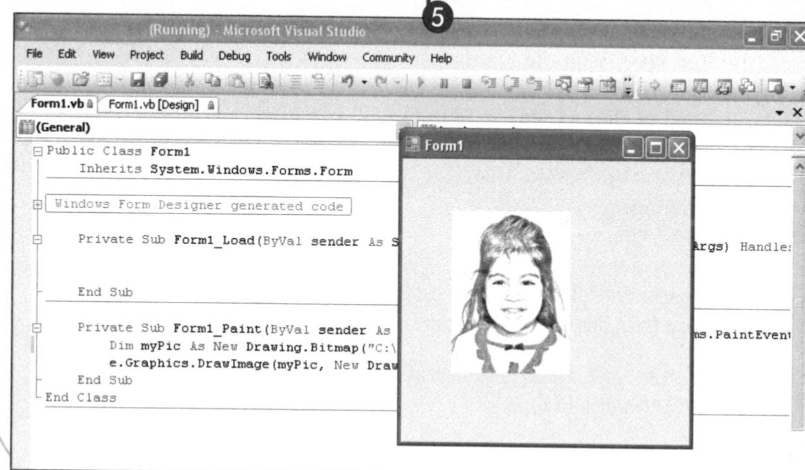

Extra

You use a metafile, a format designed to hold a list of vector commands, to make up an image. You can use a metafile image in a variety of sizes and have the image maintain its detail. Unlike raster files, metafiles, which have the extension WMF, do not contain any information about individual pixels, only information about lines and curves, shapes, and fill patterns. Pass a new instance of the `Metafile` class a WMF file and use it with the standard drawing commands to draw it onto the form. Using `DrawImage`, you can draw the metafile in any size necessary because metafiles have the capability to scale to any size. You can create metafiles in most Windows drawing applications such as Adobe Illustrator. The `Icon` class enables you to load icon files. Create a new instance of the `Icon` class and pass an icon file as the parameter. Use the `DrawIcon` method of the `Graphics` object to draw the icon. Pass the `Icon` object as the first parameter, followed by two points specifying the location to draw it. Visual Studio 2005 .NET provides many icons in the Common directory.

Example

```
Dim myIcon As New System.Drawing.Icon ("C\Explorer.ico")
e.Graphics.DrawIcon(myIcon, 100,100)
```

Draw Simple Primitives

In many cases, you need to draw borders and boxes around items in a Windows application. You can use a variety of primitives in your Windows `Forms` application to add aesthetics to parts of the form. A number of commands draw outlined objects such as lines, rectangles, and ellipses. For these commands to work, you need to create a `Pen`.

The `DrawLine` method draws a line onto the graphics region. The first parameter the method expects is a `Pen`. After the first parameter, you give the method two `Point` structures, the first specifying the starting (x, y) coordinates, and the second specifying the end (x, y) coordinates. Instead of the two `Point` objects, you can also pass four integers or four singles in the form of `x1, y1, x2, y2`. `DrawRectangle` expects a `Pen` for the first argument and a `Rectangle` object for the second argument. Instead of the `Rectangle`, you can provide four integers or singles after the `Pen` parameter. `DrawEllipse` draws an ellipse to fill a rectangular space and expects the same arguments as `DrawRectangle`.

`DrawLines` creates a connected set of line segments. When you pass a `Pen` as the first parameter with an array of `Point` objects as the second argument, the method starts at the point and connects each point together in sequence. `DrawRectangles` draws a series of rectangles with a single `Pen`. Pass the `Pen` as the first argument and an array of `Rectangle` objects as the second parameter. `DrawPolygon` draws a polygon based on a set of points. It automatically connects the first point and last point. Pass a `Pen` and an array of `Point` objects for the parameters.

Draw Simple Primitives

1. Create or open a Windows application project and double-click a form that you want to paint.
2. Click the class list and select (Base Class Events) or the control on which to draw.
3. Click the method name list and select the `Paint` event.

   The Code Editor creates the event handler.
4. Declare a new instance of a `Pen` class.
5. Type `e.Graphics.DrawEllipse` replacing `DrawEllipse` with the method name to draw.

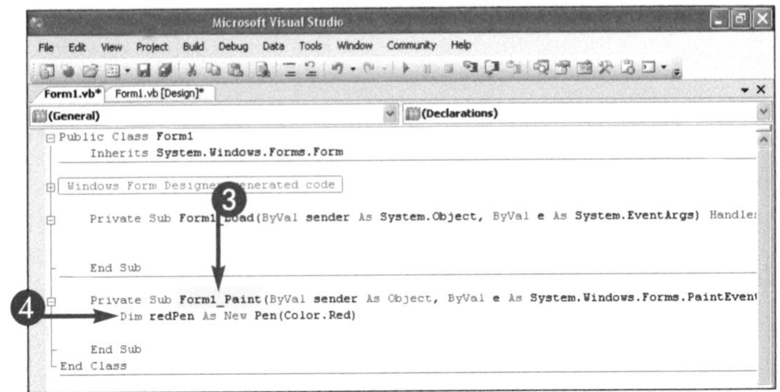

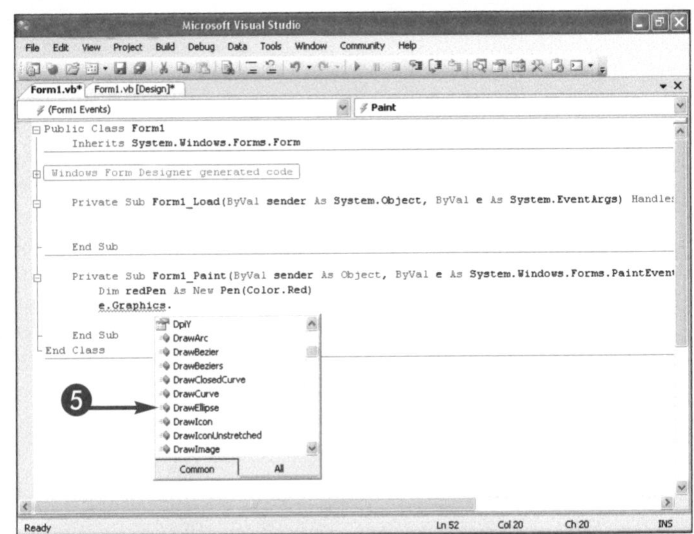

6 Type appropriate parameters inside parentheses.

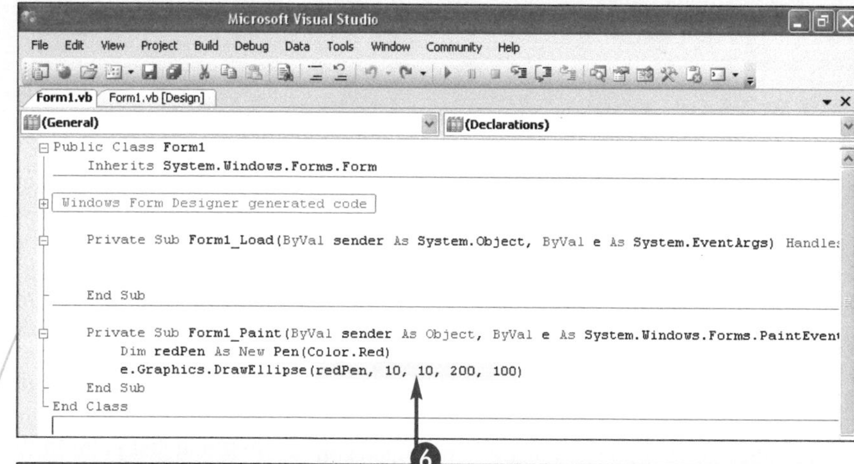

7 Press F5 to run your project.

The form draws the primitive.

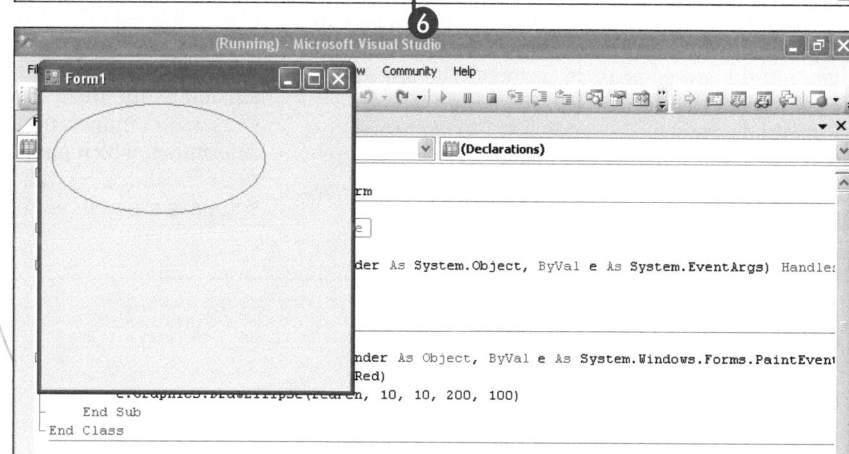

Extra

You can create filled regions using the `Graphics` object, which contains a set of methods to draw filled primitives. You can use these commands to create a primitive just like the drawing commands like `DrawLine` and `DrawEllipse`, except instead of drawing an outline, these commands fill the region. Each of these methods accepts the same parameters as their outlined counterparts, except you switch the `Pen` parameter to a `Brush`. `FillRectangle` fills a rectangular space with the supplied brush. `FillEllipse` fills an elliptical area. `FillRectangles` fills a series of rectangles. `FillPolygon` fills a polygon area based on a set of points. If you want to draw a filled region with a border, use a combination of the two commands. Draw the filled primitive first and then pass the same set of size and parameters to the outlined primitive. Calling the methods in the other order can cause the fill to overwrite the pen.

Example

```
Dim rect As New Drawing.Rectangle(50, 50, 200, 100)
Dim redBrush As Drawing.SolidBrush = System.Drawing.Brushes.Red
e.Graphics.FillEllipse(redBrush, rect)
```

Draw a Curve

Visual Basic .NET provides a set of functions to draw curves, complex line forms that use advanced algorithms to draw, given only a few reference points. You can use simple graphics primitive commands to create a variety of curved lines and shapes.

The `DrawArc` method is the simplest curve command because it draws a portion of an ellipse. You pass the method a `Pen` as the first parameter. For the next parameter, you pass either a `Rectangle` containing the size of the entire ellipse or four integers holding the dimension of the ellipse. Following these parameters, you specify the start angle and the sweep angle in degrees. The angles measure clockwise from the x-axis. The `DrawPie` and `FillPie` methods draw a pie wedge just like an arc, except two lines draw to the center of the ellipse. Because `FillPie` creates a fill region, pass it a `Brush` instead of a `Pen` as the first argument.

The `DrawCurve` method draws a curve through a specified array of points. The first parameter for the `DrawCurve` constructor is the `Pen` you use to draw the curve. The second parameter is an array of the `Point` class, which specifies the points through which you draw the curve. Another constructor takes the same two arguments plus the tension to draw the curve as the third parameter. A tension of zero creates a straight line.

`DrawClosedCurve` draws a curve with a line connecting the first and last point in the curve. The basic constructor requests only a `Pen` and `Point()`, for example, `DrawCurve`. Another constructor takes those two arguments plus the tension as the third argument and a constant from the `FillMode` enumeration for the fourth. `FillMode` determines which part of the curve encloses the section. `FillClosedCurve` fills the enclosed space of the curve. You pass a `Brush` as the first argument.

Draw a Curve

1. Create a new Windows application project or open an existing one.
2. Open the `Paint` event where the curve needs to draw.
3. Declare a `Pen` to draw the curve.

Note: To use the fill routines, you can also declare a `Brush`.

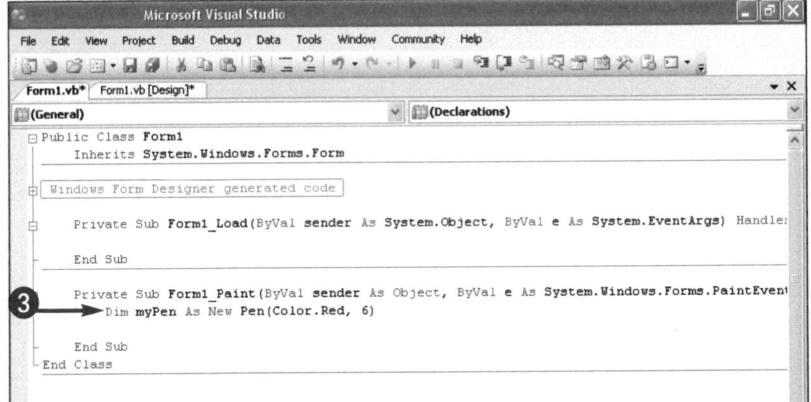

4. To draw an arc or pie, type `e.Graphics.DrawPie(myPen)`, replacing `DrawPie` with either `DrawPie` or `DrawArc` and `myPen` with the name of the `Pen` object.
5. Type a `Rectangle` object representing the size.
6. Type a comma and follow it with the start and sweep angles.

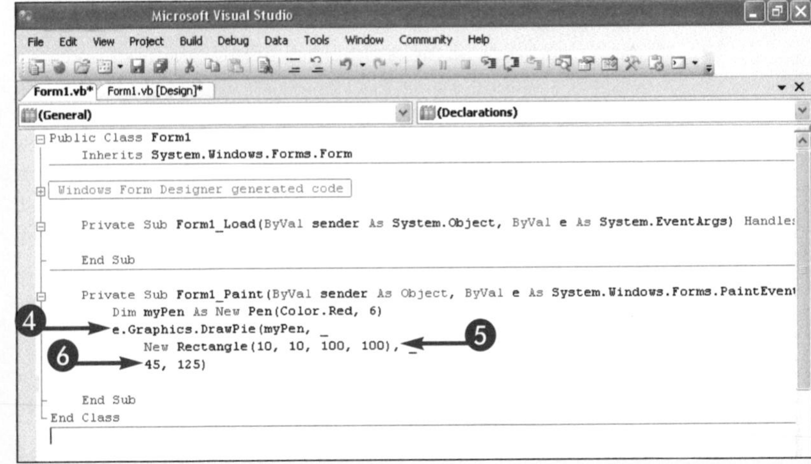

7 To draw a curve, declare an array of `Point` objects that the curve passes through.

8 Type `e.Graphics.DrawCurve (myPen, pts)`, replacing `DrawCurve` with either `DrawCurve` or `DrawClosedCurve` and `myPen` with the name of the `Pen` object and `pts` with the name of the `Point` array.

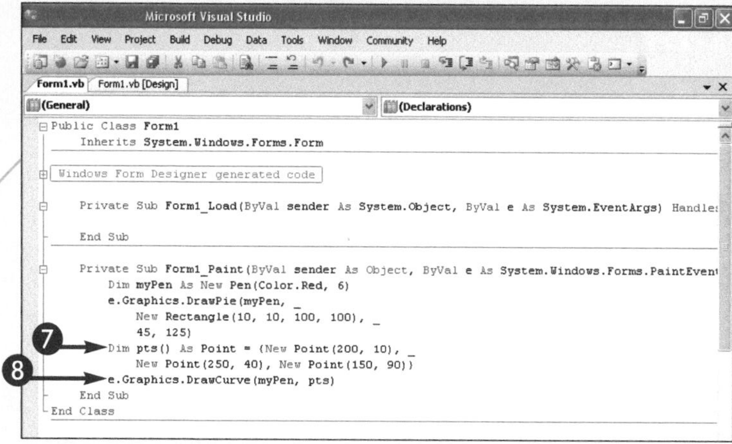

9 Press F5 to run your project.

The curve draws onto the graphics container.

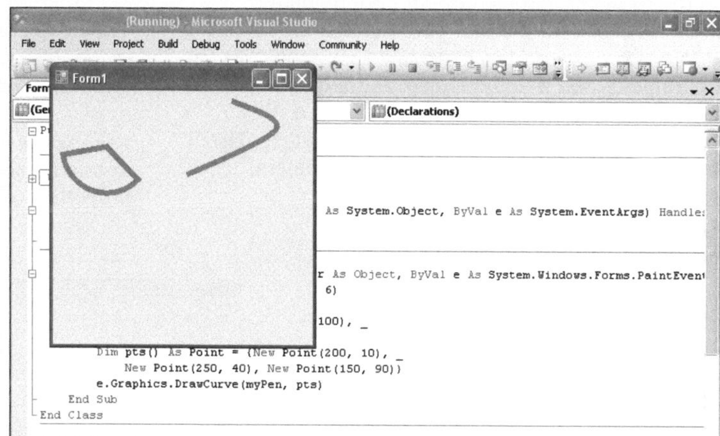

Extra

You can create different fill patterns for objects with complex shapes, such as curves, using the `FillMode` enumeration. You have two options for `FillMode`: `Winding`, and the default, `Alternate`. `Alternate` moves across the curve and alternates between filling and not filling as it hits lines of the curve. `Winding` uses the direction of the curve to determine whether to fill it. Generally, the default `Alternate` does an effective job, but you may try `Winding` when `Alternate` does not give the appropriate results.

You can use Bezier curves, a more advanced cubic curve, to specify more exact coordinates of curvature. Most professional drawing applications work with Bezier curves instead of the simpler cardinal spline curves used by `DrawCurve`. To draw a Bezier curve, you use the `DrawBezier` method, which draws only one curve defined by four points. The method requires a `Pen` object and parameters. The first and last `Point` objects make up the curve's endpoints. The two middle `Point` objects make up the two control points that create the curvature. When the curve draws, it pulls the curve out to the control points.

Example

```
e.Graphics.DrawBezier(Drawing.Pens.Red, New Point(100, 100), New Point (150,
150), New Point(150, 200), New Point (100, 250))
```

Draw Text

Most applications use text to title, label, and explain functions on a form. In some cases, a `Label` control can provide the appearance necessary. For advanced text rendering, you can use the text drawing routines that Visual Basic .NET includes in the `Graphics` object. Using the `Graphics` system, you can apply a `Brush` to your text to create text filled with a gradient, a bitmapped texture, or a hatch pattern.

The standard method of rendering text with the `Graphics` object is the `DrawString` method. In each available overloaded method call, the first parameter contains the `String` to print. `DrawString` expects a `Font` object as the second parameter and a `Brush` object as the third parameter. For the fourth parameter, you pass a `Point` object specifying the top-left point to draw the text. The simplest constructor requires these four parameters. Optionally, for a fifth parameter, you can pass a `StringFormat` object to designate how the text styles.

To provide the font to pass to `DrawString`, create a new instance of the `System.Drawing.Font` class. Depending on the data that you want to provide to the `Font` constructor, you can pass either a `FontFamily` object or a `String` to select a font family such as Arial or Times New Roman. The second parameter is the size of the font in points. Optionally, for the third parameter, specify the font style using the `FontStyle` enumeration.

The `Graphics` object exposes a method called `MeasureString`. Use this method to determine the width and height of a string that you want to draw. Pass the `String` and `Font` as the two parameters to the method. `MeasureString` returns a `SizeF` structure, contained in the `System.Drawing` namespace. The `Width` and `Height` properties of the `SizeF` contain the appropriate values.

Draw Text

1. Create a new Windows application project or open an existing one.
2. Open the `Paint` event where the curve needs to draw.

Note: This example shows the `Form1_Paint` event.

3. Declare a `Brush` object to draw the text.

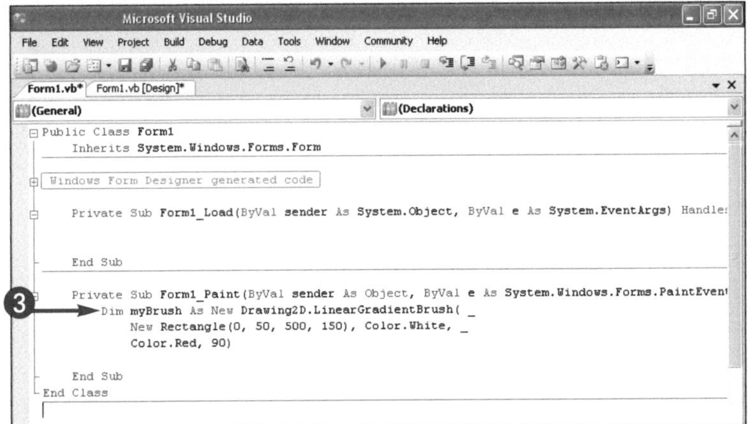

4. Type `Dim myFont As New Drawing.Font()`, replacing `myFont` with the name of the `Font` variable.
5. Inside the parentheses, type `"Arial Black",72`, replacing `Arial Black` with the font face to use and `72` with the size of the font.

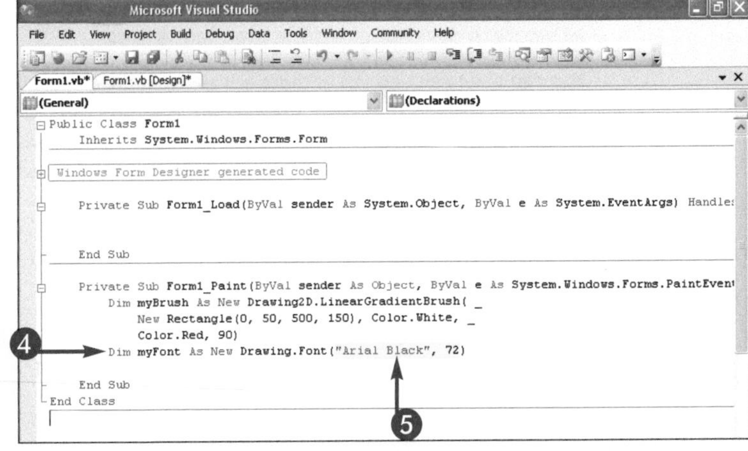

6 On a new line, type `e.Graphics.DrawString("Big text", myFont, myBrush, 20, 50)`, replacing `Big text` with the string to print or a string variable, `myFont` with the name of the `Font` variable, `myBrush` with the name of the `Brush` variable, and `20, 50` with the coordinates to draw the text.

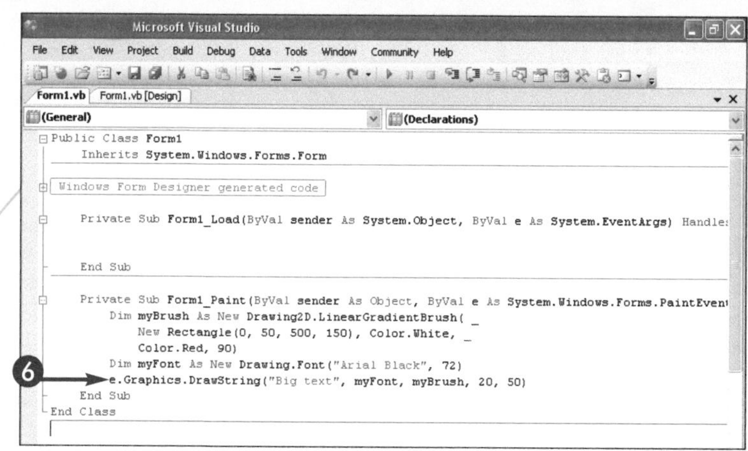

7 Press F7 to run your project.

The text renders onto the appropriate graphics container.

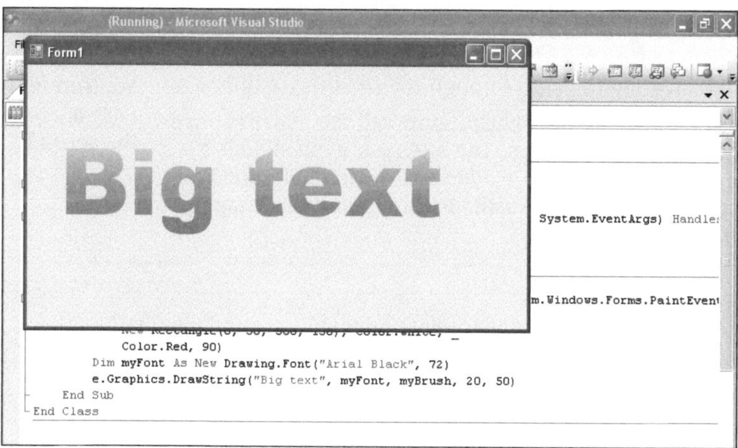

Extra

You can use the `FontStyle` enumeration to provide options for the style of font to draw. For example, you can print in a bold italics font. To do so, you can combine the constants with the `Or` operator.

MEMBER	DESCRIPTION
`Bold`	Bold text
`Italic`	Italic text
`Regular`	Normal text
`Strikeout`	Text with a line through the middle
`Underline`	Underlined text

Example

```
Dim arial As New Font("Arial", 16, FontStyle.Bold Or FontStyle.Italic)
Dim red As Brush - Brushes.Red
e.Graphics.DrawString("Bold Italic Arial Font", arial,red,10,10)
```

Create a Path

Because simple primitives may not provide the appearance that you want for your application, you can combine multiple primitives into a single object with a single fill. You use the `GraphicsPath` object to create a complex object from a number of primitives. `GraphicsPath` can also represent multiple figures, completely separate in space. A *figure* consists of an open or closed shape.

To create a `GraphicsPath`, declare a new instance of a `GraphicsPath` class with no entries passed to the constructor as parameters. The class is part of the `System.Drawing.Drawing2D` namespace. However, you may find creating the path through the constructor difficult.

To begin building an individual figure, call the `StartFigure` method with no parameters. The `AddLine` method adds a line to the figure. `AddCurve` adds a curve to the figure. You can replicate all the `Draw` methods throughout this chapter, such as `DrawEllipse` and `DrawPie`, with the prefix `Add` instead of `Draw`. The methods accept all the same parameters with the exception of the `Pen` parameter, which you leave out completely. To create a functioning path, the last point of a previous primitive and the first point of the following primitive must match.

If you want to close the figure before starting a new one, call the `CloseFigure` method. Call `StartFigure` again to the `CloseAllFigures` method with no parameters to close any open figures previously created.

To draw the path onscreen, call `DrawPath` with a `Pen` as the first argument and `GraphicsPath` as the second argument. You can fill the interior areas of a path using `FillPath`. Pass a `Brush` as the first parameter and `GraphicsPath` as the second.

Create a Path

1. Create a new Windows application project or open an existing one.
2. Open the `Paint` event where the primitive needs to draw.
3. Type `Dim myPath As New Drawing.Drawing2D.GraphicsPath()`, replacing `myPath` with the variable name for the path.
4. Type `myPath.StartFigure()`, replacing `myPath` with the path's variable name.

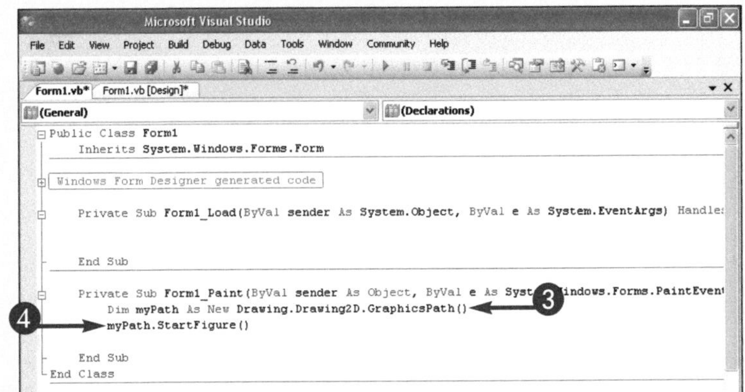

5. Type `myPath.AddLine(10,10,300,15)`, replacing `myPath` with the variable name and `AddLine(10,10,300,15)` with a primitive adding method.
6. Repeat step 5 until the figure is complete.
   - You can type `myPath.CloseFigure()`, replacing `myPath` with the path variable, to create a closed figure.
7. Repeat steps 4 to 6 to create the necessary figures.

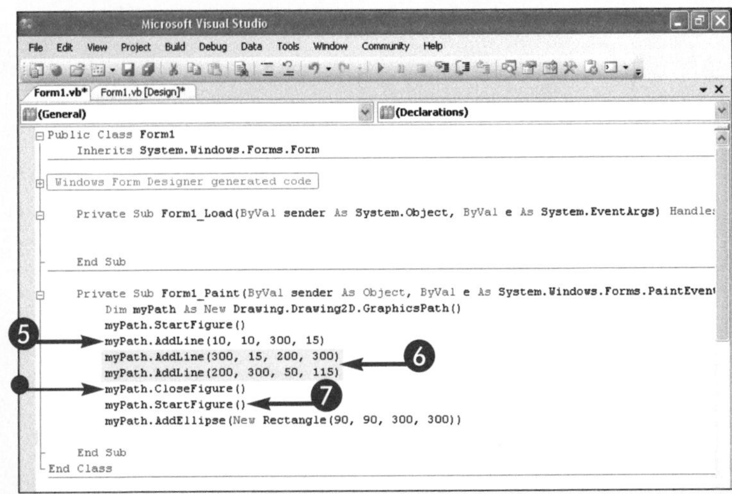

8 Declare a `Pen` to draw the path.

9 Type `e.Graphics.DrawPath(redPen, myPath)`, replacing `e.Graphics` with the name of the `Graphics` object, `redPen` with the name of the `Pen`, and `myPath` with the name of the `GraphicsPath`.

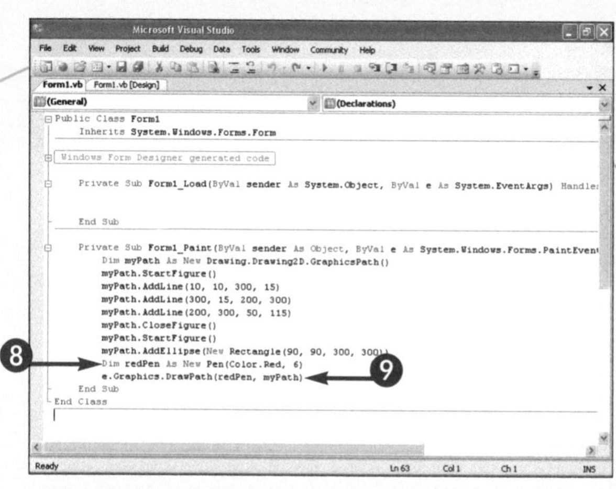

10 Press F5 to run the project.

The `GraphicsPath` draws onto the drawing region.

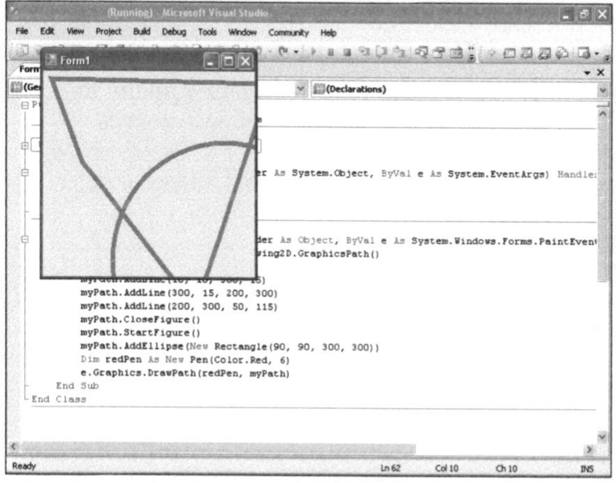

Extra

You can use the `Warp` method of the `GraphicsPath` object to warp objects. Pass a rectangle specifying the bounds of the path and an array of points making up a parallelogram into which you warp the rectangle. If you specify three points, the parallelogram adds the points and makes the lower-right point automatically. The command then warps all the points in the path to fit the shape.

Example

```
Dim myPath As New Drawing2D.GraphicsPath()
Dim srcRect As New RectangleF(0, 0, 100, 200)
myPath.AddRectangle(srcRect)
e.Graphics.DrawPath(Pens.Black, myPath)
Dim point1 - New PointF(200, 200)
Dim point2 - New PointF(400, 250)
Dim point3 - New PointF(220, 400)
Dim destPoints() As PointF - (point1, point2, point3)
myPath.Warp(destPoints, srcRect)
e.Graphics.DrawPath(Drawing.Pens.Red, myPath)
```

Using Regions

Windows GDI+ enables you to create complex areas of space defined as a region. A *region* consists of any number of rectangles and paths that build a contained area of space. The `Region` class that Visual Basic .NET provides represents a region. Windows uses a region to determine the shape of a window.

To create a region, declare a new instance of the `Region` class using `Dim` combined with the `New` operator. The class is part of the `System.Drawing` namespace. To create a simple rectangle region, pass the constructor a `Rectangle` object. To create a more complex region, you create a `GraphicsPath` object and pass it to the `Region` constructor.

The real power of regions comes from their ability to combine. Each of the two methods below expects a `GraphicsPath`, `Rectangle`, or another `Region`. `Union` takes the object from the argument and adds the object's space to the current region. `Intersect` takes the object from the argument and leaves only the part of the current region where both objects exist. `Complement` updates the current region to the portion of the specified object that does not intersect with the object. `Exclude` updates the current region to the portion of its interior that does not intersect with the specified object. `Xor` updates the current region with the union minus the intersection of itself with the object.

To draw a region, the `Graphics` object provides a `FillRegion` method. This method accepts a `Brush` as the first parameter and a `Region` as the second parameter. To use a `Region`, you create a `Clip` region in a `Graphics` object and set the `Graphics.Clip` property equal to the `Region`.

Using Regions

1. Open the `Paint` event where the primitive needs to draw.
2. Create a `GraphicsPath` object specifying a closed path.
3. Type `Dim myRegion As New Region(path)`, replacing `myRegion` with the name of the `Region` and `path` with the name of the `GraphicsPath`.

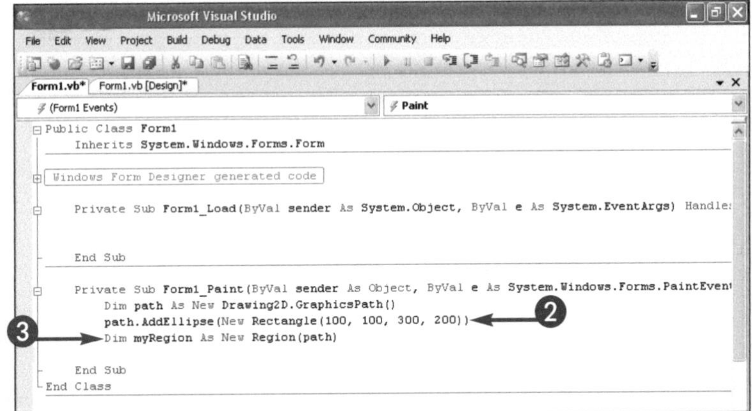

4. To combine regions, declare and initialize a new `GraphicsPath` or `Rectangle` object.
5. Type `myRegion.Xor (myRect)`, replacing `myRegion` with the name of the `Region`, `Xor` with one of the combination methods, and `myRect` with the name of the new object.

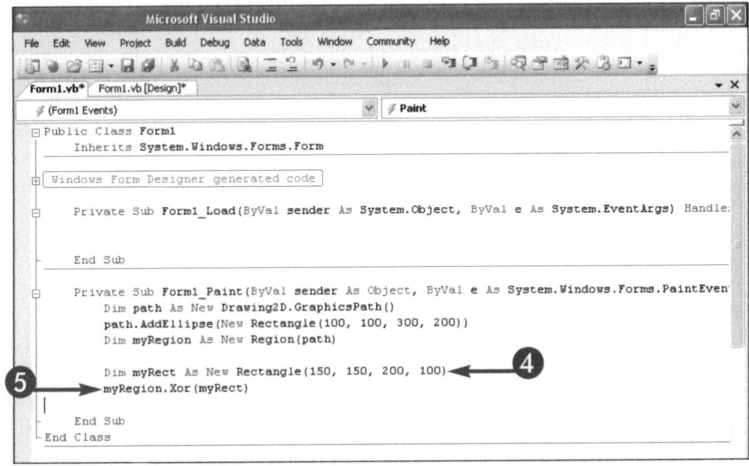

6 To draw the region, create a `Brush` object.

7 Type `e.Graphics.FillRegion(myBrush, myRegion)`, replacing `myBrush` with the name of your brush.

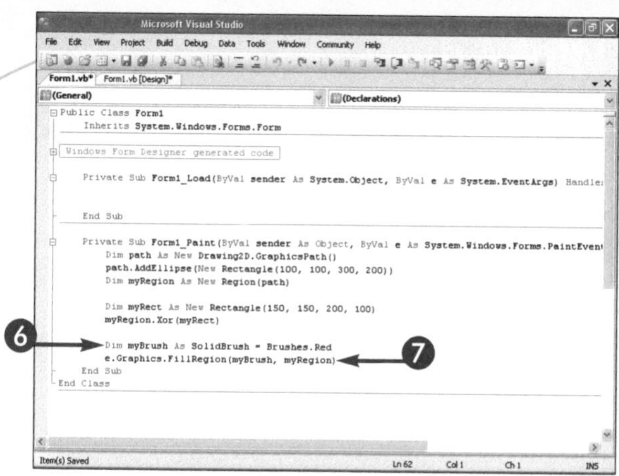

8 Press F5 to run the project.

The region accepts a range of space, combines new space, and draws to the screen.

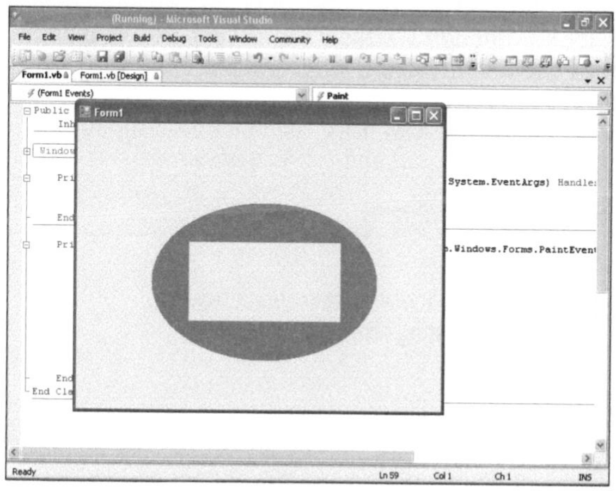

Extra

Although the coordinates of a `Region` are fixed, you can move the `Region` around when drawing it using its `Translate` method. Pass a set of integers or singles to the method that specifies the movement in the horizontal and vertical direction, respectively. The `GetBounds` property returns a `RectangleF` object that represents the smallest rectangle the `Region` fits within.

Example

```
myRegion.Translation (100, 100)
e.Graphics.FillRegion(myBrush, myRegion)\
Dim rect As RectangleF - myRegion.GetBounds(e.Graphics)
e.Graphics.DrawRectangle(Drawing.Pens.Red, rect.x, rect.Y, rect.Width, rect.Height)
```

A `RegionData` object stores the information necessary to re-create a particular `Region` object. The `RegionData` object uses an array or characters as a representation to store the region. A `Region` object's `GetRegionData` method returns a `RegionData` object that represents it. One of the constructors available for the `Region` class accepts a `RegionData` class. The example shows one `Region` object replicated into a new `Region` using the `RegionData` object.

Example

```
Dim myRegionData As Drawing2D.RegionData - myRegion.GetRegionData()
Dim myNewRegion As New Region(myRegionData)
```

Create a Shaped Window

Many utilities such as media players create a custom shaped window to resemble a real-life object. You can use a `Region` to define a shape for a window.

Defining a `Region` for a window is somewhat different than creating a drawing region or even a clip region. A `Region` object does not require you to make the shape a single enclosed object. Remember that the user still needs to use the window, so make the `Region` fairly simple.

To shape your form, set the `Form.Region` property equal to the `Region`. Although resizable forms support a Region, you must use a nonresizing `Form` and place the `Region` loading code in `Form_Load`. If you choose to create a resizable shaped window, place code based on the form's `Size` in both `Form_Load` and `Form_Resize`.

When the `Region` lies over the form, Windows uses the intersection of the actual form and the `Region` object to draw the same parts of the form that exist there. This means that if the region includes the top of the window, a title bar still draws. The code that draws the title bar does not support regions, so the caption of the window, the icon, and the buttons remain in the same corners as if you had set no region, and they cut just like the rest of the form. If your shape cuts off part of the title bar, you can hide the title bar by setting `FormBorderStyle` to `None`.

To close the window without using the form's close button, simply use a button or other control and the form's `Close` method. To minimize the window, set the `WindowState` property to `FormWindowState.Minimized`.

Create a Shaped Window

1. Create a new Windows application project or open an existing project and the form to work with.
2. In the Property window, click the `FormBorderStyle` property and then click a new value.
3. Add controls to enable the user to minimize and close the form.
4. Double-click the form.

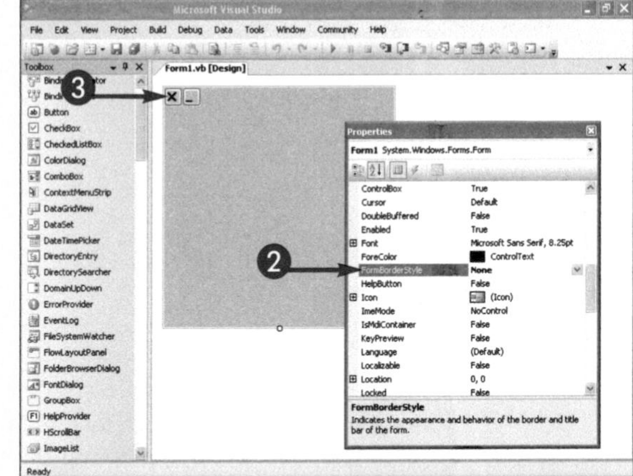

The `Form1_Load` event handler opens.

5. Create a `Region` object for the window.
6. Type `Me.Region = winReg`, replacing `winReg` with the name of the `Region` object.

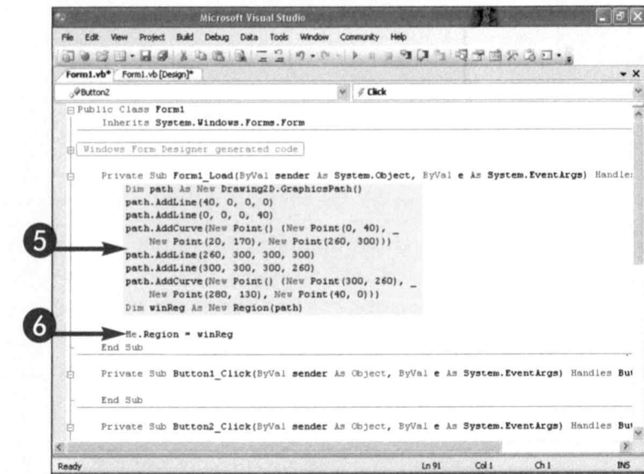

7. In the `Click` event for the Close button, type `Me.Close()`.

8. In the `Click` event for the Minimize button, type `Me.WindowState = FormWindowState.Minimized`.

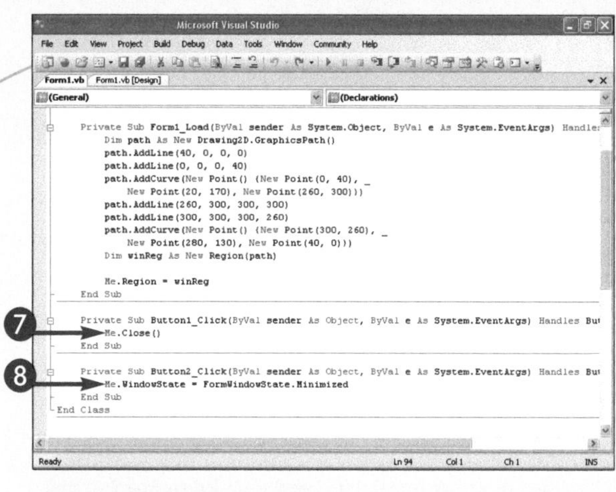

9. Press F5 to run the project.

   The window shapes to the `Region` and enables you to close and minimize the window without using the standard buttons.

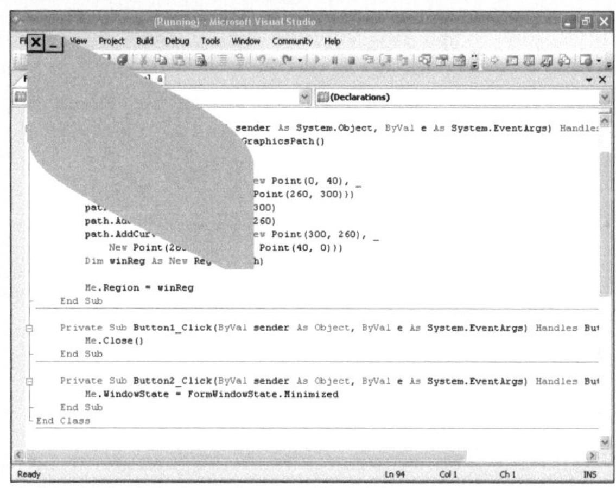

Apply It

When you create a shaped window, you often cut off the title bar or remove it completely. With the example code, which uses the Windows application programming interface (API) to access the underlying Windows system's functions, a user can move the window by clicking anywhere on the shaped form. You can change the constant for `SendMessage` to a specified constant to resize the window without using the edges of the window. You can also move the code from `Form1_MouseDown` to the mouse down event controls on the form.

TYPE THIS

```
Private Declare Function ReleaseCapture Lib "user32"() AS
Long
Private Declare Function SendMessage Lib "user32" Alias
"SendMessageA"(ByVal hwnd As IntPtr,  ByVal wMesg As
Integer, ByVal wParam As Integer, ByVal lParam as Integer)
As Integer
Const WM_NCLBUTTONDOWN - &HA1, HTCAPTION - 2, HTLEFT = 10
Const HTTOPRIGHT = 14, HTRIGHT  = 11, HTTOP = 12, HTTOPLEFT
= 13
Const HTBOTTOM - 15, HTBOTTOMLEFT = 16, HTBOTTOMRIGHT =  17
Private Sub form1_MouseDown(ByVal sender As Object, ByVal 3
As System.Windows.Forms.MouseEventArgs) Handles
MyBase.MouseDown
ReleaseCapture()
SendMessage(Me.Handle, WM_NCLBUTTONDOWN, HTCAPTION, 0)
End Sub
```

RESULT

The user can draw the window around by clicking anywhere on its surface.

Using a File Stream

Most applications provide the ability to save and load users' files. Other applications use file store configuration data. You can read or modify existing files and create new files using the `FileStream` class. The `FileStream` class does not provide the necessary functions to support reading and writing the contents of the file. You must use separate reader and writer classes to access the `FileStream`.

To set up the file stream, you must create a new instance of the `FileStream` class by placing the `New` keyword in the declaration line. When you use `New`, Visual Basic .NET calls a constructor in the class to set it up.

One of the constructors available to you requires the name of the file that you want to open or create, the file mode, the file access level, and the file sharing mode — for example, `FileStream(path, mode, access, share)`. The `FileMode` constant determines how the stream opens or creates the file. The `FileAccess` constant determines read or write access to the file. The `FileShare` constant determines if other processes can read or write to the file when this process opens it. When you call the constructor, the file opens or Visual Basic .NET creates the necessary file in the file system. Use the `Close` method to close the stream when you finish with the file.

To specify the `FileShare` constant, use a constant from the `FileShare` enumeration: `None`, `Read`, `ReadWrite`, and `Write`. If you specify `None`, no other program can access the file that you have open at the same time. `Read` enables others to read from the file while you use it, `Write` enables other programs to write to the file, and `ReadWrite` lets other files have full access.

Using a File Stream

1. Create a new project or open an existing one.

2. In the method or event where the file needs to open, type `Dim myFileStream`, replacing `myFileStream` with the variable name to assign to the stream.

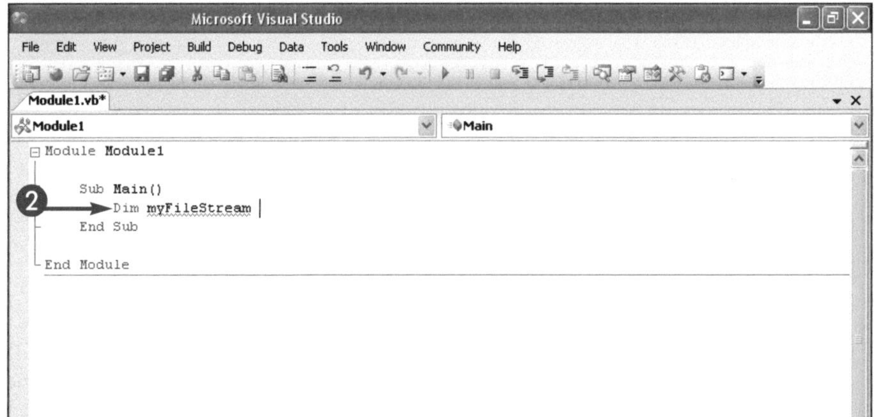

3. Type `As New IO.FileStream("C:\Test.txt")`, replacing `C:\Test.txt` with the filename that you want to open.

4. Type `IO.FileMode`.

   An IntelliSense box appears with a list of available constants.

5. Type or click a constant and follow it with a comma.

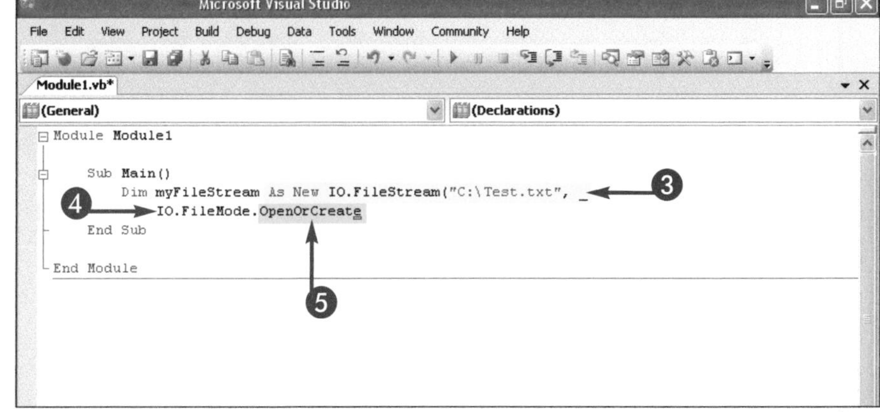

6 Type `IO.FileAccess.Read`, replacing `Read` with a constant, which you type or click.

7 Type `IO.FileShare.ReadWrite`, replacing `ReadWrite` with a constant, which you type or select.

8 Type code to access and close the stream.

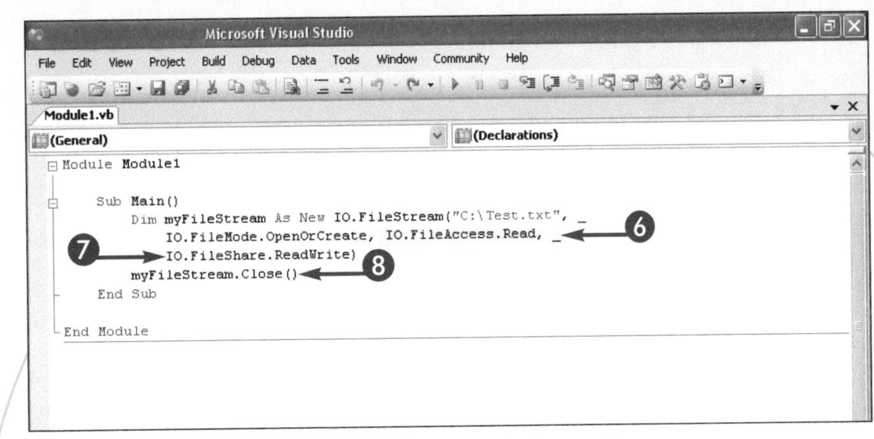

9 Press F5 to run your project.

The `FileStream` opens or creates the specified file.

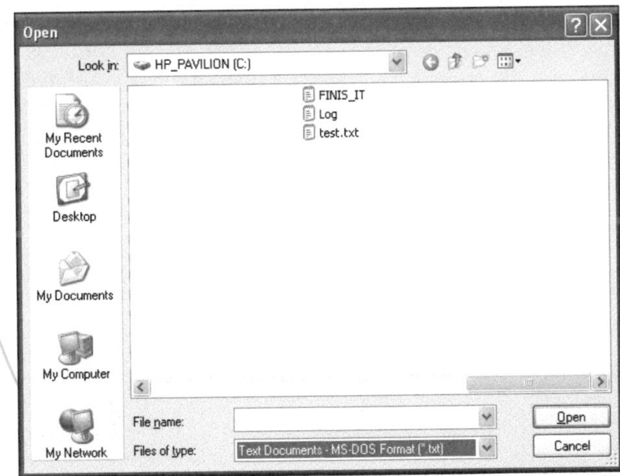

Extra

You can use the `FileMode` and `FileAccess` enumeration to specify how the stream opens the file.

The FileMode Enumeration

NAME	DESCRIPTION
`Append`	Opens the file if it exists and seeks to the end of the file, or creates a new file. Only works in conjunction with `FileAccess.Write`.
`Create`	Specifies that the operating system creates a new file. Overwrites the file if it exists.
`CreateNew`	Specifies that the operating system creates a new file. If the file exists, an error occurs.
`Open`	Specifies that the operating system opens an existing file.
`OpenOrCreate`	Specifies that the operating system opens a file if it exists; otherwise, it creates a new file.
`Truncate`	Specifies that the operating system opens an existing file and clears its contents.

The FileAccess Enumeration

NAME	DESCRIPTION
`Read`	Opens the file for reading. Allows you to read data from the file. Combine with `Write` for read/write access.
`ReadWrite`	Opens the file for reading and writing. Allows you to read data from and write data to the file.
`Write`	Opens the file for writing. Allows you to write data to the file.

Read from a Stream

A stream provides a conduit to access many different types of data with the same set of methods and properties. For example, the `FileStream` class enables you to access data in files, and the `NetworkStream` class enables you to access data from a network socket. You can use a stream reader to retrieve information from any sort of stream.

The simplest reader, `StreamReader`, works with textual information, and you can use it to read information from a text file. To declare a new instance of the class, place `New` in front of the class name and pass the constructor of the `StreamReader` class an instance of a file stream.

After creating the reader, call the `Read` method to retrieve one character out of the stream. `Read` returns the next available character from the stream as an `Integer` and moves the current position to the next character. It returns –1 if no more characters remain in the buffer. Use the `ReadLine` method to read a line out of the text file, return it as a `String`, and advance the current position to the next line. The `ReadToEnd` method retrieves all the data from the current position to the end of the stream and returns it as a `String`.

The `Peek` method extracts the character at the current position but does not consume it or advance to the next character position. Like `Read`, the `Peek` method returns –1 if the stream contains no more data. You can use `Peek` to determine if you have researched the end of the file without reading any data out of it. Always use the `Close` method after you finish reading from the file to release any resource.

Read from a Stream

1. Open a method that initializes a stream.
2. Type `Dim myReader`, replacing `myReader` with the variable name for the reader.
3. Type `As New IO.StreamReader(myStream)`, replacing `myStream` with the name of the `Stream`.
4. Type code to read from the file.

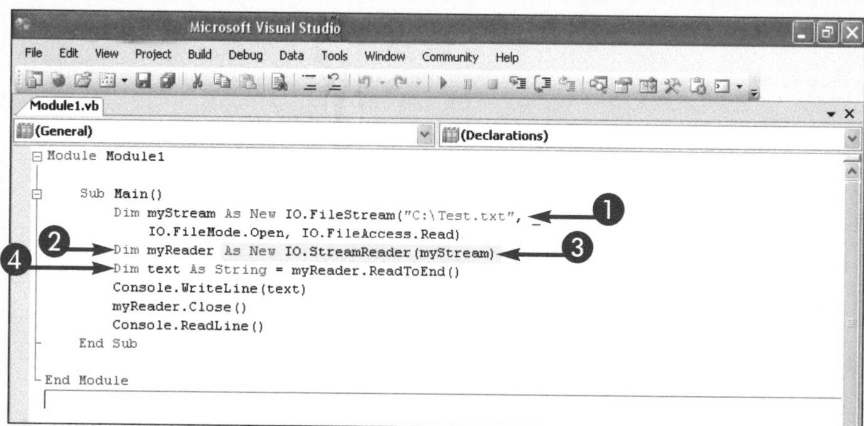

5. Press F5 to run the project.

   The stream reader processes the text in the file.

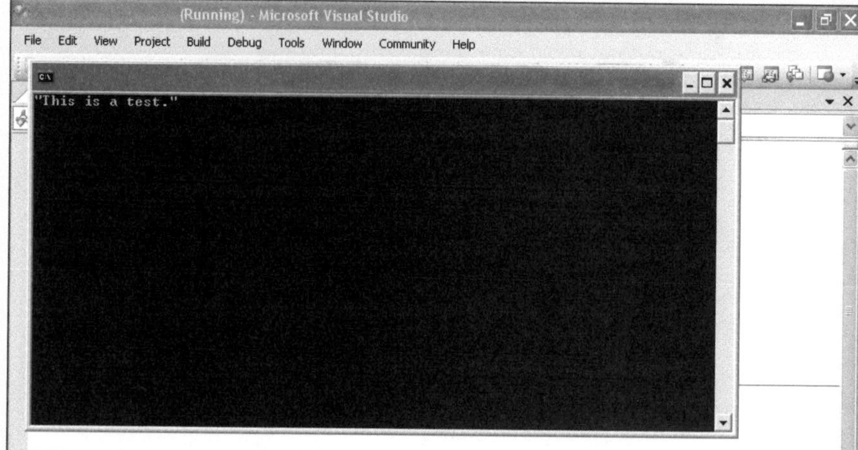

Write to a Stream

A stream works in two directions, streaming information in and out of your program. You can use a stream writer to output information to a data source. You can use a stream writer to write to a file stream that you open with write access or write data over a socket connection on a network.

A simple stream writer, the `StreamWriter` class, provides support for writing textual data. To declare a `StreamWriter`, use the `Dim` statement. To declare a new instance of the class, place `New` in front of the class name, and for the most basic constructor, pass the `StreamWriter` class an instance of the file stream.

After you initialize a `StreamWriter`, the `Write` method writes a `Char`, `Char` array, or a `String` to the stream but does not move to the next line. The variable passes in as the only parameter. The `WriteLine` method performs the same action but automatically adds a new line to the file stream.

When you call the `Write` or `WriteLine` method, the stream updates in memory only. The `Flush` method writes any new data that you store in the stream to the file. You can write a large amount of information to the stream and flush it to disk in one step. Doing a single large write to disk is more efficient because memory transfers data much faster than disks. If the data needs to move to the disk immediately after calling `Write` or `WriteLine`, use `StreamWriter.AutoFlush = True`.

The `Close` method closes the writer's connection to the file and removes any resources from memory related to the writing. Unwritten data automatically flushes to the file before the `StreamWriter` closes.

Write to a Stream

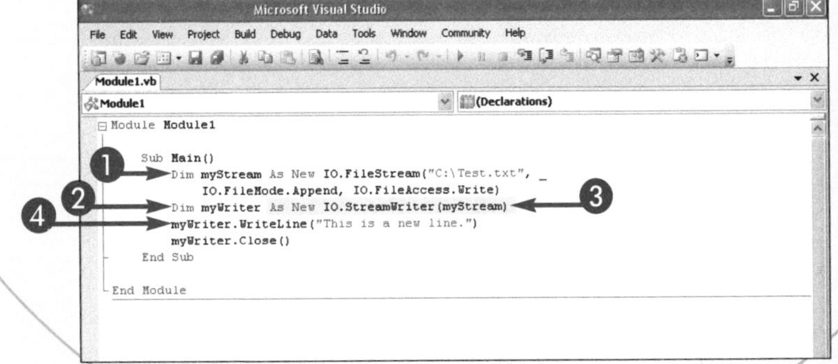

1. Open a method that initializes a stream.
2. Type `Dim myWriter`, replacing `myWriter` with the variable name for the reader.
3. Type `As New IO.StreamWriter(myStream)`, replacing `myStream` with the name of the `FileStream`.
4. Type code to read from the file.
5. Press F5 to run the project.

The stream writer processes the text in the file.

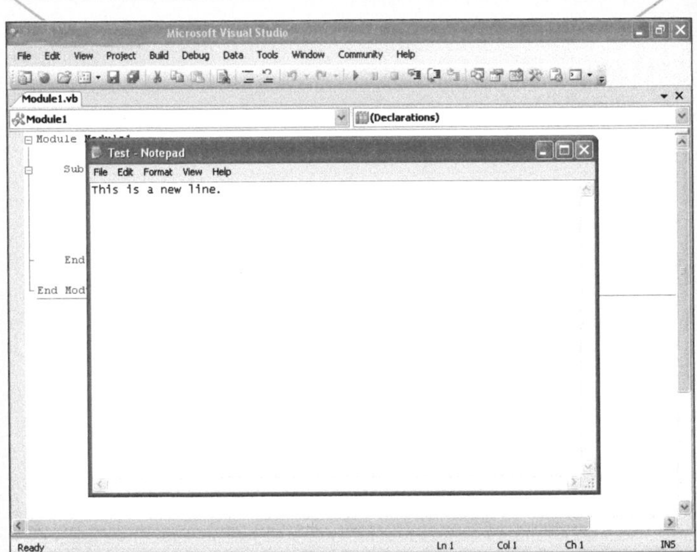

Watch for File System Changes

Windows Explorer immediately updates whenever a file saves to disk. The Windows subsystem allows programs to request notification when certain directories are updated. You can receive events using the `FileSystemWatcher` class when file system changes occur to a particular drive or directory.

You can create an instance of the `FileSystemWatcher` class, or you can add the `FileSystemWatcher` to a Windows `Form` from the `Component` category of the Toolbox. This topic assumes that you use the Windows `Form` component because of the simplicity it adds through the visual interface.

The `Path` property specifies what drive or directory the component monitors for changes. Set `IncludeSubdirectories` to include any directories under the specified `Path`. The `EnableRaisingEvents` property enables or disables the component's notification events.

The component provides four events that fire when file system changes occur: `Changed`, `Created`, `Deleted`, and `Renamed`. The `Changed` event fires when an attribute of a file changes such as the file size, last modified date, and last viewed date. You alter the `NotifyFilter` property to set conditions for when the `Changed` event fires. For example, set `NotifyFilter` to `LastWrite` to have a component fire only when an application writes to a file. The `Created` event fires when a new file or directory appears in the file system. The `Deleted` event fires when the user removes a file or directory from the file system, and the `Renamed` event fires when a file or directory name changes.

Each of the events passes a `FileSystemEventArgs` object as a variable to your event handler. The object includes a property `Name` that specifies the name of the file or directory of the change relative to the specified `Path`. The property `FullName` returns the entire path. For the `Renamed` event, the property `OldFullName` specifies the previous name of the file.

Watch for File System Changes

1. Create a new Windows application project or open an existing one.

Note: This example loads a `ListBox` control onto the form to display the output.

2. In the Toolbox, click the Components category.
3. Double-click the `FileSystemWatcher` component.

   The component loads into the form's component tray.

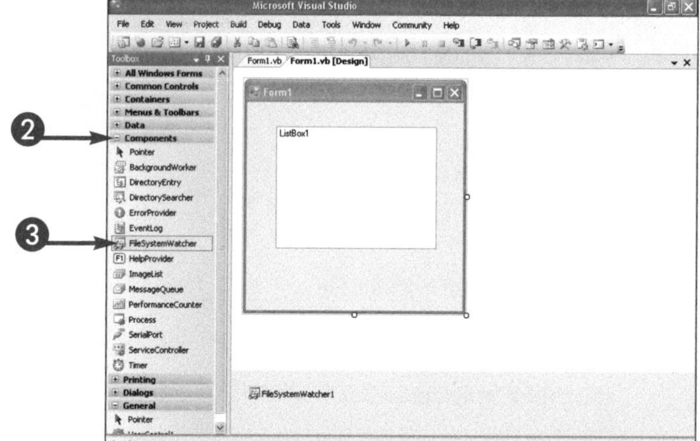

4. In the Properties window, type the path to watch in the `Path` property.
5. Set any other necessary properties.
6. Double-click the `FileSystemWatcher` in the component tray.

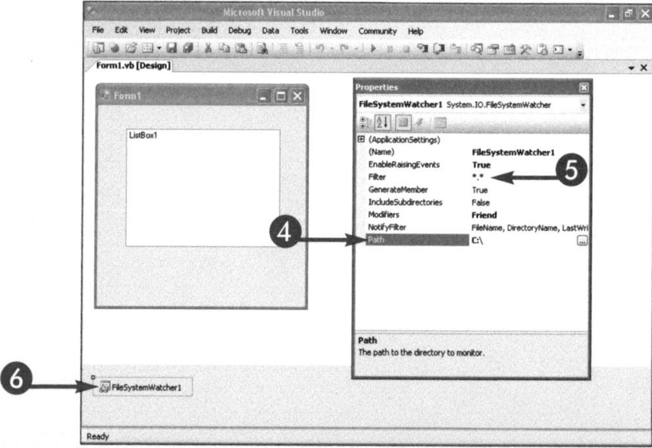

7. Type the code to respond to the `Changed` event.

Note: You can handle the `Created`, `Deleted`, or `Renamed` properties instead of `Changed` or respond to multiple events.

8. Set any other necessary properties.

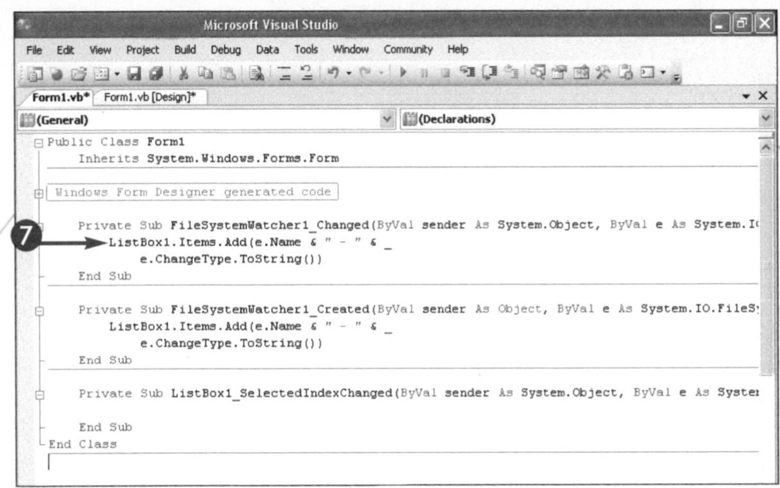

9. Press F5 to run your project.

   The `FileSystemWatcher` records changes made in the `Path`.

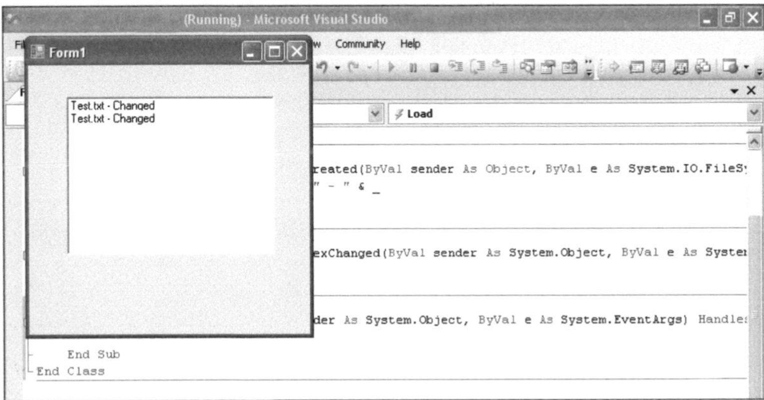

Extra

You can use a few rules to make sure that your `FileSystemWatcher` performs properly. The `FileSystemWatcher` watches disks as long as you do not switch or remove them. If network problems occur for a remote drive, the component may no longer respond to changes. The `FileSystemWatcher` does not function with CDs or DVDs because the drive content is static. `FileSystemWatcher` only works on Windows 2000 and Windows NT 4.0. Remote machines must have one of these platforms installed for the component to function properly. However, you cannot watch a remote Windows NT 4.0 computer from a Windows NT 4.0 computer.

You can alter the buffer size of the `FileSystemWatcher` depending on the size of the file system. The system notifies the component of changes through a buffer. If many changes occur in a short time, the buffer can overflow, causing the component to lose track of changes in the directory. The `InternalBufferSize` property enables you to alter the amount of memory used by the control. Increasing the size of the buffer can cause significant reduction in computer speed, so increase the buffer as little as possible. To avoid buffer overflows, use the `NotifyFilter` and `IncludeSubdirectories` properties to filter out unwanted notifications.

Access File Information

You can use the `FileInfo` class of the `IO` namespace to move through files and directories, delete and move files, and modify attributes. To link the `FileInfo` class to a file, create an instance of the class using the `New` keyword. The constructor accepts one parameter, the path and filename that you want to access. After creating the instance of class, you can begin to access properties.

The `DirectoryName` property returns the full path of the file. If you want to access properties of that directory, the `Directory` property provides access to the `DirectoryInfo` object.

The `Extension` property returns the extension of the file, the three- or four-character extension following the final period in the filename. The `Name` property specifies the name of the file with no path. `FullName` returns the entire path including the filename. The `Length` property returns a `Long` and specifies the number of bytes in the file. The `Attribute` property enables you to retrieve or change the attributes of the file.

The `CreationTime` property enables you to retrieve or change the creation date and time of a file using a `DateTime` variable. The `LastAccessTime` property enables you to retrieve or change the most recent access of the file. The `LastWriteTime` property enables you to retrieve or change the most recent write to the file.

The `Delete` method removes the file from the file system permanently and requires no parameters. `CopyTo` copies the file to a new location. Pass a string as the argument with the path of the new location. You can provide the path to copy to or a new filename for the copy. `MoveTo` performs the same action except the method copies the file to the new location and removes the original.

Access File Information

1. Create a new project or open an existing one.
2. Open the method or event where the file functions need to occur.
3. Type `Dim myFile As New IO.FileInfo("C:Text.txt")`, replacing `myFile` with the variable name and `C:\Text.txt` with the full path to the file.

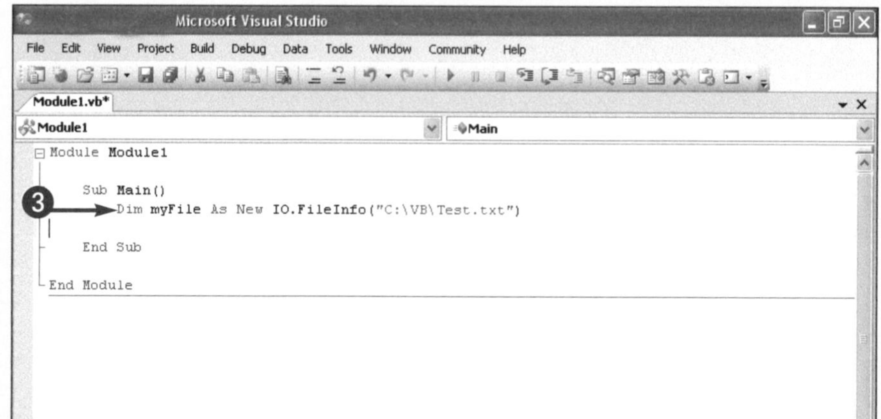

4. To modify a file's properties, type `myFile.LastWriteTime()=`, replacing `myFile` with the variable name assigned to the `FileInfo` class and `LastWriteTime` with a property.
5. Type a new value.
6. Type code to use a property.

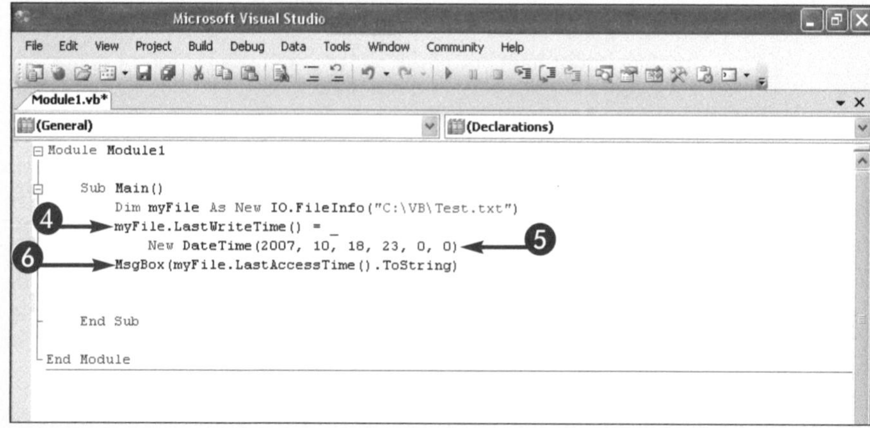

7 To perform an action on the file, type `myFile.CopyTo("C:\NewTest.txt")`, replacing `myFile` with the variable name assigned to the `FileInfo` class, and `"C:\NewTest.txt"` with the destination for the `CopyTo`.

Note: Alternatively, you can replace `CopyTo` in step 7 with `Delete` or `MoveTo`.

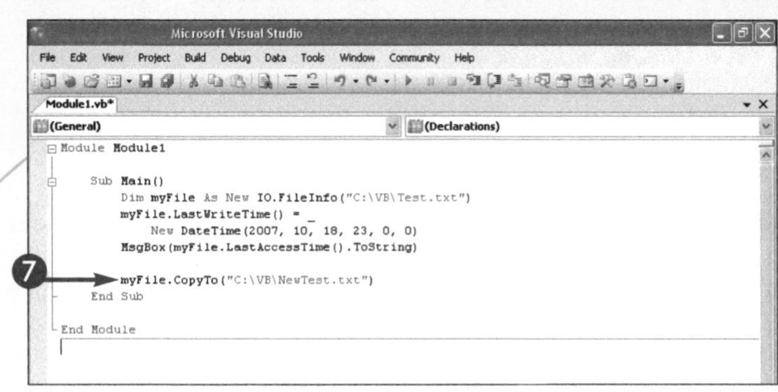

8 Press F5 to run your project.

The `FileInfo` class modifies file properties, accesses file properties, and uses methods to perform disk operations.

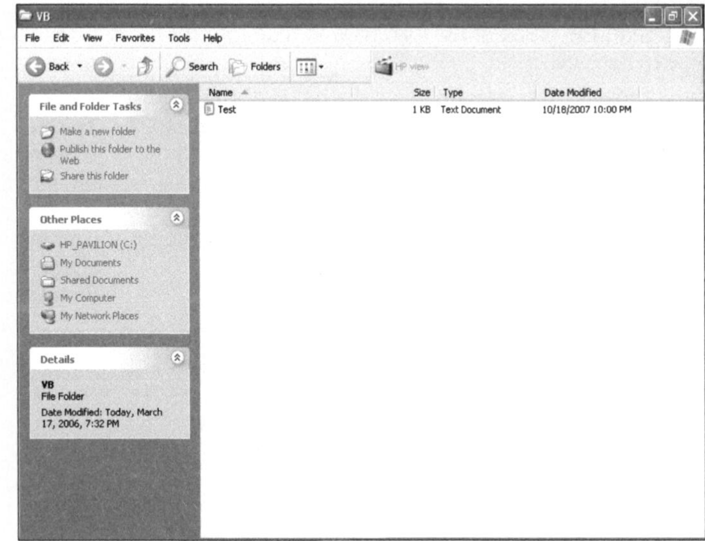

Extra

The `Attributes` property consists of a bit-wise combination of constants from the `FileAttributes` enumeration. You can use the `Attributes` property to test a file for particular attributes. To test a file, use the `And` operator combined with a constant. To set the attributes for a file, combine multiple attributes with the `Or` operator and assign the value to the `Attributes` property. A table of the most important constants in `FileAttributes` appears here. See Visual Basic .NET help for the full list.

Example

```
Dim file As New
IO.FileInfo("c:\test.txt")
' assign attributes
file.Attributes = IO.FileAttributes.Hidden
or IO.FileAttributes.Archive
Dim test As Boolean
' check attributes
test = file.Attributes And
IO.FileAtributes.Hidden
```

FileAttributes Constants

NAME	DESCRIPTION
`Archive`	Applications use this attribute to mark files for backup or removal.
`Directory`	A folder or directory.
`Hidden`	Ordinary directory listings do not list this file.
`Normal`	The file is normal and has no other attributes set.
`ReadOnly`	You cannot write to this file.
`System`	The file is part of the operating system.

Access Directory Information

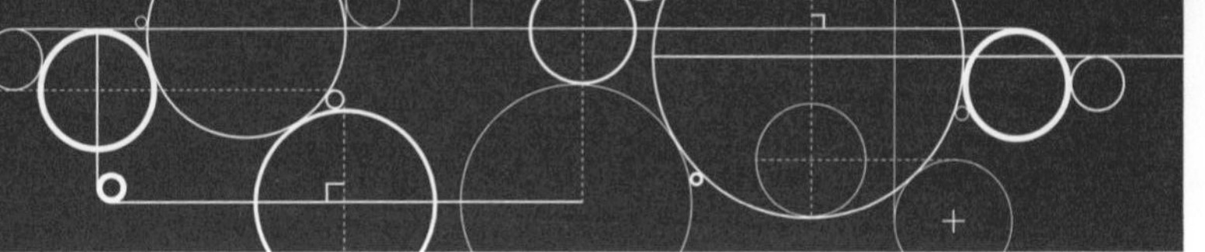

Directory listings help a user to store documents in a hierarchal, logical manner. You can view and modify disk directory structures using the `DirectoryInfo` class. The `IO` namespace contains the `DirectoryInfo` class. You declare a variable to hold the class using the `Dim` statement. To create an instance of a class, use the `New` statement. The constructor needs only one argument, the name of the directory, to load into the `DirectoryInfo` class.

The `Name` property retrieves and sets the name of the directory, and `FullName` returns the entire path including the drive letter. You can return the parent directory with the `Parent` property, which returns a `DirectoryInfo` class. The `Root` property returns the bottommost directory in the specified path. For example, if you have the directory on the local computer, `Root` returns the root drive directory as a `DirectoryInfo`.

You can use the `GetDirectories` method to return an array of `DirectoryInfo` classes representing the directory's subdirectories. The `GetFiles` method returns an array of `FileInfo` classes that represent the files in the directory. Both methods have optional parameters to specify a search pattern to filter directories or files. For example, `Getfiles("*.txt")` returns only files with a `txt` extension.

The `CreateSubdirectory` method creates a subdirectory relative to the directory loaded into `DirectoryInfo`. Pass the subdirectory path in as the only parameter. Use the `MoveTo` method to move the entire directory and all its contents to another location. Pass the new location in as the single parameter. The `Delete` method deletes the entire directory and all its contents.

Access Directory Information

1. Create a new application or open an existing one.
2. In the method or event, type `Dim myDir As New IO .DirectoryInfo("C:\")`, replacing `myDir` with the variable name, and `C:\` with the path to load into.

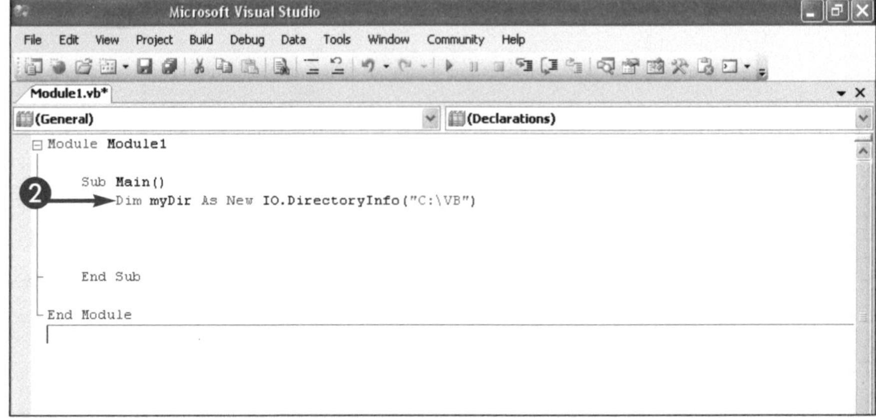

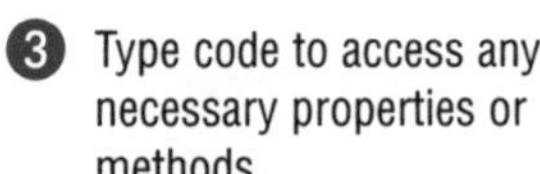

3. Type code to access any necessary properties or methods.

Note: This example creates a new subdirectory.

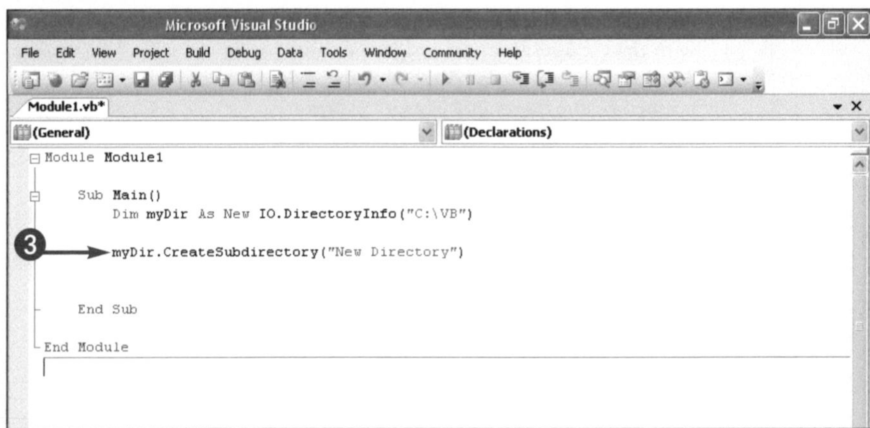

4 To list the contents of the directory, declare a storage variable and create a loop to access the contents of the directory.

Note: This example declares a `subDirectory` variable and creates a `For Each` loop.

5 Type code to access the records.

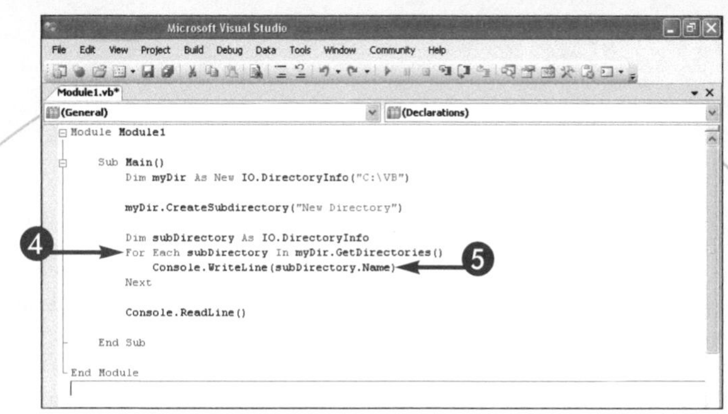

6 Press F5 to run the project.

The `DirectoryInfo` class responds with file and directory listings, and by manipulating the underlying directory structure.

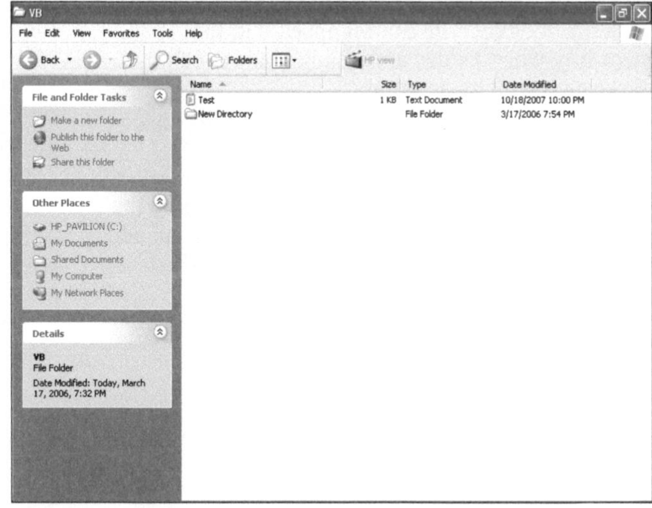

Apply It

Using a recursive method, you can build an entire directory tree using the `DirectoryInfo` component. In fact, you can use this recursive algorithm to fill a `TreeView` control and build an Explorer-like program. This example assumes that you add a `TreeView` control named `TreeView1` to the form.

TYPE THIS

```
Private Sub Form1_Load(...)
   BuildNode("My C Drive",  "C:\", TreeView1.Nodes)
End Sub
Sub BuildNode(ByVal Name As String, ByVal FullPath As String, ByVal
nodes As TreeNodeCollection)
    Dim directory As New IO.DirectoryInfo(FullPath)
    Dim newNode As TreeNode, subDir As IO.DirectoryInfo
     NewNode = nodes.Add(Name)
  Try
      For Each subDir In Directory.GetDirectories()
           BuildNode(SubDir.Name, subDir.FullName, newNode.Nodes)
      Next
   Catch
      ' an error occurred. Add a response here.
   End Try
End Sub
```

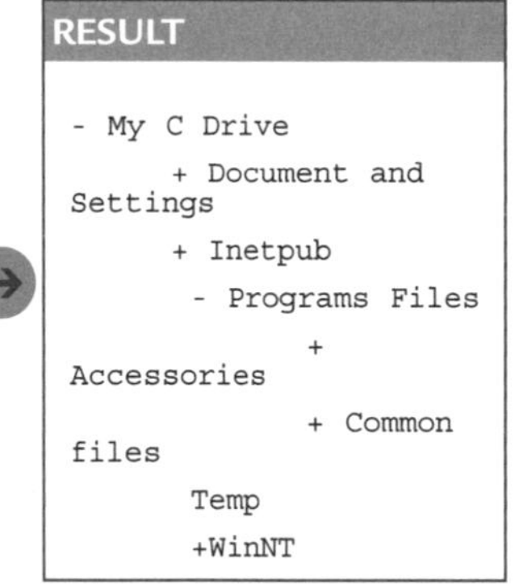

RESULT

```
- My C Drive
     + Document and
Settings
     + Inetpub
       - Programs Files
            +
Accessories
            + Common
files
         Temp
         +WinNT
```

Provide a File Dialog Box

You use the File Open and Save dialog boxes every day to work with applications. In most cases, these dialog boxes enable a user to move between applications and understand how to load and save documents in the same method. The `OpenFileDialog` and `SaveFileDialog` controls enable you to use common dialog boxes for users to select files in your application.

Both of these dialog boxes are available as Windows `Form` controls in the Toolbox. The control appears in the component tray when loaded and enables you to edit properties concerning its appearance.

The `Filter` property specifies the file types that the dialog box displays. You can specify the list of supported file formats here so that users know which files they can select. The `Filter` property contains a description followed by the format to filter separated by pipe characters (|). You can add multiple filters by placing a pipe character between them. If your application supports opening a text file format, you need to add an entry to the `Filter` property to enable the user to see only text files for selection. For example, the `Filter` may look like `"Text files (*.txt) | .txt | All files (*.*) | *.*"`. You can specify the default filter using the `FilterIndex` property with the first filter index `1`.

The `InitialDirectory` specifies the directory the dialog box loads when it appears. `ValidateNames` ensures that the user does not enter invalid characters. The `DefaultExt` property specifies an extension to add to files automatically when the user does not enter one. You must set `AddExtention` to `True` for this to occur.

To show either file dialog box, call the `ShowDialog` method. The method does not accept a parameter, but it returns a `DialogResult` specifying the user's selection of OK or Cancel.

The `FileName` property contains the full path of the file the user selects.

Provide a File Dialog Box

1. Create a new Windows application project or open an existing one.
2. In the Toolbox, double-click either the `OpenFileDialog` or `SaveFileDialog` control.

   The control appears in the component tray of the current form.

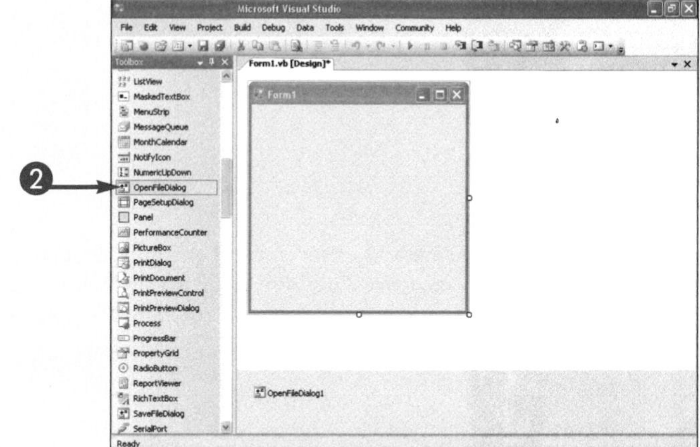

3. In the Property window, type a file filter string in the `Filter` property.
4. Edit any necessary properties.

Note: This example uses `DefaultExt = "Txt"`.

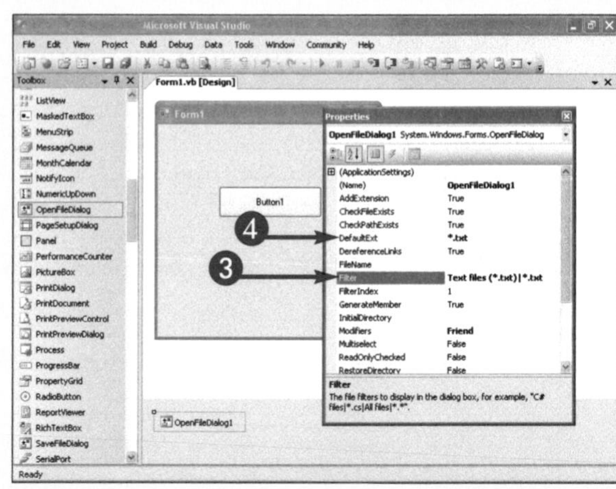

5. In the method or event where the dialog box needs to appear, declare a variable to hold the dialog box result.

6. Type `result = OpenFileDialog1.ShowDialog()`, replacing `result` with the variable name and `OpenFileDialog1` with the name of the control.

7. Type code to respond to the dialog box.

8. Press F5 to run the project.

   The file dialog box appears and allows file selection.

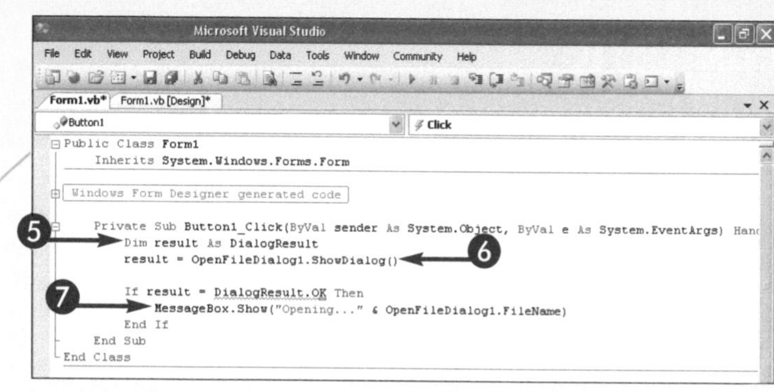

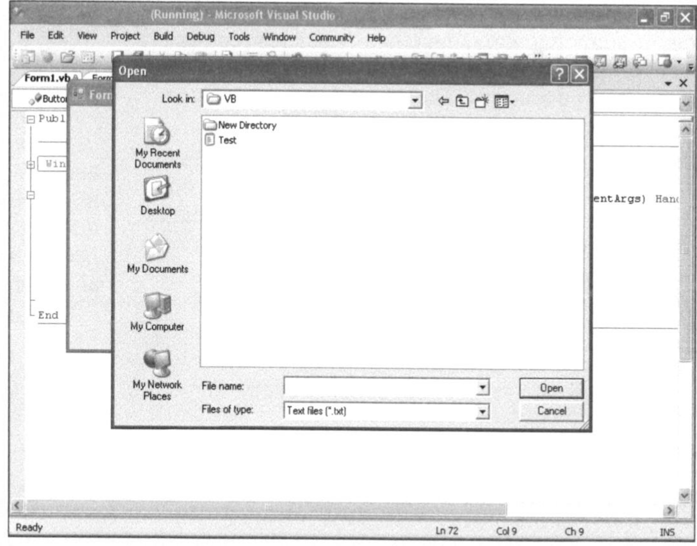

Apply It

You can enable your users to select multiple files to open with `OpenFileDialog` when you set the `MultiSelect` property to `True`. When the dialog box closes, the `Filename` property normally contains the file the user selected. For multiple selections, the `FileNames` array fills with the selected lines.

TYPE THIS

```
Private Sub Button1_Click(ByVal sender As System.Object,
ByVal e As System.EventArgs) Handles Button1.Click
    'declare a variable to hold the result
    Dim result As DialogResult
    result = OpenfileDialog1.ShowDialog()
    ' only process the file list if the user hit the OK
button
      If result - DialogResult.OK Then
          ' use a For Each loop to move through the array
           Dim filename As String
           For Each filename In OpenfileDialog1.fileName()
                  ListBox1.Items.Add(fileName)
           Next
      End If
End Sub
```

RESULT

```
C:\My Documents\Sample1.txt
C:\My Documents\Sample1.doc
C:\My Documents\Sample1.xls
```

Using the PrintDocument Control

Users expect solid printing abilities in any application. The computer monitor does not provide a resolution to make reading completely comfortable. You can use the `PrintDocument` control to provide the foundation of a printing system in your Windows `Forms` application.

Visual Basic .NET integrates all printing facilities into a combined system that works together. A `PrintDocument` control provides you with a surface to draw contents onto the pages of your document. The `PrintDocument` control appears in the Toolbox under Windows Forms.

To begin printing the document, you call the object's `Print` method. Because of the integration, a variety of dialog boxes work with the `PrintDocument` control. A Page Setup dialog box enables the user to set up margins and page sizes.

When it receives a print command, `PrintDocument` fires the `BeginPrint` event. This lets you perform initialization. After `BeginPrint` completes, the `PrintPage` event fires. You then draw the page onto the `Graphics` object provided by the event argument. The event's argument also provides a `MarginBounds` rectangle, which gives you the prescribed boundaries to print within. The `e.PageSettings` provides a list of all the settings that `PrintDocument` uses to process the print job.

When you finish drawing a page, you must determine if your application needs to print another page. Set `e.HasMorePages` equal to `True` if you need to print another page and `False` otherwise. If you set `HasMorePages` to `True`, the event fires again. The current number of the event expected to print is not available. You need to use module level variables to store information about previously printed pages.

Using the PrintDocument Control

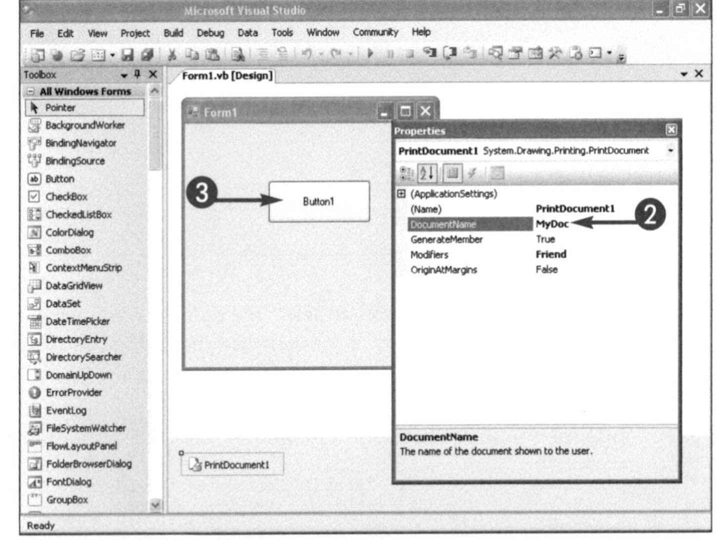

1. In a form of a Windows application project, double-click the `PrintDocument` control in the Toolbox.
2. In the Properties window, type a name for the document in the `DocumentName` property.
3. Double-click the control that you want to use to begin printing.

The default event of the control appears in the Code Editor.

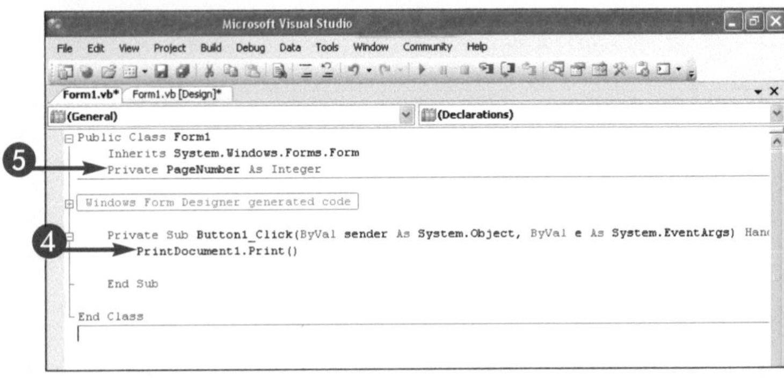

4. Type `PrintDocument1.Print()`, replacing `PrintDocument1` with the name of the control.
5. In the module level, declare necessary storage variables.
6. Click the `PrintDocument` control from the component list.
7. Click the `PrintPage` event from the event list.

Visual Basic .NET creates the event handler.

8 Declare a variable to access the `Graphics` object.

9 Type code to draw onto the page.

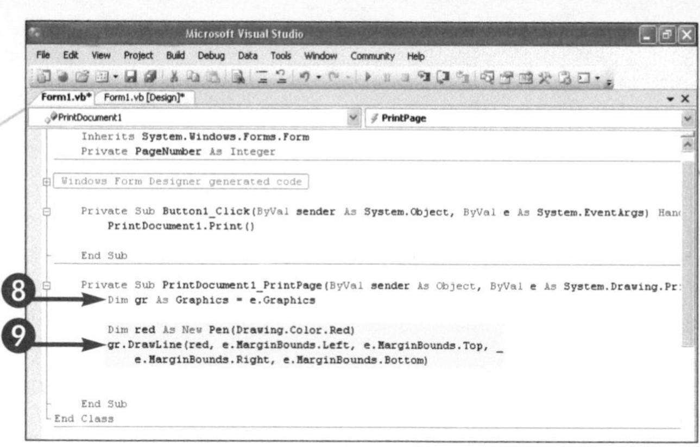

10 Type code to set `HasMorePages`.

11 Press F5 to run the project.

When the appropriate method or event runs, the pages generate and print to the printer.

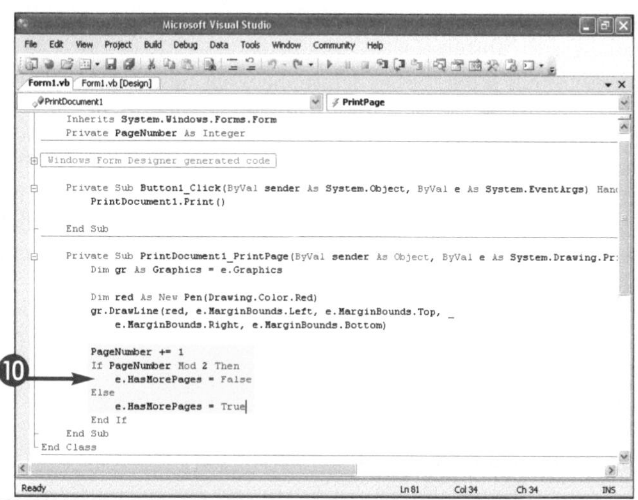

Apply It

You can create a simple text file printer using a combination of the `PrintDocument` and `Stream` commands. For this code to work, you need a button named Button1 and a `PrintDocument` named `PrintDoc`.

TYPE THIS

```
Private printFont As new Font ("Arial", 10), streamToPrint As IO.StreamReader
Private Sub Button1_Click(byVal sender As Object, ByVal e As EventArgs)
       streamToPrint = New IO.StreamReader("C:\My documents\Myfile.txt")
         printDoc.Print()
End Sub
Private Sub Printdoc_PrintPage(ByVal sender As Object, ByVal e As
system.Drawing.Printing.PrintPageEventArgs)
     Dim linesPerPage As Single = e.marginBounds.Height /
printFont.GetHeight(e.Graphics)
    Dim line As String = Nothing, count As Integer, yPos As String = 0
    For count = 0 To linesPerPage -1 'print each line of the file.
         line = streamToPrint.ReadLine()
         If line Is Nothing Then Exit for     'no more lines in file
        yPos = e.MarginBounds.Top + count * printFont.GetHeight(e.Graphics)
         e.Graphics.DrawString(line, printFont, Brushes.Black,
eMarginBounds.Left, yPos, New StringFormat()) 'output line of text
  Next
  If Not (line Is Nothing) The e.HasMorePages = True 'print another page
End Sub
```

RESULT

The text file prints to the default printer.

Using the Printer Dialog Box

Before an application prints, it often presents a `Printer` selection dialog box to let the user select which printer to use and any printer driver options, such as draft mode. You can add the `Print` dialog box to your application using the `PrintDialog` control. The `PrintDialog` control is available in the Windows Forms section of the Toolbox. A required property for the function of the `PrintDialog` control is `Document`. You must set this property to a valid `Document` provided by the `PrintDocument` control.

You can edit other properties to determine what functions to make available to the user. `AllowPrintToFile` enables or disables the Print To file check box. If `AllowPrintToFile` is `True` and the user checks the box, the `PrintToFile` property is set to `True`. `AllowSelection` enables or disables the range selector boxes, which enables the user to print only a particular range of pages. `AllowSomePages` enables or disables the box where the user can enter a selection of pages either individually or by range. If you enable these properties, the `PrintDocument` control manages the correct pages to print.

To make the dialog box appear, invoke the `ShowDialog` method with no arguments. The method returns a `DialogResult` specifying either OK or Cancel. If the user clicks OK, `PrinterDialog` sets the dialog box settings to the `PrinterSettings` of the `PrintDocument` component. If you call the `ShowDialog` method and the user does not have any defined printers, a message appears notifying the user how to add a printer, and `DialogResult` returns `Cancel`. You can use the `Reset` method to clear any previous settings the user has made and reset the dialog box to the defaults.

The example uses a `Button` control to activate the `Print` dialog box. You can use a variety of controls such as a toolbar or menu as well.

Using the Printer Dialog Box

1. Open a form in a Windows application project.
2. Add and configure a `PrintDocument` component on the form.
3. In the Toolbox, double-click the `PrintDialog` control to add it to the form.

   The control appears in the component tray.

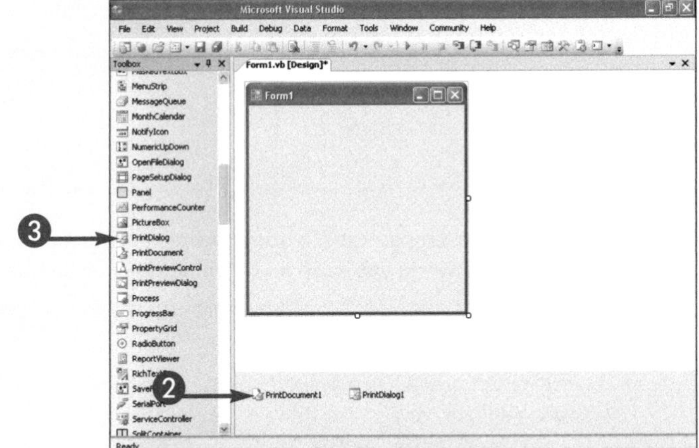

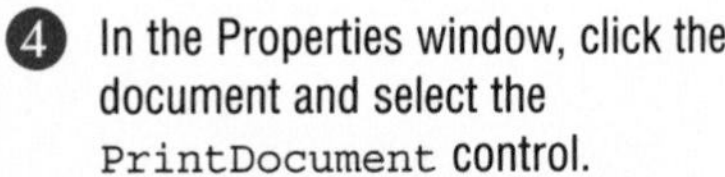

4. In the Properties window, click the document and select the `PrintDocument` control.

Note: You can optionally set other properties and toggle preference properties such as `AllowSelection` by double-clicking the property name.

5. Open the method or event where the Print dialog box needs to appear.

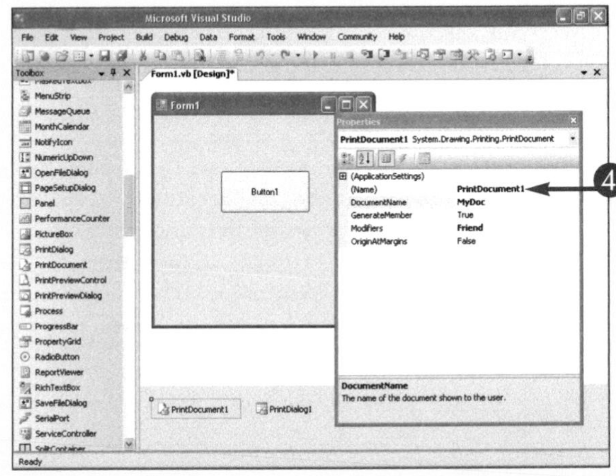

6 Type code to show the dialog box and respond to it.

- You can type `PrintDialog1.ShowDialog()` to show the dialog box, replacing `PrintDialog1` with the name of the component.

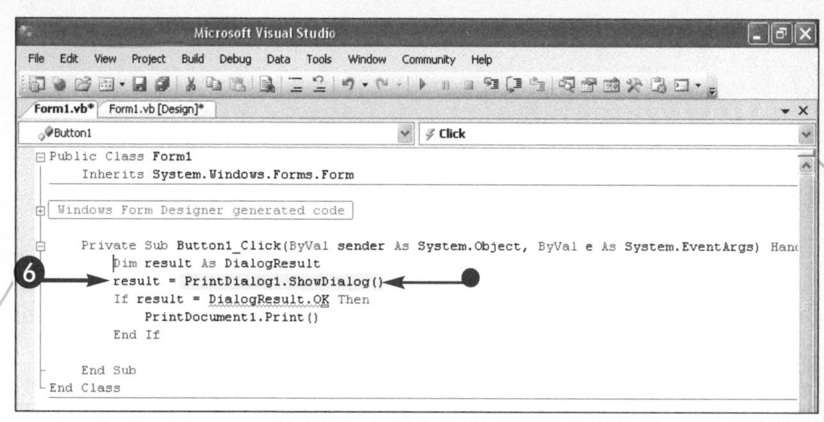

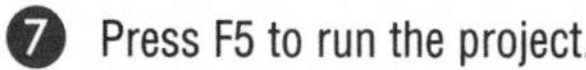

7 Press F5 to run the project.

The Print dialog box appears and allows printer selection and editing of various properties.

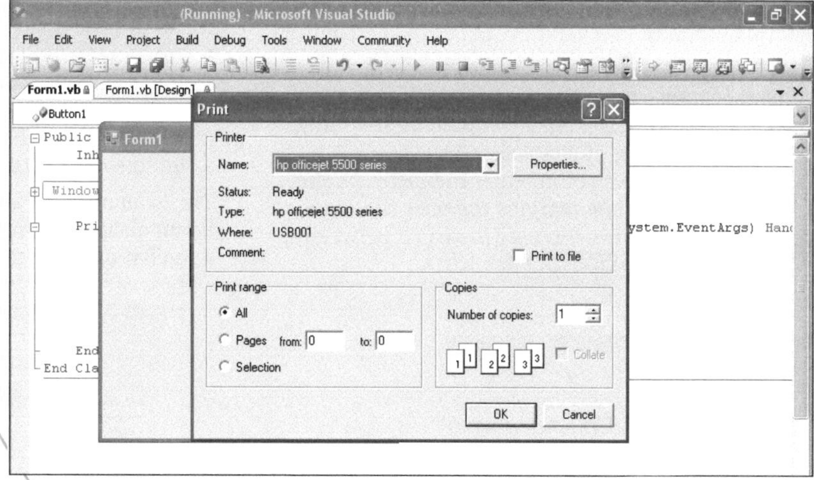

Extra

The `PrinterSettings` object of the `PrintDocument` component provides a number of properties that set up how the document prints and what features the selected printer supports. You can use the `PrinterSettings PrintRange` property to determine the print range the user selected. The property contains one of the values available in the `PrintRange` enumeration: `AllPages`, if the user selects to print all the pages in your application's document; `Selection`, to print only the information the user previously selected in the application; or `SomePages`. If the value is `SomePages`, the user entered a range he or she wants your application to print. You can access this range using the `FromPage` and `ToPage` properties of the `PrinterSettings` object. A number of properties return information about the printer the user selects. The `SupportsColor` property returns `True` if the printer supports color printing and `False` if it does not. The `PaperSizes` property maintains a collection of the paper sizes the printer supports, and `PaperSources` maintains a collection of the printer trays available for the printer. For a full list of properties available in the `PrinterSettings` object, you can search Visual Basic .NET Help by typing **PrinterSettings members**.

Using the Page Setup Dialog Box

The Page Setup dialog box enables the user to select paper sizes and page orientation using a standard interface. You can use the `PageSetupDialog` control to add this dialog box to your application. The control automatically modifies the settings of a `PrintDocument` control.

You find the `PageSetupDialog` control in the Windows Form section of the Toolbox. A required property for the function of the `PageSetupDialog` control is `Document`. You must set this property to a valid `PrintDocument` control.

The `PageSetupDialog` control provides properties to control its appearance and enable or disable functionality for the user. `AllowMargins` enables the margin-editing section of the dialog box. If enabled, `MinMargins` is a `Margin` object and allows you to enter the `Left`, `Right`, `Top`, and `Bottom` minimum margins the user can enter. `AllowOrientation` allows the user to switch between portrait and landscape orientations. `AllowPaper` enables or disables paper selection. `AllowPrinter` shows or hides the Printer button, which allows editing of the printer's settings. `ShowNetwork` shows or hides the Network button on the secondary printer dialog box. `ShowHelp` determines if the Help button is present.

To make the dialog box appear, invoke the `ShowDialog` method with no arguments. The method returns a `DialogResult` specifying either `OK` or `Cancel`. If the user clicks OK, the dialog box loads the `PageSettings` and `PrinterSettings` given by the user to the `PrintDocument` assigned to the control. This creates a totally automated printing system. Note that if you call the `ShowDialog` method and the user does not define a printer, a runtime error occurs.

The example uses a `Button` control to activate the Page Setup dialog box. You can use a variety of controls such as a toolbar or menu as well.

Using the Page Setup Dialog Box

1. Open a form in a Windows application project.
2. Add and configure a `PrintDocument` control on the form.
3. In the Toolbox, double-click the `PageSetupDialog` control to add the control to the form.

   The control appears in the component tray.

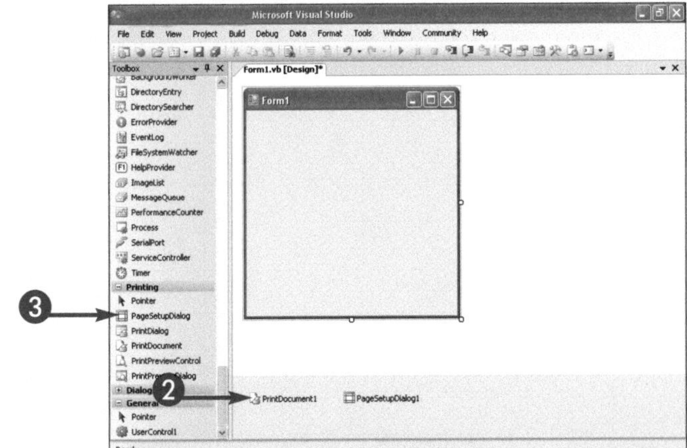

4. In the Properties window, click the document and select the `PrintDocument` control.

Note: You can optionally set other properties. Toggle preference properties such as `AllowPage` by double-clicking the property name.

5. Open the method or event where the Page Setup dialog box needs to appear.

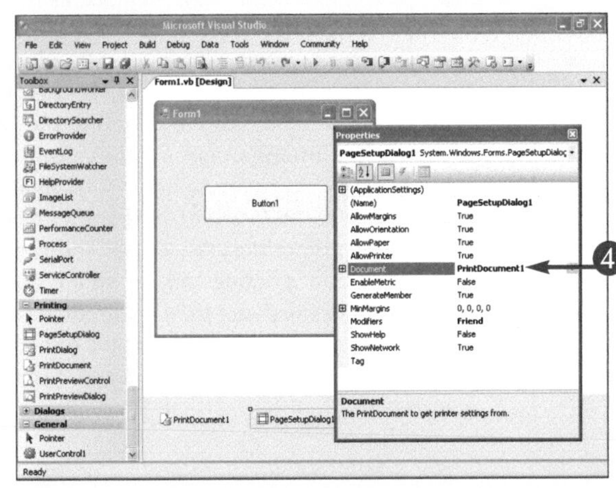

6 Add code to show the dialog box and respond to it.

- You can type `PageSetupDialog1.ShowDialog()` to show the dialog box, replacing `PageSetupdialog1` with the name of the component.

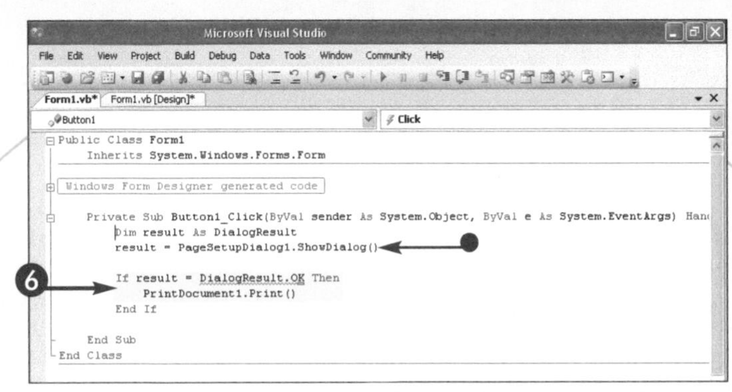

7 Press F5 to run the project.

The Page Setup dialog box appears and allows editing of various properties.

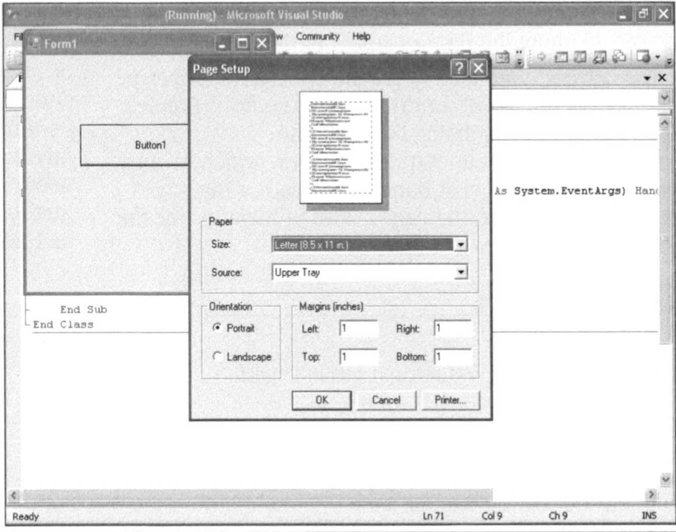

Extra

You can edit printer settings for certain requirements. Even if you provide the user with selections, you may want to check those settings. Note that you cannot make the changes while in the `PrintPage` event because the `PrintDocument` component has already built a page for you. Instead, use the `BeginPage` event. The `DefaultPageSettings` and `PrinterSettings` properties provide the settings that affect printing the page layout.

PageSettings Properties

PROPERTY	DESCRIPTION
`Bounds`	A `Rectangle` object that retrieves the bounds of the page, given the page orientation.
`Color`	A `Boolean` value that retrieves or sets whether the page prints in color.
`Landscape`	A `Boolean` value that determines whether the page prints in landscape or portrait orientation.
`Margins`	A `Margins` object that retrieves or sets the margins for the paper. Use the `MarginBounds` of the `PrintPage` event argument to specify the dimension of the printable area.
`PaperSize`	Retrieves or sets a `PaperSize` object indicating the paper size for the page.
`PaperSource`	Retrieves or sets the `PaperSource` object indicating the page's paper source (for example, the printer's upper tray).
`PrinterResolution`	Retrieves or sets the printer resolution for the page.
`PrinterSettings`	Retrieves or sets the printer settings associated with the page.

Create a Print Preview

Many modern applications enable the user to preview his or her print job before choosing to print it. You can add this powerful feature to your application using `PrintPreviewDialog`. This control takes all the pages printed by a `PrintDocument` control and maps them onto a virtual onscreen page. The `PrintPreviewDialog` control also provides an easy-to-use and familiar dialog box with a toolbar of display options and a panel to show the page or pages in the print job.

To use the control, you need to set the `Document` property to a valid `PrintDocument` control. When the Print Preview control is displayed, the dialog box calls the `PrintDocument` control to output the pages, which in turn calls your page output event handler. Instead of the pages outputting to the printer, the pages store in memory for the Print Preview dialog box to display.

The `PrintPreviewDialog` control only makes one property available: `UseAntialias`. Set the property to `True` to have the control draw the page on the screen using antialiasing to smooth the appearance of lines, shapes, and text. Keep in mind that antialiasing is an intensive process that may slow some older systems. If your application needs to run well on older machines, you may want to leave this property disabled.

To make the Print Preview dialog box appear, call the `Show` or `ShowDialog` method. When the dialog box appears, it shows a toolbar with a Print button, a Zoom button, and Column/Row selections. The control provides all the interaction with the user for the display interface. When the user clicks the Print button, the dialog box calls the `Print` method of the `PrintDocument` control assigned to the `PrintPreviewDialog`.

Create a Print Preview

1. Open a form in a Windows application project.
2. Add and configure a `PrintDocument` control on the form.
3. In the Toolbox, double-click the `PrintPreviewDialog` control to add it to the form.

   The control appears in the component tray.

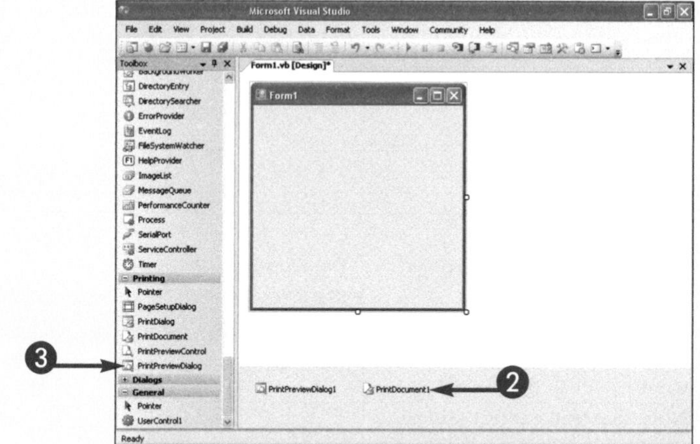

4. Click Document in the Properties window and select the `PrintDocument` control.
   - To cause the `PrintPreviewDialog` control to antialias the pages, double-click the `UseAntiAlias` property to toggle it to `True`.
5. Add a control to the form to make the dialog box appear and double-click the control to edit its default event handler.

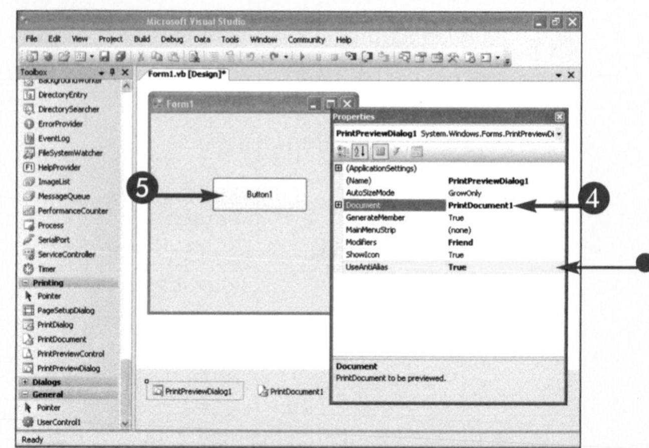

6 Type `PrintPreviewDialog1.ShowDialog()`, replacing `PrintPreviewDialog` with the name of the control.

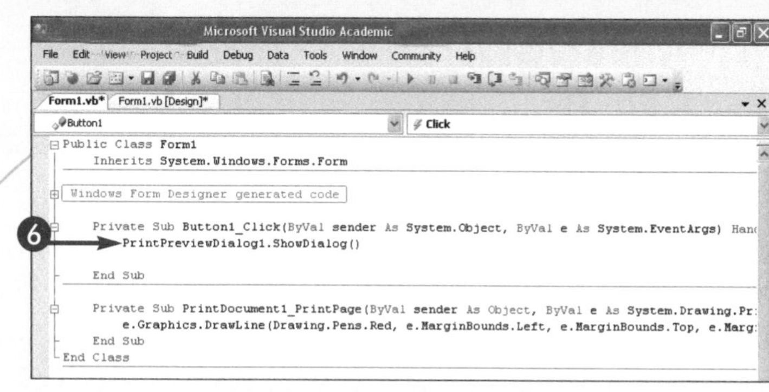

7 Press F5 to run the project.

The `PrintPreviewDialog` or `PrintPreviewControl` appears and allows you to view the document.

Note: This example uses the same `PrintPage` event handler for the `PrintDocument` as in the section "Using the `PrintDocument` Control."

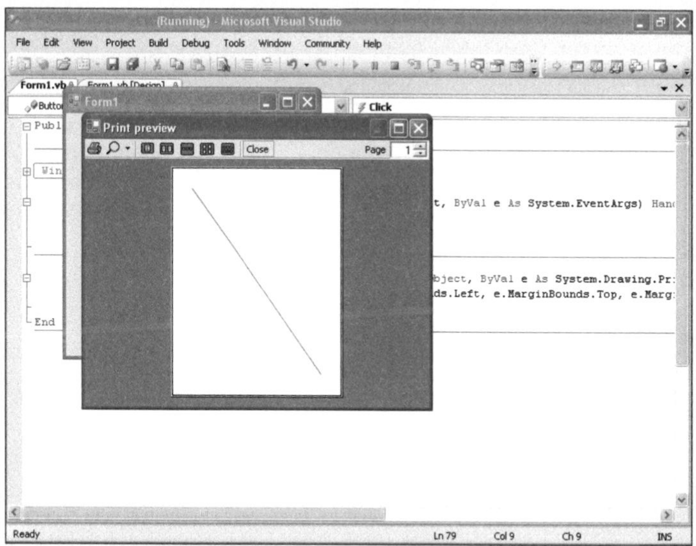

Extra

You can use the `PrintPreviewControl` to add the Print Preview pane directly to a form of your own. The `PrintPreviewDialog` control uses `PrintPreviewControl` to provide the view in the dialog box, so they appear exactly the same. If you use `PrintPreviewControl`, you must provide your own interaction with the user by setting the control properties. The `Zoom` property controls the zoom of the display. The property accepts a `Double` value, with `1.0` being full size, or 100%. To make the page appear half size, use the value `0.5`. The `Columns` property determines the number of pages to display horizontally. The `Rows` property determines the number of pages to display vertically. For example, `Print` previews in many applications and lets you switch the view to display two pages size by side or a 3 x 2 configuration of six pages. To make the control automatically size the pages to fit in the available space of the control when you alter properties such as `Columns` or `Rows`, set the `AutoZoom` property of `PrintPreviewControl` to `True`.

Download from a Web Server

Networking, clients, servers, and the Internet are important features for every application to support effectively. You can use the `WebClient` class to connect to an HTTP:// or HTTPS:// server to download and upload data. This class provides a high-level interface for accessing network sockets by working off other classes.

`WebRequest` and `WebResponse`, made to send and receive data from a server, form the basis of `WebClient`, and you can use them directly instead of `WebClient` to perform more powerful tasks. The `System.Net` namespace provides all of these classes.

To begin using `WebClient`, declare a new variable and place `As New Net.WebClient()` for the type declaration. The `New` keyword tells Visual Basic .NET to create a new instance of the class in memory and assign it the variable name that you provide.

After you create the `WebClient`, multiple methods enable you to choose the appropriate method for accessing the server. The `OpenRead` method expects one parameter, the URL to download, and returns a `Stream`. This method enables you to load the data from the server directly into your program as a string or manipulate the data in any way a `Stream` allows.

The `DownloadData` method accepts a URL as its parameter and returns a `Byte` array with the contents of the server request. The `DownloadFile` method accepts two parameters, the URL to download and the file into which you save the download. This method saves the entire contents of the URL request directly to the file. The method returns nothing.

Download from a Web Server

1. Create a new project or open an existing one.
2. In the method or event to download a file, type `Dim myWebClient As New Net.WebClient()`, replacing `myWebClient` with the variable name.

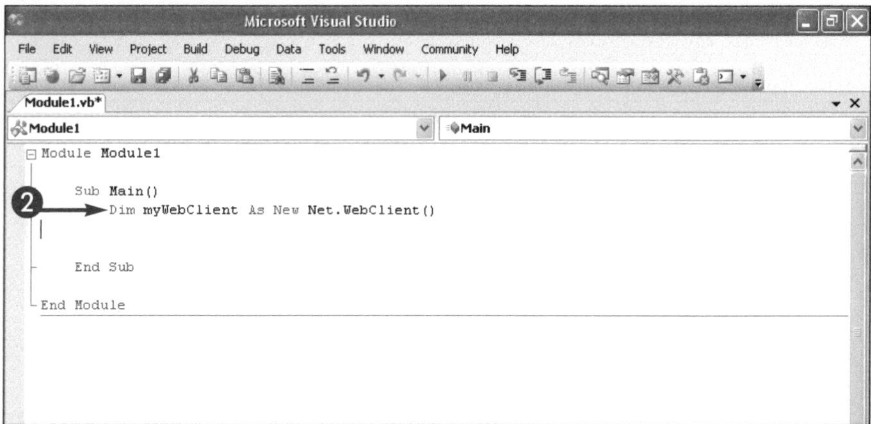

3. Type the variable name assigned to the `WebClient`.
4. Type `.OpenRead(url)`, replacing `OpenRead` with the download method to use and `url` with the appropriate parameters to the method.

Note: You can use the `DownloadData` or `DownloadFile` methods instead of `OpenRead`.

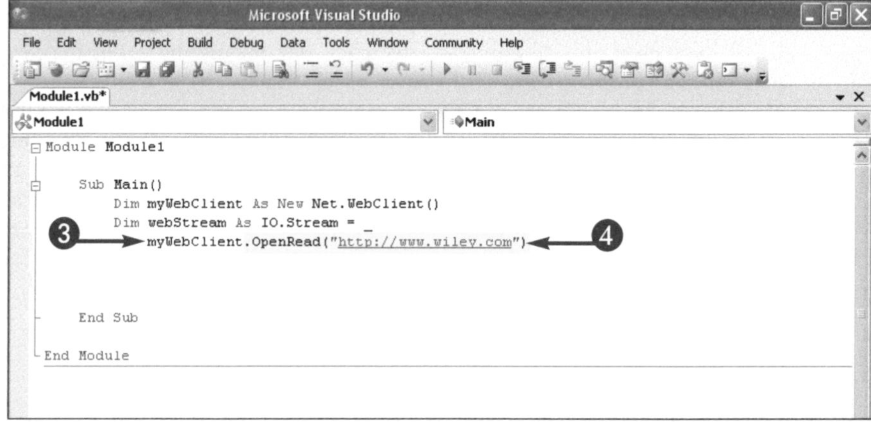

5 Type code to retrieve the data into a usable variable.

Note: The `OpenRead` method returns a stream that you can read.

6 Type code to display or use the results.

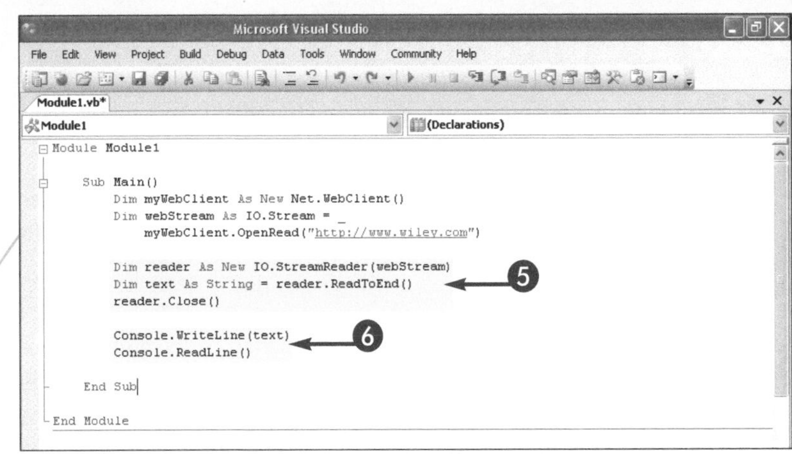

7 Press F5 to run the project.

The `WebClient` retrieves the Web page from the Web server.

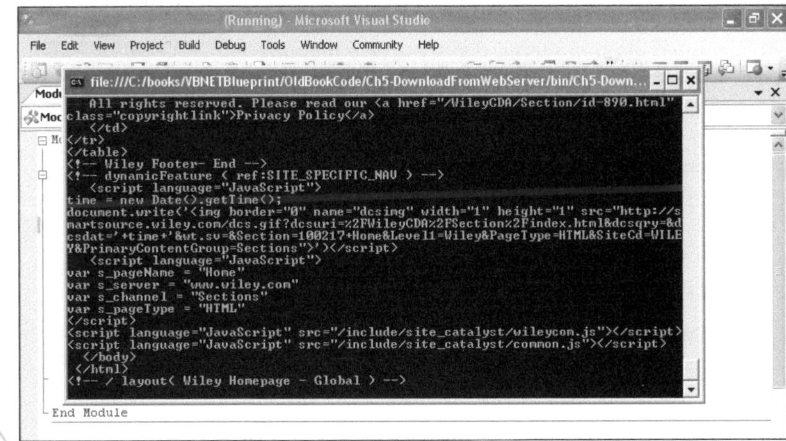

Extra

Some Web sites require users to fill out a form before they can access a particular Web page. To make your application upload form information to the server for a particular page, use the `UploadValues` method. This method accepts a URL as the first parameter and a `NameValueCollection` class as the second. The class holds a list of form values. Create a new instance of the class and use the `Add` method to specify the name and value pairs to pass to the URL.

Example

```
Dim loginForm As New Net.WebClient()
Dim loginFormElements As New System
.Collections.Specialized.NameValueCollection()
loginFormElements.Add("UserId", "rboman")
loginForm.UploadValues(http://www.sample.com/
login.asp, loginformElements)
```

Servers can lock resources on a Web site and force the browser to request a username and password. If your program needs access to a restricted directory, use the `Credentials` property of the `WebClient`. To do so, you must first create a new instance of the `CredentialCache` class in which to store the credentials. `CredentialCache` can hold any number of Web sites' credentials, and the `WebClient` selects the right one when necessary.

Example

```
Dim restrictedPage As New Net.WebClient()
Dim myCache As New Net.CredentialCache()
Dim credential As New
Net.NetworkCredential("myUser", "myPass")
MyCache.Add(New
uri(http://www.sample.com/restricted/),
"Basic", credential)
restrictedPage.Credentials - myCache.
```

Make a Connection to a Server

Although most transactions of data in your application may transfer over HTTP protocols, in some cases, you need to connect to servers that do not run HTTP protocols. In these cases, you cannot use the `WebClient` class explained in the section "Download from a Web Server." You can, however, use the `TcpClient` class to create a connection to any sort of server. Because of the flexibility of the `TcpClient` class, you may find code to support the class harder to write. If you want to create a client/server pair of applications, see the next section, "Accept Incoming Connections," for more information.

To create a connection to a server, declare a new instance of the `TcpClient` class. If you want the object to open the connection immediately, pass the server to which you want to connect as the first argument to the constructor and follow it with the port number. Leave the constructor empty to connect later. Use the `Connect` method to connect at a later time. The `Connect` method accepts the same two arguments. Use the `Close` method to close the connection.

To send and receive data, the `TcpClient` provides a `GetStream` method. The method returns a `NetworkStream` object. You can use this stream to read and write to the network socket. To use the stream the method returns, assign the stream to a variable of type `Stream`, defined in the `System.IO` namespace. You can then use this variable to create stream readers and writers to send and receive information over the network socket.

Make a Connection to a Server

1. Create a new project or open an existing one.
2. In the method or event where the connection needs to occur, type `Dim client As New Net.Sockets.TcpClient()`, replacing `client` with the variable name.

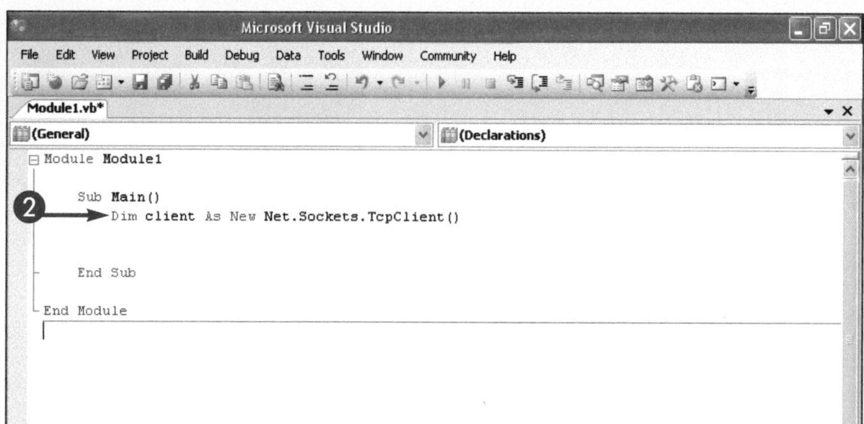

3. Inside the parentheses, type `"localhost", 90`, replacing `"localhost"` with the server and `90` with the port number.
4. Type `Dim myStream As IO.Stream = client .GetStream()`, replacing `myStream` with the variable name to store the `Stream` and `client` with the variable name of the `TcpClient`.

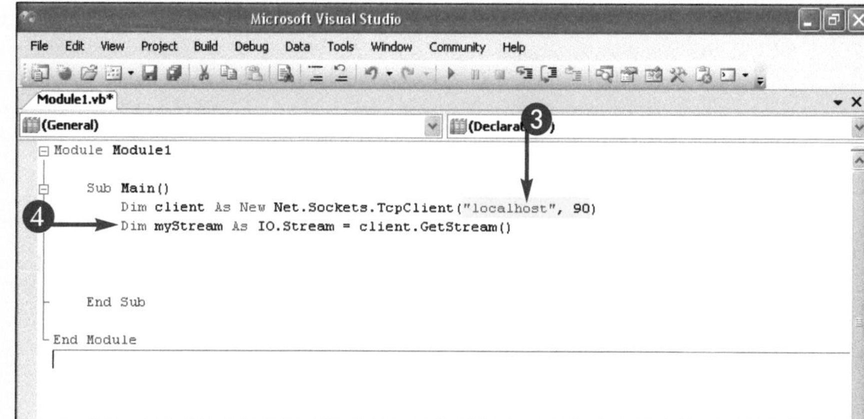

5 Read and write as appropriate to the stream.

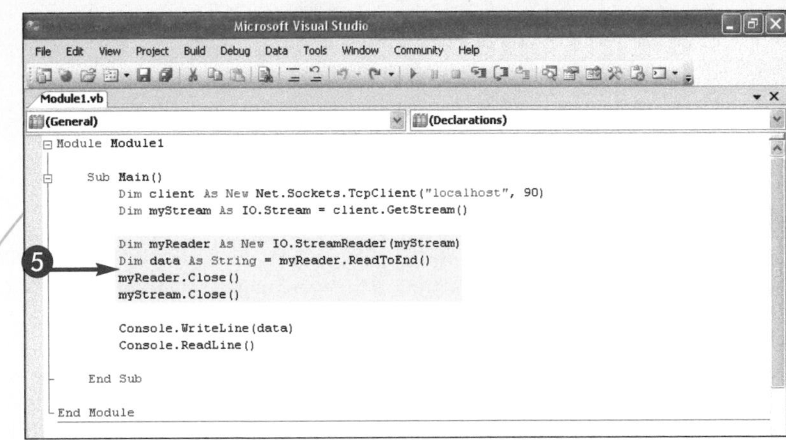

6 Press F5 to run the project.

The `TcpClient` connects to the server and exchanges data.

Note: This example shows the output of connecting to the server shown in the section "Accept Incoming Connections."

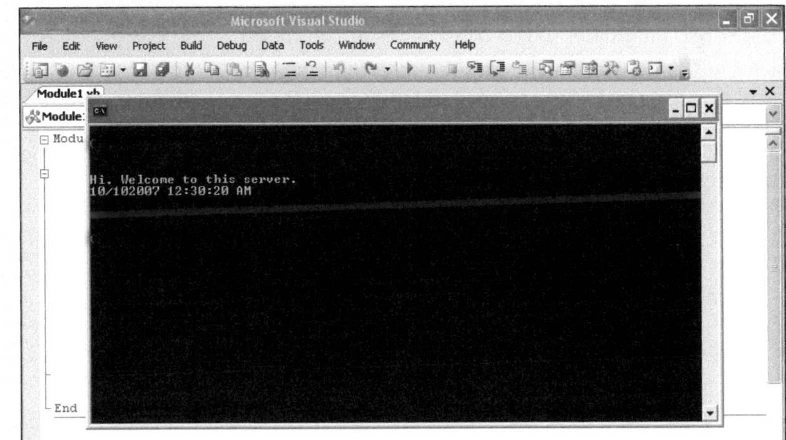

Extra

You can use a set of properties available in the `TcpClient` class to ensure that a connection remains open. The `LingerState` property represents an instance of the `LingerOption` class. Linger time is the time the connection stays open after you call the `Close` method. You can enable the `LingerState` option to make sure that your application acts like a proper client and does not disconnect in the middle of a transfer. If `LingerState.Enabled` is `True`, data continues to send over the network with a timeout of `LingerState.LingerTime`, in seconds. After your data is sent or the timeout expires, the connection closes gradually. If the `TcpClient` object finds no data in the send queue, the socket closes immediately.

Example

```
myclient.LingerState.Lingertime = 2
myclient.Lingerstate.enabled = True
```

The `TcpClient` class buffers information as it comes across a connection until you process it. You can control the buffering of the control using a set of properties. The `ReceiveBufferSize` and `SendBufferSize` properties control the size in bytes of the two respective buffers. `ReceiveTimeout` and `SendTimeout` control the amount of time the class waits for a server response in milliseconds. Set `NoDelay` to `True` to make the connection delay, if the buffers fill, so you do not lose data.

Accept Incoming Connections

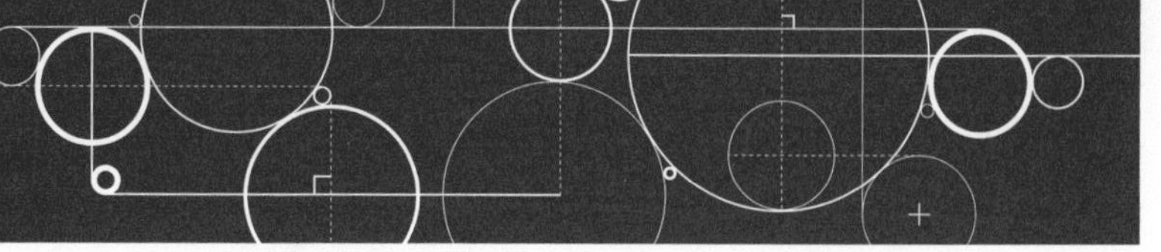

Many packages and even hardware devices provide network connections and a Web server to which you can connect to configure the package. The users can modify a setting in an application wherever their location. You can create a server by accepting incoming TCP/IP connections with the `TcpListener` class. Part of the `System.Net.Socket` namespace, this class relies heavily on the `Socket` class.

You create a `TcpListener` class by declaring a `New` instance of the class. Pass the port that you want to listen on as the single parameter to the constructor of the class.

To attach the listener to the port, call the `Start` method. At this point, the class activates the port and awaits connections. To respond to a connection, call the `AcceptSocket` method. Calling this method blocks your program until a connection occurs, so you can place code to respond to the connection directly after it. The `AcceptSocket` method returns a `Socket`, which you need to maintain a reference for reading and writing to the stream.

After you have the socket, you can freely write information to it as long as the client stays connected. To write to a socket, use the `Send` method. The first parameter of the `Send` method is the `Byte` array to send. You can optionally follow this with the length of the data and a `SocketFlags` constant. In most cases, you can safely pass a zero for `SocketFlags`.

After writing data to the socket, make sure to close it using the `Socket.Close` method. Then you can wait for another connection by invoking the `AcceptSocket` method again. Disable the `TcpListener` by calling the `Stop` method.

Accept Incoming Connections

1. Create a new project or open an existing one.
2. In the appropriate method, type `Dim server As New Net .Sockets.TcpListener(90)`, replacing `server` with the variable name and `90` with the port.
3. On a new line, type `server.Start()`, replacing `server` with the name of the `TcpListener` variable.

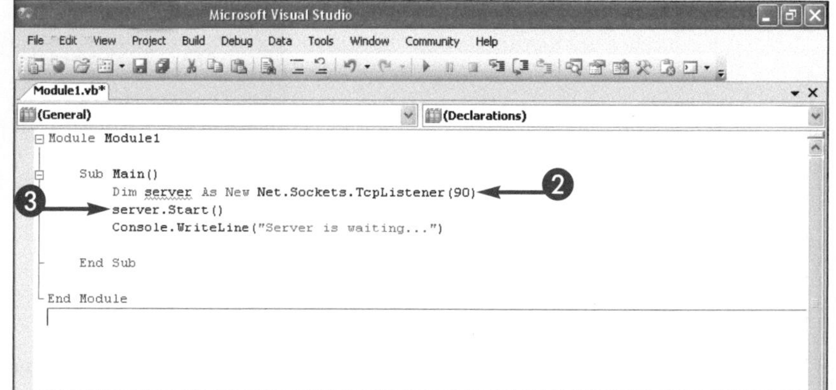

4. Type `Dim mySocket As Net.Sockets.Socket = server.AcceptSocket()`, replacing `mySocket` with the variable name to create a socket and server with the name of the `TcpListener` variable.
5. Type code to load a `Byte` array with information to send the client.
6. Type `mySocket.Send()`, replacing `mySocket` with the variable name of the socket.

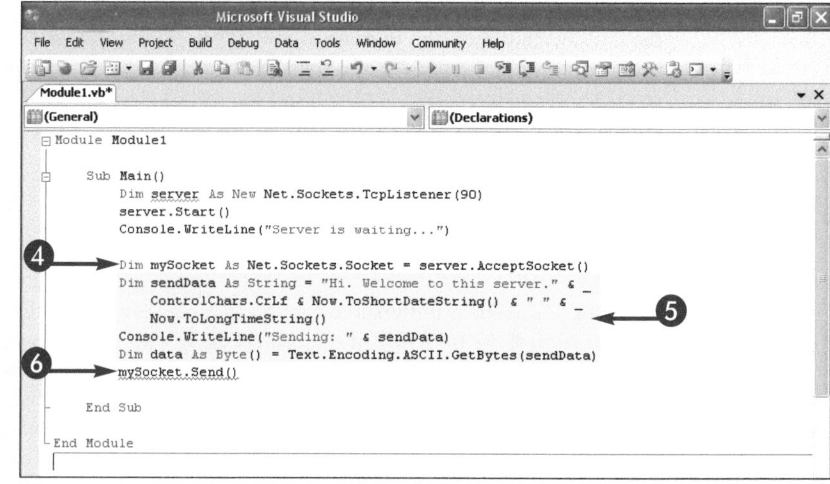

7 Inside the parentheses, type the name of the `Byte()` variable.

8 On a new line, type `mySocket.Close()`, replacing `mySocket` with the name of the variable.

9 On a new line, type `server.Stop()`, replacing `server` with the name of the `TcpListener`.

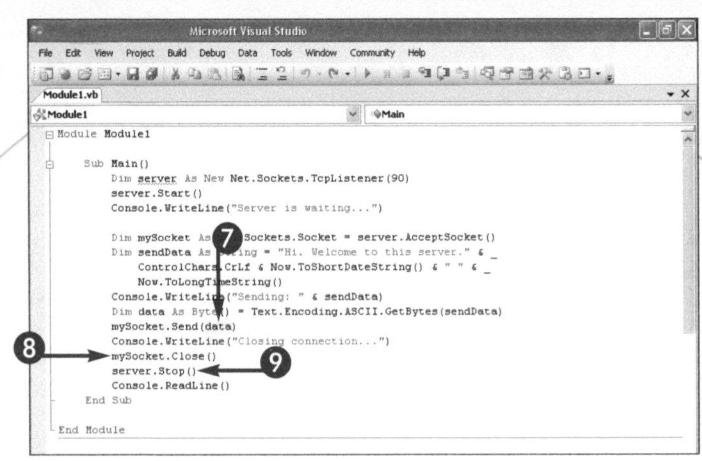

10 Press F5 to run your project.

The server loads and waits for a connection.

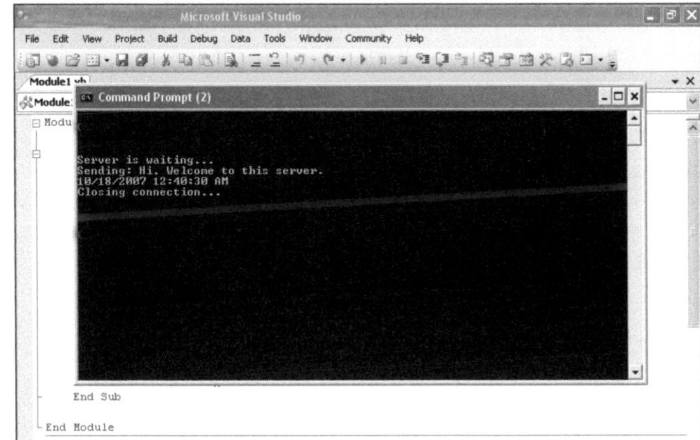

Extra

You can use the `TcpListener` class to build full-featured applications. For example, the basic function of a Web server is to wait for connections on port 80, to process the request string the browser sends to the server, and to write content back over the socket. You can retrieve information sent by the client using the `Receive` method of the `Socket` object. For the parameter to the `Receive` method, pass a `Byte` array to use the buffer. The method returns the actual number of bytes that it loads into the buffer. Call the method multiple times in sequences until all the data loads. To convert a byte array into a string, use the `Text.Encoding.ASCII.GetString` method. The example loads information until it receives a new line control character in the text.

Example

```
Dim server As New Net.Sockets.TcpListener(90)
server.Start()
Dim mySocket As Net.Sockets.Socket = server.AcceptSocket()
Dim buffer(100) As Byte, data As String = "", size As Integer = 0
Do Until InStr(headers, ControlChars.CfLf) > 0
      size = sock.Receive(buffer)
      data += Text.encoding.ASCII.GetString(buffer)
Loop
mysocket.close()
server.Stop()
Console.WriteLine("Received a carriage return.")
Console.ReadLine()
```

Create a Setup Program

A setup program is a program that installs an application on the user's computer using a wizard. The user simply runs the setup program and then responds to a few prompts, such as selecting the folder to install the application. The wizard takes care of all the installation details. You can create a setup program for your application by creating a new setup project, as shown here. When prompted, give your setup project a name that is different from the name of your application project.

The setup project has two panes. The left pane is the file system of the computer receiving your application. The right pane is the contents of the file system item selected in the left pane, called *Solution Explorer.* After you open Solution Explorer and select your application project (which will have an extension of .vbproj) in the Add Existing Project dialog box, the contents of your application project will appear in Solution Explorer.

Using the Add Project Output dialog box, you place the primary output from your Visual Basic .NET application into the Application Folder on the left pane, which is the file that will be installed on the user's computer.

Next, you build the setup program. The setup program is placed in the Debug subfolder within the setup project folder.

Create a Setup Program

1. Drag and drop a `Label` control on to a form.
2. Type text for the label, such as **Hello World**.
3. Save your project.

Note: Remember the location of the application's directory.

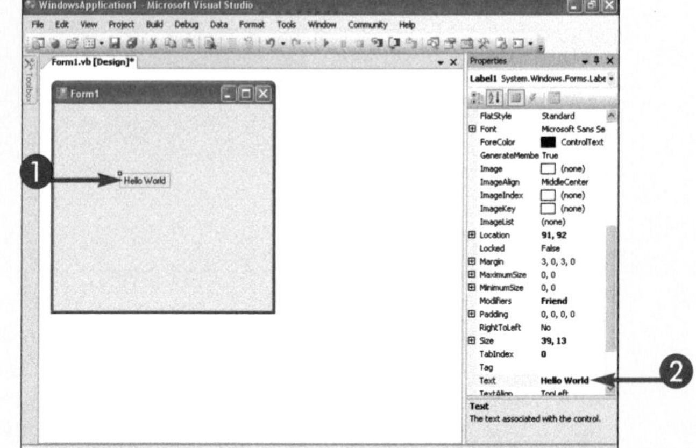

4. Click File ➔ New Project.

   The New Project dialog box appears.

5. Click the + next to Other Project Types.

   A list of other types of projects appears.

6. Click Setup and Deployment.

   - You can change the location of Setup Project if you do not want the project saved in the default directory.

7. Click OK.

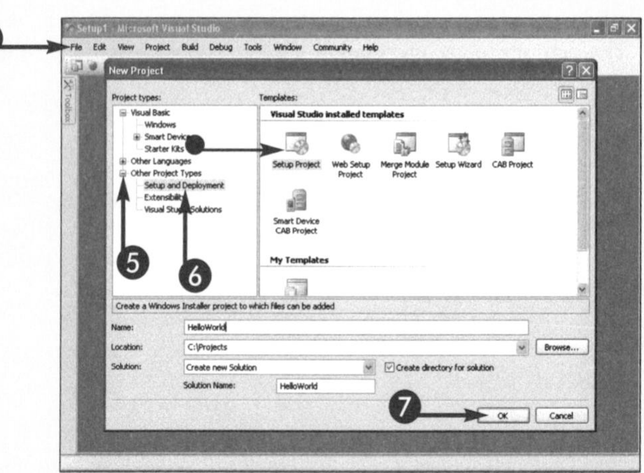

The File System screen appears.

8. Click View ➔ Solution Explorer.

   Solution Explorer appears.

9. Click File ➔ Add ➔ Existing Project.

   The Add Existing Project dialog box appears.

10. Click your project file.

11. Click Open.

    - Your project appears in Solution Explorer.

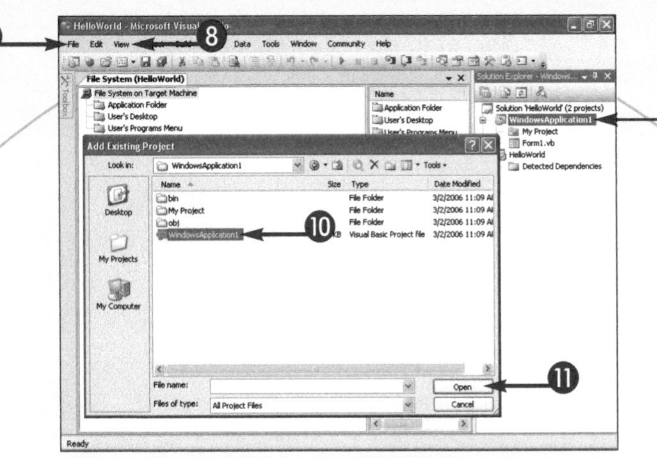

12. Right-click the setup project.

13. Click Add ➔ Project Output.

    The Add Project Output Group dialog box appears.

14. Click Primary Output.

15. Click OK.

    Your application is inserted into the setup project's application folder.

16. Right-click the setup project.

17. Click Build.

    The setup is created and placed in the Debug subfolder.

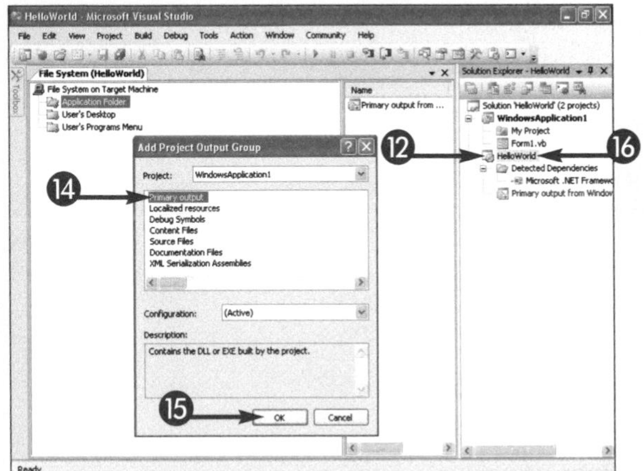

Extra

Sometimes, your project requires additional files besides those that are part of your project file. Let's say that you developed an application that tracked information about your customers. This information is likely to be stored in a database, so you will need to include the database files and install them when your application is installed. You may also want to spice up your application with graphics such as your company's logo and your client's logo. Also, you may have a customized icon to identify your application on your client's desktop. The icon and other graphics used by your application must also be installed with your application.

You can include any file in the setup project that your application requires, and those files will be installed on the user's computer along with your application. To do so, right-click the setup project in Solution Explorer and click Add ➔ File to display the Add Files dialog box. Use the Browse button to locate and select the additional needed files for your setup project.

Create a Shortcut for Your Application

Although the setup program installs your application onto the user's computer, the setup program does not automatically create a shortcut for your application. This means that you may receive a call from your user saying, "I installed your application. I looked all over the Programs folder, and I cannot find it!" You would expect that all applications would be automatically listed in the Programs folder when they are installed, but that is not how Windows works. Applications are installed in their own folder. The user must open the folder and then double-click the name of the executable to run the application.

The Programs folder contains shortcuts to applications — not executables. The name of the program that appears on the list of programs in the Programs folder points to the application's executable in the application's folder. When you click the program name on the list, Windows goes to the application's folder and runs the executable file.

You can avoid receiving the "I cannot find your application" call by having your setup program place your application on the list of programs in the Programs folder. You do this by having the setup program create a shortcut for your application when it installs your application. This is easy for you to do by simply making a few settings when creating the setup program.

Create a Shortcut for Your Application

1. Click File ➔ Open Project.

   The Open Project dialog appears.

2. Locate your setup project and click its filename.

3. Click Open.

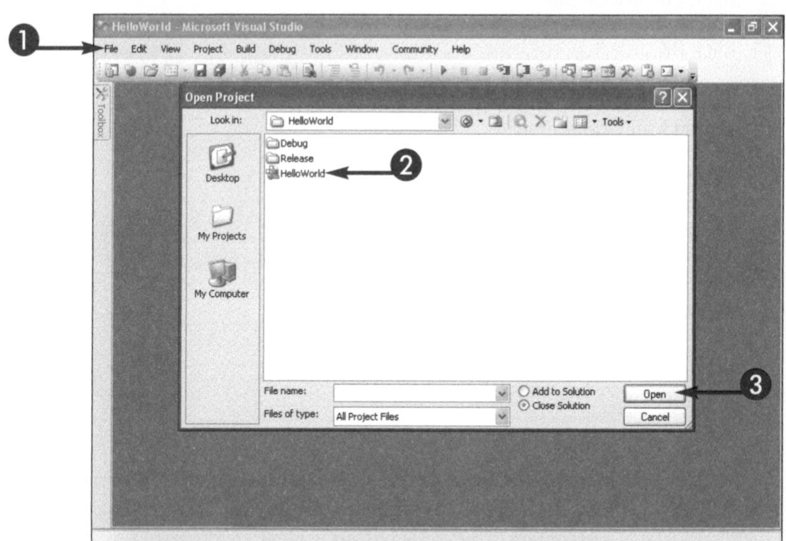

The project opens in Visual Studio 2005.

4. Click View ➔ Solution Explorer.

   Solution Explorer appears.

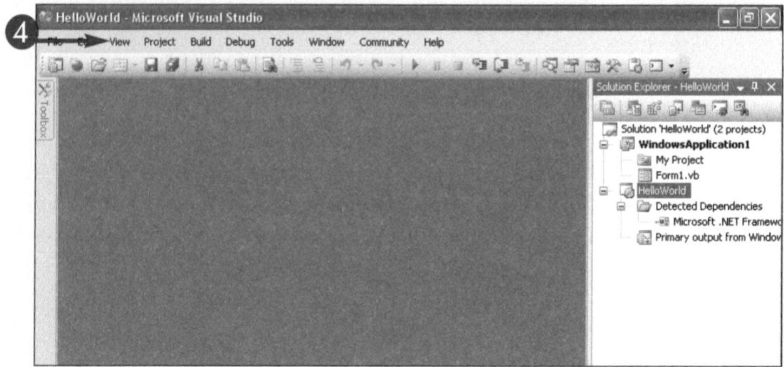

5 Click View ➔ Editor ➔ File System.

The file system of the target computer appears.

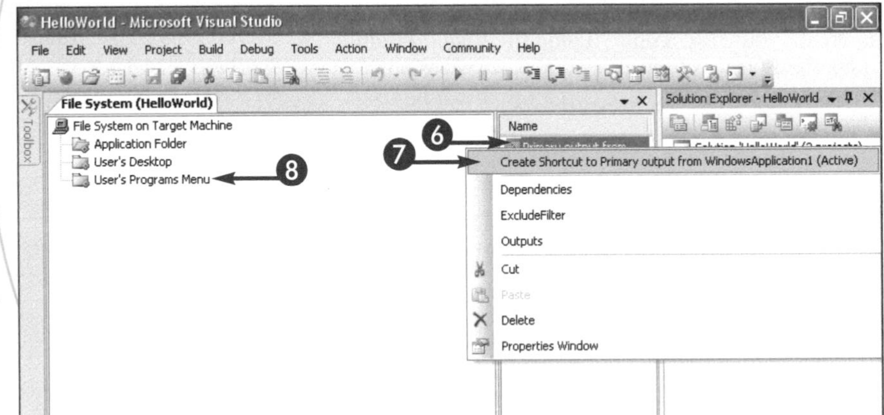

6 In the Application Folder, right-click Primary Output.

7 Click Create Shortcut.

8 Drag and drop the shortcut to the User Programs Menu folder and rename the shortcut.

9 Right-click the project name in Solution Explorer and click Build.

10 Click Start ➔ Control Panel ➔ Add/Remove Programs.

Note: You must remove the previous installation before running the updated version of the setup program.

Extra

Clicking an icon on the desktop is the most convenient way for a user to execute your application. You can have the setup program place your application on the user's desktop during installation. Here is what you need to do. First create a shortcut and then drag and drop the shortcut from the Application Folder in the right pane to the User Desktop folder in the left pane of the setup project. The setup program places your application on the desktop using the default icon. You can have the setup program place your own icon on the desktop instead; see the following section, "Create an Icon for Your Application."

Create an Icon for Your Application

Your application is assigned the default Windows icon. The icon appears when either the user or the setup program places your application on the desktop of the user's computer. You probably do not want to use the default Windows icon for your application for a number of reasons. First, the user will not be able to distinguish your application from others on the desktop that use the default Windows icon. In addition, professional developers use a unique icon to brand their application on the user's desktop.

You can create your own icon by using the Visual Studio editor (see the Extra section) or graphics software such as Photoshop, or you can purchase clip art that can be used directly as an icon or modified into an icon. If you create an icon using clip art, make sure that you have the rights to distribute it with your application. Some makers of clip art let you use it freely whereas others restrict the use to home or educational purposes even if you paid for the clip art. It is wise to ask about any restrictions before using clip art.

Icons are a little different than other graphics because their size must conform to the size of icons used by other applications. The most commonly used size is 32 x 32 pixels. This means that the image is square. Another common size 16 x 16. After you decide on an icon, you will need to incorporate the icon into your setup project.

Create an Icon for Your Application

1. Click File ➔ Open Project.

   The Open Project dialog box appears.

2. Locate your setup project and click its filename.
3. Click Open.

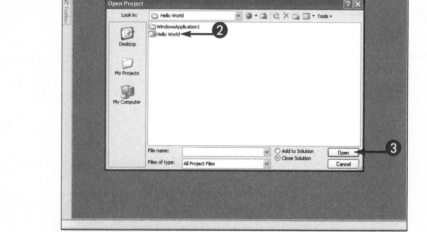

   The project opens in Visual Studio 2005.

4. Click View ➔ Solution Explorer.

   Solution Explorer appears.

5. Right-click your application project and click Properties.

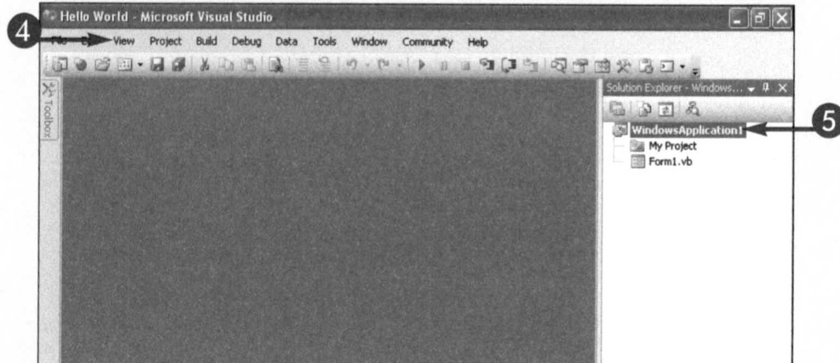

The Properties screen appears.

6. Click the Icon text box.

   A drop-down list appears.

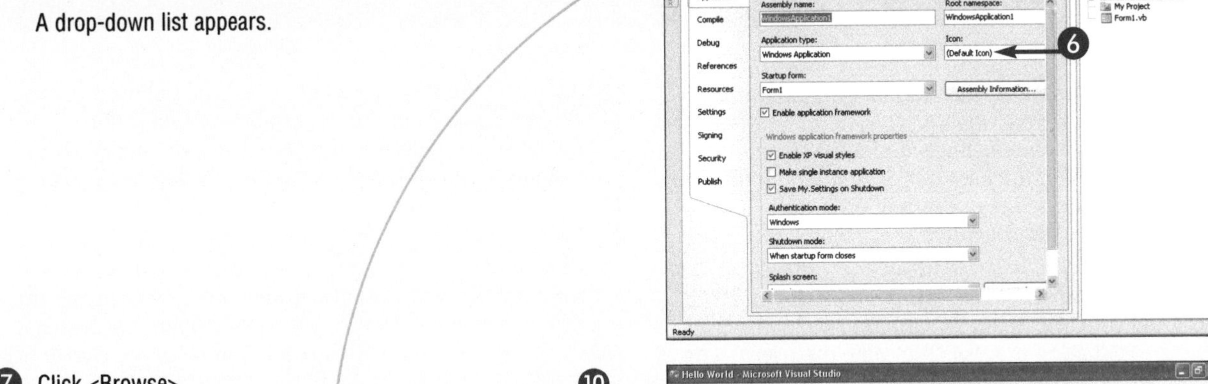

7. Click <Browse>.

8. Locate the icon on your computer and click its filename.

9. Click Open.

   The name of the icon file appears in the Icon text box.

10. Click File ➔ Save All.

    The icon is saved with your project files.

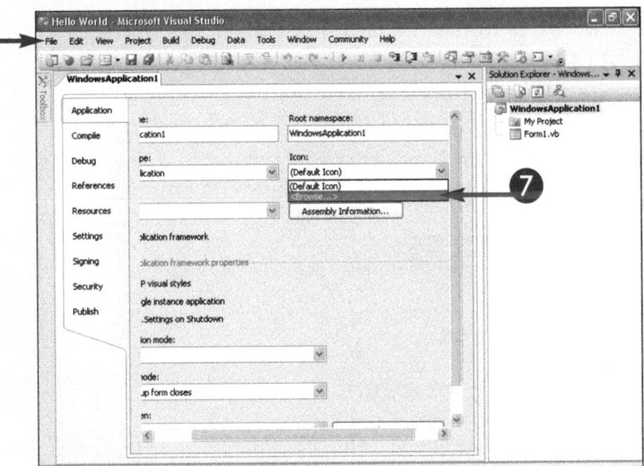

Extra

Icons can be tricky to create because their size is much smaller than other graphics that you may create. You can avoid a lot of the hassles associated with getting the right size for an icon by using the Visual Studio editor to draw it and make sure that it is the correct size. You open the Visual Studio editor by first clicking Project ➔ Add New Items, which displays a dialog box containing items that you can add to your project. You will see an Icon file. Click it to open the editor.

The editor opens the Icon tab with two 32 x 32 rather unattractive icons, and the mouse cursor changes to a pencil. The image on the left is the actual icon, and the right image is where you create your icon design using an assortment of tools available in the editor. You can see these tools by right-clicking. Changes that you make to the right image automatically appear on the left image, giving you an instantaneous look at how your icon will appear when installed with your application.

Run the Setup Program

You distribute your application by providing users with a copy of your application's setup program. The setup program can be burned to a CD or uploaded to a Web site, from which the user can download the file. The user needs to run the setup program in order to install your application on his or her computer.

The installation process is straightforward for the user. The steps for running the setup program are shown here. The setup program runs the Setup Wizard that walks the user through the installation process. Typically, the user needs to specify the folder for the application; otherwise, the user can accept the defaults. When the installation is complete, the wizard displays a message for the user.

Your application can then be run by opening the application's folder and clicking the executable. However, if you had the setup program create a shortcut, the user simply clicks Start ➔ Programs, where he will find the name of your application on the list of applications in the Programs folder. Alternatively, the user can simply select your application icon on the desktop, if you placed your shortcut in the Desktop folder; see "Create a Shortcut for Your Application."

You are able to run the setup program twice; however, the second time the setup program does not let you install the application. Instead, it gives you two options. These are to repair the application, which is a reinstall, or to remove the application. Always use the remove option of the setup program to remove your application rather than simply deleting the application files from the application folder because there may be times when the setup program places files in other folders during the installation. These files must also be removed.

Run the Setup Program

1. Click Start ➔ Run.

   The Run dialog box appears.

2. Click Browse, locate the setup program, and click its filename.

Note: The setup program is located in the Debug directory of the setup project.

3. Click Open.

   - The name of the setup file appears in the Run dialog box.

4. Click OK.

   The Setup Wizard opening screen appears.

5. Click Next.

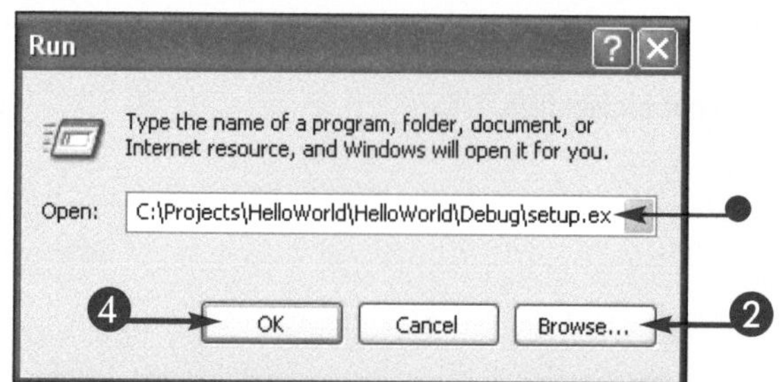

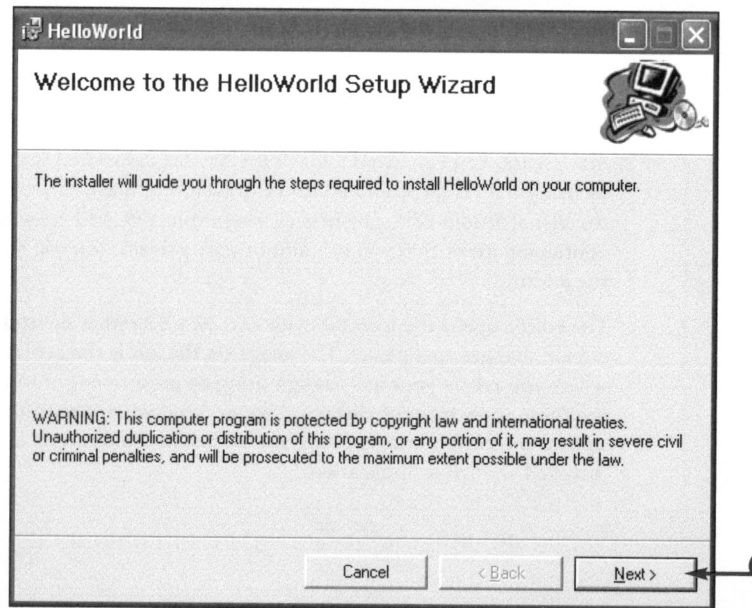

The Select Installation Folder page of the wizard appears.

6 Enter the folder name.

Note: The application will be placed in whatever folder you specify.

7 Click the radio button of who will be able to access the application.

Note: Everyone means that everyone who has a logon for your computer can execute this application. Just Me means that only your logon can access the application.

8 Click Next.

The Confirm Installation page of the wizard appears.

9 Click Next.

The application is installed on your computer.

When the installation is completed, the Install Complete screen appears.

10 Click Close.

The setup program exits.

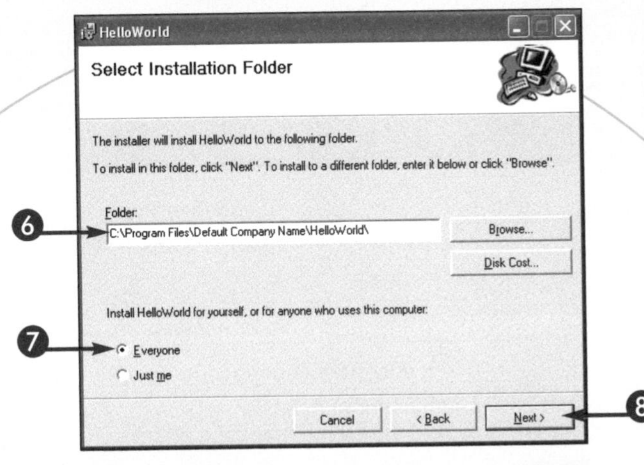

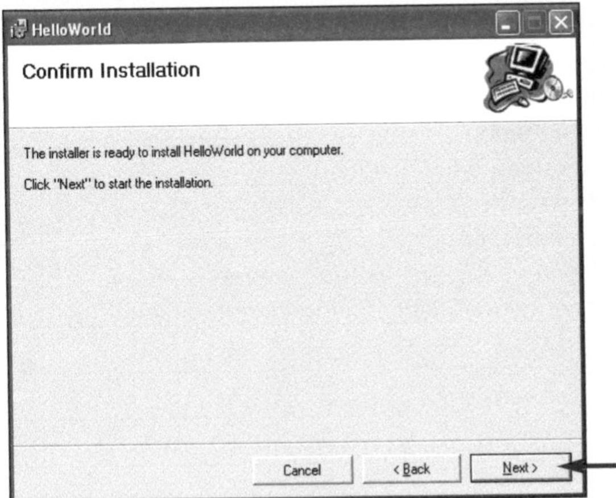

Extra

You can give your application a professional flair by starting your setup program automatically when the user loads your CD into a CD drive. This is easy to do. Windows looks for a file called AUTORUN.INF in the root directory of the CD. If the file is found, Windows follows instructions contained in it. You can create an AUTORUN.INF file and write instructions telling Windows to execute your setup program. Here is what you need to do. Open Notepad or any text editor and write the following:

```
[autorun]
Open=setup.exe
```

Save the file as AUTORUN.INF. Place this file in the root directory of your CD when you burn it.

INDEX

Symbols

INDEX

D

INDEX

E

F

INDEX

G

H

I–K

INDEX

P

INDEX

INDEX

For more professional instruction in a visual format, try these.

All designed for visual learners—just like you!

Visual® **Read Less–Learn More®**

HTML — *Your visual blueprint™ for designing Web pages with HTML, CSS, and XHTML*

0-7645-8331-X

Excel™ Data Analysis, 2nd Edition — *Your visual blueprint™ for analyzing data, charts, and PivotTables*

0-7645-9780-9

JavaScript™, 2nd Edition — *Your visual blueprint™ for building dynamic Web pages*

0-7645-7497-3

For a complete listing of *Visual Blueprint™* titles and other Visual books, go to wiley.com/go/visualtech

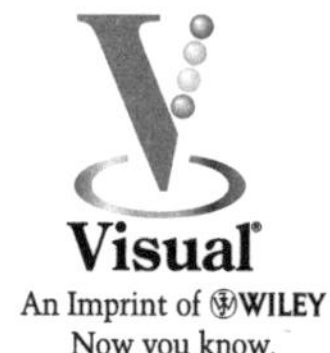